# Employment Discrimination

Carolina Academic Press
*Context and Practice Series*
Michael Hunter Schwartz
Series Editor

Administrative Law
Richard Henry Seamon

Civil Procedure for All States
Benjamin V. Madison, III

Constitutional Law
David Schwartz and Lori Ringhand

A Context and Practice Global Case File:
An Intersex Athlete's Constitiutional Challenge
*Hastings v. USATF, IAAF, and IOC*
Olivia M. Farrar

Contracts
Michael Hunter Schwartz and Denise Riebe

Current Issues in Constitutional Litigation
Sarah E. Ricks, with contributions by Evelyn M. Tenenbaum

Employment Discrimination, 2nd. Ed.
Susan Grover, Sandra F. Sperino, and Jarod S. Gonzalez

Evidence
Pavel Wonsowicz

International Business Transactions
Amy Deen Westbrook

International Women's Rights, Equality, and Justice
Christine M. Venter

The Lawyer's Practice
Kris Franklin

Professional Responsibility
Barbara Glesner Fines

Sales
Edith R. Warkentine

Torts
Paula J. Manning

Workers' Compensation Law
Michael C. Duff

# EMPLOYMENT DISCRIMINATION

## A Context and Practice Casebook

### SECOND EDITION

**Susan Grover**
WILLIAM AND MARY LAW SCHOOL

**Sandra F. Sperino**
THE UNIVERSITY OF CINCINNATI COLLEGE OF LAW

**Jarod S. Gonzalez**
TEXAS TECH UNIVERSITY SCHOOL OF LAW

CAROLINA ACADEMIC PRESS
Durham, North Carolina

ISBN 978-1-61163-308-5
LCCN 2013949335


Carolina Academic Press
700 Kent Street
Durham, North Carolina 27701
Telephone (919) 489-7486
Fax (919) 493-5668
www.cap-press.com


Printed in the United States of America

# Contents

# Table of Principal Cases

# Series Editor's Preface

Welcome to a new type of casebook. Designed by leading experts in law school teaching and learning, Context and Practice casebooks assist law professors and their students to work together to learn, minimize stress, and prepare for the rigors and joys of practicing law. **Student learning and preparation for law practice are the guiding ethics of these books.**

Why would we depart from the tried and true? Why have we abandoned the legal education model by which we were trained? Because legal education can and must improve.

In Spring 2007, the Carnegie Foundation published *Educating Lawyers: Preparation for the Practice of Law* and the Clinical Legal Education Association published *Best Practices for Legal Education*. Both works reflect in-depth efforts to assess the effectiveness of modern legal education, and both conclude that legal education, as presently practiced, falls quite short of what it can and should be. Both works criticize law professors' rigid adherence to a single teaching technique, the inadequacies of law school assessment mechanisms, and the dearth of law school instruction aimed at teaching law practice skills and inculcating professional values. Finally, the authors of both books express concern that legal education may be harming law students. Recent studies show that law students, in comparison to all other graduate students, have the highest levels of depression, anxiety and substance abuse.

**The problems with traditional law school instruction begin with the textbooks law teachers use.** Law professors cannot implement *Educating Lawyers* and *Best Practices* using texts designed for the traditional model of legal education. Moreover, even though our understanding of how people learn has grown exponentially in the past 100 years, no law school text to date even purports to have been designed with educational research in mind.

The Context and Practice Series is an effort to offer a genuine alternative. Grounded in learning theory and instructional design and written with *Educating Lawyers* and *Best Practices* in mind, Context and Practice casebooks make it easy for law professors to change.

I welcome reactions, criticisms, and suggestions; my e-mail address is mhschwartz@ualr.edu. Knowing the author(s) of these books, I know they, too, would appreciate your input; we share a common commitment to student learning. In fact, students, if your professor cares enough about your learning to have adopted this book, I bet s/he would welcome your input, too!

Professor Michael Hunter Schwartz, Series Designer and Editor
Co-Director, Institute for Law Teaching and Learning
Dean, UALR William H. Bowen School of Law

# Preface and Acknowledgments

## The Context and Practice Series

This book is part of the Context and Practice ("CAP") series, the mission of which is to support law professors' goals of becoming more effective teachers and law students' goals of becoming more effective at learning. An essential aspect of this mission is to engage students in active learning, challenging students to integrate doctrine, theory, and skills. The book uses the contextual learning emphasis of the Carnegie Foundation's EDUCATING LAWYERS (2007) and the Clinical Legal Education Association's BEST PRACTICES IN LEGAL EDUCATION (2007).

## Goals of This Casebook

This book combines traditional methodologies with an active learning approach. The traditional model of legal education centers on learning to think like a lawyer. The model tends to focus on a narrow skill set, having students derive rules of law and learn about legal reasoning by reading appellate court decisions. It is an effective approach — as far as it goes. Legal reading and analysis skills are essential to the competent lawyer, and this book, like other casebooks, challenges students to become experts at both.

At the same time, the book recognizes that students will be better prepared for professional life if they leave law school with a larger skill set, an ability to conceptualize legal theory, a sensitivity to the contexts in which legal rules operate and a concrete understanding of the lawyer's role as a professional problem solver. The casebook has been designed to give students the tools they need to understand the law and the cases, providing background reading on the history, theory, policy, and practical considerations that may impact the law's development and the outcome of particular cases. This background reading is important to help students place the cases and statutory language in their broader context. This text also tries to counter some law school courses' heavy emphasis on case law, by reminding students that statutory interpretation is an important legal reasoning device and by providing them with the tools to undertake such statutory interpretation.

The book's exercises go beyond the realm of traditional legal reasoning, providing opportunities to see how lawyers might use concepts in practice. The book asks students to view legal problems through different lenses, from the perspective of a plaintiff's lawyer, a judge, an in-house counsel, a defense attorney, a victim of discrimination, a person accused of discrimination, a human resources professional, and an employer. It tries to help students gain an understanding of what each of these individuals might consider in resolving a legal problem.

In creating the exercises for this text, special consideration was given to the skill set that a new employment discrimination attorney should possess. The authors of the book, in consultation with practitioners and professors, developed a list of skills critical to attorneys within the employment discrimination field. The following is a list highlighting those skills and identifying the exercises within the book designed to develop them:

- **Initial Case Evaluation**—Exercises 1.1, 2.4, 3.5, 5.3, 5.6, 5.9, Capstone Exercises 1 & 2
- **Client counseling**—Exercises 1.1, 1.3, 2.3, 5.8, 5.9, 5.10, 6.2, 7.4, Capstone Exercises 1 & 2
- **Forum choice**—Exercise 10.3, Capstone Exercise 1
- **Drafting a complaint or answer**—Exercises 3.8, 3.9
- **Discovery and evidence development**—Exercises 3.9, 3.12, 5.7, Capstone Exercise 3
- **Recognizing problems with statistical evidence**—Exercises 4.2, 4.3
- **Summary judgment**—Capstone Exercise 4
- **Mediation/determining value of claim**—Exercises 11.1, 11.2, 11.3, 11.4
- **Predicting the likely outcome of cases**—Exercises 3.3, 3.4, 3.5, 3.6, 4.5, 5.9, 5.10, 6.1
- **Jury instructions**—Exercises 10.1, 10.4
- **Drafting and evaluating policies**—Exercises 1.3, 2.3, 4.4, 5.11, 9.4
- **Resolution of employee complaints, employee requests, and client questions**— Exercises 1.3, 2.2, 5.8, 5.11, 7.3, 7.4, 8.5, 8.6, 8.10, Capstone Exercise 5
- **Engagement in the ADA accommodation interactive process**—Capstone Exercise 5
- **Providing training**—Exercises 5.1, 5.12, 6.3
- **Statutory Construction**—Exercise 3.1
- **Ethics**—Exercise 1.1 (Rule 11, lawyer as advisor), Exercise 2.3 (lawyer as advisor), Exercise 3.9 (Rule 11), Exercise 3.11, Capstone Exercises 1 & 2 (lawyer as advisor, speaking with represented parties, lawyer as a witness).

The exercises' fact patterns involve both litigation and transactional contexts to help students understand the multi-faceted roles of employment discrimination attorneys. When a particular exercise requires knowledge of another substantive or procedural area, the exercise provides appropriate information and direction to allow the student to practice the required skills.

Certain exercises also try to help students think about how best to learn the law. These exercises ask students to think about how they can organize material so that it is useful to them, both as students and in practice. These exercises also challenge students to synthesize material and to conceptualize it in different ways than the way the material was originally presented. The following exercises are explicitly designed to engage students in this way: Exercises 1.2, 3.2, 3.15, 4.6, 6.4, 8.13, 11.4, and 11.5.

Perhaps most importantly, this book also tries to help students understand how the policy and theory underlying discrimination law affect the doctrine. The book contains numerous problems challenging students to question the underlying theory of American employment discrimination law and to consider how the law might work differently if it were based on a different set of theoretical assumptions.

The following theoretical and policy discussions are included in Exercises:

- Whether the employment discrimination statutes should promote race-neutral decisionmaking—Exercise 2.1
- Formal v. substantive equality—Exercise 3.1
- Intersectionality—Exercise 3.7
- Whether intent should be required to prove discrimination—Exercise 3.13
- Unconscious bias—Exercise 3.14
- Affirmative action—Exercises 9.1, 9.2
- Right of personality—Exercise 9.3
- Conception of race—Exercise 9.3
- Theory of religious discrimination—Exercise 7.1
- Structural discrimination—Capstone Exercise 1.

One of the highlights of the text is the Capstone Experience. The Capstone Experience gives students an opportunity to combine the theoretical, doctrinal, historical, and practical knowledge they have gained throughout the casebook and to use that knowledge to resolve real-world problems. The Capstone Experience provides five different exercises, each focusing on a different skill set. The skills covered in the Capstone Experience are: (1) initial case evaluation from the plaintiff's attorney's perspective; (2) initial case evaluation from the defendant's attorney's perspective; (3) discovery; (4) summary judgment; and (5) resolution of employee complaints and requests.

Admittedly, this book has a lofty set of goals. At the end of the course, students should be able to identify the employment discrimination law issues implicated by a set of facts, articulate the relevant legal rules and the rationales supporting those rules, develop arguments that reasonable lawyers would make respecting a legal problem, and predict how a court might address a particular issue. Students should understand the history, policy, theory, and practical considerations relevant to employment discrimination cases, and be able to demonstrate competence in a variety of practical contexts. Further, students should develop a rich understanding of how theory molds discrimination law. At the end of the course, students should be able to use the skills taught in this course to identify gaps in the existing structure of employment discrimination law and to advocate for changes or further development of the law.

## Book Organization and Editing

The book is organized to assist students in reaching the course goals. The book uses two types of headings to do this: Core Concepts and Beyond the Basics. Here is what those headings mean.

- ✦ Core Concepts—describes foundational concepts that are required for a basic understanding of employment discrimination law.
- ➤ Beyond the Basics—describes concepts that are important, but not required, for a basic understanding of employment discrimination law.

All of the Chapters other than the Protected Traits and Special Issues Chapter (Chapter 9) and the Procedure Chapter (Chapter 10) use these headings.

Most of the cases are preceded by Focus Questions to help students identify key issues presented by the case. As described above, exercises are contained in each Chapter to test knowledge of concepts, to teach skills, and to stimulate discussion regarding theory.

To aid student reading, some internal citations within cases are omitted without notation, including citations to the case's record or the lower court's decisions.

## Acknowledgments

We could not have completed this book without help from numerous people. We appreciate Michael Schwartz' leadership in conceptualizing this book series, and Carolina Academic Press for its commitment to the series. We are grateful to our colleagues who read various drafts of the casebook and provided insightful feedback. We are also grateful to Jeffrey Hirsch for bringing us together.

Susan Grover's Acknowledgments:

Thanks to the many colleagues and students who have challenged my thinking in the areas covered by this book. Thanks to William and Mary Law School for ongoing financial and moral support. Thanks to my family and friends for putting up with my absences. Thanks to Isis for staying by my side throughout my work on this book. Thanks to Jarod Gonzalez and Sandra Sperino whose intelligence, patience, energy and creativity made this book possible.

Jarod Gonzalez's Acknowledgments:

Thank you to my wonderful wife, Leisha Dawn, and our two beautiful children, Jackson Spencer and Jamison Samuel, for your love and support. My entire family—Mom, Dad, Bonner, and Grammy—encouraged me during this process and I am grateful to all of them. Thanks to Sarah Taylor, Texas Tech University Law School, J.D. 2010, for her helpful research assistance and the Texas Tech University Law School administration and faculty for their support of this project. The Frank McDonald Research Professorship funds aided my participation in this project. Thank you to Sandra and Susan for inviting me to participate in this project and for all of your energies in striving to make a good book. Finally, my efforts on this book are for my grandfather, Grampy. He always gave me what I needed— encouragement, guidance, praise, and correction—and continues to inspire me.

Sandra Sperino's Acknowledgments:

My work on the first edition of this casebook was supported by Temple University Beasley School of Law, and my work on the second edition was supported by the University of Cincinnati College of Law, including research support from the Schott Publication Prize. I would like to thank my co-authors Susan Grover and Jarod Gonzalez for their thoughtfulness in how to approach this project, as well as their collegiality and friendship. I am also grateful for the research assistance of Tenechia Lockhart and my library liaison Ron Jones.

Words cannot properly express my love and gratitude for my family, especially my husband John and my son Joseph, who deserve much credit for all of their support while I worked on this book. I would also like to thank my mother Rita for her wisdom and her example.

# EMPLOYMENT DISCRIMINATION

# Chapter 1

# Introduction to Employment Discrimination Law

This casebook explores the principal federal protections against workplace discrimination. It focuses primarily on four statutes: Title VII of the Civil Rights Act of 1964 (Title VII), the Age Discrimination in Employment Act (ADEA), the Americans with Disabilities Act (ADA), and 42 U.S.C. § 1981 (§ 1981).

Title VII provides protections against employment discrimination based on a person's race, color, national origin, religion, or sex. As is obvious by their titles, the ADEA prohibits age discrimination in employment, and the ADA prohibits disability discrimination, with Title I of the ADA dedicated to the employment context. Section 1981 protects against race discrimination in employment and other contexts.

Many other federal statutes relate to employment discrimination, and this book will provide an overview of several of them as well. The Equal Pay Act of 1963 (EPA), as amended, prohibits wage discrimination based on sex, and the Family and Medical Leave Act (FMLA) provides certain employees with the ability to take unpaid leave in specific circumstances. You also will encounter the Genetic Information Nondiscrimination Act of 2008 (GINA), the Rehabilitation Act, and the Immigration Reform and Control Act (IRCA).

As you work your way through this book, you will learn about the kinds of discrimination prohibited under federal law, and the ways courts analyze discrimination claims. You will gain essential information about the procedures for resolving disputes and the remedies that may be available upon that resolution. Throughout the book, you will encounter exercises that ask you to apply discrimination doctrine, as well as to consider the theoretical, practical, and ethical issues that affect employment discrimination claims.

This introduction provides the groundwork for your study of employment discrimination law. It gives you an overview of the federal statutes that form the core of the subject. It introduces you to the concept of "employment at will," which is the typical common law presumption governing the employment relationship, in the absence of a contract or law to the contrary. This chapter also provides you with an overview of other federal employment statutes, so that you can understand the context in which the employment discrimination statutes operate. Finally, it considers the pragmatic factors that can affect your client's decisions about how best to resolve a discrimination dispute, including the economic and emotional costs of employment discrimination litigation.

## ✦ Core Concept: At-Will Employment

Even though this course focuses primarily on federal statutes, we begin by placing those statutes in the broader context of employment law. That context centers on a common law concept called "at-will employment." After reading the following case, you should be able to identify the core tenets of the at-will doctrine, as well as some of its exceptions.

# Howard v. Wolff Broadcasting Corp.

## 611 So. 2d 307 (Ala. 1992)

Justice Maddox.

The plaintiff was fired by Wolff Broadcasting Corporation ("Wolff") solely because she was a female. The principal question presented here is whether this court should carve out an exception to the employee-at-will doctrine [either by holding that defendant breached an implied contract or that plaintiff has a wrongful discharge cause of action because defendant's act violated public policy.]

The basic facts are not significantly disputed. In September or October 1987, the plaintiff, Patricia Williams Howard, inquired about employment with Wolff, which operated a radio station. She was unemployed at that time. Shortly thereafter, Keith Holcombe, the manager of the station, called her and set up an interview. Wolff hired Howard as a disc jockey and advertising salesperson. Howard had had no prior experience of any kind in the radio business. Howard presented evidence that, during the process of her hiring, she noted in the lobby of the station a sign stating that Wolff would not discriminate against "females, blacks, or any others." there was no written contract of employment.

On January 26, 1988, while Howard was on the air, Keith Holcombe drove to the station and informed her that she was fired. When he fired her, Holcombe told her that she was being fired because Karen Wolff, whose husband owned Wolff, did not want any females on the air. On that same night, Howard typed a letter stating that she was fired because Karen Wolff did not want females on the air....[1]

## I. Breach of Contract

Howard first argues that the trial court erred in entering the summary judgment in favor of Wolff on the claim alleging breach of contract. The determinative question on that issue is whether Howard's employment contract was terminable at will.

Employees at will can terminate their employment, or can be terminated by their employer, at any time, with or without cause or justification. Although this doctrine has been criticized as harsh, it remains the law in Alabama. If the employment is terminable at will, the employer may even act maliciously in terminating the employee.

It is undisputed that Howard was not offered lifetime employment or employment of any definite duration.... Howard contends that when she entered into her contract with Wolff, there was an implied covenant that Wolff would not discriminate against her on the basis of race, gender, religion, or national origin. [Howard bases this contention on the argument that certain regulations of the Federal Communications Commission, which apply to defendant radio station and which prohibit such discrimination, have implicitly become terms of what would otherwise be a contract for employment at will.]

---

1. When Wolff fired Howard, it had only seven employees; therefore, the Equal Employment Opportunity Commission did not have jurisdiction over Howard's complaint of discrimination. Likewise, Howard had no cause of action under federal law. *See* 42 U.S.C. § 2000e-(2) (1972).

This court has held that employment policies, especially those in writing, can become a binding promise once [they are] accepted by the employee through his continuing to work when he is not required to do so. In [one of the court's prior cases], certain employment policies were contained in an employee handbook. The court held that the provisions contained in the employee handbook, when combined with the employee's continuation of employment following the employee's receipt of the handbook, created a unilateral contract modifying the "at will" employment relationship. The court stated:

> [l]anguage contained in a handbook can be sufficient to constitute an offer to create a binding unilateral contract. The existence of such a contract is determined by applying the following analysis to the facts of each case: first, the language contained in the handbook must be examined to see if it is specific enough to constitute an offer. Second, the offer must have been communicated to the employee by the issuance of the handbook, or otherwise. Third, the employee must have accepted the offer by retaining employment after he has become generally aware of the offer. His actual performance supplies the necessary consideration. [citation omitted].

It has long been the law in Alabama that employment is terminable at will by either party for any reason unless there is an express and specific contract for lifetime employment or employment for a specific duration. "[A]bsent an agreement on a definite term, any employment is considered to be 'at-will,' and may be terminated by either party, with or without cause or justification." [citation omitted]. Furthermore, employees in Alabama bear a heavy burden of proof to establish that an employment relationship is other than "at will." ...

In view of the principle that absent an agreement on a definite term, any employment is considered to be "at-will," and may be terminated by either party, with or without cause or justification, we cannot say that the provisions of 47 C.F.R. § 73.2080 could become a binding promise once [they were] accepted by [Howard] through [her] continuing to work. In short, we cannot hold that the provisions of this federal regulation transformed Howard's at-will employment relationship with Wolff into a permanent one.

[Without further explanation, the court concluded that the FAA regulations did not modify at-will employment.]

...

### III. Public policy

Finally, Howard argues that, even assuming that a unilateral contract did not exist and that the "at-will" doctrine applies, there should be a public policy exception to that doctrine in this case.

The employment "at-will" doctrine was first recognized in Alabama in *Howard v. East Tennessee, V. & G. Ry.*, 8 So. 868 (1891). This doctrine provides "that an employment contract terminable at the will of either the employer or the employee may be terminated by either party at any time with or without cause." ... Howard argues that because the [employment at-will] doctrine is a judicially created one, the judiciary can and should abolish or modify it.

However, this court has so far declined to judicially create a public policy exception to the employment "at-will" doctrine. [T]his court has consistently chosen ... to leave the creation of exceptions to the legislature. When this court refused to create an exception [to the at-will doctrine], the legislature created a limited statutory exception permitting an employee terminated solely because he or she has made a claim for worker's compensation benefits to file an action for damages. Likewise, [one of the court's prior cases] has also been effectively overruled by the legislature's adoption of a statute preventing dismissal of an employee because the employee answered a call for jury service.

The court has consistently refused to create a cause of action for wrongful discharge on "public policy" grounds, for three reasons: (1) to do so would abrogate the inherent right of contract between employer and employee; (2) to do so would be to overrule well-established employment law; and (3) "contrary to public policy" is too vague or nebulous a standard to justify creation of a new tort.

Howard urges the court to adopt a narrow public policy exception to the employment "at-will" doctrine based on principles of non-discrimination. Indeed, many states have carved out exceptions to the employment "at-will" doctrine....

On the public policy issue, the congress of the United States has elected to exempt Wolff from the provisions of law relating to discrimination in employment. [W]e do not think, ... that we should judicially create a wrongful discharge action based on "public policy" grounds in this case[.] In refusing to adopt a "public policy" exception, we should not be understood as condoning a person's discharge because of gender. We merely hold that it is the province of the legislature to create such an exception....

---

## Further Discussion

*Howard v. Wolff Broadcasting Corp.* was decided under Alabama state law. The at-will employment doctrine is the rule that governs employment in most of the states in the United States. *But see* Mont. Code Ann. § 39-2-904(1) (statute abrogating the employment at-will doctrine in certain termination cases).

Although the exceptions to the at-will doctrine vary by state, the *Howard* decision provides a good overview of some of the exceptions that often exist under a given state's law. Some states, either through statutes or the common law, have carved out public policy-based exceptions to at-will employment. These exceptions vary widely by state, but exceptions have been recognized where an employee refuses to break the law, where an employee is performing a public obligation (such as performing jury duty), or when the employee is exercising a legal right, such as filing a worker's compensation claim or protesting unsafe working conditions.

Another exception argued by the plaintiff in *Howard* was that a policy of the employer was an implied term of the contract of employment. The *Howard* situation involved an interesting twist: the policy the plaintiff wished to incorporate was not a policy from Wolff's employee handbook, but was a policy of the federal agency with oversight responsibility for the defendant radio station. Although the particular argument the plaintiff made is not very common, it is common for a plaintiff to argue that an employee handbook or other expression of employer policy created either an express or an implied contractual obligation by the employer. In some instances, courts have found that signed handbooks or other documents are explicit contracts or are implied terms of the employment relationship. The requirements for determining whether a contract is created vary by state.

The concept of at-will employment is important because, in most states, it is the default rule governing hiring, terminations, and the terms and conditions of employment when no other law or contract applies to the employment relationship. The at-will employment concept also underlies some of the concepts applicable to federal employment discrimination law. As you encounter the business judgment rule and the various proof structures for establishing discrimination, think about how these concepts are affected by the concept of at-will employment.

Historically, the at-will presumption did not become the norm in the United States until the late 1800s and early 1900s. It replaced an English rule, where employment was presumed to be for a year or throughout all of the revolutions of the respective seasons. The at-will rule is often attributed to Horace Gay Wood, who described the rule in a treatise in the late 1800s. Some within the legal and academic community believe that Wood misstated the rule and that this misstatement then became the legal norm. *See, e.g.*, Richard Bales, *Explaining the Spread of At-will Employment as an Interjurisdictional Race to the Bottom of Employment Standards*, 75 TENN. L. REV. 453 (2008).

Consider how much power the at-will doctrine provides employers. The at-will employment concept may allow employers to control how an employee dresses, how the employee styles his or her hair, and whether the employee can date or marry co-workers. Under at-will employment, employers may be able to monitor employee communications, engage in video surveillance within the workplace, and consider an employee's personal habits and activities in making decisions. A few states have common law or statutes that prohibit an employer from engaging in some or all of these activities.

Consider whether the theoretical foundations of the employee-employer relationship, as expressed in the at-will doctrine, are flawed. Some countries recognize an employee right of privacy or right of personality. The right of personality has been described as the "right to be respected as a person, not to have one's individuality infringed, in one's right to express oneself (in appearance, writing, and speech), … and in the private and intimate areas of one's existence." Matthew W. Finkin, *Employee Privacy, American Values, and the Law*, 72 CHI-KENT L. REV. 221, 261 (1996). In countries that recognize such rights, a balancing test may be employed to weigh whether an employer intrusion into privacy or personality is justified by the employer's claimed business necessity. *See id.* Throughout this course, consider whether employment law does or should protect employee autonomy and privacy.

---

### Exercise 1.1

Imagine that you are a practicing lawyer. Sally Smith calls your office and makes an appointment to visit later in the week. Over the telephone, Sally tells you that she was terminated from her job at Acme Corporation and was told that it was because she missed two days of work without calling in. Sally tells you that, in fact, she called in and told her boss' administrative assistant that she needed two days off to attend a family funeral. She also tells you that, about a month ago, she filed a worker's compensation claim, that other employees have been retained after missing two days of work without calling in, and that all of these employees are white, while Sally is a person of color.

Prepare to interview Sally when she comes to your office. Consider the legal issues raised and any applicable rules, as well as what additional information you must obtain in order to be able to evaluate the case. Be prepared to analyze the case objectively and provide Sally with advice on how to proceed. Your advice to Sally should consider all possible solutions to Sally's problem, given the materials you have studied to date.

Determine how you will assess whether Sally's version of the events is credible. Think about how you will craft the client interview to get the most comprehensive version of the facts. In the interview you will need to consider whether Sally seems to have a good memory of the facts, whether she is omitting important facts, whether she is embellishing certain facts to enhance her story, and whether you think Sally would be a good witness if the case went to trial. Think about the documents you might need from Sally and how you might verify what she tells you.

If you decide to file a lawsuit and if that lawsuit will be filed in federal court, recall that you will be bound by the Federal Rules of Civil Procedure. Under Rule 11(b), an attorney who signs a document is representing that the claims and legal contentions are "warranted by existing law or by a nonfrivolous argument for extending, modifying or reversing existing law or for establishing new law" and that factual contentions "have evidentiary support or, if specifically so identified, will likely have evidentiary support after a reasonable opportunity for further investigation or discovery." Consider these obligations as you think about the client interview.

This exercise is designed to test your knowledge of the at-will employment doctrine and its exceptions, as well as to introduce you to skills related to conducting a client interview, gathering factual information and providing legal advice. Interviewing clients and gathering factual information are essential skills that all competent attorneys must possess. Also, it is important for you to understand the key role that fact gathering plays in lawyering.

## Exercise 1.2

One of the goals of this book is to give you an opportunity to think about the learning style or methods that will help you to best learn the material. Since employment discrimination is an upper-level course, you may have already given this issue serious thought in prior law school classes. However, many students continue to struggle in law school simply because they have been unable to learn how to learn about the law.

While this is unfortunate in law school, a failure to learn how to learn about the law can have even more serious consequences when you become a practicing lawyer. In most of the chapters, there will be an exercise or exercises to help you think about how to approach learning legal concepts or how to synthesize the material you already have learned. A list of these exercises is provided in the preface.

You have learned about the concept of at-will employment and its exceptions. Think about how to organize this material so that you can use it. Consider whether it works better for you to create a narrative description or whether a flow chart or decision tree makes more sense.

## Exercise 1.3

You are an in-house attorney for a large accounting firm. You specialize in employment law. You have been asked to provide advice regarding the conduct described below.

In crafting your advice, think about the legal issues raised, as well as what additional information you would need to evaluate the scenario. Further, think about your role as an in-house attorney. As an in-house attorney, your concern should be both about the outcome of a particular set of facts and the larger implications of the issue for the company. Think about whether each scenario raises broader concerns about company policies or practices. What implications will your advice have not only on the affected employees, but on other employees within the company? What litigation or other risks does your advice create? Also consider whether some of these decisions are business decisions for the client to make after being told about the legal and other risks.

(1) Due to an economic recession, the firm is losing clients. In response to the recession, the firm would like to take the following steps. The firm would like to cut each associate's salary by 20 percent and cancel all bonuses. Additionally, the firm has made offers for summer internship positions to 10 students. The firm originally told the students that the summer program would last 12 weeks and that the students would be paid $2,000 for each week worked. The firm wants to cut the summer program to 8 weeks. The firm believes these steps are necessary to avoid terminating current associates at the firm.

(2) The firm proposes to terminate all third-year associates, because they earn higher salaries than first- and second-year associates. Although there is an economic recession, the firm only needs to terminate associates because the partners want to increase the profits per partner. However, the firm wants to take the above steps and to use the economic recession as an excuse for terminating the associates.

(3) Prior to the recession, the firm sends a partner to conduct on-campus interviews for two available associate positions at the accounting firm. Rather than conduct substantive interviews, the partner decides to hire the first two individuals who showed up for the interviews wearing blue, pin-striped suits.

(4) Prior to the recession, a male partner at the firm hired a male associate he met during a golf tournament. The firm had not advertised that a position was available.

(5) A female associate is brutally beaten by her husband. When she reports the abuse to a partner at the firm, she is terminated. The reason given for her termination is that she was the victim of a violent crime, and the firm does not want to attract "that kind of attention."

(6) The firm is concerned about its image on social networking sites. It wants to adopt a policy of terminating the employment of any associate who posts material on a social networking site that may damage the firm's reputation or that casts any employees at the firm in a negative light. The policy would allow termination of associates who post pictures of themselves or others appearing to be inebriated, even if the conduct did not occur during work hours.

(7) An associate opposes the death penalty for social (not religious) reasons. The associate marches in an anti-death penalty rally. A partner at the firm finds out about the associate's participation in the march and recommends termination of the associate's employment.

### ✦ Core Concept: Putting the Federal Discrimination Statutes in Context

The federal employment discrimination statutes that are the central focus of this book are situated within a larger universe of state and federal laws governing the employment relationship. This section briefly introduces other important sources of law that apply to the employment relationship.

Numerous federal statutes provide protections for employees. The National Labor Relations Act (NLRA), the earliest provisions of which were enacted in 1935, guarantees many private-sector workers the right to unionize, to collectively bargain with their employers and to engage in other concerted activity. The National Labor Relations Board (NLRB) is the federal agency created by congress to administer the NLRA. A collective bargaining agreement can be an important source of rights and remedies for an employee, and employment lawyers should consider whether an employee may pursue remedies for violation of a collective bargaining agreement. Often, a collective bargaining agreement will provide mechanisms for informal resolution of disputes or for arbitration.

Further, unions have a duty of fair representation toward their members. Some employment discrimination lawsuits, therefore, raise claims against unions under both the applicable federal anti-discrimination statute and for breach of the union's duty of fair representation. *See* 29 U.S.C. § 185. These latter claims are sometimes referred to as § 301 claims, a reference to the section number of the original law.

Another major piece of federal legislation is the Fair Labor Standards Act (FLSA). The FLSA, which covers most employers in both the private and public sectors, regulates minimum wage for employees and establishes rules for the payment of overtime. The FLSA also limits the number of hours that employees under the age of 16 may work and prohibits employees under the age of 18 from working in certain dangerous jobs. The Department of Labor enforces the FLSA.

In 1963, the Equal Pay Act (EPA) amended the FLSA. The EPA prohibits certain types of pay discrimination based on sex. The sex discrimination aspects of the FLSA will be discussed in greater depth later in the book.

Enacted in 1993, the Family and Medical Leave Act (FMLA) is the federal statute that provides unpaid leave for certain workers. Only employees who meet the eligibility requirements of the FMLA are entitled to the unpaid leave, and the FMLA applies only to employees who work for local, state or federal government or who work at private employers who have 50 or more employees. FMLA leave is available if the employee has a serious health condition, if a member of the worker's immediate family has such a health condition, or for the birth or adoption of a child. The FMLA also requires the employer to continue making employer contributions to an employee's health insurance during the leave, and in many instances, requires that the employee be returned to the same or a substantially similar job upon returning from leave. Subsequent amendments to the FMLA provide unpaid leave for certain family members of individuals in the Armed Forces.

The Rehabilitation Act of 1973, a disability discrimination statute, is a precursor to the ADA. Many of the ADA's provisions were modeled on the Rehabilitation Act. In the employment context, the Rehabilitation Act prohibits certain federal employers, as well as federal contractors and entities that receive federal financial assistance, from discriminating against employees on the basis of disability.

The Immigration Reform and Control Act (IRCA) makes it illegal for employers to hire undocumented workers and requires that employers verify a worker's status to legally work within the country. In addition, IRCA prohibits discrimination on the basis of national origin. IRCA applies to employers with more than three employees. As discussed more in Chapter 2, Title VII also contains prohibitions against national origin discrimination; however, Title VII applies only to employers with 15 or more employees. Where IRCA and Title VII provide overlapping discrimination protections, IRCA requires that an employee proceed under Title VII. IRCA also prohibits citizenship discrimination against certain employees. Title VII, by contrast, does not directly prohibit citizenship discrimination.

Although this course focuses on federal anti-discrimination protections, keep in mind that state laws (and sometimes county and municipal ordinances) provide protections against workplace discrimination. In many instances an employee may bring claims under both federal and state law.

State law often plays an important role in protecting workers against discrimination. In some cases, state statutes provide greater protection than their federal counterparts. For example, the term "employer" is defined under some federal statutes as covering only those employers with a certain minimum number of employees. Employees who work for companies with fewer than fifteen employees do not fall within the employment discrimination protections of Title VII or the ADA, and a private employer must have at least fifty employees to fall within the reach of the FMLA. As a result, individuals who work for smaller employers often must rely on state statutes for discrimination protection.

Some state statutes provide protections for the same classes of individuals as the federal statutes, but define the protections differently. For example, some state disability statutes define the term "disability" more broadly than the term is defined under the ADA. *See, e.g.*, CAL. GOV'T CODE § 12926(k)(1)(b) (West 1992 & Supp. 2007) (defining a disability as, inter alia, a condition that "limits" a major life activity); CONN. GEN. STAT. § 46a-51(15) (2004) (defining disability to include "any chronic physical handicap, infirmity or impairment"). While the ADEA offers age discrimination protection only for those 40 and older, some states protect employees who are younger than 40 from age discrimination. *See, e.g.*, MINN. STAT. ANN. §§ 363a.03, 363a.08 (West 2004) (defining the protected age group to include individuals over the age of twenty-five); VT. STAT. ANN. tit. 21, § 495 (2001) (defining the protected age group to include individuals at least eighteen years of age).

In other instances, state statutes protect different categories of individuals from discrimination. For example, the state of Illinois prohibits employment discrimination because a person is a victim of domestic violence. *See* 820 Ill. Comp. Stat. 180/30 (Supp. 2008). Pennsylvania prohibits discrimination against an individual because the individual has a GED, rather than a high school diploma. *See* 43 PA. CONST. STAT. §§ 951, 955(k).

Federal and state statutes often provide different remedies. For example, a plaintiff proceeding on an ADEA discrimination claim cannot recover punitive damages or emotional distress damages; however, some state statutes allow age discrimination plaintiffs to recover both types of damages. Under Title VII, the amount of punitive and emotional distress damages that a plaintiff may obtain is limited by statutory caps. Some state discrimination regimes do not provide a statutory cap for such damages or have higher statutory caps. On the opposite end of the spectrum, some state discrimination statutes do not allow recovery of punitive damages at all, while others cap punitive damages at lower points than federal legislation. While some of the federal statutes do not allow lawsuits to proceed against individual supervisors, some state statutes provide for individual liability.

## ✦ Core Concept: Practical Realities of Employment Discrimination Claims

A discussion of the context for employment discrimination law would be incomplete without mention of the practical realities of litigation. The monetary costs of litigation are just the beginning. The time and emotional expense that litigation can extract warrant your client's serious consideration.

While litigation provides an avenue for plaintiffs to seek relief for discrimination, it can be a time-consuming, expensive, and risky endeavor for both plaintiffs and defendants. The average length of time between case filing and trial in federal court averages between one and three years, depending on the district court. State court litigation times vary widely. Years of appellate litigation may increase the time for case resolution.

For the plaintiff, taking a case to trial may mean the delay of much-needed remedies, as well as several years of life consumed by the lawsuit. For the defendant, the length of the litigation process may divert significant amounts of resources and employee time away from the employer's core business and toward the lawsuit.

The defendant is often concerned about the accrual of attorneys' fees, as defendants often pay their attorneys on an hourly basis, incurring fees for each hour of attorney time consumed. In most instances, the federal employment discrimination statutes do not allow a defendant to be reimbursed for attorney's fees, even when the defendant prevails at trial. The plaintiff's lawyer often takes cases on a contingency fee basis, which means the lawyer will not recover economically until the case has reached a resolution in favor of the plaintiff. As discussed later in the book, the federal employment discrimination statutes provide reimbursement of reasonable attorney's fees for prevailing plaintiffs in many instances; however, as discussed below, the likelihood of both getting to trial and prevailing may be small, depending on the cause of action. This financial dynamic plays an important role in decisions about whether to settle a case and in litigation strategy.

Outside of attorney costs, litigation can be expensive for other reasons. For the defendant, discovery may require making numerous witnesses available for deposition. Discovery rules often mean that the defendant is required to provide massive amounts of documents in response to discovery requests. With the advent of electronic discovery, the defendant may be required to hire an expert to ensure that it has complied with its obligations to provide computerized records. Often, significant amounts of attorney time are required to review such records. The defendant also may be faced with the prospect of being required to provide documents it had hoped to keep private. Although protective orders may be issued in some cases to protect the information from broad public disclosure, defendants are often unhappy about being required to provide such information to the opposing party.

While the plaintiff typically possesses fewer discoverable documents, the plaintiff's attorney may be required to spend large amounts of time reviewing boxes of documents produced by the defendant during discovery. Both parties may file motions to compel the production of discoverable material, as employment discrimination cases often involve disputes about the scope of discovery. For example, the plaintiff often seeks company-wide documents regarding all types of discrimination, while the defendant often attempts to limit discovery to information pertinent to the particular type of discrimination alleged by the plaintiff and the plaintiff's job unit. The defendant's lawyer often seeks broad discovery about a plaintiff's personal life, which the plaintiff's lawyer often tries to limit.

Both parties may be required to hire expert witnesses, who are typically expensive and paid by the hour for preparation time, deposition time, and court time. Doctors, psychologists, or other medical experts may be hired to establish or rebut a plaintiff's claim of emotional distress. Vocational experts may be necessary to testify about whether a plaintiff properly mitigated damages. Experts also may be necessary to assist lawyers in preparing and presenting statistical evidence or in presenting or rebutting damages calculations.

Litigation also can be expensive emotionally. The plaintiff usually believes that he or she has been discriminated against based on a protected trait or retaliated against. The defendant has been accused of discriminating, and often believes that such an accusation is unjustified.

Plaintiffs seeking emotional distress damages may be required to provide extensive information to the defendant about other sources of emotional distress. Such information may be relevant in a lawsuit because the defendant can argue that the plaintiff's emotional distress was not caused by the defendant. In many cases, defendants are able to obtain plaintiff's psychiatric records and other medical records and allowed to question the plaintiff extensively about the plaintiff's medical and psychiatric history during the deposition. Defendants also may seek information about other sources of emotional distress in a plaintiff's life, such as a divorce, a child custody battle, the death of a family member, or past job losses. In some cases, the defendant may depose the plaintiff's spouse, ex-spouse, children, or friends.

The after-acquired evidence affirmative defense, discussed later in the book, gives the defendant an incentive to investigate the plaintiff's history to uncover evidence of plaintiff's own wrongdoing. For example, the defendant may investigate whether the plaintiff made misstatements on an employment application, whether the plaintiff lied about why he or she needed time off work, or whether the plaintiff engaged in fraud. Plaintiffs who file suit to redress discrimination often feel re-victimized when they become the subjects of such investigation into their own wrongdoing.

A practicing lawyer must always keep in mind the result the client desires. A lawyer for the defendant may ultimately prevail at trial, but spend hundreds of thousands of dollars of the client's money. A plaintiff may want his or her old job back, but find that lengthy litigation has so poisoned the working relationship that a return to work is impossible. If the parties submit their dispute to the uncertainties of judicial resolution, neither side can be certain of the outcome. Studies have shown that summary judgment in favor of the defendant is granted in a high percentage of employment discrimination cases and that high damages awards are rare. Employment discrimination lawyers should always consider whether mediation or arbitration might provide better opportunities for resolving disputes and should fully counsel their clients about the range of options available for dispute resolution.

For a further discussion of likely recovery in employment discrimination cases, *see* Joseph A. Seiner, *The Failure of Punitive Damages in Employment Discrimination Cases: A Call for Change*, 50 Wm. & Mary L. Rev. 735, 741 (2008) (finding that punitive damages were awarded in slightly less than 18 percent of Title VII cases that resulted in a federal jury trial between 2004 and 2005); Kevin M. Clermont & Stewart J. Schwab, *How Employment Discrimination Plaintiffs Fare in Federal Court*, 1 J. Emp. Legal Stud. 429, 451–56 (2004); Ruth Colker, *The Americans with Disabilities Act: A Windfall for Defendants*, 34 Harv. C.R.-C.L. L. Rev. 99, 108 (1999) (reporting that either through dismissal or verdicts in ADA cases "[d]efendants prevailed in 448 of 475 cases (94%) at the trial court level and in 376 of 448 instances (84%) in which plaintiffs appealed these adverse judgments"); David Benjamin Oppenheimer, *Verdicts Matter: An Empirical Study of*

*California Employment Discrimination and Wrongful Discharge Jury Verdicts Reveal Low Success Rates for Women and Minorities*, 37 U.C. Davis L. Rev. 511, 517 (2003) (indicating low success rates for particular types of discrimination cases); Michael Selmi, *Why are Employment Discrimination Cases So Hard to Win?*, 61 La. L. Rev. 555, 556 (2001).

Understanding the remedies available for violations of discrimination laws is also fundamental knowledge for an employment discrimination attorney. A plaintiff's lawyer might consider whether the available remedies create enough of an incentive to pursue a case. The settlement value of a case often is determined by the types of damages that are available. For example, a case where punitive damages are both available and supported by the facts is likely to have a higher settlement value than one where punitive damages are not allowed by the statute under which the plaintiff is suing.

The most fundamental dynamic in an employment discrimination case is whether the plaintiff has a strong case or a weak case. To answer this question, it is important to understand the protections available under federal law, the proof structures for establishing such claims, the remedies available, and the administrative process required for claims brought under Title VII, the ADEA, and the ADA. The rest of the course focuses on these issues.

## ➤ Beyond the Basics: Statutory Interpretation and Administrative Deference

Because the foundation of federal employment discrimination law is statutory and because an administrative agency has some enforcement authority for these statutes, employment discrimination lawyers must understand basic principles of statutory interpretation and administrative deference. This section provides you with a brief and somewhat simplified overview of these two topics.

Although there are numerous statutory interpretation methodologies, three methodologies have primary importance for interpreting federal discrimination statutes: textualism, intentionalism, and purposivism.

Nearly all statutory constructions begin with an examination of the text of the statute itself. A lawyer approaching the statute from a textualist perspective is trying to discern the meaning of the statute from the terms of the statute itself. A textualist uses certain tools to discern the meaning of the statute, including canons of statutory construction, the dictionary meaning of words, the legal definitions of words, and the grammar and organization of the statutory provision and the larger statutory scheme. A pure textualist would reject the use of legislative history as an appropriate tool for discerning the meaning of a statute.

The other two methodologies of concern here consider context beyond the statutory language. An intentionalist approach to statutory interpretation seeks to determine what the legislature intended when it created the law. An intentionalist may use textualist tools to discern the meaning of a statute, but also considers legislative history to be an important tool. Statutory interpretation using a purposivist perspective seeks to construe the statute in the way that best gives effect to the statute's underlying purpose. This statutory interpretation methodology may rely on statements of policy contained within legislative history or codified within the statutes. It may also consider broader public policy arguments.

In many of the cases you read this semester you will see one or more of these methodologies being used. In some cases, each of these methodologies points to the same way to resolve a particular case. However, in the more difficult disputes, you will notice that the statutory interpretation technique espoused by the majority of the court greatly influences the case's outcome. As you read, consider the merits and drawbacks of each of these methodologies.

At times, use of statutory interpretation techniques does not provide a clear answer to the statute's meaning. In these cases, courts may turn to administrative interpretations of the statute for guidance. In such situations, courts use a body of court-made doctrine that articulates principles of administrative deference. These principles inform courts' decisions about the degree to which they should defer to an administrative agency's construction of a statute. For purposes of this class, two kinds of administrative deference are important: *Chevron* deference and *Skidmore* deference. *Chevron, U.S.A., Inc. v. Natural Resources Defense Council, Inc.*, 467 U.S. 837 (1984); *Skidmore v. Swift & Co.*, 323 U.S. 134, 140 (1994).

*Chevron* requires courts to defer to an agency's construction of a statute, when the statute's language is ambiguous and Congress has not directly spoken to the issue. *Chevron* requires deference when Congress delegated authority to the agency to make rules carrying the force of law, the agency interpretation claiming deference was promulgated in the exercise of that authority, and the agency interpretation is not procedurally defective, arbitrary or capricious in substance, or manifestly contrary to the statute. *See, e.g., U.S. v. Mead Corp.*, 533 U.S. 218, 227 (2001).

Under *Skidmore* deference, by contrast, agency interpretations are not given controlling authority, but constitute "a body of experience and informed judgments to which courts and litigants may properly resort for guidance." *Skidmore*, 323 U.S. at 140. In considering the agency's interpretation, the court will consider the thoroughness of the agency's interpretation, the validity of its reasoning, the consistency with earlier and later pronouncements and "all those factors which give it power to persuade, if lacking power to control." *Id.*

The federal agency typically charged with enforcing the employment discrimination laws is the Equal Employment Opportunity Commission (EEOC). Unfortunately, it is often difficult to determine the deference to be accorded the EEOC's interpretations of statutes. Complications arise for two separate reasons. First, Congress has granted the EEOC varying amounts of rulemaking power over Title VII, the ADEA, and the ADA. *See* 42 U.S.C. §2000e-12(a) (Title VII); 29 U.S.C. §628 (1994) (ADEA); 42 U.S.C. §12116 (ADA), ADA Amendments Act of 2008, Pub. L. No. 110-325, sec. 6(a)(2), 122 Stat. 3553, 3558. Second, the EEOC often provides its interpretations in informal mechanisms, not through more formal rulemaking. As you will see, the courts have not fully resolved when the EEOC is entitled to deference. For now, it is important to be aware that the deference to be accorded to the agency varies by statute and that deference may be affected by the mechanism through which the EEOC chooses to communicate its interpretation.

# Chapter 2

# Coverage of Statutes

In the United States, employment discrimination prohibitions have been enacted at all levels of government—municipal, county, state and federal. This casebook will focus primarily on the major federal statutory protections against employment discrimination: Title VII of the Civil Rights Act of 1964 (Title VII), the Age Discrimination in Employment Act (ADEA), the Americans with Disabilities Act (ADA), and 42 U.S.C. § 1981 (§ 1981). While this course centers on federal statutory protections, keep in mind that relief also may be available under state statutes, county or municipal ordinances, or common law or constitutional causes of action.

Not all individuals who are subjected to discrimination are entitled to proceed under the federal statutes, and not all people or entities that discriminate can be held liable under these statutes. This Chapter discusses three Core Concepts:

What traits or protected classes do the federal statutes cover?

Which individuals or entities are prohibited from discriminating or retaliating?

Which individuals do the federal statutes protect?

## ✦ Core Concept: Protected Classes

Title VII prohibits employment discrimination because of an "individual's race, color, religion, sex, or national origin." 42 U.S.C. § 2000e-2(a). In many Title VII cases, it is not disputed that the plaintiff falls into one or more of the classes protected by the statute, and in many cases, the definition of these terms is not contested. However, there have been several major controversies about the definition of certain protected traits.

In *General Elec. Co v. Gilbert*, for example, the Supreme Court interpreted Title VII's prohibition against "sex" discrimination as not including a prohibition against pregnancy discrimination. 429 U.S. 125 (1976). Congress later amended Title VII to define sex discrimination to include discrimination "because of or on the basis of pregnancy, childbirth, or related medical conditions." 42 U.S.C. § 2000e(k).

As indicated by its name, the ADEA prohibits employment discrimination based on age. 29 U.S.C. § 623(a). The ADEA does not protect all employees against age discrimination. It protects only those employees who are at least forty years old. 29 U.S.C. § 631(a). Like Title VII, ADEA cases often do not present difficult questions about whether the plaintiff falls within the protected class.

Title VII and the ADEA do not always prohibit discrimination based on the protected traits. Both statutes recognize certain affirmative defenses. For example, they both allow intentional discrimination on the basis of a protected trait, if that trait is a bona fide occupational qualification. 42 U.S.C. § 2000e-2(e); 29 U.S.C. § 623(f)(1). Although both statutes prohibit facially neutral practices that have a disparate impact on a protected group, they both permit such practices in certain cases.

Two other statutes provide additional protections against race and sex discrimination. Section 1981 prohibits certain types of race discrimination, providing that "[a]ll persons within the jurisdiction of the United States shall have the same right … to make and enforce contracts … as is enjoyed by white citizens." 42 U.S.C. § 1981. The Equal Pay Act (EPA) prohibits certain types of wage discrimination based on sex. 29 U.S.C. § 206(d)(1).

The ADA is an omnibus statute that prohibits disability discrimination in a variety of contexts. Title I of the statute applies to employment. The ADA prohibits discrimination against "a qualified individual on the basis of disability." 42 U.S.C. §§ 12102(1), 12112(a) & (b). It also protects an individual from discrimination based on his or her association with a person with a disability. 42 U.S.C § 12112(b)(4). Unlike Title VII and the ADEA, where the plaintiff's membership in a protected class is usually uncontested, ADA cases often turn on whether the plaintiff has a disability and is a "qualified individual," as those terms are defined by the ADA. Additional protection from disability discrimination is contained in the Rehabilitation Act of 1973, which applies to the federal government, programs receiving federal assistance, and federal contractors.

The primary federal statutory protections against employment discrimination are summarized in the following chart:

| Statute | Traits Protected | Notes |
|---|---|---|
| Title VII | Race, color, religion, sex, and national origin | |
| EPA | Sex | Prohibits wage discrimination |
| ADEA | Age 40 and over | |
| ADA | Disability, Association with a person with a disability | |
| Section 1981 | Race | Prohibits discrimination in the formation and performance of contracts |

Each of these statutes also prohibits retaliation in certain circumstances. An individual need not fall within a protected class to claim protection against retaliation. For example, a person is not required to have a disability to bring a claim for retaliation under the ADA.

Notice that none of the federal statutes explicitly prohibits discrimination on the basis of sexual orientation, marital status, or status as a parent. At the time of the writing of this book, Congress was giving serious consideration to enacting the Employment Non-Discrimination Act (ENDA), which would add federal protections against sexual orientation and gender-identity discrimination in employment; however, the legislation had not yet passed. Some courts have allowed sexual orientation or gender-identity discrimination claims to proceed under Title VII when the plaintiff alleges the employer engaged in sex stereotyping. Keep in mind that states, counties, and municipalities may provide more or different discrimination protections than those enumerated in the federal statutes.

The following discussion focuses on issues that arise in connection with defining protected classes under Title VII and the ADEA. This discussion is designed to present a survey of the types of issues that arise with respect to coverage. You will encounter more nuanced discussions of each of the protected traits in Chapters 7, 8 and 9, including a full discussion of religious discrimination (Chapter 7), disability discrimination (Chapter 8), and pregnancy discrimination (Chapter 9).

### Race and Color

Title VII prohibits discrimination based on an individual's race or color. Section 1981 also prohibits race discrimination. Before considering the definition of race, think about whether public policy should allow consideration of race in employment decisions.

---

### Exercise 2.1

You are the director of a private charitable organization charged with helping disadvantaged youth. Your organization focuses its efforts in a predominantly African-American neighborhood. You want to start a mentoring program for black students, and believe that black students will identify better with black mentors. When hiring mentors, should you, as a matter of public policy, be able to use race as a hiring criterion?

---

### Focus Questions: *McDonald v. Santa Fe Trail Transportation Co.*

1.  *Re-read the statutory language from Title VII and section 1981 quoted earlier in this chapter. Based on the statutory language does Title VII prohibit discrimination against white individuals? Does section 1981?*

2.  *As you read the case, consider whether the legislative history of Title VII and section 1981 answer the question posed. Do the underlying purposes of the statutes help resolve the question?*

3.  *As a matter of policy, should employment discrimination statutes prohibit so called "reverse discrimination" or should they just protect individuals who are part of historically discriminated against groups?*

4.  *Notice that certain employment discrimination claims require exhaustion of an administrative process before a claim can be filed in federal court. This administrative process will be discussed later in the book. Does section 1981 require resort to an administrative agency?*

---

## McDonald v. Santa Fe Trail Transportation Co.
### 427 U.S. 273 (1976)

Justice Marshall delivered the opinion of the Court.

[W]e must decide ... whether a complaint alleging that white employees charged with misappropriating property from their employer were dismissed from employment, while a black employee similarly charged was not dismissed, states a claim under Title VII. Second, we must decide whether section 1981, which provides that "(a)ll persons ... shall

have the same right ... to make and enforce contracts ... as is enjoyed by white citizens ..."
affords protection from racial discrimination in private employment to white persons as
well as nonwhites.

## I.

On September 26, 1970, petitioners, both white, and Charles Jackson, a Negro
employee of Santa Fe, were jointly and severally charged with misappropriating 60 one-
gallon cans of antifreeze which was part of a shipment Santa Fe was carrying for one of
its customers. Six days later, petitioners were fired by Santa Fe, while Jackson was retained.
A grievance was promptly filed with Local 988, pursuant to the collective-bargaining
agreement between the two respondents, but grievance proceedings secured no relief.
The following April, complaints were filed with the Equal Employment Opportunity
Commission (EEOC) charging that Santa Fe had discriminated against both petitioners
on the basis of their race in firing them, and that Local 988 had discriminated against
McDonald on the basis of his race in failing properly to represent his interests in the
grievance proceedings, all in violation of Title VII of the Civil Rights Act of 1964. Agency
process proved equally unavailing for petitioners, however, and the EEOC notified them
in July 1971 of their right under the Act to initiate a civil action in district court within
30 days. This suit followed, petitioners joining their section 1981 claim to their Title VII
allegations....

## II

Title VII of the Civil Rights Act of 1964 prohibits the discharge of "any individual"
because of "such individual's race," 42 U.S.C. § 2000e-2(a)(1). Its terms are not limited
to discrimination against members of any particular race. Thus, although we were not
there confronted with racial discrimination against whites, we described the Act in *Griggs
v. Duke Power Co.*, 401 U.S. 424, 431 (1971), as prohibiting "(d)iscriminatory preference
for Any (racial) group, Minority or Majority." Similarly the EEOC, whose interpretations
are entitled to great deference has consistently interpreted Title VII to proscribe racial
discrimination in private employment against whites on the same terms as racial discrimination against nonwhites, holding that to proceed otherwise would "constitute a derogation
of the Commission's Congressional mandate to eliminate all practices which operate to
disadvantage the employment opportunities of any group protected by Title VII, including
Caucasians." [citation omitted].

This conclusion is in accord with uncontradicted legislative history to the effect that
Title VII was intended to "cover white men and white women and all Americans," 110
Cong. Rec. 2578 (1964) (remarks of Rep. Celler), and create an "obligation not to
discriminate against whites," *Id.*, at 7218 (memorandum of Sen. Clark). We therefore
hold today that Title VII prohibits racial discrimination against the white petitioners in
this case upon the same standards as would be applicable were they Negroes and Jackson
white....

## III

Title 42 U.S.C. § 1981 provides in pertinent part: "All persons within the jurisdiction
of the United States shall have the same right in every State and Territory to make and
enforce contracts ... as is enjoyed by white citizens...." We have previously held, where
discrimination against Negroes was in question, that section 1981 affords a federal remedy
against discrimination in private employment on the basis of race, and respondents do
not contend otherwise....

While neither of the courts below elaborated its reasons for not applying section 1981 to racial discrimination against white persons, respondents suggest two lines of argument to support that judgment. First, they argue that by operation of the phrase "as is enjoyed by white citizens," section 1981 unambiguously limits itself to the protection of nonwhite persons against racial discrimination. Second, they contend that such a reading is consistent with the legislative history of the provision, which derives its operative language from section 1 of the Civil Rights Act of 1866.... The 1866 statute, they assert, was concerned predominantly with assuring specified civil rights to the former Negro slaves freed by virtue of the Thirteenth Amendment, and not at all with protecting the corresponding civil rights of white persons.

We find neither argument persuasive. Rather, our examination of the language and history of section 1981 convinces us that section 1981 is applicable to racial discrimination in private employment against white persons.

First, we cannot accept the view that the terms of section 1981 exclude its application to racial discrimination against white persons. On the contrary, the statute explicitly applies to "All persons," including white persons. While a mechanical reading of the phrase "as is enjoyed by white citizens" would seem to lend support to respondents' reading of the statute, we have previously described this phrase simply as emphasizing "the racial character of the rights being protected." In any event, whatever ambiguity there may be in the language of section 1981 is clarified by an examination of the legislative history of section 1981's language as it was originally forged in the Civil Rights Act of 1866. [The decision concludes with a lengthy discussion of legislative history and indicates that the legislative history supports its holding.]

While it is, of course, true that the immediate impetus for the bill was the necessity for further relief of the constitutionally emancipated former Negro slaves, the general discussion of the scope of the bill did not circumscribe its broad language to that limited goal....

---

## Notes

1. The *McDonald* case makes it possible for white workers to challenge affirmative action plans. You will learn later in the book that the law permits employers, in certain circumstances, to make race-based or sex-based decisions pursuant to valid affirmative action plans.

2. Recall that the ADA has a provision specifically prohibiting discrimination based on one's association with a person with a disability. Title VII does not technically protect individuals against discrimination based on their affiliations with other individuals. However, courts have permitted discrimination claims when an individual is discriminated against because the individual is married to a person of a different race. *See Parr v. Woodmen of World Life Ins. Co.*, 791 F.2d 888 (11th Cir. 1986).

### *National Origin*

## Focus Questions: *Saint Francis College v. Al-Khazraji*

1. *How is national origin defined? How is race defined?*

2. *Why is it so important for the Court to distinguish race and national origin?*

3.  *What methods does the Court use to determine the meaning of the term "race" in section 1981?*

4.  *Have definitions of race remained consistent over time?*

5.  *Is race biological or is race a social construct?*

---

# Saint Francis College v. Al-Khazraji

## 481 U.S. 604 (1987)

Justice White delivered the opinion of the Court.

Respondent, a citizen of the United States born in Iraq, was an associate professor at St. Francis College.... In January 1978, he applied for tenure; the Board of Trustees denied his request on February 23, 1978. He accepted a 1-year, nonrenewable contract and sought administrative reconsideration of the tenure decision, which was denied on February 6, 1979. He worked his last day at the college on May 26, 1979. In June 1979, he filed complaints with the Pennsylvania Human Relations Commission and the Equal Employment Opportunities Commission. The state agency dismissed his claim and the EEOC issued a right-to-sue letter on August 6, 1980.

On October 30, 1980, respondent filed a *pro se* complaint in the District Court alleging a violation of Title VII and claiming discrimination based on national origin, religion, and/or race. Amended complaints were filed, adding claims under 42 U.S.C. § 1981 ... and state law. The District Court dismissed the ... Title VII claims as untimely but held that the § 1981 claim [was not] barred by the Pennsylvania 6-year statute of limitations. Defendants' motion for summary judgment came up before a different judge, who construed the pleadings as asserting only discrimination on the basis of national origin and religion, which § 1981 did not cover. Even if racial discrimination was deemed to have been alleged, ... the District Court ruled that § 1981 does not reach claims of discrimination based on Arabian ancestry....

Reaching the merits, the Court of Appeals held that respondent had alleged discrimination based on race and that although under current racial classifications Arabs are Caucasians, respondent could maintain his § 1981 claim.[3] [Saint Francis College appealed.]

### II

... Section 1981 provides:

> All persons within the jurisdiction of the United States shall have the same right in every State and Territory to make and enforce contracts, to sue, be parties, give evidence, and to the full and equal benefit of all laws and proceedings for the security of persons and property as is enjoyed by white citizens, and shall be subject to like punishment, pains, penalties, taxes, licenses, and exactions of every kind, and to no other.

Although § 1981 does not itself use the word "race," the Court has construed the section to forbid all "racial" discrimination in the making of private as well as public contracts.... The issue is whether respondent has alleged *racial* discrimination within the meaning of § 1981.

---

3. The Court of Appeals also held that the individual members of the tenure committee were subject to liability under § 1981.

Petitioners contend that respondent is a Caucasian and cannot allege the kind of discrimination § 1981 forbids. Concededly, *McDonald v. Santa Fe Trail Transportation Co.*, 427 U.S. 273 (1976), held that white persons could maintain a § 1981 suit; but that suit involved alleged discrimination against a white person in favor of a black, and petitioner submits that the section does not encompass claims of discrimination by one Caucasian against another. We are quite sure that the Court of Appeals properly rejected this position.

Petitioner's submission rests on the assumption that all those who might be deemed Caucasians today were thought to be of the same race when § 1981 became law in the 19th century; and it may be that a variety of ethnic groups, including Arabs, are now considered to be within the Caucasian race.[4] The understanding of "race" in the 19th century, however, was different. Plainly, all those who might be deemed Caucasian today were not thought to be of the same race at the time § 1981 became law.

In the middle years of the 19th century, dictionaries commonly referred to race as a "continued series of descendants from a parent who is called the *stock*," N. Webster, An American Dictionary of the English Language 666 (New York 1830) (emphasis in original), "[t]he lineage of a family," 2 N. Webster, A Dictionary of the English Language 411 (New Haven 1841), or "descendants of a common ancestor," J. Donald, Chambers' Etymological Dictionary of the English Language 415 (London 1871). The 1887 edition of Webster's expanded the definition somewhat: "The descendants of a common ancestor; a family, tribe, people or nation, believed or presumed to belong to the same stock." N. Webster, Dictionary of the English Language 589 (W. Wheeler ed. 1887). It was not until the 20th century that dictionaries began referring to the Caucasian, Mongolian, and Negro races, 8 The Century Dictionary and Cyclopedia 4926 (1911), or to race as involving divisions of mankind based upon different physical characteristics. Webster's Collegiate Dictionary 794 (3d ed. 1916). Even so, modern dictionaries still include among the definitions of race "a family, tribe, people, or nation belonging to the same stock." Webster's Third New International Dictionary 1870 (1971); Webster's Ninth New Collegiate Dictionary 969 (1986).

Encyclopedias of the 19th century also described race in terms of ethnic groups, which is a narrower concept of race than petitioners urge. Encyclopedia Americana in 1858, for example, referred to various races such as Finns, gypsies, Basques, and Hebrews. The 1863 version of the New American Cyclopaedia divided the Arabs into a number of subsidiary races; represented the Hebrews as of the Semitic race, and identified numerous other groups as constituting races, including Swedes, Norwegians, Germans, Greeks, Finns, Italians, Spanish, Mongolians, Russians, and the like. The Ninth edition of the Encyclopedia Britannica also referred to Arabs, Jews, and other ethnic groups such as Germans, Hungarians, and Greeks, as separate races.

---

4. There is a common popular understanding that there are three major human races—Caucasoid, Mongoloid, and Negroid. Many modern biologists and anthropologists, however, criticize racial classifications as arbitrary and of little use in understanding the variability of human beings. It is said that genetically homogeneous populations do not exist and traits are not discontinuous between populations; therefore, a population can only be described in terms of relative frequencies of various traits. Clear-cut categories do not exist. The particular traits which have generally been chosen to characterize races have been criticized as having little biological significance. It has been found that differences between individuals of the same race are often greater than the differences between the "average" individuals of different races. These observations and others have led some, but not all, scientists to conclude that racial classifications are for the most part sociopolitical, rather than biological, in nature.

These dictionary and encyclopedic sources are somewhat diverse, but it is clear that they do not support the claim that for the purposes of § 1981, Arabs, Englishmen, Germans, and certain other ethnic groups are to be considered a single race. We would expect the legislative history of § 1981, which the Court held in *Runyon v. McCrary* had its source in the Civil Rights Act of 1866, as well as the Voting Rights Act of 1870, to reflect this common understanding, which it surely does. The debates are replete with references to the Scandinavian races, as well as the Chinese, Latin, Spanish, and Anglo-Saxon races. Jews, Mexicans, blacks, and Mongolians, were similarly categorized. Gypsies were referred to as a race.

...

The history of the 1870 Act reflects similar understanding of what groups Congress intended to protect from intentional discrimination. It is clear, for example, that the civil rights sections of the 1870 Act provided protection for immigrant groups such as the Chinese.... In the House, Representative Bingham described § 16 of the Act, part of the authority for § 1981, as declaring "that the States shall not hereafter discriminate against the immigrant from China and in favor of the immigrant from Prussia, nor against the immigrant from France and in favor of the immigrant from Ireland." [citation omitted].

Based on the history of § 1981, we have little trouble in concluding that Congress intended to protect from discrimination identifiable classes of persons who are subjected to intentional discrimination solely because of their ancestry or ethnic characteristics. Such discrimination is racial discrimination that Congress intended § 1981 to forbid, whether or not it would be classified as racial in terms of modern scientific theory. The Court of Appeals was thus quite right in holding that § 1981, "at a minimum," reaches discrimination against an individual "because he or she is genetically part of an ethnically and physiognomically distinctive sub-grouping of *homo sapiens.*" It is clear from our holding, however, that a distinctive physiognomy is not essential to qualify for § 1981 protection. If respondent on remand can prove that he was subjected to intentional discrimination based on the fact that he was born an Arab, rather than solely on the place or nation of his origin, or his religion, he will have made out a case under § 1981.

The judgment of the Court of Appeals is accordingly affirmed.

Justice Brennan, concurring.

Pernicious distinctions among individuals based solely on their ancestry are antithetical to the doctrine of equality upon which this Nation is founded. Today the Court upholds Congress' desire to rid the Nation of such arbitrary and invidious discrimination, and I concur in its opinion and judgment. I write separately only to point out that the line between discrimination based on "ancestry or ethnic characteristics," and discrimination based on "place or nation of ... origin," is not a bright one. It is true that one's ancestry— the ethnic group from which an individual and his or her ancestors are descended—is not necessarily the same as one's national origin—the country "where a person was *born*, or, more broadly, the country from which his or her ancestors *came.*" *Espinoza v. Farah Manufacturing Co.*, 414 U.S. 86, 88 (1973) (emphasis added). Often, however, the two are identical as a factual matter: one was born in the nation whose primary stock is one's own ethnic group. Moreover, national origin claims have been treated as ancestry or ethnicity claims in some circumstances. For example, in the Title VII context, the terms overlap as a legal matter. *See* 29 C.F.R. § 1606.1 (1986) (emphasis added) (national origin discrimination "includ[es], but [is] not limited to, the denial of equal employment opportunity because of an individual's, or his or her ancestor's, place of origin; *or* because an individual has the physical, cultural, or linguistic characteristics of a national origin group")....

## Note

In *Saint Francis College,* the Court construed section 1981 based on the understanding of "race" at the time Congress enacted that provision, during the 19th century. Title VII, by contrast, came into effect in the second half of the 20th century, when ideas about race had changed. Note that in some circumstances, the definition of race that applies in section 1981 cases may be different than the definition courts will apply in Title VII cases.

## Focus Questions: *Espinoza v. Farah Manufacturing Co.*

1. *Are policies to only hire United States citizens prohibited under Title VII?*

2. *What facts distinguish this case from other potential cases involving citizenship prohibitions?*

3. *What evidence does Farah Manufacturing submit to demonstrate that it does not discriminate on the basis of national origin?*

## Espinoza v. Farah Manufacturing Co.

### 414 U.S. 86 (1973)

Justice Marshall delivered the opinion of the Court.

This case involves interpretation of the phrase "national origin" in Title VII of the Civil Rights Act of 1964. Petitioner Cecilia Espinoza is a lawfully admitted resident alien who was born in and remains a citizen of Mexico. She resides in San Antonio, Texas, with her husband, Rudolfo Espinoza, a United States citizen. In July 1969, Mrs. Espinoza sought employment as a seamstress at the San Antonio division of respondent Farah Manufacturing Co. Her employment application was rejected on the basis of a longstanding company policy against the employment of aliens.... [Plaintiff exhausted her administrative remedies before the EEOC and filed suit].

[Title VII] makes it "an unlawful employment practice for an employer ... to fail or refuse to hire ... any individual ... because of such individual's race, color, religion, sex, or national origin." ... The term "national origin" on its face refers to the country where a person was born, or, more broadly, the country from which his or her ancestors came....

There are other compelling reasons to believe that Congress did not intend the term "national origin" to embrace citizenship requirements. Since 1914, the Federal Government itself, through Civil Service Commission regulations, has engaged in what amounts to discrimination against aliens by denying them the right to enter competitive examination for federal employment. But it has never been suggested that the citizenship requirement for federal employment constitutes discrimination because of national origin, even though since 1943, various Executive Orders have expressly prohibited discrimination on the basis of national origin in Federal Government employment.

... Congress itself has on several occasions since 1964 enacted statutes barring aliens from federal employment....

To interpret the term "national origin" to embrace citizenship requirements would require us to conclude that Congress itself has repeatedly flouted its own declaration of policy. This Court cannot lightly find such a breach of faith....

Suffice it to say that we cannot conclude Congress would at once continue the practice of requiring citizenship as a condition of federal employment and, at the same time, prevent private employers from doing likewise. Interpreting [Title VII] as petitioners suggest would achieve the rather bizarre result of preventing Farah from insisting on United States citizenship as a condition of employment while the very agency charged with enforcement of Title VII would itself be required by Congress to place such a condition on its own personnel.

The District Court drew primary support for its holding from an interpretative guideline issued by the Equal Employment Opportunity Commission which provides:

> Because discrimination on the basis of citizenship has the effect of discriminating on the basis of national origin, a lawfully immigrated alien who is domiciled or residing in this country may not be discriminated against on the basis of his citizenship....

29 C.F.R. § 1606.1(d) (1972).

Like the Court of Appeals, we have no occasion here to question the general validity of this guideline insofar as it can be read as an expression of the Commission's belief that there may be many situations where discrimination on the basis of citizenship would have the effect of discriminating on the basis of national origin. In some instances, for example, a citizenship requirement might be but one part of a wider scheme of unlawful national-origin discrimination. In other cases, an employer might use a citizenship test as a pretext to disguise what is in fact national-origin discrimination. Certainly Title VII prohibits discrimination on the basis of citizenship whenever it has the purpose or effect of discriminating on the basis of national origin. "The Act proscribes not only overt discrimination but also practices that are fair in form, but discriminatory in operation." *Griggs v. Duke Power Co.*, 401 U.S. 424, 431 (1971).

It is equally clear, however, that these principles lend no support to petitioners in this case. There is no indication in the record that Farah's policy against employment of aliens had the purpose or effect of discriminating against persons of Mexican national origin.[5] It is conceded that Farah accepts employees of Mexican origin, provided the individual concerned has become an American citizen. Indeed, the District Court found that persons of Mexican ancestry make up more than 96% of the employees at the company's San Antonio division, and 97% of those doing the work for which Mrs. Espinoza applied. While statistics such as these do not automatically shield an employer from a charge of unlawful discrimination, the plain fact of the matter is that Farah does not discriminate against persons of Mexican national origin with respect to employment in the job Mrs. Espinoza sought. She was denied employment, not because of the country of her origin, but because she had not yet achieved United States citizenship. In fact, the record shows that the worker hired in place of Mrs. Espinoza was a citizen with a Spanish surname.

---

5. There is no suggestion, for example, that the company refused to hire aliens of Mexican or Spanish-speaking background while hiring those of other national origins. Respondent's president informed the EEOC's Regional Director investigating the charge that once in its history the company had made a single exception to its policy against hiring aliens, but the nationality of the individual concerned is not revealed in the record. While the company asks job applicants whether they are United States citizens, it makes no inquiry as to their national origin.

The Commission's guideline may have significance for a wide range of situations, but not for a case such as this where its very premise—that discrimination on the basis of citizenship has the effect of discrimination on the basis of national origin—is not borne out.[6] ...

Finally, petitioners seek to draw support from the fact that Title VII protects all individuals from unlawful discrimination, whether or not they are citizens of the United States. We agree that aliens are protected from discrimination under the Act. That result may be derived not only from the use of the term "any individual" in section 703, but also as a negative inference from the exemption in section 702, which provides that Title VII "shall not apply to an employer with respect to the employment of aliens outside any State...." 42 U.S.C. § 2000e-1. Title VII was clearly intended to apply with respect to the employment of aliens inside any State.[7]

The question posed in the present case, however, is not whether aliens are protected from illegal discrimination under the Act, but what kinds of discrimination the Act makes illegal. Certainly it would be unlawful for an employer to discriminate against aliens because of race, color, religion, sex, or national origin—for example, by hiring aliens of Anglo-Saxon background but refusing to hire those of Mexican or Spanish ancestry. Aliens are protected from illegal discrimination under the Act, but nothing in the Act makes it illegal to discriminate on the basis of citizenship or alienage.

We agree with the Court of Appeals that neither the language of the Act, nor its history, nor the specific facts of this case indicate that respondent has engaged in unlawful discrimination because of national origin.

Justice Douglas, dissenting.

... Alienage results from one condition only: being born outside the United States. Those born within the country are citizens from birth. It could not be more clear that Farah's policy of excluding aliens is de facto a policy of preferring those who were born in this country. Therefore the construction placed upon the "national origin" provision is inconsistent with the construction this Court has placed upon the same Act's protections for persons denied employment on account of race or sex.

In connection with racial discrimination we have said that the Act prohibits "practices, procedures, or tests neutral on their face, and even neutral in terms of intent," if they create "artificial, arbitrary, and unnecessary barriers to employment when the barriers operate invidiously to discriminate on the basis of racial or other impermissible classification." *Griggs v. Duke Power Co.*, 401 U.S. 424, 430–431 (1971). There we found that the employer could not use test or diploma requirements which on their face were racially neutral, when in fact those requirements had a de facto discriminatory result and the employer was unable to justify them as related to job performance. The tests involved in *Griggs* did not eliminate all blacks seeking employment, just as the citizenship requirement here does not eliminate all applicants of foreign origin. Respondent here explicitly conceded that the citizenship requirement is imposed without regard to the alien's qualifications for the job....

---

6. It is suggested that a refusal to hire an alien always disadvantages that person because of the country of his birth. A person born in the United States, the argument goes, automatically obtains citizenship at birth, while those born elsewhere can acquire citizenship only through a long and sometimes difficult process. The answer to this argument is that it is not the employer who places the burdens of naturalization on those born outside the country, but Congress itself....

7. Title VII protects all individuals, both citizens and noncitizens, domiciled or residing in the United States, against discrimination on the basis of race, color, religion, sex, or national origin.

## Notes

1. The EEOC defines national origin discrimination to include discrimination based on (1) being from a certain place or (2) belonging to a particular national origin group.

According to the EEOC's *Compliance Manual on National Origin Discrimination*: "National origin discrimination includes discrimination because a person (or his or her ancestors) comes from a particular place. The place is usually a country or a former country, for example, Colombia or Serbia. In some cases, the place has never been a country, but is closely associated with a group of people who share a common language, culture, ancestry, and/or other similar social characteristics, for example, Kurdistan."

The *Manual* further notes: "A 'national origin group,' often referred to as an 'ethnic group,' is a group of people sharing a common language, culture, ancestry, and/or other similar social characteristics. Title VII prohibits employment discrimination against any national origin group, including larger ethnic groups, such as Hispanics and Arabs, and smaller ethnic groups, such as Kurds or Roma (Gypsies). National origin discrimination includes discrimination against American Indians or members of a particular tribe."

The EEOC further interprets the national origin prohibitions as extending to physical, linguistic, or cultural traits that are associated with a particular national origin. In-depth coverage of this type of discrimination is provided in the National Origin section of Chapter 9.

2. The Immigration Reform and Control Act ("IRCA") prohibits national origin discrimination in hiring and termination and also prohibits discrimination based on citizenship, but only in certain statutorily defined instances. 8 U.S.C. § 1324(b)(a). IRCA also makes it illegal for an employer to hire undocumented workers and requires employers to verify an employee's status to work legally. 8 U.S.C. § 1324a. If an employer asks for verification documents other than those allowed under the statute, such a request is considered to be an unlawful practice. 8 U.S.C. § 1324b(a)(6).

3. For a discussion regarding whether rules that require the speaking of English in the workplace violate Title VII, see Chapter 9.

4. Title VII contains a national security exception. This exception permits an employer to refuse to hire or continue to employ an individual if the person does not meet a requirement imposed by a statute or an executive order in the interest of national security. 42 U.S.C. § 2000e-2(g). The national security exception most commonly arises in situations where an individual does not qualify for a required security clearance.

### *Religion*

Title VII prohibits employment discrimination on the basis of religion. Under Title VII, the term "religion" includes "all aspects of religious observance and practice, as well as belief, unless an employer demonstrates that he is unable to reasonably accommodate an employee's or prospective employee's religious observance or practice without undue hardship on the conduct of the employer's business." 42 U.S.C. § 2000e(j). As discussed in more detail later in the book, the religious discrimination provisions of Title VII both prohibit discrimination based on a person's religion and also require limited accommodation of an individual's religious practice.

Title VII does not otherwise define the term "religion," and in many cases, further definition is not required, especially where the religion at issue is widely accepted as such.

The Supreme Court in a non-Title VII case defined religious belief as a sincere belief that occupies in the life of the believer a place parallel to that of God in traditional religions. *See U.S. v. Seeger*, 380 U.S. 163, 165–66 (1965).

The EEOC has provided further guidance on the definition of religious practice. The EEOC defines religious practices to include "moral or ethical beliefs as to what is right and wrong which are sincerely held with the strength of traditional religious views." *See* 29 C.F.R. § 1605.1. An individual's beliefs may be protected even though no specific religious organization espouses them. *See id.* The fact that the religious group to which an individual professes belonging does not espouse a particular belief or practice does not prohibit that belief or practice from being considered a religious one. *See id.*

In some circumstances, it is not legally important whether a person holds a particular religious belief. For example, if a person is terminated because an employer perceives him to be Jewish, whether the individual is actually Jewish is not legally relevant.

Title VII specifically allows some religious discrimination. A religious corporation, association, educational institution, or society may discriminate with respect to the employment of individuals of a particular religion to perform work connected with its activities. 42 U.S.C. § 2000e-1(a). According to the EEOC, this exemption applies to an organization "whose purpose and character" is primarily religious. EEOC COMPLIANCE MANUAL, § 2-III.B.4.b.i.

The religious organization exemption applies to all positions within an organization, not just those involving religious doctrine. Note that this provision only allows discrimination based on religious grounds. The EEOC interprets the provision as applying only to hiring and termination issues and not to other terms and conditions of employment, such as wages. EEOC COMPLIANCE MANUAL, § 2-III.B.4.b.i.

Title VII also provides an exemption for certain educational institutions. That exemption provides as follows:

> it shall not be an unlawful employment practice for a school, college, university, or educational institution or institution of learning to hire and employ employees of a particular religion if such school, college, university, or other educational institution or institution of learning is, in whole or in substantial part, owned, supported, controlled, or managed by a particular religion or by a particular religious corporation, association, or society, or if the curriculum of such school, college, university, or other educational institution or institution of learning is directed toward the propagation of a particular religion.

42 U.S.C. § 2000e-2(e)(2).

In addition to these statutory exemptions, the Supreme Court has held that clergy members and other similar employees cannot bring claims under the federal employment discrimination statutes because such claims would violate the Establishment and Free Exercise Clauses of the Constitution. *Hosanna-Tabor Evangelical Lutheran Church and School v. Equal Employment Opportunity Commission*, 565 U.S. ___ (2012). This exception is referred to as the "ministerial" exception. For more discussion of these issues, see the discussion of Religion in Chapter 7.

---

## Exercise 2.2

You work in the Human Resources department of a large company that is not a religious organization. You have been asked to evaluate several requests for accommodation. Before you can do that, you must determine whether the following constitute religious practices as that term is understood under Title VII.

(a) The Church of Body Modification was established in 1999. Its mission statement indicates the church was founded to "promote growth in mind, body, and spirit." The Church believes that its members can promote such growth by engaging in practices such as piercing, tattooing, branding, cutting, and body manipulation. An employee has numerous facial piercings and tattoos and claims that these were obtained as part of her membership in the Church of Body Modification.

(b) An employee is an atheist and does not want to attend a prayer service that is being held during work hours.

(c) An employee wants to wear a religious medallion to work and claims that the tenets of Judaism require the medallion to be worn. The religion does not require the wearing of a medallion.

(d) An employee wants a day off of work, which he claims is needed because his religion prohibits him from working on Saturdays. His religion does prohibit Saturday work; however, through conversations with other employees, you have learned the employee works a second job on Saturdays.

(e) An employee wants time off of work to attend an anti-abortion rally.

---

## Sex

The Title VII prohibition against sex discrimination gives rise to a broad variety of claims, ranging from harassment to pregnancy discrimination to pay discrimination. That full range is discussed in later chapters of the book. This introductory case, *Los Angeles v. Manhart*, provides a perspective on the Supreme Court's efforts to grapple with when discrimination is because of sex.

### Focus Questions: *City of Los Angeles, Dept. of Water & Power v. Manhart*

1. *Does Title VII prohibit discrimination based on actual differences that exist between men and women?*

2. *What statutory language within Title VII supports the Court's holding?*

# City of Los Angeles, Dept. of Water & Power v. Manhart
## 435 U.S. 702 (1978)

Justice Stevens delivered the opinion of the Court.

As a class, women live longer than men. For this reason, the Los Angeles Department of Water and Power required its female employees to make larger contributions to its pension fund than its male employees. We granted certiorari to decide whether this practice discriminated against individual female employees because of their sex in violation of § 703(a)(1) of the Civil Rights Act of 1964, as amended.

For many years the Department has administered retirement, disability, and death-benefit programs for its employees. Upon retirement each employee is eligible for a monthly retirement benefit computed as a fraction of his or her salary multiplied by years of service. The monthly benefits for men and women of the same age, seniority, and salary are equal. Benefits are funded entirely by contributions from the employees and the Department, augmented by the income earned on those contributions. No private insurance company is involved in the administration or payment of benefits.

Based on a study of mortality tables and its own experience, the Department determined that its 2,000 female employees, on the average, will live a few years longer than its 10,000 male employees. The cost of a pension for the average retired female is greater than for the average male retiree because more monthly payments must be made to the average woman. The Department therefore required female employees to make monthly contributions to the fund which were 14.84% higher than the contributions required of comparable male employees. Because employee contributions were withheld from paychecks a female employee took home less pay than a male employee earning the same salary.

… [R]espondents brought this suit in the United States District Court for the Central District of California on behalf of a class of women employed or formerly employed by the Department. They prayed for an injunction and restitution of excess contributions.

While this action was pending, the California Legislature enacted a law prohibiting certain municipal agencies from requiring female employees to make higher pension fund contributions than males. The Department therefore amended its plan, effective January 1, 1975. The current plan draws no distinction, either in contributions or in benefits, on the basis of sex. On a motion for summary judgment, the District Court held that the contribution differential violated § 703(a)(1) and ordered a refund of all excess contributions made before the amendment of the plan. The United States Court of Appeals for the Ninth Circuit affirmed.

The Department and various *amici curiae* contend that the differential in take-home pay between men and women was not discrimination within the meaning of § 703(a)(1) because it was offset by a difference in the value of the pension benefits provided to the two classes of employees.…

I

There are both real and fictional differences between women and men. It is true that the average man is taller than the average woman; it is not true that the average woman driver is more accident prone than the average man. Before the Civil Rights Act of 1964 was enacted, an employer could fashion his personnel policies on the basis of assumptions about the differences between men and women, whether or not the assumptions were valid.

It is now well recognized that employment decisions cannot be predicated on mere "stereotyped" impressions about the characteristics of males or females.[8] Myths and purely habitual assumptions about a woman's inability to perform certain kinds of work are no longer acceptable reasons for refusing to employ qualified individuals, or for paying them

---

8. "In forbidding employers to discriminate against individuals because of their sex, Congress intended to strike at the entire spectrum of disparate treatment of men and women resulting from sex stereotypes. Section 703(a)(1) subjects to scrutiny and eliminates such irrational impediments to job opportunities and enjoyment which have plagued women in the past." [citation omitted].

less. This case does not, however, involve a fictional difference between men and women. It involves a generalization that the parties accept as unquestionably true: Women, as a class, do live longer than men. The Department treated its women employees differently from its men employees because the two classes are in fact different. It is equally true, however, that all individuals in the respective classes do not share the characteristic that differentiates the average class representatives. Many women do not live as long as the average man and many men outlive the average woman. The question, therefore, is whether the existence or nonexistence of "discrimination" is to be determined by comparison of class characteristics or individual characteristics. A "stereotyped" answer to that question may not be the same as the answer that the language and purpose of the statute command.

The statute makes it unlawful "to discriminate against any *individual* with respect to his compensation, terms, conditions, or privileges of employment, because of such *individual's* race, color, religion, sex, or national origin." 42 U.S.C. § 2000e-2(a)(1) (emphasis added). The statute's focus on the individual is unambiguous. It precludes treatment of individuals as simply components of a racial, religious, sexual, or national class. If height is required for a job, a tall woman may not be refused employment merely because, on the average, women are too short. Even a true generalization about the class is an insufficient reason for disqualifying an individual to whom the generalization does not apply.

That proposition is of critical importance in this case because there is no assurance that any individual woman working for the Department will actually fit the generalization on which the Department's policy is based. Many of those individuals will not live as long as the average man. While they were working, those individuals received smaller paychecks because of their sex, but they will receive no compensating advantage when they retire.

It is true, of course, that while contributions are being collected from the employees, the Department cannot know which individuals will predecease the average woman. Therefore, unless women as a class are assessed an extra charge, they will be subsidized, to some extent, by the class of male employees. It follows, according to the Department, that fairness to its class of male employees justifies the extra assessment against all of its female employees.

But the question of fairness to various classes affected by the statute is essentially a matter of policy for the legislature to address. Congress has decided that classifications based on sex, like those based on national origin or race, are unlawful. Actuarial studies could unquestionably identify differences in life expectancy based on race or national origin, as well as sex.[9] But a statute that was designed to make race irrelevant in the employment market could not reasonably be construed to permit a take-home-pay differential based on a racial classification.

Even if the statutory language were less clear, the basic policy of the statute requires that we focus on fairness to individuals rather than fairness to classes. Practices that classify employees in terms of religion, race, or sex tend to preserve traditional assumptions about groups rather than thoughtful scrutiny of individuals. The generalization involved in this case illustrates the point. Separate mortality tables are easily interpreted as reflecting innate differences between the sexes; but a significant part of the longevity differential may be explained by the social fact that men are heavier smokers than women.

Finally, there is no reason to believe that Congress intended a special definition of discrimination in the context of employee group insurance coverage. It is true that insurance

---

9. For example, the life expectancy of a white baby in 1973 was 72.2 years; a nonwhite baby could expect to live 65.9 years, a difference of 6.3 years.

is concerned with events that are individually unpredictable, but that is characteristic of many employment decisions. Individual risks, like individual performance, may not be predicted by resort to classifications proscribed by Title VII. Indeed, the fact that this case involves a group insurance program highlights a basic flaw in the Department's fairness argument. For when insurance risks are grouped, the better risks always subsidize the poorer risks. Healthy persons subsidize medical benefits for the less healthy; unmarried workers subsidize the pensions of married workers; persons who eat, drink, or smoke to excess may subsidize pension benefits for persons whose habits are more temperate. Treating different classes of risks as though they were the same for purposes of group insurance is a common practice that has never been considered inherently unfair. To insure the flabby and the fit as though they were equivalent risks may be more common than treating men and women alike; but nothing more than habit makes one "subsidy" seem less fair than the other.[10]

[A discussion regarding the Equal Pay Act is omitted.]

### IV

The Department challenges the District Court's award of retroactive relief to the entire class of female employees and retirees. Title VII does not require a district court to grant any retroactive relief. A court that finds unlawful discrimination "may enjoin [the discrimination] ... and order such affirmative action as may be appropriate, which may include, but is not limited to, reinstatement ... with or without back pay ... or any other equitable relief as the court deems appropriate." 42 U.S.C. § 2000e-5(g). To the point of redundancy, the statute stresses that retroactive relief "may" be awarded if it is "appropriate."

...

For several reasons, we conclude that the District Court gave insufficient attention to the equitable nature of Title VII remedies. Although we now have no doubt about the application of the statute in this case, we must recognize that conscientious and intelligent administrators of pension funds, who did not have the benefit of the extensive briefs and arguments presented to us, may well have assumed that a program like the Department's was entirely lawful. The courts had been silent on the question, and the administrative agencies had conflicting views. The Department's failure to act more swiftly is a sign, not of its recalcitrance, but of the problem's complexity. As commentators have noted, pension administrators could reasonably have thought it unfair — or even illegal — to make male employees shoulder more than their "actuarial share" of the pension burden. There is no reason to believe that the threat of a backpay award is needed to cause other administrators to amend their practices to conform to this decision.

Nor can we ignore the potential impact which changes in rules affecting insurance and pension plans may have on the economy. Fifty million Americans participate in retirement plans other than Social Security. The assets held in trust for these employees are vast and

---

10. A variation on the Department's fairness theme is the suggestion that a gender-neutral pension plan would itself violate Title VII because of its disproportionately heavy impact on male employees. *Cf. Griggs v. Duke Power Co.*, 401 U.S. 424, 91 (1971). This suggestion has no force in the sex discrimination context because each retiree's total pension benefits are ultimately determined by his *actual life span*; any differential in benefits paid to men and women in the aggregate is thus "based on [a] factor other than sex," and consequently immune from challenge under the Equal Pay Act, 29 U.S.C. § 206(d). Even under Title VII itself, assuming disparate-impact analysis applies to fringe benefits, the male employees would not prevail. Even a completely neutral practice will inevitably have *some* disproportionate impact on one group or another. *Griggs* does not imply, and this Court has never held, that discrimination must always be inferred from such consequences.

growing—more than $400 billion was reserved for retirement benefits at the end of 1976 and reserves are increasing by almost $50 billion a year. These plans, like other forms of insurance depend on the accumulation of large sums to cover contingencies. The amounts set aside are determined by a painstaking assessment of the insurer's likely liability. Risks that the insurer foresees will be included in the calculation of liability, and the rates or contributions charged will reflect that calculation. The occurrence of major unforeseen contingencies, however, jeopardizes the insurer's solvency and, ultimately, the insureds' benefits. Drastic changes in the legal rules governing pension and insurance funds, like other unforeseen events, can have this effect. Consequently, the rules that apply to these funds should not be applied retroactively unless the legislature has plainly commanded that result....

There can be no doubt that the prohibition against sex-differentiated employee contributions represents a marked departure from past practice. Although Title VII was enacted in 1964, this is apparently the first litigation challenging contribution differences based on valid actuarial tables. Retroactive liability could be devastating for a pension fund. The harm would fall in large part on innocent third parties. If, as the courts below apparently contemplated, the plaintiffs' contributions are recovered from the pension fund, the administrators of the fund will be forced to meet unchanged obligations with diminished assets. If the reserve proves inadequate, either the expectations of all retired employees will be disappointed or current employees will be forced to pay not only for their own future security but also for the unanticipated reduction in the contributions of past employees....

Justice Brennan took no part in the consideration or decision of this case.

Justice Blackmun, concurring in part and concurring in the judgment.

... Given [the Court's prior decisions], the present case just cannot be an easy one for the Court. I might have thought that those decisions would have required the Court to conclude that the critical difference in the Department's pension payments was based on life expectancy, a nonstigmatizing factor that demonstrably differentiates females from males and that is not measurable on an individual basis. I might have thought, too, that there is nothing arbitrary, irrational, or "discriminatory" about recognizing the objective and accepted disparity in female-male life expectancies in computing rates for retirement plans. Moreover, it is unrealistic to attempt to force, as the Court does, an individualized analysis upon what is basically an insurance context. Unlike the possibility, for example, of properly testing job applicants for qualifications before employment, there is simply no way to determine in advance when a particular employee will die....

Chief Justice Burger, with whom Justice Rehnquist joins, concurring in part and dissenting in part.

... Gender-based actuarial tables have been in use since at least 1843, and their statistical validity has been repeatedly verified. The vast life insurance, annuity, and pension plan industry is based on these tables. As the Court recognizes, it is a fact that "women, as a class, do live longer than men." It is equally true that employers cannot know in advance when individual members of the classes will die. Yet, if they are to operate economically workable group pension programs, it is only rational to permit them to rely on statistically sound and proved disparities in longevity between men and women. Indeed, it seems to me irrational to assume Congress intended to outlaw use of the fact that, for whatever reasons or combination of reasons, women as a class outlive men.

...

The reality of differences in human mortality is what mortality experience tables reflect. The difference is the added longevity of women. All the reasons why women statistically outlive men are not clear. But categorizing people on the basis of sex, the one acknowledged immutable difference between men and women, is to take into account all of the unknown reasons, whether biologically or culturally based, or both, which give women a significantly greater life expectancy than men. It is therefore true as the Court says, "that any individual's life expectancy is based on a number of factors, of which sex is only one." But it is not true that by seizing upon the only constant, "measurable" factor, no others were taken into account. All other factors, whether known but variable — or unknown — are the elements which automatically account for the actuarial disparity. And all are accounted for when the constant factor is used as a basis for determining the costs and benefits of a group pension plan....

This is in no sense a failure to treat women as "individuals" in violation of the statute, as the Court holds. It is to treat them as individually as it is possible to do in the face of the unknowable length of each individual life. Individually, every woman has the same statistical possibility of outliving men. This is the essence of basing decisions on reliable statistics when individual determinations are infeasible or, as here, impossible.

Of course, women cannot be disqualified from, for example, heavy labor just because the generality of women are thought not as strong as men — a proposition which perhaps may sometime be statistically demonstrable, but will remain individually refutable. When, however, it is impossible to tailor a program such as a pension plan to the individual, nothing should prevent application of reliable statistical facts to the individual, for whom the facts cannot be disproved until long after planning, funding, and operating the program have been undertaken.

----

## Notes

1. Title VII does not contain any requirement of accommodation based on sex, including for childcare or other family responsibilities that may fall disproportionately on women. However, a woman may not be discriminated against based on assumptions related to her childcare or other family responsibilities. For example, Title VII would prohibit an employer from refusing to consider a recent mother for promotion because it assumes that she would not want to take on additional responsibilities while parenting a young child, while not making similar assumptions about new fathers. Further information regarding discrimination based on being a mother is contained in Chapter 9.

2. Among other things, the FMLA provides twelve weeks of unpaid leave to certain employees to care for a newborn child, to care for an adopted child, or to care for certain members of the worker's immediate family with serious health conditions. Although the FMLA provides protections for both male and female employees, the FMLA was enacted in part to alleviate workplace inequalities that existed because women traditionally bear more childcare and family care responsibilities. You will encounter these topics in more detail in Chapter 9.

3. Although some state statutes prohibit discrimination based on marital status, Title VII does not. However, Title VII does prohibit employers from treating men and women differently based on marital status. If an employer is willing to hire married men, but not married women, this refusal violates Title VII. Courts sometimes use the term, "sex-

plus" to describe such discrimination, where the protected trait PLUS an additional trait (here marriage) are being held against the employee. Many courts conclude that the fact that it is only a subset of women (the married ones) who are harmed does not keep this from being discrimination. The Second Circuit has explained that "[t]he term 'sex-plus' or 'gender plus' is simply a heuristic. It is, in other words, a judicial convenience developed in the context of Title VII to affirm that plaintiffs can, under certain circumstances, survive summary judgment even when not all members of a disfavored class are discriminated against." *Back v. Hastings on Hudson*, 365 F.3d 107, 118 (2d Cir. 2004).

4. The courts have allowed employers to implement gender-specific grooming and dress codes in certain circumstances. Grooming and dress codes are discussed in more detail in Chapter 9.

## Exercise 2.3

An employer would like to implement a policy that prohibits spouses from working in the same department. The policy would affect both new hires and individuals who become married while working at the company. The company asks you to draft a policy. Draft the policy and provide the company with advice regarding both the legality and desirability of implementing such a plan. Is such a policy legal under Title VII? Should the company implement this policy?

In some situations the law requires or prohibits certain actions; however, in other situations the law permits a wide range of options. Think about the attorney's role in these latter situations. In completing this exercise, consider an attorney's role as a counselor. Rule 2.1 of the Model Rules of Professional Conduct provides: "In representing a client, a lawyer shall exercise independent professional judgment and render candid advice. In rendering advice, a lawyer may refer not only to law but to other considerations such as moral, economic, social and political factors, that may be relevant to the client's situation."

The creation of employment policies should be an interactive process between an attorney and her client. This process can serve an important function of allowing an attorney to gain a better understanding of the needs of the employer and to communicate important information to management about legal obligations. As a client counselor, an attorney will likely need to be able to explain why a particular policy is necessary or preferred.

Of course, when creating employment policies, an attorney should consider the applicable legal standards. However, this inquiry is just the first step in crafting a policy. A good lawyer will make sure she gathers information from appropriate sources about a myriad of issues, including the structure of the workplace, the reasons supporting the policies, and the factual contexts in which the policy is likely to be implicated. The attorney should consider the employer's past practices on a particular issue and whether a new policy is warranted. Ineffective policies often result from the failure to obtain support and buy-in from affected parties during the policy drafting stage.

In many instances, an attorney will begin the drafting process by looking for comparable policies used by other employers. The drafting process should allow the client an opportunity to comment or edit the policy prior to its distribution. When drafting the policy, consider whether a procedure needs to be adopted to enforce the policy. Care should be taken to consider who will be responsible for enforcing the policy and ensuring that the policy is consistently enforced. Consideration should be given to how the policy will be communicated to employees and whether training will be given to managers or employees.

In drafting a policy, remember that most individuals reading the policy will not be lawyers. Policies should be written in plain English. Where possible, the policy should be easy to follow.

## Age

Although the ADEA prohibits discrimination on the basis of age, it protects only individuals who are at least 40 years old from such discrimination. 29 U.S.C. §631(a). Some states provide age discrimination protections for younger employees. Prior versions of the ADEA contained upper age limits after which employees would no longer be covered by the statute; Congress removed those upper age limits in 1986.

The ADEA permits an employer to require compulsory retirement for certain bona fide executives and high-level policymakers who have attained the age of 65. 29 U.S.C. §631(c). This permission extends only to individuals who have been employed as bona fide executives or in high policymaking positions for the two-year period immediately preceding retirement and who are entitled to certain levels of statutorily defined retirement benefits. *Id.*

The ADEA also permits age to be taken into account in hiring and retirement policies for firefighters and law enforcement officers in circumstances defined by the statute. 29 U.S.C. §631(j).

---

### Focus Questions: *Hazen Paper Co. v. Biggins*

1.  *What is the difference between a disparate impact claim and a disparate treatment claim?*

2.  *What correlation does the plaintiff want the court to draw? Why does the Court refuse to draw it?*

3.  *Can you think of other factors that might correlate with age?*

4.  *Notice what the Court describes as the policies that gave rise to enactment of the ADEA. Do you think these are likely to be similar to those that gave rise to enactment of Title VII?*

---

# Hazen Paper Co. v. Biggins

## 507 U.S. 604 (1993)

Justice O'Connor delivered the opinion of the Court.

… Petitioner Hazen Paper Company manufactures coated, laminated, and printed paper and paperboard. The company is owned and operated by two cousins, petitioners Robert Hazen and Thomas N. Hazen. The Hazens hired respondent Walter F. Biggins as their technical director in 1977. They fired him in 1986, when he was 62 years old.

Respondent brought suit against petitioners in the United States District Court for the District of Massachusetts, alleging a violation of the ADEA. He claimed that age had been a determinative factor in petitioners' decision to fire him....

The Courts of Appeals repeatedly have faced the question whether an employer violates the ADEA by acting on the basis of a factor, such as an employee's pension status or seniority, that is empirically correlated with age.... We now clarify that there is no disparate treatment under the ADEA when the factor motivating the employer is some feature other than the employee's age.

We long have distinguished between "disparate treatment" and "disparate impact" theories of employment discrimination. Disparate treatment is the most easily understood type of discrimination. The employer simply treats some people less favorably than others because of their race, color, religion [or other protected characteristics.] Proof of discriminatory motive is critical, although it can in some situations be inferred from the mere fact of differences in treatment.

[C]laims that stress disparate impact [by contrast] involve employment practices that are facially neutral in their treatment of different groups but that in fact fall more harshly on one group than another and cannot be justified by business necessity. Proof of discriminatory motive ... is not required under a disparate-impact theory.

The disparate treatment theory is of course available under the ADEA, as the language of that statute makes clear. "It shall be unlawful for an employer ... to fail or refuse to hire or to discharge any individual or otherwise discriminate against any individual with respect to his compensation, terms, conditions, or privileges of employment, *because of such individual's age.*" 29 U.S.C. §623(a)(1) (emphasis added)....

In a disparate treatment case, liability depends on whether the protected trait (under the ADEA, age) actually motivated the employer's decision. The employer may have relied upon a formal, facially discriminatory policy requiring adverse treatment of employees with that trait. Or the employer may have been motivated by the protected trait on an ad hoc, informal basis. Whatever the employer's decisionmaking process, a disparate treatment claim cannot succeed unless the employee's protected trait actually played a role in that process and had a determinative influence on the outcome.

Disparate treatment, thus defined, captures the essence of what Congress sought to prohibit in the ADEA. It is the very essence of age discrimination for an older employee to be fired because the employer believes that productivity and competence decline with old age.... Congress' promulgation of the ADEA was prompted by its concern that older workers were being deprived of employment on the basis of inaccurate and stigmatizing stereotypes.

"Although age discrimination rarely was based on the sort of animus motivating some other forms of discrimination, it was based in large part on stereotypes unsupported by objective fact.... Moreover, the available empirical evidence demonstrated that arbitrary age lines were in fact generally unfounded and that, as an overall matter, the performance of older workers was at least as good as that of younger workers." [citation omitted].

Thus the ADEA commands that "employers are to evaluate [older] employees ... on their merits and not their age." *Western Air Lines, Inc. v. Criswell,* 472 U.S. 400, 422 (1985). The employer cannot rely on age as a proxy for an employee's remaining characteristics, such as productivity, but must instead focus on those factors directly.

When the employer's decision *is* wholly motivated by factors other than age, the problem of inaccurate and stigmatizing stereotypes disappears. This is true even if the motivating factor is correlated with age, as pension status typically is. Pension plans typically provide that an employee's accrued benefits will become nonforfeitable, or vested, once the employee completes a certain number of years of service with the employer. On average, an older employee has had more years in the work force than a younger employee, and thus may well have accumulated more years of service with a particular employer. Yet an employee's age is analytically distinct from his years of service. An employee who is younger than 40, and therefore outside the class of older workers as defined by the ADEA, *see* 29 U.S.C. §631(a), may have worked for a particular employer his entire career, while an older worker may have been newly hired. Because age and years of service are analytically distinct, an employer can take account of one while ignoring the other, and thus it is incorrect to say that a decision based on years of service is necessarily "age based."

The instant case is illustrative. Under the Hazen Paper pension plan, as construed by the Court of Appeals, an employee's pension benefits vest after the employee completes 10 years of service with the company. Perhaps it is true that older employees of Hazen Paper are more likely to be "close to vesting" than younger employees. Yet a decision by the company to fire an older employee solely because he has nine-plus years of service and therefore is "close to vesting" would not constitute discriminatory treatment on the basis of age. The prohibited stereotype ("Older employees are likely to be ___") would not have figured in this decision, and the attendant stigma would not ensue. The decision would not be the result of an inaccurate and denigrating generalization about age, but would rather represent an *accurate* judgment about the employee—that he indeed is "close to vesting."

We do not mean to suggest that an employer *lawfully* could fire an employee in order to prevent his pension benefits from vesting. Such conduct is actionable under §510 of ERISA, as the Court of Appeals rightly found in affirming judgment for respondent under that statute.

We do not preclude the possibility that an employer who targets employees with a particular pension status on the assumption that these employees are likely to be older thereby engages in age discrimination. Pension status may be a proxy for age, not in the sense that the ADEA makes the two factors equivalent, but in the sense that the employer may suppose a correlation between the two factors and act accordingly. Nor do we rule out the possibility of dual liability under ERISA and the ADEA where the decision to fire the employee was motivated both by the employee's age and by his pension status. Finally, we do not consider the special case where an employee is about to vest in pension benefits as a result of his *age,* rather than years of service, and the employer fires the employee in order to prevent vesting. That case is not presented here. Our holding is simply that an employer does not violate the ADEA just by interfering with an older employee's pension benefits that would have vested by virtue of the employee's years of service.

The judgment of the Court of Appeals is vacated, and the case is remanded for further proceedings consistent with this opinion.

*So ordered.*

[A concurring opinion by Justice Kennedy is omitted.]

---

## Note

In a concurring opinion, Justice Kennedy noted that the plaintiff had not asserted a disparate impact claim and that the Supreme Court had not yet decided whether disparate impact claims would be available under the ADEA. You will see subsequent developments in this issue in Chapter 4.

## ✦ Core Concept: The Proper Defendant

The federal employment discrimination statutes not only specify the types of discrimination that are prohibited, they also specify the individuals or entities that can be liable for such discrimination. It is important to be able to identify individuals or entities that might be held liable for discrimination under each statutory regime.

Title VII, the ADEA, and the ADA all prohibit discrimination by certain employers, employment agencies, and labor organizations. Joint labor-management committees also are barred from discriminating in certain circumstances. This textbook focuses largely on discrimination caused by employers; however, before proceeding with a further discussion of the term "employer," a brief discussion of employment agencies and labor organizations is warranted.

### Employment Agencies and Labor Organizations

Under Title VII it is unlawful for an employment agency "to fail or refuse to refer for employment, or otherwise to discriminate against, any individual because of his race, color, religion, sex, or national origin, or to classify or refer for employment any individual on the basis of his race, color, religion, sex, or national origin." 42 U.S.C. § 2000e-2(b). A similar age-based proscription is found within the ADEA. 29 U.S.C. § 623(b).

Under Title VII, certain labor organizations are prohibited from excluding or expelling from their membership, or otherwise discriminating against any individual because of his race, color, religion, sex, or national origin. 42 U.S.C. § 2000e-2(c). A labor organization also cannot "limit, segregate, or classify its membership or applicants for membership, or ... classify or fail or refuse to refer for employment any individual, in any way which would deprive or tend to deprive any individual of employment opportunities, or would limit such employment opportunities or otherwise adversely affect his status as an employee or as an applicant for employment, because of such individual's race, color, religion, sex, or national origin." *Id.* Labor organizations also are prohibited from causing or attempting to cause an employer to discriminate against an individual in violation of Title VII. *Id.* Similar age-based provisions are found in the ADEA. 29 U.S.C. § 623(c).

The ADA, whose statutory provisions are structured differently, prohibits a "covered entity" from discriminating in certain ways enumerated by the statute. 42 U.S.C. § 12112(a) & (b). The term "covered entity" is defined to include employment agencies and labor organizations. 42 U.S.C. § 12111(2). The ADA covers a broad array of disability discrimination, including discrimination in public accommodations, but this book focuses on the portions of the Act that relate to employment discrimination.

### Private Employers

Many cases brought under the federal employment discrimination statutes are brought against private employers. Title VII defines an employer as "a person engaged in an industry affecting commerce who has fifteen or more employees ... and any agent of such person[.]" 42 U.S.C. § 2000e(b). The term "person" does not mean *person* in the word's normal sense. Rather, the term is defined in another statutory section to include various individuals and entities, including corporations and partnerships. 42 U.S.C. § 2000e(a). The ADA has a similar definition of the term "employer." 42 U.S.C. § 12111(5)(A). The ADEA defines an employer as "a person engaged in an industry affecting commerce who has twenty or more employees … [including] (1) any agent of such a person[.]"

To determine whether an individual or an entity is an employer, it is necessary to ascertain whether the putative employer employs enough people to fall within a particular statute's coverage provisions. Congress chose to exempt the smallest employers from coverage under Title VII, the ADA, and the ADEA. The Supreme Court has indicated that small employers are exempted from such coverage to spare them "from the potentially crushing expense of mastering the intricacies of the antidiscrimination laws, establishing procedures to assure compliance, and defending against suits when efforts at compliance fail." *Clackamas Gastroenterology Associates, P. C. v. Wells*, 538 U.S. 440, 447 (2003).

At times, the employees of two different enterprises can be counted together for purposes of satisfying the minimum employee requirement for statutory coverage. Under the concept of enterprise liability, the business of two or more employers may be so intertwined that they can be considered one entity for coverage purposes. A separate concept is that of joint employers. The term "joint employer" applies when two or more employers are "unrelated or … are not sufficiently related to qualify as an integrated enterprise, but that each exercise sufficient control of an individual to qualify as his/her employer." EEOC COMPLIANCE MANUAL, § 2-III.B.1.a.iii(a).

There are many cases where victims of discrimination have no recourse under federal law because their employers are too small. Keep in mind that state, county, or municipal anti-discrimination provisions often apply to smaller employers. In addition, tort and contract laws sometimes provide remedies.

The general rule under the federal employment discrimination statutes is that the employer is liable for discriminatory employment actions taken by supervisors. *See Faragher v. Boca Raton*, 524 U.S. 775, 790 (1998). You will learn about an important exception to this principle in Chapter 5, which discusses discriminatory harassment. In harassment cases, the question of whether the employer is to be held liable for the acts of its supervisors can become quite complicated. In some circumstances, the employer may also be held liable for harassment committed by co-workers and others.

### Individual Supervisors and Co-Workers

A question that often arises under Title VII, the ADA, and the ADEA is whether individual supervisors or other co-workers can be held personally liable under these statutes. Simply reading the statutory provisions may lead to the conclusion that such individuals are proper defendants. However, the majority view among circuit courts is that individual supervisors or co-workers are not personally liable, unless the individual in question also otherwise falls within the definition of person within each statute. For example, an individual wrongdoer who is the sole proprietor of a business would be a proper defendant under the statutes. The Supreme Court has not determined whether Title VII, the ADA, or the ADEA allow individual liability. Section 1981 provides for individual liability, as do some state, county, and municipal anti-discrimination provisions.

### Government Employers

Title VII, the ADA, and the ADEA all apply to state governments and their agencies and subdivisions. However, the numerosity requirements vary by statute. Title VII and the ADA's employment discrimination provisions apply to such entities or agencies that employ at least 15 employees. 42 U.S.C. § 2000e(a) & (b). Courts have reached contrary decisions regarding whether the ADEA's numerosity requirements apply to state governments or their political subdivisions. *See* 29 U.S.C. § 630(b); *see also Kimel v. Fla. Bd. of Regents*, 528 U.S. 62 (2000) (holding that the ADEA does not abrogate a state's sovereign immunity).

Further, there may be limits imposed by the Eleventh Amendment regarding suits against state governments brought under the ADA, ADEA, and section 1981. In *Board of Trustees of Univ. of Ala. v. Garrett*, 531 U.S. 356 (2001), the Supreme Court held that the Eleventh Amendment bars private suits seeking money damages for state violations of Title I of the ADA. In *Kimel v. Florida Bd. of Regents*, 528 U.S. 62, 91 (2000), the Court held that Congress did not validly abrogate the States' sovereign immunity to suits by private individuals under the ADEA. Likewise, some courts have held that the Eleventh Amendment applies in section 1981 cases. *See, e.g., Singletary v. Mo. Dep't of Corrections*, 423 F.3d 886, 890 (8th Cir. 2005). These same restrictions do not apply in Title VII cases.

As originally enacted, neither Title VII nor the ADEA prohibited discrimination by the federal government. However, later amendments to these statutes prohibit most federal agencies and organizations from discriminating on the basis of the protected traits, including the legislative branch of the federal government. *See, e.g.*, 42 U.S.C. § 2000e-16; 29 U.S.C. § 633a(a); 2 U.S.C. § 1302 (2000).

The Congressional Accountability Act provides that Title I of the ADA applies to the legislative branch of the Federal Government. *See* 2 U.S.C. § 1302 (2000). The ADA does not include most other federal government employers within its coverage provisions; however, disability discrimination provisions applicable to the federal government can be found in the Rehabilitation Act, a precursor to the ADA.

Section 1981 claims may not be asserted against the federal government. *See Brown v. General Services Administration*, 425 U.S. 820 (1976).

### *Major Exceptions*

Title VII, the ADEA, and the ADA all explicitly exempt certain types of entities from some or all of their provisions. This section discusses the major exceptions to these statutes.

By statute, Indian tribes are not bound by the provisions of Title VII or the ADA. 42 U.S.C. § 2000e(b); 42 U.S.C. § 12111(5)(B). Additionally, Title VII permits businesses or enterprises on or near an Indian reservation to have employment practices that give preferential treatment to an individual because he is an Indian living on or near a reservation. 42 U.S.C. § 2000e-2(i). Neither the ADEA nor section 1981 contains explicit exemptions for Indian tribes; however, courts have held that these statutes do not apply to Indian tribes. *See, e.g., EEOC v. Fond du Lac Heavy Equipment and Construction Co., Inc.*, 986 F.2d 246, 250 (8th Cir. 1993) (regarding ADEA); *Wardle v. Ute Indian Tribe*, 623 F.2d 670, 673 (10th Cir. 1980) (regarding section 1981); *but see Aleman v. Chugach Support Serv., Inc.*, 485 F.3d 206 (4th Cir. 2007) (not extending protection to Alaska Native corporation).

Certain tax-exempt bona fide private membership clubs also are excluded from coverage under the ADA and Title VII. 42 U.S.C. § 2000e(b); 42 U.S.C. § 12111(5)(B). Following EEOC Guidance, courts have required entities trying to fit within the private membership club exemption to establish that the club "(1) is a club in the ordinary sense of the word, (2) is private, and (3) requires meaningful conditions of limited membership." *Richard* *v. Friar's Club*, 1997 WL 579146, at *1 (9th Cir. 1997). Other courts have phrased the requirements differently. *Roman v. Concharty Council of Girl Scouts, Inc.*, 195 F. Supp. 2d 1377, 1379 (M.D. Ga. 2002) (considering the group's selectivity in membership, historically unique existence, distinct purpose, and non-profit status.) Neither the ADEA nor section 1981 contains explicit exceptions for private membership clubs.

Generally, foreign employers operating within the United States are governed by the employment discrimination statutes to the same extent as domestic employers. However, in limited circumstances, foreign employers may be permitted to discriminate, if a treaty allows the foreign company to prefer its own nationals for such employment.

American entities operating within foreign countries also are prohibited from discriminating against American citizens under Title VII, the ADEA, and the ADA. *See, e.g.*, 42 U.S.C. §2000e(f) (Title VII); 29 U.S.C. §630(f) (ADEA); 42 U.S.C. §12111(4) (ADA). This limitation usually applies to employers that are incorporated in the United States, as well as employers with sufficient connections to the United States to be considered an American employer. Section 1981 does not apply outside of the United States. 42 U.S.C. §1981(a). American entities operating within foreign countries are not required to comply with the anti-discrimination statutes if the law of the foreign country in which the employer is operating would prohibit such compliance. *See, e.g.*, 42 U.S.C. §2000e-1(b) (Title VII); 29 U.S.C. §623(f)(1) (ADEA); 42 U.S.C. §12112(c) (ADA).

## ✦ Core Concept: Protected Individuals

As this Chapter demonstrates, not all individuals who are discriminated against or retaliated against in the employment context are protected by the federal discrimination statutes. In addition to the limitations discussed earlier in the Chapter, the federal statutes impose several express limitations on the kinds of individuals protected by the statutes.

In most circumstances, an individual alleging prohibited discrimination by an employer under Title VII, the ADEA, and the ADA must be an "employee" to be protected, and this protection extends to potential employees, such as applicants for employment, and former employees in certain instances. Unfortunately, the definition of the term "employee" is perhaps the most unhelpful statutory definition on record. An employee is defined as "an individual employed by an employer." 42 U.S.C. §2000e(f); 42 U.S.C. §12111(4); *see also* 29 U.S.C. §627(f). In the ADA context, the Supreme Court has noted the definition of employee "qualifies as a mere nominal definition that is completely circular and explains nothing." *Clackamas Gastroenterology Associates, P. C. v. Wells*, 538 U.S. 440, 444 (2003). Independent contractors, volunteers, partners, shareholders, and others who are not employees may not receive the protections of Title VII, the ADEA, or the ADA.

However, courts and the EEOC often look beyond the labels assigned to describe certain relationships to determine whether an individual really is an employee. An individual is not required to receive monetary compensation to be considered to be an employee. Other significant, non-monetary remuneration may qualify an individual as an employee.

In *Clackamas Gastroenterology Associates, P. C. v. Wells*, the Supreme Court considered whether physicians who were practitioners in and shareholders of a professional corporation were employees. The Court considered six factors: (1) whether the organization can hire or fire the individual or set the rules and regulations of the individual's work; (2) whether and, if so, to what extent the organization supervises the individual's work; (3) whether the individual reports to someone higher in the organization; (4) whether and, if so, to what extent the individual is able to influence the organization; (5) whether the parties intended that the individual be an employee, as expressed in written agreements or contracts; and (6) whether the individual shares in the profits, losses, and liabilities of the organization. 538 U.S. 440, 449–50 (2003). No one factor is determinative regarding whether an individual is an employee.

Section 1981 does not require that an individual be an employee to fall within its protections.

---

### Focus Questions: *Hishon v. King & Spalding*

1. *What is the employment practice that is being contested here? Notice the importance of the way the plaintiff characterized her claim.*

2. *Would the plaintiff be protected if she was a lateral candidate for partnership from another law firm?*

---

# Hishon v. King & Spalding
## 467 U.S. 69 (1984)

Chief Justice Burger delivered the opinion of the Court.

We granted certiorari to determine whether the District Court properly dismissed a Title VII complaint alleging that a law partnership discriminated against petitioner, a woman lawyer employed as an associate, when it failed to invite her to become a partner.

### I
### A

In 1972 petitioner Elizabeth Anderson Hishon accepted a position as an associate with respondent, a large Atlanta law firm established as a general partnership. When this suit was filed in 1980, the firm had more than 50 partners and employed approximately 50 attorneys as associates. Up to that time, no woman had ever served as a partner at the firm.

Petitioner alleges that the prospect of partnership was an important factor in her initial decision to accept employment with respondent. She alleges that respondent used the possibility of ultimate partnership as a recruiting device to induce petitioner and other young lawyers to become associates at the firm. According to the complaint, respondent represented that advancement to partnership after five or six years was "a matter of course" for associates "who receive[d] satisfactory evaluations" and that associates were promoted to partnership "on a fair and equal basis." Petitioner alleges that she relied on these representations when she accepted employment with respondent. The complaint further alleges that respondent's promise to consider her on a "fair and equal basis" created a binding employment contract.

In May 1978 the partnership considered and rejected Hishon for admission to the partnership; one year later, the partners again declined to invite her to become a partner. Once an associate is passed over for partnership at respondent's firm, the associate is notified to begin seeking employment elsewhere. Petitioner's employment as an associate terminated on December 31, 1979.

## B

[A discussion of the administrative process is omitted.]

... The District Court dismissed the complaint on the ground that Title VII was inapplicable to the selection of partners by a partnership....

## II

At this stage of the litigation, we must accept petitioner's allegations as true. A court may dismiss a complaint only if it is clear that no relief could be granted under any set of facts that could be proved consistent with the allegations. The issue before us is whether petitioner's allegations state a claim under Title VII, the relevant portion of which provides as follows:

(a) It shall be an unlawful employment practice for an employer—

(1) to fail or refuse to hire or to discharge any individual, or otherwise to discriminate against any individual with respect to his compensation, terms, conditions, or privileges of employment, because of such individual's race, color, religion, sex, or national origin.

42 U.S.C. § 2000e-2(a) (emphasis added).

## A

Petitioner alleges that respondent is an "employer" to whom Title VII is addressed. She then asserts that consideration for partnership was one of the "terms, conditions, or privileges of employment" as an associate with respondent. *See* § 2000e-2(a)(1). If this is correct, respondent could not base an adverse partnership decision on "race, color, religion, sex, or national origin."

Once a contractual relationship of employment is established, the provisions of Title VII attach and govern certain aspects of that relationship. In the context of Title VII, the contract of employment may be written or oral, formal or informal; an informal contract of employment may arise by the simple act of handing a job applicant a shovel and providing a workplace. The contractual relationship of employment triggers the provision of Title VII governing "terms, conditions, or privileges of employment." Title VII in turn forbids discrimination on the basis of "race, color, religion, sex, or national origin."

Because the underlying employment relationship is contractual, it follows that the "terms, conditions, or privileges of employment" clearly include benefits that are part of an employment contract. Here, petitioner in essence alleges that respondent made a contract to consider her for partnership.[11] Indeed, this promise was allegedly a key contractual provision which induced her to accept employment. If the evidence at trial establishes that the parties contracted to have petitioner considered for partnership, that promise clearly was a term, condition, or privilege of her employment. Title VII would then bind respondent to consider petitioner for partnership as the statute provides, *i.e.*, without regard to petitioner's sex. The contract she alleges would lead to the same result.

---

11. Petitioner alleges not only that respondent promised to consider her for partnership, but also that it promised to consider her on a "fair and equal basis." This latter promise is not necessary to petitioner's Title VII claim. Even if the employment contract did not afford a basis for an implied condition that the ultimate decision would be fairly made on the merits, Title VII itself would impose such a requirement. If the promised consideration for partnership is a term, condition, or privilege of employment, then the partnership decision must be without regard to "race, color, religion, sex, or national origin."

Petitioner's claim that a contract was made, however, is not the only allegation that would qualify respondent's consideration of petitioner for partnership as a term, condition, or privilege of employment. An employer may provide its employees with many benefits that it is under no obligation to furnish by any express or implied contract. Such a benefit, though not a contractual right of employment, may qualify as a "privileg[e]" of employment under Title VII. A benefit that is part and parcel of the employment relationship may not be doled out in a discriminatory fashion, even if the employer would be free under the employment contract simply not to provide the benefit at all. Those benefits that comprise the "incidents of employment," or that form "an aspect of the relationship between the employer and employees," may not be afforded in a manner contrary to Title VII. [citations omitted].

Several allegations in petitioner's complaint would support the conclusion that the opportunity to become a partner was part and parcel of an associate's status as an employee at respondent's firm, independent of any allegation that such an opportunity was included in associates' employment contracts. Petitioner alleges that respondent's associates could regularly expect to be considered for partnership at the end of their "apprenticeships," and it appears that lawyers outside the firm were not routinely so considered.[12] Thus, the benefit of partnership consideration was allegedly linked directly with an associate's status as an employee, and this linkage was far more than coincidental: petitioner alleges that respondent explicitly used the prospect of ultimate partnership to induce young lawyers to join the firm. Indeed, the importance of the partnership decision to a lawyer's status as an associate is underscored by the allegation that associates' employment is terminated if they are not elected to become partners. These allegations, if proved at trial, would suffice to show that partnership consideration was a term, condition, or privilege of an associate's employment at respondent's firm, and accordingly that partnership consideration must be without regard to sex.

B

Respondent contends that advancement to partnership may never qualify as a term, condition, or privilege of employment for purposes of Title VII. First, respondent asserts that elevation to partnership entails a change in status from an "employee" to an "employer." However, even if respondent is correct that a partnership invitation is not itself an offer of employment, Title VII would nonetheless apply and preclude discrimination on the basis of sex. The benefit a plaintiff is denied need not be employment to fall within Title VII's protection; it need only be a term, condition, or privilege of employment. It is also of no consequence that employment as an associate necessarily ends when an associate becomes a partner. A benefit need not accrue before a person's employment is completed to be a term, condition, or privilege of that employment relationship. Pension benefits, for example, qualify as terms, conditions, or privileges of employment even though they are received only after employment terminates. Accordingly, nothing in the change in status that advancement to partnership might entail means that partnership consideration falls outside the terms of the statute.

Second, respondent argues that Title VII categorically exempts partnership decisions from scrutiny. However, respondent points to nothing in the statute or the legislative history that would support such a per se exemption. When Congress wanted to grant an employer complete immunity, it expressly did so.

---

12. Respondent's own submissions indicate that most of respondent's partners in fact were selected from the ranks of associates who had spent their entire prepartnership legal careers (excluding judicial clerkships) with the firm.

Third, respondent argues that application of Title VII in this case would infringe constitutional rights of expression or association. Although we have recognized that the activities of lawyers may make a "distinctive contribution ... to the ideas and beliefs of our society," *NAACP v. Button*, 371 U.S. 415, 431 (1963), respondent has not shown how its ability to fulfill such a function would be inhibited by a requirement that it consider petitioner for partnership on her merits. Moreover, as we have held in another context, "[i]nvidious private discrimination may be characterized as a form of exercising freedom of association protected by the First Amendment, but it has never been accorded affirmative constitutional protections." *Norwood v. Harrison*, 413 U.S. 455, 470 (1973).

III

We conclude that petitioner's complaint states a claim cognizable under Title VII. Petitioner therefore is entitled to her day in court to prove her allegations. The judgment of the Court of Appeals is reversed, and the case is remanded for further proceedings consistent with this opinion.

Justice Powell, concurring.

I join the Court's opinion holding that petitioner's complaint alleges a violation of Title VII and that the motion to dismiss should not have been granted. Petitioner's complaint avers that the law firm violated its promise that she would be considered for partnership on a "fair and equal basis" within the time span that associates generally are so considered. Petitioner is entitled to the opportunity to prove these averments.

I write to make clear my understanding that the Court's opinion should not be read as extending Title VII to the management of a law firm by its partners. The reasoning of the Court's opinion does not require that the relationship among partners be characterized as an "employment" relationship to which Title VII would apply. The relationship among law partners differs markedly from that between employer and employee—including that between the partnership and its associates.[13] The judgmental and sensitive decisions that must be made among the partners embrace a wide range of subjects.[14] The essence of the law partnership is the common conduct of a shared enterprise. The relationship among law partners contemplates that decisions important to the partnership normally will be made by common agreement or consent among the partners.

Respondent contends that for these reasons application of Title VII to the decision whether to admit petitioner to the firm implicates the constitutional right to association. But here it is alleged that respondent as an employer is obligated by contract to consider petitioner for partnership on equal terms without regard to sex. I agree that enforcement of this obligation, voluntarily assumed, would impair no right of association.[15]

---

13. Of course, an employer may not evade the strictures of Title VII simply by labeling its employees as "partners." Law partnerships usually have many of the characteristics that I describe generally here.

14. These decisions concern such matters as participation in profits and other types of compensation; work assignments; approval of commitments in bar association, civic, or political activities; questions of billing; acceptance of new clients; questions of conflicts of interest; retirement programs; and expansion policies. Such decisions may affect each partner of the firm. Divisions of partnership profits, unlike shareholders' rights to dividends, involve judgments as to each partner's contribution to the reputation and success of the firm. This is true whether the partner's participation in profits is measured in terms of points or percentages, combinations of salaries and points, salaries and bonuses, and possibly in other ways.

15. The Court's opinion properly reminds us that "invidious private discrimination ... has never been accorded affirmative constitutional protections." [citation omitted]. This is not to say, however, that enforcement of laws that ban discrimination will always be without cost to other values, including

In admission decisions made by law firms, it is now widely recognized—as it should be—that in fact neither race nor sex is relevant. The qualities of mind, capacity to reason logically, ability to work under pressure, leadership, and the like are unrelated to race or sex. This is demonstrated by the success of women and minorities in law schools, in the practice of law, on the bench, and in positions of community, state, and national leadership. Law firms—and, of course, society—are the better for these changes.

---

## Exercise 2.4

A law firm, facing financial pressures, decides to terminate a small, but significant, portion of its partners. All of the individuals terminated are over the age of 40. The law firm has 200 lawyers. Many of the decisions related to the firm are made by a management committee comprised of five partners. The partners at the firm fall within one of two categories: non-equity partners and equity partners. All members of the management committee are equity partners. Each partner has entered into an agreement indicating that he or she is not an employee of the law firm.

Non-equity partners are entitled to receive certain financial and other information about the firm and are able to attend some meetings related to firm decisionmaking. The non-equity partners are not allowed to vote at these meetings. The non-equity partners are paid a monthly salary. Although non-equity partners manage their own client's legal work and the work of associates, non-equity partners also are expected to work on legal teams with other firm partners.

Equity partners who are not on the management committee have the following rights and responsibilities. Each equity partner has contributed a certain amount of money to the partnership and is responsible for its losses and shares in its profits. While the equity partners are allowed votes regarding some areas of firm management, many of the decisions have been delegated to the management committee. All of the equity partners vote on whether a person is made partner and on whether to terminate a relationship with a partner. However, in practice, the firm always follows the leadership of the management committee.

A non-equity partner and an equity partner go to separate plaintiff's law firms to seek advice regarding a potential claim. Should the law firms take the cases? You should consider all legal arguments and practical reasons that might affect your decision.

---

constitutional rights. Such laws may impede the exercise of personal judgment in choosing one's associates or colleagues. Impediments to the exercise of one's right to choose one's associates can violate the right of association protected by the First and Fourteenth Amendments. With respect to laws that prevent discrimination, much depends upon the standards by which the courts examine private decisions that are an exercise of the right of association. For example, the Courts of Appeals generally have acknowledged that respect for academic freedom requires some deference to the judgment of schools and universities as to the qualifications of professors, particularly those considered for tenured positions. The present case, before us on a motion to dismiss for lack of subject-matter jurisdiction, does not present such an issue.

## Exercise 2.5

Shelly is a waitress at a local restaurant. Larry is her supervisor and Danny is a waiter at the restaurant. On a daily basis, Larry and Danny sexually harass Shelly by groping her and by asking her out on dates. Larry and Danny also make racially insensitive and harassing comments to her in a joking manner. You are an associate at a plaintiff's law firm, and Shelly has come to your law firm seeking legal advice. A partner has asked you to write a brief memo discussing the claims that Shelly should pursue and against whom Shelly should file suit. You should assume that Shelly has exhausted any administrative requirements, and you should assume that the harassment by Larry and Danny constitutes discrimination in the terms and conditions of her employment. If you need further information, your memo should indicate what further information is needed.

Later in the course, you will learn that an employer may be liable for the acts of its employees and even non-employees, in certain circumstances. For now, focus on who is the proper defendant in this case, not on agency issues.

# Chapter 3

# Disparate Treatment

This Chapter begins the exploration of the analytical frameworks that are used to consider employment discrimination claims. As a preliminary matter, the Chapter considers the primary operative language of Title VII, the ADA, and the ADEA, as well as the history of these statutes. It then examines a type of discrimination the courts refer to as "disparate treatment."

In Chapter 4, you will learn about a very different type of discrimination: disparate impact. Disparate impact analysis imposes liability where a facially neutral practice has a disparate impact on a protected group and is not justified by a sufficient reason. In subsequent chapters, you will learn about other modes of analysis, those used in cases involving harassment, retaliation and requests for religious or disability accommodation. The following chart will help you to visualize the types of discrimination that will be discussed.

| Type of Conduct | Applicable Major Statutes | Coverage in Book |
| --- | --- | --- |
| Individual Disparate Treatment | Title VII, ADEA, ADA, § 1981 | Chapter 3 |
| Pattern or Practice | Title VII, ADEA, ADA, § 1981 | Chapter 3 |
| Disparate Impact | Title VII, ADEA, ADA | Chapter 4 |
| Harassment | Title VII, ADEA, ADA, § 1981 | Chapter 5 |
| Retaliation | Title VII, ADEA, ADA, § 1981 | Chapter 6 |
| Failure to Accommodate | Title VII (religion), ADA | Chapter 7 (religion); Chapter 8 (disability) |

By the end of the course, you should understand the tests that the courts use to evaluate discrimination claims, as well as the circumstances under which a court will apply a particular test.

In thinking about disparate treatment, it is important to start with the applicable statutory language and its history. Title VII is the cornerstone of federal employment discrimination protections. Title VII was enacted as part of a much larger piece of civil rights legislation, the Civil Rights Act of 1964, which contained discrimination protections in areas such as voting, schools, public accommodations and access to government services. The debate regarding passage of such comprehensive discrimination protections was long and contentious.

Title VII has been amended several times since its original enactment, and these amendments will be discussed in detail as they become relevant. Section 703(a) of Title VII currently provides:

(a) Employer practices

It shall be an unlawful employment practice for an employer—

(1) to fail or refuse to hire or to discharge any individual, or otherwise to discriminate against any individual with respect to his compensation, terms, conditions, or privileges of employment, because of such individual's race, color, religion, sex, or national origin; or

(2) to limit, segregate, or classify his employees or applicants for employment in any way which would deprive or tend to deprive any individual of employment opportunities or otherwise adversely affect his status as an employee, because of such individual's race, color, religion, sex, or national origin.

42 U.S.C. § 2000e-2.

Events during Congress' consideration of Title VII led to the subsequent enactment of the ADEA. During the debate leading to the passage of Title VII, Congress considered adding provisions to the statute to prohibit age discrimination. Instead of amending Title VII, Congress directed Secretary of Labor Willard Wirtz to report back to Congress on the causes and effects of age discrimination in the workplace and to propose remedial legislation.

Wirtz's report to Congress recognized that age discrimination existed and proposed that Congress take action to prohibit this type of discrimination. However, Wirtz also made two observations about age discrimination that are important to the development of the ADEA. First, Wirtz concluded that unlike discrimination based on race or other protected traits, age discrimination was typically not a result of animus or intolerance for the protected group. Rather, the most problematic type of discrimination facing older workers was discrimination based on unsupported general assumptions about the effect of age on ability. Second, Wirtz noted that many legitimate, non-discriminatory factors used to make employment decisions correlate with age. These factors include: declining health among older workers that might make them less able or unable to perform job functions; lack of skills or educational credentials required for jobs; and an outdated skill set caused by rapid technological advances.

In 1967, Congress enacted the ADEA. In its current iteration, the ADEA provides:

It shall be unlawful for an employer—

(1) to fail or refuse to hire or to discharge any individual or otherwise discriminate against any individual with respect to his compensation, terms, conditions, or privileges of employment, because of such individual's age;

(2) to limit, segregate, or classify his employees in any way which would deprive or tend to deprive any individual of employment opportunities or otherwise adversely affect his status as an employee, because of such individual's age; or

(3) to reduce the wage rate of any employee in order to comply with this chapter.

29 U.S.C. § 623(a). The ADEA also contains some very important language of limitation: "It shall not be unlawful for an employer, employment agency, or labor organization—(1) to take any action otherwise prohibited under subsections (a) ... where the differentiation is based on reasonable factors other than age." 29 U.S.C. § 623(f)(1). Courts refer to this latter provision as the "reasonable factor other than age" (RFOA) provision.

In the first few decades of the ADEA's enforcement, it was often assumed that its discrimination provisions worked in the same way that Title VII's discrimination provisions do and that the proof structures used for Title VII could simply be imported into ADEA cases. While this is still true in some instances, in other instances, the courts interpret the ADEA's discrimination provisions differently. The RFOA provision plays a significant role in the differentiation of Title VII and the ADEA. You should consider whether the conclusions within the Wirtz Report are correct as you read cases in this chapter in which the Supreme Court relies on the report to interpret the ADEA and to distinguish it from other discrimination statutes.

The Americans with Disabilities Act was not enacted until 1990. Although it prohibits discrimination against a qualified individual on the basis of disability, its operative discrimination provisions look different from the provisions found in the ADEA and Title VII, with a longer list of enumerated prohibited acts. Notice that the ADA also requires accommodation of disability in certain circumstances. The ADA provides as follows:

(a) General rule

No covered entity shall discriminate against a qualified individual on the basis of disability in regard to job application procedures, the hiring, advancement, or discharge of employees, employee compensation, job training, and other terms, conditions, and privileges of employment.

(b) Construction

As used in subsection (a) of this section, the term "discriminate against a qualified individual on the basis of disability" includes —

(1) limiting, segregating, or classifying a job applicant or employee in a way that adversely affects the opportunities or status of such applicant or employee because of the disability of such applicant or employee;

(2) participating in a contractual or other arrangement or relationship that has the effect of subjecting a covered entity's qualified applicant or employee with a disability to the discrimination prohibited by this subchapter (such relationship includes a relationship with an employment or referral agency, labor union, an organization providing fringe benefits to an employee of the covered entity, or an organization providing training and apprenticeship programs);

(3) utilizing standards, criteria, or methods of administration —

   (A) that have the effect of discrimination on the basis of disability; or

   (B) that perpetuate the discrimination of others who are subject to common administrative control;

(4) excluding or otherwise denying equal jobs or benefits to a qualified individual because of the known disability of an individual with whom the qualified individual is known to have a relationship or association;

(5) (A) not making reasonable accommodations to the known physical or mental limitations of an otherwise qualified individual with a disability who is an applicant or employee, unless such covered entity can demonstrate that the accommodation would impose an undue hardship on the operation of the business of such covered entity; or

   (B) denying employment opportunities to a job applicant or employee who is an otherwise qualified individual with a disability, if such denial is based on the need of such covered entity to make reasonable accommodation to the physical or mental impairments of the employee or applicant;

(6) using qualification standards, employment tests or other selection criteria that screen out or tend to screen out an individual with a disability or a class of individuals with disabilities unless the standard, test or other selection criteria, as used by the covered entity, is shown to be job-related for the position in question and is consistent with business necessity; and

(7) failing to select and administer tests concerning employment in the most effective manner to ensure that, when such test is administered to a job applicant or employee who has a disability that impairs sensory, manual, or speaking skills, such test results accurately reflect the skills, aptitude, or whatever other factor of such applicant or employee that such test purports to measure, rather than reflecting the impaired sensory, manual, or speaking skills of such employee or applicant (except where such skills are the factors that the test purports to measure).

42 U.S.C. § 12112.

When interpreting the discrimination provisions of the ADA, courts often use the proof structures developed under Title VII. Unless otherwise noted, the Title VII proof structures discussed in this Chapter can be used in the ADA context. However, given the courts' willingness to read the statutory provisions of Title VII and the ADEA as requiring separate analytical frameworks, at least in some cases, good employment discrimination lawyers should always be prepared to argue that differences in the statutory language between Title VII and the ADA require different treatment.

Section 1981 provides as follows:

(a) All persons within the jurisdiction of the United States shall have the same right in every State and Territory to make and enforce contracts, … as is enjoyed by white citizens[.]

(b) "Make and enforce contracts" defined

For purposes of this section, the term "make and enforce contracts" includes the making, performance, modification, and termination of contracts, and the enjoyment of all benefits, privileges, terms, and conditions of the contractual relationship.

42 U.S.C. § 1981.

In many instances the courts also use Title VII proof structures to interpret Section 1981. However, there are some important differences between Section 1981 and Title VII that will be discussed throughout the book. For example, Section 1981 does not have a statutory cap on remedies, it does not require a plaintiff to exhaust administrative remedies, it has a different statute of limitations, and provides a cause of action for individuals (such as independent contractors) who may not be covered by Title VII. These differences often influence plaintiffs' decisions about which statute to invoke. In some instances, both statutes can be invoked.

Title VII, the ADEA, the ADA and § 1981 also prohibit retaliation, which will be discussed in Chapter 6. On questions of retaliation, the courts very often read the statutes *in pari materia*, meaning that precedent under one statute often guides courts in their decisions under other statutes.

Throughout this course, you should think about the theoretical underpinnings of employment discrimination law. In Chapter 1, you learned about the concept of personal privacy or right to personality, the idea that an individual has certain inherent rights that the employer may infringe only if the employer has a substantial interest in doing so. This idea contrasts with the concept of at-will employment, in which the employer is presumed to be able to make decisions that affect the employee for any reason or no reason, absent a contract or other law to the contrary. Recall that at-will employment is the conception of the employee-employer relationship that applies in most states.

Two other concepts are important to this theoretical foundation. These are the concepts of "formal equality" and "substantive equality." Proponents of formal equality argue that similarly situated people should be treated equally, without regard to their protected traits.

For example, an employer not covered by the Family and Medical Leave Act (FMLA) may provide employees with no sick leave and have the no-leave policy apply equally to men and women. Proponents of substantive equality argue that the concern of the law should be equality of results, considering that underlying social structures and realities sometimes undermine the ability of formal equality to achieve just results. Proponents of substantive equality might argue that a no-leave policy discriminates against women who are pregnant and would need to take leave to have a child.

As you learn more about employment discrimination, consider whether either of these theoretical foundations is present in the courts' interpretation of the federal discrimination statutes. Also consider which theories should be manifest in these interpretations. Is either more consistent with your concept of justice?

---

## Exercise 3.1

Even though the operative provisions of Title VII are important, Congress only described the prohibited actions in broad terms. Re-read the primary operative provisions of Title VII. Based on that language, list the elements of the plaintiff's case for discrimination under Title VII. In other words, as you understand the statutory language, what should a plaintiff have to prove in order to win a case? Also, based on that language, what kinds of discriminatory conduct does Title VII seem to prohibit?

In thinking about Title VII, consider whether it should be read as ensuring formal equality or substantive equality. Think about whether men and women are inherently different or inherently the same. Consider whether differences in societal expectations or differences based on biology make formal equality insufficient as an underlying theory for employment discrimination. Think about whether race affects an individual's opportunities and whether and how any lack of opportunities should be addressed by federal discrimination law.

---

## ✦ Core Concept: Individual Disparate Treatment

Individual disparate treatment claims are the most common kinds of discrimination claims that arise under the employment discrimination statutes. These cases typically involve an individual or a group of individuals alleging differential treatment based on a protected trait.

At the time that Title VII was enacted, it was lawful in many states for companies to have explicit policies relating to employees based on protected traits. Thus, some companies maintained segregated work forces, in which certain jobs were reserved strictly for white men. Some employers also prohibited women from working in particular jobs or required women to leave employment when they married or became pregnant. Some employers also engaged in wage discrimination, paying different wages for identical work depending on an employee's race or gender.

Some companies maintained these policies even after Title VII's enactment. Further, because explicit discrimination was not as socially shunned as it is today, employers sometimes provided employees with blatantly discriminatory reasons for their actions. For example, a supervisor might tell a job applicant that she was not hired because she is a woman.

Courts began referring to this type of proof of discrimination as direct evidence of discrimination. Although rules of evidence do not draw a distinction between direct evidence and circumstantial evidence, this dichotomy plays an important role in how courts evaluate individual disparate treatment claims.

Direct evidence cases are evaluated in a fairly straightforward way. If the plaintiff is able to demonstrate through direct evidence that an employer took an action because of a protected trait, the employer usually is unable to avoid liability unless it has a defense or affirmative defense or can show that the statute does not apply to the situation at hand. For example, the employer might argue that it is not large enough to be covered by Title VII.

As employers began to develop policies prohibiting discrimination and as explicit discrimination became less socially acceptable, the types of evidence plaintiffs relied on to prove their cases began to change. Many plaintiffs began to rely on circumstantial evidence. "Circumstantial evidence" allows the jury to infer that a fact is true, rather than directly supporting the truth of that fact. For example, evidence that the ground was wet supports the *inference* that rain fell (though other sources of the moisture are possible). Whereas testimony that the witness saw rain falling *directly* supports the conclusion that it rained. Although some direct evidence cases are still brought, these types of cases are fairly rare.

In *McDonnell-Douglas v. Green*, the Supreme Court developed the first test designed to assist courts in evaluating individual disparate treatment claims based on circumstantial evidence. This may be the most important case you will read all semester, and it is critical to your understanding of employment discrimination law.

## ✦ Core Concept: The *McDonnell-Douglas* Test

### Focus Questions: *McDonnell Douglas Corp. v. Green*

1.  *What analytical framework does the Court create and how does it work?*

2.  *What is the first step of the analytical framework supposed to accomplish?*

3.  *In thinking about this case and the reading following it, consider what the difference is between a burden of production and a burden of persuasion.*

4.  *Does the Court hold that subjective employment criteria are inherently suspect? Should subjective criteria be viewed skeptically by a court?*

5.  *Is the analytical framework provided in this case going to have the same components in every case?*

# McDonnell Douglas Corp. v. Green

## 411 U.S. 792 (1973)

Justice Powell delivered the opinion of the Court.

The case before us raises significant questions as to the proper order and nature of proof in actions under Title VII of the Civil Rights Act of 1964.

Petitioner, McDonnell Douglas Corp., is an aerospace and aircraft manufacturer headquartered in St. Louis, Missouri, where it employs over 30,000 people. Respondent, a black citizen of St. Louis, worked for petitioner as a mechanic and laboratory technician from 1956 until August 28, 1964, when he was laid off in the course of a general reduction in petitioner's work force.

Respondent, a long-time activist in the civil rights movement, protested vigorously that his discharge and the general hiring practices of petitioner were racially motivated. As part of this protest, respondent and other members of the Congress on Racial Equality illegally stalled their cars on the main roads leading to petitioner's plant for the purpose of blocking access to it at the time of the morning shift change....

Acting under the "stall in" plan, plaintiff (respondent in the present action) drove his car onto Brown Road, a McDonnell access road, at approximately 7:00 a.m., at the start of the morning rush hour. Plaintiff was aware of the traffic problems that would result.... Plaintiff's car was towed away by the police, and he was arrested for obstructing traffic. Plaintiff pleaded guilty to the charge of obstructing traffic and was fined.

On July 2, 1965, a "lock-in" took place wherein a chain and padlock were placed on the front door of a building to prevent the occupants, certain of petitioner's employees, from leaving. Though respondent apparently knew beforehand of the "lock-in," the full extent of his involvement remains uncertain.

Some three weeks following the "lock-in," on July 25, 1965, petitioner publicly advertised for qualified mechanics, respondent's trade, and respondent promptly applied for re-employment. Petitioner turned down respondent, basing its rejection on respondent's participation in the "stall-in" and "lock-in." Shortly thereafter, respondent filed a formal complaint with the Equal Employment Opportunity Commission, claiming that petitioner had refused to rehire him because of his race and persistent involvement in the civil rights movement, in violation of §§ 703(a)(1) and 704(a) of the Civil Rights Act of 1964, 42 U.S.C. §§ 2000e-2(a)(1) and 2000e-3(a). The former section generally prohibits racial discrimination in any employment decision while the latter forbids discrimination against applicants or employees for attempting to protest or correct allegedly discriminatory conditions of employment.

[A discussion of the administrative procedure is omitted.] The District Court also found that petitioner's refusal to rehire respondent was based solely on his participation in the illegal demonstrations and not on his legitimate civil rights activities. The court concluded that nothing in Title VII or § 704 protected such activity as employed by the plaintiff in the "stall in" and "lock in" demonstrations.

On appeal, the Eighth Circuit affirmed that unlawful protests were not protected activities under § 704(a).... [However, the] court ordered the case remanded for trial of respondent's claim under § 703(a)(1).

In remanding, the Court of Appeals attempted to set forth standards to govern the consideration of respondent's claim. The majority noted that respondent had established a prima facie case of racial discrimination; that petitioner's refusal to rehire respondent rested on "subjective" criteria which carried little weight in rebutting charges of discrimination; that, though respondent's participation in the unlawful demonstrations might indicate a lack of a responsible attitude toward performing work for that employer, respondent should be given the opportunity to demonstrate that petitioner's reasons for refusing to rehire him were mere pretext. In order to clarify the standards governing the disposition of an action challenging employment discrimination, we granted certiorari....

## II

The critical issue before us concerns the order and allocation of proof in a private, non-class action challenging employment discrimination. The language of Title VII makes plain the purpose of Congress to assure equality of employment opportunities and to eliminate those discriminatory practices and devices which have fostered racially stratified job environments to the disadvantage of minority citizens....

There are societal as well as personal interests on both sides of this equation. The broad, overriding interest, shared by employer, employee, and consumer, is efficient and trustworthy workmanship assured through fair and racially neutral employment and personnel decisions. In the implementation of such decisions, it is abundantly clear that Title VII tolerates no racial discrimination, subtle or otherwise.

In this case respondent, the complainant below, charges that he was denied employment "because of his involvement in civil rights activities' and 'because of his race and color.'" Petitioner denied discrimination of any kind, asserting that its failure to re-employ respondent was based upon and justified by his participation in the unlawful conduct against it. Thus, the issue at the trial on remand is framed by those opposing factual contentions. The two opinions of the Court of Appeals and the several opinions of the three judges of that court attempted, with a notable lack of harmony, to state the applicable rules as to burden of proof and how this shifts upon the making of a prima facie case. We now address this problem.

The complainant in a Title VII trial must carry the initial burden under the statute of establishing a prima facie case of racial discrimination. This may be done by showing (i) that he belongs to a racial minority; (ii) that he applied and was qualified for a job for which the employer was seeking applicants; (iii) that, despite his qualifications, he was rejected; and (iv) that, after his rejection, the position remained open and the employer continued to seek applicants from persons of complainant's qualifications.[13] In the instant case, we agree with the Court of Appeals that respondent proved a prima facie case. Petitioner sought mechanics, respondent's trade, and continued to do so after respondent's rejection. Petitioner, moreover, does not dispute respondent's qualifications[14] and acknowledges that his past work performance in petitioner's employ was satisfactory.

The burden then must shift to the employer to articulate some legitimate, nondiscriminatory reason for the employee's rejection. We need not attempt in the instant case to detail every matter which fairly could be recognized as a reasonable basis for a refusal to hire. Here petitioner has assigned respondent's participation in unlawful conduct against it as the cause for his rejection. We think that this suffices to discharge petitioner's burden of proof at this stage and to meet respondent's prima facie case of discrimination.

The Court of Appeals intimated, however, that petitioner's stated reason for refusing to rehire respondent was a "subjective" rather than objective criterion which "carr[ies] little weight in rebutting charges of discrimination." This was among the statements which caused the dissenting judge to read the opinion as taking "the position that such unlawful acts as Green committed against McDonnell would not legally entitle McDonnell to refuse to hire him, even though no racial motivation was involved...." Regardless of whether this was the intended import of the opinion, we think the court below seriously under-

---

13. The facts necessarily will vary in Title VII cases, and the specification above of the prima facie proof required from respondent is not necessarily applicable in every respect to differing factual situations.

14. We note that the issue of what may properly be used to test qualifications for employment is not present in this case. Where employers have instituted employment tests and qualifications with an exclusionary effect on minority applicants, such requirements must be "shown to bear a demonstrable relationship to successful performance of the jobs" for which they were used, *Griggs v. Duke Power Co.*, 401 U.S. 424, 431 (1971).

estimated the rebuttal weight to which petitioner's reasons were entitled. Respondent admittedly had taken part in a carefully planned "stall-in," designed to tie up access to and egress from petitioner's plant at a peak traffic hour. Nothing in Title VII compels an employer to absolve and rehire one who has engaged in such deliberate, unlawful activity against it. . . .

Petitioner's reason for rejection thus suffices to meet the prima facie case, but the inquiry must not end here. While Title VII does not, without more, compel rehiring of respondent, neither does it permit petitioner to use respondent's conduct as a pretext for the sort of discrimination prohibited by § 703(a)(1). On remand, respondent must, as the Court of Appeals recognized, be afforded a fair opportunity to show that petitioner's stated reason for respondent's rejection was in fact pretext. Especially relevant to such a showing would be evidence that white employees involved in acts against petitioner of comparable seriousness to the "stall-in" were nevertheless retained or rehired. Petitioner may justifiably refuse to rehire one who was engaged in unlawful, disruptive acts against it, but only if this criterion is applied alike to members of all races.

Other evidence that may be relevant to any showing of pretext includes facts as to the petitioner's treatment of respondent during his prior term of employment; petitioner's reaction, if any, to respondent's legitimate civil rights activities; and petitioner's general policy and practice with respect to minority employment. On the latter point, statistics as to petitioner's employment policy and practice may be helpful to a determination of whether petitioner's refusal to rehire respondent in this case conformed to a general pattern of discrimination against blacks. In short, on the retrial respondent must be given a full and fair opportunity to demonstrate by competent evidence that the presumptively valid reasons for his rejection were in fact a coverup for a racially discriminatory decision. . . .

If the evidence on retrial is substantially in accord with that before us in this case, we think that plaintiff carried his burden of establishing a prima facie case of racial discrimination and that defendant successfully rebutted that case. But this does not end the matter. On retrial, plaintiff must be afforded a fair opportunity to demonstrate that defendant's assigned reason for refusing to re-employ was a pretext or discriminatory in its application. . . .

The cause is hereby remanded to the District Court for reconsideration in accordance with this opinion.

---

## Subsequent Developments

After *McDonnell-Douglas*, significant confusion existed about the three-part burden-shifting framework. Two subsequent cases clarified (and some would say altered) how the *McDonnell-Douglas* test operates. These cases are *Texas Dept. of Community Affairs v. Burdine*, 450 U.S. 248 (1981), and *St. Mary's Honor Center v. Hicks*, 509 U.S. 502 (1993). At times, the three-part burden-shifting framework is referred to as the *McDonnell-Douglas/Burdine* test or the *McDonnell-Douglas/Burdine/Hicks* test.

In *Burdine*, the Court indicated that "the burden of establishing a prima facie case of disparate treatment is not onerous." 450 U.S. at 253. The prima facie case, the Court explained, serves the function of "eliminat[ing] the most common nondiscriminatory reasons for the plaintiff's rejection." *Id.* at 254. "The prima facie case 'raises an inference of discrimination only because we presume these acts, if otherwise unexplained, are more likely than not based on the consideration of impermissible factors.'" *Id.* (quoting *Furnco*

*Construction Corp. v. Walters*, 438 U.S. 567, 577 (1978)). The Court further explained the effect of establishing a prima facie case: "If the trier of fact believes the plaintiff's evidence, and if the employer is silent in the face of the presumption, the court must enter judgment for the plaintiff because no issue of fact remains in the case." *Id.*

Thus, if the plaintiff makes a prima facie case, the defendant is required to articulate a legitimate, non-discriminatory reason for its actions. The Court clarified that the defendant's burden at this second step is a burden of production. "Placing this burden of production on the defendant thus serves simultaneously to meet the plaintiff's prima facie case by presenting a legitimate reason for the action and to frame the factual issue with sufficient clarity so that the plaintiff will have a full and fair opportunity to demonstrate pretext." *Id.* at 255–56. The defendant must meet this burden of production with admissible evidence.

After defendant has articulated a legitimate, non-discriminatory reason, the plaintiff has the opportunity to demonstrate that the proffered reason was not the true reason for the employment decision. The *Burdine* Court indicated that "[t]his burden now merges with the ultimate burden of persuading the court that she has been the victim of intentional discrimination. She may succeed in this either directly by persuading the court that a discriminatory reason more likely motivated the employer or indirectly by showing that the employer's proffered explanation is unworthy of credence." *Id.* at 256. The Court held that the "ultimate burden of persuading the trier of fact that the defendant intentionally discriminated against the plaintiff remains at all times with the plaintiff." *Id.*

In *Hicks*, the Court considered whether the factfinder's rejection of the employer's asserted reason for its action mandated a finding for the plaintiff. Before answering that question, the Court explained again how the *McDonnell-Douglas* framework operates. It noted: "[E]stablishment of the prima facie case in effect creates a presumption that the employer unlawfully discriminated against the employee. To establish a presumption is to say that a finding of the predicate fact (here, the prima facie case) produces a required conclusion in the absence of explanation (here, the finding of unlawful discrimination)." *Hicks*, 509 U.S. at 507 (citations omitted).

The Court further explained the rebuttable presumption created by the prima facie case, indicating that it operates like all presumptions, as described in Federal Rule of Evidence 301:

> In all civil actions and proceedings not otherwise provided for by Act of Congress or by these rules, a presumption imposes on the party against whom it is directed the burden of going forward with evidence to rebut or meet the presumption, but does not shift to such party the burden of proof in the sense of the risk of nonpersuasion, which remains throughout the trial upon the party on whom it was originally cast.

*Id.* (citations omitted). Regarding the burden of production that shifts to the defendant, the Court noted: "In the nature of things, the determination that a defendant has met its burden of production (and has thus rebutted any legal presumption of intentional discrimination) can involve no credibility assessment." *Id.* at 509.

In *Hicks*, the District Court found that the employer provided false reasons for its demotion and discharge of the plaintiff. *Id.* at 508. However, it found that the real reason for the plaintiff's discharge was a personal vendetta against him, and not his race. *Id.* The Supreme Court held that while the factfinder's rejection of the employer's proffered reason permits the factfinder to infer discrimination, it does not compel such a finding. *Id.* at 510–11.

Stated another way, the Court in *Hicks* recognized that an employer may proffer a false reason for its actions because it is engaging in illegal discrimination or for other reasons. Because Title VII requires that an action be taken because of a protected trait, a finding of discrimination is not compelled simply because the employer's proffered reason for its conduct is disbelieved. However, a factfinder may infer discrimination based on evidence that the employer lied about the reason for its action.

In subsequent cases, courts have held that the employer may be mistaken regarding its reason for acting and still be able to articulate its mistaken reason as a legitimate, non-discriminatory reason for its actions, and ultimately prevail in the case. As one court indicated:

> The normal rule in discrimination cases is that if an employer honestly believes that an employee is terminated for misconduct, but it turns out later that the employer was mistaken about whether the employee violated a workplace rule, the employer cannot be liable for discrimination. If the employer takes an adverse action based on a good faith belief that an employee engaged in misconduct, then the employer has acted because of perceived misconduct, not because of protected status or activity. The relevant inquiry is whether the [employer] *believed* [the employee] was guilty of the conduct justifying discharge.

*See Richey v. City of Independence*, 540 F.3d 779, 784 (8th Cir. 2008).

Some judges are becoming skeptical of the continued usefulness of the *McDonnell-Douglas* test. Consider the following concurrence in a 2012 case.

> The original *McDonnell Douglas* decision was designed to clarify and to simplify the plaintiff's task in presenting such a case. Over the years, unfortunately, both of those goals have gone by the wayside.... [W]e engage in an allemande worthy of the 16th century, carefully executing the first four steps of the dance for the *prima facie* case, shifting over to the partner for the "articulation" interlude, and then concluding with the examination of evidence of pretext. But, as my colleagues correctly point out, evidence relevant to one of the initial four steps is often (and is here) equally helpful for showing pretext.
>
> Perhaps *McDonnell Douglas* was necessary nearly 40 years ago, when Title VII litigation was still relatively new in the federal courts. By now, however, as this case well illustrates, the various tests that we insist lawyers use have lost their utility. Courts manage tort litigation every day without the ins and outs of these methods of proof, and I see no reason why employment discrimination litigation (including cases alleging retaliation) could not be handled in the same straight-forward way. In order to defeat summary judgment, the plaintiff one way or the other must present evidence showing that she is in a class protected by the statute, that she suffered the requisite adverse action (depending on her theory), and that a rational jury could conclude that the employer took that adverse action on account of her protected class, not for any non-invidious reason.

*Coleman v. Donahoe*, 667 F.3d 835, 863 (7th Cir. 2012) (Wood, J., concurring).

The *McDonnell-Douglas* framework, as modified by the subsequent cases, has been applied in cases brought under the ADA, the ADEA, and section 1981. However, federal circuits disagree about whether juries should be instructed using the *McDonnell-Douglas* framework, with the majority view being that the framework should not be used. There are two main rationales for not using the framework in jury instructions. Some courts articulate that the framework is too confusing for juries, while others note that applying the framework at the end of a trial does not make sense because in most cases, the defendant has submitted evidence of its legitimate, non-discriminatory reason for acting, and thus, having the jury consider the prima facie case does not make sense.

---

## Focus Question: *Reeves v. Sanderson Plumbing Products, Inc.*

*Did the Supreme Court decide that the* McDonnell-Douglas *framework should be used in the ADEA context?*

---

# Reeves v. Sanderson Plumbing Products, Inc.

### 530 U.S. 133 (2000)

Justice O'Connor delivered the opinion of the Court.

This case concerns the kind and amount of evidence necessary to sustain a jury's verdict that an employer unlawfully discriminated on the basis of age. Specifically, we must resolve whether a defendant is entitled to judgment as a matter of law when the plaintiff's case consists exclusively of a prima facie case of discrimination and sufficient evidence for the trier of fact to disbelieve the defendant's legitimate, nondiscriminatory explanation for its action. We must also decide whether the employer was entitled to judgment as a matter of law under the particular circumstances presented here.

### I

In October 1995, petitioner Roger Reeves was 57 years old and had spent 40 years in the employ of respondent, Sanderson Plumbing Products, Inc., a manufacturer of toilet seats and covers. Petitioner worked in a department known as the "Hinge Room," where he supervised the "regular line." Joe Oswalt, in his mid-thirties, supervised the Hinge Room's "special line," and Russell Caldwell, the manager of the Hinge Room and age 45, supervised both petitioner and Oswalt. Petitioner's responsibilities included recording the attendance and hours of those under his supervision, and reviewing a weekly report that listed the hours worked by each employee.

In the summer of 1995, Caldwell informed Powe Chesnut, the director of manufacturing and the husband of company president Sandra Sanderson, that production was down in the Hinge Room because employees were often absent and were coming in late and leaving early. Because the monthly attendance reports did not indicate a problem, Chesnut ordered an audit of the Hinge Room's timesheets for July, August, and September of that year. According to Chesnut's testimony, that investigation revealed "numerous timekeeping errors and misrepresentations on the part of Caldwell, Reeves, and Oswalt." Following the audit, Chesnut, along with Dana Jester, vice president of human resources, and Tom Whitaker, vice president of operations, recommended to company president Sanderson that petitioner and Caldwell be fired. In October 1995, Sanderson followed the recommendation and discharged both petitioner and Caldwell.

In June 1996, petitioner filed suit in the United States District Court for the Northern District of Mississippi, contending that he had been fired because of his age in violation of the Age Discrimination in Employment Act of 1967. At trial, respondent contended that it had fired petitioner due to his failure to maintain accurate attendance records, while petitioner attempted to demonstrate that respondent's explanation was pretext for age discrimination. Petitioner introduced evidence that he had accurately recorded the attendance and hours of the employees under his supervision, and that Chesnut, whom Oswalt described as wielding "absolute power" within the company, had demonstrated age-based animus in his dealings with petitioner.

During the trial, the District Court twice denied oral motions by respondent for judgment as a matter of law under Rule 50 of the Federal Rules of Civil Procedure, and the case went to the jury. The court instructed the jury that "[i]f the plaintiff fails to prove age was a determinative or motivating factor in the decision to terminate him, then your verdict shall be for the defendant." So charged, the jury returned a verdict in favor of petitioner....

The Court of Appeals for the Fifth Circuit reversed, holding that petitioner had not introduced sufficient evidence to sustain the jury's finding of unlawful discrimination. After noting respondent's proffered justification for petitioner's discharge, the court acknowledged that petitioner "very well may" have offered sufficient evidence for "a reasonable jury [to] have found that [respondent's] explanation for its employment decision was pretextual." The court explained, however, that this was "not dispositive" of the ultimate issue—namely, "whether Reeves presented sufficient evidence that his age motivated [respondent's] employment decision." Addressing this question, the court weighed petitioner's additional evidence of discrimination against other circumstances surrounding his discharge. Specifically, the court noted that Chesnut's age-based comments "were not made in the direct context of Reeves's termination"; there was no allegation that the two other individuals who had recommended that petitioner be fired (Jester and Whitaker) were motivated by age; two of the decisionmakers involved in petitioner's discharge (Jester and Sanderson) were over the age of 50; all three of the Hinge Room supervisors were accused of inaccurate recordkeeping; and several of respondent's management positions were filled by persons over age 50 when petitioner was fired. On this basis, the court concluded that petitioner had not introduced sufficient evidence for a rational jury to conclude that he had been discharged because of his age....

## II

Under the ADEA, it is "unlawful for an employer ... to fail or refuse to hire or to discharge any individual or otherwise discriminate against any individual with respect to his compensation, terms, conditions, or privileges of employment, because of such individual's age." 29 U.S.C. § 623(a)(1). When a plaintiff alleges disparate treatment, "liability depends on whether the protected trait (under the ADEA, age) actually motivated the employer's decision." *Hazen Paper Co. v. Biggins*, 507 U.S. 604, 610 (1993). That is, the plaintiff's age must have "actually played a role in [the employer's decisionmaking] process and had a determinative influence on the outcome." *Ibid.* Recognizing that "the question facing triers of fact in discrimination cases is both sensitive and difficult," and that "[t]here will seldom be 'eyewitness' testimony as to the employer's mental processes," [citation omitted], the Courts of Appeals, including the Fifth Circuit in this case, have employed some variant of the framework articulated in *McDonnell Douglas* to analyze ADEA claims that are based principally on circumstantial evidence. This Court has not squarely addressed whether the *McDonnell Douglas* framework, developed to assess claims brought under ... Title VII ... also applies to ADEA actions. Because the parties do not dispute the issue, we shall assume, *arguendo,* that the *McDonnell Douglas* framework is fully applicable here.

*McDonnell Douglas* and subsequent decisions have "established an allocation of the burden of production and an order for the presentation of proof in ... discriminatory-treatment cases." *St. Mary's Honor Center v. Hicks,* 509 U.S. 502, 506 (1993). First, the plaintiff must establish a prima facie case of discrimination. *Ibid.; Texas Dept. of Community Affairs v. Burdine,* 450 U.S. 248, 252–253 (1981). It is undisputed that petitioner satisfied this burden here: (i) at the time he was fired, he was a member of the class protected by the ADEA ("individuals who are at least 40 years of age," 29 U.S.C. §631(a)), (ii) he was otherwise qualified for the position of Hinge Room supervisor, (iii) he was discharged by respondent, and (iv) respondent successively hired three persons in their thirties to fill petitioner's position. The burden therefore shifted to respondent to "produc[e] evidence that the plaintiff was rejected, or someone else was preferred, for a legitimate, nondiscriminatory reason." *Burdine, supra,* at 254. This burden is one of production, not persuasion; it "can involve no credibility assessment." *St. Mary's Honor Center, supra,* at 509. Respondent met this burden by offering admissible evidence sufficient for the trier of fact to conclude that petitioner was fired because of his failure to maintain accurate attendance records. Accordingly, "the *McDonnell Douglas* framework—with its presumptions and burdens"—disappeared, *St. Mary's Honor Center, supra,* at 510, and the sole remaining issue was "discrimination *vel non.*"

Although intermediate evidentiary burdens shift back and forth under this framework, "[t]he ultimate burden of persuading the trier of fact that the defendant intentionally discriminated against the plaintiff remains at all times with the plaintiff." *Burdine,* 450 U.S., at 253. And in attempting to satisfy this burden, the plaintiff—once the employer produces sufficient evidence to support a nondiscriminatory explanation for its decision—must be afforded the "opportunity to prove by a preponderance of the evidence that the legitimate reasons offered by the defendant were not its true reasons, but were a pretext for discrimination." *Ibid.* That is, the plaintiff may attempt to establish that he was the victim of intentional discrimination "by showing that the employer's proffered explanation is unworthy of credence." *Burdine, supra,* at 256. Moreover, although the presumption of discrimination "drops out of the picture" once the defendant meets its burden of production, *St. Mary's Honor Center, supra,* at 511, the trier of fact may still consider the evidence establishing the plaintiff's prima facie case "and inferences properly drawn therefrom … on the issue of whether the defendant's explanation is pretextual," *Burdine, supra,* at 255.

In this case, the evidence supporting respondent's explanation for petitioner's discharge consisted primarily of testimony by Chesnut and Sanderson and documentation of petitioner's alleged "shoddy record keeping." … Petitioner, however, made a substantial showing that respondent's explanation was false. First, petitioner offered evidence that he had properly maintained the attendance records. Most of the timekeeping errors cited by respondent involved employees who were not marked late but who were recorded as having arrived at the plant at 7 a.m. for the 7 a.m. shift. Respondent contended that employees arriving at 7 a.m. could not have been at their workstations by 7 a.m., and therefore must have been late. But both petitioner and Oswalt testified that the company's automated timeclock often failed to scan employees' timecards, so that the timesheets would not record any time of arrival. On these occasions, petitioner and Oswalt would visually check the workstations and record whether the employees were present at the start of the shift. They stated that if an employee arrived promptly but the timesheet contained no time of arrival, they would reconcile the two by marking "7 a.m." as the employee's arrival time, even if the employee actually arrived at the plant earlier. On cross-examination, Chesnut acknowledged that the timeclock sometimes malfunctioned, and that if "people were there at their work station[s]" at the start of the shift, the supervisor "would write in seven o'clock."

Petitioner similarly cast doubt on whether he was responsible for any failure to discipline late and absent employees. Petitioner testified that his job only included reviewing the daily and weekly attendance reports, and that disciplinary writeups were based on the monthly reports, which were reviewed by Caldwell. Sanderson admitted that Caldwell, and not petitioner, was responsible for citing employees for violations of the company's attendance policy....

Based on this evidence, the Court of Appeals concluded that petitioner "very well may be correct" that "a reasonable jury could have found that [respondent's] explanation for its employment decision was pretextual." Nonetheless, the court held that this showing, standing alone, was insufficient to sustain the jury's finding of liability.... And in making this determination, the Court of Appeals ignored the evidence supporting petitioner's prima facie case and challenging respondent's explanation for its decision.... That is, the Court of Appeals proceeded from the assumption that a prima facie case of discrimination, combined with sufficient evidence for the trier of fact to disbelieve the defendant's legitimate, nondiscriminatory reason for its decision, is insufficient as a matter of law to sustain a jury's finding of intentional discrimination.

In so reasoning, the Court of Appeals misconceived the evidentiary burden borne by plaintiffs who attempt to prove intentional discrimination through indirect evidence. This much is evident from our decision in *St. Mary's Honor Center.* There we held that the factfinder's rejection of the employer's legitimate, nondiscriminatory reason for its action does not *compel* judgment for the plaintiff. 509 U.S. at 511. The ultimate question is whether the employer intentionally discriminated, and proof that "the employer's proffered reason is unpersuasive, or even obviously contrived, does not necessarily establish that the plaintiff's proffered reason ... is correct." *Id.* at 524. In other words, "[i]t is not enough ... to *dis*believe the employer; the factfinder must *believe* the plaintiff's explanation of intentional discrimination." *Id.* at 519.

In reaching this conclusion, however, we reasoned that it is *permissible* for the trier of fact to infer the ultimate fact of discrimination from the falsity of the employer's explanation. Specifically, we stated:

> The factfinder's disbelief of the reasons put forward by the defendant (particularly if disbelief is accompanied by a suspicion of mendacity) may, together with the elements of the prima facie case, suffice to show intentional discrimination. Thus, rejection of the defendant's proffered reasons will *permit* the trier of fact to infer the ultimate fact of intentional discrimination.

*Id.* at 511.

Proof that the defendant's explanation is unworthy of credence is simply one form of circumstantial evidence that is probative of intentional discrimination, and it may be quite persuasive. In appropriate circumstances, the trier of fact can reasonably infer from the falsity of the explanation that the employer is dissembling to cover up a discriminatory purpose. Such an inference is consistent with the general principle of evidence law that the factfinder is entitled to consider a party's dishonesty about a material fact as "affirmative evidence of guilt." ...

This is not to say that such a showing by the plaintiff will *always* be adequate to sustain a jury's finding of liability. Certainly there will be instances where, although the plaintiff has established a prima facie case and set forth sufficient evidence to reject the defendant's explanation, no rational factfinder could conclude that the action was discriminatory. For instance, an employer would be entitled to judgment as a matter of law if the record conclusively revealed some other, nondiscriminatory reason for the employer's decision, or if the plaintiff created only a weak issue of fact as to whether the employer's reason was untrue and there was abundant and uncontroverted independent evidence that no discrimination had occurred....

[It] is apparent that respondent was not entitled to judgment as a matter of law. In this case, in addition to establishing a prima facie case of discrimination and creating a jury issue as to the falsity of the employer's explanation, petitioner introduced additional evidence that Chesnut was motivated by age-based animus and was principally responsible for petitioner's firing. Petitioner testified that Chesnut had told him that he "was so old [he] must have come over on the Mayflower" and, on one occasion when petitioner was having difficulty starting a machine, that he "was too damn old to do [his] job." ... Oswalt, roughly 24 years younger than petitioner, corroborated that there was an "obvious difference" in how Chesnut treated them. He stated that, although he and Chesnut "had [their] differences," "it was nothing compared to the way [Chesnut] treated Roger." Oswalt explained that Chesnut "tolerated quite a bit" from him even though he "defied" Chesnut "quite often," but that Chesnut treated petitioner "[i]n a manner, as you would ... treat ... a child when ... you're angry with [him]." ...

The ultimate question in every employment discrimination case involving a claim of disparate treatment is whether the plaintiff was the victim of intentional discrimination.... Given that petitioner established a prima facie case of discrimination, introduced enough evidence for the jury to reject respondent's explanation, and produced additional evidence of age-based animus, there was sufficient evidence for the jury to find that respondent had intentionally discriminated. The District Court was therefore correct to submit the case to the jury, and the Court of Appeals erred in overturning its verdict.

For these reasons, the judgment of the Court of Appeals is reversed.

[A concurrence by Justice Ginsburg is omitted.]

---

## Exercise 3.2

Write out the *McDonnell-Douglas* framework. You may do this in the form of a flow-chart, a diagram or in simple text. Now, think about whether you actually understand how it works. Does this framework make sense for answering the question of whether a person was discriminated against based on a protected trait?

---

## Exercise 3.3

Susan Smith is Hispanic. She applies for a managerial position at a department store. The managerial position requires that applicants (1) possess a high school diploma; and (2) have at least two years of experience working at a department store. Susan will testify that she applied for the position in question, that she has a high school diploma, and that she worked at another department store for five years. Susan did not get the managerial position and a non-Hispanic woman was hired for the job. After exhausting administrative requirements, Susan files a claim of race discrimination under Title VII.

Has Susan made out a prima facie case under *McDonnell-Douglas*? If so, what happens as a result? Note that, with respect to the second prong of the prima facie case—applied and was qualified—courts have held that the plaintiff must show she meets the objective, minimum qualifications of the position. *See Carter v. Three Springs Residential Treatment*, 132 F.3d 635, 643–44 (11th Cir. 1998).

The employer's lawyer argues at the hearing on the summary judgment motion that the reason that Susan was not chosen for the position was that the candidate who was chosen was more qualified for the position. In whose favor should this case be resolved, Susan's or the employer's?

Now assume that the department store has additional job requirements — that the applicant possess superior communication skills and be energetic. The department store employee who interviewed Susan testifies that during the interview Susan was not energetic and that her communication skills were average. Can Susan establish her prima facie case?

## Exercise 3.4

Joseph Satish is originally from India. His employment is terminated because his supervisor claims he was late for work for five days in a row. Employees at the company are required to punch in for work, and the time sheet records actually demonstrate that Joseph was on time each of the five days and that his supervisor is lying about Joseph being late. After Joseph is terminated, his supervisor hires a white male for Joseph's old position. Can Joseph establish his prima facie case?

Now assume a change in the facts. Instead of being terminated for tardiness, Joseph is terminated because he failed to return client phone calls. Joseph has evidence that other employees within his department did not return client phone calls and maintained their jobs. The employer presents evidence that Joseph did not return client phone calls and articulates that this was the legitimate, non-discriminatory reason for its actions. No one has been hired to replace Joseph. How should the prima facie case be articulated in this case? Who should prevail on this set of facts?

## ✦ Core Concept: Comparators — Similarly Situated Employees Outside of Plaintiff's Protected Class

The actual prima facie case announced in *McDonnell-Douglas* was specific to the facts of that case, which involved a failure to hire and the employer continuing to seek applicants of plaintiff's qualifications. Courts have frequently accepted the *McDonnell-Douglas* Court's invitation to tailor the test to differing factual situations. 411 U.S. 782, 802 n.13 (1973). Courts often modify the fourth prong of the *McDonnell-Douglas* test to allow plaintiffs to proceed if they can establish that similarly situated employees outside the protected class received better treatment than plaintiff. *See, e.g., Chuang v. Univ. of Cal. Davis Bd. of Trustees*, 225 F.3d 1115, 1123 (9th Cir. 2000). Exercise 3.4 above, involving Joseph Satish, illustrates the kind of case in which the test might be so modified, allowing Joseph to use evidence that other workers received better treatment than he did to create an inference that his race motivated the differential treatment.

The use of comparators to create an inference of discriminatory intent raises two questions. First, what does it mean for employees to be similarly situated? Second, in the age discrimination context, what does it mean for the comparators to fall outside of the protected class?

Courts have held that for employees to be considered similarly situated, they must be comparable "in all material respects, such as dealing with the same supervisor, engaging in similar conduct, and being subject to the same standards." *Timm v. Illinois Dept. of Corrections*, No. 07-3697, 2009 WL 1845641, at *4 (7th Cir. June 29, 2009). While some courts strictly adhere to the similarly situated requirement, others have "cautioned against a hyper-technical approach to this prong." *Id.* These latter courts look "for enough common features to allow for a meaningful comparison between substantially similar employees." *Id.*

The following case addresses whether a comparator who is over the age of forty and thus within the protected class can nevertheless be used as a comparator in the age discrimination context.

# O'Connor v. Consolidated Coin Caterers Corp.

## 517 U.S. 308 (1996)

Justice Scalia delivered the opinion of the Court.

This case presents the question whether a plaintiff alleging that he was discharged in violation of the Age Discrimination in Employment Act of 1967 (ADEA) must show that he was replaced by someone outside the age group protected by the ADEA to make out a prima facie case under the framework established by *McDonnell Douglas Corp. v. Green*, 411 U.S. 792 (1973).

Petitioner James O'Connor was employed by respondent Consolidated Coin Caterers Corporation from 1978 until August 10, 1990, when, at age 56, he was fired. Claiming that he had been dismissed because of his age in violation of the ADEA, petitioner brought suit in the United States District Court for the Western District of North Carolina. After discovery, the District Court granted respondent's motion for summary judgment, and petitioner appealed. The Court of Appeals for the Fourth Circuit stated that petitioner could establish a prima facie case under *McDonnell Douglas* only if he could prove that (1) he was in the age group protected by the ADEA; (2) he was discharged or demoted; (3) at the time of his discharge or demotion, he was performing his job at a level that met his employer's legitimate expectations; and (4) following his discharge or demotion, he was replaced by someone of comparable qualifications outside the protected class. Since petitioner's replacement was 40 years old, the Court of Appeals concluded that the last element of the prima facie case had not been made out. Finding that petitioner's claim could not survive a motion for summary judgment without benefit of the *McDonnell Douglas* presumption (*i.e.*, "under the ordinary standards of proof used in civil cases,"), the Court of Appeals affirmed the judgment of dismissal. We granted O'Connor's petition for certiorari.

In *McDonnell Douglas*, we "established an allocation of the burden of production and an order for the presentation of proof in Title VII discriminatory-treatment cases." We held that a plaintiff alleging racial discrimination in violation of Title VII could establish a prima facie case by showing "(i) that he belongs to a racial minority; (ii) that he applied and was qualified for a job for which the employer was seeking applicants; (iii) that, despite his qualifications, he was rejected; and (iv) that, after his rejection, the position remained open and the employer continued to seek applicants from persons of [the] complainant's qualifications." Once the plaintiff has met this initial burden, the burden of production shifts to the employer "to articulate some legitimate, nondiscriminatory reason for the employee's rejection." [citation omitted]. If the trier of fact finds that the elements of the prima facie case are supported by a preponderance of the evidence and the employer remains silent, the court must enter judgment for the plaintiff.

In assessing claims of age discrimination brought under the ADEA, the Fourth Circuit, like others, has applied some variant of the basic evidentiary framework set forth in *McDonnell Douglas*. We have never had occasion to decide whether that application of the Title VII rule to the ADEA context is correct, but since the parties do not contest that point, we shall assume it. On that assumption, the question presented for our determination is what elements must be shown in an ADEA case to establish the prima facie case that triggers the employer's burden of production.

As the very name "prima facie case" suggests, there must be at least a logical connection between each element of the prima facie case and the illegal discrimination for which it establishes a "legally mandatory, rebuttable presumption." [citation omitted]. The element of replacement by someone under 40 fails this requirement. The discrimination prohibited by the ADEA is discrimination "because of [an] individual's age," 29 U.S.C. §623(a)(1), though the prohibition is "limited to individuals who are at least 40 years of age," §631(a). This language does not ban discrimination against employees because they are aged 40 or older; it bans discrimination against employees because of their age, but limits the protected class to those who are 40 or older. The fact that one person in the protected class has lost out to another person in the protected class is thus irrelevant, so long as he has lost out *because of his age.* Or to put the point more concretely, there can be no greater inference of *age* discrimination (as opposed to "40 or over" discrimination) when a 40-year-old is replaced by a 39-year-old than when a 56-year-old is replaced by a 40-year-old. Because it lacks probative value, the fact that an ADEA plaintiff was replaced by someone outside the protected class is not a proper element of the *McDonnell Douglas* prima facie case.

Perhaps some courts have been induced to adopt the principle urged by respondent in order to avoid creating a prima facie case on the basis of very thin evidence—for example, the replacement of a 68-year-old by a 65-year-old. While the respondent's principle theoretically permits such thin evidence (consider the example above of a 40-year-old replaced by a 39-year-old), as a practical matter it will rarely do so, since the vast majority of age-discrimination claims come from older employees. In our view, however, the proper solution to the problem lies not in making an utterly irrelevant factor an element of the prima facie case, but rather in recognizing that the prima facie case requires "*evidence adequate to create an inference that an employment decision was based on a[n] [illegal] discriminatory criterion....*" *Teamsters v. United States,* 431 U.S. 324, 358 (1977) (emphasis added). In the age-discrimination context, such an inference cannot be drawn from the replacement of one worker with another worker insignificantly younger. Because the ADEA prohibits discrimination on the basis of age and not class membership, the fact that a replacement is substantially younger than the plaintiff is a far more reliable indicator of age discrimination than is the fact that the plaintiff was replaced by someone outside the protected class.

The judgment of the Fourth Circuit is reversed, and the case is remanded for proceedings consistent with this opinion.

------------

## Further Discussion

As you can see from the prior *O'Connor* case, courts may be required to alter the *McDonnell-Douglas* framework to fit the particular circumstances of a case. These alterations and the way that they are articulated may vary from circuit to circuit, and circuit splits often exist regarding whether certain formulations of the test are acceptable. Lawyers on both sides of an employment discrimination case where the *McDonnell-Douglas* framework will be used should consider whether modifications to the framework are necessary given the circumstances of a particular case and should be ready to advocate for those changes. However, as the appellate decision in *O'Connor* case suggests, courts may be reluctant to make changes to the framework, and attorneys should also be ready to proceed under a previously accepted version of the test.

The *McDonnell-Douglas* framework is commonly modified in two other circumstances: reverse discrimination cases and reduction-in-force cases. Some courts require that those seeking to prove a case of reverse discrimination establish " 'background circumstances' sufficient to demonstrate that the particular employer has 'reason or inclination to discriminate invidiously against whites' or evidence that 'there is something "fishy" about the facts at hand.' " *See, e.g., Hague v. Thompson Distrib. Co.*, 436 F.3d 816, 821 (7th Cir. 2006). Courts base this added requirement on the assumption that reverse discrimination seldom happens. Thus, members of the majority who wish to benefit from the *McDonnell-Douglas* inference must add some additional evidence to warrant the inference. As one court indicated: "Invidious racial discrimination against whites is relatively uncommon in our society, and so there is nothing inherently suspicious in an employer's decision to promote a qualified minority applicant instead of a qualified white applicant." *Id.*

Some courts have rejected the idea that reverse discrimination plaintiffs must prove more than others to proceed through the *McDonnell-Douglas* framework. *See, e.g., Iadimarco v. Runyon*, 190 F.3d 151, 161 (3d Cir. 1999). Still, other courts have used a test that appears to combine the two positions, allowing a reverse-discrimination plaintiff to prevail either by showing additional background circumstances or "indirect evidence sufficient to support a reasonable probability, that but for the plaintiff's status the challenged employment decision would have favored the plaintiff." *See, e.g., Lyons v. Red Roof Inns, Inc.*, 130 Fed. App'x 953, 954 (10th Cir. 2005).

In the reduction-in-force context, iterations of the *McDonnell-Douglas* framework that require replacement by a person outside the plaintiff's protected class often do not make sense because the employer is reducing the number of employees. Some courts have modified the test to require that there be other evidence suggesting a discriminatory motive. Some courts modify the test because there often are not replacement employees in a reduction-in-force context. *See, e.g., Diaz v. Eagle Produce Ltd. Partnership*, 521 F.3d 1201, 1208 (9th Cir. 2008). Others reason that, "because the most common legitimate reason for the discharge of a plaintiff in a [reduction in force] situation is the work force reduction, the plaintiff must provide additional direct, circumstantial, or statistical evidence tending to indicate that the employer singled out the plaintiff for discharge for impermissible reasons." *Geiger v. Tower Automotive*, 579 F.3d 614, 624 (6th Cir. 2004).

## ✦ Core Concept: Stray Remarks

Plaintiffs often proffer evidence of discriminatory remarks within the workplace to support their discrimination claims. Courts may decline to consider some remarks as relevant to the plaintiff's case, if the comments are made by individuals who were not part of the decisionmaking process, if the comments are removed in time from the decision at issue, if the comments are not about the type of discrimination alleged by the plaintiff, or if there are other reasons why the comments do not relate to plaintiff's claim. Courts often justify such exclusion by claiming that comments are "stray remarks," using a phrase coined by Justice Sandra O'Connor in *Price Waterhouse v. Hopkins*, 490 U.S. 228, 277 (1989) (O'Connor, J., concurring).

A few examples clarify this concept. For example, assume a woman claims that she was terminated because of her sex. The woman has evidence that the individual who decided she should be fired made derogatory comments about other employees based on their religion or that the same individual made a derogatory comment about women ten years prior to the plaintiff's termination. The court may exclude consideration of these comments, finding they are merely stray remarks and too attenuated from the issues in the woman's case.

In one sense, the stray remarks doctrine attempts to prevent the jury from being unduly swayed by discriminatory comments that have little relationship to the plaintiff's claim of discrimination. Critics of the stray remarks doctrine note that courts may use the doctrine excessively and exclude evidence that shows the context in which a particular decision is being made. Although this concept is not limited to circumstances in which the *McDonnell-Douglas* framework is used, the concept is discussed within this section of the text, because it commonly arises in this context.

## ✦ Core Concept: Business Judgment

Remember that in many states, the at-will employment rule is the default rule for determining whether an employer may take an action. The rules of at-will employment provide the employer with significant leeway in making decisions. The federal anti-discrimination statutes do not completely disrupt the at-will employment concept, and employers still retain discretion to make decisions, as long as those decisions do not violate the statutes (or some other source of law or contract).

In some instances, a court will defer to an employer's prerogative to make certain decisions and indicate that the federal anti-discrimination statutes do not allow the courts to second-guess the employer's business judgment or to act as a super personnel department. For example, in a reduction-in-force case, a plaintiff may try to claim that other companies in the same economic circumstances would not have chosen to undertake a reduction. Or the employee may argue that the employer had more onerous job requirements than other employers. Courts may choose not to consider such arguments because the federal anti-discrimination statutes do not take away an employer's ability to make decisions, even bad decisions, as long as those decisions do not otherwise violate the statutes.

It is difficult to characterize how the business judgment concept fits within the discrimination framework. Some judges appear to use it simply as another reason to explain a decision to grant summary judgment in the employer's favor. Other courts use it as a way to describe why the plaintiff's evidence of pretext is insufficient.

## ✦ Core Concept: Same Decisionmaker and Same Class Inferences

In some employment discrimination cases, an individual makes a positive decision related to an employee, and then later that same individual makes a negative decision related to that same employee. At times, the courts infer that discrimination is not the likely explanation for the negative decision because the same decisionmaker earlier made a positive decision related to the same individual. In other words, it is unlikely that a person who harbors discriminatory animus toward a protected trait would have made the earlier positive employment decision in favor of the employee who is now alleging discrimination.

A related concept is whether discriminatory motive is at work where the decisionmaker is in the same protected class as the plaintiff. Some courts are disinclined to find discrimination where, for example, a female plaintiff alleges sex discrimination by a supervisor who is also female. Some courts infer that discrimination is not the likely explanation for conduct by the decisionmaker.

As with the concept of business judgment, many courts use these inferences to bolster a decision a judge already has made on other grounds. No matter how the inferences are used in a technical manner, they point to powerful assumptions being made by judges (and perhaps juries) about the circumstances under which discrimination does and does not occur. Can you think of instances in which these inferences do not make sense?

## ✦ Core Concept: Direct vs. Circumstantial Evidence

The *McDonnell-Douglas* Court explained that the framework it was creating was for analyzing cases lacking direct evidence. The idea was that plaintiffs had limited access to information about the defendant's motives, so the *McDonnell-Douglas* analysis would help to ferret out the truth. Direct evidence cases, presumably, would proceed in accordance with the regular rules of evidence and procedure just like any civil action. As discussed earlier, courts, as a result, tend to use the *McDonnell-Douglas* framework in cases involving circumstantial evidence of discrimination, but not in cases consisting primarily of direct evidence. Over the years, some of the circuit courts have recognized that pushing all circumstantial claims into the *McDonnell-Douglas* framework may not be appropriate; others continue to maintain the direct/circumstantial evidence dichotomy. Thus, there are two important issues that confront courts and litigants. First, what exactly is the difference between direct and circumstantial evidence? Second, will the court consider a case through the direct evidence framework even if the plaintiff possesses circumstantial evidence?

Outside of the context of facially discriminatory policies, courts have had a difficult time defining direct evidence, and definitions regarding what constitutes direct evidence vary. Direct evidence of discrimination can be described as "evidence, that, if believed, proves the existence of a fact in issue without inference or presumption ... [and] is composed of only the most blatant remarks, whose intent could be nothing other than to discriminate on the basis of some impermissible factor." *Rojas v. Fla.*, 285 F.3d 1339, 1342 n. 2 (11th Cir. 2002) (per curiam). One court has described direct evidence as that which "essentially requires an admission by the employer," and explained that "such evidence is rare." *Argyropoulos v. City of Alton*, 539 F.3d 724, 733 (7th Cir. 2008). "A statement that can plausibly be interpreted two different ways—one discriminatory and the other benign—does not directly reflect illegal animus, and, thus, does not constitute direct evidence." *Vaughn v. Epworth Villa*, 537 F.3d 1147, 1154–55 (10th Cir. 2008).

Evidence that is not considered to be direct evidence of discrimination is labeled as circumstantial evidence. Circumstantial evidence "allows the trier of fact to *infer* intentional discrimination by the decisionmaker, typically through a longer chain of inferences." *Caskey v. Colgate-Palmolive Co.*, 535 F.3d 585, 593 (7th Cir. 2008).

Given the ambiguity inherent in these definitions, courts have been unable when faced with various factual scenarios to consistently determine when evidence rises to the level of direct evidence and when it constitutes circumstantial evidence. The use of powerful racial epithets is often seen as direct evidence of discrimination. *See Kendall v. Block,* 821 F.2d 1142 (5th Cir. 1987) (using the term "n*****" may be direct evidence of discrimination); *Brewer v. Muscle Shoals Bd. of Educ.,* 790 F.2d 1515 (11th Cir. 1986) (school superintendent's comment that he did not want to appoint plaintiff to an administrative position because he did not want to see the school system "n*****-rigged" is direct evidence of discriminatory animus, even though the comment was made with regard to an incident occurring after the alleged violation).

However, the use of epithets in other contexts may not be regarded as direct evidence. For example, in one case a plaintiff argued that she had direct evidence of discrimination because she was referred to as a "bitch" in written evaluations. *Neuren v. Adduci, Mastriani, Meeks & Schill,* 43 F.3d 1507, 1513 (D.C. Cir. 1995). The court disagreed. "Although this pejorative term may support an inference that an employment decision is discriminatory under different circumstances, *see Walsdorf v. Board of Commissioners for the East Jefferson Levee District,* 857 F.2d 1047, 1049, 1054 (granting Title VII relief to female employee based upon evidence which included statement by supervisor that 'Ain't no bitch going to get this job.'), in itself, the term is not always conclusive of sex discrimination." *Neuren,* 43 F.3d at 1513.

At times, courts consider negative statements made by the decisionmaker and referencing a protected trait to be direct evidence of discrimination. *EEOC v. Alton Packaging Corp.,* 901 F.2d 920 (11th Cir. 1990) (general manager's statement that if it were his company he would not hire blacks is direct evidence of discriminatory animus in failing to promote the plaintiff). At times, the courts require these statements to be made at or near the time of the allegedly discriminatory action to constitute direct evidence.

While the difference between direct and circumstantial evidence continues to be important in discrimination cases, some circuits will allow a plaintiff to make a case of discrimination without resorting to *McDonnell Douglas,* if the plaintiff has "either direct or circumstantial evidence that supports an inference of intentional discrimination." *See, e.g., Coffman v. Indianapolis Fire Dept.,* 578 F.3d 559, 563 (7th Cir. 2009). Whether circumstantial evidence rises to the level to create the required inference of discrimination seems to vary depending on how a particular court interprets the facts of the case before it.

---

## Exercise 3.5

Sheila works at XYZ Motors for several years as a welder. XYZ Motors makes customized motorcycles. Sheila is the only woman who works at XYZ Motors. The shop floor has a locker room atmosphere, and employees constantly make fun of one another. Sheila enjoys the atmosphere and often joins in name calling and practical jokes. On her 50th birthday, Sheila receives a birthday card that describes all of the reasons that she is "Over the Hill." Everyone writes age-related comments in the card, including her supervisor Bill. Bill writes in the card: "It is all downhill from here, you Old Fart." After the party, Bill and other co-workers continue to reference Sheila's age by calling her Old Fart or the old lady. Several weeks later, Sheila is terminated from her position. Bill tells Sheila that he no longer needs her services and that it is time for her to move on.

You are a plaintiff's attorney and Sheila comes to your office seeking advice on whether she has a valid claim. What framework do you think a court would use to evaluate Sheila's claim? Would Sheila prevail under such a framework? Identify any additional information you need to answer these questions.

## ✦ Core Concept: Adverse Actions

Recall that the first portion of Title VII's operative language prohibits an employer from "fail[ing] or refus[ing] to hire or to discharge any individual, or otherwise to discriminate against any individual with respect to his compensation, terms, conditions, or privileges of employment" because of a protected trait. 42 U.S.C. § 2000e-2(1). Although this statutory language seems to encompass any discrimination, regardless of how minor, many courts require that an action rise to a certain level of seriousness to be cognizable under the federal employment discrimination statutes. Courts have sometimes embodied this requirement of seriousness in the concept of "adverse action" or "adverse employment action." Such courts would say that only adverse actions are cognizable under the employment discrimination laws.

Certain discriminatory actions, such as failure to hire, termination, failure to promote, or demotion, are always serious enough to create potential liability under the federal anti-discrimination statutes. Some conduct, such as minor social slights, never rises to the required level of seriousness. In between these two extremes is a gray area. Actions such as changing an employee's working conditions without changing the employee's pay or placing a negative evaluation in an employee's file may or may not affect the "terms and conditions" of employment, as that term is understood in a legal sense. *See, e.g., Cooper v. United Parcel Service, Inc.,* No. 09-30864, 2010 WL 610047, at *4 (5th Cir. Feb. 22, 2010) (indicating that lateral transfer is not cognizable).

A minority of circuits use the term "ultimate employment action" to define the required level of seriousness. This latter term is stricter than the term "adverse action," and requires an action such as a failure to hire, a discharge, a failure to promote, or a compensation decision. *Lee v. Department of Veterans Affairs,* 247 Fed. Appx. 472, 477 (5th Cir. 2007).

Later when you read about the "materially adverse action" concept in the retaliation context, consider whether the term means the same thing in that context as it does in the discrimination context. Also, be careful to distinguish the term "adverse action" from the term "tangible employment action," which you will study in Chapter 5. Before leaving this section, consider what types of harm the discrimination statutes should protect employees from. If an employer places a negative evaluation in an employee's file or gives the employee an undesirable office based on a protected trait, should the employee be able to file a discrimination claim?

## ✦ Core Concept: Mixed Motive

The *McDonnell-Douglas* case and the analytical framework it produced envisioned a single-motive paradigm: was Green's race the reason why defendant rejected Green's application, or was the reason some other "legitimate, nondiscriminatory" factor. *McDonnell-Douglas* simply said nothing on the question of how courts should treat cases where the defendant has two reasons for taking the challenged action, one legitimate reason and one discriminatory reason. Thus, after *McDonnell-Douglas,* it remained unclear whether a plaintiff was required to prove that an employment decision was taken solely because of a protected trait or whether a plaintiff could prevail on an employment discrimination claim if the employer was motivated both by legitimate and discriminatory motives. The following case recognized a mixed-motive analysis under Title VII and set forth a framework for handling such claims. After reading the case, you should be able to articulate the proof structure the Supreme Court created.

---

### Focus Questions: *Price Waterhouse v. Hopkins*

1. *What framework does the Supreme Court establish for evaluating mixed-motive cases?*

2. *Does this test favor plaintiffs or defendants? Why?*

3. *Does the test require a plaintiff to have direct evidence of discrimination?*

4. *Count the votes. Is there a majority opinion in this case? If not, what kind of opinion is this and what kind of precedential value does it have? What is the holding of the Court?*

5. *Based on your reading of the facts, did the employer have both legitimate and discriminatory reasons for acting? Is it possible to disentangle the legitimate from the discriminatory reasons?*

---

# Price Waterhouse v. Hopkins
### 490 U.S. 228 (1989)

Justice Brennan, announced the judgment of the Court and delivered an opinion, in which Justices Marshall, Blackmun and Stevens joined. Justices White and O'Connor filed opinions concurring in the judgment. Justice Kennedy filed a dissenting opinion, in which Chief Justice Rehnquist and Justice Scalia joined.

Ann Hopkins was a senior manager in an office of Price Waterhouse when she was proposed for partnership in 1982. She was neither offered nor denied admission to the partnership; instead, her candidacy was held for reconsideration the following year. When the partners in her office later refused to repropose her for partnership, she sued Price Waterhouse under Title VII, charging that the firm had discriminated against her on the basis of sex in its decisions regarding partnership.... We granted certiorari to resolve a conflict among the Courts of Appeals concerning the respective burdens of proof of a defendant and plaintiff in a suit under Title VII when it has been shown that an employment decision resulted from a mixture of legitimate and illegitimate motives.

I

At Price Waterhouse, a nationwide professional accounting partnership, a senior manager becomes a candidate for partnership when the partners in her local office submit her name as a candidate. All of the other partners in the firm are then invited to submit written comments on each candidate — either on a "long" or a "short" form, depending on the partner's degree of exposure to the candidate. Not every partner in the firm submits comments on every candidate. After reviewing the comments and interviewing the partners who submitted them, the firm's Admissions Committee makes a recommendation to the

Policy Board. This recommendation will be either that the firm accept the candidate for partnership, put her application on "hold," or deny her the promotion outright. The Policy Board then decides whether to submit the candidate's name to the entire partnership for a vote, to "hold" her candidacy, or to reject her. The recommendation of the Admissions Committee, and the decision of the Policy Board, are not controlled by fixed guidelines: a certain number of positive comments from partners will not guarantee a candidate's admission to the partnership, nor will a specific quantity of negative comments necessarily defeat her application. Price Waterhouse places no limit on the number of persons whom it will admit to the partnership in any given year.

Ann Hopkins had worked at Price Waterhouse's Office of Government Services in Washington, D.C., for five years when the partners in that office proposed her as a candidate for partnership. Of the 662 partners at the firm at that time, 7 were women. Of the 88 persons proposed for partnership that year, only 1—Hopkins—was a woman. Forty-seven of these candidates were admitted to the partnership, 21 were rejected, and 20—including Hopkins—were "held" for reconsideration the following year.[15] Thirteen of the 32 partners who had submitted comments on Hopkins supported her bid for partnership. Three partners recommended that her candidacy be placed on hold, eight stated that they did not have an informed opinion about her, and eight recommended that she be denied partnership.

In a jointly prepared statement supporting her candidacy, the partners in Hopkins' office showcased her successful 2-year effort to secure a $25 million contract with the De-partment of State, labeling it "an outstanding performance" and one that Hopkins carried out "virtually at the partner level." Despite Price Waterhouse's attempt at trial to minimize her contribution to this project, Judge Gesell specifically found that Hopkins had "played a key role in Price Waterhouse's successful effort to win a multi-million dollar contract with the Department of State." Indeed, he went on, "[n]one of the other partnership can-didates at Price Waterhouse that year had a comparable record in terms of successfully securing major contracts for the partnership."

The partners in Hopkins' office praised her character as well as her accomplishments, describing her in their joint statement as "an outstanding professional" who had a "deft touch," a "strong character, independence and integrity." Clients appear to have agreed with these assessments. At trial, one official from the State Department described her as "extremely competent, intelligent," "strong and forthright, very productive, energetic and creative." Another high-ranking official praised Hopkins' decisiveness, broadmindedness, and "intellectual clarity"; she was, in his words, "a stimulating conversationalist." Evaluations such as these led Judge Gesell to conclude that Hopkins "had no difficulty dealing with clients and her clients appear to have been very pleased with her work" and that she "was generally viewed as a highly competent project leader who worked long hours, pushed vigorously to meet deadlines and demanded much from the multidisciplinary staffs with which she worked."

On too many occasions, however, Hopkins' aggressiveness apparently spilled over into abrasiveness. Staff members seem to have borne the brunt of Hopkins' brusqueness. Long before her bid for partnership, partners evaluating her work had counseled her to improve her relations with staff members. Although later evaluations indicate an improvement,

---

15. Before the time for reconsideration came, two of the partners in Hopkins' office withdrew their support for her, and the office informed her that she would not be reconsidered for partnership. Hopkins then resigned. Price Waterhouse does not challenge the Court of Appeals' conclusion that the refusal to repropose her for partnership amounted to a constructive discharge....

Hopkins' perceived shortcomings in this important area eventually doomed her bid for partnership. Virtually all of the partners' negative remarks about Hopkins—even those of partners supporting her—had to do with her "interpersonal skills." Both "[s]upporters and opponents of her candidacy," stressed Judge Gesell, "indicated that she was sometimes overly aggressive, unduly harsh, difficult to work with and impatient with staff."

There were clear signs, though, that some of the partners reacted negatively to Hopkins' personality because she was a woman. One partner described her as "macho"; another suggested that she "overcompensated for being a woman"; a third advised her to take "a course at charm school[.]" Several partners criticized her use of profanity; in response, one partner suggested that those partners objected to her swearing only "because it's a lady using foul language." Another supporter explained that Hopkins "ha[d] matured from a tough-talking somewhat masculine hard-nosed mgr to an authoritative, formidable, but much more appealing lady ptr candidate." But it was the man who, as Judge Gesell found, bore responsibility for explaining to Hopkins the reasons for the Policy Board's decision to place her candidacy on hold who delivered the *coup de grace:* in order to improve her chances for partnership, Thomas Beyer advised, Hopkins should "walk more femininely, talk more femininely, dress more femininely, wear make-up, have her hair styled, and wear jewelry."

Dr. Susan Fiske, a social psychologist and Associate Professor of Psychology at Carnegie-Mellon University, testified at trial that the partnership selection process at Price Waterhouse was likely influenced by sex stereotyping. Her testimony focused not only on the overtly sex-based comments of partners but also on gender-neutral remarks, made by partners who knew Hopkins only slightly, that were intensely critical of her. One partner, for example, baldly stated that Hopkins was "universally disliked" by staff, and another described her as "consistently annoying and irritating"; yet these were people who had had very little contact with Hopkins. According to Fiske, Hopkins' uniqueness (as the only woman in the pool of candidates) and the subjectivity of the evaluations made it likely that sharply critical remarks such as these were the product of sex stereotyping— although Fiske admitted that she could not say with certainty whether any particular comment was the result of stereotyping. Fiske based her opinion on a review of the submitted comments, explaining that it was commonly accepted practice for social psychologists to reach this kind of conclusion without having met any of the people involved in the decisionmaking process.

In previous years, other female candidates for partnership also had been evaluated in sex-based terms. As a general matter, Judge Gesell concluded, "[c]andidates were viewed favorably if partners believed they maintained their femin[in]ity while becoming effective professional managers"; in this environment, "[t]o be identified as a 'women's lib[b]er' was regarded as [a] negative comment." In fact, the judge found that in previous years "[o]ne partner repeatedly commented that he could not consider any woman seriously as a partnership candidate and believed that women were not even capable of functioning as senior managers—yet the firm took no action to discourage his comments and recorded his vote in the overall summary of the evaluations."

Judge Gesell found that Price Waterhouse legitimately emphasized interpersonal skills in its partnership decisions, and also found that the firm had not fabricated its complaints about Hopkins' interpersonal skills as a pretext for discrimination. Moreover, he concluded, the firm did not give decisive emphasis to such traits only because Hopkins was a woman; although there were male candidates who lacked these skills but who were admitted to partnership, the judge found that these candidates possessed other, positive traits that Hopkins lacked.

The judge went on to decide, however, that some of the partners' remarks about Hopkins stemmed from an impermissibly cabined view of the proper behavior of women, and that Price Waterhouse had done nothing to disavow reliance on such comments. He held that Price Waterhouse had unlawfully discriminated against Hopkins on the basis of sex by consciously giving credence and effect to partners' comments that resulted from sex stereotyping. Noting that Price Waterhouse could avoid equitable relief by proving by clear and convincing evidence that it would have placed Hopkins' candidacy on hold even absent this discrimination, the judge decided that the firm had not carried this heavy burden.

The Court of Appeals affirmed the District Court's ultimate conclusion, but departed from its analysis in one particular: it held that even if a plaintiff proves that discrimination played a role in an employment decision, the defendant will not be found liable if it proves, by clear and convincing evidence, that it would have made the same decision in the absence of discrimination. Under this approach, an employer is not deemed to have violated Title VII if it proves that it would have made the same decision in the absence of an impermissible motive, whereas under the District Court's approach, the employer's proof in that respect only avoids equitable relief. We decide today that the Court of Appeals had the better approach, but that both courts erred in requiring the employer to make its proof by clear and convincing evidence.

## II

The specification of the standard of causation under Title VII is a decision about the kind of conduct that violates that statute. According to Price Waterhouse, an employer violates Title VII only if it gives decisive consideration to an employee's gender, race, national origin, or religion in making a decision that affects that employee. On Price Waterhouse's theory, even if a plaintiff shows that her gender played a part in an employment decision, it is still her burden to show that the decision would have been different if the employer had not discriminated. In Hopkins' view, on the other hand, an employer violates the statute whenever it allows one of these attributes to play any part in an employment decision. Once a plaintiff shows that this occurred, according to Hopkins, the employer's proof that it would have made the same decision in the absence of discrimination can serve to limit equitable relief but not to avoid a finding of liability. We conclude that, as often happens, the truth lies somewhere in between.

## A

In passing Title VII, Congress made the simple but momentous announcement that sex, race, religion, and national origin are not relevant to the selection, evaluation, or compensation of employees.[16] Yet, the statute does not purport to limit the other qualities and characteristics that employers *may* take into account in making employment decisions. The converse, therefore, of "for cause" legislation, Title VII eliminates certain bases for distinguishing among employees while otherwise preserving employers' freedom of choice. This balance between employee rights and employer prerogatives turns out to be decisive in the case before us.

Congress' intent to forbid employers to take gender into account in making employment decisions appears on the face of the statute. In now-familiar language, the statute forbids an employer to "fail or refuse to hire or to discharge any individual, or otherwise to dis-

---

16. We disregard, for purposes of this discussion, the special context of affirmative action.

criminate with respect to his compensation, terms, conditions, or privileges of employment," or to "limit, segregate, or classify his employees or applicants for employment in any way which would deprive or tend to deprive any individual of employment opportunities or otherwise adversely affect his status as an employee, *because of* such individual's ... sex." 42 U.S.C. §§ 2000e-2(a)(1), (2) (emphasis added). We take these words to mean that gender must be irrelevant to employment decisions. To construe the words "because of" as colloquial shorthand for "but-for causation," as does Price Waterhouse, is to misunderstand them.

But-for causation is a hypothetical construct. In determining whether a particular factor was a but-for cause of a given event, we begin by assuming that that factor was present at the time of the event, and then ask whether, even if that factor had been absent, the event nevertheless would have transpired in the same way. The present, active tense of the operative verbs of § 703(a)(1) ("to fail or refuse"), in contrast, turns our attention to the actual moment of the event in question, the adverse employment decision. The critical inquiry, the one commanded by the words of § 703(a)(1), is whether gender was a factor in the employment decision *at the moment it was made.* Moreover, since we know that the words "because of" do not mean "*solely* because of," we also know that Title VII meant to condemn even those decisions based on a mixture of legitimate and illegitimate considerations. When, therefore, an employer considers both gender and legitimate factors at the time of making a decision, that decision was "because of" sex and the other, legitimate considerations—even if we may say later, in the context of litigation, that the decision would have been the same if gender had not been taken into account.

To attribute this meaning to the words "because of" does not, as the dissent asserts, divest them of causal significance. A simple example illustrates the point. Suppose two physical forces act upon and move an object, and suppose that either force acting alone would have moved the object. As the dissent would have it, *neither* physical force was a "cause" of the motion unless we can show that but for one or both of them, the object would not have moved; apparently both forces were simply "in the air" unless we can identify at least one of them as a but-for cause of the object's movement. Events that are causally overdetermined, in other words, may not have any "cause" at all. This cannot be so.

We need not leave our common sense at the doorstep when we interpret a statute. It is difficult for us to imagine that, in the simple words "because of," Congress meant to obligate a plaintiff to identify the precise causal role played by legitimate and illegitimate motivations in the employment decision she challenges. We conclude, instead, that Congress meant to obligate her to prove that the employer relied upon sex-based considerations in coming to its decision.

Our interpretation of the words "because of" also is supported by the fact that Title VII does identify one circumstance in which an employer may take gender into account in making an employment decision, namely, when gender is a "bona fide occupational qualification (BFOQ) reasonably necessary to the normal operation of th[e] particular business or enterprise." 42 U.S.C. § 2000e-2(e). The only plausible inference to draw from this provision is that, in all other circumstances, a person's gender may not be considered in making decisions that affect her. Indeed, Title VII even forbids employers to make gender an indirect stumbling block to employment opportunities. An employer may not, we have held, condition employment opportunities on the satisfaction of facially neutral tests or qualifications that have a disproportionate, adverse impact on members of protected groups when those tests or qualifications are not required for performance of the job.

To say that an employer may not take gender into account is not, however, the end of the matter, for that describes only one aspect of Title VII. The other important aspect of the statute is its preservation of an employer's remaining freedom of choice. We conclude that the preservation of this freedom means that an employer shall not be liable if it can prove that, even if it had not taken gender into account, it would have come to the same decision regarding a particular person. The statute's maintenance of employer prerogatives is evident from the statute itself and from its history, both in Congress and in this Court.

To begin with, the existence of the BFOQ exception shows Congress' unwillingness to require employers to change the very nature of their operations in response to the statute. And our emphasis on "business necessity" in disparate-impact cases, and on "legitimate, nondiscriminatory reason[s]" in disparate-treatment cases, see *McDonnell Douglas Corp. v. Green*, 411 U.S. 792, 802 (1973), results from our awareness of Title VII's balance between employee rights and employer prerogatives. In *McDonnell Douglas*, we described as follows Title VII's goal to eradicate discrimination while preserving workplace efficiency: "The broad, overriding interest, shared by employer, employee, and consumer, is efficient and trustworthy workmanship assured through fair and racially neutral employment and personnel decisions. In the implementation of such decisions, it is abundantly clear that Title VII tolerates no racial discrimination, subtle or otherwise." ...

Our holding casts no shadow on *Burdine*, in which we decided that, even after a plaintiff has made out a prima facie case of discrimination under Title VII, the burden of persuasion does not shift to the employer to show that its stated legitimate reason for the employment decision was the true reason. [S]ince we hold that the plaintiff retains the burden of persuasion on the issue whether gender played a part in the employment decision, the situation before us is not the one of "shifting burdens" that we addressed in *Burdine*. Instead, the employer's burden is most appropriately deemed an affirmative defense: the plaintiff must persuade the factfinder on one point, and then the employer, if it wishes to prevail, must persuade it on another.[17]

... Where a decision was the product of a mixture of legitimate and illegitimate motives, however, it simply makes no sense to ask whether the legitimate reason was "*the* true reason." [citations omitted].[18] Oblivious to this last point, the dissent would insist that *Burdine's* framework perform work that it was never intended to perform. It would require a plaintiff who challenges an adverse employment decision in which both legitimate and illegitimate considerations played a part to pretend that the decision, in fact, stemmed from a single source—for the premise of *Burdine* is that *either* a legitimate *or* an illegitimate set of considerations led to the challenged decision. To say that *Burdine's* evidentiary

---

17. Given that both the plaintiff and defendant bear a burden of proof in cases such as this one, it is surprising that the dissent insists that our approach requires the employer to bear "the ultimate burden of proof." It is, moreover, perfectly consistent to say *both* that gender was a factor in a particular decision when it was made *and* that, when the situation is viewed hypothetically and after the fact, the same decision would have been made even in the absence of discrimination. Thus, we do not see the "internal inconsistency" in our opinion that the dissent perceives.

18. Nothing in this opinion should be taken to suggest that a case must be correctly labeled as either a "pretext" case or a "mixed-motives" case from the beginning in the District Court; indeed, we expect that plaintiffs often will allege, in the alternative, that their cases are both. Discovery often will be necessary before the plaintiff can know whether both legitimate and illegitimate considerations played a part in the decision against her. At some point in the proceedings, of course, the District Court must decide whether a particular case involves mixed-motives. If the plaintiff fails to satisfy the factfinder that it is more likely than not that a forbidden characteristic played a part in the employment decision, then she may prevail only if she proves, following *Burdine*, that the employer's stated reason for its decision is pretextual....

scheme will not help us decide a case admittedly involving *both* kinds of considerations is not to cast aspersions on the utility of that scheme in the circumstances for which it was designed.

## B

In deciding as we do today, we do not traverse new ground. We have in the past confronted Title VII cases in which an employer has used an illegitimate criterion to distinguish among employees, and have held that it is the employer's burden to justify decisions resulting from that practice. When an employer has asserted that gender is a BFOQ within the meaning of § 703(e), for example, we have assumed that it is the employer who must show why it must use gender as a criterion in employment.... [O]ur assumption always has been that if an employer allows gender to affect its decisionmaking process, then it must carry the burden of justifying its ultimate decision. We have not in the past required women whose gender has proved relevant to an employment decision to establish the negative proposition that they would not have been subject to that decision had they been men, and we do not do so today.

...

[We conclude] that the plaintiff who shows that an impermissible motive played a motivating part in an adverse employment decision has thereby placed upon the defendant the burden to show that it would have made the same decision in the absence of the unlawful motive. Our decision today treads this well-worn path.

## C

In saying that gender played a motivating part in an employment decision, we mean that, if we asked the employer at the moment of the decision what its reasons were and if we received a truthful response, one of those reasons would be that the applicant or employee was a woman. In the specific context of sex stereotyping, an employer who acts on the basis of a belief that a woman cannot be aggressive, or that she must not be, has acted on the basis of gender.

Although the parties do not overtly dispute this last proposition, the placement by Price Waterhouse of "sex stereotyping" in quotation marks throughout its brief seems to us an insinuation either that such stereotyping was not present in this case or that it lacks legal relevance. We reject both possibilities. As to the existence of sex stereotyping in this case, we are not inclined to quarrel with the District Court's conclusion that a number of the partners' comments showed sex stereotyping at work. As for the legal relevance of sex stereotyping, we are beyond the day when an employer could evaluate employees by assuming or insisting that they matched the stereotype associated with their group, for "[i]n forbidding employers to discriminate against individuals because of their sex, Congress intended to strike at the entire spectrum of disparate treatment of men and women resulting from sex stereotypes." [citations omitted]. An employer who objects to aggressiveness in women but whose positions require this trait places women in an intolerable and impermissible catch 22: out of a job if they behave aggressively and out of a job if they do not. Title VII lifts women out of this bind.

Remarks at work that are based on sex stereotypes do not inevitably prove that gender played a part in a particular employment decision. The plaintiff must show that the employer actually relied on her gender in making its decision. In making this showing, stereotyped remarks can certainly be *evidence* that gender played a part. In any event, the stereotyping in this case did not simply consist of stray remarks. On the contrary, Hopkins proved that Price Waterhouse invited partners to submit comments; that some of the comments stemmed from sex stereotypes; that an important part of the Policy Board's decision on Hopkins was an assessment of the submitted comments; and that Price Waterhouse in no way disclaimed reliance on the sex-linked evaluations. This is not, as Price Waterhouse suggests, "discrimination in the air"; rather, it is, as Hopkins puts it, "discrimination brought to ground and visited upon" an employee....

As to the employer's proof, in most cases, the employer should be able to present some objective evidence as to its probable decision in the absence of an impermissible motive. Moreover, proving "that the same decision would have been justified ... is not the same as proving that the same decision would have been made." [citation omitted]. An employer may not, in other words, prevail in a mixed-motives case by offering a legitimate and sufficient reason for its decision if that reason did not motivate it at the time of the decision. Finally, an employer may not meet its burden in such a case by merely showing that at the time of the decision it was motivated only in part by a legitimate reason. The very premise of a mixed-motives case is that a legitimate reason was present, and indeed, in this case, Price Waterhouse already has made this showing by convincing Judge Gesell that Hopkins' interpersonal problems were a legitimate concern. The employer instead must show that its legitimate reason, standing alone, would have induced it to make the same decision.

## III

The courts below held that an employer who has allowed a discriminatory impulse to play a motivating part in an employment decision must prove by clear and convincing evidence that it would have made the same decision in the absence of discrimination. We are persuaded that the better rule is that the employer must make this showing by a preponderance of the evidence....

## IV

Price Waterhouse also charges that Hopkins produced no evidence that sex stereotyping played a role in the decision to place her candidacy on hold. As we have stressed, however, Hopkins showed that the partnership solicited evaluations from all of the firm's partners; that it generally relied very heavily on such evaluations in making its decision; that some of the partners' comments were the product of stereotyping; and that the firm in no way disclaimed reliance on those particular comments, either in Hopkins' case or in the past. Certainly a plausible—and, one might say, inevitable—conclusion to draw from this set of circumstances is that the Policy Board in making its decision did in fact take into account all of the partners' comments, including the comments that were motivated by stereotypical notions about women's proper deportment....

Nor is the finding that sex stereotyping played a part in the Policy Board's decision undermined by the fact that many of the suspect comments were made by supporters rather than detractors of Hopkins. A negative comment, even when made in the context of a generally favorable review, nevertheless may influence the decisionmaker to think less highly of the candidate; the Policy Board, in fact, did not simply tally the "yeses" and "noes" regarding a candidate, but carefully reviewed the content of the submitted comments. The additional suggestion that the comments were made by "persons outside the decisionmaking chain"—and therefore could not have harmed Hopkins—simply ignores the critical role that partners' comments played in the Policy Board's partnership decisions.

Price Waterhouse appears to think that we cannot affirm the factual findings of the trial court without deciding that, instead of being overbearing and aggressive and curt, Hopkins is, in fact, kind and considerate and patient. If this is indeed its impression, petitioner misunderstands the theory on which Hopkins prevailed. The District Judge acknowledged that Hopkins' conduct justified complaints about her behavior as a senior manager. But he also concluded that the reactions of at least some of the partners were reactions to her as a *woman* manager. Where an evaluation is based on a subjective assessment of a person's strengths and weaknesses, it is simply not true that each evaluator will focus on, or even mention, the same weaknesses. Thus, even if we knew that Hopkins had "personality problems," this would not tell us that the partners who cast their evaluations of Hopkins in sex-based terms would have criticized her as sharply (or criticized her at all) if she had been a man. It is not our job to review the evidence and decide that the negative reactions to Hopkins were based on reality; our perception of Hopkins' character is irrelevant. We sit not to determine whether Ms. Hopkins is nice, but to decide whether the partners reacted negatively to her personality because she is a woman.

V

We hold that when a plaintiff in a Title VII case proves that her gender played a motivating part in an employment decision, the defendant may avoid a finding of liability only by proving by a preponderance of the evidence that it would have made the same decision even if it had not taken the plaintiff's gender into account. Because the courts below erred by deciding that the defendant must make this proof by clear and convincing evidence, we reverse the Court of Appeals' judgment against Price Waterhouse on liability and remand the case to that court for further proceedings.

[The concurring opinion of Justice White is omitted.]

Justice O'Connor, concurring in the judgment.

...

[T]here is mounting evidence in the decisions of the lower courts that respondent here is not alone in her inability to pinpoint discrimination as the precise cause of her injury, despite having shown that it played a significant role in the decisional process. Many of these courts, which deal with the evidentiary issues in Title VII cases on a regular basis, have concluded that placing the risk of nonpersuasion on the defendant in a situation where uncertainty as to causation has been created by its consideration of an illegitimate criterion makes sense as a rule of evidence and furthers the substantive command of Title VII.... Particularly in the context of the professional world, where decisions are often made by collegial bodies on the basis of largely subjective criteria, requiring the plaintiff to prove that *any* one factor was the definitive cause of the decisionmakers' action may be tantamount to declaring Title VII inapplicable to such decisions....

I believe there are significant differences between shifting the burden of persuasion to the employer in a case resting purely on statistical proof as in the disparate impact setting and shifting the burden of persuasion in a case like this one, where an employee has demonstrated by direct evidence that an illegitimate factor played a substantial role in a particular employment decision. First, the explicit consideration of race, color, religion, sex, or national origin in making employment decisions "was the most obvious evil Congress had in mind when it enacted Title VII." [citation omitted]. While the prima facie case under *McDonnell Douglas* and the statistical showing of imbalance involved in a disparate impact case may both be indicators of discrimination or its "functional equivalent," they are not, in and of themselves, the evils Congress sought to eradicate from the employment setting. Second, shifting the burden of persuasion to the employer in a situation like this one creates no incentive to preferential treatment in violation of § 2000e-2(j). To avoid bearing the burden of justifying its decision, the employer need not seek racial or sexual balance in its work force; rather, all it need do is avoid substantial reliance on forbidden criteria in making its employment decisions....

In my view, in order to justify shifting the burden on the issue of causation to the defendant, a disparate treatment plaintiff must show by direct evidence that an illegitimate criterion was a substantial factor in the decision. As the Court of Appeals noted below: "While most circuits have not confronted the question squarely, the consensus among those that have is that once a Title VII plaintiff has demonstrated by direct evidence that discriminatory animus played a significant or substantial role in the employment decision, the burden shifts to the employer to show that the decision would have been the same absent discrimination." Requiring that the plaintiff demonstrate that an illegitimate factor played a substantial role in the employment decision identifies those employment situations where the deterrent purpose of Title VII is most clearly implicated. As an evidentiary matter, where a plaintiff has made this type of strong showing of illicit motivation, the factfinder is entitled to presume that the employer's discriminatory animus made a difference to the outcome, absent proof to the contrary from the employer. Where a disparate treatment plaintiff has made such a showing, the burden then rests with the employer to convince the trier of fact that it is more likely than not that the decision would have been the same absent consideration of the illegitimate factor. The employer need not isolate the sole cause for the decision; rather it must demonstrate that with the illegitimate factor removed from the calculus, sufficient business reasons would have induced it to take the same employment action. This evidentiary scheme essentially requires the employer to place the employee in the same position he or she would have occupied absent discrimination. If the employer fails to carry this burden, the factfinder is justified in concluding that the decision was made "because of" consideration of the illegitimate factor and the substantive standard for liability under the statute is satisfied.

Thus, stray remarks in the workplace, while perhaps probative of sexual harassment, see *Meritor Savings Bank v. Vinson*, 477 U.S. 57, 63–69 (1986), cannot justify requiring the employer to prove that its hiring or promotion decisions were based on legitimate criteria. Nor can statements by nondecisionmakers, or statements by decisionmakers unrelated to the decisional process itself, suffice to satisfy the plaintiff's burden in this regard.... Race and gender always "play a role" in an employment decision in the benign sense that these are human characteristics of which decisionmakers are aware and about which they may comment in a perfectly neutral and nondiscriminatory fashion. For example, in the context of this case, a mere reference to "a lady candidate" might show that gender "played a role" in the decision, but by no means could support a rational factfinder's inference that the decision was made "because of" sex. What is required is what Ann Hopkins showed here: direct evidence that decisionmakers placed substantial negative reliance on an illegitimate criterion in reaching their decision....

In sum, because of the concerns outlined above, and because I believe that the deterrent purpose of Title VII is disserved by a rule which places the burden of proof on plaintiffs on the issue of causation in all circumstances, I would retain but supplement the framework we established in *McDonnell Douglas* and subsequent cases. The structure of the presentation of evidence in an individual disparate treatment case should conform to the general outlines we established in *McDonnell Douglas* and *Burdine*. First, the plaintiff must establish the *McDonnell Douglas* prima facie case by showing membership in a protected group, qualification for the job, rejection for the position, and that after rejection the employer continued to seek applicants of complainant's general qualifications. The plaintiff should also present any direct evidence of discriminatory animus in the decisional process. The defendant should then present its case, including its evidence as to legitimate, nondiscriminatory reasons for the employment decision. As the dissent notes, under this framework, the employer "has every incentive to convince the trier of fact that the decision was lawful." [footnote omitted]. Once all the evidence has been received, the court should determine whether the *McDonnell Douglas* or *Price Waterhouse* framework properly applies to the evidence before it. If the plaintiff has failed to satisfy the *Price Waterhouse* threshold, the case should be decided under the principles enunciated in *McDonnell Douglas* and *Burdine,* with the plaintiff bearing the burden of persuasion on the ultimate issue whether the employment action was taken because of discrimination. In my view, such a system is both fair and workable, and it calibrates the evidentiary requirements demanded of the parties to the goals behind the statute itself....

Justice Kennedy, with whom Chief Justice Rehnquist and Justice Scalia join, dissenting.

Today the Court manipulates existing and complex rules for employment discrimination cases in a way certain to result in confusion. Continued adherence to the evidentiary scheme established in *McDonnell Douglas Corp. v. Green,* 411 U.S. 792, (1973), and *Texas Dept. of Community Affairs v. Burdine,* 450 U.S. 248 (1981), is a wiser course than creation of more disarray in an area of the law already difficult for the bench and bar, and so I must dissent....

---

## Subsequent Developments

After *Price Waterhouse,* Congress passed the Civil Rights Act of 1991, which amended Title VII. Among other things, the 1991 Act affected mixed-motive analysis in two important ways. First, the amendment explicitly recognized that mixed-motive analysis was appropriate under Title VII. The amended statutory language, found at 42 U.S.C. § 2000e-2(m), reads as follows:

(m) Impermissible consideration of race, color, religion, sex, or national origin in employment practices

Except as otherwise provided in this subchapter, an unlawful employment practice is established when the complaining party demonstrates that race, color, religion, sex, or national origin was a motivating factor for any employment practice, even though other factors also motivated the practice.

Second, the amendment changed the structure for establishing a mixed motive under Title VII. The amended language reads as follows:

(B) On a claim in which an individual proves a violation under section 2000e-2(m) of this title and a respondent demonstrates that the respondent would have taken the same action in the absence of the impermissible motivating factor, the court—

(i) may grant declaratory relief, injunctive relief (except as provided in clause (ii)), and attorney's fees and costs demonstrated to be directly attributable only to the pursuit of a claim under section 2000e-2(m) of this title; and

(ii) shall not award damages or issue an order requiring any admission, reinstatement, hiring, promotion, or payment, described in subparagraph (A).

42 U.S.C. § 2000e-5(g)(2). The 1991 Act defined the term "demonstrates" to mean "meets the burdens of production and persuasion." 42 U.S.C. § 2000e(m).

What important change does this amendment make to the framework set forth in *Price Waterhouse*? Importantly, Congress did not amend the ADEA, section 1981, or the ADA when it amended Title VII. We will explore the implications of this in Exercise 3.6 and the cases following it.

---

### Focus Question: *Desert Palace, Inc. v. Costa*

*Why was it necessary for the Supreme Court to resolve the issue raised in this case?*

---

# Desert Palace, Inc. v. Costa

## 539 U.S. 90 (2003)

Justice Thomas delivered the opinion of the Court.

The question before us in this case is whether a plaintiff must present direct evidence of discrimination in order to obtain a mixed-motive instruction under Title VII, as amended by the Civil Rights Act of 1991 (1991 Act). We hold that direct evidence is not required.

### I
### A

Since 1964, Title VII has made it an "unlawful employment practice for an employer ... to discriminate against any individual..., *because of* such individual's race, color, religion, sex, or national origin." 42 U.S.C. § 2000e-2(a)(1) (emphasis added). In *Price Waterhouse v. Hopkins*, 490 U.S. 228 (1989), the Court considered whether an employment decision is made "because of" sex in a "mixed-motive" case, *i.e.*, where both legitimate and illegitimate reasons motivated the decision. The Court concluded that, under § 2000e-2(a)(1), an employer could "avoid a finding of liability ... by proving that it would have made the same decision even if it had not allowed gender to play such a role." The Court was divided, however, over the predicate question of when the burden of proof may be shifted to an employer to prove the affirmative defense.

Justice Brennan, writing for a plurality of four Justices, ... did not "suggest a limitation on the possible ways of proving that [gender] stereotyping played a motivating role in an employment decision."

... [U]nder Justice O'Connor's [concurring] view, "the burden on the issue of causation" would shift to the employer only where "a disparate treatment plaintiff [could] show by *direct evidence* that an illegitimate criterion was a substantial factor in the decision." [citation omitted].

Two years after *Price Waterhouse*, Congress passed the 1991 Act "in large part [as] a response to a series of decisions of this Court interpreting the Civil Rights Acts of 1866 and 1964." [citation omitted]. In particular, § 107 of the 1991 Act, which is at issue in this case, "respond[ed]" to *Price Waterhouse* by "setting forth standards applicable in 'mixed motive' cases" in two new statutory provisions.[19] ...

---

19. This case does not require us to decide when, if ever, § 107 applies outside of the mixed-motive context.

Since the passage of the 1991 Act, the Courts of Appeals have divided over whether a plaintiff must prove by direct evidence that an impermissible consideration was a "motivating factor" in an adverse employment action. *See* 42 U.S.C. § 2000e-2(m). Relying primarily on Justice O'Connor's concurrence in *Price Waterhouse,* a number of courts have held that direct evidence is required to establish liability under § 2000e-2(m).

## B

Petitioner Desert Palace, Inc., dba Caesar's Palace Hotel & Casino of Las Vegas, Nevada, employed respondent Catharina Costa as a warehouse worker and heavy equipment operator. Respondent was the only woman in this job and in her local Teamsters bargaining unit.

Respondent experienced a number of problems with management and her co-workers that led to an escalating series of disciplinary sanctions, including informal rebukes, a denial of privileges, and suspension. Petitioner finally terminated respondent after she was involved in a physical altercation in a warehouse elevator with fellow Teamsters member Herbert Gerber. Petitioner disciplined both employees because the facts surrounding the incident were in dispute, but Gerber, who had a clean disciplinary record, received only a 5-day suspension.

Respondent subsequently filed this lawsuit against petitioner in the United States District Court for the District of Nevada, asserting claims of sex discrimination and sexual harassment under Title VII. The District Court dismissed the sexual harassment claim, but allowed the claim for sex discrimination to go to the jury. At trial, respondent presented evidence that (1) she was singled out for "intense stalking" by one of her supervisors, (2) she received harsher discipline than men for the same conduct, (3) she was treated less favorably than men in the assignment of overtime, and (4) supervisors repeatedly "stack[ed]" her disciplinary record and "frequently used or tolerated" sex-based slurs against her.

Based on this evidence, the District Court denied petitioner's motion for judgment as a matter of law, and submitted the case to the jury with instructions, two of which are relevant here. First, without objection from petitioner, the District Court instructed the jury that "[t]he plaintiff has the burden of proving ... by a preponderance of the evidence that she suffered adverse work conditions and that her sex was a motivating factor in any such work conditions imposed upon her."

Second, the District Court gave the jury the following mixed-motive instruction:

> You have heard evidence that the defendant's treatment of the plaintiff was motivated by the plaintiff's sex and also by other lawful reasons. If you find that the plaintiff's sex was a motivating factor in the defendant's treatment of the plaintiff, the plaintiff is entitled to your verdict, even if you find that the defendant's conduct was also motivated by a lawful reason.

> However, if you find that the defendant's treatment of the plaintiff was motivated by both gender and lawful reasons, you must decide whether the plaintiff is entitled to damages. The plaintiff is entitled to damages unless the defendant proves by a preponderance of the evidence that the defendant would have treated plaintiff similarly even if the plaintiff's gender had played no role in the employment decision.

Petitioner unsuccessfully objected to this instruction, claiming that respondent had failed to adduce "direct evidence" that sex was a motivating factor in her dismissal or in any of the other adverse employment actions taken against her. The jury rendered a verdict for respondent, awarding backpay, compensatory damages, and punitive damages. The District Court denied petitioner's renewed motion for judgment as a matter of law.

[The Ninth Circuit Court of Appeals sitting en banc] saw no need to decide whether Justice O'Connor's concurrence in *Price Waterhouse* controlled because it concluded that Justice O'Connor's references to "direct evidence" had been "wholly abrogated" by the 1991 Act. And, turning "to the language" of § 2000e-2(m), the court observed that the statute "imposes no special [evidentiary] requirement and does not reference 'direct evidence.'" Accordingly, the court concluded that a "plaintiff ... may establish a violation through a preponderance of evidence (whether direct or circumstantial) that a protected characteristic played 'a motivating factor.'" Based on that standard, the Court of Appeals held that respondent's evidence was sufficient to warrant a mixed-motive instruction and that a reasonable jury could have found that respondent's sex was a "motivating factor in her treatment." ...

## II

This case provides us with the first opportunity to consider the effects of the 1991 Act on jury instructions in mixed-motive cases. Specifically, we must decide whether a plaintiff must present direct evidence of discrimination in order to obtain a mixed-motive instruction under 42 U.S.C. § 2000e-2(m). Petitioner's argument on this point proceeds in three steps: (1) Justice O'Connor's opinion is the holding of *Price Waterhouse;* (2) Justice O'Connor's *Price Waterhouse* opinion requires direct evidence of discrimination before a mixed-motive instruction can be given; and (3) the 1991 Act does nothing to abrogate that holding. Like the Court of Appeals, we see no need to address which of the opinions in *Price Waterhouse* is controlling: the third step of petitioner's argument is flawed, primarily because it is inconsistent with the text of § 2000e-2(m).

Our precedents make clear that the starting point for our analysis is the statutory text. And where, as here, the words of the statute are unambiguous, the "judicial inquiry is complete." [citation omitted]. Section 2000e-2(m) unambiguously states that a plaintiff need only "demonstrat[e]" that an employer used a forbidden consideration with respect to "any employment practice." On its face, the statute does not mention, much less require, that a plaintiff make a heightened showing through direct evidence....

Moreover, Congress explicitly defined the term "demonstrates" in the 1991 Act, leaving little doubt that no special evidentiary showing is required. Title VII defines the term "demonstrates" as to "mee[t] the burdens of production and persuasion." § 2000e(m). If Congress intended the term "demonstrates" to require that the "burdens of production and persuasion" be met by direct evidence or some other heightened showing, it could have made that intent clear by including language to that effect in § 2000e(m). Its failure to do so is significant, for Congress has been unequivocal when imposing heightened proof requirements in other circumstances, including in other provisions of Title 42. *See, e.g.,* 8 U.S.C. § 1158(a)(2)(B) (stating that an asylum application may not be filed unless an alien "demonstrates by clear and convincing evidence" that the application was filed within one year of the alien's arrival in the United States); 42 U.S.C. § 5851(b)(3)(D) (providing that "[r]elief may not be ordered" against an employer in retaliation cases involving whistleblowers under the Atomic Energy Act where the employer is able to "*demonstrat[e] by clear and convincing evidence* that it would have taken the same unfavorable personnel action in the absence of such behavior" (emphasis added)); *cf. Price Waterhouse,* 490 U.S. at 253 (plurality opinion) ("Only rarely have we required clear and convincing proof where the action defended against seeks only conventional relief").

In addition, Title VII's silence with respect to the type of evidence required in mixed-motive cases also suggests that we should not depart from the "[c]onventional rul[e] of civil litigation [that] generally appl[ies] in Title VII cases." [citation omitted]. That rule requires a plaintiff to prove his case "by a preponderance of the evidence," using "direct or circumstantial evidence." [citation omitted]. We have often acknowledged the utility of circumstantial evidence in discrimination cases. For instance, in *Reeves v. Sanderson Plumbing Products, Inc.*, 530 U.S. 133 (2000), we recognized that evidence that a defendant's explanation for an employment practice is "unworthy of credence" is "one form of *circumstantial evidence* that is probative of intentional discrimination." The reason for treating circumstantial and direct evidence alike is both clear and deep rooted: "Circumstantial evidence is not only sufficient, but may also be more certain, satisfying and persuasive than direct evidence." [citation omitted].

The adequacy of circumstantial evidence also extends beyond civil cases; we have never questioned the sufficiency of circumstantial evidence in support of a criminal conviction, even though proof beyond a reasonable doubt is required. And juries are routinely instructed that "[t]he law makes no distinction between the weight or value to be given to either direct or circumstantial evidence." [citation omitted]. It is not surprising, therefore, that neither petitioner nor its *amici curiae* can point to any other circumstance in which we have restricted a litigant to the presentation of direct evidence absent some affirmative directive in a statute.

Finally, the use of the term "demonstrates" in other provisions of Title VII tends to show further that § 2000e-2(m) does not incorporate a direct evidence requirement. *See, e.g.,* 42 U.S.C. §§ 2000e-2(k)(1)(A)(i), 2000e-5(g)(2)(B). For instance, § 2000e-5(g)(2)(B) requires an employer to "demonstrat[e] that [it] would have taken the same action in the absence of the impermissible motivating factor" in order to take advantage of the partial affirmative defense. Due to the similarity in structure between that provision and § 2000e-2(m), it would be logical to assume that the term "demonstrates" would carry the same meaning with respect to both provisions. But when pressed at oral argument about whether direct evidence is required before the partial affirmative defense can be invoked, petitioner did not "agree that … the defendant or the employer has any heightened standard" to satisfy. Absent some congressional indication to the contrary, we decline to give the same term in the same Act a different meaning depending on whether the rights of the plaintiff or the defendant are at issue....

In order to obtain an instruction under § 2000e-2(m), a plaintiff need only present sufficient evidence for a reasonable jury to conclude, by a preponderance of the evidence, that "race, color, religion, sex, or national origin was a motivating factor for any employment practice." Because direct evidence of discrimination is not required in mixed-motive cases, the Court of Appeals correctly concluded that the District Court did not abuse its discretion in giving a mixed-motive instruction to the jury. Accordingly, the judgment of the Court of Appeals is affirmed.

---

## Exercise 3.6

Tom, who is white, applies to be the director of a program for at-risk youth. The particular program is designed to help kids in a neighborhood where the children or their parents come predominantly from Eastern European countries. Tom is interviewed for the position by five individuals, one of whom is a friend of his. Tom is not selected for the director's position. Tom's friend tells him that he interviewed poorly and that during the decisionmaking process one of the interviewers was concerned that Tom might not connect with the community because he lacks communication skills and because he did not have an Eastern

European background. Assuming that the program cannot establish that national origin is a bona fide occupational qualification for the position, how would this case be analyzed under the *Price Waterhouse* framework? How would it be analyzed under the 1991 amendments to Title VII?

Now, change the facts of the case slightly. Tom is 56. Tom's friend tells him that he interviewed poorly and that during the decisionmaking process one of the interviewers was concerned that Tom's age might make him less able to connect with at-risk youth. Assume that the case is being argued directly after the 1991 amendments were made to Title VII. Recall that those amendments expressly modified Title VII, but made no reference to the ADEA. What framework should the court use in analyzing this ADEA case? Should *Price Waterhouse* control?

As an attorney, one of your important roles is to be able to predict the likely legal outcome of a case based on your knowledge of the underlying law even where the courts have not yet decided the particular issue that your case presents. This skill is crucial for several reasons. Predicting the likely outcome of a case will help you advise your client regarding the strength of the case and whether to proceed with litigation. It also will be critical to determining the value of the case for purposes of settlement. In making predictions about a case, it is important that you consider the strengths and weaknesses of the case from various perspectives. For each portion of the hypothetical, think of the arguments that you would make if you were the plaintiff's counsel. What if you were the defendant's counsel? How should the court rule?

---

### Focus Questions: *Gross v. FBL Financial Services, Inc.*

1.  *What does this case mean for mixed-motive cases under the ADEA?*

2.  *Are you satisfied by the Court's reasoning?*

3.  *Do you think Congress intended this difference between Title VII and the ADEA? Do you think such a difference makes sense?*

---

## Gross v. FBL Financial Services, Inc.
### 557 U.S. 167 (2009)

Justice Thomas delivered the opinion of the Court.

The question presented by the petitioner in this case is whether a plaintiff must present direct evidence of age discrimination in order to obtain a mixed-motives jury instruction in a suit brought under the Age Discrimination in Employment Act of 1967 (ADEA). Because we hold that such a jury instruction is never proper in an ADEA case, we vacate the decision below.

#### I

Petitioner Jack Gross began working for respondent FBL Financial Group, Inc. (FBL), in 1971. As of 2001, Gross held the position of claims administration director. But in 2003, when he was 54 years old, Gross was reassigned to the position of claims project coordinator. At that same time, FBL transferred many of Gross' job responsibilities to a newly created position—claims administration manager. That position was given to Lisa Kneeskern, who had previously been supervised by Gross and who was then in her early forties. Although Gross (in his new position) and Kneeskern received the same compensation, Gross considered the reassignment a demotion because of FBL's reallocation of his former job responsibilities to Kneeskern.

In April 2004, Gross filed suit in District Court, alleging that his reassignment to the position of claims project coordinator violated the ADEA, which makes it unlawful for an employer to take adverse action against an employee "because of such individual's age." 29 U.S.C. §623(a). The case proceeded to trial, where Gross introduced evidence suggesting that his reassignment was based at least in part on his age. FBL defended its decision on the grounds that Gross' reassignment was part of a corporate restructuring and that Gross' new position was better suited to his skills.

At the close of trial, and over FBL's objections, the District Court instructed the jury that it must return a verdict for Gross if he proved, by a preponderance of the evidence, that FBL "demoted [him] to claims projec[t] coordinator" and that his "age was a motivating factor" in FBL's decision to demote him. The jury was further instructed that Gross' age would qualify as a "'motivating factor,' if [it] played a part or a role in [FBL]'s decision to demote [him]." The jury was also instructed regarding FBL's burden of proof. According to the District Court, the "verdict must be for [FBL] … if it has been proved by the preponderance of the evidence that [FBL] would have demoted [Gross] regardless of his age." The jury returned a verdict for Gross, awarding him $46,945 in lost compensation.

FBL challenged the jury instructions on appeal. The United States Court of Appeals for the Eighth Circuit reversed and remanded for a new trial, holding that the jury had been incorrectly instructed under the standard established in *Price Waterhouse v. Hopkins,* 490 U.S. 228 (1989)…. In accordance with Circuit precedent, the Court of Appeals identified Justice O'Connor's [*Price Waterhouse*] opinion as controlling. Applying that standard, the Court of Appeals found that Gross needed to present "[d]irect evidence … sufficient to support a finding by a reasonable fact finder that an illegitimate criterion actually motivated the adverse employment action." In the Court of Appeals' view, "direct evidence" is only that evidence that "show[s] a specific link between the alleged discriminatory animus and the challenged decision." Only upon a presentation of such evidence, the Court of Appeals held, should the burden shift to the employer "to convince the trier of fact that it is more likely than not that the decision would have been the same absent consideration of the illegitimate factor."

The Court of Appeals thus concluded that the District Court's jury instructions were flawed because they allowed the burden to shift to FBL upon a presentation of a preponderance of *any* category of evidence showing that age was a motivating factor—not just "direct evidence" related to FBL's alleged consideration of age. Because Gross conceded that he had not presented direct evidence of discrimination, the Court of Appeals held that the District Court should not have given the mixed-motives instruction. Rather, Gross should have been held to the burden of persuasion applicable to typical, non-mixed-motives claims; the jury thus should have been instructed only to determine whether Gross had carried his burden of "prov[ing] that age was the determining factor in FBL's employment action."

## II

The parties have asked us to decide whether a plaintiff must "present direct evidence of discrimination in order to obtain a mixed-motive instruction in a non-Title VII discrimination case." Before reaching this question, however, we must first determine whether the burden of persuasion ever shifts to the party defending an alleged mixed-motives discrimination claim brought under the ADEA. We hold that it does not.

A

Petitioner relies on this Court's decisions construing Title VII for his interpretation of the ADEA. Because Title VII is materially different with respect to the relevant burden of persuasion, however, these decisions do not control our construction of the ADEA.

In *Price Waterhouse*, a plurality of the Court and two Justices concurring in the judgment determined that once a "plaintiff in a Title VII case proves that [the plaintiff's membership in a protected class] played a motivating part in an employment decision, the defendant may avoid a finding of liability only by proving by a preponderance of the evidence that it would have made the same decision even if it had not taken [that factor] into account." But as we explained in *Desert Palace, Inc. v. Costa*, 539 U.S. 90, 94–95 (2003), Congress has since amended Title VII by explicitly authorizing discrimination claims in which an improper consideration was "a motivating factor" for an adverse employment decision.

This Court has never held that this burden-shifting framework applies to ADEA claims. And, we decline to do so now. When conducting statutory interpretation, we "must be careful not to apply rules applicable under one statute to a different statute without careful and critical examination." [citation omitted]. Unlike Title VII, the ADEA's text does not provide that a plaintiff may establish discrimination by showing that age was simply a motivating factor. Moreover, Congress neglected to add such a provision to the ADEA when it amended Title VII to add §§ 2000e-2(m) and 2000e-5(g)(2)(B), even though it contemporaneously amended the ADEA in several ways[.]

We cannot ignore Congress' decision to amend Title VII's relevant provisions but not make similar changes to the ADEA. When Congress amends one statutory provision but not another, it is presumed to have acted intentionally. Furthermore, as the Court has explained, "negative implications raised by disparate provisions are strongest" when the provisions were "considered simultaneously when the language raising the implication was inserted." [citations omitted]. As a result, the Court's interpretation of the ADEA is not governed by Title VII decisions such as *Desert Palace* and *Price Waterhouse*.[20]

B

Our inquiry therefore must focus on the text of the ADEA to decide whether it authorizes a mixed-motives age discrimination claim. It does not. "Statutory construction must begin with the language employed by Congress and the assumption that the

---

20. Justice Stevens argues that the Court must incorporate its past interpretations of Title VII into the ADEA because "the substantive provisions of the ADEA were derived *in haec verba* from Title VII," and because the Court has frequently applied its interpretations of Title VII to the ADEA. But the Court's approach to interpreting the ADEA in light of Title VII has not been uniform. In *General Dynamics Land Systems, Inc. v. Cline*, 540 U.S. 581 (2004), for example, the Court declined to interpret the phrase "because of ... age" in 29 U.S.C. § 623(a) to bar discrimination against people of all ages, even though the Court had previously interpreted "because of ... race [or] sex" in Title VII to bar discrimination against people of all races and both sexes. And the Court has not definitively decided whether the evidentiary framework of *McDonnell Douglas Corp. v. Green*, 411 U.S. 792 (1973), utilized in Title VII cases is appropriate in the ADEA context. *See Reeves v. Sanderson Plumbing Products, Inc.*, 530 U.S. 133, 142 (2000); *O'Connor v. Consolidated Coin Caterers Corp.*, 517 U.S. 308, 311 (1996). In this instance, it is the textual differences between Title VII and the ADEA that prevent us from applying *Price Waterhouse* and *Desert Palace* to federal age discrimination claims.

ordinary meaning of that language accurately expresses the legislative purpose." [citation omitted]. The ADEA provides, in relevant part, that "[i]t shall be unlawful for an employer ... to fail or refuse to hire or to discharge any individual or otherwise discriminate against any individual with respect to his compensation, terms, conditions, or privileges of employment, *because of* such individual's age." 29 U.S.C. §623(a)(1) (emphasis added).

The words "because of" mean "by reason of: on account of." 1 Webster's Third New International Dictionary 194 (1966); *see also* 1 Oxford English Dictionary 746 (1933) (defining "because of" to mean "By reason *of,* on account *of*" (italics in original)); The Random House Dictionary of the English Language 132 (1966) (defining "because" to mean "by reason; on account"). Thus, the ordinary meaning of the ADEA's requirement that an employer took adverse action "because of" age is that age was the "reason" that the employer decided to act. To establish a disparate-treatment claim under the plain language of the ADEA, therefore, a plaintiff must prove that age was the "but-for" cause of the employer's adverse decision....

It follows, then, that under §623(a)(1), the plaintiff retains the burden of persuasion to establish that age was the "but-for" cause of the employer's adverse action. Indeed, we have previously held that the burden is allocated in this manner in ADEA cases. And nothing in the statute's text indicates that Congress has carved out an exception to that rule for a subset of ADEA cases. Where the statutory text is "silent on the allocation of the burden of persuasion," we "begin with the ordinary default rule that plaintiffs bear the risk of failing to prove their claims." [citations omitted]. We have no warrant to depart from the general rule in this setting.

Hence, the burden of persuasion necessary to establish employer liability is the same in alleged mixed-motives cases as in any other ADEA disparate-treatment action. A plaintiff must prove by a preponderance of the evidence (which may be direct or circumstantial), that age was the "but-for" cause of the challenged employer decision....

### III

Finally, we reject petitioner's contention that our interpretation of the ADEA is controlled by *Price Waterhouse,* which initially established that the burden of persuasion shifted in alleged mixed-motives Title VII claims. In any event, it is far from clear that the Court would have the same approach were it to consider the question today in the first instance.

Whatever the deficiencies of *Price Waterhouse* in retrospect, it has become evident in the years since that case was decided that its burden-shifting framework is difficult to apply. For example, in cases tried to a jury, courts have found it particularly difficult to craft an instruction to explain its burden-shifting framework. Thus, even if *Price Waterhouse* was doctrinally sound, the problems associated with its application have eliminated any perceivable benefit to extending its framework to ADEA claims.

### IV

We hold that a plaintiff bringing a disparate-treatment claim pursuant to the ADEA must prove, by a preponderance of the evidence, that age was the "but-for" cause of the challenged adverse employment action. The burden of persuasion does not shift to the employer to show that it would have taken the action regardless of age, even when a plaintiff has produced some evidence that age was one motivating factor in that decision. Accordingly, we vacate the judgment of the Court of Appeals and remand the case for further proceedings consistent with this opinion.

Justice Stevens, with whom Justice Souter, Justice Ginsburg, and Justice Breyer join, dissenting.

The Age Discrimination in Employment Act of 1967 (ADEA), makes it unlawful for an employer to discriminate against any employee "because of" that individual's age. The most natural reading of this statutory text prohibits adverse employment actions motivated in whole or in part by the age of the employee. The "but-for" causation standard endorsed by the Court today was advanced in Justice Kennedy's dissenting opinion in *Price Waterhouse v. Hopkins*, 490 U.S. 228, 279 (1989), a case construing identical language in Title VII. Not only did the Court reject the but-for standard in that case, but so too did Congress when it amended Title VII in 1991. Given this unambiguous history, it is particularly inappropriate for the Court, on its own initiative, to adopt an interpretation of the causation requirement in the ADEA that differs from the established reading of Title VII. I disagree not only with the Court's interpretation of the statute, but also with its decision to engage in unnecessary lawmaking. I would simply answer the question presented by the certiorari petition and hold that a plaintiff need not present direct evidence of age discrimination to obtain a mixed-motives instruction.

I

... Unfortunately, the majority's inattention to prudential Court practices is matched by its utter disregard of our precedent and Congress' intent. The ADEA provides that "[i]t shall be unlawful for an employer ... to fail or refuse to hire or to discharge any individual or otherwise discriminate against any individual with respect to his compensation, terms, conditions, or privileges of employment, *because of* such individual's age." As we recognized in *Price Waterhouse* when we construed the identical "because of" language of Title VII, see 42 U.S.C. § 2000e-2(a)(1) (making it unlawful for an employer "to fail or refuse to hire or to discharge any individual ... with respect to his compensation, terms, conditions, or privileges of employment, *because of* such individual's race, color, religion, sex, or national origin" (emphasis added)), the most natural reading of the text proscribes adverse employment actions motivated in whole or in part by the age of the employee.

In *Price Waterhouse*, we concluded that the words " 'because of' such individual's ... sex ... mean that gender must be irrelevant to employment decisions." [citations omitted]. To establish a violation of Title VII, we therefore held, a plaintiff had to prove that her sex was a motivating factor in an adverse employment decision....

Today, however, the Court interprets the words "because of" in the ADEA "as colloquial shorthand for 'but-for' causation." That the Court is construing the ADEA rather than Title VII does not justify this departure from precedent. The relevant language in the two statutes is identical, and we have long recognized that our interpretations of Title VII's language apply "with equal force in the context of age discrimination, for the substantive provisions of the ADEA 'were derived *in haec verba* from Title VII.' " [citation omitted]....

Because the 1991 Act amended only Title VII and not the ADEA with respect to mixed-motives claims, the Court reasonably declines to apply the amended provisions to the ADEA. But it proceeds to ignore the conclusion compelled by this interpretation of the Act: *Price Waterhouse*'s construction of "because of" remains the governing law for ADEA claims.

... To the contrary, the fact that Congress endorsed this Court's interpretation of the "because of" language in *Price Waterhouse* (even as it rejected the employer's affirmative defense to liability) provides all the more reason to adhere to that decision's motivating-factor test. Indeed, Congress emphasized in passing the 1991 Act that the motivating-factor test was consistent with its original intent in enacting Title VII....

The Court's resurrection of the but-for causation standard is unwarranted. *Price Waterhouse* repudiated that standard 20 years ago, and Congress' response to our decision further militates against the crabbed interpretation the Court adopts today. The answer to the question the Court has elected to take up—whether a mixed-motives jury instruction is ever proper in an ADEA case—is plainly yes.

### III

Although the Court declines to address the question we granted certiorari to decide, I would answer that question by following our unanimous opinion in *Desert Palace, Inc. v. Costa*, 539 U.S. 90 (2003). I would accordingly hold that a plaintiff need not present direct evidence of age discrimination to obtain a mixed-motives instruction....

Justice Breyer, with whom Justice Souter and Justice Ginsburg join, dissenting.

I agree with Justice Stevens that mixed-motive instructions are appropriate in the Age Discrimination in Employment Act context. And I join his opinion. The Court rejects this conclusion on the ground that the words "because of" require a plaintiff to prove that age was the "but-for" cause of his employer's adverse employment action. But the majority does not explain why this is so. The words "because of" do not inherently require a showing of "but-for" causation, and I see no reason to read them to require such a showing.

It is one thing to require a typical tort plaintiff to show "but-for" causation. In that context, reasonably objective scientific or commonsense theories of physical causation make the concept of "but-for" causation comparatively easy to understand and relatively easy to apply. But it is an entirely different matter to determine a "but-for" relation when we consider, not physical forces, but the mind-related characterizations that constitute motive. Sometimes we speak of *determining* or *discovering* motives, but more often we *ascribe* motives, after an event, to an individual in light of the individual's thoughts and other circumstances present at the time of decision. In a case where we characterize an employer's actions as having been taken out of multiple motives, say, both because the employee was old and because he wore loud clothing, to apply "but-for" causation is to engage in a hypothetical inquiry about what would have happened if the employer's thoughts and other circumstances had been different. The answer to this hypothetical inquiry will often be far from obvious, and, since the employee likely knows less than does the employer about what the employer was thinking at the time, the employer will often be in a stronger position than the employee to provide the answer.

All that a plaintiff can know for certain in such a context is that the forbidden motive did play a role in the employer's decision. And the fact that a jury has found that age did play a role in the decision justifies the use of the word "because," *i.e.*, the employer dismissed the employee because of his age (and other things). *See Price Waterhouse v. Hopkins*, 490 U.S. 228, 239–242 (1989) (plurality opinion). I therefore would see nothing wrong in concluding that the plaintiff has established a violation of the statute.

But the law need not automatically assess liability in these circumstances. In *Price Waterhouse*, the plurality recognized an affirmative defense where the defendant could show that the employee would have been dismissed regardless. The law permits the employer this defense, not because the forbidden motive, age, had no role in the *actual* decision, but because the employer can show that he would have dismissed the employee anyway in the *hypothetical* circumstance in which his age-related motive was absent. And it makes sense that this would be an affirmative defense, rather than part of the showing of a violation, precisely because the defendant is in a better position than the plaintiff to establish how he would have acted in this hypothetical situation. . . .

---

## Subsequent Developments

You have now learned many different ways to think about how the causation inquiry works in discrimination claims. One question that remained unanswered after *Gross* is what standard a plaintiff would be required to prove to establish a retaliation claim under Title VII. In 2013, the Supreme Court answered this question in *University of Texas Southwestern Medical Center v. Nassar*, a case that is contained in Chapter 6.

## ➤ Beyond the Basics: Mixed Motive in the ADA Context

The Supreme Court has not considered the question of whether mixed-motive claims are allowed under the ADA. Consider the implications of *Gross* for the ADA. Re-read the ADA's statutory language, and you will notice that its operative provisions are different from those found in Title VII and the ADEA. Think about how these differences might impact a court's interpretation of the mixed-motive question under the ADA. When you read the *Nassar* case in Chapter 6, see if this case changes your answer.

Also, the ADA has a provision that makes available to ADA plaintiffs the same "powers, remedies, and procedures" set forth in 42 U.S.C. § 2000e-5. *See* 42 U.S.C. § 12117(a). Thus, the ADA cross-references the remedies set forth for Title VII mixed-motive claims, which are found at 42 U.S.C. § 2000e-5(g)(2)(B). However, the ADA does not reference the Title VII provision, § 2000e-2(m), which provides the substantive standard for considering allegations of mixed motive.

## ➤ Beyond the Basics: Intersectionality

Mixed-motive analysis was conceived to cover situations when two motives are at work — a legitimate motive and a discriminatory one. Another concept that involves dual motives is called "intersectionality." Sometimes plaintiffs allege that discrimination was the result of more than one protected trait. For example, a person might claim that he was discriminated against because of his race and his disability. Such claims are sometimes referred to as "intersectional" claims. Consider how multiple protected traits might affect a claim in the following exercise.

---

### Exercise 3.7

You are a plaintiff's lawyer, and a client seeks your advice on the following set of facts. Mary Ann is a 50-year-old woman. She was terminated from her job. Throughout her two years of employment, Mary Ann's supervisor, who made the decision to fire her, referred to her as "the old lady" and repeatedly said that he doubted "old women like her could keep up their performance." He also noted that older men do not seem to suffer from the same issue. What claims would you suggest the plaintiff raise and what problems do you anticipate?

Recall that one way that a plaintiff often seeks to establish her case is by the use of comparator employees. If Mary Ann wants to use such evidence in addition to the discriminatory comments, should she have to show that she was treated differently from younger men? From men generally? From younger women?

> ## ➤ Beyond the Basics: The Intersection of Mixed-Motive and Single-Motive Cases

A particular set of facts may potentially implicate both single-motive and mixed-motive frameworks. In these cases, complicated questions arise regarding what a plaintiff is required to plead, whether the defendant can proceed on a mixed-motive framework if the plaintiff asserts her claim as a single-motive case, and what standards courts should use at summary judgment and at trial. The lower courts have been inconsistent in their responses to these issues.

It also remains unclear how and whether the *McDonnell-Douglas* standard intersects with the mixed-motive framework. The Fifth Circuit Court of Appeals uses a modified *McDonnell-Douglas* framework, described as follows:

> Under this approach, the plaintiff must first establish a prima facie case of discrimination by showing that (1) he is a member of a protected class; (2) he is qualified for the position at issue; (3) he suffered an adverse employment action; and (4) he was replaced by someone outside the protected class or was treated less favorably than similarly-situated employees outside the protected class. If the plaintiff establishes a prima facie case, the burden shifts to the defendant to proffer a legitimate, nondiscriminatory reason for its action. If the defendant satisfies its burden of production, the burden then shifts back to the plaintiff to offer sufficient evidence to create a genuine issue of material fact that either (1) the defendant's reason is false and is a pretext for discrimination, or (2) that the employer's reason, while true, is only one of the reasons for its conduct, and the plaintiff's protected characteristic was a motivating factor in its decision. If the plaintiff demonstrates that the protected characteristic was a motivating factor in the employment decision, it then falls to the defendant to prove that the same adverse employment decision would have been made regardless of discriminatory animus. If the employer fails to carry this burden, the plaintiff prevails.

*Taylor v. Peerless Industries Inc.*, 322 Fed. Appx. 355, 361, 2009 WL 837326, at *5 (5th Cir. 2009) (citations and quotations omitted). Some circuit courts consider the mixed-motive and single-motive frameworks to be separate tests and decline to conflate them. *See, e.g., Diamond v. Colonial Life & Accident Ins. Co.*, 416 F.3d 310, 318 (4th Cir. 2005).

It is possible that the addition of "motivating factor" language in Title VII means that a plaintiff should be required only to show that a protected trait was a motivating factor for the decision, whether the plaintiff believes a single factor motivated the decision or multiple factors did. After *Desert Palace*, there also is a good argument that the courts' consideration of single-motive cases using direct and indirect frameworks is no longer appropriate. Recall that the Supreme Court, in *Desert Palace*, held that direct evidence was not required in mixed-motive cases because the 1991 amendment to Title VII did not draw a distinction regarding the type of evidence needed in mixed-motive cases. The same argument can be made regarding the primary operative language of Title VII, which does not make a distinction between direct and circumstantial evidence.

Many commentators believe that these changes in the statutory regime spell the end of the *McDonnell-Douglas* framework. *See, e.g.,* Henry L. Chambers, Jr., *The Effect of Eliminating Distinctions Among Title VII Disparate Treatment Cases,* 57 SMU L. REV. 83 (2004); William R. Corbett, *An Allegory of the Cave and the* Desert Palace, 41 HOUS. L. REV. 1549 (2005); William R. Corbett, McDonnell Douglas, *1972–2003, May You Rest in Peace?,* 6 U. PA. J. LAB. & EMPL. L. 199 (2003); Jeffrey A. Van Detta, *"Le Roi Est Mort; Vive Le Roi!": An Essay on the Quiet Demise of* McDonnell Douglas *and the Transformation of Every Title VII Case After* Desert Palace, Inc. v. Costa *into a "Mixed-Motives" Case,* 52 DRAKE L. REV. 71, 76 (2003); Michael J. Zimmer, *The New Discrimination Law:* Price Waterhouse *is Dead, Whither* McDonnell Douglas?, 53 EMORY L.J. 1887 (2004). However, courts still continue to use the *McDonnell-Douglas* framework and the questions introduced by the recognition of mixed-motive claims have not been resolved.

---

## Exercise 3.8

Consider the following set of facts. Beth and John get into a fight at work. Beth punches John and John deflects the punch by pushing Beth. Beth is fired as a result of the fight and John is not. Beth decides to sue for sex discrimination. Does this set of facts fall under a single-motive framework or a mixed-motive framework? Will the plaintiff want to present the facts as a single-motive case or a mixed-motive case? How will the defendant want to present the facts?

Consider how the complaint should be drafted. Should the plaintiff's attorney use the words "single motive" and/or "mixed motive" in the complaint? Should her attorney cite all of the applicable statutory provisions for both mixed-motive and single-motive claims? Should the defendant raise the same decision defense in the answer even if the plaintiff does not mention mixed motive in the complaint? Keep in mind that the Federal Rules of Civil Procedure require the defendant to plead affirmative defenses or risk losing them. At summary judgment, which framework or frameworks should the defendant use in arguing its motion? How should the plaintiff respond? How should the court rule?

In completing this exercise, think about an attorney's role in crafting claims, pleading claims, and developing evidence. Keep in mind that the client, in consultation with her lawyers, has the power to decide which legal claims to pursue and how to develop those claims factually.

Model Rule of Professional Conduct 1.4 requires lawyers to "promptly inform the client of any decision or circumstance with respect to which the client's informed consent" is necessary and "reasonably consult with the client about the means by which the client's objectives are to be accomplished." The Rule further requires lawyers to "explain a matter to the extent reasonably necessary to permit the client to make informed decisions regarding the representation." In thinking about the choices implicated in this exercise, consider your duty to discuss these choices with your client. In Beth's case, presumably you will begin by determining how the circuit where the case will be filed treats mixed-motive and single-motive cases. You will then need to help your client understand the implications of your circuit's doctrine — often no easy matter, even for those with legal training!

## ✦ Core Concept: Pattern or Practice

Courts often distinguish between individual disparate treatment cases and systemic disparate treatment cases. The Supreme Court has described the difference between these types of cases as follows: "The inquiry regarding an individual's claim is the reason for a particular employment decision, while at the liability stage of a pattern-or-practice trial the focus often will not be on individual hiring decisions, but on a pattern of discriminatory decisionmaking." *Cooper v. Federal Reserve Bank of Richmond*, 467 U.S. 867, 876 (1984). As described in the case below, the allegation in a pattern or practice case is that the employer systematically discriminates against employees on the basis of a protected trait.

Pattern or practice cases are often brought on behalf of classes of individuals, either by private plaintiffs or by the government. Some courts have held that the proof structure provided for pattern or practice claims is not available in claims brought by individual plaintiffs. *See, e.g., Celestine v. Petroleos de Venezuella SA*, 266 F.3d 343, 356 (5th Cir. 2001) ("While the Supreme Court has not explicitly stated that the pattern and practice method of proof may never be used in private non-class suits, other courts have reached this conclusion.") Special rules allow the government to proceed on a pattern or practice claim without meeting class action requirements provided in the Federal Rules of Civil Procedure. 42 U.S.C. § 2000e-6(a).

Even in circuits where the pattern or practice framework cannot be used in individual cases, evidence of patterns of discriminatory conduct may be admissible to prove an individual disparate treatment case.

---

### Focus Questions: *International Broth. of Teamsters v. U.S.*

1.  How is a pattern or practice case different than an individual disparate treatment case?

2.  Focus on the evidence used by the parties.

---

# International Broth. of Teamsters v. U.S.

## 431 U.S. 324 (1977)

Justice Stewart delivered the opinion of the Court.

This litigation brings here several important questions under Title VII. The issues grow out of alleged unlawful employment practices engaged in by an employer and a union. The employer is a common carrier of motor freight with nationwide operations, and the union represents a large group of its employees. The District Court and the Court of Appeals held that the employer had violated Title VII by engaging in a pattern and practice of employment discrimination against Negroes and Spanish-surnamed Americans, and that the union had violated the Act by agreeing with the employer to create and maintain a seniority system that perpetuated the effects of past racial and ethnic discrimination....

I

The United States brought an action in a Tennessee federal court against the petitioner T.I.M.E.-D.C., Inc. (company), pursuant to § 707(a) of the Civil Rights Act of 1964, 42

U.S.C. § 2000e-6(a).[21] The complaint charged that the company had followed discriminatory hiring, assignment, and promotion policies against Negroes at its terminal in Nashville, Tenn. The Government brought a second action against the company almost three years later in a Federal District Court in Texas, charging a pattern and practice of employment discrimination against Negroes and Spanish-surnamed persons throughout the company's transportation system. The petitioner International Brotherhood of Teamsters (union) was joined as a defendant in that suit. The two actions were consolidated for trial in the Northern District of Texas.

The central claim in both lawsuits was that the company had engaged in a pattern or practice of discriminating against minorities in hiring so-called line drivers. Those Negroes and Spanish-surnamed persons who had been hired, the Government alleged, were given lower paying, less desirable jobs as servicemen or local city drivers, and were thereafter discriminated against with respect to promotions and transfers.[22] In this connection the complaint also challenged the seniority system established by the collective-bargaining agreements between the employer and the union. The Government sought a general injunctive remedy and specific "make whole" relief for all individual discriminatees, which would allow them an opportunity to transfer to line-driver jobs with full company seniority for all purposes.

The cases went to trial and the District Court found that the Government had shown "by a preponderance of the evidence that T.I.M.E.-D.C. and its predecessor companies were engaged in a plan and practice of discrimination in violation of Title VII...."[23] The court further found that the seniority system contained in the collective-bargaining contracts between the company and the union violated Title VII because it "operate(d) to impede the free transfer of minority groups into and within the company." Both the company and the union were enjoined from committing further violations of Title VII....

The Court of Appeals for the Fifth Circuit agreed with the basic conclusions of the District Court: that the company had engaged in a pattern or practice of employment discrimination and that the seniority system in the collective-bargaining agreements violated Title VII as applied to victims of prior discrimination. The appellate court held, however, that the relief ordered by the District Court was inadequate....

... We granted both the company's and the union's petitions for certiorari to consider the significant questions presented under the Civil Rights Act of 1964.

## II

In this Court the company and the union contend that their conduct did not violate Title VII in any respect, asserting first that the evidence introduced at trial was insufficient to show that the company engaged in a "pattern or practice" of employment discrimination. The union further contends that the seniority system contained in the collective-bargaining

---

21. Section 707 was amended to give the Equal Employment Opportunity Commission, rather than the Attorney General, the authority to bring "pattern or practice" suits under that section against private-sector employers.

22. Line drivers, also known as over-the-road drivers, engage in long-distance hauling between company terminals. They compose a separate bargaining unit at the company.

23. Following the receipt of evidence, but before decision, the Government and the company consented to the entry of a Decree in Partial Resolution of Suit.... The Decree in Partial Resolution of Suit narrowed the scope of the litigation, but the District Court still had to determine whether unlawful discrimination had occurred. If so, the court had to identify the actual discriminatees entitled to fill future job vacancies under the decree. The validity of the collective-bargaining contract's seniority system also remained for decision....

agreements in no way violated Title VII. If these contentions are correct, it is unnecessary, of course, to reach any of the issues concerning remedies that so occupied the attention of the Court of Appeals.

## A

Consideration of the question whether the company engaged in a pattern or practice of discriminatory hiring practices involves controlling legal principles that are relatively clear. The Government's theory of discrimination was simply that the company, in violation of § 703(a) of Title VII, regularly and purposefully treated Negroes and Spanish-surnamed Americans less favorably than white persons. The disparity in treatment allegedly involved the refusal to recruit, hire, transfer, or promote minority group members on an equal basis with white people, particularly with respect to line-driving positions. The ultimate factual issues are thus simply whether there was a pattern or practice of such disparate treatment and, if so, whether the differences were "racially premised." *McDonnell Douglas Corp. v. Green*, 411 U.S. 792, 805 n. 18 (1973).[24]

As the plaintiff, the Government bore the initial burden of making out a prima facie case of discrimination. And, because it alleged a systemwide pattern or practice of resistance to the full enjoyment of Title VII rights, the Government ultimately had to prove more than the mere occurrence of isolated or "accidental" or sporadic discriminatory acts. It had to establish by a preponderance of the evidence that racial discrimination was the company's standard operating procedure, the regular rather than the unusual practice.

We agree with the District Court and the Court of Appeals that the Government carried its burden of proof. As of March 31, 1971, shortly after the Government filed its complaint alleging systemwide discrimination, the company had 6,472 employees. Of these, 314 (5%) were Negroes and 257 (4%) were Spanish-surnamed Americans. Of the 1,828 line drivers, however, there were only 8 (0.4%) Negroes and 5 (0.3%) Spanish-surnamed persons, and all of the Negroes had been hired after the litigation had commenced. With one exception a man who worked as a line driver at the Chicago terminal from 1950 to 1959 the company and its predecessors did not employ a Negro on a regular basis as a line driver until 1969. And, as the Government showed, even in 1971 there were terminals in areas of substantial Negro population where all of the company's line drivers were white.[25] A great majority of the Negroes (83%) and Spanish-surnamed Americans (78%) who did work for the company held the lower paying city operations and serviceman jobs, whereas only 39% of the nonminority employees held jobs in those categories.

---

24. "Disparate treatment" such as is alleged in the present case is the most easily understood type of discrimination. The employer simply treats some people less favorably than others because of their race, color, religion, sex, or national origin. Proof of discriminatory motive is critical, although it can in some situations be inferred from the mere fact of differences in treatment. Undoubtedly disparate treatment was the most obvious evil Congress had in mind when it enacted Title VII. Claims of disparate treatment may be distinguished from claims that stress "disparate impact." The latter involve employment practices that are facially neutral in their treatment of different groups but that in fact fall more harshly on one group than another and cannot be justified by business necessity. Proof of discriminatory motive, we have held, is not required under a disparate-impact theory. Either theory may, of course, be applied to a particular set of facts.

25. In Atlanta, for instance, Negroes composed 22.35% of the population in the surrounding metropolitan area and 51.31% of the population in the city proper. The company's Atlanta terminal employed 57 line drivers. All were white. In Los Angeles, 10.84% of the greater metropolitan population and 17.88% of the city population were Negro. But at the company's two Los Angeles terminals there was not a single Negro among the 374 line drivers. The proof showed similar disparities in San Francisco, Denver, Nashville, Chicago, Dallas, and at several other terminals.

The Government bolstered its statistical evidence with the testimony of individuals who recounted over 40 specific instances of discrimination. Upon the basis of this testimony the District Court found that "(n)umerous qualified black and Spanish-surnamed American applicants who sought line driving jobs at the company over the years, either had their requests ignored, were given false or misleading information about requirements, opportunities, and application procedures, or were not considered and hired on the same basis that whites were considered and hired." Minority employees who wanted to transfer to line-driver jobs met with similar difficulties.[26]

The company's principal response to this evidence is that statistics can never in and of themselves prove the existence of a pattern or practice of discrimination, or even establish a prima facie case shifting to the employer the burden of rebutting the inference raised by the figures. But, as even our brief summary of the evidence shows, this was not a case in which the Government relied on "statistics alone." The individuals who testified about their personal experiences with the company brought the cold numbers convincingly to life.

In any event, our cases make it unmistakably clear that "(s)tatistical analyses have served and will continue to serve an important role" in cases in which the existence of discrimination is a disputed issue. We have repeatedly approved the use of statistical proof, where it reached proportions comparable to those in this case, to establish a prima facie case of racial discrimination in jury selection cases. Statistics are equally competent in proving employment discrimination.[27] We caution only that statistics are not irrefutable;

---

26. Two examples are illustrative: George Taylor, a Negro, worked for the company as a city driver in Los Angeles, beginning late in 1966. In 1968, after hearing that a white city driver had transferred to a line-driver job, he told the terminal manager that he also would like to consider line driving. The manager replied that there would be "a lot of problems on the road ... with different people, Caucasian, et cetera," and stated: "I don't feel that the company is ready for this right now.... Give us a little time. It will come around, you know." Mr. Taylor made similar requests some months later and got similar responses. He was never offered a line-driving job or an application. Feliberto Trujillo worked as a dockman at the company's Denver terminal. When he applied for a line-driver job in 1967, he was told by a personnel officer that he had one strike against him. He asked what that was and was told: "You're a Chicano, and as far as we know, there isn't a Chicano driver in the system."

27. Petitioners argue that statistics, at least those comparing the racial composition of an employer's work force to the composition of the population at large, should never be given decisive weight in a Title VII case because to do so would conflict with § 703(j) of the Act, 42 U.S.C. § 2000e-2(j). That section provides: "Nothing contained in this subchapter shall be interpreted to require any employer ... to grant preferential treatment to any individual or to any group because of the race ... or national origin of such individual or group on account of an imbalance which may exist with respect to the total number or percentage of persons of any race ... or national origin employed by any employer ... in comparison with the total number or percentage of persons of such race ... or national origin in any community, State, section, or other area, or in the available work force in any community, State, section, or other area." The argument fails in this case because the statistical evidence was not offered or used to support an erroneous theory that Title VII requires an employer's work force to be racially balanced. Statistics showing racial or ethnic imbalance are probative in a case such as this one only because such imbalance is often a telltale sign of purposeful discrimination; absent explanation, it is ordinarily to be expected that nondiscriminatory hiring practices will in time result in a work force more or less representative of the racial and ethnic composition of the population in the community from which employees are hired. Evidence of longlasting and gross disparity between the composition of a work force and that of the general population thus may be significant even though § 703(j) makes clear that Title VII imposes no requirement that a work force mirror the general population. Considerations such as small sample size may, of course, detract from the value of such evidence, and evidence showing that the figures for the general population might not accurately reflect the pool of qualified job applicants would also be relevant. "Since the passage of the Civil Rights Act of 1964, the courts have frequently relied upon statistical evidence to prove a violation.... In many cases the only available avenue of proof is the use of racial statistics to uncover clandestine and covert discrimination by the employer or union involved." [citations omitted].

they come in infinite variety and, like any other kind of evidence, they may be rebutted. In short, their usefulness depends on all of the surrounding facts and circumstances.

In addition to its general protest against the use of statistics in Title VII cases, the company claims that in this case the statistics revealing racial imbalance are misleading because they fail to take into account the company's particular business situation as of the effective date of Title VII. The company concedes that its line drivers were virtually all white in July 1965, but it claims that thereafter business conditions were such that its work force dropped. Its argument is that low personnel turnover, rather than post-Act discrimination, accounts for more recent statistical disparities. It points to substantial minority hiring in later years, especially after 1971, as showing that any pre-Act patterns of discrimination were broken.

The argument would be a forceful one if this were an employer who, at the time of suit, had done virtually no new hiring since the effective date of Title VII. But it is not. Although the company's total number of employees apparently dropped somewhat during the late 1960's, the record shows that many line drivers continued to be hired throughout this period, and that almost all of them were white. To be sure, there were improvements in the company's hiring practices. The Court of Appeals commented that "T.I.M.E.-D.C.'s recent minority hiring progress stands as a laudable good faith effort to eradicate the effects of past discrimination in the area of hiring and initial assignment." But the District Court and the Court of Appeals found upon substantial evidence that the company had engaged in a course of discrimination that continued well after the effective date of Title VII. The company's later changes in its hiring and promotion policies could be of little comfort to the victims of the earlier post-Act discrimination, and could not erase its previous illegal conduct or its obligation to afford relief to those who suffered because of it.

The District Court and the Court of Appeals, on the basis of substantial evidence, held that the Government had proved a prima facie case of systematic and purposeful employment discrimination, continuing well beyond the effective date of Title VII. The company's attempts to rebut that conclusion were held to be inadequate. For the reasons we have summarized, there is no warrant for this Court to disturb the findings of the District Court and the Court of Appeals on this basic issue.

B

The District Court and the Court of Appeals also found that the seniority system contained in the collective-bargaining agreements between the company and the union operated to violate Title VII of the Act.

For purposes of calculating benefits, such as vacations, pensions, and other fringe benefits, an employee's seniority under this system runs from the date he joins the company, and takes into account his total service in all jobs and bargaining units. For competitive purposes, however, such as determining the order in which employees may bid for particular jobs, are laid off, or are recalled from layoff, it is bargaining-unit seniority that controls. Thus, a line driver's seniority, for purposes of bidding for particular runs and protection against layoff, takes into account only the length of time he has been a line driver at a particular terminal. The practical effect is that a city driver or serviceman who transfers to a line-driver job must forfeit all the competitive seniority he has accumulated in his previous bargaining unit and start at the bottom of the line drivers' "board."

The vice of this arrangement, as found by the District Court and the Court of Appeals, was that it "locked" minority workers into inferior jobs and perpetuated prior discrimination by discouraging transfers to jobs as line drivers. While the disincentive applied to all workers, including whites, it was Negroes and Spanish-surnamed persons who, those courts found, suffered the most because many of them had been denied the equal opportunity to become line drivers when they were initially hired, whereas whites either had not sought or were refused line-driver positions for reasons unrelated to their race or national origin.

The linchpin of the theory embraced by the District Court and the Court of Appeals was that a discriminatee who must forfeit his competitive seniority in order finally to obtain a line-driver job will never be able to "catch up" to the seniority level of his contemporary who was not subject to discrimination. Accordingly, this continued, built-in disadvantage to the prior discriminatee who transfers to a line-driver job was held to constitute a continuing violation of Title VII, for which both the employer and the union who jointly created and maintain the seniority system were liable.

The union, while acknowledging that the seniority system may in some sense perpetuate the effects of prior discrimination, asserts that the system is immunized from a finding of illegality by reason of § 703(h) of Title VII, 42 U.S.C. § 2000e-2(h), which provides in part: "Notwithstanding any other provision of this subchapter, it shall not be an unlawful employment practice for an employer to apply different standards of compensation, or different terms, conditions, or privileges of employment pursuant to a bona fide seniority ... system, ... provided that such differences are not the result of an intention to discriminate because of race ... or national origin...."

It argues that the seniority system in this case is "bona fide" within the meaning of § 703(h) when judged in light of its history, intent, application, and all of the circumstances under which it was created and is maintained. More specifically, the union claims that the central purpose of § 703(h) is to ensure that mere perpetuation of pre-Act discrimination is not unlawful under Title VII. And, whether or not § 703(h) immunizes the perpetuation of post-Act discrimination, the union claims that the seniority system in this litigation has no such effect. Its position in this Court, as has been its position throughout this litigation, is that the seniority system presents no hurdle to post-Act discriminates who seek retroactive seniority to the date they would have become line drivers but for the company's discrimination. Indeed, the union asserts that under its collective-bargaining agreements the union will itself take up the cause of the post-Act victim and attempt, through grievance procedures, to gain for him full "make whole" relief, including appropriate seniority.

The Government responds that a seniority system that perpetuates the effects of prior discrimination pre-Act or post-Act can never be "bona fide" under § 703(h); at a minimum Title VII prohibits those applications of a seniority system that perpetuate the effects on incumbent employees of prior discriminatory job assignments....

What remains for review is the judgment that the seniority system unlawfully perpetuated the effects of pre-Act discrimination. We must decide, in short, whether § 703(h) validates otherwise bona fide seniority systems that afford no constructive seniority to victims discriminated against prior to the effective date of Title VII, and it is to that issue that we now turn....

One kind of practice "fair in form, but discriminatory in operation" is that which perpetuates the effects of prior discrimination....

Were it not for § 703(h), the seniority system in this case would seem to fall under the *Griggs* rationale. The heart of the system is its allocation of the choicest jobs, the greatest protection against layoffs, and other advantages to those employees who have been line drivers for the longest time. Where, because of the employer's prior intentional discrimination, the line drivers with the longest tenure are without exception white, the advantages of the seniority system flow disproportionately to them and away from Negro and Spanish-surnamed employees who might by now have enjoyed those advantages had not the employer discriminated before the passage of the Act. This disproportionate distribution of advantages does in a very real sense "operate to 'freeze' the status quo of prior discriminatory employment practices." But both the literal terms of §703(h) and the legislative history of Title VII demonstrate that Congress considered this very effect of many seniority systems and extended a measure of immunity to them.

Throughout the initial consideration of H.R. 7152, later enacted as the Civil Rights Act of 1964, critics of the bill charged that it would destroy existing seniority rights. The consistent response of Title VII's congressional proponents and of the Justice Department was that seniority rights would not be affected, even where the employer had discriminated prior to the Act....

It is apparent that §703(h) was drafted with an eye toward meeting the earlier criticism on this issue with an explicit provision embodying the understanding and assurances of the Act's proponents, namely, that Title VII would not outlaw such differences in treatment among employees as flowed from a bona fide seniority system that allowed for full exercise of seniority accumulated before the effective date of the Act....

In sum, the unmistakable purpose of §703(h) was to make clear that the routine application of a bona fide seniority system would not be unlawful under Title VII. As the legislative history shows, this was the intended result even where the employer's pre-Act discrimination resulted in whites having greater existing seniority rights than Negroes. Although a seniority system inevitably tends to perpetuate the effects of pre-Act discrimination in such cases, the congressional judgment was that Title VII should not outlaw the use of existing seniority lists and thereby destroy or water down the vested seniority rights of employees simply because their employer had engaged in discrimination prior to the passage of the Act.

To be sure, §703(h) does not immunize all seniority systems. It refers only to "bona fide" systems, and a proviso requires that any differences in treatment not be "the result of an intention to discriminate because of race ... or national origin[.]"... Accordingly, we hold that an otherwise neutral, legitimate seniority system does not become unlawful under Title VII simply because it may perpetuate pre-Act discrimination. Congress did not intend to make it illegal for employees with vested seniority rights to continue to exercise those rights, even at the expense of pre-Act discriminatees....

The seniority system in this litigation is entirely bona fide. It applies equally to all races and ethnic groups. To the extent that it "locks" employees into non-line-driver jobs, it does so for all. The city drivers and servicemen who are discouraged from transferring to line-driver jobs are not all Negroes or Spanish-surnamed Americans; to the contrary, the overwhelming majority are white. The placing of line drivers in a separate bargaining unit from other employees is rational in accord with the industry practice, and consistent with National Labor Relations Board precedents. It is conceded that the seniority system did not have its genesis in racial discrimination, and that it was negotiated and has been maintained free from any illegal purpose. In these circumstances, the single fact that the system extends no retroactive seniority to pre-Act discriminatees does not make it unlawful....

Because the seniority system was protected by §703(h), the union's conduct in agreeing to and maintaining the system did not violate Title VII. On remand, the District Court's injunction against the union must be vacated.

### III

Our conclusion that the seniority system does not violate Title VII will necessarily affect the remedy granted to individual employees on remand of this litigation to the District Court. Those employees who suffered only pre-Act discrimination are not entitled to relief, and no person may be given retroactive seniority to a date earlier than the effective date of the Act....

### A

The petitioners' first contention is in substance that the Government's burden of proof in a pattern-or-practice case must be equivalent to that outlined in *McDonnell Douglas v. Green*. Since the Government introduced specific evidence of company discrimination against only some 40 employees, they argue that the District Court properly refused to award retroactive seniority to the remainder of the class of minority incumbent employees.

In *McDonnell Douglas* the Court considered "the order and allocation of proof in a private, non-class action challenging employment discrimination." 411 U.S. at 800. We held that an individual Title VII complainant must carry the initial burden of proof by establishing a prima facie case of racial discrimination. On the specific facts there involved, we concluded that this burden was met by showing that a qualified applicant, who was a member of a racial minority group, had unsuccessfully sought a job for which there was a vacancy and for which the employer continued thereafter to seek applicants with similar qualifications. This initial showing justified the inference that the minority applicant was denied an employment opportunity for reasons prohibited by Title VII, and therefore shifted the burden to the employer to rebut that inference by offering some legitimate, nondiscriminatory reason for the rejection.

The company and union seize upon the *McDonnell Douglas* pattern as the only means of establishing a prima facie case of individual discrimination. Our decision in that case, however, did not purport to create an inflexible formulation. We expressly noted that "(t)he facts necessarily will vary in Title VII cases, and the specification ... of the prima facie proof required from (a plaintiff) is not necessarily applicable in every respect to differing factual situations." *Id.* at 802 n. 13. The importance of *McDonnell Douglas* lies, not in its specification of the discrete elements of proof there required, but in its recognition of the general principle that any Title VII plaintiff must carry the initial burden of offering evidence adequate to create an inference that an employment decision was based on a discriminatory criterion illegal under the Act.

In *Franks v. Bowman Transportation Co.*, the Court applied this principle in the context of a class action. The *Franks* plaintiffs proved, to the satisfaction of a District Court, that Bowman Transportation Co. "had engaged in a pattern of racial discrimination in various company policies, including the hiring, transfer, and discharge of employees." 424 U.S. at 751. Despite this showing, the trial court denied seniority relief to certain members of the class of discriminatees because not every individual had shown that he was qualified for the job he sought and that a vacancy had been available. We held that the trial court had erred in placing this burden on the individual plaintiffs. By "demonstrating the existence of a discriminatory hiring pattern and practice" the plaintiffs had made out a prima facie case of discrimination against the individual class members; the burden therefore shifted to the employer "to prove that individuals who reapply were not in fact victims of previous hiring discrimination." *Id.* at 772. The *Franks* case thus illustrates another means by which a Title VII plaintiff's initial burden of proof can be met. The class there alleged a broad-based policy of employment discrimination; upon proof of that allegation there were reasonable grounds to infer that individual hiring decisions were made in pursuit of the discriminatory policy and to require the employer to come forth with evidence dispelling that inference.[28]

Although not all class actions will necessarily follow the *Franks* model, the nature of a pattern-or-practice suit brings it squarely within our holding in *Franks*. The plaintiff in a pattern-or-practice action is the Government, and its initial burden is to demonstrate that unlawful discrimination has been a regular procedure or policy followed by an employer or group of employers. At the initial, "liability" stage of a pattern-or-practice suit the Government is not required to offer evidence that each person for whom it will ultimately seek relief was a victim of the employer's discriminatory policy. Its burden is to establish a prima facie case that such a policy existed. The burden then shifts to the employer to defeat the prima facie showing of a pattern or practice by demonstrating that the Government's proof is either inaccurate or insignificant. An employer might show, for example, that the claimed discriminatory pattern is a product of pre-Act hiring rather than unlawful post-Act discrimination, or that during the period it is alleged to have pursued a discriminatory policy it made too few employment decisions to justify the inference that it had engaged in a regular practice of discrimination.[29]

If an employer fails to rebut the inference that arises from the Government's prima facie case, a trial court may then conclude that a violation has occurred and determine the appropriate remedy. Without any further evidence from the Government, a court's finding of a pattern or practice justifies an award of prospective relief. Such relief might take the form of an injunctive order against continuation of the discriminatory practice, an order that the employer keep records of its future employment decisions and file periodic reports with the court, or any other order "necessary to ensure the full enjoyment of the rights" protected by Title VII.

When the Government seeks individual relief for the victims of the discriminatory practice, a district court must usually conduct additional proceedings after the liability phase of the trial to determine the scope of individual relief. The petitioners' contention in this case is that if the Government has not, in the course of proving a pattern or practice, already brought forth specific evidence that each individual was discriminatorily denied

---

28. The holding in *Franks* that proof of a discriminatory pattern and practice creates a rebuttable presumption in favor of individual relief is consistent with the manner in which presumptions are created generally. Presumptions shifting the burden of proof are often created to reflect judicial evaluations of probabilities and to conform with a party's superior access to the proof. These factors were present in *Franks*. Although the prima facie case did not conclusively demonstrate that all of the employer's decisions were part of the proved discriminatory pattern and practice, it did create a greater likelihood that any single decision was a component of the overall pattern. Moreover, the finding of a pattern or practice changed the position of the employer to that of a proved wrongdoer. Finally, the employer was in the best position to show why any individual employee was denied an employment opportunity. Insofar as the reasons related to available vacancies or the employer's evaluation of the applicant's qualifications, the company's records were the most relevant items of proof. If the refusal to hire was based on other factors, the employer and its agents knew best what those factors were and the extent to which they influenced the decision-making process.

29. The employer's defense must, of course, be designed to meet the prima facie case of the Government. We do not mean to suggest that there are any particular limits on the type of evidence an employer may use. The point is that at the liability stage of a pattern-or-practice trial the focus often will not be on individual hiring decisions, but on a pattern of discriminatory decisionmaking. While a pattern might be demonstrated by examining the discrete decisions of which it is composed, the Government's suits have more commonly involved proof of the expected result of a regularly followed discriminatory policy.

an employment opportunity, it must carry that burden at the second, "remedial" stage of trial. That basic contention was rejected in the *Franks* case. As was true of the particular facts in *Franks*, and as is typical of Title VII pattern-or-practice suits, the question of individual relief does not arise until it has been proved that the employer has followed an employment policy of unlawful discrimination. The force of that proof does not dissipate at the remedial stage of the trial. The employer cannot, therefore, claim that there is no reason to believe that its individual employment decisions were discriminatorily based; it has already been shown to have maintained a policy of discriminatory decisionmaking.

The proof of the pattern or practice supports an inference that any particular employment decision, during the period in which the discriminatory policy was in force, was made in pursuit of that policy. The Government need only show that an alleged individual discriminatee unsuccessfully applied for a job and therefore was a potential victim of the proved discrimination. As in *Franks*, the burden then rests on the employer to demonstrate that the individual applicant was denied an employment opportunity for lawful reasons....

The question whether seniority relief may be awarded to nonapplicants was left open by our decision in *Franks*, since the class at issue in that case was limited to "identifiable applicants who were denied employment ... after the effective date ... of Title VII." [citation omitted]. We now decide that an incumbent employee's failure to apply for a job is not an inexorable bar to an award of retroactive seniority. Individual nonapplicants must be given an opportunity to undertake their difficult task of proving that they should be treated as applicants and therefore are presumptively entitled to relief accordingly.

... The effects of and the injuries suffered from discriminatory employment practices are not always confined to those who were expressly denied a requested employment opportunity. A consistently enforced discriminatory policy can surely deter job applications from those who are aware of it and are unwilling to subject themselves to the humiliation of explicit and certain rejection.

If an employer should announce his policy of discrimination by a sign reading "Whites Only" on the hiring-office door, his victims would not be limited to the few who ignored the sign and subjected themselves to personal rebuffs. The same message can be communicated to potential applicants more subtly but just as clearly by an employer's ... consistent discriminatory treatment of actual applicants, by the manner in which he publicizes vacancies, his recruitment techniques, his responses to casual or tentative inquiries, and even by the racial or ethnic composition of that part of his work force from which he has discriminatorily excluded members of minority groups. When a person's desire for a job is not translated into a formal application solely because of his unwillingness to engage in a futile gesture he is as much a victim of discrimination as is he who goes through the motions of submitting an application....

The denial of Title VII relief on the ground that the claimant had not formally applied for the job could exclude from the Act's coverage the victims of the most entrenched forms of discrimination. Victims of gross and pervasive discrimination could be denied relief precisely because the unlawful practices had been so successful as totally to deter job applications from members of minority groups. A per se prohibition of relief to nonapplicants could thus put beyond the reach of equity the most invidious effects of employment discrimination.... Such a per se limitation on the equitable powers granted to courts by Title VII would be manifestly inconsistent with the "historic purpose of equity to 'secur(e) complete justice' and with the duty of courts in Title VII cases 'to render a decree which will so far as possible eliminate the discriminatory effects of the past.'" [citation omitted].

... A nonapplicant must show that he was a potential victim of unlawful discrimination. Because he is necessarily claiming that he was deterred from applying for the job by the employer's discriminatory practices, his is the not always easy burden of proving that he would have applied for the job had it not been for those practices....[30]

...

The task remaining for the District Court on remand will not be a simple one. Initially, the court will have to make a substantial number of individual determinations in deciding which of the minority employees were actual victims of the company's discriminatory practices. After the victims have been identified, the court must, as nearly as possible, "recreate the conditions and relationships that would have been had there been no unlawful discrimination." [citation omitted]....

Moreover, after the victims have been identified and their rightful place determined, the District Court will again be faced with the delicate task of adjusting the remedial interests of discriminatees and the legitimate expectations of other employees innocent of any wrongdoing....

For all the reasons we have discussed, the judgment of the Court of Appeals is vacated, and the cases are remanded to the District Court for further proceedings consistent with this opinion.

\* \* \*

---

## Focus Questions: *Hazelwood School Dist. v. U.S.*

1. *Focus on the attorney's role to develop the factual record and the types of evidence used in this case. What should each party's attorneys have done differently?*

2. *Look at a map of St. Louis City and St. Louis County. Notice that the two are distinct legal entities. Why is it important to understand where St. Louis City lies in comparison to Hazelwood?*

3. *What does the term "standard deviation" mean?*

4. *Do you believe that the facts establish intentional discrimination? Why or why not?*

---

# Hazelwood School Dist. v. U.S.

### 433 U.S. 299 (1977)

Justice Stewart delivered the opinion of the Court.

The petitioner Hazelwood School District covers 78 square miles in the northern part of St. Louis County, Mo. In 1973 the [United States] brought this lawsuit against Hazel-

---

30. Inasmuch as the purpose of the nonapplicant's burden of proof will be to establish that his status is similar to that of the applicant, he must bear the burden of coming forward with the basic information about his qualifications that he would have presented in an application. As in *Franks*, and in accord with Part III-A, supra, the burden then will be on the employer to show that the nonapplicant was nevertheless not a victim of discrimination. For example, the employer might show that there were other, more qualified persons who would have been chosen for a particular vacancy, or that the nonapplicant's stated qualifications were insufficient.

wood ... alleging that they were engaged in a "pattern or practice" of employment discrimination in violation of Title VII of the Civil Rights Act of 1964, as amended, 42 U.S.C. § 2000e *et seq.* The complaint asked for an injunction requiring Hazelwood to cease its discriminatory practices, to take affirmative steps to obtain qualified Negro faculty members, and to offer employment and give backpay to victims of past illegal discrimination.

Hazelwood was formed from 13 rural school districts between 1949 and 1951 by a process of annexation. By the 1967–1968 school year, 17,550 students were enrolled in the district, of whom only 59 were Negro; the number of Negro pupils increased to 576 of 25,166 in 1972–1973, a total of just over 2%.

From the beginning, Hazelwood followed relatively unstructured procedures in hiring its teachers. Every person requesting an application for a teaching position was sent one, and completed applications were submitted to a central personnel office, where they were kept on file.[31] ... The personnel office ... select[ed] anywhere from 3 to 10 applicants for interviews at the school where the vacancy existed. The personnel office did not substantively screen the applicants in determining which of them to send for interviews, other than to ascertain that each applicant, if selected, would be eligible for state certification by the time he began the job....

Interviews were conducted by a department chairman, program coordinator, or the principal at the school where the teaching vacancy existed. Although those conducting the interviews did fill out forms rating the applicants in a number of respects, it is undisputed that each school principal possessed virtually unlimited discretion in hiring teachers for his school. The only general guidance given to the principals was to hire the "most competent" person available, and such intangibles as "personality, disposition, appearance, poise, voice, articulation, and ability to deal with people" counted heavily....

In the early 1960's Hazelwood found it necessary to recruit new teachers, and for that purpose members of its staff visited a number of colleges and universities in Missouri and bordering States. All the institutions visited were predominantly white, and Hazelwood did not seriously recruit at either of the two predominantly Negro four-year colleges in Missouri. As a buyer's market began to develop for public school teachers, Hazelwood curtailed its recruiting efforts. For the 1971–1972 school year, 3,127 persons applied for only 234 teaching vacancies; for the 1972–1973 school year, there were 2,373 applications for 282 vacancies. A number of the applicants who were not hired were Negroes.

Hazelwood hired its first Negro teacher in 1969. The number of Negro faculty members gradually increased in successive years: 6 of 957 in the 1970 school year; 16 of 1,107 by the end of the 1972 school year; 22 of 1,231 in the 1973 school year. By comparison, according to 1970 census figures, of more than 19,000 teachers employed in that year in the St. Louis area, 15.4% were Negro. That percentage figure included the St. Louis City School District, which in recent years has followed a policy of attempting to maintain a 50% Negro teaching staff. Apart from that school district, 5.7% of the teachers in the county were Negro in 1970.

Drawing upon these historic facts, the Government mounted its pattern or practice attack in the District Court upon four different fronts. It adduced evidence of (1) a history of alleged racially discriminatory practices, (2) statistical disparities in hiring, (3) the standardless and largely subjective hiring procedures, and (4) specific instances of alleged

---

31. Before 1954 Hazelwood's application forms required designation of race, and those forms were in use as late as the 1962–1963 school year.

discrimination against 55 unsuccessful Negro applicants for teaching jobs. Hazelwood offered virtually no additional evidence in response, relying instead on evidence introduced by the Government, perceived deficiencies in the Government's case, and its own officially promulgated policy "to hire all teachers on the basis of training, preparation and recommendations, regardless of race, color or creed."

The District Court ruled that the Government had failed to establish a pattern or practice of discrimination. The court was unpersuaded by the alleged history of discrimination.... The statistics showing that relatively small numbers of Negroes were employed as teachers were found nonprobative, on the ground that the percentage of Negro pupils in Hazelwood was similarly small. The court found nothing illegal or suspect in the teacher-hiring procedures that Hazelwood had followed. Finally, the court reviewed the evidence in the 55 cases of alleged individual discrimination, and after stating that the burden of proving intentional discrimination was on the Government, it found that this burden had not been sustained in a single instance. Hence, the court entered judgment for the defendants.

The Court of Appeals for the Eighth Circuit reversed.... [T]he Court of Appeals rejected the trial court's analysis of the statistical data as resting on an irrelevant comparison of Negro teachers to Negro pupils in Hazelwood. The proper comparison, in the appellate court's view, was one between Negro teachers in Hazelwood and Negro teachers in the relevant labor market area. Selecting St. Louis County and St. Louis City as the relevant area, the Court of Appeals compared the 1970 census figures, showing that 15.4% of teachers in that area were Negro, to the racial composition of Hazelwood's teaching staff. In the 1972–1973 and 1973–1974 school years, only 1.4% and 1.8%, respectively, of Hazelwood's teachers were Negroes. This statistical disparity, particularly when viewed against the background of the teacher-hiring procedures that Hazelwood had followed, was held to constitute a prima facie case of a pattern or practice of racial discrimination.

... [T]he appellate court found 16 cases of individual discrimination, which buttressed the statistical proof. Because Hazelwood had not rebutted the Government's prima facie case of a pattern or practice of racial discrimination, the Court of Appeals directed judgment for the Government and prescribed the remedial order to be entered.

We granted certiorari....

The petitioners primarily attack the judgment of the Court of Appeals for its reliance on "undifferentiated work force statistics to find an unrebutted prima facie case of employment discrimination."

This Court's recent consideration in *International Brotherhood of Teamsters v. United States*, 431 U.S. 324, of the role of statistics in pattern-or-practice suits under Title VII provides substantial guidance in evaluating the arguments advanced by the petitioners. In that case we stated that it is the Government's burden to "establish by a preponderance of the evidence that racial discrimination was the (employer's) standard operating procedure, the regular rather than the unusual practice." *Id.* at 336. We also noted that statistics can be an important source of proof in employment discrimination cases, since

> absent explanation, it is ordinarily to be expected that nondiscriminatory hiring practices will in time result in a work force more or less representative of the racial and ethnic composition of the population in the community from which employees are hired. Evidence of long-lasting and gross disparity between the composition of a work force and that of the general population thus may be significant even though § 703(j) makes clear that Title VII imposes no requirement that a work force mirror the general population.

*Id.* at 340 n. 20. Where gross statistical disparities can be shown, they alone may in a proper case constitute prima facie proof of a pattern or practice of discrimination. *Id.* at 339.

There can be no doubt, in light of the *Teamsters* case, that the District Court's comparison of Hazelwood's teacher work force to its student population fundamentally misconceived the role of statistics in employment discrimination cases. The Court of Appeals was correct in the view that a proper comparison was between the racial composition of Hazelwood's teaching staff and the racial composition of the qualified public school teacher population in the relevant labor market.[32] The percentage of Negroes on Hazelwood's teaching staff in 1972–1973 was 1.4% and in 1973–1974 it was 1.8%. By contrast, the percentage of qualified Negro teachers in the area was, according to the 1970 census, at least 5.7%.[33] Although these differences were on their face substantial, the Court of Appeals erred in substituting its judgment for that of the District Court and holding that the Government had conclusively proved its "pattern or practice" lawsuit.

The Court of Appeals totally disregarded the possibility that this prima facie statistical proof in the record might at the trial court level be rebutted by statistics dealing with Hazelwood's hiring after it became subject to Title VII. Racial discrimination by public employers was not made illegal under Title VII until March 24, 1972. A public employer who from that date forward made all its employment decisions in a wholly nondiscriminatory way would not violate Title VII even if it had formerly maintained an all-white work force by purposefully excluding Negroes.[34] For this reason, the Court cautioned in the *Teamsters* opinion that once a prima facie case has been established by statistical work-force disparities, the employer must be given an opportunity to show that "the claimed discriminatory pattern is a product of pre-Act hiring rather than unlawful post-Act discrimination." [citation omitted].

The record in this case showed that for the 1972–1973 school year, Hazelwood hired 282 new teachers, 10 [of] whom (3.5%) were Negroes; for the following school year it hired 123 new teachers, 5 of whom (4.1%) were Negroes. Over the two-year period,

---

32. In *Teamsters*, the comparison between the percentage of Negroes on the employer's work force and the percentage in the general areawide population was highly probative, because the job skill there involved the ability to drive a truck is one that many persons possess or can fairly readily acquire. When special qualifications are required to fill particular jobs, comparisons to the general population (rather than to the smaller group of individuals who possess the necessary qualifications) may have little probative value.

33. As is discussed below, the Government contends that a comparative figure of 15.4%, rather than 5.7%, is the appropriate one. But even assuming, arguendo, that the 5.7% figure urged by the petitioners is correct, the disparity between that figure and the percentage of Negroes on Hazelwood's teaching staff would be more than fourfold for the 1972–1973 school year, and threefold for the 1973–1974 school year. Using the 5.7% figure as the basis for calculating the expected value, the expected number of Negroes on the Hazelwood teaching staff would be roughly 63 in 1972–1973 and 70 in 1973–1974. The observed number in those years was 16 and 22, respectively. The difference between the observed and expected values was more than six standard deviations in 1972–1973 and more than five standard deviations in 1973–1974. "(A)s a general rule for such large samples, if the difference between the expected value and the observed number is greater than two or three standard deviations," then the hypothesis that teachers were hired without regard to race would be suspect. [citation omitted].

34. This is not to say that evidence of pre-Act discrimination can never have any probative force. Proof that an employer engaged in racial discrimination prior to the effective date of Title VII might in some circumstances support the inference that such discrimination continued, particularly where relevant aspects of the decisionmaking process had undergone little change....

Negroes constituted a total of 15 of the 405 new teachers hired (3.7%). Although the Court of Appeals briefly mentioned these data in reciting the facts, it wholly ignored them in discussing whether the Government had shown a pattern or practice of discrimination. And it gave no consideration at all to the possibility that post-Act data as to the number of Negroes hired compared to the total number of Negro applicants might tell a totally different story.

What the hiring figures prove obviously depends upon the figures to which they are compared. The Court of Appeals accepted the Government's argument that the relevant comparison was to the labor market area of St. Louis County and the city of St. Louis, in which, according to the 1970 census, 15.4% of all teachers were Negro. The propriety of that comparison was vigorously disputed by the petitioners, who urged that because the city of St. Louis has made special attempts to maintain a 50% Negro teaching staff, inclusion of that school district in the relevant market area distorts the comparison. Were that argument accepted, the percentage of Negro teachers in the relevant labor market area (St. Louis County alone) as shown in the 1970 census would be 5.7% rather than 15.4%.

The difference between these figures may well be important; the disparity between 3.7% (the percentage of Negro teachers hired by Hazelwood in 1972–1973 and 1973–1974) and 5.7% may be sufficiently small to weaken the Government's other proof, while the disparity between 3.7% and 15.4% may be sufficiently large to reinforce it. In determining which of the two figures or, very possibly, what intermediate figure provides the most accurate basis for comparison to the hiring figures at Hazelwood, it will be necessary to evaluate such considerations as (i) whether the racially based hiring policies of the St. Louis City School District were in effect as far back as 1970, the year in which the census figures were taken; (ii) to what extent those policies have changed the racial composition of that district's teaching staff from what it would otherwise have been; (iii) to what extent St. Louis' recruitment policies have diverted to the city, teachers who might otherwise have applied to Hazelwood; (iv) to what extent Negro teachers employed by the city would prefer employment in other districts such as Hazelwood; and (v) what the experience in other school districts in St. Louis County indicates about the validity of excluding the City School District from the relevant labor market.

It is thus clear that a determination of the appropriate comparative figures in this case will depend upon further evaluation by the trial court. As this Court admonished in *Teamsters*: "(S)tatistics ... come in infinite variety.... (T)heir usefulness depends on all of the surrounding facts and circumstances." 431 U.S. at 340. Only the trial court is in a position to make the appropriate determination after further findings. And only after such a determination is made can a foundation be established for deciding whether or not Hazelwood engaged in a pattern or practice of racial discrimination in its employment practices in violation of the law.

We hold, therefore, that the Court of Appeals erred in disregarding the post-Act hiring statistics in the record, and that it should have remanded the case to the District Court for further findings as to the relevant labor market area and for an ultimate determination of whether Hazelwood engaged in a pattern or practice of employment discrimination after March 24, 1972. Accordingly, the judgment is vacated, and the case is remanded to the District Court for further proceedings consistent with this opinion.

It is so ordered.

[A concurring opinion by Justice Brennan is omitted, as is a dissenting opinion by Justice Stevens.]

## Exercise 3.9

Sims is a large national retail chain. You are a plaintiff's attorney. A disgruntled former employee in Sims' human resources office comes to you and gives you documents. From these documents, you learn that, on average, a female manager at Sims make $2,000 less a year than a male manager. You also learn that only 40 percent of the managers for Sims are women. The disgruntled former employee tells you that Sims hires from within and that it requires people to move from store to store, often in different states, to gain successively higher levels of managerial experience. When selecting managers, the store director at each location is given complete discretion to hire. Store managers are selected by the regional director for the particular area of the country, who likewise is given complete discretion to hire. Assume for purposes of this exercise that the information given to you is completely accurate.

Think about an attorney's role to gather admissible evidence to support a claim of discrimination and also think about the mistakes that attorneys can make in pattern or practice cases in this critical role. What kinds of information would you need to support a pattern or practice case based on these facts?

Recall that under Fed. R. Civ. P. 11(b)(3), an attorney filing a complaint in federal court certifies that "the factual contentions have evidentiary support or, if specifically so identified, will likely have evidentiary support after a reasonable opportunity for further investigation or discovery." Think about what information you are likely to possess at the time the complaint is filed and what evidence you will need to obtain through discovery. How contentious (and expensive) do you think the discovery process will be? Will you need experts to help you craft the case? Does the necessity of expert witnesses change the calculation regarding whether to file the case?

## ✦ Core Concept: Affirmative Action

In some cases, a decision can be based on a protected trait and still be legal under the federal employment discrimination statutes. One such instance is when an employer argues that its actions were taken pursuant to an appropriate voluntary affirmative action plan. *See United Steelworkers v. Weber*, 443 U.S. 193 (1979). Affirmative action as a defense is discussed in detail in Chapter 9. At this point it is important for you simply to recognize affirmative action as a potential affirmative defense in discrimination cases. You will learn later, when discussing remedies, that a court that finds that discrimination occurred, may order affirmative action as a remedy.

## ✦ Core Concept: BFOQ

Title VII contains a statutory provision that reads as follows:

Notwithstanding any other provision of this subchapter, (1) it shall not be an unlawful employment practice for an employer to hire and employ employees, for an employment agency to classify, or refer for employment any individual, for a labor organization to classify its membership or to classify or refer for employment any individual, or for an employer, labor organization, or joint labor-management committee controlling apprenticeship or other training or retraining programs to admit or employ any individual in any such program, on the basis of his religion, sex, or national origin in those certain instances where religion, sex, or national origin is a bona fide occupational qualification reasonably necessary to the normal operation of that particular business or enterprise....

42 U.S.C. § 2000e-2(e). This provision is known as the BFOQ provision and allows certain protected traits to be taken into consideration in employment decisions. The ADEA contains a similar provision. 29 U.S.C. § 623(f)(1). Recall that the ADEA also contains the RFOA (reasonable factor other than age) provision, in addition to a defense for BFOQ. Section 1981 does not contain a BFOQ provision. While the ADA does not contain a BFOQ provision, other concepts under the ADA allow an employer to make employment decisions related to disability. Chapter 8 discusses these concepts.

The following case outlines the contours of the BFOQ defense in the context of age.

---

### Focus Questions: *Western Air Lines, Inc. v. Criswell*

1. *What are the contours of the BFOQ defense?*

2. *Does the airline present a convincing factual argument?*

---

# Western Air Lines, Inc. v. Criswell
## 472 U.S. 400 (1985)

Justice Stevens delivered the opinion of the Court.

The petitioner, Western Air Lines, Inc., requires that its flight engineers retire at age 60. Although the Age Discrimination in Employment Act of 1967, 29 U.S.C. §§ 621–634, generally prohibits mandatory retirement..., the Act provides an exception "where age is a bona fide occupational qualification [BFOQ] reasonably necessary to the normal operation of the particular business." A jury concluded that Western's mandatory retirement rule did not qualify as a BFOQ even though it purportedly was adopted for safety reasons. The question here is whether the jury was properly instructed on the elements of the BFOQ defense.

I

In its commercial airline operations, Western operates ... aircraft [that] require three crew members in the cockpit: a captain, a first officer, and a flight engineer. "The 'captain' is the pilot and controls the aircraft. He is responsible for all phases of its operation. The 'first officer' is the copilot and assists the captain. The 'flight engineer' usually monitors a side-facing instrument panel. He does not operate the flight controls unless the captain and the first officer become incapacitated."

A regulation of the Federal Aviation Administration (FAA) prohibits any person from serving as a pilot or first officer on a commercial flight "if that person has reached his

60th birthday." 14 C.F.R. § 121.383(c) (1985). The FAA has justified the retention of mandatory retirement for pilots on the theory that "incapacitating medical events" and "adverse psychological, emotional, and physical changes" occur as a consequence of aging. "The inability to detect or predict with precision an individual's risk of sudden or subtle incapacitation, in the face of known age-related risks, counsels against relaxation of the rule." [citation omitted].

At the same time, the FAA has refused to establish a mandatory retirement age for flight engineers. "While a flight engineer has important duties which contribute to the safe operation of the airplane, he or she may not assume the responsibilities of the pilot in command." [citation omitted]. Moreover, available statistics establish that flight engineers have rarely been a contributing cause or factor in commercial aircraft "accidents" or "incidents."

In 1978, respondents Criswell and Starley were captains ... for Western. Both men celebrated their 60th birthdays in July 1978. Under the collective-bargaining agreement in effect between Western and the union, cockpit crew members could obtain open positions by bidding in order of seniority. In order to avoid mandatory retirement under the FAA's under-age-60 rule for pilots, Criswell and Starley applied for reassignment as flight engineers. Western denied both requests, ostensibly on the ground that both employees were members of the company's retirement plan which required all crew members to retire at age 60. For the same reason, respondent Ron, a career flight engineer, was also retired in 1978 after his 60th birthday.

Criswell, Starley, and Ron brought this action against Western contending that the under-age-60 qualification for the position of flight engineer violated the ADEA. In the District Court, Western defended, in part, on the theory that the age-60 rule is a BFOQ "reasonably necessary" to the safe operation of the airline.[35] All parties submitted evidence concerning the nature of the flight engineer's tasks, the physiological and psychological traits required to perform them, and the availability of those traits among persons over age 60.

As the District Court summarized, the evidence at trial established that the flight engineer's "normal duties are less critical to the safety of flight than those of a pilot." The flight engineer, however, does have critical functions in emergency situations and, of course, might cause considerable disruption in the event of his own medical emergency.

The actual capabilities of persons over age 60, and the ability to detect disease or a precipitous decline in their faculties, were the subject of conflicting medical testimony. Western's expert witness, a former FAA Deputy Federal Air Surgeon, was especially concerned about the possibility of a "cardiovascular event" such as a heart attack. He testified that "with advancing age the likelihood of onset of disease increases and that in persons over age 60 it could not be predicted whether and when such diseases would occur."

The plaintiffs' experts, on the other hand, testified that physiological deterioration is caused by disease, not aging, and that "it was feasible to determine on the basis of individual medical examinations whether flight deck crew members, including those over age 60, were physically qualified to continue to fly." These conclusions were corroborated by the nonmedical evidence:

> The record also reveals that both the FAA and the airlines have been able to deal with the health problems of pilots on an individualized basis. Pilots who have

---

35. Western also contended that its denials of the downbids by pilots Starley and Criswell were based on "reasonable factors other than age." 29 U.S.C. § 623(f)(1).

been grounded because of alcoholism or cardiovascular disease have been recertified by the FAA and allowed to resume flying. Pilots who were unable to pass the necessary examination to maintain their FAA first class medical certificates, but who continued to qualify for second class medical certificates were allowed to "down-grade" from pilot to [flight engineer]. There is nothing in the record to indicate that these flight deck crew members are physically better able to perform their duties than flight engineers over age 60 who have not experienced such events or that they are less likely to become incapacitated.

Moreover, several large commercial airlines have flight engineers over age 60 "flying the line" without any reduction in their safety record.

The jury was instructed that the "BFOQ defense is available only if it is reasonably necessary to the normal operation or essence of defendant's business." [citation omitted]. The jury was informed that "the essence of Western's business is the safe transportation of their passengers." The jury was also instructed:

One method by which defendant Western may establish a BFOQ in this case is to prove:

(1) That in 1978, when these plaintiffs were retired, it was highly impractical for Western to deal with each second officer over age 60 on an individualized basis to determine his particular ability to perform his job safely; and

(2) That some second officers over age 60 possess traits of a physiological, psychological or other nature which preclude safe and efficient job performance that cannot be ascertained by means other than knowing their age.

In evaluating the practicability to defendant Western of dealing with second officers over age 60 on an individualized basis, with respect to the medical testimony, you should consider the state of the medical art as it existed in July 1978.

The jury rendered a verdict for the plaintiffs, and awarded damages. After trial, the District Court granted equitable relief, explaining in a written opinion why it found no merit in Western's BFOQ defense to the mandatory retirement rule.

On appeal, Western made various arguments attacking the verdict and judgment below, but the Court of Appeals affirmed in all respects. In particular, the Court of Appeals rejected Western's contention that the instruction on the BFOQ defense was insufficiently deferential to the airline's legitimate concern for the safety of its passengers. We granted certiorari to consider the merits of this question.[36]

---

36. One of Western's claims in the trial court was that its refusal to allow pilots to serve as flight engineers after they reached age 60 was based on "reasonable factors other than age" (RFOA), namely, a facially neutral policy embodied in its collective-bargaining agreement which prohibited downbidding. The jury rejected this defense in its verdict. On appeal, Western claimed that the instructions had improperly required it to bear the burden of proof on the RFOA issue inasmuch as the burden of persuasion on the issue of age discrimination is at all times on the plaintiff. The Court of Appeals rejected this claim on the merits. We granted certiorari to consider the merits of this question, but as we read the instructions the burden *was* placed on the plaintiffs on the RFOA issue. The general instruction on the question of discrimination provided that the "burden of proof is on the plaintiffs to show discriminatory treatment on the basis of age." The instructions expressly informed the jury when the burden shifted to the defendant to prove [business necessity and BFOQ] but did not so inform the jury in the RFOA instruction. Because the plaintiffs were assigned the burden of proof, we need not consider whether it would have been error to assign it to the defendant. [Ed. Note: In a subsequent case involving disparate impact, the Court held that RFOA is an affirmative defense for the employer to establish. *Meacham v. Knolls Atomic Power Laboratory*, 554 U.S. 84 (2008).]

II

Throughout the legislative history of the ADEA, one empirical fact is repeatedly emphasized: the process of psychological and physiological degeneration caused by aging varies with each individual. "The basic research in the field of aging has established that there is a wide range of individual physical ability regardless of age." [footnote omitted]. As a result, many older American workers perform at levels equal or superior to their younger colleagues.

In 1965, the Secretary of Labor reported to Congress that despite these well-established medical facts there "is persistent and widespread use of age limits in hiring that in a great many cases can be attributed only to arbitrary discrimination against older workers on the basis of age and regardless of ability." Two years later, the President recommended that Congress enact legislation to abolish arbitrary age limits on hiring. Such limits, the President declared, have a devastating effect on the dignity of the individual and result in a staggering loss of human resources vital to the national economy.

"In economic terms, this is a serious—and senseless—loss to a nation on the move. But the greater loss is the cruel sacrifice in happiness and well-being which joblessness imposes on these citizens and their families." [citation omitted].

After further study, Congress responded with the enactment of the ADEA. The preamble declares that the purpose of the ADEA is "to promote employment of older persons based on their ability rather than age [and] to prohibit arbitrary age discrimination in employment." ...

... "Increasingly, it is being recognized that mandatory retirement based solely upon age is arbitrary and that chronological age alone is a poor indicator of ability to perform a job. Mandatory retirement does not take into consideration actual differing abilities and capacities. Such forced retirement can cause hardships for older persons through loss of roles and loss of income. Those older persons who wish to be re-employed have a much more difficult time finding a new job than younger persons.

"Society, as a whole, suffers from mandatory retirement as well. As a result of mandatory retirement, skills and experience are lost from the work force resulting in reduced GNP. Such practices also add a burden to Government income maintenance programs such as social security." [citations omitted].

In the 1978 Amendments, Congress narrowed an exception to the ADEA which had previously authorized involuntary retirement under limited circumstances.... In both 1967 and 1978, however, Congress recognized that classifications based on age, like classifications based on religion, sex, or national origin, may sometimes serve as a necessary proxy for neutral employment qualifications essential to the employer's business. The diverse employment situations in various industries, however, forced Congress to adopt a "case-by-case basis ... as the underlying rule in the administration of the legislation." [citation omitted]. Congress offered only general guidance on when an age classification might be permissible by borrowing a concept and statutory language from Title VII and providing that such a classification is lawful "where age is a bona fide occupational qualification reasonably necessary to the normal operation of the particular business." 29 U.S.C. §623(f)(1).

Shortly after the passage of the Act, the Secretary of Labor, who was at that time charged with its enforcement, adopted regulations declaring that the BFOQ exception to the ADEA has only "limited scope and application" and "must be construed narrowly." The Equal Employment Opportunity Commission (EEOC) adopted the same narrow construction of the BFOQ exception after it was assigned authority for enforcing the statute. The restrictive language of the statute and the consistent interpretation of the administrative agencies charged with enforcing the statute convince us that, like its Title VII counterpart, the BFOQ exception "was in fact meant to be an extremely narrow exception to the general prohibition" of age discrimination contained in the ADEA.

## III

In *Usery v. Tamiami Trail Tours, Inc.*, 531 F.2d 224 (1976), the Court of Appeals for the Fifth Circuit was called upon to evaluate the merits of a BFOQ defense to a claim of age discrimination. Tamiami Trail Tours, Inc., had a policy of refusing to hire persons over-age-40 as intercity bus drivers. At trial, the bus company introduced testimony supporting its theory that the hiring policy was a BFOQ based upon safety considerations—the need to employ persons who have a low risk of accidents. In evaluating this contention, the Court of Appeals drew on its Title VII precedents, and concluded that two inquiries were relevant.

First, the court recognized that some job qualifications may be so peripheral to the central mission of the employer's business that *no* age discrimination can be "reasonably *necessary* to the normal operation of the particular business."[37] The bus company justified the age qualification for hiring its drivers on safety considerations, but the court concluded that this claim was to be evaluated under an objective standard:

"[T]he job qualifications which the employer invokes to justify his discrimination must be *reasonably necessary* to the essence of his business—here, the *safe* transportation of bus passengers from one point to another. The greater the safety factor, measured by the likelihood of harm and the probable severity of that harm in case of an accident, the more stringent may be the job qualifications designed to insure safe driving."

This inquiry "adjusts to the safety factor" by ensuring that the employer's restrictive job qualifications are "reasonably necessary" to further the overriding interest in public safety. [citation omitted]. In *Tamiami*, the court noted that no one had seriously challenged the bus company's safety justification for hiring drivers with a low risk of having accidents.

Second, the court recognized that the ADEA requires that age qualifications be something more than "convenient" or "reasonable"; they must be "reasonably necessary ... to the particular business," and this is only so when the employer is compelled to rely on age as a proxy for the safety-related job qualifications validated in the first inquiry. [citation omitted]. This showing could be made in two ways. The employer could establish that it "had reasonable cause to believe, that is, a factual basis for believing, that all or substantially all [persons over the age qualifications] would be unable to perform safely and efficiently the duties of the job involved." [citation omitted]. In *Tamiami*, the employer did not seek to justify its hiring qualification under this standard.

Alternatively, the employer could establish that age was a legitimate proxy for the safety-related job qualifications by proving that it is "impossible or highly impractical"

---

37. *Diaz v. Pan American World Airways, Inc.*, 442 F.2d 385 (5th Cir. 1971), provided authority for this proposition. In *Diaz* the court had rejected Pan American's claim that a female-only qualification for the position of in-flight cabin attendant was a BFOQ under Title VII. The District Court had upheld the qualification as a BFOQ finding that the airline's passengers preferred the "pleasant environment" and the "cosmetic effect" provided by female attendants, and that most men were unable to perform effectively the "non-mechanical functions" of the job. The Court of Appeals rejected the BFOQ defense concluding that these considerations "are tangential to the essence of the business involved." 442 F.2d. at 388.

to deal with the older employees on an individualized basis. [citation omitted]. "One method by which the employer can carry this burden is to establish that some members of the discriminated-against class possess a trait precluding safe and efficient job performance that cannot be ascertained by means other than knowledge of the applicant's membership in the class." [citation omitted]....

... Considering the narrow language of the BFOQ exception, the parallel treatment of such questions under Title VII, and the uniform application of the standard by the federal courts, the EEOC, and Congress, we conclude that this two-part inquiry properly identifies the relevant considerations for resolving a BFOQ defense to an age-based qualification purportedly justified by considerations of safety.

An employer asserting a BFOQ defense has the burden of proving that (1) the age limit is reasonably necessary to the essence of the business, and either (2) that all or substantially all individuals excluded from the job involved are in fact disqualified, or (3) that some of the individuals so excluded possess a disqualifying trait that cannot be ascertained except by reference to age. If the employer's objective in asserting a BFOQ is the goal of public safety, the employer must prove that the challenged practice does indeed effectuate that goal and that there is no acceptable alternative which would better advance it or equally advance it with less discriminatory impact.

## IV

In the trial court, Western preserved an objection to any instruction in the *Tamiami* mold, claiming that "any instruction pertaining to the statutory phrase 'reasonably necessary to the normal operation of [defendant's] business'... is irrelevant to and confusing for the deliberations of the jury." Western proposed an instruction that would have allowed it to succeed on the BFOQ defense by proving that "in 1978, when these plaintiffs were retired, there existed a *rational basis in fact* for defendant to believe that use of [flight engineers] over age 60 on its DC-10 airliners would increase the likelihood of risk to its passengers." The proposed instruction went on to note that the jury might rely on the FAA's age-60 rule for pilots to establish a BFOQ under this standard "without considering any other evidence." It also noted that the medical evidence submitted by the parties might provide a "rational basis in fact."

The airline now acknowledges that the *Tamiami* standard identifies the relevant general inquiries that must be made in evaluating the BFOQ defense. However, Western claims that in several respects the instructions given below were insufficiently protective of public safety. Western urges that we interpret or modify the *Tamiami* standard to weigh these concerns in the balance.

Reasonably Necessary Job Qualifications

Western relied on two different kinds of job qualifications to justify its mandatory retirement policy. First, it argued that flight engineers should have a low risk of incapacitation or psychological and physiological deterioration. At this vague level of analysis respondents have not seriously disputed — nor could they — that the qualification of good health for a vital crew member is reasonably necessary to the essence of the airline's operations. Instead, they have argued that age is not a necessary proxy for that qualification.

On a more specific level, Western argues that flight engineers must meet the same stringent qualifications as pilots, and that it was therefore quite logical to extend to flight engineers the FAA's age-60 retirement rule for pilots. Although the FAA's rule for pilots, adopted for safety reasons, is relevant evidence in the airline's BFOQ defense, it is not to be accorded conclusive weight. The extent to which the rule is probative varies with the weight of the evidence supporting its safety rationale and "the congruity between the ... occupations at issue." In this case, the evidence clearly established that the FAA, Western, and other airlines all recognized that the qualifications for a flight engineer were less rigorous than those required for a pilot.

... Western nevertheless argues that the jury should have been instructed to defer to "Western's selection of job qualifications for the position of [flight engineer] that are reasonable in light of the safety risks." This proposal is plainly at odds with Congress' decision, in adopting the ADEA, to subject such management decisions to a test of objective justification in a court of law. The BFOQ standard adopted in the statute is one of "reasonable necessity," not reasonableness.

In adopting that standard, Congress did not ignore the public interest in safety. That interest is adequately reflected in instructions that track the language of the statute. When an employer establishes that a job qualification has been carefully formulated to respond to documented concerns for public safety, it will not be overly burdensome to persuade a trier of fact that the qualification is "reasonably necessary" to safe operation of the business. The uncertainty implicit in the concept of managing safety risks always makes it "reasonably necessary" to err on the side of caution in a close case. The employer cannot be expected to establish the risk of an airline accident "to a certainty, for certainty would require running the risk until a tragic accident would prove that the judgment was sound." [citation omitted]. When the employer's argument has a credible basis in the record, it is difficult to believe that a jury of laypersons—many of whom no doubt have flown or could expect to fly on commercial air carriers—would not defer in a close case to the airline's judgment. Since the instructions in this case would not have prevented the airline from raising this contention to the jury in closing argument, we are satisfied that the verdict is a consequence of a defect in Western's proof rather than a defect in the trial court's instructions....

Age as a Proxy for Job Qualifications

Western contended below that the ADEA only requires that the employer establish "a rational basis in fact" for believing that identification of those persons lacking suitable qualifications cannot occur on an individualized basis.

... Western argues that a "rational basis" standard should be adopted because medical disputes can never be proved "to a certainty" and because juries should not be permitted "to resolve bona fide conflicts among medical experts respecting the adequacy of individualized testing." The jury, however, need not be convinced beyond all doubt that medical testing is impossible, but only that the proposition is true "on a preponderance of the evidence." Moreover, Western's attack on the wisdom of assigning the resolution of complex questions to 12 laypersons is inconsistent with the structure of the ADEA. Congress expressly decided that problems involving age discrimination in employment should be resolved on a "case-by-case basis" by proof to a jury.

The "rational basis" standard is also inconsistent with the preference for individual evaluation expressed in the language and legislative history of the ADEA. Under the Act, employers are to evaluate employees ... on their merits and not their age. In the BFOQ defense, Congress provided a limited exception to this general principle, but required that employers validate any discrimination as "reasonably necessary to the normal operation of the particular business." It might well be "rational" to require mandatory retirement at *any* age less than 70, but that result would not comply with Congress' direction that employers must justify the rationale for the age chosen. Unless an employer can establish a substantial basis for believing that all or nearly all employees above an age lack the qualifications required for the position, the age selected for mandatory retirement … must be an age at which it is highly impractical for the employer to insure by individual testing that its employees will have the necessary qualifications for the job.

Western argues that its lenient standard is necessary because "where qualified experts disagree as to whether persons over a certain age can be dealt with on an individual basis, an employer must be allowed to resolve that controversy in a conservative manner." This argument incorrectly assumes that all expert opinion is entitled to equal weight, and virtually ignores the function of the trier of fact in evaluating conflicting testimony. In this case, the jury may well have attached little weight to the testimony of Western's expert witness. A rule that would require the jury to defer to the judgment of any expert witness testifying for the employer, no matter how unpersuasive, would allow some employers to give free reign to the stereotype of older workers that Congress decried in the legislative history of the ADEA.

… Even in cases involving public safety, the ADEA plainly does not permit the trier of fact to give complete deference to the employer's decision.

---

### Focus Questions: *Dothard v. Rawlinson*

1. *Compare this case with the 1985 case of* Western Air Lines v. Criswell *immediately above. Are they consistent? Is the BFOQ defense to be construed broadly or narrowly?*

2. *Is the holding in this case likely to be applied in other factual contexts? In other prison contexts?*

---

# Dothard v. Rawlinson
## 433 U.S. 321 (1977)

Justice Stewart delivered the opinion of the Court.

Appellee Dianne Rawlinson sought employment with the Alabama Board of Corrections as a prison guard.… After her application was rejected, she brought this class suit under Title VII and under 42 U.S.C. § 1983, alleging that she had been denied employment because of her sex in violation of federal law.…

### I

At the time she applied for a position as correctional counselor trainee, Rawlinson was a 22-year-old college graduate whose major course of study had been correctional psychology. She was refused employment because she failed to meet the minimum 120-pound weight requirement established by an Alabama statute. The statute also establishes a height minimum of 5 feet 2 inches. [The plaintiff's disparate impact claim is considered in Chapter 4].

While the disparate impact suit was pending, the Alabama Board of Corrections adopted Administrative Regulation 204, establishing gender criteria for assigning correctional counselors to maximum-security institutions for "contact positions," that is, positions requiring continual close physical proximity to inmates of the institution.[38] Rawlinson amended her class-action complaint by adding a challenge to regulation 204 as also violative of Title VII and the Fourteenth Amendment.

... Like most correctional facilities in the United States, Alabama's prisons are segregated on the basis of sex. Currently the Alabama Board of Corrections operates four major all-male penitentiaries Holman Prison, Kilby Corrections Facility, G. K. Fountain Correction Center, and Draper Correctional Center. The Board also operates the Julia Tutwiler Prison for Women, the Frank Lee Youth Center, the Number Four Honor Camp, the State Cattle Ranch, and nine Work Release Centers, one of which is for women. The Julia Tutwiler Prison for Women and the four male penitentiaries are maximum-security institutions. Their inmate living quarters are for the most part large dormitories, with communal showers and toilets that are open to the dormitories and hallways. The Draper and Fountain penitentiaries carry on extensive farming operations, making necessary a large number of strip searches for contraband when prisoners re-enter the prison buildings.

... Because most of Alabama's prisoners are held at the four maximum-security male penitentiaries, 336 of ... 435 correctional counselor jobs were in those institutions, a majority of them concededly in the "contact" classification. Thus, even though meeting the statutory height and weight requirements, women applicants could under Regulation 204 compete equally with men for only about 25% of the correctional counselor jobs available in the Alabama prison system....

III

... Regulation 204 explicitly discriminates against women on the basis of their sex. In defense of this overt discrimination, the appellants rely on § 703(e) of Title VII, 42 U.S.C. § 2000e-2(e), which permits sex-based discrimination "in those certain instances where ... sex ... is a bona fide occupational qualification reasonably necessary to the normal operation of that particular business or enterprise."

The District Court rejected the bona-fide occupational-qualification (bfoq) defense, relying on the virtually uniform view of the federal courts that § 703(e) provides only the

---

38. Administrative Regulation 204 provides in pertinent part as follows:
    ... PROCEDURE 8. Institutional Wardens and Directors will identify each institutional Correctional Counselor I position which they feel requires selective certification and will request that it be so designated in writing to the Associate Commissioner for Administration for his review, evaluation, and submission to the Commissioner for final decision.
    9. The request will contain the exact duties and responsibilities of the position and will utilize and identify the following criteria to establish that selective certification is necessary; A. That the presence of the opposite sex would cause disruption of the orderly running and security of the institution. B. That the position would require contact with the inmates of the opposite sex without the presence of others. C. That the position would require patrolling dormitories, restrooms, or showers while in use, frequently, during the day or night. D. That the position would require search of inmates of the opposite sex on a regular basis. E. That the position would require that the Correctional Counselor Trainee not be armed with a firearm.
    10. All institutional Correctional Counselor I positions which are not approved for selective certification will be filled from Correctional Counselor Trainee registers without regard to sex.
Although Regulation 204 is not limited on its face to contact positions in maximum-security institutions, the District Court found that it did not preclude ... (women) from serving in contact positions in the all-male institutions other than the penitentiaries. Appellants similarly defended the regulation as applying only to maximum-security facilities.

narrowest of exceptions to the general rule requiring equality of employment opportunities. This view has been variously formulated. [T]he Court of Appeals for the Fifth Circuit held that "discrimination based on sex is valid only when the essence of the business operation would be undermined by not hiring members of one sex exclusively." In an earlier case, ... the same court said that an employer could rely on the bfoq exception only by proving "that he had reasonable cause to believe, that is, a factual basis for believing, that all or substantially all women would be unable to perform safely and efficiently the duties of the job involved." But whatever the verbal formulation, the federal courts have agreed that it is impermissible under Title VII to refuse to hire an individual woman or man on the basis of stereotyped characterizations of the sexes, and the District Court in the present case held in effect that Regulation 204 is based on just such stereotypical assumptions.

We are persuaded by the restrictive language of § 703(e), the relevant legislative history, and the consistent interpretation of the Equal Employment Opportunity Commission that the bfoq exception was in fact meant to be an extremely narrow exception to the general prohibition of discrimination on the basis of sex. In the particular factual circumstances of this case, however, we conclude that the District Court erred in rejecting the State's contention that Regulation 204 falls within the narrow ambit of the bfoq exception.

The environment in Alabama's penitentiaries is a peculiarly inhospitable one for human beings of whatever sex. Indeed, a Federal District Court has held that the conditions of confinement in the prisons of the State, characterized by "rampant violence" and a "jungle atmosphere," are constitutionally intolerable. *Pugh v. Locke*, 406 F. Supp. 318, 325 (M.D. Ala. 1976). The record in the present case shows that because of inadequate staff and facilities, no attempt is made in the four maximum-security male penitentiaries to classify or segregate inmates according to their offense or level of dangerousness—a procedure that, according to expert testimony, is essential to effective penological administration. Consequently, the estimated 20% of the male prisoners who are sex offenders are scattered throughout the penitentiaries' dormitory facilities.

In this environment of violence and disorganization, it would be an oversimplification to characterize Regulation 204 as an exercise in "romantic paternalism." In the usual case, the argument that a particular job is too dangerous for women may appropriately be met by the rejoinder that it is the purpose of Title VII to allow the individual woman to make that choice for herself. More is at stake in this case, however, than an individual woman's decision to weigh and accept the risks of employment in a "contact" position in a maximum-security male prison.

The essence of a correctional counselor's job is to maintain prison security. A woman's relative ability to maintain order in a male, maximum-security, unclassified penitentiary of the type Alabama now runs could be directly reduced by her womanhood. There is a basis in fact for expecting that sex offenders who have criminally assaulted women in the past would be moved to do so again if access to women were established within the prison. There would also be a real risk that other inmates, deprived of a normal heterosexual environment, would assault women guards because they were women.[39] In a prison system where violence is the order of the day, where inmate access to guards is facilitated by dormitory living arrangements, where every institution is understaffed, and where a substantial portion of the inmate population is composed of sex offenders mixed at

---

39. The record contains evidence of an attack on a female clerical worker in an Alabama prison, and of an incident involving a woman student who was taken hostage during a visit to one of the maximum-security institutions.

random with other prisoners, there are few visible deterrents to inmate assaults on women custodians.

Appellee Rawlinson's own expert testified that dormitory housing for aggressive inmates poses a greater security problem than single-cell lockups, and further testified that it would be unwise to use women as guards in a prison where even 10% of the inmates had been convicted of sex crimes and were not segregated from the other prisoners.[40] The likelihood that inmates would assault a woman because she was a woman would pose a real threat not only to the victim of the assault but also to the basic control of the penitentiary and protection of its inmates and the other security personnel. The employee's very womanhood would thus directly undermine her capacity to provide the security that is the essence of a correctional counselor's responsibility.

There was substantial testimony from experts on both sides of this litigation that the use of women as guards in "contact" positions under the existing conditions in Alabama maximum-security male penitentiaries would pose a substantial security problem, directly linked to the sex of the prison guard. On the basis of that evidence, we conclude that the District Court was in error in ruling that being male is not a bona fide occupational qualification for the job of correctional counselor in a contact position in an Alabama male maximum-security penitentiary.

The judgment is accordingly affirmed in part and reversed in part, and the case is remanded to the District Court for further proceedings consistent with this opinion.

Justice Marshall, with whom Justice Brennan joins, concurring in part and dissenting in part.

… The Court is unquestionably correct when it holds "that the bfoq exception was in fact meant to be an extremely narrow exception to the general prohibition of discrimination on the basis of sex." I must, however, respectfully disagree with the Court's application of the bfoq exception in this case.

The Court properly rejects two proffered justifications for denying women jobs as prison guards. It is simply irrelevant here that a guard's occupation is dangerous and that some women might be unable to protect themselves adequately. Those themes permeate the testimony of the state officials below, but as the Court holds, "the argument that a particular job is too dangerous for women" is refuted by the "purpose of Title VII to allow the individual woman to make that choice for herself." Some women, like some men, undoubtedly are not qualified and do not wish to serve as prison guards, but that does not justify the exclusion of all women from this employment opportunity. Thus, in the usual case, the Court's interpretation of the bfoq exception would mandate hiring qualified women for guard jobs in maximum-security institutions. The highly successful experiences of other States allowing such job opportunities, confirm that absolute disqualification of women is not, in the words of Title VII, "reasonably necessary to the normal operation" of a maximum security prison.

What would otherwise be considered unlawful discrimination against women is justified by the Court, however, on the basis of the barbaric and inhumane conditions in Alabama prisons, conditions so bad that state officials have conceded that they violate the

---

40. Alabama's penitentiaries are evidently not typical. Appellee Rawlinson's two experts testified that in a normal, relatively stable maximum-security prison characterized by control over the inmates, reasonable living conditions, and segregation of dangerous offenders women guards could be used effectively and beneficially. Similarly, an amicus brief filed by the State of California attests to that State's success in using women guards in all-male penitentiaries.

Constitution. To me, this analysis sounds distressingly like saying two wrongs make a right. It is refuted by the plain words of § 703(e). The statute requires that a bfoq be "reasonably necessary to the normal operation of that particular business or enterprise." ... A prison system operating in blatant violation of the Eighth Amendment is an exception that should be remedied with all possible speed[.] In the meantime, the existence of such violations should not be legitimatized by calling them "normal." Nor should the Court accept them as justifying conduct that would otherwise violate a statute intended to remedy age-old discrimination.

The Court's error in statutory construction is less objectionable, however, than the attitude it displays toward women. Though the Court recognizes that possible harm to women guards is an unacceptable reason for disqualifying women, it relies instead on an equally speculative threat to prison discipline supposedly generated by the sexuality of female guards. There is simply no evidence in the record to show that women guards would create any danger to security in Alabama prisons significantly greater than that which already exists. All of the dangers with one exception discussed below are inherent in a prison setting, whatever the gender of the guards.

The Court first sees women guards as a threat to security because "there are few visible deterrents to inmate assaults on women custodians." In fact, any prison guard is constantly subject to the threat of attack by inmates, and "invisible" deterrents are the guard's only real protection. No prison guard relies primarily on his or her ability to ward off an inmate attack to maintain order. Guards are typically unarmed and sheer numbers of inmates could overcome the normal complement. Rather, like all other law enforcement officers, prison guards must rely primarily on the moral authority of their office and the threat of future punishment for miscreants. As one expert testified below, common sense, fairness, and mental and emotional stability are the qualities a guard needs to cope with the dangers of the job. Well qualified and properly trained women, no less than men, have these psychological weapons at their disposal.

The particular severity of discipline problems in the Alabama maximum-security prisons is also no justification for the discrimination sanctioned by the Court. The District Court found in *Pugh v. Locke, supra*, that guards "must spend all their time attempting to maintain control or to protect themselves." If male guards face an impossible situation, it is difficult to see how women could make the problem worse, unless one relies on precisely the type of generalized bias against women that the Court agrees Title VII was intended to outlaw. For example, much of the testimony of appellants' witnesses ignores individual differences among members of each sex and reads like "ancient canards about the proper role of women." [citation omitted]. The witnesses claimed that women guards are not strict disciplinarians; that they are physically less capable of protecting themselves and subduing unruly inmates; that inmates take advantage of them as they did their mothers, while male guards are strong father figures who easily maintain discipline, and so on. Yet the record shows that the presence of women guards has not led to a single incident amounting to a serious breach of security in any Alabama institution.[41] And, in any event, guards rarely enter the cell blocks and dormitories, where the danger of inmate attacks is the greatest.

---

41. The Court refers to two incidents involving potentially dangerous attacks on women in prisons. But these did not involve trained corrections officers; one victim was a clerical worker and the other a student visiting on a tour.

It appears that the real disqualifying factor in the Court's view is "(t)he employee's very womanhood." The Court refers to the large number of sex offenders in Alabama prisons, and to "(t)he likelihood that inmates would assault a woman because she was a woman." In short, the fundamental justification for the decision is that women as guards will generate sexual assaults. With all respect, this rationale regrettably perpetuates one of the most insidious of the old myths about women that women, wittingly or not, are seductive sexual objects. The effect of the decision, made I am sure with the best of intentions, is to punish women because their very presence might provoke sexual assaults. It is women who are made to pay the price in lost job opportunities for the threat of depraved conduct by prison inmates. Once again, "(t)he pedestal upon which women have been placed has..., upon closer inspection, been revealed as a cage." [citation omitted]. It is particularly ironic that the cage is erected here in response to feared misbehavior by imprisoned criminals.

The Court points to no evidence in the record to support the asserted "likelihood that inmates would assault a woman because she was a woman." ... But the danger in this emotionally laden context is that common sense will be used to mask the "romantic paternalism" and persisting discriminatory attitudes that the Court properly eschews. To me, the only matter of innate recognition is that the incidence of sexually motivated attacks on guards will be minute compared to the likelihood that inmates will assault a guard because he or she is a guard.

The proper response to inevitable attacks on both female and male guards is not to limit the employment opportunities of lawabiding women who wish to contribute to their community, but to take swift and sure punitive action against the inmate offenders. Presumably, one of the goals of the Alabama prison system is the eradication of inmates' antisocial behavior patterns so that prisoners will be able to live one day in free society. Sex offenders can begin this process by learning to relate to women guards in a socially acceptable manner. To deprive women of job opportunities because of the threatened behavior of convicted criminals is to turn our social priorities upside down.[42]

Although I do not countenance the sex discrimination condoned by the majority, it is fortunate that the Court's decision is carefully limited to the facts before it. I trust the lower courts will recognize that the decision was impelled by the shockingly inhuman conditions in Alabama prisons, and thus that the "extremely narrow (bfoq) exception" recognized here, will not be allowed to swallow the rule against sex discrimination. Expansion of today's decision beyond its narrow factual basis would erect a serious roadblock to economic equality for women.

---

42. The appellants argue that restrictions on employment of women are also justified by consideration of inmates' privacy. It is strange indeed to hear state officials who have for years been violating the most basic principles of human decency in the operation of their prisons suddenly become concerned about inmate privacy. It is stranger still that these same officials allow women guards in contact positions in a number of nonmaximum-security institutions, but strive to protect inmates' privacy in the prisons where personal freedom is most severely restricted.... I have no doubt on this record that appellants' professed concern is nothing but a feeble excuse for discrimination. As the District Court suggested, it may well be possible, once a constitutionally adequate staff is available, to rearrange work assignments so that legitimate inmate privacy concerns are respected without denying jobs to women. Finally, if women guards behave in a professional manner at all times, they will engender reciprocal respect from inmates, who will recognize that their privacy is being invaded no more than if a woman doctor examines them. The suggestion implicit in the privacy argument that such behavior is unlikely on either side is an insult to the professionalism of guards and the dignity of inmates.

---

### Focus Questions: *UAW v. Johnson Controls, Inc.*

1.  *Is the Court correct in minimizing concerns about Johnson Control's potential tort liability for birth defects?*

2.  *Is it possible to reconcile this case with* Dothard?

---

# International Union, United Auto., Aerospace and Agr. Implement Workers of America, UAW v. Johnson Controls, Inc.
### 499 U.S. 187 (1991)

Justice Blackmun delivered the opinion of the Court.

In this case we are concerned with an employer's gender-based fetal-protection policy. May an employer exclude a fertile female employee from certain jobs because of its concern for the health of the fetus the woman might conceive?

#### I

Respondent Johnson Controls, Inc., manufactures batteries. In the manufacturing process, the element lead is a primary ingredient. Occupational exposure to lead entails health risks, including the risk of harm to any fetus carried by a female employee.

Before the Civil Rights Act of 1964 became law, Johnson Controls did not employ any woman in a battery-manufacturing job. In June 1977, however, it announced its first official policy concerning its employment of women in lead-exposure work:

> [P]rotection of the health of the unborn child is the immediate and direct responsibility of the prospective parents. While the medical profession and the company can support them in the exercise of this responsibility, it cannot assume it for them without simultaneously infringing their rights as persons.

> ... Since not all women who can become mothers wish to become mothers (or will become mothers), it would appear to be illegal discrimination to treat all who are capable of pregnancy as though they will become pregnant.

Consistent with that view, Johnson Controls "stopped short of excluding women capable of bearing children from lead exposure," but emphasized that a woman who expected to have a child should not choose a job in which she would have such exposure. The company also required a woman who wished to be considered for employment to sign a statement that she had been advised of the risk of having a child while she was exposed to lead. The statement informed the woman that although there was evidence "that women exposed to lead have a higher rate of abortion," this evidence was "not as clear ... as the relationship between cigarette smoking and cancer," but that it was, "medically speaking, just good sense not to run that risk if you want children and do not want to expose the unborn child to risk, however small...."

Five years later, in 1982, Johnson Controls shifted from a policy of warning to a policy of exclusion. Between 1979 and 1983, eight employees became pregnant while maintaining blood lead levels in excess of 30 micrograms per deciliter. This appeared to be the critical level noted by the Occupational Safety and Health Administration (OSHA) for a worker who was planning to have a family. *See* 29 C.F.R. § 1910.1025 (1990). The company responded by announcing a broad exclusion of women from jobs that exposed them to lead:

> ... [I]t is [Johnson Controls'] policy that women who are pregnant or who are capable of bearing children will not be placed into jobs involving lead exposure or which could expose them to lead through the exercise of job bidding, bumping, transfer or promotion rights.

The policy defined "women ... capable of bearing children" as "[a]ll women except those whose inability to bear children is medically documented." It further stated that an unacceptable work station was one where, "over the past year," an employee had recorded a blood lead level of more than 30 micrograms per deciliter or the work site had yielded an air sample containing a lead level in excess of 30 micrograms per cubic meter.

## II

In April 1984, petitioners filed in the United States District Court for the Eastern District of Wisconsin a class action challenging Johnson Controls' fetal-protection policy as sex discrimination that violated Title VII. Among the individual plaintiffs were petitioners Mary Craig, who had chosen to be sterilized in order to avoid losing her job, Elsie Nason, a 50-year-old divorcee, who had suffered a loss in compensation when she was transferred out of a job where she was exposed to lead, and Donald Penney, who had been denied a request for a leave of absence for the purpose of lowering his lead level because he intended to become a father. Upon stipulation of the parties, the District Court certified a class consisting of "all past, present and future production and maintenance employees" in United Auto Workers bargaining units at nine of Johnson Controls' plants "who have been and continue to be affected by [the employer's] Fetal Protection Policy implemented in 1982."

The District Court granted summary judgment for defendant-respondent Johnson Controls. [T]he District Court concluded that while "there is a disagreement among the experts regarding the effect of lead on the fetus," the hazard to the fetus through exposure to lead was established by "a considerable body of opinion"; that although "[e]xpert opinion has been provided which holds that lead also affects the reproductive abilities of men and women ... [and] that these effects are as great as the effects of exposure of the fetus ... a great body of experts are of the opinion that the fetus is more vulnerable to levels of lead that would not affect adults"; and that petitioners had "failed to establish that there is an acceptable alternative policy which would protect the fetus." ...

The Court of Appeals for the Seventh Circuit, sitting en banc, affirmed the summary judgment by a 7-to-4 vote. [T]he court proceeded to discuss the BFOQ defense and concluded that Johnson Controls met that test[.] The en banc majority ruled that industrial safety is part of the essence of respondent's business, and that the fetal-protection policy is reasonably necessary to further that concern. Quoting *Dothard v. Rawlinson*, the majority emphasized that, in view of the goal of protecting the unborn, "more is at stake" than simply an individual woman's decision to weigh and accept the risks of employment....

## III

The bias in Johnson Controls' policy is obvious. Fertile men, but not fertile women, are given a choice as to whether they wish to risk their reproductive health for a particular job. Section 703(a) of the Civil Rights Act of 1964, as amended, 42 U.S.C. § 2000e-2(a), prohibits sex-based classifications in terms and conditions of employment, in hiring and discharging decisions, and in other employment decisions that adversely affect an employee's status. Respondent's fetal-protection policy explicitly discriminates against women on the basis of their sex. The policy excludes women with childbearing capacity from lead-exposed jobs and so creates a facial classification based on gender....

Nevertheless, the Court of Appeals assumed, as did the two appellate courts that already had confronted the issue, that sex-specific fetal-protection policies do not involve facial discrimination. These courts analyzed the policies as though they were facially neutral, and had only a discriminatory effect upon the employment opportunities of women. Consequently, the courts looked to see if each employer in question had established that its policy was justified as a business necessity [which is the appropriate defense in cases of disparate impact]. The business necessity standard is more lenient for the employer than the statutory BFOQ defense.... The court assumed that because the asserted reason for the sex-based exclusion (protecting women's unconceived offspring) was ostensibly benign, the policy was not sex-based discrimination. That assumption, however, was incorrect.

First, Johnson Controls' policy classifies on the basis of gender and childbearing capacity, rather than fertility alone. Respondent does not seek to protect the unconceived children of all its employees. Despite evidence in the record about the debilitating effect of lead exposure on the male reproductive system, Johnson Controls is concerned only with the harms that may befall the unborn offspring of its female employees.... Johnson Controls' policy is facially discriminatory because it requires only a female employee to produce proof that she is not capable of reproducing.

Our conclusion is bolstered by the Pregnancy Discrimination Act (PDA), 42 U.S.C. §2000e(k), in which Congress explicitly provided that, for purposes of Title VII, discrimination "on the basis of sex" includes discrimination "because of or on the basis of pregnancy, childbirth, or related medical conditions." The Pregnancy Discrimination Act has now made clear that, for all Title VII purposes, discrimination based on a woman's pregnancy is, on its face, discrimination because of her sex. In its use of the words "capable of bearing children" in the 1982 policy statement as the criterion for exclusion, Johnson Controls explicitly classifies on the basis of potential for pregnancy. Under the PDA, such a classification must be regarded, for Title VII purposes, in the same light as explicit sex discrimination. Respondent has chosen to treat all its female employees as potentially pregnant; that choice evinces discrimination on the basis of sex.

We concluded above that Johnson Controls' policy is not neutral because it does not apply to the reproductive capacity of the company's male employees in the same way as it applies to that of the females. Moreover, the absence of a malevolent motive does not convert a facially discriminatory policy into a neutral policy with a discriminatory effect. Whether an employment practice involves disparate treatment through explicit facial discrimination does not depend on why the employer discriminates but rather on the explicit terms of the discrimination.... The beneficence of an employer's purpose does not undermine the conclusion that an explicit gender-based policy is sex discrimination under §703(a) and thus may be defended only as a BFOQ.

... We hold that Johnson Controls' fetal-protection policy is sex discrimination forbidden under Title VII unless respondent can establish that sex is a "bona fide occupational qualification."

## IV

Under §703(e)(1) of Title VII, an employer may discriminate on the basis of "religion, sex, or national origin in those certain instances where religion, sex, or national origin is a bona fide occupational qualification reasonably necessary to the normal operation of that particular business or enterprise." 42 U.S.C. §2000e-2(e)(1). We therefore turn to the question whether Johnson Controls' fetal-protection policy is one of those "certain instances" that come within the BFOQ exception.

The BFOQ defense is written narrowly, and this Court has read it narrowly. We have read the BFOQ language of §4(f) of the Age Discrimination in Employment Act of 1967 (ADEA), as amended, 29 U.S.C. §623(f)(1), which tracks the BFOQ provision in Title VII, just as narrowly. Our emphasis on the restrictive scope of the BFOQ defense is grounded on both the language and the legislative history of §703.

The wording of the BFOQ defense contains several terms of restriction that indicate that the exception reaches only special situations. The statute thus limits the situations in which discrimination is permissible to "certain instances" where sex discrimination is "reasonably necessary" to the "normal operation" of the "particular" business. Each one of these terms—certain, normal, particular—prevents the use of general subjective standards and favors an objective, verifiable requirement. But the most telling term is "occupational"; this indicates that these objective, verifiable requirements must concern job-related skills and aptitudes.

... Johnson Controls argues that its fetal-protection policy falls within the so-called safety exception to the BFOQ. Our cases have stressed that discrimination on the basis of sex because of safety concerns is allowed only in narrow circumstances. In *Dothard v. Rawlinson,* this Court indicated that danger to a woman herself does not justify discrimination. We there allowed the employer to hire only male guards in contact areas of maximum-security male penitentiaries only because more was at stake than the "individual woman's decision to weigh and accept the risks of employment." We found sex to be a BFOQ inasmuch as the employment of a female guard would create real risks of safety to others if violence broke out because the guard was a woman. Sex discrimination was tolerated because sex was related to the guard's ability to do the job—maintaining prison security....

Similarly, some courts have approved airlines' layoffs of pregnant flight attendants at different points during the first five months of pregnancy on the ground that the employer's policy was necessary to ensure the safety of passengers.

We considered safety to third parties in *Western Airlines, Inc. v. Criswell,* in the context of the ADEA.... Our safety concerns were not independent of the individual's ability to perform the assigned tasks, but rather involved the possibility that, because of age-connected debility, a flight engineer might not properly assist the pilot, and might thereby cause a safety emergency. Furthermore, although we considered the safety of third parties in *Dothard* and *Criswell,* those third parties were indispensable to the particular business at issue. In *Dothard,* the third parties were the inmates; in *Criswell,* the third parties were the passengers on the plane. We stressed that in order to qualify as a BFOQ, a job qualification must relate to the "essence," *Dothard,* 433 U.S. at 333 (emphasis deleted), or to the "central mission of the employer's business," *Criswell,* 472 U.S. at 413.

Justice White ignores the "essence of the business" test and so concludes that "protecting fetal safety while carrying out the duties of battery manufacturing is as much a legitimate concern as is safety to third parties in guarding prisons (*Dothard*) or flying airplanes (*Criswell*)." By limiting his discussion to cost and safety concerns and rejecting the "essence of the business" test that our case law has established, he seeks to expand what is now the narrow BFOQ defense.... Third-party safety considerations properly entered into the BFOQ analysis in *Dothard* and *Criswell* because they went to the core of the employee's job performance. Moreover, that performance involved the central purpose of the enterprise. *Dothard,* 433 U.S. at 335 ("The essence of a correctional counselor's job is to maintain prison security"); *Criswell,* 472 U.S. at 413 (the central mission of the airline's business was the safe transportation of its passengers). [Justice White's concurrence] attempts to transform this case into one of customer safety. The unconceived fetuses of Johnson Controls' female employees, however, are neither customers nor third parties whose safety is essential to the business of battery manufacturing. No one can disregard the possibility of injury to future children; the BFOQ, however, is not so broad that it transforms this deep social concern into an essential aspect of battery making.

Our case law, therefore, makes clear that the safety exception is limited to instances in which sex or pregnancy actually interferes with the employee's ability to perform the job. This approach is consistent with the language of the BFOQ provision itself, for it suggests that permissible distinctions based on sex must relate to ability to perform the duties of the job. Johnson Controls suggests, however, that we expand the exception to allow fetal-protection policies that mandate particular standards for pregnant or fertile women. We decline to do so. Such an expansion contradicts not only the language of the BFOQ and the narrowness of its exception, but also the plain language and history of the PDA.

The PDA's amendment to Title VII contains a BFOQ standard of its own: Unless pregnant employees differ from others "in their ability or inability to work," they must be "treated the same" as other employees "for all employment-related purposes." 42 U.S.C. § 2000e(k). This language clearly sets forth Congress' remedy for discrimination on the basis of pregnancy and potential pregnancy. Women who are either pregnant or potentially pregnant must be treated like others "similar in their ability ... to work." [citation omitted]. In other words, women as capable of doing their jobs as their male counterparts may not be forced to choose between having a child and having a job....

The legislative history confirms what the language of the PDA compels. Both the House and Senate Reports accompanying the legislation indicate that this statutory standard was chosen to protect female workers from being treated differently from other employees simply because of their capacity to bear children....

This history counsels against expanding the BFOQ to allow fetal-protection policies. The Senate Report quoted above states that employers may not require a pregnant woman to stop working at any time during her pregnancy unless she is unable to do her work. Employment late in pregnancy often imposes risks on the unborn child, but Congress indicated that the employer may take into account only the woman's ability to get her job done. With the PDA, Congress made clear that the decision to become pregnant or to work while being either pregnant or capable of becoming pregnant was reserved for each individual woman to make for herself.

We conclude that the language of both the BFOQ provision and the PDA which amended it, as well as the legislative history and the case law, prohibit an employer from discriminating against a woman because of her capacity to become pregnant unless her reproductive potential prevents her from performing the duties of her job. We reiterate our holdings in *Criswell* and *Dothard* that an employer must direct its concerns about a woman's ability to perform her job safely and efficiently to those aspects of the woman's job-related activities that fall within the "essence" of the particular business.[43]

---

43. Justice White predicts that our reaffirmation of the narrowness of the BFOQ defense will preclude considerations of privacy as a basis for sex-based discrimination. We have never addressed privacy-based sex discrimination and shall not do so here because the sex-based discrimination at issue today does not involve the privacy interests of Johnson Controls' customers. Nothing in our

## V

We have no difficulty concluding that Johnson Controls cannot establish a BFOQ. Fertile women, as far as appears in the record, participate in the manufacture of batteries as efficiently as anyone else. Johnson Controls' professed moral and ethical concerns about the welfare of the next generation do not suffice to establish a BFOQ of female sterility. Decisions about the welfare of future children must be left to the parents who conceive, bear, support, and raise them rather than to the employers who hire those parents. Congress has mandated this choice through Title VII, as amended by the PDA. Johnson Controls has attempted to exclude women because of their reproductive capacity. Title VII and the PDA simply do not allow a woman's dismissal because of her failure to submit to sterilization.

Nor can concerns about the welfare of the next generation be considered a part of the "essence" of Johnson Controls' business. Judge Easterbrook in this case pertinently observed: "It is word play to say that 'the job' at Johnson [Controls] is to make batteries without risk to fetuses in the same way 'the job' at Western Air Lines is to fly planes without crashing."

Johnson Controls argues that it must exclude all fertile women because it is impossible to tell which women will become pregnant while working with lead. This argument is somewhat academic in light of our conclusion that the company may not exclude fertile women at all; it perhaps is worth noting, however, that Johnson Controls has shown no "factual basis for believing that all or substantially all women would be unable to perform safely and efficiently the duties of the job involved." Even on this sparse record, it is apparent that Johnson Controls is concerned about only a small minority of women. Of the eight pregnancies reported among the female employees, it has not been shown that any of the babies have birth defects or other abnormalities. The record does not reveal the birth rate for Johnson Controls' female workers, but national statistics show that approximately nine percent of all fertile women become pregnant each year. The birthrate drops to two percent for blue collar workers over age 30. Johnson Controls' fear of prenatal injury, no matter how sincere, does not begin to show that substantially all of its fertile women employees are incapable of doing their jobs.

## VI

A word about tort liability and the increased cost of fertile women in the workplace is perhaps necessary. One of the dissenting judges in this case expressed concern about an employer's tort liability and concluded that liability for a potential injury to a fetus is a social cost that Title VII does not require a company to ignore. It is correct to say that Title VII does not prevent the employer from having a conscience. The statute, however, does prevent sex-specific fetal-protection policies. These two aspects of Title VII do not conflict.

More than 40 States currently recognize a right to recover for a prenatal injury based either on negligence or on wrongful death. According to Johnson Controls, however, the company complies with the lead standard developed by OSHA and warns its female employees about the damaging effects of lead. It is worth noting that OSHA gave the problem of lead lengthy consideration and concluded that "there is no basis whatsoever for the claim that women of childbearing age should be excluded from the workplace in order to protect the fetus or the course of pregnancy." 43 Fed.Reg. 52952, 52966 (1978). Instead, OSHA established a series of mandatory protections which, taken together, "should effectively minimize any risk to the fetus and newborn child. Without negligence,

---

discussion of the "essence of the business test," however, suggests that sex could not constitute a BFOQ when privacy interests are implicated.

it would be difficult for a court to find liability on the part of the employer. If, under general tort principles, Title VII bans sex-specific fetal-protection policies, the employer fully informs the woman of the risk, and the employer has not acted negligently, the basis for holding an employer liable seems remote at best.

Although the issue is not before us, Justice White observes that "it is far from clear that compliance with Title VII will pre-empt state tort liability." ... When it is impossible for an employer to comply with both state and federal requirements, this Court has ruled that federal law pre-empts that of the States. ...

If state tort law furthers discrimination in the workplace and prevents employers from hiring women who are capable of manufacturing the product as efficiently as men, then it will impede the accomplishment of Congress' goals in enacting Title VII. Because Johnson Controls has not argued that it faces any costs from tort liability, not to mention crippling ones, the pre-emption question is not before us. We therefore say no more than that the concurrence's speculation appears unfounded as well as premature.

The tort-liability argument reduces to two equally unpersuasive propositions. First, Johnson Controls attempts to solve the problem of reproductive health hazards by resorting to an exclusionary policy. Title VII plainly forbids illegal sex discrimination as a method of diverting attention from an employer's obligation to police the workplace. Second, the specter of an award of damages reflects a fear that hiring fertile women will cost more. The extra cost of employing members of one sex, however, does not provide an affirmative Title VII defense for a discriminatory refusal to hire members of that gender. Indeed, in passing the PDA, Congress considered at length the considerable cost of providing equal treatment of pregnancy and related conditions, but made the "decision to forbid special treatment of pregnancy despite the social costs associated therewith."

We, of course, are not presented with, nor do we decide, a case in which costs would be so prohibitive as to threaten the survival of the employer's business. We merely reiterate our prior holdings that the incremental cost of hiring women cannot justify discriminating against them.

## VII

Our holding today that Title VII, as so amended, forbids sex-specific fetal-protection policies is neither remarkable nor unprecedented. Concern for a woman's existing or potential offspring historically has been the excuse for denying women equal employment opportunities. Congress in the PDA prohibited discrimination on the basis of a woman's ability to become pregnant. We do no more than hold that the PDA means what it says.

It is no more appropriate for the courts than it is for individual employers to decide whether a woman's reproductive role is more important to herself and her family than her economic role. Congress has left this choice to the woman as hers to make.

The judgment of the Court of Appeals is reversed, and the case is remanded for further proceedings consistent with this opinion.

Justice White, with whom the Chief Justice and Justice Kennedy join, concurring in part and concurring in the judgment.

The Court properly holds that Johnson Controls' fetal-protection policy overtly discriminates against women, and thus is prohibited by Title VII unless it falls within the bona fide occupational qualification (BFOQ) exception, set forth at 42 U.S.C. § 2000e-2(e). The Court erroneously holds, however, that the BFOQ defense is so narrow that it could never justify a sex-specific fetal-protection policy. ...

… [A] fetal-protection policy would be justified under the terms of the statute if, for example, an employer could show that exclusion of women from certain jobs was reasonably necessary to avoid substantial tort liability. Common sense tells us that it is part of the normal operation of business concerns to avoid causing injury to third parties, as well as to employees, if for no other reason than to avoid tort liability and its substantial costs. This possibility of tort liability is not hypothetical; every State currently allows children born alive to recover in tort for prenatal injuries caused by third parties, and an increasing number of courts have recognized a right to recover even for prenatal injuries caused by torts committed prior to conception.

The Court dismisses the possibility of tort liability by no more than speculating that if "Title VII bans sex-specific fetal-protection policies, the employer fully informs the woman of the risk, and the employer has not acted negligently, the basis for holding an employer liable seems remote at best." Such speculation will be small comfort to employers. First, it is far from clear that compliance with Title VII will pre-empt state tort liability, and the Court offers no support for that proposition. Second, although warnings may preclude claims by injured *employees,* they will not preclude claims by injured children because the general rule is that parents cannot waive causes of action on behalf of their children, and the parents' negligence will not be imputed to the children. Finally, although state tort liability for prenatal injuries generally requires negligence, it will be difficult for employers to determine in advance what will constitute negligence. Compliance with OSHA standards, for example, has been held not to be a defense to state tort or criminal liability. Moreover, it is possible that employers will be held strictly liable, if, for example, their manufacturing process is considered "abnormally dangerous." *See* Restatement (Second) of Torts § 869, Comment *b* (1979).

Prior decisions construing the BFOQ defense confirm that the defense is broad enough to include considerations of cost and safety of the sort that could form the basis for an employer's adoption of a fetal-protection policy.…

*Dothard* and *Criswell* make clear that avoidance of substantial safety risks to third parties is *inherently* part of both an employee's ability to perform a job and an employer's "normal operation" of its business.…

*Dothard* and *Criswell* also confirm that costs are relevant in determining whether a discriminatory policy is reasonably necessary for the normal operation of a business. In *Dothard,* the safety problem that justified exclusion of women from the prison guard positions was largely a result of inadequate staff and facilities.… If the cost of employing women could not be considered, the employer there should have been required to hire more staff and restructure the prison environment rather than exclude women. Similarly, in *Criswell* the airline could have been required to hire more pilots and install expensive monitoring devices rather than discriminate against older employees. The BFOQ statute, however, reflects "Congress' unwillingness to require employers to change the very nature of their operations." [citation omitted].…

The Court's narrow interpretation of the BFOQ defense in this case, however, means that an employer cannot exclude even *pregnant* women from an environment highly toxic to their fetuses. It is foolish to think that Congress intended such a result, and neither the language of the BFOQ exception nor our cases require it.[44]

---

44. The Court's cramped reading of the BFOQ defense is also belied by the legislative history of Title VII, in which three examples of permissible sex discrimination were mentioned—a female nurse hired to care for an elderly woman, an all-male professional baseball team, and a masseur. In none

The Court's interpretation of the BFOQ standard also would seem to preclude considerations of privacy as a basis for sex-based discrimination, since those considerations do not relate directly to an employee's physical ability to perform the duties of the job. The lower federal courts, however, have consistently recognized that privacy interests may justify sex-based requirements for certain jobs.

II

Despite my disagreement with the Court concerning the scope of the BFOQ defense, I concur in reversing the Court of Appeals because that court erred in affirming the District Court's grant of summary judgment in favor of Johnson Controls. First, the Court of Appeals erred in failing to consider the level of risk avoidance that was part of Johnson Controls' "normal operation." Although the court did conclude that there was a "substantial risk" to fetuses from lead exposure in fertile women, it merely meant that there was a high risk that *some* fetal injury would occur absent a fetal-protection policy. That analysis, of course, fails to address the *extent* of fetal injury that is likely to occur. If the fetal-protection policy insists on a risk-avoidance level substantially higher than other risk levels tolerated by Johnson Controls such as risks to employees and consumers, the policy should not constitute a BFOQ.[45]

Second, even without more information about the normal level of risk at Johnson Controls, the fetal-protection policy at issue here reaches too far. This is evident both in its presumption that, absent medical documentation to the contrary, all women are fertile regardless of their age, and in its exclusion of presumptively fertile women from positions that might result in a promotion to a position involving high lead exposure. There has been no showing that either of those aspects of the policy is reasonably necessary to ensure safe and efficient operation of Johnson Controls' battery-manufacturing business. Of course, these infirmities in the company's policy do not warrant invalidating the entire fetal-protection program.

Third, it should be recalled that until 1982 Johnson Controls operated without an exclusionary policy, and it has not identified any grounds for believing that its current policy is reasonably necessary to its normal operations. Although it is now more aware of some of the dangers of lead exposure, it has not shown that the risks of fetal harm or the costs associated with it have substantially increased.

---

## Notes

1. The employer bears the burden of persuasion of proving the existence of a bona fide occupational qualification.

2. The EEOC has issued regulations pertaining to the contours of the BFOQ defense in various contexts. As examples of situations that do not warrant application of BFOQ based on gender, the EEOC provides the following:

---

of those situations would gender "actually interfer[e] with the employee's ability to perform the job," as required today by the Court.

45. It is possible, for example, that alternatives to exclusion of women, such as warnings combined with frequent blood testings, would sufficiently minimize the risk such that it would be comparable to other risks tolerated by Johnson Controls.

(i)   The refusal to hire a woman because of her sex based on assumptions of the comparative employment characteristics of women in general. For example, the assumption that the turnover rate among women is higher than among men.

(ii)  The refusal to hire an individual based on stereotyped characterizations of the sexes. Such stereotypes include, for example, that men are less capable of assembling intricate equipment; that women are less capable of aggressive sales-manship. The principle of nondiscrimination requires that individuals be considered on the basis of individual capacities and not on the basis of any char-acteristics generally attributed to the group.

(iii) The refusal to hire an individual because of the preferences of coworkers, the employer, clients or customers except as covered specifically in paragraph (a)(2) of this section.

29 C.F.R. § 1604.2(a). The regulations further provide: "Where it is necessary for the purpose of authenticity or genuineness, the Commission will consider sex to be a bona fide occupational qualification, *e.g.*, an actor or actress." *Id.* at § 1604.2(a)(2).

---

## Exercise 3.10

Write a list of the business interests that the courts or the EEOC have identified as being a proper basis for finding that a protected trait is a BFOQ.

Consider whether an employer would be able to establish BFOQ in the following circumstances.

1. A gym needs to hire an attendant to work in a ladies' locker room. It considers only women for the open position.

2. A company needs to hire a salesman to negotiate customer contracts in the Middle East. It refuses to hire people of the Jewish faith for the position because it fears for their safety during required travel to the Middle East, and it fears customers will respond poorly.

3. Tanya is a counselor in a program to prevent teen-age pregnancy. Tanya is 19 and counsels young girls on how to avoid pregnancy. Tanya becomes pregnant. Can the counseling program fire Tanya because she does not set a good example for the students enrolled in the program?

4. A Chinese restaurant wants to be known for its authentic food. It thinks that this interest in authenticity will be served if it hires only employees who appear to be Chinese. Can the restaurant have such a hiring policy?

5. A clothing store's image is based on selling trendy clothes to teenagers. Although not an explicit policy, managers know not to hire anyone who is older than 25 to work in customer-contact positions in the stores.

6. An airline believes that customers prefer to be pampered by flight attendants. It wants to hire women for flight attendant positions because it believes they are better at pampering.

7. Tattlers is a restaurant that serves hot wings and other bar food. Its entire brand revolves around its sexy waitresses in tight outfits. Its commercials feature the Tattlers Girls. Tattlers refuses to hire men for wait staff positions at its restaurants.

## Exercise 3.11

You are a corporate partner at a large law firm and Excel Corporation is your primary client. Excel Corporation spends $2 million a year in legal fees with your firm and its business played a significant role in the firm's decision to make you partner. Excel Corporation has been sued in a products liability suit regarding alleged defects in one of its core product lines. The lawsuit is the most important case being defended by Excel.

You think the best litigator to handle the lawsuit's defense is Robert Jones. Robert is not white. The General Counsel of Excel Corporation has several telephone conferences with Robert. The General Counsel expresses no concerns about Robert's performance. Later, the General Counsel meets with Robert and you in person. After the meeting, the General Counsel calls you and says that he is uncomfortable with Robert litigating the case because the General Counsel is concerned that juries in the area might harbor racial animus and that animus might be transferred from Robert to the company. How do you respond to the General Counsel?

Now change the facts of the case slightly. You believe the best person to litigate the case is Amanda Simpson. After a meeting with Amanda, the General Counsel expresses reservations that she is "too meek" and that the General Counsel would like to see an aggressive, dominant personality in the courtroom. Do you take Amanda off the case?

## ✦ Core Concept: After-Acquired Evidence

Although the following case is presented in the context of age discrimination, after-acquired evidence may also be used to limit remedies under Title VII, the ADA, and section 1981.

### Focus Questions: *McKennon v. Nashville Banner Pub. Co.*

1. *What does an employer need to prove to get the benefit of the after-acquired evidence defense?*

2. *If an employer prevails on an after-acquired evidence defense, what is the result?*

3. *Can you foresee any negative consequences that the after-acquired evidence doctrine might create?*

## McKennon v. Nashville Banner Pub. Co.

### 513 U.S. 352 (1995)

Justice Kennedy delivered the opinion of the Court.

The question before us is whether an employee discharged in violation of the Age Discrimination in Employment Act of 1967 is barred from all relief when, after her discharge, the employer discovers evidence of wrongdoing that, in any event, would have led to the employee's termination on lawful and legitimate grounds.

## I

For some 30 years, petitioner Christine McKennon worked for respondent Nashville Banner Publishing Company. She was discharged, the Banner claimed, as part of a work force reduction plan necessitated by cost considerations. McKennon, who was 62 years old when she lost her job, thought another reason explained her dismissal: her age. She filed suit in the United States District Court for the Middle District of Tennessee, alleging that her discharge violated the Age Discrimination in Employment Act of 1967....

McKennon sought a variety of legal and equitable remedies available under the ADEA, including backpay.

In preparation of the case, the Banner took McKennon's deposition. She testified that, during her final year of employment, she had copied several confidential documents bearing upon the company's financial condition. She had access to these records as secretary to the Banner's comptroller. McKennon took the copies home and showed them to her husband. Her motivation, she averred, was an apprehension she was about to be fired because of her age. When she became concerned about her job, she removed and copied the documents for "insurance" and "protection." A few days after these deposition disclosures, the Banner sent McKennon a letter declaring that removal and copying of the records was in violation of her job responsibilities and advising her (again) that she was terminated. The Banner's letter also recited that had it known of McKennon's misconduct it would have discharged her at once for that reason.

For purposes of summary judgment, the Banner conceded its discrimination against McKennon. The District Court granted summary judgment for the Banner, holding that McKennon's misconduct was grounds for her termination and that neither backpay nor any other remedy was available to her under the ADEA. The United States Court of Appeals for the Sixth Circuit affirmed on the same rationale. We granted certiorari to resolve conflicting views among the Courts of Appeals on the question whether all relief must be denied when an employee has been discharged in violation of the ADEA and the employer later discovers some wrongful conduct that would have led to discharge if it had been discovered earlier. We now reverse.

## II

We shall assume, as summary judgment procedures require us to assume, that the sole reason for McKennon's initial discharge was her age, a discharge violative of the ADEA. Our further premise is that the misconduct revealed by the deposition was so grave that McKennon's immediate discharge would have followed its disclosure in any event. The District Court and the Court of Appeals found no basis for contesting that proposition, and for purposes of our review we need not question it here. We do question the legal conclusion reached by those courts that after-acquired evidence of wrongdoing which would have resulted in discharge bars employees from any relief under the ADEA. That ruling is incorrect.

The Court of Appeals considered McKennon's misconduct, in effect, to be supervening grounds for termination. That may be so, but it does not follow, as the Court of Appeals said in citing one of its own earlier cases, that the misconduct renders it "irrelevant whether or not [McKennon] was discriminated against." We conclude that a violation of the ADEA cannot be so altogether disregarded....

When confronted with a violation of the ADEA, a district court is authorized to afford relief by means of reinstatement, backpay, injunctive relief, declaratory judgment, and attorney's fees. In the case of a willful violation of the Act, the ADEA authorizes an award of liquidated damages equal to the backpay award. 29 U.S.C. §626(b). The Act also gives federal courts the discretion to "grant such legal or equitable relief as may be appropriate to effectuate the purposes of [the Act]."

The ADEA and Title VII share common substantive features and also a common purpose: "the elimination of discrimination in the workplace." [citation omitted]. Congress designed the remedial measures in these statutes to serve as a "spur or catalyst" to cause employers "to self-examine and to self-evaluate their employment practices and to endeavor to eliminate, so far as possible, the last vestiges" of discrimination. [citation omitted]. Deterrence is one object of these statutes. Compensation for injuries caused by the prohibited discrimination is another. The ADEA, in keeping with these purposes, contains a vital element found in both Title VII and the Fair Labor Standards Act: It grants an injured employee a right of action to obtain the authorized relief. 29 U.S.C. §626(c). The private litigant who seeks redress for his or her injuries vindicates both the deterrence and the compensation objectives of the ADEA. It would not accord with this scheme if after-acquired evidence of wrongdoing that would have resulted in termination operates, in every instance, to bar all relief for an earlier violation of the Act.

The objectives of the ADEA are furthered when even a single employee establishes that an employer has discriminated against him or her. The disclosure through litigation of incidents or practices that violate national policies respecting nondiscrimination in the work force is itself important, for the occurrence of violations may disclose patterns of noncompliance resulting from a misappreciation of the Act's operation or entrenched resistance to its commands, either of which can be of industry-wide significance. The efficacy of its enforcement mechanisms becomes one measure of the success of the Act....

Our inquiry is not at an end, however, for even though the employer has violated the Act, we must consider how the after-acquired evidence of the employee's wrongdoing bears on the specific remedy to be ordered. Equity's maxim that a suitor who engaged in his own reprehensible conduct in the course of the transaction at issue must be denied equitable relief because of unclean hands, a rule which in conventional formulation operated *in limine* to bar the suitor from invoking the aid of the equity court, has not been applied where Congress authorizes broad equitable relief to serve important national policies. We have rejected the [equitable] unclean hands defense "where a private suit serves important public purposes." [citation omitted]. That does not mean, however, the employee's own misconduct is irrelevant to all the remedies otherwise available under the statute.... In giving effect to the ADEA, we must recognize the duality between the legitimate interests of the employer and the important claims of the employee.... The employee's wrongdoing must be taken into account, we conclude, lest the employer's legitimate concerns be ignored. The ADEA, like Title VII, is not a general regulation of the workplace but a law which prohibits discrimination. The statute does not constrain employers from exercising significant other prerogatives and discretions in the course of the hiring, promoting, and discharging of their employees. In determining appropriate remedial action, the employee's wrongdoing becomes relevant not to punish the employee, or out of concern "for the relative moral worth of the parties," [citation omitted], but to take due account of the lawful prerogatives of the employer in the usual course of its business and the corresponding equities that it has arising from the employee's wrongdoing.

The proper boundaries of remedial relief in the general class of cases where, after termination, it is discovered that the employee has engaged in wrongdoing must be addressed by the judicial system in the ordinary course of further decisions, for the factual permutations and the equitable considerations they raise will vary from case to case. We do conclude that here, and as a general rule in cases of this type, neither reinstatement nor front pay is an appropriate remedy. It would be both inequitable and pointless to order the reinstatement of someone the employer would have terminated, and will terminate, in any event and upon lawful grounds.

The proper measure of backpay presents a more difficult problem. Resolution of this question must give proper recognition to the fact that an ADEA violation has occurred which must be deterred and compensated without undue infringement upon the employer's rights and prerogatives. The object of compensation is to restore the employee to the position he or she would have been in absent the discrimination, but that principle is difficult to apply with precision where there is after-acquired evidence of wrongdoing that would have led to termination on legitimate grounds had the employer known about it. Once an employer learns about employee wrongdoing that would lead to a legitimate discharge, we cannot require the employer to ignore the information, even if it is acquired during the course of discovery in a suit against the employer and even if the information might have gone undiscovered absent the suit. The beginning point in the trial court's formulation of a remedy should be calculation of backpay from the date of the unlawful discharge to the date the new information was discovered. In determining the appropriate order for relief, the court can consider taking into further account extraordinary equitable circumstances that affect the legitimate interests of either party. An absolute rule barring any recovery of backpay, however, would undermine the ADEA's objective of forcing employers to consider and examine their motivations, and of penalizing them for employment decisions that spring from age discrimination.

Where an employer seeks to rely upon after-acquired evidence of wrongdoing, it must first establish that the wrongdoing was of such severity that the employee in fact would have been terminated on those grounds alone if the employer had known of it at the time of the discharge. The concern that employers might as a routine matter undertake extensive discovery into an employee's background or performance on the job to resist claims under the Act is not an insubstantial one, but we think the authority of the courts to award attorney's fees, mandated under the statute, 29 U.S.C. §§ 216(b), 626(b), and to invoke the appropriate provisions of the Federal Rules of Civil Procedure will deter most abuses.

The judgment is reversed, and the case is remanded to the Court of Appeals for the Sixth Circuit for further proceedings consistent with this opinion.

## Exercise 3.12

To prove a claim or a defense, an attorney must present admissible evidence. Under Fed. R. Civ. P. 26(b)(1), a party may obtain discovery "regarding any nonprivileged matter that is relevant to any party's claim or defense — including the existence, description, nature, custody, condition, and location of any documents or other tangible things and the identity and location of persons who know of any discoverable matter."

During discovery in federal court, parties have several discovery tools at their disposal, including depositions, document requests, and interrogatories. An interrogatory is a written question seeking information. Physical or mental examinations of parties also can be requested when the physical or mental condition of a party is in controversy. States often have similar rules for proceedings in state court.

Think about the kinds of discovery that might be warranted by the concept of after-acquired evidence in a simple discriminatory termination case. Make a list of the interrogatories and document requests that the employer might propound related to after-acquired evidence. Make a list of individuals who might have relevant information related to after-acquired evidence and the types of questions these individuals might be asked.

## ✦ Core Concept: Intent

The courts often use the terms "disparate treatment" and "intentional discrimination" interchangeably. As discussed earlier, the Supreme Court has considered the term "because of" in the federal anti-discrimination statutes to refer to causation, in the sense that the protected trait played a part in the decision, regardless of whether the decisionmaker was aware it. Although *Johnson Controls* and other Supreme Court decisions make it clear that a plaintiff need not show that animus or malice formed part of the decisionmaker's thinking, some courts require that discriminatory acts be taken with "intent" in the sense that the decisionmaker is conscious that the protected trait is motivating the decision.

Whether intent is required to establish an individual disparate treatment claim is not an issue in many cases because the plaintiff often uses biased statements by a decisionmaker to prove a case. However, in some circumstances whether intent must be proven is critical.

One area in which this concept frequently appears is in so-called cat's paw cases. The name "cat's paw" is based on a story in which a monkey wants to get nuts off of a fire. The monkey convinces a cat to obtain the nuts, then steals them, with the result that the monkey obtains the nuts and the cat ends up with a burnt paw. The term "cat's paw" refers to one person being used as the tool of another.

In cat's paw cases, the employer alleges that it cannot be held liable for discrimination because a person acting without intent actually made the employment decision. The plaintiff typically argues that the decisionmaker relied on biased information, served as a conduit for the discrimination of others, or merely rubber stamped a discriminatory decision made by another person. In other words, while "intent" is present in these cases, the ultimate decisionmaker is not the person who possesses such intent.

Another interesting issue about intent and causation arose in *Staub v. Proctor Hospital* (reprinted below). When defining these concepts, where should the courts look for meaning? In *Staub*, the Supreme Court relies on tort law. Consider whether the use of tort law to define concepts in federal discrimination law is appropriate. Have the courts always relied on tort concepts to define discrimination concepts? How does the use of tort law affect the substantive discrimination doctrine?

## Exercise 3.13

Jeanette's new supervisor is Bob. On several occasions, Bob asks Jeanette out on dates and appears angry when she refuses. Jeannette, who previously received good job performance evaluations from prior supervisors, starts receiving bad performance reviews. Bob tells Jeanette that he has to rate someone lower, and he knows that women will complain less than men, so he picked Jeanette to get a bad review. Jeanette complains to Human Resources. Bob is required to attend discrimination training, and Jeannette agrees to transfer to another department at the same rate of pay and job responsibilities.

Several years later, Bob gets promoted to a new job, in which he is in charge of auditing the performance of employees in numerous departments. Bob audits Jeanette's work and finds mistakes with her work, which he describes in several audit reports. Jeanette is not aware of the audit reports.

A year later the company restructures its operations and terminates some employees. Tammy is in charge of making the decision regarding which employees will lose their jobs. Tammy decides to fire the individuals who have received the lowest scores on performance audits. Jeanette is fired. Tammy has never met Jeanette, has only met Bob socially, and is not aware of the earlier incident between Bob and Jeanette.

Should the company be liable for discrimination in this instance? Consider the argument from Jeanette's perspective and the company's. Should Title VII provide a remedy in this instance? Do you need more information to make a decision? If so, what additional information is needed?

---

### Focus Questions: *Staub v. Proctor Hosp.*

1. *Could the plaintiff prevail if he was required to show that the decisionmaker took an action because of a protected trait?*

2. *Is the decisionmaker's decision separate from the animus of the supervisors? Consider whether the plaintiff was singled out for further scrutiny because of his military service.*

3. *What exactly is the plaintiff required to prove to prevail? Do you see any ambiguity in the holding?*

4. *Notice that the Court uses the term "proximate cause." In the prior cases, the Court has not used this terminology in discrimination frameworks.*

---

# Staub v. Proctor Hosp.
### 131 S.Ct. 1186 (2011)

Justice Scalia, delivered the opinion of the Court. Kagan, J., took no part in the consideration or decision of the case.

We consider the circumstances under which an employer may be held liable for employment discrimination based on the discriminatory animus of an employee who influenced, but did not make, the ultimate employment decision.

### I

Petitioner Vincent Staub worked as an angiography technician for respondent Proctor Hospital until 2004, when he was fired. Staub and Proctor hotly dispute the facts surrounding the firing, but because a jury found for Staub in his claim of employment discrimination against Proctor, we describe the facts viewed in the light most favorable to him.

While employed by Proctor, Staub was a member of the United States Army Reserve, which required him to attend drill one weekend per month and to train full time for two to three weeks a year. Both Janice Mulally, Staub's immediate supervisor, and Michael Korenchuk, Mulally's supervisor, were hostile to Staub's military obligations. Mulally scheduled Staub for additional shifts without notice so that he would "pa[y] back the department for everyone else having to bend over backwards to cover [his] schedule for the Reserves." She also informed Staub's co-worker, Leslie Sweborg, that Staub's "military duty had been a strain on th[e] department," and asked Sweborg to help her "get rid of him." Korenchuk referred to Staub's military obligations as "a b[u]nch of smoking and joking and [a] waste of taxpayers['] money." He was also aware that Mulally was "out to get" Staub.

In January 2004, Mulally issued Staub a "Corrective Action" disciplinary warning for purportedly violating a company rule requiring him to stay in his work area whenever he was not working with a patient. The Corrective Action included a directive requiring Staub to report to Mulally or Korenchuk "when [he] ha[d] no patients and [the angio] cases [we]re complete[d]." According to Staub, Mulally's justification for the Corrective Action was false for two reasons: First, the company rule invoked by Mulally did not exist; and second, even if it did, Staub did not violate it.

On April 2, 2004, Angie Day, Staub's co-worker, complained to Linda Buck, Proctor's vice president of human resources, and Garrett McGowan, Proctor's chief operating officer, about Staub's frequent unavailability and abruptness. McGowan directed Korenchuk and Buck to create a plan that would solve Staub's "availability problems." But three weeks later, before they had time to do so, Korenchuk informed Buck that Staub had left his desk without informing a supervisor, in violation of the January Corrective Action. Staub now contends this accusation was false: he had left Korenchuk a voice-mail notification that he was leaving his desk. Buck relied on Korenchuk's accusation, however, and after reviewing Staub's personnel file, she decided to fire him. The termination notice stated that Staub had ignored the directive issued in the January 2004 Corrective Action.

Staub challenged his firing through Proctor's grievance process, claiming that Mulally had fabricated the allegation underlying the Corrective Action out of hostility toward his military obligations. Buck did not follow up with Mulally about this claim. After discussing the matter with another personnel officer, Buck adhered to her decision.

Staub sued Proctor under the Uniformed Services Employment and Reemployment Rights Act of 1994, 38 U.S.C. § 4301 *et seq.*, claiming that his discharge was motivated by hostility to his obligations as a military reservist. His contention was not that Buck had any such hostility but that Mulally and Korenchuk did, and that their actions influenced Buck's ultimate employment decision. A jury found that Staub's "military status was a motivating factor in [Proctor's] decision to discharge him," and awarded $57,640 in damages.

The Seventh Circuit reversed, holding that Proctor was entitled to judgment as a matter of law. The court observed that Staub had brought a "cat's paw case," meaning that he sought to hold his employer liable for the animus of a supervisor who was not charged with making the ultimate employment decision.[46] It explained that under Seventh Circuit

---

46. The term "cat's paw" derives from a fable conceived by Aesop, put into verse by La Fontaine in 1679, and injected into United States employment discrimination law by Posner in 1990. See *Shager v. Upjohn Co.*, 913 F.2d 398, 405 (7th Cir. 1990). In the fable, a monkey induces a cat by flattery to extract roasting chestnuts from the fire. After the cat has done so, burning its paws in the process,

precedent, a "cat's paw" case could not succeed unless the nondecisionmaker exercised such "singular influence" over the decisionmaker that the decision to terminate was the product of "blind reliance." It then noted that "Buck looked beyond what Mulally and Korenchuk said," relying in part on her conversation with Day and her review of Staub's personnel file. The court "admit[ted] that Buck's investigation could have been more robust," since it "failed to pursue Staub's theory that Mulally fabricated the write-up." But the court said that the "singular influence" rule "does not require the decisionmaker to be a paragon of independence": "It is enough that the decisionmaker is not wholly dependent on a single source of information and conducts her own investigation into the facts relevant to the decision." Because the undisputed evidence established that Buck was not wholly dependent on the advice of Korenchuk and Mulally, the court held that Proctor was entitled to judgment.

We granted certiorari.

## II

The Uniformed Services Employment and Reemployment Rights Act (USERRA) provides in relevant part as follows:

> A person who is a member of ... or has an obligation to perform service in a uniformed service shall not be denied initial employment, reemployment, retention in employment, promotion, or any benefit of employment by an employer on the basis of that membership, ... or obligation.

38 U.S.C. §4311(a). It elaborates further:

> An employer shall be considered to have engaged in actions prohibited ... under subsection (a), if the person's membership ... is a motivating factor in the employer's action, unless the employer can prove that the action would have been taken in the absence of such membership.

§4311(c). The statute is very similar to Title VII, which prohibits employment discrimination "because of ... race, color, religion, sex, or national origin" and states that such discrimination is established when one of those factors "was a motivating factor for any employment practice, even though other factors also motivated the practice." 42 U.S.C. §§2000e-2(a), (m).

The central difficulty in this case is construing the phrase "motivating factor in the employer's action." When the company official who makes the decision to take an adverse employment action is personally acting out of hostility to the employee's membership in or obligation to a uniformed service, a motivating factor obviously exists. The problem we confront arises when that official has no discriminatory animus but is influenced by previous company action that is the product of a like animus in someone else.

In approaching this question, we start from the premise that when Congress creates a federal tort it adopts the background of general tort law. *See Burlington N. & S.F.R. Co. v. United States,* 556 U.S. ___, ___, 129 S.Ct. 1870, 1880–1881 (2009); *Burlington Industries, Inc. v. Ellerth,* 524 U.S. 742, 764 (1998). Intentional torts such as this, "as distinguished from negligent or reckless torts, ... generally require that the actor intend 'the *consequences*' of an act, not simply 'the act itself.'" *Kawaauhau v. Geiger,* 523 U.S. 57, 61–62 (1998).

---

the monkey makes off with the chestnuts and leaves the cat with nothing. A coda to the fable (relevant only marginally, if at all, to employment law) observes that the cat is similar to princes who, flattered by the king, perform services on the king's behalf and receive no reward.

Staub contends that the fact that an unfavorable entry on the plaintiff's personnel record was caused to be put there, with discriminatory animus, by Mulally and Korenchuk, suffices to establish the tort, even if Mulally and Korenchuk did not intend to cause his dismissal. But discrimination was no part of Buck's reason for the dismissal; and while Korenchuk and Mulally acted with discriminatory animus, the act they committed—the mere making of the reports—was not a denial of "initial employment, reemployment, retention in employment, promotion, or any benefit of employment," as liability under USERRA requires. If dismissal was not the object of Mulally's and Korenchuk's reports, it may have been their result, or even their foreseeable consequence, but that is not enough to render Mulally or Korenchuk responsible.

Here, however, Staub is seeking to hold liable not Mulally and Korenchuk, but their employer. Perhaps, therefore, the discriminatory motive of one of the employer's agents (Mulally or Korenchuk) can be aggregated with the act of another agent (Buck) to impose liability on Proctor. Again we consult general principles of law, agency law, which form the background against which federal tort laws are enacted. Here, however, the answer is not so clear. The Restatement of Agency suggests that the malicious mental state of one agent cannot generally be combined with the harmful action of another agent to hold the principal liable for a tort that requires both. *See* Restatement (Second) Agency § 275, Illustration 4 (1958). Some of the cases involving federal torts apply that rule. But another case involving a federal tort, and one involving a federal crime, hold to the contrary. Ultimately, we think it unnecessary in this case to decide what the background rule of agency law may be, since the former line of authority is suggested by the governing text, which requires that discrimination be "a motivating factor" *in the adverse action*. When a decision to fire is made with no unlawful animus on the part of the firing agent, but partly on the basis of a report prompted (unbeknownst to that agent) by discrimination, discrimination might perhaps be called a "factor" or a "causal factor" in the decision; but it seems to us a considerable stretch to call it "a motivating factor."

Proctor, on the other hand, contends that the employer is not liable unless the *de facto* decisionmaker (the technical decisionmaker or the agent for whom he is the "cat's paw") is motivated by discriminatory animus. This avoids the aggregation of animus and adverse action, but it seems to us not the only application of general tort law that can do so. Animus and responsibility for the adverse action can both be attributed to the earlier agent (here, Staub's supervisors) if the adverse action is the intended consequence of that agent's discriminatory conduct. So long as the agent intends, for discriminatory reasons, that the adverse action occur, he has the scienter required to be liable under USERRA. And it is axiomatic under tort law that the exercise of judgment by the decisionmaker does not prevent the earlier agent's action (and hence the earlier agent's discriminatory animus) from being the proximate cause of the harm. Proximate cause requires only "some direct relation between the injury asserted and the injurious conduct alleged," and excludes only those "link[s] that are too remote, purely contingent, or indirect." We do not think that the ultimate decisionmaker's exercise of judgment automatically renders the link to the supervisor's bias "remote" or "purely contingent." The decisionmaker's exercise of judgment is *also* a proximate cause of the employment decision, but it is common for injuries to have multiple proximate causes. Nor can the ultimate decisionmaker's judgment be deemed a superseding cause of the harm. A cause can be thought "superseding" only if it is a "cause of independent origin that was not foreseeable."

Moreover, the approach urged upon us by Proctor gives an unlikely meaning to a provision designed to prevent employer discrimination. An employer's authority to reward, punish, or dismiss is often allocated among multiple agents. The one who makes the ultimate decision does so on the basis of performance assessments by other supervisors. Proctor's view would have the improbable consequence that if an employer isolates a personnel official from an employee's supervisors, vests the decision to take adverse employment actions in that official, and asks that official to review the employee's personnel file before taking the adverse action, then the employer will be effectively shielded from discriminatory acts and recommendations of supervisors that were *designed and intended* to produce the adverse action. That seems to us an implausible meaning of the text, and one that is not compelled by its words.

Proctor suggests that even if the decisionmaker's mere exercise of independent judgment does not suffice to negate the effect of the prior discrimination, at least the decisionmaker's independent investigation (and rejection) of the employee's allegations of discriminatory animus ought to do so. We decline to adopt such a hard-and-fast rule. As we have already acknowledged, the requirement that the biased supervisor's action be a causal factor of the ultimate employment action incorporates the traditional tort-law concept of proximate cause. Thus, if the employer's investigation results in an adverse action for reasons unrelated to the supervisor's original biased action (by the terms of USERRA it is the employer's burden to establish that), then the employer will not be liable. But the supervisor's biased report may remain a causal factor if the independent investigation takes it into account without determining that the adverse action was, apart from the supervisor's recommendation, entirely justified. We are aware of no principle in tort or agency law under which an employer's mere conduct of an independent investigation has a claim-preclusive effect. Nor do we think the independent investigation somehow relieves the employer of "fault." The employer is at fault because one of its agents committed an action based on discriminatory animus that was intended to cause, and did in fact cause, an adverse employment decision.

Justice Alito claims that our failure to adopt a rule immunizing an employer who performs an independent investigation reflects a "stray[ing] from the statutory text." We do not understand this accusation. Since a supervisor is an agent of the employer, when he causes an adverse employment action the employer causes it; and when discrimination is a motivating factor in his doing so, it is a "motivating factor in the employer's action," precisely as the text requires. Justice Alito suggests that the employer should be held liable only when it "should be regarded as having delegated part of the decisionmaking power" to the biased supervisor. But if the independent investigation relies on facts provided by the biased supervisor—as is necessary in any case of cat's-paw liability—then the employer (either directly or through the ultimate decisionmaker) will have effectively delegated the factfinding portion of the investigation to the biased supervisor. Contrary to Justice Alito's suggestion, the biased supervisor is not analogous to a witness at a bench trial. The mere witness is not an actor in the events that are the subject of the trial. The biased supervisor and the ultimate decisionmaker, however, acted as agents of the entity that the plaintiff seeks to hold liable; each of them possessed supervisory authority delegated by their employer and exercised it in the interest of their employer. In sum, we do not see how "fidelity to the statutory text," requires the adoption of an independent-investigation defense that appears nowhere in the text. And we find both speculative and implausible Justice Alito's prediction that our Nation's employers will systematically disfavor members of the armed services in their hiring decisions to avoid the possibility of cat's-paw liability, a policy that would violate USERRA in any event.

We therefore hold that if a supervisor performs an act motivated by antimilitary animus that is *intended* by the supervisor to cause an adverse employment action,[3] and if that act is a proximate cause of the ultimate employment action, then the employer is liable under USERRA.[4]

## III

Applying our analysis to the facts of this case, it is clear that the Seventh Circuit's judgment must be reversed. Both Mulally and Korenchuk were acting within the scope of their employment when they took the actions that allegedly caused Buck to fire Staub. A "reprimand ... for workplace failings" constitutes conduct within the scope of an agent's employment. *Faragher v. Boca Raton,* 524 U.S. 775, 798–799 (1998). As the Seventh Circuit recognized, there was evidence that Mulally's and Korenchuk's actions were motivated by hostility toward Staub's military obligations. There was also evidence that Mulally's and Korenchuk's actions were causal factors underlying Buck's decision to fire Staub. Buck's termination notice expressly stated that Staub was terminated because he had "ignored" the directive in the Corrective Action. Finally, there was evidence that both Mulally and Korenchuk had the specific intent to cause Staub to be terminated. Mulally stated she was trying to "get rid of" Staub, and Korenchuk was aware that Mulally was "out to get" Staub. Moreover, Korenchuk informed Buck, Proctor's personnel officer responsible for terminating employees, of Staub's alleged noncompliance with Mulally's Corrective Action, and Buck fired Staub immediately thereafter; a reasonable jury could infer that Korenchuk intended that Staub be fired. The Seventh Circuit therefore erred in holding that Proctor was entitled to judgment as a matter of law.

It is less clear whether the jury's verdict should be reinstated or whether Proctor is entitled to a new trial. The jury instruction did not hew precisely to the rule we adopt today; it required only that the jury find that "military status was a motivating factor in [Proctor's] decision to discharge him." Whether the variance between the instruction and our rule was harmless error or should mandate a new trial is a matter the Seventh Circuit may consider in the first instance.

The judgment of the Seventh Circuit is reversed, and the case is remanded for further proceedings consistent with this opinion.

Justice Alito, with whom Justice Thomas joins, concurring in the judgment.

I agree with the Court that the decision of the Court of Appeals must be reversed, but I would do so based on the statutory text, rather than principles of agency and tort law that do not speak directly to the question presented here.

The relevant statutory provision states:

> An employer shall be considered to have engaged in [prohibited discrimination against a member of one of the uniformed services] if the person's membership ...

---

3. Under traditional tort law, "intent ... denote[s] that the actor desires to cause consequences of his act, or that he believes that the consequences are substantially certain to result from it."

4. Needless to say, the employer would be liable only when the supervisor acts within the scope of his employment, or when the supervisor acts outside the scope of his employment and liability would be imputed to the employer under traditional agency principles. *See Burlington Industries, Inc. v. Ellerth,* 524 U.S. 742, 758 (1998). We express no view as to whether the employer would be liable if a co-worker, rather than a supervisor, committed a discriminatory act that influenced the ultimate employment decision. We also observe that Staub took advantage of Proctor's grievance process, and we express no view as to whether Proctor would have an affirmative defense if he did not. *Cf. Pennsylvania State Police v. Suders,* 542 U.S. 129, 148–149 (2004).

is *a motivating factor in the employer's action,* unless the employer can prove that the action would have been taken in the absence of such membership....

38 U.S.C. §4311(c)(1) (emphasis added).

For present purposes, the key phrase is "a motivating factor in the employer's action." A "motivating factor" is a factor that "provide[s] ... a motive." *See* Webster's Third New International Dictionary 1475 (1971) (defining "motivate"). A "motive," in turn, is "something within a person ... that incites him to action." *Ibid.* Thus, in order for discrimination to be "a motivating factor in [an] employer's action," discrimination must be present "within," *i.e.,* in the mind of, the person who makes the decision to take that action. And "the employer's action" here is the decision to fire petitioner. Thus, petitioner, in order to recover, was required to show that discrimination motivated *that* action.

The Court, however, strays from the statutory text by holding that it is enough for an employee to show that discrimination motivated *some other action* and that this latter action, in turn, caused the termination decision. That is simply not what the statute says.

The Court fears this interpretation of the statute would allow an employer to escape liability by assigning formal decisionmaking authority to an officer who may merely rubberstamp the recommendation of others who are motivated by antimilitary animus. But fidelity to the statutory text does not lead to this result. Where the officer with formal decisionmaking authority merely rubberstamps the recommendation of others, the employer, I would hold, has actually delegated the decisionmaking responsibility to those whose recommendation is rubberstamped. I would reach a similar conclusion where the officer with the formal decisionmaking authority is put on notice that adverse information about an employee may be based on antimilitary animus but does not undertake an independent investigation of the matter. In that situation, too, the employer should be regarded as having delegated part of the decisionmaking power to those who are responsible for memorializing and transmitting the adverse information that is accepted without examination. The same cannot be said, however, where the officer with formal decisionmaking responsibility, having been alerted to the possibility that adverse information may be tainted, undertakes a reasonable investigation and finds insufficient evidence to dispute the accuracy of that information.

Nor can the employer be said to have "effectively delegated" decisionmaking authority any time a decisionmaker "relies on facts provided by [a] biased supervisor." A decisionmaker who credits information provided by another person — for example, a judge who credits the testimony of a witness in a bench trial — does not thereby delegate a portion of the decisionmaking authority to the person who provides the information.

This interpretation of §4311(c)(1) heeds the statutory text and would provide fair treatment for both employers and employees who are members of the uniformed services. It would also encourage employers to establish internal grievance procedures similar to those that have been adopted following our decisions in *Burlington Industries, Inc. v. Ellerth,* 524 U.S. 742 (1998), and *Faragher v. Boca Raton,* 524 U.S. 775 (1998). Such procedures would often provide relief for employees without the need for litigation, and they would provide protection for employers who proceed in good faith.

The Court's contrary approach, by contrast, is almost certain to lead to confusion and is likely to produce results that will not serve the interests of either employers or employees who are members of the uniformed services. The Court's holding will impose liability unfairly on employers who make every effort to comply with the law, and it may have the perverse effect of discouraging employers from hiring applicants who are members of the Reserves or the National Guard. In addition, by leaving open the possibility that an employer may be held liable if it innocently takes into account adverse information provided, not by a supervisor, but by a low-level employee, the Court increases the confusion that its decision is likely to produce.

For these reasons, I cannot accept the Court's interpretation of § 4311(c)(1), but I nevertheless agree that the decision below must be reversed. There was sufficient evidence to support a finding that at least Korenchuk was actually delegated part of the decisionmaking authority in this case. Korenchuk was the head of the unit in which Staub worked and it was Korenchuk who told Buck that Staub left his work area without informing his supervisors. There was evidence that Korenchuk's accusation formed the basis of Buck's decision to fire Staub, and that Buck simply accepted the accusation at face value. According to one version of events, Buck fired Staub immediately after Korenchuk informed her of Staub's alleged misconduct, and she cited only that misconduct in the termination notice provided to Staub. All of this is enough to show that Korenchuk was in effect delegated some of Buck's termination authority. There was also evidence from which it may be inferred that displeasure with Staub's Reserve responsibilities was a motivating factor in Korenchuk's actions.

## Exercise 3.14

Some academics and social science researchers argue that some employment discrimination is the result of unconscious bias. In other words, a person who claims to not take a protected trait into consideration when making a decision may actually be unknowingly doing so. Must a decisionmaker be aware of the discriminatory motive or is unconscious bias enough?

What if the supervisor who made the decision *thought* he was deciding based on the merits—that Joe performed better than Jill—but in fact was influenced by an unconscious stereotype/bias against women? Assume that this bias is simply something that the supervisor learned as a child from his parents or from societal norms and of which the supervisor is totally unaware. What are the arguments in favor of holding employers responsible for the unconscious motives of the supervisors they employ? Opposed? How can a plaintiff prove what motivated the supervisor in a case where the supervisor is not aware of the motivation?

## Exercise 3.15

In this chapter, you have started to learn about various frameworks courts might use to think about discrimination. Think about how to organize this information, so that it will be useful to you. You might think about creating a flow-chart or other visual aide for each of the frameworks. Other students might find it helpful to make a list, followed by a narrative description of the frameworks.

Whichever method works best for your learning style, take care to ensure that your organizational tool is complete and articulates the frameworks in a legally correct way. As you learn additional frameworks in subsequent chapters, add to your chart, list or narrative description.

# Chapter 4

# Disparate Impact

Disparate impact claims allege that a facially neutral practice has a disparate impact on a protected group. Such claims are available under Title VII, the ADEA, and the ADA. Section 1981 does not recognize disparate impact as a cognizable theory. *See General Bldg. Contractors Ass'n, Inc. v. Pennsylvania*, 458 U.S. 375 (1982).

The Supreme Court first recognized the availability of disparate impact analysis in the 1971 case of *Griggs v. Duke Power*, which is set forth below. Since that time, the analytical frameworks for disparate impact have become increasingly complex. This Chapter begins by discussing the theoretical basis for disparate impact claims, and then proceeds with a series of cases (and in some instances, statutory amendments) that altered disparate impact analysis.

The Core Concepts discussed in this Chapter include the theory and structure of disparate impact claims, the size of disparity required, the correct comparisons for proving disparity and the concept of job-related and consistent with business necessity. The Chapter ends with a discussion of how ADEA disparate impact claims differ from those under Title VII and how disparate impact claims interact with disparate treatment claims.

When considering disparate impact, think again about the theoretical basis for discrimination claims. Should such claims focus on formal equality or substantive equality? Recall that formal equality is the idea that similar people should be treated equally, without regard to their protected traits. Under substantive equality, anti-discrimination law should be concerned with equality of results, considering that underlying social structures undermine the ability of formal equality to achieve just results.

## ✦ Core Concept: Disparate Impact, Its Theory and Structure

### Focus Questions: *Griggs v. Duke Power Co.*

1. What is the underlying rationale for disparate impact claims?

2. Does disparate impact focus on the intent of the employer or the consequences of its business practices?

3. Is the following case a case of intentional discrimination?

4. Does a high school diploma reflect an employee's ability to do a job? What about intelligence tests?

5. If you are not familiar with the fable discussed in the opinion, do basic research so that you understand the parallel being drawn.

# Griggs v. Duke Power Co.

## 401 U.S. 424 (1971)

Chief Justice Burger delivered the opinion of the Court.

We granted the writ in this case to resolve the question whether an employer is prohibited by Title VII from requiring a high school education or passing of a standardized general intelligence test as a condition of employment in or transfer to jobs when (a) neither standard is shown to be significantly related to successful job performance, (b) both requirements operate to disqualify Negroes at a substantially higher rate than white applicants, and (c) the jobs in question formerly had been filled only by white employees as part of a longstanding practice of giving preference to whites.

Congress provided, in Title VII, for class actions for enforcement of provisions of the Act and this proceeding was brought by a group of incumbent Negro employees against Duke Power Company. All the petitioners are employed at the Company's Dan River Steam Station, a power generating facility located at Draper, North Carolina. At the time this action was instituted, the Company had 95 employees at the Dan River Station, 14 of whom were Negroes; 13 of these are petitioners here.

The District Court found that prior to July 2, 1965, the effective date of the Civil Rights Act of 1964, the Company openly discriminated on the basis of race in the hiring and assigning of employees at its Dan River plant. The plant was organized into five operating departments: (1) Labor, (2) Coal Handling, (3) Operations, (4) Maintenance, and (5) Laboratory and Test. Negroes were employed only in the Labor Department where the highest paying jobs paid less than the lowest paying jobs in the other four "operating" departments in which only whites were employed. Promotions were normally made within each department on the basis of job seniority. Transferees into a department usually began in the lowest position.

In 1955 the Company instituted a policy of requiring a high school education for initial assignment to any department except Labor, and for transfer from the Coal Handling to any "inside" department (Operations, Maintenance, or Laboratory). When the Company abandoned its policy of restricting Negroes to the Labor Department in 1965, completion of high school also was made a prerequisite to transfer from Labor to any other department. From the time the high school requirement was instituted to the time of trial, however, white employees hired before the time of the high school education requirement continued to perform satisfactorily and achieve promotions in the "operating" departments. Findings on this score are not challenged.

The Company added a further requirement for new employees on July 2, 1965, the date on which Title VII became effective. To qualify for placement in any but the Labor Department it became necessary to register satisfactory scores on two professionally prepared aptitude tests, as well as to have a high school education. Completion of high school alone continued to render employees eligible for transfer to the four desirable departments from which Negroes had been excluded if the incumbent had been employed prior to the time of the new requirement. In September 1965 the Company began to permit incumbent employees who lacked a high school education to qualify for transfer from Labor or Coal Handling to an "inside" job by passing two tests—the Wonderlic Personnel Test, which purports to measure general intelligence, and the Bennett Mechanical Comprehension Test. Neither was directed or intended to measure the ability to learn to perform a particular job or category of jobs. The requisite scores used for both initial hiring and transfer approximated the national median for high school graduates.[3]

The District Court had found that while the Company previously followed a policy of overt racial discrimination in a period prior to the Act, such conduct had ceased. The District Court also concluded that Title VII was intended to be prospective only and, consequently, the impact of prior inequities was beyond the reach of corrective action authorized by the Act.

The Court of Appeals was confronted with a question of first impression, as are we, concerning the meaning of Title VII. After careful analysis a majority of that court concluded that a subjective test of the employer's intent should govern, particularly in a close case, and that in this case there was no showing of a discriminatory purpose in the adoption of the diploma and test requirements. On this basis, the Court of Appeals concluded there was no violation of the Act.

The Court of Appeals reversed the District Court in part, rejecting the holding that residual discrimination arising from prior employment practices was insulated from remedial action. The Court of Appeals noted, however, that the District Court was correct in its conclusion that there was no showing of a racial purpose or invidious intent in the adoption of the high school diploma requirement or general intelligence test and that these standards had been applied fairly to whites and Negroes alike. It held that, in the absence of a discriminatory purpose, use of such requirements was permitted by the Act. In so doing, the Court of Appeals rejected the claim that because these two requirements operated to render ineligible a markedly disproportionate number of Negroes, they were unlawful under Title VII unless shown to be job related....

The objective of Congress in the enactment of Title VII is plain from the language of the statute. It was to achieve equality of employment opportunities and remove barriers that have operated in the past to favor an identifiable group of white employees over other employees. Under the Act, practices, procedures, or tests neutral on their face, and even neutral in terms of intent, cannot be maintained if they operate to freeze the status quo of prior discriminatory employment practices.

The Court of Appeals' opinion, and the partial dissent, agreed that, on the record in the present case, "whites register far better on the Company's alternative requirements" than Negroes.... This consequence would appear to be directly traceable to race. Basic intelligence must have the means of articulation to manifest itself fairly in a testing process. Because they are Negroes, petitioners have long received inferior education in segregated schools and this Court expressly recognized these differences in *Gaston County v. United States*, 395 U.S. 285 (1969). There, because of the inferior education received by Negroes in North Carolina, this Court barred the institution of a literacy test for voter registration on the ground that the test would abridge the right to vote indirectly on account of race. Congress did not intend by Title VII, however, to guarantee a job to every person regardless of qualifications. In short, the Act does not command that any person be hired simply because he was formerly the subject of discrimination, or because he is a member of a minority group. Discriminatory preference for any group, minority or majority, is precisely and only what Congress has proscribed. What is required by Congress is the removal of

---

3. The test standards are thus more stringent than the high school requirement, since they would screen out approximately half of all high school graduates.

artificial, arbitrary, and unnecessary barriers to employment when the barriers operate invidiously to discriminate on the basis of racial or other impermissible classification.

Congress has now provided that tests or criteria for employment or promotion may not provide equality of opportunity merely in the sense of the fabled offer of milk to the stork and the fox. On the contrary, Congress has now required that the posture and condition of the job-seeker be taken into account. It has—to resort again to the fable—provided that the vessel in which the milk is proffered be one all seekers can use. The Act proscribes not only overt discrimination but also practices that are fair in form, but discriminatory in operation. The touchstone is business necessity. If an employment practice which operates to exclude Negroes cannot be shown to be related to job performance, the practice is prohibited.

On the record before us, neither the high school completion requirement nor the general intelligence test is shown to bear a demonstrable relationship to successful performance of the jobs for which it was used. Both were adopted, as the Court of Appeals noted, without meaningful study of their relationship to job-performance ability. Rather, a vice president of the Company testified, the requirements were instituted on the Company's judgment that they generally would improve the overall quality of the work force.

The evidence, however, shows that employees who have not completed high school or taken the tests have continued to perform satisfactorily and make progress in departments for which the high school and test criteria are now used. The promotion record of present employees who would not be able to meet the new criteria thus suggests the possibility that the requirements may not be needed even for the limited purpose of preserving the avowed policy of advancement within the Company. In the context of this case, it is unnecessary to reach the question whether testing requirements that take into account capability for the next succeeding position or related future promotion might be utilized upon a showing that such long range requirements fulfill a genuine business need. In the present case the Company has made no such showing.

The Court of Appeals held that the Company had adopted the diploma and test requirements without any "intention to discriminate against Negro employees." We do not suggest that either the District Court or the Court of Appeals erred in examining the employer's intent; but good intent or absence of discriminatory intent does not redeem employment procedures or testing mechanisms that operate as "built-in headwinds" for minority groups and are unrelated to measuring job capability.

The Company's lack of discriminatory intent is suggested by special efforts to help the undereducated employees through Company financing of two-thirds the cost of tuition for high school training. But Congress directed the thrust of the Act to the consequences of employment practices, not simply the motivation. More than that, Congress has placed on the employer the burden of showing that any given requirement must have a manifest relationship to the employment in question.

The facts of this case demonstrate the inadequacy of broad and general testing devices as well as the infirmity of using diplomas or degrees as fixed measures of capability. History is filled with examples of men and women who rendered highly effective performance without the conventional badges of accomplishment in terms of certificates, diplomas, or degrees. Diplomas and tests are useful servants, but Congress has mandated the commonsense proposition that they are not to become masters of reality.

The Company contends that its general intelligence tests are specifically permitted by §703(h) of the Act.[8] That section authorizes the use of "any professionally developed ability test" that is not "designed, intended or used to discriminate because of race...."

...

Nothing in the Act precludes the use of testing or measuring procedures; obviously they are useful. What Congress has forbidden is giving these devices and mechanisms controlling force unless they are demonstrably a reasonable measure of job performance. Congress has not commanded that the less qualified be preferred over the better qualified simply because of minority origins. Far from disparaging job qualifications as such, Congress has made such qualifications the controlling factor, so that race, religion, nationality, and sex become irrelevant. What Congress has commanded is that any tests used must measure the person for the job and not the person in the abstract.

---

## Subsequent Developments

While *Griggs* recognized disparate impact claims, it did not provide a fully functional account of how courts should consider such claims. Four years after *Griggs*, the Court issued an opinion that created confusion about how a disparate impact framework would operate. *Albemarle Paper Co. v. Moody*, 422 U.S. 405, 425 (1975). In *Albemarle*, the Supreme Court indicated that after the plaintiff established a prima facie case, the employer would then have the burden of proving that its tests are job-related. *Id.* at 425. The Court cited *McDonnell Douglas* in its discussion, but did not clarify what it meant that the employer would have the burden of proving the second step. *Id.* Did the Court mean that the employer had a burden of production or one of both production and persuasion? The Court indicated that after the second step in the analysis, the employee could rebut the employer's showing by proving that "other tests or selection devices, without a similarly undesirable racial effect, would serve the employer's interest in efficient and trusty workmanship." 422 U.S. at 425 (citation and quotation omitted).

Later, the Court clarified (some would argue modified) the test to be applied to disparate impact claims in two cases: *Watson v. Fort Worth Bank & Trust*, 487 U.S. 977 (1988), and *Wards Cove Packing Co. v. Atonio* (provided below). In *Watson*, the Court indicated that to prove a disparate impact the plaintiff must identify "the specific employment practice that is challenged" and must establish statistical evidence of a kind and degree sufficient to show that the protected trait caused the disparity. 487 U.S. at 994 (portion of the opinion joined by a plurality). The burden of production then shifts to the defendant to show that "its employment practices are based on legitimate business reasons." *Id.* at 998. Once the defendant meets this burden, the plaintiff can prevail by making the showing discussed in *Albemarle*. *Id.*

In *Watson*, the Supreme Court also held that disparate-impact analysis could be applied to subjective hiring practices. 487 U.S. at 991.

In *Wards Cove*, the Supreme Court specifically addressed the analytical framework for disparate impact claims under Title VII. Portions of *Wards Cove* remain good law; however, portions of its disparate impact analysis have undergone modifications as a result of amendments in the 1991 Civil Rights Act, excerpts of which follow the case.

---

8. Section 703(h) applies only to tests. It has no applicability to the high school diploma requirement.

---

## Focus Questions: *Wards Cove Packing Co., Inc. v. Atonio*

1.  *What problems existed with the plaintiff's evidence?*
2.  *What structure did the Court apply to disparate impact claims?*

---

# Wards Cove Packing Co., Inc. v. Atonio

### 490 U.S. 642 (1989)

Justice White delivered the opinion of the Court.

Title VII makes it an unfair employment practice for an employer to discriminate against any individual with respect to hiring or the terms and condition[s] of employment because of such individual's race, color, religion, sex, or national origin; or to limit, segregate, or classify his employees in ways that would adversely affect any employee because of the employee's race, color, religion, sex, or national origin. *Griggs v. Duke Power Co.,* 401 U.S. 424, 431 (1971), construed Title VII to proscribe "not only overt discrimination but also practices that are fair in form but discriminatory in practice." Under this basis for liability, which is known as the "disparate-impact" theory and which is involved in this case, a facially neutral employment practice may be deemed violative of Title VII without evidence of the employer's subjective intent to discriminate that is required in a "disparate-treatment" case.

### I

The claims before us are disparate-impact claims, involving the employment practices of petitioners, two companies that operate salmon canneries in remote and widely separated areas of Alaska. The canneries operate only during the salmon runs in the summer months. They are inoperative and vacant for the rest of the year. In May or June of each year, a few weeks before the salmon runs begin, workers arrive and prepare the equipment and facilities for the canning operation. Most of these workers possess a variety of skills. When salmon runs are about to begin, the workers who will operate the cannery lines arrive, remain as long as there are fish to can, and then depart. The canneries are then closed down, winterized, and left vacant until the next spring. During the off-season, the companies employ only a small number of individuals at their headquarters in Seattle and Astoria, Oregon, plus some employees at the winter shipyard in Seattle.

The length and size of salmon runs vary from year to year, and hence the number of employees needed at each cannery also varies. Estimates are made as early in the winter as possible; the necessary employees are hired, and when the time comes, they are transported to the canneries. Salmon must be processed soon after they are caught, and the work during the canning season is therefore intense. For this reason, and because the canneries are located in remote regions, all workers are housed at the canneries and have their meals in company-owned mess halls.

Jobs at the canneries are of two general types: "cannery jobs" on the cannery line, which are unskilled positions; and "noncannery jobs," which fall into a variety of classifications. Most noncannery jobs are classified as skilled positions.[3] Cannery jobs are

---

3. The noncannery jobs were described as follows by the Court of Appeals: "Machinists and engineers are hired to maintain the smooth and continuous operation of the canning equipment. Quality control personnel conduct the FDA-required inspections and recordkeeping. Tenders are

filled predominantly by nonwhites: Filipinos and Alaska Natives. The Filipinos are hired through, and dispatched by, Local 37 of the International Longshoremen's and Warehousemen's Union pursuant to a hiring hall agreement with the local. The Alaska Natives primarily reside in villages near the remote cannery locations. Noncannery jobs are filled with predominantly white workers, who are hired during the winter months from the companies' offices in Washington and Oregon. Virtually all of the noncannery jobs pay more than cannery positions. The predominantly white noncannery workers and the predominantly nonwhite cannery employees live in separate dormitories and eat in separate mess halls.

In 1974, respondents, a class of nonwhite cannery workers who were (or had been) employed at the canneries, brought this Title VII action against petitioners. Respondents alleged that a variety of petitioners' hiring/promotion practices—*e.g.*, nepotism, a rehire preference, a lack of objective hiring criteria, separate hiring channels, a practice of not promoting from within—were responsible for the racial stratification of the work force and had denied them and other nonwhites employment as noncannery workers on the basis of race. Respondents also complained of petitioners' racially segregated housing and dining facilities. All of respondents' claims were advanced under both the disparate-treatment and disparate-impact theories of Title VII liability.

The District Court held a bench trial, after which it entered 172 findings of fact. It then rejected all of respondents' disparate-treatment claims. It also rejected the disparate-impact challenges involving the subjective employment criteria used by petitioners to fill these noncannery positions, on the ground that those criteria were not subject to attack under a disparate-impact theory. Petitioners' "objective" employment practices (*e.g.*, an English language requirement, alleged nepotism in hiring, failure to post noncannery openings, the rehire preference, *etc.*) were found to be subject to challenge under the disparate-impact theory, but these claims were rejected for failure of proof. Judgment was entered for petitioners.

On appeal, a panel of the Ninth Circuit affirmed, but that decision was vacated when the Court of Appeals agreed to hear the case en banc.... [Sitting en banc, the Ninth Circuit concluded that subjective hiring practices are subject to disparate impact analysis and that,] "[o]nce the plaintiff class has shown disparate impact caused by specific, identifiable employment practices or criteria, the burden shifts to the employer," to [prove the business necessity] of the challenged practice.

... Neither the en banc court nor the panel disturbed the District Court's rejection of the disparate-treatment claims....

## II

In holding that respondents had made out a prima facie case of disparate impact, the Court of Appeals relied solely on respondents' statistics showing a high percentage of nonwhite workers in the cannery jobs and a low percentage of such workers in the noncannery positions. Although statistical proof can alone make out a prima facie case, the Court of Appeals' ruling here misapprehends our precedents and the purposes of Title VII, and we therefore reverse.

... It is a comparison—between the racial composition of the qualified persons in the labor market and the persons holding at-issue jobs—that generally forms the proper basis

---

staffed with a crew necessary to operate the vessel. A variety of support personnel are employed to operate the entire cannery community, including, for example, cooks, carpenters, store-keepers, bookkeepers, beach gangs for dock yard labor and construction, etc."

for the initial inquiry in a disparate-impact case. Alternatively, in cases where such labor market statistics will be difficult if not impossible to ascertain, we have recognized that certain other statistics—such as measures indicating the racial composition of "otherwise-qualified applicants" for at-issue jobs—are equally probative for this purpose.[6]

It is clear to us that the Court of Appeals' acceptance of the comparison between the racial composition of the cannery work force and that of the noncannery work force, as probative of a prima facie case of disparate impact in the selection of the latter group of workers, was flawed for several reasons. Most obviously, with respect to the skilled noncannery jobs at issue here, the cannery work force in no way reflected "the pool of *qualified* job applicants" or the "*qualified* population in the labor force." Measuring alleged discrimination in the selection of accountants, managers, boat captains, electricians, doctors, and engineers—and the long list of other "skilled" noncannery positions found to exist by the District Court—by comparing the number of nonwhites occupying these jobs to the number of nonwhites filling cannery worker positions is nonsensical. If the absence of minorities holding such skilled positions is due to a dearth of qualified nonwhite applicants (for reasons that are not petitioners' fault),[7] petitioners' selection methods or employment practices cannot be said to have had a "disparate impact" on nonwhites.

One example illustrates why this must be so. Respondents' own statistics concerning the noncannery work force at one of the canneries at issue here indicate that approximately 17% of the new hires for medical jobs, and 15% of the new hires for officer worker positions, were nonwhite. If it were the case that less than 15 to 17% of the applicants for these jobs were nonwhite and that nonwhites made up a lower percentage of the relevant qualified labor market, it is hard to see how respondents, without more would have made out a prima facie case of disparate impact. Yet, under the Court of Appeals' theory, simply because nonwhites comprise 52% of the cannery workers at the cannery in question, respondents would be successful in establishing a prima facie case of racial discrimination under Title VII.

Such a result cannot be squared with our cases or with the goals behind the statute. The Court of Appeals' theory, at the very least, would mean that any employer who had a segment of his work force that was—for some reason—racially imbalanced, could be haled into court and forced to engage in the expensive and time-consuming task of defending the "business necessity" of the methods used to select the other members of his work force. The only practicable option for many employers would be to adopt racial quotas, insuring that no portion of their work forces deviated in racial composition from the other portions thereof; this is a result that Congress expressly rejected in drafting Title VII. *See* 42 U.S.C. § 2000e-2(j). The Court of Appeals' theory would "leave the employer little choice ... but to engage in a subjective quota system of employment selection. This, of course, is far from the intent of Title VII." [citation omitted].

The Court of Appeals also erred with respect to the unskilled noncannery positions. Racial imbalance in one segment of an employer's work force does not, without more, establish a prima facie case of disparate impact with respect to the selection of workers for the employer's other positions, even where workers for the different positions may

---

6. In fact, where "figures for the general population might ... accurately reflect the pool of qualified job applicants," *cf. Teamsters v. United States,* 431 U.S. 324, 340, n. 20 (1977), we have even permitted plaintiffs to rest their prima facie case on such statistics as well. *See, e.g., Dothard v. Rawlinson,* 431 U.S. 321, 329–330 (1977).

7. Obviously, the analysis would be different if it were found that the dearth of qualified nonwhite applicants was due to practices on petitioners' part which—expressly or implicitly—deterred minority group members from applying for noncannery positions.

have somewhat fungible skills (as is arguably the case for cannery and unskilled noncannery workers). As long as there are no barriers or practices deterring qualified nonwhites from applying for noncannery positions, if the percentage of selected applicants who are nonwhite is not significantly less than the percentage of qualified applicants who are nonwhite, the employer's selection mechanism probably does not operate with a disparate impact on minorities. Where this is the case, the percentage of nonwhite workers found in other positions in the employer's labor force is irrelevant to the question of a prima facie statistical case of disparate impact. As noted above, a contrary ruling on this point would almost inexorably lead to the use of numerical quotas in the workplace, a result that Congress and this Court have rejected repeatedly in the past.

Moreover, isolating the cannery workers as the potential "labor force" for unskilled non-cannery positions is at once both too broad and too narrow in its focus. It is too broad because the vast majority of these cannery workers did not seek jobs in unskilled noncannery positions; there is no showing that many of them would have done so even if none of the arguably "deterring" practices existed. Thus, the pool of cannery workers cannot be used as a surrogate for the class of qualified job applicants because it contains many persons who have not (and would not) be noncannery job applicants. Conversely, if respondents propose to use the cannery workers for comparison purposes because they represent the "qualified labor population" generally, the group is too narrow because there are obviously many qualified persons in the labor market for noncannery jobs who are not cannery workers.

The peculiar facts of this case further illustrate why a comparison between the percentage of nonwhite cannery workers and nonwhite noncannery workers is an improper basis for making out a claim of disparate impact. Here, the District Court found that nonwhites were "overrepresent[ed]" among cannery workers because petitioners had contracted with a predominantly nonwhite union (local 37) to fill these positions. As a result, if petitioners (for some permissible reason) ceased using local 37 as its hiring channel for cannery positions, it appears (according to the District Court's findings) that the racial stratification between the cannery and noncannery workers might diminish to statistical insignificance. Under the Court of Appeals' approach, therefore, it is possible that *with no change whatsoever* in their hiring practices for noncannery workers—the jobs at issue in this lawsuit—petitioners could make respondents' prima facie case of disparate impact "disappear." But *if* there would be no prima facie case of disparate impact in the selection of noncannery workers absent petitioners' use of local 37 to hire cannery workers, surely petitioners' reliance on the union to fill the cannery jobs ... (and its resulting "overrepresentation" of nonwhites in those positions) does not—standing alone—make out a prima facie case of disparate impact. Yet it is precisely such an ironic result that the Court of Appeals reached below.

Consequently, we reverse the Court of Appeals' ruling that a comparison between the percentage of cannery workers who are nonwhite and the percentage of noncannery workers who are nonwhite makes out a prima facie case of disparate impact....

### III

... Because we remand for further proceedings, however, on whether a prima facie case of disparate impact has been made in defensible fashion in this case, we address two other challenges petitioners have made to the decision of the Court of Appeals.

### A

First is the question of causation in a disparate-impact case. The law in this respect was correctly stated by Justice O'Connor's opinion last Term in *Watson v. Fort Worth Bank & Trust,* 487 U.S. at 994:

[W]e note that the plaintiff's burden in establishing a prima facie case goes beyond the need to show that there are statistical disparities in the employer's work force. The plaintiff must begin by identifying the specific employment practice that is challenged.... Especially in cases where an employer combines subjective criteria with the use of more rigid standardized rules or tests, the plaintiff is in our view responsible for isolating and identifying the specific employment practices that are allegedly responsible for any observed statistical disparities.

Our disparate-impact cases have always focused on the impact of *particular* hiring practices on employment opportunities for minorities.... As a general matter, a plaintiff must demonstrate that it is the application of a specific or particular employment practice that has created the disparate impact under attack. Such a showing is an integral part of the plaintiff's prima facie case in a disparate-impact suit under Title VII.

... Here, respondents have alleged that several "objective" employment practices (*e.g.*, nepotism, separate hiring channels, rehire preferences), as well as the use of "subjective decision making" to select noncannery workers, have had a disparate impact on nonwhites. Respondents base this claim on statistics that allegedly show a disproportionately low percentage of nonwhites in the at-issue positions. However, even if on remand respondents can show that nonwhites are underrepresented in the at-issue jobs in a manner that is acceptable under the standards set forth in Part II, *supra*, this alone will *not* suffice to make out a prima facie case of disparate impact. Respondents will also have to demonstrate that the disparity they complain of is the result of one or more of the employment practices that they are attacking here, specifically showing that each challenged practice has a significantly disparate impact on employment opportunities for whites and nonwhites. To hold otherwise would result in employers being potentially liable for "the myriad of innocent causes that may lead to statistical imbalances in the composition of their work forces." [citation omitted].

Some will complain that this specific causation requirement is unduly burdensome on Title VII plaintiffs. But liberal civil discovery rules give plaintiffs broad access to employers' records in an effort to document their claims. Also, employers falling within the scope of the Uniform Guidelines on Employee Selection Procedures, 29 C.F.R. § 1607.1 *et seq.* (1988), are required to "maintain ... records or other information which will disclose the impact which its tests and other selection procedures have upon employment opportunities of persons by identifiable race, sex, or ethnic group[s]." *See* § 1607.4(A). This includes records concerning "the individual components of the selection process" where there is a significant disparity in the selection rates of whites and nonwhites. *See* § 1607.4(C). Plaintiffs as a general matter will have the benefit of these tools to meet their burden of showing a causal link between challenged employment practices and racial imbalances in the work force....

Consequently, on remand, the courts below are instructed to require, as part of respondents' prima facie case, a demonstration that specific elements of the petitioners' hiring process have a significantly disparate impact on nonwhites.

B

If, on remand, respondents meet the proof burdens outlined above, and establish a prima facie case of disparate impact with respect to any of petitioners' employment practices, the case will shift to any business justification petitioners offer for their use of these practices. This phase of the disparate-impact case contains two components: first, a consideration of the justifications an employer offers for his use of these practices; and second, the availability of alternative practices to achieve the same business ends, with less racial impact....

(1)

Though we have phrased the query differently in different cases, it is generally well established that at the justification stage of such a disparate-impact case, the dispositive issue is whether a challenged practice serves, in a significant way, the legitimate employment goals of the employer. The touchstone of this inquiry is a reasoned review of the employer's justification for his use of the challenged practice. A mere insubstantial justification in this regard will not suffice, because such a low standard of review would permit discrimination to be practiced through the use of spurious, seemingly neutral employment practices. At the same time, though, there is no requirement that the challenged practice be "essential" or "indispensable" to the employer's business for it to pass muster....

In this phase, the employer carries the burden of producing evidence of a business justification for his employment practice. The burden of persuasion, however, remains with the disparate-impact plaintiff. To the extent that the Ninth Circuit held otherwise in its en banc decision in this case, or in the panel's decision on remand—suggesting that the persuasion burden should shift to petitioners once respondents established a prima facie case of disparate impact—its decisions were erroneous. "[T]he ultimate burden of proving that discrimination against a protected group has been caused by a specific employment practice remains with the plaintiff *at all times.*" [citation omitted]. This rule conforms with the usual method for allocating persuasion and production burdens in the federal courts, *see* Fed. Rule Evid. 301, and more specifically, it conforms to the rule in disparate-treatment cases that the plaintiff bears the burden of disproving an employer's assertion that the adverse employment action or practice was based solely on a legitimate neutral consideration. We acknowledge that some of our earlier decisions can be read as suggesting otherwise. But to the extent that those cases speak of an employers' "burden of proof" with respect to a legitimate business justification defense, *see, e.g., Dothard v. Rawlinson,* 433 U.S. 321, 329 (1977), they should have been understood to mean an employer's production—but not persuasion—burden. The persuasion burden here must remain with the plaintiff, for it is he who must prove that it was "because of such individual's race, color," *etc.,* that he was denied a desired employment opportunity. *See* 42 U.S.C. § 2000e-2(a).

(2)

Finally, if on remand the case reaches this point, and respondents cannot persuade the trier of fact on the question of petitioners' business necessity defense, respondents may still be able to prevail. To do so, respondents will have to persuade the factfinder that "other tests or selection devices, without a similarly undesirable racial effect, would also serve the employer's legitimate [hiring] interest[s]"; by so demonstrating, respondents would prove that "[petitioners were] using [their] tests merely as a 'pretext' for discrimination." [citations omitted]. If respondents, having established a prima facie case, come forward with alternatives to petitioners' hiring practices that reduce the racially disparate impact of practices currently being used, and petitioners refuse to adopt these alternatives, such a refusal would belie a claim by petitioners that their incumbent practices are being employed for nondiscriminatory reasons.

Of course, any alternative practices which respondents offer up in this respect must be equally effective as petitioners' chosen hiring procedures in achieving petitioners' legitimate employment goals. Moreover, "[f]actors such as the cost or other burdens of proposed alternative selection devices are relevant in determining whether they would be equally as effective as the challenged practice in serving the employer's legitimate business goals." [citation omitted]. "Courts are generally less competent than employers to restructure business practices," [citation omitted]; consequently, the judiciary should proceed with care before mandating that an employer must adopt a plaintiff's alternative selection or hiring practice in response to a Title VII suit.

Justice Blackmun, with whom Justice Brennan and Justice Marshall join, dissenting.

I fully concur in Justice Stevens' analysis of this case. Today a bare majority of the Court takes three major strides backwards in the battle against race discrimination. It reaches out to make last Term's plurality opinion in *Watson v. Fort Worth Bank & Trust*, 487 U.S. 977 (1988), the law, thereby upsetting the longstanding distribution of burdens of proof in Title VII disparate-impact cases. It bars the use of internal work force comparisons in the making of a prima facie case of discrimination, even where the structure of the industry in question renders any other statistical comparison meaningless. And it requires practice-by-practice statistical proof of causation, even where, as here, such proof would be impossible.

The harshness of these results is well demonstrated by the facts of this case. The salmon industry as described by this record takes us back to a kind of overt and institutionalized discrimination we have not dealt with in years: a total residential and work environment organized on principles of racial stratification and segregation, which, as Justice Stevens points out, resembles a plantation economy. This industry long has been characterized by a taste for discrimination of the old-fashioned sort: a preference for hiring nonwhites to fill its lowest level positions, on the condition that they stay there. The majority's legal rulings essentially immunize these practices from attack under a Title VII disparate-impact analysis.

Sadly, this comes as no surprise. One wonders whether the majority still believes that race discrimination—or, more accurately, race discrimination against nonwhites—is a problem in our society, or even remembers that it ever was.

Justice Stevens, with whom Justice Brennan, Justice Marshall, and Justice Blackmun join, dissenting.

Fully 18 years ago, this Court unanimously held that Title VII prohibits employment practices that have discriminatory effects as well as those that are intended to discriminate. Federal courts and agencies consistently have enforced that interpretation, thus promoting our national goal of eliminating barriers that define economic opportunity not by aptitude and ability but by race, color, national origin, and other traits that are easily identified but utterly irrelevant to one's qualification for a particular job. Regrettably, the Court retreats from these efforts in its review of an interlocutory judgment respecting the "peculiar facts" of this lawsuit. Turning a blind eye to the meaning and purpose of Title VII, the majority's opinion perfunctorily rejects a longstanding rule of law and underestimates the probative value of evidence of a racially stratified work force.[4] I cannot join this latest sojourn into judicial activism.

---

4. Respondents constitute a class of present and former employees of petitioners, two Alaskan salmon canning companies. The class members, described by the parties as "nonwhite," include persons of Samoan, Chinese, Filipino, Japanese, and Alaska Native descent, all but one of whom are United States citizens. Fifteen years ago they commenced this suit, alleging that petitioners engage in hiring, job assignment, housing, and messing practices that segregate nonwhites from whites in violation of Title VII. Evidence included this response in 1971 by a foreman to a college student's inquiry about cannery employment: "We are not in a position to take many young fellows to our Bristol Bay canneries as they do not have the background for our type of employees. Our cannery labor is either Eskimo or Filipino and we do not have the facilities to mix others with these groups." Some characteristics of the Alaska salmon industry described in this litigation—in particular, the segregation of housing and

## Subsequent Developments

In the Civil Rights Act of 1991, Congress, among other things, codified a structure for disparate impact claims under Title VII that differed in some respects from the structure enunciated by the Supreme Court in *Wards Cove*. Congress did not amend the ADEA or ADA relating to disparate impact claims, when it made these changes to Title VII. The amended statutory language, which is codified at 42 U.S.C. §2000e-2(k), reads as follows:

(1)(A) An unlawful employment practice based on disparate impact is established under this subchapter only if—

(i) a complaining party demonstrates that a respondent uses a particular employment practice that causes a disparate impact on the basis of race, color, religion, sex, or national origin and the respondent fails to demonstrate that the challenged practice is job related for the position in question and consistent with business necessity; or

(ii) the complaining party makes the demonstration described in subparagraph (C) with respect to an alternative employment practice and the respondent refuses to adopt such alternative employment practice.

(B)(i) With respect to demonstrating that a particular employment practice causes a disparate impact as described in subparagraph (A)(i), the complaining party shall demonstrate that each particular challenged employment practice causes a disparate impact, except that if the complaining party can demonstrate to the court that the elements of a respondent's decisionmaking process are not capable of separation for analysis, the decisionmaking process may be analyzed as one employment practice.

(ii) If the respondent demonstrates that a specific employment practice does not cause the disparate impact, the respondent shall not be required to demonstrate that such practice is required by business necessity.

(C) The demonstration referred to by subparagraph (A)(ii) shall be in accordance with the law as it existed on June 4, 1989, with respect to the concept of "alternative employment practice".

(2) A demonstration that an employment practice is required by business necessity may not be used as a defense against a claim of intentional discrimination under this subchapter.

(3) Notwithstanding any other provision of this subchapter, a rule barring the employment of an individual who currently and knowingly uses or possesses a controlled substance, as defined in schedules I and II of section 102(6) of the Controlled Substances Act (21 U.S.C. §802(6)), other than the use or possession of a drug taken under the supervision of a licensed health care professional, or any other use or possession authorized by the Controlled Substances Act [21 U.S.C. §801 *et seq.*] or any other provision of Federal law, shall be considered

dining facilities and the stratification of jobs along racial and ethnic lines—bear an unsettling resemblance to aspects of a plantation economy. Indeed the maintenance of inferior, segregated facilities for housing and feeding nonwhite employees, strikes me as a form of discrimination that, although it does not necessarily fit neatly into a disparate-impact or disparate-treatment mold, nonetheless violates Title VII. Respondents, however, do not press this theory before us....

an unlawful employment practice under this subchapter only if such rule is adopted or applied with an intent to discriminate because of race, color, religion, sex, or national origin.

The 1991 Act defined the term "demonstrates" to mean "meets the burdens of production and persuasion." 42 U.S.C. § 2000e(m). In what ways do the amendments to Title VII alter the *Wards Cove* analysis? Do these changes make it easier or more difficult for the plaintiff to make a disparate impact case?

---

## Exercise 4.1

ABC Company has a policy that prohibits women from working in its steel manufacturing department because it believes women cannot lift some of the equipment, which weighs 50 pounds. If a plaintiff filed suit based on this set of facts, would a disparate impact analysis be appropriate?

Change the facts slightly. ABC Company has a policy that requires all individuals who work within its steel manufacturing department to be at least 6 feet tall and to weigh at least 175 pounds. It believes these individuals are more likely to be able to lift the equipment used in the department, some of which weighs 50 pounds. What kinds of individuals might file suit to protest such a policy? Write out the structure that a court would use to evaluate such a claim, and the reasoning you think it would use. Which party do you think will ultimately prevail?

---

## ✦ Core Concept: Defining Disparity

One of the questions left unanswered by the statutory articulation of disparate impact is how disparate the results of a practice need to be to constitute a legally actionable claim. The EEOC regulations provide as follows:

> A selection rate for any race, sex, or ethnic group which is less than four-fifths (4/5) (or eighty percent) of the rate for the group with the highest rate will generally be regarded by the Federal enforcement agencies as evidence of adverse impact, while a greater than four-fifths rate will generally not be regarded by Federal enforcement agencies as evidence of adverse impact.

29 C.F.R. § 1607.4(D).

The regulations also indicate that smaller differences may constitute a disparate impact "where they are significant in both statistical and practical terms or where a user's actions have discouraged applicants disproportionately on grounds of race, sex, or ethnic group." *Id.* On the other hand, "[g]reater differences in selection rate may not constitute adverse impact where the differences are based on small numbers and are not statistically significant, or where special recruiting or other programs cause the pool of minority or female candidates to be atypical of the normal pool of applicants from that group." *Id.*

The regulations continue:

> Where the user's evidence concerning the impact of a selection procedure indicates adverse impact but is based upon numbers which are too small to be reliable, evidence concerning the impact of the procedure over a longer period of time

and/or evidence concerning the impact which the selection procedure had when used in the same manner in similar circumstances elsewhere may be considered in determining adverse impact.

*Id.*

In *Watson v. Fort Worth Bank & Trust*, the Supreme Court indicated that the EEOC's 80 percent standard is "a rule of thumb" for the courts, but is not binding on them as a standard for evaluating disparate impact. 487 U.S. 977, 995 n.3 (1988) (plurality opinion). The Supreme Court refused to adopt any particular standard for evaluating when an impact is large enough.

The EEOC also requires that certain employers maintain records of whether their tests and selection criteria create a disparate impact. 29 C.F.R. § 1607.4(A) & (B). When an employer does not maintain such records, the EEOC "may draw an inference of adverse impact of the selection process from the failure of the user to maintain such data, if the user has an underutilization of a group in the job category, as compared to the group's representation in the relevant labor market or, in the case of jobs filled from within, the applicable work force." 29 C.F.R. § 1607.4(D).

### Bottom-Line Defense

With the development of the disparate impact theory, employers began to argue that they could not be held liable for disparate impact if a practice created a disparate impact, which the employer then ameliorated. In *Connecticut v. Teal*, 457 U.S. 440 (1982), the Supreme Court determined that employers may not use the so-called "bottom line" defense to avoid liability for disparate impact. In *Connecticut v. Teal*, an employer had a multi-step process for promoting individuals to be supervisors. The first step in the process required passing a written exam. Only individuals who passed the exam were placed on an eligibility list for promotion to supervisor. African-American candidates for supervisor passed the test at a rate that was 68% of the passing rate for white candidates. Black employees who failed the exam filed suit, alleging that the test created a disparate impact and was not consistent with business necessity.

The employer argued that it chose a higher percentage of black candidates than white candidates from the eligibility list, so, when taken as a whole, the process did not result in a disparate impact. The Supreme Court rejected this "bottom line" defense. It reasoned that measuring disparate impact only at the "bottom line" ignored that Title VII's guarantees apply to individual employees and that the individuals who failed the exam should be given the opportunity to compete equally with white workers on the basis of job-related criteria. Discrimination against these individuals was not remedied simply because other people in the same protected class ultimately benefited from the second step in the process. The employer violated Title VII as to the plaintiffs unless the employer could demonstrate that the examination in question was not an artificial, arbitrary, or unnecessary barrier, but measured skills related to effective performance as a supervisor.

The EEOC has indicated that in most circumstances where a multi-step process results in a bottom line of no disparate impact, the EEOC will not use its enforcement authority to challenge those procedures. 29 C.F.R. § 1607.4 (C). However, the EEOC has cautioned that it may use its enforcement authority in bottom line cases if a practice "is a significant factor in the continuation of patterns of assignments of incumbent employees caused by prior discriminatory employment practices," "where the weight of court decisions or administrative interpretations hold that a specific procedure (such as height or weight requirements or no-arrest records) is not job related in the same or similar circumstances," or in other "unusual circumstances." *Id.* at § 1607.4(C)(1)-(2).

---

## Exercise 4.2

A company uses a standardized test to determine which of its applicants will be hired. Three out of five women pass the test and are eligible to be hired. All male applicants pass the test. Considering only the first prong of the disparate impact analysis, does this fact scenario create the required disparate impact?

---

## ✦ Core Concept: The Correct Comparison

Recall that a key issue in *Wards Cove* was whether the plaintiffs had submitted proper proof of a disparate impact by presenting meaningful comparisons for the court to consider. What mistake did the plaintiffs in *Wards Cove* make?

A key problem for plaintiffs in disparate impact cases is providing the court with statistical comparisons that assist the court in determining whether a particular practice causes a disparate impact based on a protected trait. The appropriate comparison in a disparate impact case may vary depending on the particular factual circumstances of the jobs and job market at issue in a particular case.

To prove disparate impact, plaintiffs often hire statistical experts and experts in local economic and labor conditions to help them develop and present their case. Likewise, a defendant in such a case also may hire experts to refute the evidence offered by the plaintiff and to establish that a disparate impact does not exist. Expert advice is often expensive as the parties usually pay experts for their time in evaluating and collecting data, in creating any expert reports required by civil procedure rules, in preparing for and testifying at depositions, and in preparing for and testifying in court.

---

## Exercise 4.3

You are an associate at a law firm. You are handed a document by a partner and asked to consider the possibility of establishing a disparate impact claim based on the following facts.

The Montgomery County School District hires teachers for its elementary schools in the following way. It has an Internet-based application procedure through which applicants initially apply. If an applicant has submitted a complete application and possesses a valid teaching certificate for teaching elementary school, the applicant is placed into a pool of eligible applicants.

Eligible applicants are invited to attend a job fair held twice a year, in which all eligible applicants are interviewed by an individual from the District's Human Resources Department. Those interviewed are rated on a scale of one to five, with five being the best score. When an elementary school within the district has a job opening, the applications of all individuals who scored a four or a five in the interview (and who have not already been hired by the district) are sent to the school's principal. The principal then selects five individuals to interview. After the interviews, the principal selects one individual to receive a job offer.

The largest city in Montgomery County is Maryville. Given its size, the city of Maryville has its own school district. All other cities and areas within the county are a part of the Montgomery County School District.

Twenty percent of the elementary school teachers in the Montgomery County School District are Hispanic and eighty percent of the teachers are white. Half of the teachers in the Maryville elementary schools are Hispanic and half of the teachers are white.

Half of the elementary school students in Montgomery County are Hispanic and the other half are white. Montgomery County is within the fictional state of Springfield. Forty percent of the people who live within the state of Springfield are Hispanic. Forty percent of the working-age adults in the state are Hispanic, as are forty percent of the working adults within Montgomery County itself. Within Montgomery County, there are equal numbers of white and Hispanic individuals who possess teaching certificates to teach elementary school. Eighty percent of the Hispanic individuals who possess teaching certificates reside in Maryville.

Using these facts, could a plaintiff successfully argue that Montgomery County School District's hiring policy has a disparate impact based on race? Which information listed above would be helpful for a plaintiff in making such a case? Which information would be irrelevant? If you believe additional information is necessary, list what that information would be.

---

## ✦ Core Concept: Job-Related and Consistent with Business Necessity

Under Title VII, the second prong of the disparate impact analysis requires the defendant to establish that the "challenged practice is job related for the position in question and consistent with business necessity." 42 U.S.C. § 2000e-2(k)(1)(A)(i). Courts have had a difficult time analyzing the second prong in a consistent manner across different factual scenarios. Certain employment criteria, such as height or weight requirements or a requirement that a person not have an arrest record, are typically held not to meet this second prong.

The EEOC has indicated that an employer can meet the standard by showing that a selection procedure is "necessary to the safe and efficient performance of the job. The challenged policy or practice should therefore be associated with the skills needed to perform the job successfully. In contrast to a general measurement of applicants' or employees' skills, the challenged policy or practice must evaluate an individual's skills as related to the particular job in question." EEOC Fact Sheet on Employment Tests and Selection Procedures. The following case helps to illustrate the concept.

---

### Focus Questions: *Dothard v. Rawlinson*

1.  *What evidence does the plaintiff use to establish disparate impact?*

2.  *Why is the prison's policy not job-related and consistent with business necessity?*

---

# Dothard v. Rawlinson

## 433 U.S. 321 (1977)

Justice Stewart delivered the opinion of the Court.

... Appellee Dianne Rawlinson sought employment with the Alabama Board of Corrections as a prison guard[.] After her application was rejected, she brought this class suit under Title VII and under 42 U.S.C. § 1983, alleging that she had been denied employment because of her sex in violation of federal law....

... She was refused employment because she failed to meet the minimum 120-pound weight requirement established by an Alabama statute. The statute also establishes a height minimum of 5 feet 2 inches.

In enacting Title VII, Congress required "the removal of artificial, arbitrary, and unnecessary barriers to employment when the barriers operate invidiously to discriminate on the basis of racial or other impermissible classification." [citation omitted]. The District Court found that the minimum statutory height and weight requirements that applicants for employment as correctional counselors must meet constitute the sort of arbitrary barrier to equal employment opportunity that Title VII forbids. The appellants assert that the District Court erred both in finding that the height and weight standards discriminate against women, and in its refusal to find that, even if they do, these standards are justified as "job related." ...

The gist of the claim that the statutory height and weight requirements discriminate against women does not involve an assertion of purposeful discriminatory motive. It is asserted, rather, that these facially neutral qualification standards work in fact disproportionately to exclude women from eligibility for employment by the Alabama Board of Corrections....

Although women 14 years of age or older compose 52.75% of the Alabama population and 36.89% of its total labor force, they hold only 12.9% of its correctional counselor positions. In considering the effect of the minimum height and weight standards on this disparity in rate of hiring between the sexes, the District Court found that the 5'2"-requirement would operate to exclude 33.29% of the women in the United States between the ages of 18–79, while excluding only 1.28% of men between the same ages. The 120-pound weight restriction would exclude 22.29% of the women and 2.35% of the men in this age group. When the height and weight restrictions are combined, Alabama's statutory standards would exclude 41.13% of the female population while excluding less than 1% of the male population. Accordingly, the District Court found that Rawlinson had made out a prima facie case of unlawful sex discrimination.

The appellants argue that a showing of disproportionate impact on women based on generalized national statistics should not suffice to establish a prima facie case. They point in particular to Rawlinson's failure to adduce comparative statistics concerning actual applicants for correctional counselor positions in Alabama. There is no requirement, however, that a statistical showing of disproportionate impact must always be based on analysis of the characteristics of actual applicants. The application process might itself not adequately reflect the actual potential applicant pool, since otherwise qualified people might be discouraged from applying because of a self-recognized inability to meet the very standards challenged as being discriminatory. A potential applicant could easily determine her height and weight and conclude that to make an application would be futile. Moreover, reliance on general population demographic data was not misplaced where there was no reason to suppose that physical height and weight characteristics of Alabama men and women differ markedly from those of the national population.

... If the employer discerns fallacies or deficiencies in the data offered by the plaintiff, he is free to adduce countervailing evidence of his own. In this case no such effort was made....

We turn, therefore, to the appellants' argument that they have rebutted the prima facie case of discrimination by showing that the height and weight requirements are job related. These requirements, they say, have a relationship to strength, a sufficient but unspecified amount of which is essential to effective job performance as a correctional counselor. In the District Court, however, the appellants produced no evidence correlating the height and weight requirements with the requisite amount of strength thought essential to good job performance. Indeed, they failed to offer evidence of any kind in specific justification of the statutory standards.

If the job-related quality that the appellants identify is bona fide, their purpose could be achieved by adopting and validating a test for applicants that measures strength directly. Such a test, fairly administered, would fully satisfy the standards of Title VII because it would be one that "measure(s) the person for the job and not the person in the abstract." [citation omitted]. But nothing in the present record even approaches such a measurement....

Justice Rehnquist, with whom the Chief Justice and Justice Blackmun join, concurring in the result and concurring in part.

... The Court's conclusion..., holding that the District Court was "not in error" in holding the statutory height and weight requirements in this case to be invalidated by Title VII, [is] bound to arise so frequently that I feel obliged to separately state the reasons for my agreement with its result. I view affirmance of the District Court in this respect as essentially dictated by the peculiarly limited factual and legal justifications offered below by appellants on behalf of the statutory requirements. For that reason, I do not believe and do not read the Court's opinion as holding that all or even many of the height and weight requirements imposed by States on applicants for a multitude of law enforcement agency jobs are pretermitted by today's decision.

I agree that the statistics relied upon in this case are sufficient, absent rebuttal, to sustain a finding of a prima facie violation of § 703(a)(2), in that they reveal a significant discrepancy between the numbers of men, as opposed to women, who are automatically disqualified by reason of the height and weight requirements. The fact that these statistics are national figures of height and weight, as opposed to statewide or pool-of-labor-force statistics, does not seem to me to require us to hold that the District Court erred as a matter of law in admitting them into evidence....

If the defendants in a Title VII suit believe there to be reason to discredit plaintiffs' statistics that does not appear on their face, the opportunity to challenge them is available to the defendants just as in any other lawsuit. They may endeavor to impeach the reliability of the statistical evidence, they may offer rebutting evidence, or they may disparage in arguments or in briefs the probative weight which the plaintiffs' evidence should be accorded. Since I agree with the Court that appellants made virtually no such effort, I also agree with it that the District Court cannot be said to have erred as a matter of law in finding that a prima facie case had been made out in the instant case.

While the District Court's conclusion is by no means required by the proffered evidence, I am unable to conclude that the District Court's finding in that respect was clearly erroneous. In other cases there could be different evidence which could lead a district court to conclude that height and weight are in fact an accurate enough predictor of strength to justify, under all the circumstances, such minima. Should the height and weight requirements be found to advance the job-related qualification of strength sufficiently to rebut the prima facie case, then, under our cases, the burden would shift back to appellee Rawlinson to demonstrate that other tests, without such disparate effect, would also meet that concern. But, here, the District Court permissibly concluded that appellants had not shown enough of a nexus even to rebut the inference.

The District Court was confronted, however, with only one suggested job-related reason for the qualification that of strength. Appellants argued only the job-relatedness of actual physical strength; they did not urge that an equally job-related qualification for prison guards is the appearance of strength. As the Court notes, the primary job of correctional counselor in Alabama prisons "is to maintain security and control of the inmates...," a function that I at least would imagine is aided by the psychological impact on prisoners of the presence of tall and heavy guards. If the appearance of strength had been urged upon the District Court here as a reason for the height and weight minima, I think that the District Court would surely have been entitled to reach a different result than it did. For, even if not perfectly correlated, I would think that Title VII would not preclude a State from saying that anyone under 5'2" or 120 pounds, no matter how strong in fact, does not have a sufficient appearance of strength to be a prison guard.

---

## Note

A safety rationale is often accepted by courts as being job-related and consistent with business necessity. For example, in *Fitzpatrick v. City of Atlanta*, twelve African-American firefighters filed suit arguing that the city's no beard policy disproportionately affected black men. 2 F.3d 1112, 1114 (11th Cir. 1993). The plaintiffs argued that black men are more prone than others to have pseudofolliculitis barbae, a bacterial disorder which causes men's faces to become infected if they shave them. Without ruling on whether the plaintiffs had established a disparate impact, the Eleventh Circuit held that the employer could establish that the rule was job-related and consistent with business necessity because evidence showed that facial hair could prevent a firefighter's respirator from maintaining a good seal and could pose a danger to the firefighter. *Id.* at 1120–21.

## Further Exploration of "Job-Related" and "Consistent with Business Necessity"

Title VII does not prohibit an employer from acting "upon the results of any professionally developed ability test provided that such test, its administration or action upon the results is not designed, intended or used to discriminate because of race, color, religion, sex or national origin." 42 U.S.C. § 2000e-2(h). However, if a selection test or procedure creates a disparate impact, the EEOC Uniform Guidelines on Employee Selection Procedures direct that the test or procedure must be validated pursuant to the Guidelines. 29 C.F.R. § 1607.1., *et seq.* The Guidelines do not require a user to conduct validity studies of selection procedures where no adverse impact results. 29 C.F.R. § 1607.1.

Courts are not bound by the EEOC Guidelines when considering the appropriateness of a test or procedure, and formal validation is not required in every instance. *See, e.g.,* *Gulino v. New York State Educ. Dept.*, 460 F.3d 361, 383–84 (2d Cir. 2006). Some courts have indicated that the Guidelines are the "primary yardstick" by which a defendant's attempts to validate a test or procedure will be evaluated. *Id.* at 384.

The following provides a general overview of the Guidelines, which can be quite complex in their application. The Guidelines "apply only to persons subject to Title VII, Executive Order 11246, or other equal employment opportunity requirements of Federal law" and not to the ADEA, the ADA or certain sections of the Rehabilitation Act. 29 C.F.R. § 1607.2(D).

Employment decisions that fall within the Guidelines include but are not limited to "hiring, promotion, demotion, membership (for example, in a labor organization), referral, retention, and licensing and certification, to the extent that licensing and certification may be covered by Federal equal employment opportunity law. Other selection decisions, such as selection for training or transfer, may also be considered employment decisions if they lead to any of the decisions listed above." 29 C.F.R. § 1607.2. The Guidelines define "selection procedures" to include "the full range of assessment techniques from traditional paper and pencil tests, performance tests, training programs, or probationary periods and physical, educational, and work experience requirements through informal or casual interviews and unscored application forms." 29 C.F.R. § 1607.16(Q). A validation study may not be required for informal or unscored procedures; however, the Guidelines note that if such procedures create a disparate impact, they should be modified. 29 C.F.R. § 1607.6(B)(1).

The Guidelines allow validation by several methods: criterion-related validity studies, content validity studies, or construct validity studies. 29 C.F.R. § 1607.5(A). Determining which kind of validation is required is important because it is more difficult to validate a test under some methodologies than others. For example, content validation is "generally much easier to achieve than construct validation." *Gulino v. New York State Educ. Dept.*, 460 F.3d 361, 384 (2d Cir. 2006). In some circumstances, it may be difficult to determine the types of validation that may appropriately be used for a certain test or selection device.

Criterion-related validity uses empirical data to demonstrate that "the selection procedure is predictive of or significantly correlated with important elements of job performance." 29 C.F.R. § 1607.5(B). For example, data might be gathered to show that individuals who performed at a certain level on a test were consistently able to perform their jobs at a successful level, while individuals who performed below that level could not.

A content validity study consists of "data showing that the content of the selection procedure is representative of important aspects of performance on the job for which the candidates are to be evaluated." *Id.* Content-based tests are those that measure the knowledge, skills, or abilities required for a particular job. A common example of a content-based test would be a typing test given to an individual whose job would require typing.

A construct validity study shows "that the procedure measures the degree to which candidates have identifiable characteristics which have been determined to be important in successful performance in the job for which the candidates are to be evaluated." *Id.* Construct tests seek information about mental processes or traits, such as intelligence, personality, or diligence. For example, if certain managerial positions require leadership ability, an employer might be able to use a test or selection device to measure leadership.

In validating a test or procedure, it also is important to consider any cut-off score used. Title VII prohibits having different cut-off scores for members of different protected classes. 42 U.S.C. § 2000e-2(l). Under the Guidelines, where cutoff scores are used, "they should normally be set so as to be reasonable and consistent with normal expectations of acceptable proficiency within the work force." 29 C.F.R. § 1607.5(H). A test that is otherwise valid may fail because a cut-off score is set too high.

In certain circumstances, an employer may use a selection device that is intended to yield information regarding whether an individual is qualified for a higher-level job than the one for which the individual is currently being considered. "If job progression structures are so established that employees will probably, within a reasonable period of time and in a majority of cases, progress to a higher level, it may be considered that the applicants are being evaluated for a job or jobs at the higher level." 29 C.F.R. § 1607.5(J). "However, where job progression is not so nearly automatic, or the time span is such that higher level jobs or employees' potential may be expected to change in significant ways, it should be considered that applicants are being evaluated for a job at or near the entry level." *Id.*

The validation process should include consideration of other alternative methods that create no or a lesser disparate impact. 29 C.F.R. § 1607.3(B). If an "equally valid" alternative method that creates less disparate impact is available, it should be adopted. 29 C.F.R. § 1607.3(B).

The Guidelines allow for the interim use of tests and selection devices that have not been validated if "the user has available substantial evidence of validity" and the user conducts the required study within a reasonable time. 29 C.F.R. § 1607.5(J). The Guidelines also require that the validity of a study be kept current. 29 C.F.R. § 1607.5(K). Under certain circumstances, an employer or other entity may use a test that it has not validated, but that has been validated elsewhere. 29 C.F.R. § 1607.7(A).

The Guidelines require maintenance of records regarding the impact of tests and other selection devices. 29 C.F.R. § 1607.3(A). The Guidelines contain specific details about the types of information that are to be retained. 29 C.F.R. § 1607.3.

## Other Considerations

If a selection procedure has been properly validated pursuant to EEOC Guidelines, it is likely that a defendant will be able to demonstrate that the test is job-related and consistent with business necessity. As indicated earlier, courts may not require formal validation studies in all instances. Although the term "job related" is fairly self-explanatory, the courts have described "consistent with business necessity" in various ways.

Title VII does not require that the practice be absolutely essential or indispensable to the continued operation of the employer to constitute a business necessity. Some courts appear not to examine the concept of business necessity at all, indicating that the entire affirmative defense requires the proponent to show that the test or procedure in question has "a manifest relationship to the employment." *Phillips v. Gates*, 329 Fed.Appx. 577, 580–81 (6th Cir. 2009). Others have argued that the term "business necessity" is a separate inquiry from "job related" and requires that the task in question must be necessary to a business goal and that the goal must be essential to the business in some way.

It is important to be able to recognize the following common circumstances when a selection device may not be job-related and consistent with business necessity:

(1) it concerns traits or skills that are not related to the job in question;

(2) it requires demonstration of traits or skills at a level higher than that required for the job in question or a job that the individual is reasonably likely to possess within a reasonable time;

(3) it is adopted based on assumptions about its validity, with no effort to find out whether such assumptions are correct;

(4) it does not actually reveal whether the candidate has the required traits or skills;

(5) it concerns traits or skills that are a small and/or insignificant part of an individual's job;

(6) it has been validated with respect to another job, but the job in question differs in material respects from the job for which the test was validated.

Even if a test or selection device does not create a disparate impact or if the disparate impact is legally permissible, users of such selection criteria should make sure that they comply with other legal restrictions regarding employee testing. For example, the Genetic Information Nondiscrimination Act of 2008 ("GINA") prohibits the improper use of genetic information in employment and other contexts. The Employee Polygraph Protection Act of 1988 ("EPPA") prohibits, in certain circumstances, employers from using, requiring or requesting prospective employees to submit to lie detector tests. 29 U.S.C. § 2002, *et seq.* Even when polygraph tests are allowed, EPPA contains restrictions on the types of questions that may be asked. *Id.* As discussed later in this book, the ADA also prohibits testing in certain circumstances.

An employer may also be able to argue that it is not liable for a disparate impact because it is complying with the terms of a bona fide seniority or merit system. *See* 42 U.S.C. § 2000e-2(h).

---

## Exercise 4.4

Assuming that the following create a disparate impact based on a protected trait, at least under some circumstances, evaluate problems the employer might have in establishing that the practice is job-related and consistent with business necessity.

a. A large employer has jobs open for janitors, administrative assistants, factory workers, engineers, and management. It requires all employees to possess at least two years of college education to be hired.

b. Same as (a), except the employer instead has a minimum requirement of a high-school education.

c. An employer will not hire any individual who has been convicted of a crime.

d. An airline has a requirement that all employees who fly on aircraft have a weight proportional to their height. The requirement is necessary in order for the airline to reduce fuel costs by minimizing the weight it carries on each flight. Female employees are required to fall within the low end of the weight range for their height. Men can fall within the low or medium range of weight for their height.

e. All administrative assistants at a company have typing responsibilities as part of their job. The company administers a test that requires all candidates for the position of administrative assistant to type from dictation. If the administrative assistant candidate cannot type 60 words per minute, the individual is not considered for an open position.

f. A predominantly white municipality requires all of its employees to live within the city limits.

g. The New York City Police Department has validated a physical fitness test for police candidates. A fire department in a small rural community relies on this validation to use the test for potential job candidates.

## ✦ Core Concept: Disparate Impact — ADEA

When Congress amended Title VII in 1991 to codify the disparate impact framework, it did not insert a similar provision into the ADEA. The question remained whether disparate impact claims were cognizable under the ADEA. The Supreme Court answered that question in the following case.

In answering this question, a particular statutory provision in the ADEA was important, the so-called RFOA (reasonable factor other than age) provision. The statutory text provides: "It shall not be unlawful for an employer, employment agency, or labor organization — (1) to take any action otherwise prohibited under subsections (a) ... where the differentiation is based on reasonable factors other than age." 29 U.S.C. § 623(f)(1).

---

### Focus Questions: *Smith v. City of Jackson, Miss.*

1. *How do disparate impact claims under the ADEA differ from those under Title VII?*

2. *What reasoning does the Court use to reach its decision?*

3. *Does this decision favor plaintiffs or defendants?*

4. *Does this set of facts present a compelling disparate impact case?*

---

# Smith v. City of Jackson, Miss.
## 544 U.S. 228 (2005)

Justice Stevens announced the judgment of the Court and delivered the opinion of the Court with respect to Parts I, II, and IV, and an opinion with respect to Part III, in which Justice Souter, Justice Ginsburg, and Justice Breyer join.

Petitioners, police and public safety officers employed by the city of Jackson, Mississippi (hereinafter City), contend that salary increases received in 1999 violated the Age Discrimination in Employment Act of 1967 (ADEA) because they were less generous to officers over the age of 40 than to younger officers. Their suit raises the question whether the "disparate-impact" theory of recovery announced in *Griggs v. Duke Power Co.*, 401 U.S. 424 (1971), for cases brought under Title VII, is cognizable under the ADEA. Despite the age of the ADEA, it is a question that we have not yet addressed.

I

On October 1, 1998, the City adopted a pay plan granting raises to all City employees. The stated purpose of the plan was to "attract and retain qualified people, provide incentive for performance, maintain competitiveness with other public sector agencies and ensure equitable compensation to all employees regardless of age, sex, race and/or disability." On May 1, 1999, a revision of the plan, which was motivated, at least in part, by the City's desire to bring the starting salaries of police officers up to the regional average, granted raises to all police officers and police dispatchers. Those who had less than five years of tenure received proportionately greater raises when compared to their former pay than those with more seniority. Although some officers over the age of 40 had less than five years of service, most of the older officers had more.

We granted the officers' petition for certiorari, and now hold that the ADEA does authorize recovery in "disparate-impact" cases comparable to *Griggs*. Because, however, we conclude that petitioners have not set forth a valid disparate-impact claim, we affirm.

## II

During the deliberations that preceded the enactment of the Civil Rights Act of 1964, Congress considered and rejected proposed amendments that would have included older workers among the classes protected from employment discrimination. Congress did, however, request the Secretary of Labor to "make a full and complete study of the factors which might tend to result in discrimination in employment because of age and of the consequences of such discrimination on the economy and individuals affected." [citation omitted]. The Secretary's report, submitted in response to Congress' request, noted that there was little discrimination arising from dislike or intolerance of older people, but that "arbitrary" discrimination did result from certain age limits ... [and] that discriminatory effects resulted from "[i]nstitutional arrangements that indirectly restrict the employment of older workers." [citation omitted].

In response to that report Congress directed the Secretary to propose remedial legislation and then acted favorably on his proposal. As enacted in 1967, § 4(a)(2) of the ADEA, now codified as 29 U.S.C. § 623(a)(2), provided that it shall be unlawful for an employer "to limit, segregate, or classify his employees in any way which would deprive or tend to deprive any individual of employment opportunities or otherwise adversely affect his status as an employee, because of such individual's age...." Except for substitution of the word "age" for the words "race, color, religion, sex, or national origin," the language of that provision in the ADEA is identical to that found in § 703(a)(2) of the Civil Rights Act of 1964 (Title VII). Other provisions of the ADEA also parallel the earlier statute. Unlike Title VII, however, § 4(f)(1) of the ADEA contains language that significantly narrows its coverage by permitting any "otherwise prohibited" action "where the differentiation is based on reasonable factors other than age" (hereinafter RFOA provision).

## III

In determining whether the ADEA authorizes disparate-impact claims, we begin with the premise that when Congress uses the same language in two statutes having similar purposes, particularly when one is enacted shortly after the other, it is appropriate to presume that Congress intended that text to have the same meaning in both statutes. We have consistently applied that presumption to language in the ADEA that was "derived *in haec verba* from Title VII." [citation omitted]. Our unanimous interpretation of § 703(a)(2) of Title VII in *Griggs* is therefore a precedent of compelling importance.

...

*Griggs*, which interpreted the identical text at issue here, thus strongly suggests that a disparate-impact theory should be cognizable under the ADEA. Indeed, for over two decades after our decision in *Griggs*, the Courts of Appeals uniformly interpreted the ADEA as authorizing recovery on a "disparate-impact" theory in appropriate cases. It was only after our decision in *Hazen Paper Co. v. Biggins*, 507 U.S. 604 (1993), that some of those courts concluded that the ADEA did not authorize a disparate-impact theory of liability. Our opinion in *Hazen Paper*, however, did not address or comment on the issue we decide today. In that case, we held that an employee's allegation that he was discharged shortly before his pension would have vested did not state a cause of action under a *disparate-treatment* theory. The motivating factor was not, we held, the employee's age, but rather his years of service, a factor that the ADEA did not prohibit an employer from considering when terminating an employee....

... As we have already explained, we think the history of the enactment of the ADEA, with particular reference to the Wirtz Report, supports the pre-*Hazen Paper* consensus concerning disparate-impact liability. And *Hazen Paper* itself contains the response to the concern over the RFOA provision.

The RFOA provision provides that it shall not be unlawful for an employer "to take any action otherwise prohibited under subsectio[n] (a) ... where the differentiation is based on reasonable factors other than age...." In most disparate-treatment cases, if an employer in fact acted on a factor other than age, the action would not be prohibited under subsection (a) in the first place. *See Hazen Paper,* 507 U.S., at 609 ("[T]here is no disparate treatment under the ADEA when the factor motivating the employer is some feature other than the employee's age"). In those disparate-treatment cases, such as in *Hazen Paper* itself, the RFOA provision is simply unnecessary to avoid liability under the ADEA, since there was no prohibited action in the first place....

In disparate-impact cases, however, the allegedly "otherwise prohibited" activity is not based on age. It is, accordingly, in cases involving disparate-impact claims that the RFOA provision plays its principal role by precluding liability if the adverse impact was attributable to a nonage factor that was "reasonable." Rather than support an argument that disparate impact is unavailable under the ADEA, the RFOA provision actually supports the contrary conclusion.[11]

Finally, we note that both the Department of Labor, which initially drafted the legislation, and the EEOC, which is the agency charged by Congress with responsibility for implementing the statute have consistently interpreted the ADEA to authorize relief on a disparate-impact theory. The initial regulations, while not mentioning disparate impact by name, nevertheless permitted such claims if the employer relied on a factor that was not related to age.

The text of the statute, as interpreted in *Griggs,* the RFOA provision, and the EEOC regulations all support petitioners' view. We therefore conclude that it was error for the Court of Appeals to hold that the disparate-impact theory of liability is categorically unavailable under the ADEA.

## IV

Two textual differences between the ADEA and Title VII make it clear that even though both statutes authorize recovery on a disparate-impact theory, the scope of disparate-impact liability under the ADEA is narrower than under Title VII. The first is the RFOA provision, which we have already identified. The second is the amendment to Title VII contained in the Civil Rights Act of 1991. One of the purposes of that amendment was to modify the Court's holding in *Wards Cove Packing Co. v. Atonio,* 490 U.S. 642 (1989), a case in which we narrowly construed the employer's exposure to liability on a disparate-

---

11. We note that if Congress intended to prohibit all disparate-impact claims, it certainly could have done so. For instance, in the Equal Pay Act of 1963, 29 U.S.C. § 206(d)(1), Congress barred recovery if a pay differential was based "on any other factor" — reasonable or unreasonable — "other than sex." The fact that Congress provided that employers could use only *reasonable* factors in defending a suit under the ADEA is therefore instructive.

impact theory. While the relevant 1991 amendments expanded the coverage of Title VII, they did not amend the ADEA or speak to the subject of age discrimination. Hence, *Wards Cove's* pre-1991 interpretation of Title VII's identical language remains applicable to the ADEA.

Congress' decision to limit the coverage of the ADEA by including the RFOA provision is consistent with the fact that age, unlike race or other classifications protected by Title VII, not uncommonly has relevance to an individual's capacity to engage in certain types of employment. To be sure, Congress recognized that this is not always the case, and that society may perceive those differences to be larger or more consequential than they are in fact. However, as Secretary Wirtz noted in his report, "certain circumstances ... unquestionably affect older workers more strongly, as a group, than they do younger workers." Thus, it is not surprising that certain employment criteria that are routinely used may be reasonable despite their adverse impact on older workers as a group. Moreover, intentional discrimination on the basis of age has not occurred at the same levels as discrimination against those protected by Title VII. While the ADEA reflects Congress' intent to give older workers employment opportunities whenever possible, the RFOA provision reflects this historical difference.

Turning to the case before us, we initially note that petitioners have done little more than point out that the pay plan at issue is relatively less generous to older workers than to younger workers. They have not identified any specific test, requirement, or practice within the pay plan that has an adverse impact on older workers. As we held in *Wards Cove,* it is not enough to simply allege that there is a disparate impact on workers, or point to a generalized policy that leads to such an impact. Rather, the employee is "responsible for isolating and identifying the *specific* employment practices that are allegedly responsible for any observed statistical disparities." [citation omitted]. Petitioners have failed to do so. Their failure to identify the specific practice being challenged is the sort of omission that could "result in employers being potentially liable for 'the myriad of innocent causes that may lead to statistical imbalances....'" [citation omitted]. In this case not only did petitioners thus err by failing to identify the relevant practice, but it is also clear from the record that the City's plan was based on reasonable factors other than age.

The plan divided each of five basic positions—police officer, master police officer, police sergeant, police lieutenant, and deputy police chief—into a series of steps and half-steps. The wage for each range was based on a survey of comparable communities in the Southeast. Employees were then assigned a step (or half-step) within their position that corresponded to the lowest step that would still give the individual a 2% raise. Most of the officers were in the three lowest ranks; in each of those ranks there were officers under age 40 and officers over 40. In none did their age affect their compensation. The few officers in the two highest ranks are all over 40. Their raises, though higher in dollar amount than the raises given to junior officers, represented a smaller percentage of their salaries, which of course are higher than the salaries paid to their juniors. They are members of the class complaining of the "disparate impact" of the award.

Petitioners' evidence established two principal facts: First, almost two-thirds (66.2%) of the officers under 40 received raises of more than 10% while less than half (45.3%) of those over 40 did. Second, the average percentage increase for the entire class of officers with less than five years of tenure was somewhat higher than the percentage for those with more seniority. Because older officers tended to occupy more senior positions, on average they received smaller increases when measured as a percentage of their salary. The basic explanation for the differential was the City's perceived need to raise the salaries of junior officers to make them competitive with comparable positions in the market.

Thus, the disparate impact is attributable to the City's decision to give raises based on seniority and position. Reliance on seniority and rank is unquestionably reasonable given the City's goal of raising employees' salaries to match those in surrounding communities. In sum, we hold that the City's decision to grant a larger raise to lower echelon employees for the purpose of bringing salaries in line with that of surrounding police forces was a decision based on a "reasonable facto[r] other than age" that responded to the City's legitimate goal of retaining police officers.

While there may have been other reasonable ways for the City to achieve its goals, the one selected was not unreasonable. Unlike the business necessity test, which asks whether there are other ways for the employer to achieve its goals that do not result in a disparate impact on a protected class, the reasonableness inquiry includes no such requirement. Accordingly, while we do not agree with the Court of Appeals' holding that the disparate-impact theory of recovery is never available under the ADEA, we affirm its judgment.

The Chief Justice took no part in the decision of this case.

Justice Scalia, concurring in part and concurring in the judgment.

I concur in the judgment of the Court, and join all except Part III of its opinion. As to that Part, I agree with all of the Court's reasoning, but would find it a basis, not for independent determination of the disparate-impact question, but for deferral to the reasonable views of the Equal Employment Opportunity Commission (EEOC or Commission) pursuant to *Chevron U.S.A. Inc. v. Natural Resources Defense Council, Inc.,* 467 U.S. 837 (1984).

This is an absolutely classic case for deference to agency interpretation. The ADEA, 29 U.S.C. § 621 *et seq.,* confers upon the EEOC authority to issue "such rules and regulations as it may consider necessary or appropriate for carrying out" the ADEA. 29 U.S.C. § 628. Pursuant to this authority, the EEOC promulgated, after notice-and-comment rulemaking, a regulation that reads as follows: "When an employment practice, including a test, is claimed as a basis for different treatment of employees or applicants for employment on the grounds that it is a 'factor other than' age, and such a practice has an adverse impact on individuals within the protected age group, it can only be justified as a business necessity." 29 C.F.R. § 1625.7(d) (2004).

. . .

The EEOC has express authority to promulgate rules and regulations interpreting the ADEA. It has exercised that authority to recognize disparate-impact claims. And, for the reasons given by the plurality opinion, its position is eminently reasonable. In my view, that is sufficient to resolve this case.

Justice O'Connor, with whom Justice Kennedy and Justice Thomas join, concurring in the judgment.

. . . I would instead affirm the judgment below on the ground that disparate impact claims are not cognizable under the ADEA. The ADEA's text, legislative history, and purposes together make clear that Congress did not intend the statute to authorize such claims. Moreover, the significant differences between the ADEA and Title VII counsel against transposing to the former our construction of the latter in *Griggs v. Duke Power Co.,* 401 U.S. 424 (1971). Finally, the agencies charged with administering the ADEA have never authoritatively construed the statute's prohibitory language to impose disparate impact liability. Thus, on the precise question of statutory interpretation now before us, there is no reasoned agency reading of the text to which we might defer.

[A discussion of the statutory text is omitted.]

The legislative history of the ADEA confirms what its text plainly indicates—that Congress never intended the statute to authorize disparate impact claims. The drafters of the ADEA and the Congress that enacted it understood that age discrimination was qualitatively different from the kinds of discrimination addressed by Title VII, and that many legitimate employment practices would have a disparate impact on older workers. Accordingly, Congress determined that the disparate impact problem would best be addressed through noncoercive measures, and that the ADEA's prohibitory provisions should be reserved for combating intentional age-based discrimination.

The Wirtz Report reached two conclusions of central relevance to the question presented by this case. First, the Report emphasized that age discrimination is qualitatively different from the types of discrimination prohibited by Title VII (*i.e.,* race, color, religion, sex, and national origin discrimination). Most importantly—in stark contrast to the types of discrimination addressed by Title VII—the Report found no evidence that age discrimination resulted from intolerance or animus toward older workers. Rather, age discrimination was based primarily upon unfounded assumptions about the relationship between an individual's age and her ability to perform a job. In addition, whereas ability is nearly always completely unrelated to the characteristics protected by Title VII, the Report found that, in some cases, "there is in fact a relationship between [an individual's] age and his ability to perform the job."

Second, the Wirtz Report drew a sharp distinction between "arbitrary discrimination" (which the Report clearly equates with disparate treatment) and circumstances or practices having a disparate impact on older workers. The Report defined "arbitrary" discrimination as adverse treatment of older workers "because of assumptions about the effect of age on their ability to do a job *when there is in fact no basis for these assumptions.*" While the "most obvious kind" of arbitrary discrimination is the setting of unjustified maximum age limits for employment, naturally the Report's definition encompasses a broad range of disparate treatment.

The Report distinguished such "arbitrary" (*i.e.,* intentional and unfounded) discrimination from two other phenomena. One involves differentiation of employees based on a genuine relationship between age and ability to perform a job. In this connection, the Report examined "circumstances which unquestionably affect older workers more strongly, as a group, than they do younger workers," including questions of health, educational attainment, and technological change. In addition, the Report assessed "institutional arrangements"—such as seniority rules, workers' compensation laws, and pension plans—which, though intended to benefit older workers, might actually make employers less likely to hire or retain them.

… Congress' decision not to authorize disparate impact claims is understandable in light of the questionable utility of such claims in the age-discrimination context. No one would argue that older workers have suffered disadvantages as a result of entrenched historical patterns of discrimination, like racial minorities have. Accordingly, disparate impact liability under the ADEA cannot be justified, and is not necessary, as a means of redressing the cumulative results of past discrimination.

Moreover, the Wirtz Report correctly concluded that—unlike the classifications protected by Title VII—there often *is* a correlation between an individual's age and her ability to perform a job. That is to be expected, for "physical ability generally declines with age." [citation omitted]. Perhaps more importantly, advances in technology and increasing access to formal education often leave older workers at a competitive disadvantage vis-á-vis younger workers. Beyond these performance-affecting factors, there is also the fact that many employment benefits, such as salary, vacation time, and so forth, increase as an employee gains experience and seniority. Accordingly, many employer decisions that are intended to cut costs or respond to market forces will likely have a disproportionate effect on older workers. Given the myriad ways in which legitimate business practices can have a disparate impact on older workers, it is hardly surprising that Congress declined to subject employers to civil liability based solely on such effects....

## Subsequent Developments

Although the *City of Jackson* case recognized disparate impact claims were cognizable under the ADEA, it was unclear how courts should analyze these claims. In *Meacham v. Knolls Atomic Power Laboratory*, 554 U.S. 84 (2008), the Court discussed whether the *Wards Cove* framework would apply in ADEA cases.

The Court explained:

> Although *City of Jackson* contains the statement that "*Wards Cove*'s pre-1991 inter-pretation of Title VII's identical language remains applicable to the ADEA," *City of Jackson* made only two specific references to aspects of the *Wards Cove* interpretation of Title VII that might have "remain[ed] applicable" in ADEA cases. One was to the existence of disparate-impact liability, which *City of Jackson* explained was narrower in ADEA cases than under Title VII. The other was to a plaintiff-employee's burden of identifying which particular practices allegedly cause an observed disparate impact, which is the employee's burden under both the ADEA and the pre-1991 Title VII.

*Id.* at 98.

The Court reiterated that the business necessity inquiry should have no place in ADEA disparate impact cases. *Id.* Instead, once the plaintiff has proven the existence of the disparate impact, the defendant bears the burden of establishing that the practice or policy is based on a reasonable factor other than age. *Id.* In other words, the reasonable factor other than age inquiry is an affirmative defense, on which the employer bears the burdens of production and persuasion.

In 2012, the EEOC issued new regulations explaining how it construes the reasonable factor other than age defense. Those regulations provide as follows:

> (e)(1) A reasonable factor other than age is a non-age factor that is objectively reasonable when viewed from the position of a prudent employer mindful of its responsibilities under the ADEA under like circumstances. Whether a differentiation is based on reasonable factors other than age must be decided on the basis of all the particular facts and circumstances surrounding each individual situation. To establish the RFOA defense, an employer must show that the employment practice was both reasonably designed to further or achieve a legitimate business purpose and administered in a way that reasonably achieves that purpose in light of the particular facts and circumstances that were known, or should have been known, to the employer.

> (2) Considerations that are relevant to whether a practice is based on a reasonable factor other than age include, but are not limited to:

> (i) The extent to which the factor is related to the employer's stated business purpose;

(ii) The extent to which the employer defined the factor accurately and applied the factor fairly and accurately, including the extent to which managers and supervisors were given guidance or training about how to apply the factor and avoid discrimination;

(iii) The extent to which the employer limited supervisors' discretion to assess employees subjectively, particularly where the criteria that the supervisors were asked to evaluate are known to be subject to negative age-based stereotypes;

(iv) The extent to which the employer assessed the adverse impact of its employment practice on older workers; and

(v) The degree of the harm to individuals within the protected age group, in terms of both the extent of injury and the numbers of persons adversely affected, and the extent to which the employer took steps to reduce the harm, in light of the burden of undertaking such steps.

(3) No specific consideration or combination of considerations need be present for a differentiation to be based on reasonable factors other than age. Nor does the presence of one of these considerations automatically establish the defense.

29 U.S.C. § 1625.7.

The regulation further provides that a differentiation based on the average cost of employing older workers is also unlawful under the ADEA, except as to employee benefit plans. *Id.* at § 1625.7(f). As of the printing of this book, there has been no significant litigation considering how and whether courts will apply the EEOC's interpretation.

---

## Exercise 4.5

Targo is a company that makes parts for naval nuclear reactors. Since the end of the Cold War, the demand for such reactors has continually decreased. Targo undertakes a reduction-in-force to make the size of its work force compatible with the demand for its products. To determine which employees would be subjected to the reduction-in-force, the company told its managers to score subordinates on three dimensions: performance, flexibility, and critical skills. The scores were totaled, along with points for years of service. Individuals with the lowest total scores were fired.

The performance score was based on the worker's two most recent appraisals. To rate flexibility, the managers were instructed to do the following: "Rate the employee's flexibility within the Company. Can his or her documented skills be used in other assignments that will add value to current or future Company work? Is the employee retrainable for other Company assignments?" To assess critical skills, managers were instructed to determine how critical the employee's skills were to continuing work of the Company and whether the skills the employee had were possessed by others in the Company or generally available from the external market.

Of the 31 salaried employees laid off, 30 were at least 40 years old. The workers have statistical expert evidence that results so skewed according to age could rarely occur by chance; and that the scores for flexibility and criticality, over which managers had the most discretionary judgment, had the closest statistical ties to the outcomes.

You are an associate at a plaintiff's law firm. A partner at the firm has asked you to *write* a short memo assessing the workers' case. What test will a court use to assess the workers' claims? What are the strengths and weaknesses of the workers' case? What other information would you need to proceed? Do you think the workers can prevail on a disparate impact claim?

Now change the facts slightly for a second memo. What if the same set of facts applied, except 30 of the individuals laid off were women? Assess the same issues contained in the prior paragraph. Do the workers have a better chance of prevailing if they proceed on an age claim or a sex claim? Why?

---

## ➤ Beyond the Basics: Disparate Impact and the ADA

A disparate impact claim is cognizable under the ADA; however, courts have not fully explored the analytical framework that would be applied to such claims. When Congress codified the disparate impact framework for Title VII in 1991, it did not make similar amendments to the ADA.

However, the ADA has different statutory language than Title VII that likely impacts how courts would approach such claims. The ADA prohibits the use of "qualification standards, employment tests or other selection criteria that screen out or tend to screen out an individual with a disability or a class of individuals with disabilities unless the standard, test or other selection criteria, as used by the covered entity, is shown to be job-related for the position in question and is consistent with business necessity." 42 U.S.C. § 12112(b)(6). Also the ADA requires that tests be administered and selected "in the most effective manner to ensure that, when such test is administered to a job applicant or employee who has a disability that impairs sensory, manual, or speaking skills, such test results accurately reflect the skills, aptitude, or whatever other factor of such applicant or employee that such test purports to measure, rather than reflecting the impaired sensory, manual, or speaking skills of such employee or applicant (except where such skills are the factors that the test purports to measure)." 42 U.S.C. § 12112(b)(7).

Attorneys litigating an ADA disparate impact claim should be prepared to argue for the imposition of whatever framework best supports the case, knowing that the attorney may need to be flexible and prepared to argue his or her case under numerous frameworks.

---

## ✦ Core Concept: Choices Made to Avoid Disparate Impact Liability May Lead to Disparate Treatment Claims

### Focus Questions: *Ricci v. DeStefano*

1. *What practical problems with disparate impact analysis does this case highlight?*

2. *Why does the Court detail Ricci's preparation for the test and note that he has dyslexia?*

3. *Does this case represent a change from the assumptions that motivated the Supreme Court's decision in* Griggs?

4.  *Are you satisfied by the way that the Court applied the test it announced in this case to the facts of the case?*

5.  *What does the firefighter's test examine?*

---

# Ricci v. DeStefano

## 557 U.S. 557 (2009)

Justice Kennedy delivered the opinion of the Court.

... In 2003, 118 New Haven firefighters took examinations to qualify for promotion to the rank of lieutenant or captain. Promotion examinations in New Haven (or City) were infrequent, so the stakes were high. The results would determine which firefighters would be considered for promotions during the next two years, and the order in which they would be considered. Many firefighters studied for months, at considerable personal and financial cost.

When the examination results showed that white candidates had outperformed minority candidates, the mayor and other local politicians opened a public debate that turned rancorous. Some firefighters argued the tests should be discarded because the results showed the tests to be discriminatory. They threatened a discrimination lawsuit if the City made promotions based on the tests. Other firefighters said the exams were neutral and fair. And they, in turn, threatened a discrimination lawsuit if the City, relying on the statistical racial disparity, ignored the test results and denied promotions to the candidates who had performed well. In the end the City took the side of those who protested the test results. It threw out the examinations.

Certain white and Hispanic firefighters who likely would have been promoted based on their good test performance sued the City and some of its officials. Theirs is the suit now before us. The suit alleges that, by discarding the test results, the City and the named officials discriminated against the plaintiffs based on their race, in violation of both Title VII and the Equal Protection Clause of the Fourteenth Amendment. The City and the officials defended their actions, arguing that if they had certified the results, they could have faced liability under Title VII for adopting a practice that had a disparate impact on the minority firefighters. The District Court granted summary judgment for the defendants, and the Court of Appeals affirmed.

We conclude that race-based action like the City's in this case is impermissible under Title VII unless the employer can demonstrate a strong basis in evidence that, had it not taken the action, it would have been liable under the disparate-impact statute. The respondents, we further determine, cannot meet that threshold standard. As a result, the City's action in discarding the tests was a violation of Title VII. In light of our ruling under the statutes, we need not reach the question whether respondents' actions may have violated the Equal Protection Clause.

I

...

A

When the City of New Haven undertook to fill vacant lieutenant and captain positions in its fire department (Department), the promotion and hiring process was governed by the city charter, in addition to federal and state law. The charter establishes a merit system. That system requires the City to fill vacancies in the classified civil-service ranks with the most qualified individuals, as determined by job-related examinations. After each examination, the New Haven Civil Service Board (CSB) certifies a ranked list of applicants who passed the test. Under the charter's "rule of three," the relevant hiring authority must fill each vacancy by choosing one candidate from the top three scorers on the list. Certified promotional lists remain valid for two years.

The City's contract with the New Haven firefighters' union specifies additional requirements for the promotion process. Under the contract, applicants for lieutenant and captain positions were to be screened using written and oral examinations, with the written exam accounting for 60 percent and the oral exam 40 percent of an applicant's total score. To sit for the examinations, candidates for lieutenant needed 30 months' experience in the Department, a high-school diploma, and certain vocational training courses. Candidates for captain needed one year's service as a lieutenant in the Department, a high-school diploma, and certain vocational training courses.

After reviewing bids from various consultants, the City hired Industrial/Organizational Solutions, Inc. (IOS) to develop and administer the examinations, at a cost to the City of $100,000. IOS is an Illinois company that specializes in designing entry-level and promotional examinations for fire and police departments. In order to fit the examinations to the New Haven Department, IOS began the test-design process by performing job analyses to identify the tasks, knowledge, skills, and abilities that are essential for the lieutenant and captain positions. IOS representatives interviewed incumbent captains and lieutenants and their supervisors. They rode with and observed other on-duty officers. Using information from those interviews and ride-alongs, IOS wrote job-analysis questionnaires and administered them to most of the incumbent battalion chiefs, captains, and lieutenants in the Department. At every stage of the job analyses, IOS, by deliberate choice, oversampled minority firefighters to ensure that the results—which IOS would use to develop the examinations—would not unintentionally favor white candidates.

With the job-analysis information in hand, IOS developed the written examinations to measure the candidates' job-related knowledge. For each test, IOS compiled a list of training manuals, Department procedures, and other materials to use as sources for the test questions. IOS presented the proposed sources to the New Haven fire chief and assistant fire chief for their approval. Then, using the approved sources, IOS drafted a multiple-choice test for each position. Each test had 100 questions, as required by CSB rules, and was written below a 10th-grade reading level. After IOS prepared the tests, the City opened a 3-month study period. It gave candidates a list that identified the source material for the questions, including the specific chapters from which the questions were taken.

IOS developed the oral examinations as well. These concentrated on job skills and abilities. Using the job-analysis information, IOS wrote hypothetical situations to test incident-command skills, firefighting tactics, interpersonal skills, leadership, and management ability, among other things. Candidates would be presented with these hypotheticals and asked to respond before a panel of three assessors.

IOS assembled a pool of 30 assessors who were superior in rank to the positions being tested. At the City's insistence (because of controversy surrounding previous examinations), all the assessors came from outside Connecticut. IOS submitted the assessors' resumes to City officials for approval. They were battalion chiefs, assistant chiefs, and chiefs from departments of similar sizes to New Haven's throughout the country. Sixty-six percent of the panelists were minorities, and each of the nine three-member assessment panels contained two minority members. IOS trained the panelists for several hours on the day before it administered the examinations, teaching them how to score the candidates' responses consistently using checklists of desired criteria.

Candidates took the examinations in November and December 2003. Seventy-seven candidates completed the lieutenant examination—43 whites, 19 blacks, and 15 Hispanics. Of those, 34 candidates passed—25 whites, 6 blacks, and 3 Hispanics. Eight lieutenant positions were vacant at the time of the examination. As the rule of three operated, this meant that the top 10 candidates were eligible for an immediate promotion to lieutenant. All 10 were white. Subsequent vacancies would have allowed at least 3 black candidates to be considered for promotion to lieutenant.

Forty-one candidates completed the captain examination—25 whites, 8 blacks, and 8 Hispanics. Of those, 22 candidates passed—16 whites, 3 blacks, and 3 Hispanics. Seven captain positions were vacant at the time of the examination. Under the rule of three, 9 candidates were eligible for an immediate promotion to captain—7 whites and 2 Hispanics.

### B

[I]n January 2004, ... City officials, including the City's counsel, Thomas Ude, convened a meeting with IOS Vice President Chad Legel. (Legel was the leader of the IOS team that developed and administered the tests.) Based on the test results, the City officials expressed concern that the tests had discriminated against minority candidates. [On behalf of IOS,] Legel defended the examinations' validity, stating that any numerical disparity between white and minority candidates was likely due to various external factors and was in line with results of the Department's previous promotional examinations.

Several days after the meeting, Ude sent a letter to the CSB purporting to outline its duties with respect to the examination results. Ude stated that under federal law, "a statistical demonstration of disparate impact," standing alone, "constitutes a sufficiently serious claim of racial discrimination to serve as a predicate for employer-initiated, voluntar[y] remedies—even ... race-conscious remedies."

### 1

[A series of meetings was held to discuss the test results.] Although they did not know whether they had passed or failed, some firefighter-candidates spoke at the first CSB meeting in favor of certifying the test results. Michael Blatchley stated that "[e]very one" of the questions on the written examination "came from the [study] material.... [I]f you read the materials and you studied the material, you would have done well on the test." Frank Ricci stated that the test questions were based on the Department's own rules and procedures and on "nationally recognized" materials that represented the "accepted standard[s]" for firefighting. Ricci stated that he had "several learning disabilities," including dyslexia; that he had spent more than $1,000 to purchase the materials and pay his neighbor to read them on tape so he could "give it [his] best shot"; and that he had studied "8 to 13 hours a day to prepare" for the test. "I don't even know if I made it," Ricci told the CSB, "[b]ut the people who passed should be promoted. When your life's on the line, second best may not be good enough."

Other firefighters spoke against certifying the test results. They described the test questions as outdated or not relevant to firefighting practices in New Haven. Gary Tinney stated that source materials "came out of New York.... Their makeup of their city and everything is totally different than ours." And they criticized the test materials, a full set of which cost about $500, for being too expensive and too long.

2

At a second CSB meeting, on February 5, the president of the New Haven firefighters' union asked the CSB to perform a validation study to determine whether the tests were job-related. Petitioners' counsel in this action argued that the CSB should certify the results. A representative of the International Association of Black Professional Firefighters, Donald Day from neighboring Bridgeport, Connecticut, "beseech[ed]" the CSB "to throw away that test," which he described as "inherently unfair" because of the racial distribution of the results. Another Bridgeport-based representative of the association, Ronald Mackey, stated that a validation study was necessary. He suggested that the City could "adjust" the test results to "meet the criteria of having a certain amount of minorities get elevated to the rank of Lieutenant and Captain."

[Section 3, which discusses a third meeting, is omitted.]

4

At the next meeting, on March 11, the CSB heard from three witnesses it had selected to "tell us a little bit about their views of the testing, the process, [and] the methodology." The first, Christopher Hornick, spoke to the CSB by telephone. Hornick is an industrial/ organizational psychologist from Texas who operates a consulting business that "direct[ly]" competes with IOS. Hornick, who had not "stud[ied] the test at length or in detail" and had not "seen the job analysis data," told the CSB that the scores indicated a "relatively high adverse impact." He stated that "[n]ormally, whites outperform ethnic minorities on the majority of standardized testing procedures," but that he was "a little surprised" by the disparity in the candidates' scores—although "[s]ome of it is fairly typical of what we've seen in other areas of the countr[y] and other tests." Hornick stated that the "adverse impact on the written exam was somewhat higher but generally in the range that we've seen professionally."

When asked to explain the New Haven test results, Hornick opined in the telephone conversation that the collective-bargaining agreement's requirement of using written and oral examinations with a 60/40 composite score might account for the statistical disparity. He also stated that "[b]y not having anyone from within the [D]epartment review" the tests before they were administered—a limitation the City had imposed to protect the security of the exam questions—"you inevitably get things in there" that are based on the source materials but are not relevant to New Haven. Hornick suggested that testing candidates at an "assessment center" rather than using written and oral examinations "might serve [the City's] needs better." Hornick stated that assessment centers, where candidates face real-world situations and respond just as they would in the field, allow candidates "to demonstrate how they would address a particular problem as opposed to just verbally saying it or identifying the correct option on a written test."

...

The second witness was Vincent Lewis, a fire program specialist for the Department of Homeland Security and a retired fire captain from Michigan. Lewis, who is black, had looked "extensively" at the lieutenant exam and "a little less extensively" at the captain exam. He stated that the candidates "should know that material." In Lewis's view, the "questions were relevant for both exams," and the New Haven candidates had an advantage because the study materials identified the particular book chapters from which the questions were taken. In other departments, by contrast, "you had to know basically the ... entire book." Lewis concluded that any disparate impact likely was due to a pattern that "usually whites outperform some of the minorities on testing," or that "more whites ... take the exam."

Janet Helms, a professor at Boston College whose "primary area of expertise" is "not with firefighters per se" but in "race and culture as they influence performance on tests and other assessment procedures," expressly declined to review the examinations, [and stated] that no matter what test the City had administered, it would have revealed "a disparity between blacks and whites, Hispanics and whites," particularly on a written test.

### 5

At the final CSB meeting, on March 18, Ude (the City's counsel) argued against certifying the examination results.... Ude focused the CSB on determining "whether there are other ways to test for ... those positions that are equally valid with less adverse impact." Ude described Hornick as having said that the written examination "had one of the most severe adverse impacts that he had seen." ... and that "there are much better alternatives to identifying [firefighting] skills." Ude offered his "opinion that promotions ... as a result of these tests would not be consistent with federal law, would not be consistent with the purposes of our Civil Service Rules or our Charter[,] nor is it in the best interests of the firefighters ... who took the exams." He stated that previous Department exams "have not had this kind of result," and that previous results had not been "challenged as having adverse impact, whereas we are assured that these will be."

...

Karen DuBois-Walton, the City's chief administrative officer, spoke on behalf of Mayor John DeStefano and argued against certifying the results.... DuBois-Walton also relied on Hornick's testimony, asserting that Hornick "made it extremely clear that ... there are more appropriate ways to assess one's ability to serve" as a captain or lieutenant.

Burgett (the human resources director) asked the CSB to discard the examination results. She, too, relied on Hornick's statement to show the existence of alternative testing methods....

Other witnesses addressed the CSB. They included the president of the New Haven firefighters' union, who supported certification. He reminded the CSB that Hornick "also concluded that the tests were reasonable and fair and under the current structure to certify them." Firefighter Frank Ricci again argued for certification; he stated that although "assessment centers in some cases show less adverse impact," they were not available alternatives for the current round of promotions.... It would take several years, Ricci explained, for the Department to develop an assessment-center protocol and the accompanying training materials....

At the close of witness testimony, the CSB voted on a motion to certify the examinations. With one member recused, the CSB deadlocked 2 to 2, resulting in a decision not to certify the results....

### C

The CSB's decision not to certify the examination results led to this lawsuit. The plaintiffs—who are the petitioners here—are 17 white firefighters and 1 Hispanic firefighter who passed the examinations but were denied a chance at promotions....

Petitioners sued the City ... asserting that the City violated the disparate-treatment prohibition contained in Title VII.

The parties filed cross-motions for summary judgment. Respondents asserted they had a good-faith belief that they would have violated the disparate-impact prohibition in Title VII had they certified the examination results. It follows, they maintained, that they cannot be held liable under Title VII's disparate-treatment provision for attempting to comply with Title VII's disparate-impact bar. Petitioners countered that respondents' good-faith belief was not a valid defense to allegations of disparate treatment and unconstitutional discrimination.

The District Court granted summary judgment for respondents.... It concluded that respondents' actions were not "based on race" because "all applicants took the same test, and the result was the same for all because the test results were discarded and nobody was promoted." ...

## II

Petitioners raise a statutory claim, under the disparate-treatment prohibition of Title VII, and a constitutional claim, under the Equal Protection Clause of the Fourteenth Amendment. A decision for petitioners on their statutory claim would provide the relief sought, so we consider it first.

## A

... The Civil Rights Act of 1964 did not include an express prohibition on policies or practices that produce a disparate impact. But in *Griggs v. Duke Power Co.,* 401 U.S. 424 (1971), the Court interpreted the Act to prohibit, in some cases, employers' facially neutral practices that, in fact, are "discriminatory in operation." ...

Twenty years after *Griggs,* the Civil Rights Act of 1991 [codified] the prohibition on disparate-impact discrimination.... Under the disparate-impact statute, a plaintiff establishes a prima facie violation by showing that an employer uses "a particular employment practice that causes a disparate impact on the basis of race, color, religion, sex, or national origin." 42 U.S.C. § 2000e-2(k)(1)(A)(i). An employer may defend against liability by demonstrating that the practice is "job related for the position in question and consistent with business necessity." Even if the employer meets that burden, however, a plaintiff may still succeed by showing that the employer refuses to adopt an available alternative employment practice that has less disparate impact and serves the employer's legitimate needs.

## B

Petitioners allege that when the CSB refused to certify the captain and lieutenant exam results based on the race of the successful candidates, it discriminated against them in violation of Title VII's disparate-treatment provision. The City counters that its decision was permissible because the tests "appear[ed] to violate Title VII's disparate-impact provisions." Our analysis begins with this premise: The City's actions would violate the disparate-treatment prohibition of Title VII absent some valid defense. All the evidence demonstrates that ... the City rejected the test results because "too many whites and not enough minorities would be promoted were the lists to be certified." Without some other justification, this express, race-based decisionmaking violates Title VII.

... Whatever the City's ultimate aim—however well intentioned or benevolent it might have seemed—the City made its employment decision because of race. The City rejected the test results solely because the higher scoring candidates were white. The question is not whether that conduct was discriminatory but whether the City had a lawful justification for its race-based action.

...

We consider, therefore, whether the purpose to avoid disparate-impact liability excuses what otherwise would be prohibited disparate-treatment discrimination....

With these principles in mind, we turn to the parties' proposed means of reconciling the statutory provisions. Petitioners take a strict approach, arguing that under Title VII, it cannot be permissible for an employer to take race-based adverse employment actions in order to avoid disparate-impact liability—even if the employer knows its practice violates the disparate-impact provision.... That assertion, however, ignores the fact that, by codifying the disparate-impact provision in 1991, Congress has expressly prohibited both types of discrimination. We must interpret the statute to give effect to both provisions where possible. We cannot accept petitioners' broad and inflexible formulation.

Petitioners next suggest that an employer in fact must be in violation of the disparate-impact provision before it can use compliance as a defense in a disparate-treatment suit. Again, this is overly simplistic and too restrictive of Title VII's purpose. The rule petitioners offer would run counter to what we have recognized as Congress's intent that "voluntary compliance" be "the preferred means of achieving the objectives of Title VII." [citation omitted]. Forbidding employers to act unless they know, with certainty, that a practice violates the disparate-impact provision would bring compliance efforts to a near standstill. Even in the limited situations when this restricted standard could be met, employers likely would hesitate before taking voluntary action for fear of later being proven wrong in the course of litigation and then held to account for disparate treatment.

At the opposite end of the spectrum, respondents and the Government assert that an employer's good-faith belief that its actions are necessary to comply with Title VII's disparate-impact provision should be enough to justify race-conscious conduct.... When Congress codified the disparate-impact provision in 1991, it made no exception to disparate-treatment liability for actions taken in a good-faith effort to comply with the new, disparate-impact provision.... Allowing employers to violate the disparate-treatment prohibition based on a mere good-faith fear of disparate-impact liability would encourage race-based action at the slightest hint of disparate impact. A minimal standard could cause employers to discard the results of lawful and beneficial promotional examinations even where there is little if any evidence of disparate-impact discrimination. That would amount to a *de facto* quota system, in which a "focus on statistics ... could put undue pressure on employers to adopt inappropriate prophylactic measures." [citation omitted]. Even worse, an employer could discard test results (or other employment practices) with the intent of obtaining the employer's preferred racial balance. That operational principle could not be justified, for Title VII is express in disclaiming any interpretation of its requirements as calling for outright racial balancing. § 2000e-2(j). The purpose of Title VII "is to promote hiring on the basis of job qualifications, rather than on the basis of race or color." [citation omitted].

In [the context of constitutional challenges to affirmative action,] this Court ... has held that certain government actions to remedy past racial discrimination—actions that are themselves based on race—are constitutional only where there is a "strong basis in evidence" that the remedial actions were necessary. [citation omitted]. This suit does not call on us to consider whether the statutory constraints under Title VII must be parallel in all respects to those under the Constitution. That does not mean the constitutional authorities are irrelevant, however....

Writing for a plurality in *Wygant* [*v. Jackson Board of Education*, 476 U.S. 267 (1986)] and announcing the strong-basis-in-evidence standard, Justice Powell recognized the tension between eliminating segregation and discrimination on the one hand and doing away with all governmentally imposed discrimination based on race on the other. The plurality stated that those "related constitutional duties are not always harmonious," and that "reconciling them requires ... employers to act with extraordinary care." [citation omitted]. The plurality required a strong basis in evidence because "[e]videntiary support for the conclusion that remedial action is warranted becomes crucial when the remedial program is challenged in court by nonminority employees." [citation omitted]. The Court applied the same standard in [*City of Richmond v. Croson,* 488 U.S. 469 (1989)], observing that "an amorphous claim that there has been past discrimination … cannot justify the use of an unyielding racial quota." [citation omitted].

The same interests are at work in the interplay between the disparate-treatment and disparate-impact provisions of Title VII.… Applying the strong-basis-in-evidence standard to Title VII gives effect to both the disparate-treatment and disparate-impact provisions, allowing violations of one in the name of compliance with the other only in certain, narrow circumstances. The standard leaves ample room for employers' voluntary compliance efforts, which are essential to the statutory scheme and to Congress's efforts to eradicate workplace discrimination. And the standard appropriately constrains employers' discretion in making race-based decisions: It limits that discretion to cases in which there is a strong basis in evidence of disparate-impact liability, but it is not so restrictive that it allows employers to act only when there is a provable, actual violation.

Resolving the statutory conflict in this way allows the disparate-impact prohibition to work in a manner that is consistent with other provisions of Title VII, including the prohibition on adjusting employment-related test scores on the basis of race. *See* § 2000e-2(*l*). Examinations like those administered by the City create legitimate expectations on the part of those who took the tests. As is the case with any promotion exam, some of the firefighters here invested substantial time, money, and personal commitment in preparing for the tests. Employment tests can be an important part of a neutral selection system that safeguards against the very racial animosities Title VII was intended to prevent. Here, however, the firefighters saw their efforts invalidated by the City in sole reliance upon race-based statistics.

If an employer cannot rescore a test based on the candidates' race, § 2000e-2(*l*), then it follows *a fortiori* that it may not take the greater step of discarding the test altogether to achieve a more desirable racial distribution of promotion-eligible candidates—absent a strong basis in evidence that the test was deficient and that discarding the results is necessary to avoid violating the disparate-impact provision. Restricting an employer's ability to discard test results (and thereby discriminate against qualified candidates on the basis of their race) also is in keeping with Title VII's express protection of bona fide promotional examinations.

For the foregoing reasons, we adopt the strong-basis-in-evidence standard as a matter of statutory construction to resolve any conflict between the disparate-treatment and disparate-impact provisions of Title VII.

. . .

Title VII does not prohibit an employer from considering, before administering a test or practice, how to design that test or practice in order to provide a fair opportunity for all individuals, regardless of their race. And when, during the test-design stage, an employer invites comments to ensure the test is fair, that process can provide a common ground for open discussions toward that end. We hold only that, under Title VII, before an employer can engage in intentional discrimination for the asserted purpose of avoiding or remedying an unintentional disparate impact, the employer must have a strong basis in evidence to believe it will be subject to disparate-impact liability if it fails to take the race-conscious, discriminatory action.

## C

The City argues that, even under the strong-basis-in-evidence standard, its decision to discard the examination results was permissible under Title VII. That is incorrect. Even if respondents were motivated as a subjective matter by a desire to avoid committing disparate-impact discrimination, the record makes clear there is no support for the conclusion that respondents had an objective, strong basis in evidence to find the tests inadequate, with some consequent disparate-impact liability in violation of Title VII.

... The racial adverse impact here was significant, and petitioners do not dispute that the City was faced with a prima facie case of disparate-impact liability.... The pass rates of minorities, which were approximately one-half the pass rates for white candidates, fall well below the 80-percent standard....

The problem for respondents is that a prima facie case of disparate-impact liability — essentially, a threshold showing of a significant statistical disparity, *Connecticut v. Teal*, 457 U.S. 440, 446 (1982), and nothing more — is far from a strong basis in evidence that the City would have been liable under Title VII had it certified the results. That is because the City could be liable for disparate-impact discrimination only if the examinations were not job related and consistent with business necessity, or if there existed an equally valid, less-discriminatory alternative that served the City's needs but that the City refused to adopt. We conclude there is no strong basis in evidence to establish that the test was deficient in either of these respects....

1

There is no genuine dispute that the examinations were job-related and consistent with business necessity. The City's assertions to the contrary are "blatantly contradicted by the record." ... Of the outside witnesses who appeared before the CSB, only one, Vincent Lewis, had reviewed the examinations in any detail, and he was the only one with any firefighting experience. Lewis stated that the "questions were relevant for both exams." The only other witness who had seen any part of the examinations, Christopher Hornick (a competitor of IOS's), criticized the fact that no one within the Department had reviewed the tests — a condition imposed by the City to protect the integrity of the exams in light of past alleged security breaches. But Hornick stated that the exams "appea[r] to be ... reasonably good" and recommended that the CSB certify the results.

... The City, moreover, turned a blind eye to evidence that supported the exams' validity.... IOS stood ready to provide respondents with detailed information to establish the validity of the exams, but respondents did not accept that offer.

2

Respondents also lacked a strong basis in evidence of an equally valid, less-discriminatory testing alternative that the City, by certifying the examination results, would necessarily have refused to adopt. Respondents raise three arguments to the contrary, but each argument fails. First, respondents refer to testimony before the CSB that a different composite-score calculation — weighting the written and oral examination scores 30/70 — would have allowed the City to consider two black candidates for then-open lieutenant positions and one black candidate for then-open captain positions. (The City used a 60/40 weighting as required by its contract with the New Haven firefighters' union.) But respondents have produced no evidence to show that the 60/40 weighting was indeed arbitrary. In fact, because that formula was the result of a union-negotiated collective-bargaining agreement, we presume the parties negotiated that weighting for a rational reason. Nor does the record contain any evidence that the 30/70 weighting would be an equally valid way to determine whether candidates possess the proper mix of job knowledge and situational skills to earn promotions. Changing the weighting formula, moreover, could well have violated Title VII's prohibition of altering test scores on the basis of race. *See* § 2000e-2(*l*). On this record, there is no basis to conclude that a 30/70 weighting was an equally valid alternative the City could have adopted.

. . .

[R]espondents refer to statements by Hornick in his telephone interview with the CSB regarding alternatives to the written examinations. Hornick stated his "belie[f]" that an "assessment center process," which would have evaluated candidates' behavior in typical job tasks, "would have demonstrated less adverse impact." [citation omitted]. But Hornick's brief mention of alternative testing methods, standing alone, does not raise a genuine issue of material fact that assessment centers were available to the City at the time of the examinations and that they would have produced less adverse impact. Other statements to the CSB indicated that the Department could not have used assessment centers for the 2003 examinations.... Especially when it is noted that the strong-basis-in-evidence standard applies, respondents cannot create a genuine issue of fact based on a few stray (and contradictory) statements in the record. And there is no doubt respondents fall short of the mark by relying entirely on isolated statements by Hornick. Hornick had not "stud[ied] the test at length or in detail." And as he told the CSB, he is a "direct competitor" of IOS's. The remainder of his remarks showed that Hornick's primary concern — somewhat to the frustration of CSB members — was marketing his services for the future, not commenting on the results of the tests the City had already administered. Hornick's hinting had its intended effect: The City has since hired him as a consultant. As for the other outside witnesses who spoke to the CSB, Vincent Lewis (the retired fire captain) thought the CSB should certify the test results. And Janet Helms (the Boston College professor) declined to review the examinations and told the CSB that, as a society, "we need to develop a new way of assessing people." That task was beyond the reach of the CSB, which was concerned with the adequacy of the test results before it.

. . .

Justice Alito, with whom Justice Scalia and Justice Thomas join, concurring.

... As initially described by the dissent, the process by which the City reached the decision not to accept the test results was open, honest, serious, and deliberative. But even the District Court admitted that "a jury could rationally infer that city officials worked behind the scenes to sabotage the promotional examinations because they knew that, were the exams certified, the Mayor would incur the wrath of [Rev. Boise] Kimber and other influential leaders of New Haven's African-American community." [citations to record omitted throughout].

This admission finds ample support in the record. Reverend Boise Kimber, to whom the District Court referred, is a politically powerful New Haven pastor and a self-professed "kingmaker." On one occasion, "[i]n front of TV cameras, he threatened a race riot during the murder trial of the black man arrested for killing white Yalie Christian Prince. He continues to call whites racist if they question his actions."

Reverend Kimber's personal ties with seven-term New Haven Mayor John DeStefano (Mayor) stretch back more than a decade....

Almost immediately after the test results were revealed in "early January" 2004, Rev. Kimber called the City's Chief Administrative Officer, Karen Dubois-Walton, who "acts 'on behalf of the Mayor.'" Dubois-Walton and Rev. Kimber met privately in her office because he wanted "to express his opinion" about the test results and "to have some influence" over the City's response. As discussed in further detail below, Rev. Kimber adamantly opposed certification of the test results—a fact that he or someone in the Mayor's office eventually conveyed to the Mayor.

... [O]n January 13, 2004, Chad Legel, who had designed the tests, flew from Chicago to New Haven to meet with Dubois-Walton, Burgett, and Thomas Ude, the City's corporate counsel. "Legel outlined the merits of the examination and why city officials should be confident in the validity of the results." But according to Legel, Dubois-Walton was "argumentative" and apparently had already made up her mind that the tests were "discriminatory." Again according to Legel, "[a] theme" of the meeting was "the political and racial overtones of what was going on in the City." "Legel came away from the January 13, 2004 meeting with the impression that defendants were already leaning toward discarding the examination results."

On January 22, 2004, the Civil Service Board (CSB or Board) convened its first public meeting. Almost immediately, Rev. Kimber began to exert political pressure on the CSB. He began a loud, minutes-long outburst that required the CSB Chairman to shout him down and hold him out of order three times.

Four days after the CSB's first meeting, Mayor DeStefano's executive aide sent an e-mail to Dubois-Walton, Burgett, and Ude. The message clearly indicated that the Mayor had made up his mind to oppose certification of the test results (but nevertheless wanted to conceal that fact from the public): "I wanted to make sure we are all on the same page for this meeting tomorrow.... *[L]et's remember, that these folks are not against certification yet. So we can't go in and tell them that is our position;* we have to deliberate and arrive there as the fairest and most cogent outcome."

On February 5, 2004, the CSB convened its second public meeting. Reverend Kimber again testified and threatened the CSB with political recriminations if they voted to certify the test results: "I look at this [Board] tonight. I look at three whites and one Hispanic and no blacks.... I would hope that you would not put yourself in this type of position, *a political ramification that may come back upon you* as you sit on this [Board] and decide the future of a department and the future of those who are being promoted."

...

One of Rev. Kimber's "friends and allies," Lieutenant Gary Tinney, also exacerbated racial tensions before the CSB. After some firefighters applauded in support of certifying the test results, "Lt. Tinney exclaimed, 'Listen to the Klansmen behind us.'"

... Taking into account all the evidence in the summary judgment record, a reasonable jury could find the following. Almost as soon as the City disclosed the racial makeup of the list of firefighters who scored the highest on the exam, the City administration was lobbied by an influential community leader to scrap the test results, and the City administration decided on that course of action before making any real assessment of the possibility of a disparate-impact violation. To achieve that end, the City administration concealed its internal decision but worked—as things turned out, successfully—to persuade the CSB that acceptance of the test results would be illegal and would expose the City to disparate-impact liability. Taking this view of the evidence, a reasonable jury could easily find that the City's real reason for scrapping the test results was not a concern about violating the disparate-impact provision of Title VII but a simple desire to please a politically important racial constituency. It is noteworthy that the Solicitor General—whose position on the principal legal issue in this case is largely aligned with the dissent—concludes that "[n]either the district court nor the court of appeals ... adequately considered whether, viewing the evidence in the light most favorable to petitioners, a genuine issue of material fact remained whether respondents' claimed purpose to comply with Title VII was a pretext for intentional racial discrimination...."

...

Justice Ginsburg, with whom Justice Stevens, Justice Souter, and Justice Breyer join, dissenting.

In assessing claims of race discrimination, "[c]ontext matters." [citation omitted]. In 1972, Congress extended Title VII to cover public employment. At that time, municipal fire departments across the country, including New Haven's, pervasively discriminated against minorities. The extension of Title VII to cover jobs in firefighting effected no overnight change. It took decades of persistent effort, advanced by Title VII litigation, to open firefighting posts to members of racial minorities.

The white firefighters who scored high on New Haven's promotional exams understandably attract this Court's sympathy. But they had no vested right to promotion. Nor have other persons received promotions in preference to them. New Haven maintains that it refused to certify the test results because it believed, for good cause, that it would be vulnerable to a Title VII disparate-impact suit if it relied on those results. The Court today holds that New Haven has not demonstrated "a strong basis in evidence" for its plea. In so holding, the Court pretends that "[t]he City rejected the test results solely because the higher scoring candidates were white." That pretension, essential to the Court's disposition, ignores substantial evidence of multiple flaws in the tests New Haven used. The Court similarly fails to acknowledge the better tests used in other cities, which have yielded less racially skewed outcomes.[1]

## I
## A

... The Court's recitation of the facts leaves out important parts of the story. Firefighting is a profession in which the legacy of racial discrimination casts an especially long shadow. In extending Title VII to state and local government employers in 1972, Congress took note of a U.S. Commission on Civil Rights (USCCR) report finding racial discrimination in municipal employment even "more pervasive than in the private sector." According to the report, overt racism was partly to blame, but so too was a failure on the part of municipal employers to apply merit-based employment principles. In making hiring and promotion decisions, public employers often "rel[ied] on criteria unrelated to job performance," including nepotism or political patronage. Such flawed selection methods served to entrench preexisting racial hierarchies. The USCCR report singled out police and fire departments for having "[b]arriers to equal employment ... greater ... than in any other area of State or local government," with African-Americans "hold[ing] almost no positions in the officer ranks."

The city of New Haven (City) was no exception. In the early 1970's, African-Americans and Hispanics composed 30 percent of New Haven's population, but only 3.6 percent of the City's 502 firefighters. The racial disparity in the officer ranks was even more pronounced: "[O]f the 107 officers in the Department only one was black, and he held the lowest rank above private."

---

1. Never mind the flawed tests New Haven used and the better selection methods used elsewhere, Justice Alito's concurring opinion urges. Overriding all else, racial politics, fired up by a strident African-American pastor, were at work in New Haven. Even a detached and disinterested observer, however, would have every reason to ask: Why did such racially skewed results occur in New Haven, when better tests likely would have produced less disproportionate results?

Following a lawsuit and settlement agreement, the City initiated efforts to increase minority representation in the New Haven Fire Department (Department). Those litigation-induced efforts produced some positive change. New Haven's population includes a greater proportion of minorities today than it did in the 1970's: Nearly 40 percent of the City's residents are African-American and more than 20 percent are Hispanic. Among entry-level firefighters, minorities are still underrepresented, but not starkly so. As of 2003, African-Americans and Hispanics constituted 30 percent and 16 percent of the City's fire-fighters, respectively. In supervisory positions, however, significant disparities remain. Overall, the senior officer ranks (captain and higher) are nine percent African-American and nine percent Hispanic. Only one of the Department's 21 fire captains is African-American. It is against this backdrop of entrenched inequality that the promotion process at issue in this litigation should be assessed.

B

... New Haven, the record indicates, did not closely consider what sort of "practical" examination would "fairly measure the relative fitness and capacity of the applicants to discharge the duties" of a fire officer. Instead, the City simply adhered to the testing regime outlined in its two-decades-old contract with the local firefighters' union: a written exam, which would account for 60 percent of an applicant's total score, and an oral exam, which would account for the remaining 40 percent. In soliciting bids from exam development companies, New Haven made clear that it would entertain only "proposals that include a written component that will be weighted at 60%, and an oral component that will be weighted at 40%." Chad Legel, a representative of the winning bidder, Industrial/Organizational Solutions, Inc. (IOS), testified during his deposition that the City never asked whether alternative methods might better measure the qualities of a successful fire officer, including leadership skills and command presence.

[A discussion of the meetings held in New Haven is omitted.] A representative of the Northeast Region of the International Association of Black Professional Firefighters, Donald Day, also spoke at the second meeting. Statistical disparities, he told the CSB, had been present in the Department's previous promotional exams. On earlier tests, however, a few minority candidates had fared well enough to earn promotions. Day contrasted New Haven's experience with that of nearby Bridgeport, where minority firefighters held one-third of lieutenant and captain positions. Bridgeport, Day observed, had once used a testing process similar to New Haven's, with a written exam accounting for 70 percent of an applicant's score, an oral exam for 25 percent, and seniority for the remaining five percent. Bridgeport recognized, however, that the oral component, more so than the written component, addressed the sort of "real-life scenarios" fire officers encounter on the job. Accordingly, that city "changed the relative weights" to give primacy to the oral exam. Since that time, Day reported, Bridgeport had seen minorities "fairly represented" in its exam results.

... At its fourth meeting, CSB solicited the views of three individuals with testing-related expertise. Dr. Christopher Hornick, an industrial/organizational psychology consultant with 25 years' experience with police and firefighter testing, described the exam results as having "relatively high adverse impact." ... Hornick downplayed the notion of "facial neutrality." It was more important, he advised the CSB, to consider "the broader issue of how your procedures and your rules and the types of tests that you are using are contributing to the adverse impact."

Specifically, Hornick questioned New Haven's union-prompted 60/40 written/oral examination structure, noting the availability of "different types of testing procedures that are much more valid in terms of identifying the best potential supervisors in [the] fire department." He suggested, for example, "an assessment center process, which is essentially an opportunity for candidates ... to demonstrate how they would address a particular problem as opposed to just verbally saying it or identifying the correct option on a written test." Such selection processes, Hornick said, better "identif[y] the best possible people" and "demonstrate dramatically less adverse impacts." Hornick added: "I've spoken to at least 10,000, maybe 15,000 firefighters in group settings in my consulting practice and I have never one time ever had anyone in the fire service say to me, 'Well, the person who answers—gets the highest score on a written job knowledge, multiple-guess test makes the best company officer.' We know that it's not as valid as other procedures that exist."

...

Asked whether he thought the City should certify the results, Hornick hedged: "There is adverse impact in the test. That will be identified in any proceeding that you have. You will have industrial psychology experts, if it goes to court, on both sides. And it will not be a pretty or comfortable position for anyone to be in." Perhaps, he suggested, New Haven might certify the results but immediately begin exploring "alternative ways to deal with these issues" in the future.

...

As a result of today's decision, an employer who discards a dubious selection process can anticipate costly disparate-treatment litigation in which its chances for success—even for surviving a summary-judgment motion—are highly problematic. Concern about exposure to disparate-impact liability, however well grounded, is insufficient to insulate an employer from attack. Instead, the employer must make a "strong" showing that (1) its selection method was "not job related and consistent with business necessity," or (2) that it refused to adopt "an equally valid, less-discriminatory alternative." [citation omitted]. It is hard to see how these requirements differ from demanding that an employer establish "a provable, actual violation" *against itself.* [citation omitted].

... The Court stacks the deck further by denying respondents any chance to satisfy the newly announced strong-basis-in-evidence standard. When this Court formulates a new legal rule, the ordinary course is to remand and allow the lower courts to apply the rule in the first instance. I see no good reason why the Court fails to follow that course in this case. Indeed, the sole basis for the Court's peremptory ruling is the demonstrably false pretension that respondents showed "nothing more" than "a significant statistical disparity."[9]

This case presents an unfortunate situation, one New Haven might well have avoided had it utilized a better selection process in the first place. But what this case does not present is race-based discrimination in violation of Title VII. I dissent from the Court's judgment, which rests on the false premise that respondents showed "a significant statistical disparity," but "nothing more."

## ✦ Core Concept: The Adequacy of the Frameworks

The last two chapters covered many of the key analytical structures the courts use for considering discrimination claims. The question remains whether these frameworks

---

9. The Court's refusal to remand for further proceedings also deprives respondents of an opportunity to invoke 42 U.S.C. § 2000e-12(b) [providing for no liability if an employer acts in good faith, in conformity with, and in reliance on any written interpretation or opinion of the EEOC] as a shield to liability....

account for all workplace treatment that happens because of a person's protected trait. As you read the following case, consider whether some or all of the plaintiffs' allegations would fall within the existing structures for discrimination claims.

---

### Focus Questions: *Wal-Mart Stores, Inc. v. Dukes*

1. *What are the plaintiffs alleging? Is it discrimination for a company to be aware of hiring and pay differences between men and women but not take appropriate action to find out why they are happening or to correct them?*

2. *Is this case about class action certification or about substantive anti-discrimination law?*

3. *If the plaintiffs are not able to proceed through a class action does this affect the strength of their substantive claims? If one of the plaintiffs sues as an individual do you think the court would allow the use of nationwide statistics?*

4. *Does the majority opinion present a different version of the facts than that offered in the partial concurrence and dissent?*

---

# Wal-Mart Stores, Inc. v. Dukes

## 131 S.Ct. 2541 (2011)

Justice Scalia delivered the opinion of the Court.

We are presented with one of the most expansive class actions ever. The District Court and the Court of Appeals approved the certification of a class comprising about one and a half million plaintiffs, current and former female employees of petitioner Wal-Mart who allege that the discretion exercised by their local supervisors over pay and promotion matters violates Title VII by discriminating against women. In addition to injunctive and declaratory relief, the plaintiffs seek an award of backpay. We consider whether the certification of the plaintiff class was consistent with Federal Rules of Civil Procedure 23(a) and (b)(2).

### I
### A

Petitioner Wal-Mart is the Nation's largest private employer. It operates four types of retail stores throughout the country: Discount Stores, Supercenters, Neighborhood Markets, and Sam's Clubs. Those stores are divided into seven nationwide divisions, which in turn comprise 41 regions of 80 to 85 stores apiece. Each store has between 40 and 53 separate departments and 80 to 500 staff positions. In all, Wal-Mart operates approximately 3,400 stores and employs more than one million people.

Pay and promotion decisions at Wal-Mart are generally committed to local managers' broad discretion, which is exercised "in a largely subjective manner." [citation omitted.] Local store managers may increase the wages of hourly employees (within limits) with only limited corporate oversight. As for salaried employees, such as store managers and their deputies, higher corporate authorities have discretion to set their pay within pre-established ranges.

Promotions work in a similar fashion. Wal-Mart permits store managers to apply their own subjective criteria when selecting candidates as "support managers," which is the first step on the path to management. Admission to Wal-Mart's management training program, however, does require that a candidate meet certain objective criteria, including an above-average performance rating, at least one year's tenure in the applicant's current position, and a willingness to relocate. But except for those requirements, regional and district managers have discretion to use their own judgment when selecting candidates for management training. Promotion to higher office — e.g., assistant manager, co-manager, or store manager — is similarly at the discretion of the employee's superiors after prescribed objective factors are satisfied.

## B

The named plaintiffs in this lawsuit, representing the 1.5 million members of the certified class, are three current or former Wal-Mart employees who allege that the company discriminated against them on the basis of their sex by denying them equal pay or promotions, in violation of Title VII of the Civil Rights Act of 1964.

Betty Dukes began working at a Pittsburgh, California, Wal-Mart in 1994. She started as a cashier, but later sought and received a promotion to customer service manager. After a series of disciplinary violations, however, Dukes was demoted back to cashier and then to greeter. Dukes concedes she violated company policy, but contends that the disciplinary actions were in fact retaliation for invoking internal complaint procedures and that male employees have not been disciplined for similar infractions. Dukes also claims two male greeters in the Pittsburgh store are paid more than she is.

Christine Kwapnoski has worked at Sam's Club stores in Missouri and California for most of her adult life. She has held a number of positions, including a supervisory position. She claims that a male manager yelled at her frequently and screamed at female employees, but not at men. The manager in question "told her to 'doll up,' to wear some makeup, and to dress a little better."

The final named plaintiff, Edith Arana, worked at a Wal-Mart store in Duarte, California, from 1995 to 2001. In 2000, she approached the store manager on more than one occasion about management training, but was brushed off. Arana concluded she was being denied opportunity for advancement because of her sex. She initiated internal complaint procedures, whereupon she was told to apply directly to the district manager if she thought her store manager was being unfair. Arana, however, decided against that and never applied for management training again. In 2001, she was fired for failure to comply with Wal-Mart's timekeeping policy.

These plaintiffs, respondents here, do not allege that Wal-Mart has any express corporate policy against the advancement of women. Rather, they claim that their local managers' discretion over pay and promotions is exercised disproportionately in favor of men, leading to an unlawful disparate impact on female employees, see 42 U.S.C. § 2000e-2(k). And, respondents say, because Wal-Mart is aware of this effect, its refusal to cabin its managers' authority amounts to disparate treatment, see § 2000e-2(a). Their complaint seeks injunctive and declaratory relief, punitive damages, and backpay. It does not ask for compensatory damages.

Importantly for our purposes, respondents claim that the discrimination to which they have been subjected is common to *all* Wal-Mart's female employees. The basic theory of their case is that a strong and uniform "corporate culture" permits bias against women to infect, perhaps subconsciously, the discretionary decisionmaking of each one of Wal-

Mart's thousands of managers—thereby making every woman at the company the victim of one common discriminatory practice. Respondents therefore wish to litigate the Title VII claims of all female employees at Wal-Mart's stores in a nationwide class action.

## C

Class certification is governed by Federal Rule of Civil Procedure 23. Under Rule 23(a), the party seeking certification must demonstrate, first, that:

(1) the class is so numerous that joinder of all members is impracticable,

(2) there are questions of law or fact common to the class,

(3) the claims or defenses of the representative parties are typical of the claims or defenses of the class, and

(4) the representative parties will fairly and adequately protect the interests of the class.

Second, the proposed class must satisfy at least one of the three requirements listed in Rule 23(b). Respondents rely on Rule 23(b)(2), which applies when "the party opposing the class has acted or refused to act on grounds that apply generally to the class, so that final injunctive relief or corresponding declaratory relief is appropriate respecting the class as a whole."

Invoking these provisions, respondents moved the District Court to certify a plaintiff class consisting of "[a]ll women employed at any Wal-Mart domestic retail store at any time since December 26, 1998, who have been or may be subjected to Wal-Mart's challenged pay and management track promotions policies and practices." [citation omitted.] As evidence that there were indeed "questions of law or fact common to" all the women of Wal-Mart, as Rule 23(a)(2) requires, respondents relied chiefly on three forms of proof: statistical evidence about pay and promotion disparities between men and women at the company, anecdotal reports of discrimination from about 120 of Wal-Mart's female employees, and the testimony of a sociologist, Dr. William Bielby, who conducted a "social framework analysis" of Wal-Mart's "culture" and personnel practices, and concluded that the company was "vulnerable" to gender discrimination. . . .

## D

[The trial court certified the class, and the divided en banc Court of Appeals substantially affirmed that certification order.] The majority concluded that respondents' evidence of commonality was sufficient to "raise the common question whether Wal-Mart's female employees nationwide were subjected to a single set of corporate policies (not merely a number of independent discriminatory acts) that may have worked to unlawfully discriminate against them in violation of Title VII." It also agreed with the District Court that the named plaintiffs' claims were sufficiently typical of the class as a whole to satisfy Rule 23(a)(3), and that they could serve as adequate class representatives, see Rule 23(a)(4). With respect to the Rule 23(b)(2) question, the Ninth Circuit held that respondents' backpay claims could be certified as part of a (b)(2) class because they did not "predominat[e]" over the requests for declaratory and injunctive relief, meaning they were not "superior in strength, influence, or authority" to the nonmonetary claims.

Finally, the Court of Appeals determined that the action could be manageably tried as a class action because the District Court could adopt the approach the Ninth Circuit approved in *Hilao v. Estate of Marcos*, 103 F.3d 767, 782–787 (9th Cir. 1996). There compensatory damages for some 9,541 class members were calculated by selecting 137 claims at random, referring those claims to a special master for valuation, and then extrapolating the validity and value of the untested claims from the sample set. *See* 603 F.3d at 625–26. The Court of Appeals "s[aw] no reason why a similar procedure to that used in *Hilao* could not be employed in this case." *Id.* at 627. It would allow Wal-Mart "to present individual defenses in the randomly selected 'sample cases,' thus revealing the approximate percentage of class members whose unequal pay or nonpromotion was due to something other than gender discrimination." *Id.* at 627 n.56 (emphasis deleted).

We granted certiorari.

## II

The class action is "an exception to the usual rule that litigation is conducted by and on behalf of the individual named parties only." *Califano v. Yamasaki,* 442 U.S. 682, 700–01 (1979). In order to justify a departure from that rule, "a class representative must be part of the class and 'possess the same interest and suffer the same injury' as the class members." [citation omitted.] Rule 23(a) ensures that the named plaintiffs are appropriate representatives of the class whose claims they wish to litigate. The Rule's four requirements — numerosity, commonality, typicality, and adequate representation — "effectively 'limit the class claims to those fairly encompassed by the named plaintiff's claims.'" [citation omitted.]

## A

The crux of this case is commonality — the rule requiring a plaintiff to show that "there are questions of law or fact common to the class." Rule 23(a)(2). That language is easy to misread, since "[a]ny competently crafted class complaint literally raises common 'questions.'" Nagareda, *Class Certification in the Age of Aggregate Proof,* 84 N.Y.U. L. Rev. 97, 131–132 (2009). For example: Do all of us plaintiffs indeed work for Wal-Mart? Do our managers have discretion over pay? Is that an unlawful employment practice? What remedies should we get? Reciting these questions is not sufficient to obtain class certification. Commonality requires the plaintiff to demonstrate that the class members "have suffered the same injury." [citation omitted.] This does not mean merely that they have all suffered a violation of the same provision of law. Title VII, for example, can be violated in many ways — by intentional discrimination, or by hiring and promotion criteria that result in disparate impact, and by the use of these practices on the part of many different superiors in a single company. Quite obviously, the mere claim by employees of the same company that they have suffered a Title VII injury, or even a disparate-impact Title VII injury, gives no cause to believe that all their claims can productively be litigated at once. Their claims must depend upon a common contention — for example, the assertion of discriminatory bias on the part of the same supervisor. That common contention, moreover, must be of such a nature that it is capable of classwide resolution — which means that determination of its truth or falsity will resolve an issue that is central to the validity of each one of the claims in one stroke.

"What matters to class certification ... is not the raising of common 'questions' — even in droves — but, rather the capacity of a classwide proceeding to generate common *answers* apt to drive the resolution of the litigation. Dissimilarities within the proposed class are what have the potential to impede the generation of common answers."

Rule 23 does not set forth a mere pleading standard. A party seeking class certification must affirmatively demonstrate his compliance with the Rule — that is, he must be prepared to prove that there are *in fact* sufficiently numerous parties, common questions of law or fact, etc....

In this case, proof of commonality necessarily overlaps with respondents' merits contention that Wal-Mart engages in a *pattern or practice* of discrimination. That is so because, in resolving an individual's Title VII claim, the crux of the inquiry is "the reason for a particular employment decision," *Cooper v. Federal Reserve Bank of Richmond,* 467 U.S. 867, 876 (1984). Here respondents wish to sue about literally millions of employment decisions at once. Without some glue holding the alleged *reasons* for all those decisions together, it will be impossible to say that examination of all the class members' claims for relief will produce a common answer to the crucial question *why was I disfavored.*

...

B

This Court's opinion in *Falcon* describes how the commonality issue must be approached. There an employee who claimed that he was deliberately denied a promotion on account of race obtained certification of a class comprising all employees wrongfully denied promotions and all applicants wrongfully denied jobs. 457 U.S. at 152. We rejected that composite class for lack of commonality and typicality, explaining:

> Conceptually, there is a wide gap between (a) an individual's claim that he has been denied a promotion [or higher pay] on discriminatory grounds, and his otherwise unsupported allegation that the company has a policy of discrimination, and (b) the existence of a class of persons who have suffered the same injury as that individual, such that the individual's claim and the class claim will share common questions of law or fact and that the individual's claim will be typical of the class claims.

*Id.,* at 157–58.

*Falcon* suggested two ways in which that conceptual gap might be bridged. First, if the employer "used a biased testing procedure to evaluate both applicants for employment and incumbent employees, a class action on behalf of every applicant or employee who might have been prejudiced by the test clearly would satisfy the commonality and typicality requirements of Rule 23(a)." *Id.,* at 159, n. 15. Second, "[s]ignificant proof that an employer operated under a general policy of discrimination conceivably could justify a class of both applicants and employees if the discrimination manifested itself in hiring and promotion practices in the same general fashion, such as through entirely subjective decisionmaking processes." *Ibid.* We think that statement precisely describes respondents' burden in this case. The first manner of bridging the gap obviously has no application here; Wal-Mart has no testing procedure or other companywide evaluation method that can be charged with bias. The whole point of permitting discretionary decisionmaking is to avoid evaluating employees under a common standard.

The second manner of bridging the gap requires "significant proof" that Wal-Mart "operated under a general policy of discrimination." That is entirely absent here. Wal-Mart's announced policy forbids sex discrimination, ... The only evidence of a "general policy of discrimination" respondents produced was the testimony of Dr. William Bielby, their sociological expert. Relying on "social framework" analysis, Bielby testified that Wal-Mart has a "strong corporate culture," that makes it "vulnerable" to "gender bias." He could not, however, "determine with any specificity how regularly stereotypes play a meaningful role in employment decisions at Wal-Mart. At his deposition ... Dr. Bielby conceded that he could not calculate whether 0.5 percent or 95 percent of the employment decisions at Wal-Mart might be determined by stereotyped thinking." The parties dispute whether Bielby's testimony even met the standards for the admission of expert testimony under

Federal Rule of Civil Procedure 702 and our *Daubert* case, see *Daubert v. Merrell Dow Pharmaceuticals, Inc.,* 509 U.S. 579 (1993).[8] The District Court concluded that *Daubert* did not apply to expert testimony at the certification stage of class-action proceedings. We doubt that is so, but even if properly considered, Bielby's testimony does nothing to advance respondents' case. "[W]hether 0.5 percent or 95 percent of the employment decisions at Wal-Mart might be determined by stereotyped thinking" is the essential question on which respondents' theory of commonality depends. If Bielby admittedly has no answer to that question, we can safely disregard what he has to say. It is worlds away from "significant proof" that Wal-Mart "operated under a general policy of discrimination."

## C

The only corporate policy that the plaintiffs' evidence convincingly establishes is Wal-Mart's "policy" of *allowing discretion* by local supervisors over employment matters. On its face, of course, that is just the opposite of a uniform employment practice that would provide the commonality needed for a class action; it is a policy *against having* uniform employment practices. It is also a very common and presumptively reasonable way of doing business—one that we have said "should itself raise no inference of discriminatory conduct," *Watson v. Fort Worth Bank & Trust,* 487 U.S. 977, 990 (1988).

To be sure, we have recognized that, "in appropriate cases," giving discretion to lower-level supervisors can be the basis of Title VII liability under a disparate-impact theory— since "an employer's undisciplined system of subjective decisionmaking [can have] precisely the same effects as a system pervaded by impermissible intentional discrimination." But the recognition that this type of Title VII claim "can" exist does not lead to the conclusion that every employee in a company using a system of discretion has such a claim in common. To the contrary, left to their own devices most managers in any corporation—and surely most managers in a corporation that forbids sex discrimination—would select sex-neutral, performance-based criteria for hiring and promotion that produce no actionable disparity at all. Others may choose to reward various attributes that produce disparate impact— such as scores on general aptitude tests or educational achievements, see *Griggs v. Duke Power Co.,* 401 U.S. 424, 431–32 (1971). And still other managers may be guilty of intentional discrimination that produces a sex-based disparity. In such a company, demonstrating the invalidity of one manager's use of discretion will do nothing to demonstrate the invalidity of another's. A party seeking to certify a nationwide class will be unable to show that all the employees' Title VII claims will in fact depend on the answers to common questions.

Respondents have not identified a common mode of exercising discretion that pervades the entire company—aside from their reliance on Dr. Bielby's social frameworks analysis that we have rejected. In a company of Wal-Mart's size and geographical scope, it is quite unbelievable that all managers would exercise their discretion in a common way without some common direction. Respondents attempt to make that showing by means of statistical and anecdotal evidence, but their evidence falls well short.

The statistical evidence consists primarily of regression analyses performed by Dr. Richard Drogin, a statistician, and Dr. Marc Bendick, a labor economist. Drogin conducted his analysis region-by-region, comparing the number of women promoted into management positions with the percentage of women in the available pool of hourly workers. After

---

8. Bielby's conclusions in this case have elicited criticism from the very scholars on whose conclusions he relies for his social-framework analysis. *See* Monahan, Walker, & Mitchell, *Contextual Evidence of Gender Discrimination: The Ascendance of "Social Frameworks,"* 94 Va. L. Rev. 1715, 1747 (2008)....

considering regional and national data, Drogin concluded that "there are statistically significant disparities between men and women at Wal-Mart ... [and] these disparities ... can be explained only by gender discrimination." Bendick compared work-force data from Wal-Mart and competitive retailers and concluded that Wal-Mart "promotes a lower percentage of women than its competitors."

Even if they are taken at face value, these studies are insufficient to establish that respondents' theory can be proved on a classwide basis. In *Falcon,* we held that one named plaintiff's experience of discrimination was insufficient to infer that "discriminatory treatment is typical of [the employer's employment] practices." 457 U.S. at 158. A similar failure of inference arises here. As Judge Ikuta observed in her dissent, "[i]nformation about disparities at the regional and national level does not establish the existence of disparities at individual stores, let alone raise the inference that a company-wide policy of discrimination is implemented by discretionary decisions at the store and district level." A regional pay disparity, for example, may be attributable to only a small set of Wal-Mart stores, and cannot by itself establish the uniform, store-by-store disparity upon which the plaintiffs' theory of commonality depends.

There is another, more fundamental, respect in which respondents' statistical proof fails. Even if it established (as it does not) a pay or promotion pattern that differs from the nationwide figures or the regional figures in *all* of Wal-Mart's 3,400 stores, that would still not demonstrate that commonality of issue exists. Some managers will claim that the availability of women, or qualified women, or interested women, in their stores' area does not mirror the national or regional statistics. And almost all of them will claim to have been applying some sex-neutral, performance-based criteria—whose nature and effects will differ from store to store. In the landmark case of ours which held that giving discretion to lower-level supervisors can be the basis of Title VII liability under a disparate-impact theory, the plurality opinion *conditioned* that holding on the corollary that merely proving that the discretionary system has produced a racial or sexual disparity *is not enough*. "[T]he plaintiff must begin by identifying the specific employment practice that is challenged." *Watson,* 487 U.S., at 994. That is all the more necessary when a class of plaintiffs is sought to be certified. Other than the bare existence of delegated discretion, respondents have identified no "specific employment practice"—much less one that ties all their 1.5 million claims together. Merely showing that Wal-Mart's policy of discretion has produced an overall sex-based disparity does not suffice.

Respondents' anecdotal evidence suffers from the same defects, and in addition is too weak to raise any inference that all the individual, discretionary personnel decisions are discriminatory. In *Teamsters v. United States,* 431 U.S. 324, (1977), in addition to substantial statistical evidence of company-wide discrimination, the Government (as plaintiff) produced about 40 specific accounts of racial discrimination from particular individuals. That number was significant because the company involved had only 6,472 employees, of whom 571 were minorities, and the class itself consisted of around 334 persons. The 40 anecdotes thus represented roughly one account for every eight members of the class. Moreover, the Court of Appeals noted that the anecdotes came from individuals "spread throughout" the company who "for the most part" worked at the company's operational centers that employed the largest numbers of the class members. Here, by contrast, respondents filed some 120 affidavits reporting experiences of discrimination—about 1 for every 12,500 class members—relating to only some 235 out of Wal-Mart's 3,400 stores. More than half of these reports are concentrated in only six States (Alabama, California, Florida, Missouri, Texas, and Wisconsin); half of all States have only one or two anecdotes; and 14 States have no anecdotes about Wal-Mart's operations at all. Even if every single one of these accounts is true, that would not demonstrate that the entire company "operate[s] under a general policy of discrimination," *Falcon, supra,* at 159, n. 15, which is what respondents must show to certify a companywide class....

In sum, we agree with Chief Judge Kozinski that the members of the class:

> held a multitude of different jobs, at different levels of Wal-Mart's hierarchy, for variable lengths of time, in 3,400 stores, sprinkled across 50 states, with a kaleidoscope of supervisors (male and female), subject to a variety of regional policies that all differed.... Some thrived while others did poorly. They have little in common but their sex and this lawsuit.

603 F.3d at 652 (dissenting opinion).

## III

We also conclude that respondents' claims for backpay were improperly certified under Federal Rule of Civil Procedure 23(b)(2)....

### A

Rule 23(b)(2) allows class treatment when "the party opposing the class has acted or refused to act on grounds that apply generally to the class, so that final injunctive relief or corresponding declaratory relief is appropriate respecting the class as a whole." One possible reading of this provision is that it applies *only* to requests for such injunctive or declaratory relief and does not authorize the class certification of monetary claims at all. We need not reach that broader question in this case, because we think that, at a minimum, claims for *individualized* relief (like the backpay at issue here) do not satisfy the Rule. The key to the (b)(2) class is "the indivisible nature of the injunctive or declaratory remedy warranted — the notion that the conduct is such that it can be enjoined or declared unlawful only as to all of the class members or as to none of them." Nagareda, 84 N.Y.U. L. Rev., at 132. In other words, Rule 23(b)(2) applies only when a single injunction or declaratory judgment would provide relief to each member of the class. It does not authorize class certification when each individual class member would be entitled to a *different* injunction or declaratory judgment against the defendant. Similarly, it does not authorize class certification when each class member would be entitled to an individualized award of monetary damages.

That interpretation accords with the history of the Rule. Because Rule 23 "stems from equity practice" that predated its codification, *Amchem Products, Inc. v. Windsor,* 521 U.S. 591, 613 (1997), in determining its meaning we have previously looked to the historical models on which the Rule was based, *Ortiz v. Fibreboard Corp.,* 527 U.S. 815, 841–45 (1999). As we observed in *Amchem,* "[c]ivil rights cases against parties charged with unlawful, class-based discrimination are prime examples" of what (b)(2) is meant to capture. 521 U.S. at 614. In particular, the Rule reflects a series of decisions involving challenges to racial segregation — conduct that was remedied by a single classwide order. In none of the cases cited by the Advisory Committee as examples of (b)(2)'s antecedents did the plaintiffs combine any claim for individualized relief with their classwide injunction....

Permitting the combination of individualized and classwide relief in a (b)(2) class is also inconsistent with the structure of Rule 23(b). Classes certified under (b)(1) and (b)(2) share the most traditional justifications for class treatment — that individual adjudications would be impossible or unworkable, as in a (b)(1) class, or that the relief sought must perforce affect the entire class at once, as in a (b)(2) class. For that reason these are also mandatory classes: The Rule provides no opportunity for (b)(1) or (b)(2) class members to opt out, and does not even oblige the District Court to afford them notice of the action. Rule 23(b)(3), by contrast, is an "adventuresome innovation" of the 1966 amendments ... It allows class certification in a much wider set of circumstances but with greater procedural protections. Its only prerequisites are that "the questions of law or fact common to class members predominate over any questions affecting only individual members, and that a class action is superior to other available methods for fairly and efficiently adjudicating the controversy." Rule 23(b)(3). And unlike (b)(1) and (b)(2) classes, the (b)(3) class is not mandatory; class members are entitled to receive "the best notice that is practicable under the circumstances" and to withdraw from the class at their option. *See* Rule 23(c)(2)(B).

Given that structure, we think it clear that individualized monetary claims belong in Rule 23(b)(3). The procedural protections attending the (b)(3) class—predominance, superiority, mandatory notice, and the right to opt out—are missing from (b)(2) not because the Rule considers them unnecessary, but because it considers them unnecessary *to a (b)(2) class.* When a class seeks an indivisible injunction benefitting all its members at once, there is no reason to undertake a case-specific inquiry into whether class issues predominate or whether class action is a superior method of adjudicating the dispute. Predominance and superiority are self-evident. But with respect to each class member's individualized claim for money, that is not so—which is precisely why (b)(3) requires the judge to make findings about predominance and superiority before allowing the class. Similarly, (b)(2) does not require that class members be given notice and optout rights, presumably because it is thought (rightly or wrongly) that notice has no purpose when the class is mandatory, and that depriving people of their right to sue in this manner complies with the Due Process Clause. In the context of a class action predominantly for money damages we have held that absence of notice and opt-out violates due process. See *Phillips Petroleum Co. v. Shutts,* 472 U.S. 797, 812 (1985). While we have never held that to be so where the monetary claims do not predominate, the serious possibility that it may be so provides an additional reason not to read Rule 23(b)(2) to include the monetary claims here.

B

Against that conclusion, respondents argue that their claims for backpay were appropriately certified as part of a class under Rule 23(b)(2) because those claims do not "predominate" over their requests for injunctive and declaratory relief. They rely upon the Advisory Committee's statement that Rule 23(b)(2) "does not extend to cases in which the appropriate final relief relates *exclusively or predominantly* to money damages." ...

Respondents' predominance test, moreover, creates perverse incentives for class representatives to place at risk potentially valid claims for monetary relief. In this case, for example, the named plaintiffs declined to include employees' claims for compensatory damages in their complaint. That strategy of including only backpay claims made it more likely that monetary relief would not "predominate." But it also created the possibility (if the predominance test were correct) that individual class members' compensatory-damages claims would be *precluded* by litigation they had no power to hold themselves apart from. If it were determined, for example, that a particular class member is not entitled to backpay because her denial of increased pay or a promotion was *not* the product of discrimination, that employee might be collaterally estopped from independently seeking compensatory damages based on that same denial. That possibility underscores the need for plaintiffs with individual monetary claims to decide *for themselves* whether to tie their fates to the class representatives' or go it alone—a choice Rule 23(b)(2) does not ensure that they have.

...

Finally, respondents argue that their backpay claims are appropriate for a (b)(2) class action because a backpay award is equitable in nature. The latter may be true, but it is irrelevant. The Rule does not speak of "equitable" remedies generally but of injunctions and declaratory judgments. As Title VII itself makes pellucidly clear, backpay is neither. *See* 42 U.S.C. § 2000e-5(g)(2)(B)(i) and (ii) (distinguishing between declaratory and injunctive relief and the payment of "backpay," *see* § 2000e-5(g)(2)(A)).

C

...

Contrary to the Ninth Circuit's view, Wal-Mart is entitled to individualized determinations of each employee's eligibility for backpay. Title VII includes a detailed remedial scheme. If a plaintiff prevails in showing that an employer has discriminated against him in violation of the statute, the court "may enjoin the respondent from engaging in such unlawful employment practice, and order such affirmative action as may be appropriate, [including] reinstatement or hiring of employees, with or without backpay ... or any other equitable relief as the court deems appropriate." § 2000e-5(g)(1). But if the employer can show that it took an adverse employment action against an employee for any reason other than discrimination, the court cannot order the "hiring, reinstatement, or promotion of an individual as an employee, or the payment to him of any backpay." § 2000e-5(g)(2)(A).

We have established a procedure for trying pattern-or-practice cases that gives effect to these statutory requirements. When the plaintiff seeks individual relief such as reinstatement or backpay after establishing a pattern or practice of discrimination, "a district court must usually conduct additional proceedings ... to determine the scope of individual relief." *Teamsters,* 431 U.S. at 361. At this phase, the burden of proof will shift to the company, but it will have the right to raise any individual affirmative defenses it may have, and to "demonstrate that the individual applicant was denied an employment opportunity for lawful reasons." *Id.* at 362.

The Court of Appeals believed that it was possible to replace such proceedings with Trial by Formula. A sample set of the class members would be selected, as to whom liability for sex discrimination and the backpay owing as a result would be determined in depositions supervised by a master. The percentage of claims determined to be valid would then be applied to the entire remaining class, and the number of (presumptively) valid claims thus derived would be multiplied by the average backpay award in the sample set to arrive at the entire class recovery—without further individualized proceedings. We disapprove that novel project....

The judgment of the Court of Appeals is *reversed.*

Justice Ginsburg, with whom Justice Breyer, Justice Sotomayor, and Justice Kagan join, concurring in part and dissenting in part.

The class in this case, I agree with the Court, should not have been certified under Federal Rule of Civil Procedure 23(b)(2). The plaintiffs, alleging discrimination in violation of Title VII, 42 U.S.C. § 2000e *et seq.,* seek monetary relief that is not merely incidental to any injunctive or declaratory relief that might be available. A putative class of this type may be certifiable under Rule 23(b)(3), if the plaintiffs show that common class questions "predominate" over issues affecting individuals—*e.g.,* qualification for, and the amount of, backpay or compensatory damages—and that a class action is "superior" to other modes of adjudication.

Whether the class the plaintiffs describe meets the specific requirements of Rule 23(b)(3) is not before the Court, and I would reserve that matter for consideration and decision on remand. The Court, however, disqualifies the class at the starting gate, holding that the plaintiffs cannot cross the "commonality" line set by Rule 23(a)(2). In so ruling, the Court imports into the Rule 23(a) determination concerns properly addressed in a Rule 23(b)(3) assessment.

[In part I.A., the opinion discusses the requirements of Rule 23.]

### B

The District Court, recognizing that "one significant issue common to the class may be sufficient to warrant certification," found that the plaintiffs easily met that test....

The District Court certified a class of "[a]ll women employed at any Wal-Mart domestic retail store at any time since December 26, 1998." The named plaintiffs, led by Betty Dukes, propose to litigate, on behalf of the class, allegations that Wal-Mart discriminates on the basis of gender in pay and promotions. They allege that the company "[r]eli[es] on gender stereotypes in making employment decisions such as ... promotion[s][and] pay." Wal-Mart permits those prejudices to infect personnel decisions, the plaintiffs contend, by leaving pay and promotions in the hands of "a nearly all male managerial workforce" using "arbitrary and subjective criteria." Further alleged barriers to the advancement of female employees include the company's requirement, "as a condition of promotion to management jobs, that employees be willing to relocate." Absent instruction otherwise, there is a risk that managers will act on the familiar assumption that women, because of their services to husband and children, are less mobile than men. *See* Dept. of Labor, Federal Glass Ceiling Commission, Good for Business: Making Full Use of the Nation's Human Capital 151 (1995).

Women fill 70 percent of the hourly jobs in the retailer's stores but make up only "33 percent of management employees." "[T]he higher one looks in the organization the lower the percentage of women." The plaintiffs' "largely uncontested descriptive statistics" also show that women working in the company's stores "are paid less than men in every region" and "that the salary gap widens over time even for men and women hired into the same jobs at the same time."

The District Court identified "systems for ... promoting in-store employees" that were "sufficiently similar across regions and stores" to conclude that "the manner in which these systems affect the class raises issues that are common to all class members." The selection of employees for promotion to in-store management "is fairly characterized as a 'tap on the shoulder' process," in which managers have discretion about whose shoulders to tap. Vacancies are not regularly posted; from among those employees satisfying minimum qualifications, managers choose whom to promote on the basis of their own subjective impressions.

Wal-Mart's compensation policies also operate uniformly across stores, the District Court found. The retailer leaves open a $2 band for every position's hourly pay rate. Wal-Mart provides no standards or criteria for setting wages within that band, and thus does nothing to counter unconscious bias on the part of supervisors.

Wal-Mart's supervisors do not make their discretionary decisions in a vacuum. The District Court reviewed means Wal-Mart used to maintain a "carefully constructed ... corporate culture," such as frequent meetings to reinforce the common way of thinking, regular transfers of managers between stores to ensure uniformity throughout the company, monitoring of stores "on a close and constant basis," and "Wal-Mart TV," "broadcas[t] ... into all stores."

The plaintiffs' evidence, including class members' tales of their own experiences, suggests that gender bias suffused Wal-Mart's company culture. Among illustrations, senior management often refer to female associates as "little Janie Qs." One manager told an employee that "[m]en are here to make a career and women aren't." A committee of female Wal-Mart executives concluded that "[s]tereotypes limit the opportunities offered to women."

Finally, the plaintiffs presented an expert's appraisal to show that the pay and promotions disparities at Wal-Mart "can be explained only by gender discrimination and not by ... neutral variables." ...

## C

The District Court's identification of a common question, whether Wal-Mart's pay and promotions policies gave rise to unlawful discrimination, was hardly infirm. The practice of delegating to supervisors large discretion to make personnel decisions, uncontrolled by formal standards, has long been known to have the potential to produce disparate effects. Managers, like all humankind, may be prey to biases of which they are unaware.[6] The risk of discrimination is heightened when those managers are predominantly of one sex, and are steeped in a corporate culture that perpetuates gender stereotypes.

The plaintiffs' allegations resemble those in one of the prototypical cases in this area, *Leisner v. New York Tel. Co.*, 358 F. Supp. 359, 364–65 (S.D.N.Y. 1973). In deciding on promotions, supervisors in that case were to start with objective measures; but ultimately, they were to "look at the individual as a total individual." *Id.* at 365 (internal quotation marks omitted). The final question they were to ask and answer: "Is this person going to be successful in our business?" *Ibid.* (internal quotation marks omitted). It is hardly surprising that for many managers, the ideal candidate was someone with characteristics similar to their own.

We have held that "discretionary employment practices" can give rise to Title VII claims, not only when such practices are motivated by discriminatory intent but also when they produce discriminatory results. *See Watson v. Fort Worth Bank & Trust,* 487 U.S. 977, 988, 991 (1988)....

Aware of "the problem of subconscious stereotypes and prejudices," we held that the employer's "undisciplined system of subjective decisionmaking" was an "employment practic[e]" that "may be analyzed under the disparate impact approach." *Id.,* at 990–991.

## II

[The opinion continues with a discussion of Rule 23.]

Wal-Mart's delegation of discretion over pay and promotions is a policy uniform throughout all stores. The very nature of discretion is that people will exercise it in various ways. A system of delegated discretion, *Watson* held, is a practice actionable under Title

---

6. An example vividly illustrates how subjective decisionmaking can be a vehicle for discrimination. Performing in symphony orchestras was long a male preserve. Goldin and Rouse, *Orchestrating Impartiality: The Impact of "Blind" Auditions on Female Musicians,* 90 Am. Econ. Rev. 715, 715–716 (2000). In the 1970's orchestras began hiring musicians through auditions open to all comers. *Id.,* at 716. Reviewers were to judge applicants solely on their musical abilities, yet subconscious bias led some reviewers to disfavor women. Orchestras that permitted reviewers to see the applicants hired far fewer female musicians than orchestras that conducted blind auditions, in which candidates played behind opaque screens. *Id.,* at 738.

VII when it produces discriminatory outcomes. 487 U.S., at 990–991. A finding that Wal-Mart's pay and promotions practices in fact violate the law would be the first step in the usual order of proof for plaintiffs seeking individual remedies for company-wide discrimination. *Teamsters v. United States,* 431 U.S. 324, 359 (1977); *see Albemarle Paper Co. v. Moody,* 422 U.S. 405, 415–23 (1975). That each individual employee's unique circumstances will ultimately determine whether she is entitled to backpay or damages, § 2000e-5(g)(2)(A) (barring backpay if a plaintiff "was refused ... advancement ... for any reason other than discrimination"), should not factor into the Rule 23(a)(2) determination.

\* \* \*

The Court errs in importing a "dissimilarities" notion suited to Rule 23(b)(3) into the Rule 23(a) commonality inquiry. I therefore cannot join Part II of the Court's opinion.

---

### Exercise 4.6

In thinking about whether you understand the material studied so far, consider the similarities and differences between the types of discrimination you have learned about and the frameworks used by courts for evaluating these claims.

# Chapter 5

# Discriminatory Harassment

Federal law prohibits workplace harassment that is discriminatory—motivated by sex, race or another protected trait. All of the protected traits that you have learned about in this course may support claims for discriminatory harassment. Thus, for example, an employee subjected to harassment because of disability or because she is elderly may have a claim. People sometimes lose sight of the availability of such claims because sexual harassment has had such a high profile in our society that it overshadows the other types of discriminatory harassment. Keep in mind, now and with your future clients, that harassment based on any legally protected trait may be unlawful. Remember, too, that, in addition to suits under the federal employment discrimination statutes, a plaintiff may be able to bring a discriminatory harassment suit under state or municipal law, under the state or federal constitution (if a government employee) and under tort or even contract law.

This Chapter begins with an explanation of the types of harassment and then continues with a more in-depth examination, first of *quid pro quo* harassment and then of *hostile environment* claims. The hostile environment discussion encompasses the following concepts:

- Unwelcomeness
- Because of
- Severe or Pervasive
- Motive v. Content

The Chapter ends with a discussion of employer liability, including the concept of *tangible employment action*.

## ✦ Core Concept: Types of Harassment

There are two types of discriminatory harassment: hostile environment and quid pro quo. Most cases of discriminatory harassment fit within the hostile environment framework, where unwelcome, offensive words or conduct create an intimidating, hostile, or offensive working environment. In quid pro quo harassment, by contrast, typically a supervisor demands sexual favors from a subordinate employee, threatening negative consequences if the employee fails to comply or promising benefits if the subordinate does comply. Quid pro quo harassment is thus typically restricted to sex-motivated cases.

## ✦ Core Concept: Quid Pro Quo Harassment

"Quid pro quo" is a Latin term meaning approximately "something for something" or "this for that." It connotes an invitation to bargain for an exchange. In the context of harassment law, "quid pro quo" occurs when someone in a position of authority demands sexual favors from someone in a subordinate position, and then bases employment decisions on how the subordinate responds. 29 C.F.R. § 1604.11(a)(2). Typically, the quid pro quo harasser threatens the target with a negative consequence if the target does not submit to the demands, although, in theory, it also is possible for the harasser to promise benefits if the target submits to sexual requests.

Quid pro quo harassment was the earliest form of harassment recognized by the courts. Its contours were not always well-defined, but courts generally agreed during the decades following enactment of Title VII that such harassment was actionable. In more recent years, because of developments in the Supreme Court, the boundaries between quid pro quo and hostile environment harassment have become murkier. In particular, as you will read later on, the cases of *Faragher v. City of Boca Raton*, 524 U.S. 775 (1998), and *Burlington Industries, Inc. v. Ellerth*, 524 U.S. 742 (1998), arguably realigned the boundaries so that the essential distinction is between harassment that culminates in a "tangible employment action" and that which does not, rather than between quid pro quo harassment and hostile work environment harassment. *See Gregory v. Daly*, 243 F.3d 687, 698 (2d Cir. 2001).

To the extent courts continue to recognize the quid pro quo claim, it makes sense to distinguish it from hostile environment harassment because the latter can be much more burdensome to prove. *See Burlington Industries, Inc., v. Ellerth*, 524 U.S. at 753. As discussed below, the hostile environment plaintiff must prove that abuse was unwelcome, severe or pervasive, and motivated by the claimant's sex or other protected trait. By contrast, if a plaintiff proves that a supervisor made an unwelcome demand, that the plaintiff declined the demand, and that adverse employment action resulted from the declined demand, the plaintiff may establish a sex-based harassment claim without going to the trouble of proving all of the elements of hostile environment. "A plaintiff making a quid pro quo claim need not prove that the conduct was severe or pervasive enough to create a hostile or abusive work environment, 'because any carried-out threat is itself deemed an actionable change in the terms or conditions of employment.'" *Anderson v. Family Dollar Stores of Ark. Inc.*, 579 F.3d 858, 863 (8th Cir. 2009). The quid pro quo plaintiff "must show that [the harasser] 'explicitly or implicitly condition[ed] a job, a job benefit, or the absence of a job detriment, upon [the] employee's acceptance of sexual conduct.'" If a plaintiff is able to make such a showing, the employer is strictly liable for the supervisor's conduct." *Craig v. M & O Agencies, Inc.*, 496 F.3d 1047, 1054 (9th Cir. 2007) (employers held strictly accountable if they place in positions of authority persons who extract sexual favors from those over whom they exercise power). *See Faragher v. City of Boca Raton*, 524 U.S. at 790–91 (noting unanimous rule that employers held liable when supervisor bases tangible employment action on subordinate's rejection of sexual advances); *Burlington Industries, Inc. v. Ellerth*, 524 U.S. at 753–54 (proving that tangible employment action resulted from refusal to submit to supervisor's sexual demands establishes that the employment decision itself constitutes a change in the terms and conditions of employment that is actionable under Title VII).

Typically, courts require the quid pro quo plaintiff to prove that

- a supervisor requested sexual favors;
- the subordinate employee rejected that request;
- the supervisor took adverse action against the subordinate; and
- the subordinate's rejection of the request caused/motivated the adverse action.

*See, e.g., Moser v. MCC Outdoor, L.L.C.*, 256 Fed. Appx. 634, 642 (4th Cir. 2007) (citing *Burlington Indus. Inc. v. Ellerth*, 524 U.S. 742, 753 (1998)). In the words of the Tenth

Circuit Court of Appeals, "[t]he gravamen of a *quid pro quo* sexual harassment claim is that tangible job benefits are conditioned on an employee's submission to conduct of a sexual nature and that adverse job consequences result from the employee's refusal to submit to the conduct." *Hicks v. Gates Rubber Co.*, 833 F.2d 1406, 1414 (10th Cir. 1987).

Regardless of how the courts articulate the standards for quid pro quo harassment, problems of proof are likely to revolve around two issues: whether sexual demands were actually made and whether the adverse action was caused or motivated by a rejection of those advances. The first of these is problematic because sexual demands, if they are made, usually are made in private. The absence of witnesses causes the evidence on this issue to devolve into a "he said-she said" situation. The plaintiff may prove the causal connection by direct or indirect evidence. Direct evidence is rare and might consist of an admission (written or oral) that the supervisor acted because of the plaintiff's rejection of the advance. Indirect proof might consist of any evidence that permits an inference that plaintiff's rejection of the sexual advance is what motivated the adverse action. For example, the plaintiff may introduce evidence of a close temporal proximity between the rejection of a proven sexual advance and the adverse employment action, accompanied by the employer's inability to articulate a legitimate nondiscriminatory reason for the action taken against the plaintiff.

Historically, the term "quid pro quo" was used to describe every situation in which a supervisor combined sexual demands with threats for non-compliance. In the early years, courts sometimes recognized a right to recover for such harassment even where no adverse action ensued. *See Jansen v. Packaging Corp. of America*, 123 F.3d 490 (7th Cir. 1997); *Karibian v. Columbia Univ.*, 14 F.3d 773 (3d Cir. 1994). Today, threats without adverse action do not suffice to prove a quid pro quo claim. If demands are made and the worker is not fired or otherwise penalized, then the claim is treated as a hostile environment claim, requiring proof of the elements of that claim. *Burlington Industries, Inc. v. Ellerth*, 524 U.S. 742, 754 (1998).

What if the harasser lacks authority to fire the worker? In *Ford v. Colson Caster Corp.*, an employee who refused a supervisor's advances alleged quid pro quo sexual harassment after she was denied a promised promotion and was eventually terminated. The harassing supervisor was not the decisionmaker on the promotion or termination, and the court granted summary judgment to the employer. 353 F. Supp. 2d 991, 998, 1002 (2005). "The operative question is whether the harassing employee 'had sufficient control over the plaintiff to be considered her supervisor.'" *Wright-Simmons v. City of Okla. City*, 155 F.3d 1264, 1271 (10th Cir. 1998). On the other hand, "an employer may be vicariously liable when the harassing employee has apparent authority—gives the false impression that the actor was a supervisor, when he in fact was not, and the victim's mistaken conclusion was a reasonable one." *Wilson v. Muckala*, 303 F.3d 1207, 1220 (10th Cir. 2002). For further discussion of this issue, see the case of *Vance v. Ball State University*, *infra*.

## ✦ Core Concept: Hostile Work Environment Harassment

The 1986 Supreme Court decision in *Meritor Savings Bank, FSB v. Vinson* established the availability and contours of the hostile work environment harassment cause of action. Before *Meritor*, some courts had refused to recognize hostile work environment cases, because they believed that Title VII required plaintiffs to establish economic harm, such as firing, reduced pay, or failure to hire, in order to win a Title VII case. *Meritor* established that hostile work environment claims are actionable, despite the absence of economic harm.

---

### Focus Questions: *Meritor Savings Bank, FSB v. Vinson*

1.  *How did the defendant define "terms, conditions and privileges of employment"?*

2.  *What degree of deference does the* Meritor *Court give to the EEOC Guidelines?*

3.  *Do you see room under* Meritor *for sex-motivated hostile environment harassment that is not sexual in content?*

4.  *What does the* Meritor *Court decide on the question of how trial courts should treat evidence of the victim's "provocative dress and demeanor" in harassment cases?*

---

# Meritor Savings Bank, FSB v. Vinson

### 477 U.S. 57 (1986)

Justice Rehnquist delivered the opinion of the Court.

This case presents important questions concerning claims of workplace "sexual harassment" brought under Title VII of the Civil Rights Act of 1964.

In 1974, respondent Mechelle Vinson met Sidney Taylor, a vice president of what is now petitioner Meritor Savings Bank and manager of one of its branch offices.... With Taylor as her supervisor, respondent started as a teller-trainee, and thereafter was promoted to teller, head teller, and assistant branch manager. She worked at the same branch for four years, and it is undisputed that her advancement there was based on merit alone. In September 1978, respondent notified Taylor that she was taking sick leave for an indefinite period. On November 1, 1978, the bank discharged her for excessive use of that leave.

Respondent brought this action against Taylor and the bank, claiming that during her four years at the bank she had "constantly been subjected to sexual harassment" by Taylor in violation of Title VII. She sought injunctive relief, compensatory and punitive damages against Taylor and the bank, and attorney's fees.

At the 11-day bench trial, the parties presented conflicting testimony about Taylor's behavior during respondent's employment. Respondent testified that during her probationary period as a teller-trainee, Taylor treated her in a fatherly way and made no sexual advances. Shortly thereafter, however, he invited her out to dinner and, during the course of the meal, suggested that they go to a motel to have sexual relations. At first she refused, but out of what she described as fear of losing her job she eventually agreed. According to respondent, Taylor thereafter made repeated demands upon her for sexual favors, usually at the branch, both during and after business hours; she estimated that over the next several years she had intercourse with him some 40 or 50 times. In addition, respondent testified that Taylor fondled her in front of other employees, followed her into the women's restroom when she went there alone, exposed himself to her, and even forcibly raped her on several occasions. These activities ceased after 1977, respondent stated, when she started going with a steady boyfriend....

[R]espondent testified that because she was afraid of Taylor she never reported his harassment to any of his supervisors and never attempted to use the bank's complaint procedure.

Taylor denied respondent's allegations of sexual activity, testifying that he never fondled her, never made suggestive remarks to her, never engaged in sexual intercourse with her, and never asked her to do so. He contended instead that respondent made her accusations in response to a business-related dispute. The bank also denied respondent's allegations and asserted that any sexual harassment by Taylor was unknown to the bank and engaged in without its consent or approval.

The District Court denied relief, but did not resolve the conflicting testimony about the existence of a sexual relationship between respondent and Taylor. It found instead that "[i]f [respondent] and Taylor did engage in an intimate or sexual relationship during the time of [respondent's] employment with [the bank], that relationship was a voluntary one having nothing to do with her continued employment at [the bank] or her advancement or promotions at that institution."

... The Court of Appeals for the District of Columbia Circuit reversed....

Respondent argues, and the Court of Appeals held, that unwelcome sexual advances that create an offensive or hostile working environment violate Title VII. Without question, when a supervisor sexually harasses a subordinate because of the subordinate's sex, that supervisor "discriminate[s]" on the basis of sex. Petitioner apparently does not challenge this proposition. It contends instead that in prohibiting discrimination with respect to "compensation, terms, conditions, or privileges" of employment, Congress was concerned with what defendant describes as "tangible loss" of "an economic character," not "purely psychological aspects of the workplace environment."

We reject defendant's view. First, the language of Title VII is not limited to "economic" or "tangible" discrimination. The phrase "terms, conditions, or privileges of employment" evinces a congressional intent " 'to strike at the entire spectrum of disparate treatment of men and women' " in employment.... Second, in 1980 the EEOC issued Guidelines specifying that "sexual harassment," as there defined, is a form of sex discrimination prohibited by Title VII. As an "administrative interpretation of the Act by the enforcing agency," these Guidelines, " 'while not controlling upon the courts by reason of their authority, do constitute a body of experience and informed judgment to which courts and litigants may properly resort for guidance.' " [citations omitted].... In defining "sexual harassment," the Guidelines first describe the kinds of workplace conduct that may be actionable under Title VII. These include "[u]nwelcome sexual advances, requests for sexual favors, and other verbal or physical conduct of a sexual nature." Relevant to the charges at issue in this case, the Guidelines provide that such sexual misconduct constitutes prohibited "sexual harassment," whether or not it is directly linked to the grant or denial of an economic *quid pro quo*, where "such conduct has the purpose or effect of unreasonably interfering with an individual's work performance or creating an intimidating, hostile, or offensive working environment."

In concluding that so-called "hostile environment" (*i.e.*, non-*quid pro quo*) harassment violates Title VII, the EEOC drew upon a substantial body of judicial decisions and EEOC precedent holding that Title VII affords employees the right to work in an environment free from discriminatory intimidation, ridicule, and insult. *Rogers v. EEOC*, 454 F.2d 234 (5th Cir. 1971), *cert. denied*, 406 U.S. 957 (1972). In *Rogers*, the Court of Appeals for the Fifth Circuit held that a Hispanic complainant could establish a Title VII violation by demonstrating that her employer created an offensive work environment for employees by giving discriminatory service to its Hispanic clientele....

Defendant [also] contends that ... the Court of Appeals erred in stat[ing] that testimony about plaintiff's "dress and personal fantasies," which the District Court apparently admitted into evidence, "had no place in this litigation." ... [A] complainant's sexually provocative speech or dress [may be] relevant [to a determination of] whether he or she found particular sexual advances unwelcome.... The EEOC Guidelines emphasize that the trier of fact must determine the existence of sexual harassment in light of "the record as a whole" and "the totality of circumstances, such as the nature of the sexual advances and the context in which the alleged incidents occurred." 29 C.F.R. § 1604.11(b) (1985). Plaintiff's claim that any marginal relevance of the evidence in question was outweighed by the potential for unfair prejudice is the sort of argument properly addressed to the District Court. In this case the District Court concluded that the evidence should be admitted, and the Court of Appeals' contrary conclusion was based upon the erroneous, categorical view that testimony about provocative dress and publicly expressed sexual fantasies "had no place in this litigation." While the District Court must carefully weigh the applicable considerations in deciding whether to admit evidence of this kind, there is no *per se* rule against its admissibility.

In sum, we hold that a claim of "hostile environment" sex discrimination is actionable under Title VII, that the District Court's findings were insufficient to dispose of respondent's hostile environment claim, and that the District Court did not err in admitting testimony about respondent's sexually provocative speech and dress. As to employer liability, we conclude that the Court of Appeals was wrong to entirely disregard agency principles and impose absolute liability on employers for the acts of their supervisors, regardless of the circumstances of a particular case. [Ed. Note: *Meritor* left open the question of when the employer would be liable for harassment. The next segment of *Meritor*, which discusses, but does not resolve, the employer liability issue, is included, *infra*, in the section on employer liability for workplace harassment.]

## Exercise 5.1

The *Meritor* Court concluded that sex-motivated hostile environment harassment qualifies as sex discrimination, and thus violates Title VII. To reach this conclusion, the Court relied on the case of *Rogers v. EEOC*, brought by a Hispanic complainant, for the proposition that Title VII affords employees the right to work in an environment free from discriminatory intimidation, ridicule, and insult. Although the *Meritor* Court did not set the exact contours of employer liability for toxic environments, it made clear that such liability accrues in some cases, thus creating an incentive for employers to "clean up" the workplace. This Exercise asks you to consider the obligation Title VII imposes on employers to hire supervisors capable of and willing to maintain a harassment-free workplace.

You are in-house counsel at McDuffy's Corporation, owner/operator of a chain of thirty hamburger outlets. Every year, you provide training to all supervisors about discriminatory harassment. Nevertheless, McDuffy's has recently received complaints about hostile treatment of women and racial minorities in McDuffy's outlets. The complaints have come from employees and customers alike, with special emphasis on the failure of store supervisors to take action when the treatment occurs.

As in-house counsel, you have been tasked with expanding the company's effort. In addition to continuing with an enhanced training program, the company wants you to assure that all applicants for supervisor positions are screened for sensitivity on the issue of discriminatory harassment. How will you help the hiring mangers identify and hire those applicants who are likely to respond effectively to complaints of harassment? Draft a list of questions to be asked by hiring managers that will help them determine which job applicants are likely to be sensitive to the problem. Is this screening effort likely to have the desired effect? Are there other steps that you would recommend?

For several years after the Supreme Court decided the *Meritor* case, lower courts struggled to devise the proper standards for determining what constitutes a discriminatorily abusive working environment. In the next case, the Court provided some answers. As you read *Harris*, consider whether the standard announced provided clear guidance to trial courts and whether questions about the proper standards remain open after *Harris*.

### Focus Questions: *Harris v. Forklift Systems, Inc.*

1. *The magistrate found that Hardy's treatment of Harris did not cause psychological injury or impair Harris' ability to do her job. Why did the Supreme Court nevertheless conclude that actionable harassment had occurred?*

2. *What does the Supreme Court decide on the subject of point of view? Whose point of view matters on the question of whether the abuse is sufficiently severe or pervasive to alter plaintiff's work conditions: the defendant's, the plaintiff's or the reasonable person's?*

# Harris v. Forklift Systems, Inc.

## 510 U.S. 17 (1993)

Justice O'Connor delivered the opinion of the Court.

In this case we consider the definition of a discriminatorily "abusive work environment" (also known as a "hostile work environment") under Title VII of the Civil Rights Act of 1964.

### I

Teresa Harris worked as a manager at Forklift Systems, Inc., an equipment rental company, from April 1985 until October 1987. Charles Hardy was Forklift's president.

The Magistrate found that, throughout Harris' time at Forklift, Hardy often insulted her because of her gender and often made her the target of unwanted sexual innuendos. Hardy told Harris on several occasions, in the presence of other employees, "You're a woman, what do you know" and "We need a man as the rental manager"; at least once, he told her she was "a dumb ass woman." Again in front of others, he suggested that the two of them "go to the Holiday Inn to negotiate [Harris'] raise." Hardy occasionally asked Harris and other female employees to get coins from his front pants pocket. He threw objects on the ground in front of Harris and other women, and asked them to pick the objects up. He made sexual innuendos about Harris' and other women's clothing.

In mid-August 1987, Harris complained to Hardy about his conduct. Hardy said he was surprised that Harris was offended, claimed he was only joking, and apologized. He also promised he would stop, and based on this assurance Harris stayed on the job. But in early September, Hardy began anew: While Harris was arranging a deal with one of Forklift's customers, he asked her, again in front of other employees, "What did you do, promise the guy ... some [sex] Saturday night?" On October 1, Harris collected her paycheck and quit.

Harris then sued Forklift, claiming that Hardy's conduct had created an abusive work environment for her because of her gender. The United States District Court for the Middle District of Tennessee, adopting the report and recommendation of the Magistrate, found this to be "a close case," but held that Hardy's conduct did not create an abusive environment. The court found that some of Hardy's comments "offended [Harris], and would offend the reasonable woman," but that they were not "so severe as to be expected to seriously affect [Harris'] psychological well-being. A reasonable woman manager under like circumstances would have been offended by Hardy, but his conduct would not have risen to the level of interfering with that person's work performance. [Nor was Harris] subjectively so offended that she suffered injury.... Although Hardy may at times have genuinely offended [Harris], ... [he did not create] a working environment so poisoned as to be intimidating or abusive to [Harris]."

... We granted certiorari to resolve a conflict among the Circuits on whether conduct, to be actionable as "abusive work environment" harassment (no *quid pro quo* harassment issue is present here), must "seriously affect [an employee's] psychological well-being" or lead the plaintiff to "suffe[r] injury."

## II

Title VII of the Civil Rights Act of 1964 makes it "an unlawful employment practice for an employer ... to discriminate against any individual with respect to his compensation, terms, conditions, or privileges of employment, because of such individual's race, color, religion, sex, or national origin." As we made clear in *Meritor Savings Bank, FSB v. Vinson,* 477 U.S. 57 (1986), this language "is not limited to 'economic' or 'tangible' discrimination. The phrase 'terms, conditions, or privileges of employment' evinces a congressional intent 'to strike at the entire spectrum of disparate treatment of men and women' in employment," which includes requiring people to work in a discriminatorily hostile or abusive environment. When the workplace is permeated with "discriminatory intimidation, ridicule, and insult," that is "sufficiently severe or pervasive to alter the conditions of the victim's employment and create an abusive working environment," Title VII is violated.

This standard, which we reaffirm today, takes a middle path between making actionable any conduct that is merely offensive and requiring the conduct to cause a tangible psychological injury. As we pointed out in *Meritor,* "mere utterance of an ... epithet which engenders offensive feelings in a employee," does not sufficiently affect the conditions of employment to implicate Title VII. Conduct that is not severe or pervasive enough to create an objectively hostile or abusive work environment—an environment that a reasonable person would find hostile or abusive—is beyond Title VII's purview. Likewise, if the victim does not subjectively perceive the environment to be abusive, the conduct has not actually altered the conditions of the victim's employment, and there is no Title VII violation.

But Title VII comes into play before the harassing conduct leads to a nervous breakdown. A discriminatorily abusive work environment, even one that does not seriously affect employees' psychological well-being, can and often will detract from employees' job performance, discourage employees from remaining on the job, or keep them from advancing in their careers. Moreover, even without regard to these tangible effects, the very fact that the discriminatory conduct was so severe or pervasive that it created a work environment abusive to employees because of their race, gender, religion, or national origin offends Title VII's broad rule of workplace equality. The appalling conduct alleged in *Meritor,* and the reference in that case to environments "so heavily polluted with discrimination as to destroy completely the emotional and psychological stability of minority group workers," merely present some especially egregious examples of harassment. They do not mark the boundary of what is actionable.

We therefore believe the District Court erred in relying on whether the conduct "seriously affect[ed] plaintiff's psychological well-being" or led her to "suffe[r] injury." Such an inquiry may needlessly focus the factfinder's attention on concrete psychological harm, an element Title VII does not require. Certainly Title VII bars conduct that would seriously affect a reasonable person's psychological well-being, but the statute is not limited to such conduct. So long as the environment would reasonably be perceived, and is perceived, as hostile or abusive, there is no need for it also to be psychologically injurious.

[W]hether an environment is "hostile" or "abusive" can be determined only by looking at all the circumstances. These may include the frequency of the discriminatory conduct; its severity; whether it is physically threatening or humiliating, or a mere offensive utterance; and whether it unreasonably interferes with an employee's work performance. The effect on the employee's psychological well-being is, of course, relevant to determining whether the plaintiff actually found the environment abusive. But while psychological harm, like any other relevant factor, may be taken into account, no single factor is required.

### III

…

We therefore reverse the judgment of the Court of Appeals, and remand the case for further proceedings consistent with this opinion.

*So ordered.*

Justice Scalia, concurring.

…

"Abusive" (or "hostile," which in this context I take to mean the same thing) does not seem to me a very clear standard — and I do not think clarity is at all increased by adding the adverb "objectively" or by appealing to a "reasonable person['s]" notion of what the vague word means…. Be that as it may, I know of no alternative to the course the Court today has taken. One of the factors mentioned in the Court's nonexhaustive list — whether the conduct unreasonably interferes with an employee's work performance — would, if it were made an absolute test, provide greater guidance to juries and employers. But I see no basis for such a limitation in the language of the statute.

Justice Ginsburg, concurring.

… [T]he adjudicator's inquiry should center, dominantly, on whether the discriminatory conduct has unreasonably interfered with the plaintiff's work performance. To show such interference, "the plaintiff need not prove that his or her tangible productivity has declined as a result of the harassment." [citation omitted]. It suffices to prove that a reasonable person subjected to the discriminatory conduct would find, as the plaintiff did, that the harassment so altered working conditions as to "ma[k]e it more difficult to do the job." [citation omitted].

---

## Further Discussion

Relying on *Meritor* and *Harris,* courts generally require the hostile environment harassment plaintiff to prove that (1) plaintiff belongs to a protected group; (2) plaintiff was subjected to unwelcome harassment; (3) the harassment was because of a protected trait; and (4) the harassment affected a term, condition, or privilege of employment. *See Harvil v. Westwood Comms., L.L.C.,* 433 F.3d 428, 434 (5th Cir. 2005). The test may be articulated differently, however, depending on the circuit. For example, in the context of sex-motivated hostile environment harassment, the First Circuit requires the plaintiff to establish "(1) that plaintiff is a member of a protected class; (2) that plaintiff was subjected to unwelcome sexual harassment; (3) that the harassment was based upon sex; (4) that the harassment was sufficiently severe or pervasive to alter the conditions of plaintiff's employment and create an abusive work environment; and (5) that sexually objectionable conduct was both objectively and subjectively offensive, such that a reasonable person would find it hostile or abusive and the victim in fact did perceive it to be so." *Agusty-Reyes v. Dept. of Educ. of Puerto Rico,* 601 F.3d 45, 53 (1st Cir. 2010).

In virtually every hostile environment case, no matter how the court organizes the elements, the question of whether actionable harassment occurred usually turns on three issues: whether the conduct was *unwelcome,* whether the conduct was *because of* a protected trait, and whether the conduct was *severe or pervasive* enough to alter the terms or conditions of employment. The question of whether plaintiff is a member of a protected group is unlikely to be litigated since reverse discrimination is actionable.

The essential elements for proving harassment are explored in more detail below. Before that discussion, though, it is worth mentioning that these elements of harassment remain the same, regardless of who the harasser is. Whether the accused harasser is a supervisor, a co-worker, a customer or even a member of the general public, the occurrence of harassment usually must be proven through the elements described above. Although the harasser's identity does not always affect the elements for purposes of proving that harassment occurred, *but cf.* Susan Grover and Kimberly Piro, *Consider The Source: When The Harasser Is The Boss,* 79 Fordham L. Rev. 499 (2010), harasser identity does have significance for establishing whether the employer will be held liable for a particular instance of workplace harassment once proven. We will discuss the standards for holding the employer liable for harassment later in this Chapter. For now, keep in mind that the question of whether harassment occurred is separate from the question of whether an employer is held liable for any harassment that did occur.

## ✦ Core Concept: Because of a Protected Trait

The *Meritor* Court recognized the availability of claims for both hostile environment harassment and quid pro quo harassment. As to both types of harassment, the Court emphasized that plaintiffs may prevail only by proving the harassment was *because of* or *motivated by* the target's sex or other protected trait. In a case where the harassment involves sexual demands or is otherwise sexual in content, it may often be easy to conclude that harassment is *because of* sex. For harassment cases involving sheer hostility with little or no ostensible sexual content, however, proving that a protected trait motivated the abuse can be less obvious.

# Oncale v. Sundowner Offshore Services

## 523 U.S. 75 (1998)

Justice Scalia delivered the opinion of the Court.

This case presents the question whether workplace harassment can violate Title VII's prohibition against "discriminat[ion] … because of … sex," when the harasser and the harassed employee are of the same sex.

## I

The District Court having granted summary judgment for respondents, we must assume the facts to be as alleged by petitioner Joseph Oncale. The precise details are irrelevant to the legal point we must decide, and in the interest of both brevity and dignity we shall describe them only generally. In late October 1991, Oncale was working for respondent Sundowner Offshore Services, Inc., on a Chevron U.S.A., Inc., oil platform in the Gulf of Mexico. He was employed as a roustabout on an eight-man crew which included respondents John Lyons, Danny Pippen, and Brandon Johnson. Lyons, the crane operator, and Pippen, the driller, had supervisory authority. On several occasions, Oncale was forcibly subjected to sex-related, humiliating actions against him by Lyons, Pippen, and Johnson in the presence of the rest of the crew. Pippen and Lyons also physically assaulted Oncale in a sexual manner, and Lyons threatened him with rape.

Oncale's complaints to supervisory personnel produced no remedial action; in fact, the company's Safety Compliance Clerk, Valent Hohen, told Oncale that Lyons and Pippen "picked [on] him all the time too," and called him a name suggesting homosexuality. Oncale eventually quit—asking that his pink slip reflect that he "voluntarily left due to sexual harassment and verbal abuse." When asked at his deposition why he left Sundowner, Oncale stated: "I felt that if I didn't leave my job, that I would be raped or forced to have sex."

Oncale filed a complaint against Sundowner in the United States District Court for the Eastern District of Louisiana, alleging that he was discriminated against in his employment because of his sex. [T]he District Court held that "Mr. Oncale, a male, has no cause of action under Title VII for harassment by male co-workers." On appeal, a panel of the Fifth Circuit affirmed. We granted certiorari.

## II

Title VII of the Civil Rights Act of 1964 provides, in relevant part, that "[i]t shall be an unlawful employment practice for an employer … to discriminate against any individual with respect to his compensation, terms, conditions, or privileges of employment, because of such individual's race, color, religion, sex, or national origin." We have held that this not only covers "terms" and "conditions" in the narrow contractual sense, but "evinces a congressional intent to strike at the entire spectrum of disparate treatment of men and women in employment." *Meritor Savings Bank, FSB v. Vinson,* 477 U.S. 57, 64 (1986). "When the workplace is permeated with discriminatory intimidation, ridicule, and insult that is sufficiently severe or pervasive to alter the conditions of the victim's employment and create an abusive working environment, Title VII is violated." *Harris v. Forklift Systems, Inc.,* 510 U.S. 17, 21 (1993).

Title VII's prohibition of discrimination "because of … sex" protects men as well as women, *Newport News Shipbuilding & Dry Dock Co. v. EEOC,* 462 U.S. 669, 682 (1983), and in the related context of racial discrimination in the workplace we have rejected any conclusive presumption that an employer will not discriminate against members of his own race. "Because of the many facets of human motivation, it would be unwise to presume as a matter of law that human beings of one definable group will not discriminate against other members of their group." [citation omitted].... If our precedents leave any doubt on the question, we hold today that nothing in Title VII necessarily bars a claim of discrimination "because of ... sex" merely because the plaintiff and the defendant (or the person charged with acting on behalf of the defendant) are of the same sex.

Courts have had little trouble with that principle ... where an employee claims to have been passed over for a job or promotion. But when the issue arises in the context of a "hostile environment" sexual harassment claim, the state and federal courts have taken a bewildering variety of stances. Some, like the Fifth Circuit in this case, have held that same-sex sexual harassment claims are never cognizable under Title VII. Other decisions say that such claims are actionable only if the plaintiff can prove that the harasser is homosexual (and thus presumably motivated by sexual desire). Still others suggest that workplace harassment that is sexual in content is always actionable, regardless of the harasser's sex, sexual orientation, or motivations.

We see no justification in the statutory language or our precedents for a categorical rule excluding same-sex harassment claims from the coverage of Title VII. As some courts have observed, male-on-male sexual harassment in the workplace was assuredly not the principal evil Congress was concerned with when it enacted Title VII. But statutory prohibitions often go beyond the principal evil to cover reasonably comparable evils, and it is ultimately the provisions of our laws rather than the principal concerns of our legislators by which we are governed. Title VII prohibits "discriminat[ion] ... because of ... sex" in the "terms" or "conditions" of employment. Our holding that this includes sexual harassment must extend to sexual harassment of any kind that meets the statutory requirements.

Respondents and their *amici* contend that recognizing liability for same-sex harassment will transform Title VII into a general civility code for the American workplace. But that risk is no greater for same-sex than for opposite-sex harassment, and is adequately met by careful attention to the requirements of the statute. Title VII does not prohibit all verbal or physical harassment in the workplace; it is directed only at "*discriminat[ion] ... because of ... sex.*" We have never held that workplace harassment, even harassment between men and women, is automatically discrimination because of sex merely because the words used have sexual content or connotations. "The critical issue, Title VII's text indicates, is whether members of one sex are exposed to disadvantageous terms or conditions of employment to which members of the other sex are not exposed." [citation omitted].

Courts and juries have found the inference of discrimination easy to draw in most male-female sexual harassment situations, because the challenged conduct typically involves explicit or implicit proposals of sexual activity; it is reasonable to assume those proposals would not have been made to someone of the same sex. The same chain of inference would be available to a plaintiff alleging same-sex harassment, if there were credible evidence that the harasser was homosexual. But harassing conduct need not be motivated by sexual desire to support an inference of discrimination on the basis of sex. A trier of fact might reasonably find such discrimination, for example, if a female victim is harassed in such sex-specific and derogatory terms by another woman as to make it clear that the harasser is motivated by general hostility to the presence of women in the workplace. A same-sex harassment plaintiff may also, of course, offer direct comparative evidence about how the alleged harasser treated members of both sexes in a mixed-sex workplace. Whatever evidentiary route the plaintiff chooses to follow, he or she must always prove that the conduct at issue was not merely tinged with offensive sexual connotations, but actually constituted *"discrimina[tion] … because of … sex."*

And there is another requirement that prevents Title VII from expanding into a general civility code: As we emphasized in *Meritor* and *Harris*, the statute does not reach genuine but innocuous differences in the ways men and women routinely interact with members of the same sex and of the opposite sex. The prohibition of harassment on the basis of sex requires neither asexuality nor androgyny in the workplace; it forbids only behavior so objectively offensive as to alter the "conditions" of the victim's employment. "Conduct that is not severe or pervasive enough to create an objectively hostile or abusive work environment—an environment that a reasonable person would find hostile or abusive—is beyond Title VII's purview." [citation omitted]. We have always regarded that requirement as crucial, and as sufficient to ensure that courts and juries do not mistake ordinary socializing in the workplace—such as male-on-male horseplay or intersexual flirtation—for discriminatory "conditions of employment."

We have emphasized, moreover, that the objective severity of harassment should be judged from the perspective of a reasonable person in the plaintiff's position, considering "all the circumstances." [citation omitted]. In same-sex (as in all) harassment cases, that inquiry requires careful consideration of the social context in which particular behavior occurs and is experienced by its target. A professional football player's working environment is not severely or pervasively abusive, for example, if the coach smacks him on the buttocks as he heads onto the field—even if the same behavior would reasonably be experienced as abusive by the coach's secretary (male or female) back at the office. The real social impact of workplace behavior often depends on a constellation of surrounding circumstances, expectations, and relationships which are not fully captured by a simple recitation of the words used or the physical acts performed. Common sense, and an appropriate sensitivity to social context, will enable courts and juries to distinguish between simple teasing or roughhousing among members of the same sex, and conduct which a reasonable person in the plaintiff's position would find severely hostile or abusive.

### III

Because we conclude that sex discrimination consisting of same-sex sexual harassment is actionable under Title VII, the judgment of the Court of Appeals for the Fifth Circuit is reversed, and the case is remanded for further proceedings consistent with this opinion.

---

## Notes

1. Because sexual orientation claims are not cognizable under Title VII, harassment claims related to sexual orientation are often raised in the context of sex discrimination. Some courts have held that harassing comments made regarding an individual's sex or the individual's conformance with sex stereotypes can lead to liability under Title VII. Other courts have held that such comments do not create liability under Title VII, because they are motivated by sexual orientation, not sex.

2. Because the federal anti-discrimination laws require a showing that harassment is motivated by a protected trait, those laws do not protect against generic (nondiscriminatory) harassment. For this reason, there is currently a move in some legal circles to expand statutory protections against nondiscriminatory bullying in the workplace, at school, on the internet and elsewhere. *See* David Yamada, *Crafting a Legislative Response to Workplace Bullying*, 8

EMP. RTS. & EMP. POL'Y J. 475 (2004). In response to grass roots movements across the country, "Healthy Workplace" bills have been introduced in numerous state legislatures.

---

## Exercise 5.2

Steve is the supervisor of the department. Steve is a bad manager. He routinely yells at all employees in the office, male or female. When he yells, he often uses demeaning language, telling women that "women shouldn't even be working outside the home" and telling men "that if they were more of a man, they would not mess up so many projects." Steve often uses explicitly gender-stereotyped language and epithets to both male and female employees. Can a female employee prove a sex-based harassment case against Steve?

---

## ✦ Core Concept: Unwelcomeness

In order to establish unlawful harassment, the plaintiff must prove that the alleged abuse was *unwelcome*. The Ninth Circuit has explained that the plaintiff must prove unwelcomeness "in the sense that the employee did not solicit or incite it, and in the sense that the employee regarded the conduct as undesirable or offensive." *Henson v. City of Dundee*, 682 F.2d 897, 903 (9th Cir. 1982). Proving unwelcomeness can be difficult in cases where the conduct is ostensibly romantic in nature or where the plaintiff seems a willing participant in workplace banter that is later challenged as abusive. In other cases, where harassment consists of overtly abusive conduct in which the plaintiff clearly did not acquiesce, it is often safe to assume that the target did not welcome the behavior.

Difficulties of proving unwelcomeness are common when the harassment involves sexual advances. This is because the challenged conduct might be perfectly acceptable in some other context or between some other people. In some circumstances, especially those involving consensual conduct that later becomes unwelcome, courts may require the plaintiff to demonstrate that the plaintiff clearly signaled to the alleged harasser that the conduct was unwelcome. *Chamberlin v. 101 Realty, Inc.*, 915 F.2d 777 (1st Cir. 1990).

Title VII does not prohibit all conduct of a sexual nature in the workplace. Consensual relationships do not constitute hostile environment harassment if the conduct is welcome. When the consensual relationship ends, however, a claim may arise if now-unwelcome conduct persists in the face of communication by plaintiff that the conduct is unwelcome. *See, e.g., Green v. Adm'rs of the Tulane Educ. Fund.*, 284 F.3d 642 (5th Cir. 2002).

Many employers have policies against consensual amorous relationships between co-workers, even if the law permits them. If the employer is a government employer, thus bound by the First Amendment, might such a prohibition violate that amendment's free association clause? In *Kukla v. Antioch*, two employees of a municipality were dating and eventually living together. Upon discovering their relationship, the employer terminated both employees under a municipal policy prohibiting amorous relationships between co-workers. The co-workers sued for a violation of their First Amendment right to free association. The court granted summary judgment for defendant, balancing the plaintiff's associational interests against the municipality's interests embodied in the amorous relationship policy. 647 F. Supp. 799 (N.D. Ill. 1986). *See also* Gary M. Kramer, *Limited License to Fish off the Company Pier: Toward Express Employer Policies on Supervisor-Subordinate Fraternization*, 22 W. New Eng. L. Rev. 77, 112–115 (2000).

If a consensual amorous relationship exists between a supervisor and a subordinate employee, and the subordinate gains job advantages as a result, should other workers who do not have the opportunity to gain such advantages be able to recover for sex discrimination? What if a male complains because women have a chance to sleep their way to the top and men do not? In the case of *Miller v. Department of Corrections*, the advantages reaped by the supervisor's sexual partners became so great that "sleeping with the boss" became viewed as the only way for women to advance in the workplace, thus giving rise to a discrimination claim. 115 P.3d 77 (Cal. 2005).

Even in the absence of romantic involvement, the line between welcomeness and unwelcomeness may be unclear. Consider this: a supervisor sends a subordinate funny emails or instant messages that are welcome and reciprocated at first, but that become unwelcome with increasing sexual content. What must the subordinate employee do to "undo" the welcomeness she expressed at the outset? In *Kraus v. Howroyd-Wright Employment Agency*, an employee initially engaged in consensual, flirty "Instant Message" communications, but became increasingly uncomfortable with the conduct. After a threatening encounter, the employee resigned and filed a claim of sexual harassment. The court granted defendant's motion for summary judgment, finding no conduct rising to the level of a hostile work environment. No. 06-975, 2008 U.S. Dist. LEXIS 1254, at *31–32 (E.D. Pa. Jan. 8, 2008).

Although a plaintiff's apparent complicity in the challenged conduct, such as telling sexist or racist jokes, may create skepticism about the conduct's unwelcomeness, such a plaintiff may still be able to demonstrate the alleged harassment was unwelcome. The plaintiff may be able to show that the challenged conduct was of a type or degree different from the conduct in which the plaintiff participated. In *Horney v. Westfield Gage Co., Inc.*, for example, the court observed that the jury might reasonably distinguish between the plaintiff's "joking references to sexual material" and "her supervisor's screamed obscenities, offensive and derogatory comments regarding whether she or her mother were engaging in sex acts with particular co-workers, and statements about women's role at Westfield." 77 Fed. Appx. 24, 30 (1st Cir. 2003).

Some plaintiffs have successfully argued that they engaged in offensive behavior as a coping mechanism in response to harassment. Thus, in *Garcez v. Freightliner Corp.*, the court concluded that a reasonable jury could find that racially motivated conduct and comments directed at the plaintiff were subjectively unwelcome even though plaintiff had engaged in some similar conduct as a coping mechanism. 72 P.3d 78, 86 (2003).

---

## Exercise 5.3

Frank Labit works in an environment where practical jokes are normal. Frank is good friends with Bob Anderson (Frank's supervisor) and Terry Polen. The three men often take hunting and fishing trips together and are considered to be the "life of the party" at work social events. Frequently, Bob, Terry and Frank engage in horseplay and practical jokes at work. Frank once filled Terry's office with balloons, and on several occasions Bob and Terry hid Frank's lunch in odd places around the worksite.

As a result of a childhood accident, Frank lost his right arm and uses a prosthesis. On numerous occasions, Bob and Terry have made jokes about Frank's amputation. In response, Frank would tease Bob and Terry about their height and weight. At one Halloween party, Bob dressed up as Frank, and his costume included a prosthetic arm that spewed blood if anyone shook his hand.

Last month, Frank received a suspension without pay for violation of company policies. After the suspension, Frank complained to the Human Resources Office about the disability-related jokes. Frank did not complain about this conduct until after receiving the suspension. You are now a plaintiff's lawyer. Based on the applicable law, would you take Frank's case?

## Exercise 5.4

During lunch with her male and female work friends, Jane often makes jokes of a sexual nature. These lunch gatherings do not include another co-worker, Steve, who is not a friend of Jane's. Every day, when Steve sees Jane in the hall, Steve makes jokes of a sexual nature. Occasionally he sends Jane bawdy e-mail messages containing nudity. Jane says nothing when Steve jokes with her in the hall and does nothing in response to the e-mails. Will Jane's silence preclude her demonstrating unwelcomeness? Can evidence of her lunch-time joking be used against her if she challenges Steve's behavior as harassment?

## ✦ Core Concept: Severe or Pervasive

In order to be cognizable as discriminatory harassment, the challenged conduct must be severe or pervasive enough to alter the terms and conditions of a plaintiff's employment. Note that this standard is disjunctive: the plaintiff need *not* show both severity and pervasiveness. The *Harris* Court indicated that, in making this inquiry, courts should consider: "the frequency of the discriminatory conduct; its severity; whether it is physically threatening or humiliating, or a mere offensive utterance; and whether it unreasonably interferes with an employee's work performance." Note that there are two points of view that matter for purposes of the standard: the plaintiff's and the reasonable person's. The harassment must be so severe or pervasive that (1) it causes the plaintiff to find the work environment abusive (subjective standard), and (2) it would cause a reasonable person to find the work environment abusive (objective standard).

In determining whether an employee subjectively views the harassment as severe or pervasive, courts can consider the effect of the conduct on the employee's psychological well-being. As *Harris* demonstrates, however, psychological harm is not required to establish cognizable harassment. Regarding the objective prong, requiring that a reasonable person would find the workplace to be hostile or abusive, some courts deem the "reasonable person" to mean a reasonable person of plaintiff's gender. *See, e.g., Ellison v. Brady,* 924 F. 2d 872 (9th Cir. 1991); *cf. Oncale v. Sundowner Offshore Services, Inc.* 523 U.S. 75, 82 (1998) (describing standard as "reasonable person in plaintiff's position"). Can you think of circumstances where a case might depend on whether the conduct was viewed through the lens of a reasonable man or a reasonable woman?

## Exercise 5.5

Would the requirement of severity or pervasiveness be met in the following instances?

- A co-worker or supervisor rapes Jane one time.
- A co-worker or supervisor hangs nude centerfolds around the workplace where Jane necessarily sees them.
- A co-worker or supervisor compliments Jane's new hairstyle.
- A co-worker or supervisor invites Jane to lunch.

## Exercise 5.6

You are an attorney in private practice, specializing in employment discrimination and representing primarily plaintiffs. A new client, Fran Freeburn, comes to your office to talk to you about a situation she has been experiencing at work. Fran is the only female on a team of oil rig workers. She describes an ongoing tirade of abuse, replete with vulgarities and sexual content inflicted upon her daily by her immediate superior and coworkers on her team. As she recounts the story, Fran surprises you by using a number of expletives. None of these is sexual in content, but her manner of speaking makes you believe that Fran is probably somewhat hardened to the abuse likely to be exchanged by workers on an oil rig. What questions will you ask Ms. Freeburn to assess whether the facts of her case would support a finding that the abuse was both objectively and subjectively sufficiently severe or pervasive to support a claim for harassment?

## Exercise 5.7

At trial, when the plaintiff and his or her witnesses take the stand, what sorts of facts might they recount to prove that the plaintiff perceived the conduct as abusive (subjective test) and was reasonable in perceiving it that way (objective test)?

The following case considers whether plaintiff Ranee Tademy's facts are sufficient to prove the severe or pervasive element in a racial harassment case. Because the trial court granted summary judgment for the employer, the only question the appellate court must decide is whether a reasonable jury *could* conclude that the abuse was severe or pervasive.

### Focus Questions: *Tademy v. Union Pacific Corporation*

1. *Are courts likely to treat claims of racial harassment identically to how they treat claims of sex-based harassment, or are they likely to discriminate between the two types of claims?*

2. *Do you think that Mr. Tademy did everything within his power to mitigate the problem, or should he have made a greater effort to inform management of the situation?*

3. *If you were in-house counsel at Union Pacific, would you approve the decision to have Cagle conduct equal opportunity training for other employees? What do you view as the objectives of training exercises, and how can they best be achieved in this situation?*

---

# Tademy v. Union Pacific Corporation
### 520 F.3d 1149 (10th Cir. 2008)

Circuit Judge Henry.

I. Background

...

The events supporting Mr. Tademy's claim began in 1995, when he was working as a foreman and one of his crew members, Shane Marvin, seemed to ignore his radio communications. When Mr. Tademy asked Bud Sadler, a coworker, if he had any idea why Mr. Marvin was not responding, he told Mr. Tademy that "Shane doesn't like black people." Mr. Tademy approached Mr. Marvin during a break and asked him if he was ignoring his radio communications because he harbored racial animosity. Mr. Marvin responded by rising out of his chair and approaching Mr. Tademy in a physically threatening manner. Mr. Tademy avoided a physical altercation by walking away and telling the manager of yard operations. Union Pacific never talked to Mr. Marvin about the incident.

In 1996, Mr. Tademy found the word "N*****" etched into his locker. He covered the word with a sticker and reported the graffiti to the yard manager on duty, Scott Wagner. In response, Mr. Wagner mentioned that his daughter dated an African American who played football for the University of Utah. He assured Mr. Tademy, "No matter what anybody says about you, Ranee, you're all right with me." Union Pacific made no effort to find the culprit.

In 1997, Mr. Tademy found the words "N***** go home" written on his locker. He also discovered two racist cartoons posted on company billboards. One was a crude cartoon drawing of a simian figure with an "Afro" hairstyle labeled "monkey" posted on a company billboard. Mr. Tademy removed the first cartoon himself and reported the second one to a union representative.

In 1998, Mr. Tademy saw the word "N*****" on a restroom wall. He reported it to Manager of Operations Lyndon Raphael, who told him that he had removed it.

In 1999, in Mr. Tademy's presence, Mark Bleckert, a Union Pacific employee, referred to Lyndon Raphael, an African-American Union Pacific manager, as "F* * *ing Kunta Kinte," presumably an allusion to the character in Alex Haley's *Roots* who was brought from Africa to America as a slave. Mr. Tademy reported the incident to Mr. Raphael and the superintendent, Ted Lewis. Union Pacific did not conduct an investigation and did not discipline Mr. Bleckert.

In 2000, Mr. Tademy discovered the words "N***** swimming pool" with an arrow pointing at the toilet along with a "Sambo" character drawn on a restroom wall. Mr. Tademy again reported the incident to the yard manager, Mr. Raphael, who described it to someone up the Union Pacific chain of command, but Union Pacific merely removed the graffiti without investigation.

On January 29, 2001, Mr. Tademy reported for a shift approximately five minutes late, and David Cagle, another yard manager, asked Mr. Tademy, "What time does this job go to work, boy?" in the presence of at least two other employees. Mr. Tademy was offended by Mr. Cagle's use of the word "boy," and he reported the incident to his yard manager and called Union Pacific's Equal Employment Opportunity (EEO) hotline. This time, in response to Mr. Tademy's report, Norris Wiseman, Mr. Cagle's supervisor, and Yvonne Method-Walker, Union Pacific's manager of EEO compliance, conducted an investigation. In conjunction with that investigation, Cameron Scott, Union Pacific's superintendent of the Salt Lake City unit, determined that Mr. Cagle should take a 30-day fully paid leave of absence. The company also mandated that he attend a diversity workshop in Omaha, Nebraska, and required Mr. Cagle to conduct EEO sessions at different locations in the company's various units in Salt Lake City.

… In some instances, Mr. Tademy's decision to report Mr. Cagle's comment became a point of contention between Mr. Tademy and other Union Pacific employees. One Union Pacific manager told Mr. Tademy, "the railroad is watching you because you made that charge against Cagle, and you better watch out because they're watching you."

In June of 2001, after what Mr. Tademy believed was a lackluster response to the Cagle incident, he filed a charge of discrimination with the Utah Antidiscrimination & Labor Division (UALD). In his complaint, Mr. Tademy listed his threatening confrontation with Mr. Marvin, the "N*****" etching on his locker, the "Kunte Kinte" incident, the "N***** swimming pool" and the Sambo graffiti, along with the Cagle incident. In addition, during the course of the Cagle investigation, and after he filed his discrimination claim, Mr. Tademy learned from Mr. Raphael that he had found and erased graffiti reading "hang all N*****s and jews" in the bathroom wall of the north shanty. Mr. Raphael cleaned up the graffiti, but the company never attempted to discover the perpetrator. Mr. Tademy included this incident in his UALD complaint.

In January 2002, while Mr. Tademy's discrimination charge was pending, a Union Pacific employee, Charlie White, hacked into a manager's e-mail account and sent an e-mail from the manager's account to a significant number of Union Pacific employees admonishing them to "Keep an eye on the slaves, seriously." Although Mr. White did not send the e-mail to Mr. Tademy, he saw it when a recipient printed out copies and posted them all over Union Pacific's facilities. Union Pacific investigated the incident and terminated Mr. White. However, the company reinstated Mr. White four to six months later.

After receiving a right-to-sue letter in August of 2002, Mr. Tademy met with Mr. Scott (the superintendent of the Salt Lake City unit) and expressed a desire to avoid litigation "[b]ecause all [he] ever wanted was to be able to continue working without being subject to ongoing harassment." Ultimately, Mr. Tademy "agreed not to pursue a lawsuit against Union Pacific if the company promised it would incorporate annual EEO training into the mandatory Session B trainings." In addition, Union Pacific promised that it would "do on-going annual EEO training." However, according to the Superintendent of Union Pacific's Salt Lake Service Unit, the company cancelled the training in 2003 for financial reasons.

In 2003, Mr. Tademy was required to undergo random drug testing for three consecutive weeks. Although a white co-worker, Richard Puffer, was tested along with Mr. Tademy on each occasion, Mr. Tademy alleges that these drug tests were conducted in retaliation for his discrimination claim.

Finally, on July 4, 2003, Mr. Tademy entered Union Pacific's south shanty and was immediately struck by what appeared to be a life-size hangman's noose prominently suspended from a large industrial wall clock. The sight of the noose caused Mr. Tademy to become so nauseated that he vomited. He immediately attempted to notify the yard manager on duty. When none was available, he worked his shift, found yard manager Mike Simmons, and reported the noose. He also notified the Union Pacific EEO office as well as his union representative, Blaine Bailey. Mr. Simmons contacted Mr. Scott, who sent Mark Rowley, a Union Pacific special agent, to investigate. After Mr. Rowley and a Union Pacific manager viewed the noose and interviewed employees, Jan Erickson, a Union Pacific employee, confessed to placing the rope above the clock, but denied any malicious intent. Instead, Mr. Erickson explained that he found the rope in the rail yard and placed it over the clock so that he would remember to take it for use on his truck.

After conducting a hearing, Union Pacific terminated Mr. Erickson's employment. However, Mr. Erickson appealed the decision to a public law board, which ordered his restatement after a year's suspension without pay. Union Pacific held several town hall meetings to discuss how a hanging noose could violate the EEO policy. However, the company did not require Mr. Erickson to undergo any EEO training.

In the fall of 2003, Mr. Tademy was placed on disability retirement after a specialist diagnosed him with major depression, post-traumatic stress disorder, and anxiety disorder. In January 2004, Mr. Tademy filed a second charge of discrimination with the UALD. After receiving his right-to-sue letter, Mr. Tademy filed suit in the United States District Court for the District of Utah under Title VII of the 1964 Civil Rights Act and 42 U.S.C. § 1981. The district court granted summary judgment for Union Pacific, and this appeal followed.

II. Discussion

… Taking all of the hostile environment factors into account … and, again, drawing all reasonable inferences in Mr. Tademy's favor, as we must, we hold that a reasonable jury could find that Mr. Tademy was subjected to a racially hostile work environment in violation of Title VII.

…

2. Severity or Pervasiveness

… [W]e [must] assess whether a reasonable jury could conclude that "[Mr. Tademy's] workplace [was] permeated with discriminatory intimidation, ridicule, and insult, that [was] sufficiently severe or pervasive to alter the conditions of [his] employment and create an abusive working environment." We have stated that "[p]ervasiveness and severity are independent and equal grounds" upon which a plaintiff may establish this element of a hostile environment claim…. Nevertheless, those two grounds "are, to a certain degree inversely related; a sufficiently severe episode may occur as rarely as once…, while a relentless pattern of lesser harassment that extends over a long period of time also violates the statute." [citations omitted].

"In making this determination, we consider the work atmosphere both objectively and subjectively, looking at all the circumstances from the perspective of a reasonable person in the plaintiff's position." [citation omitted]. We may consider the conduct's frequency and severity; "whether it is physically threatening or humiliating, or a mere offensive utterance"; and whether it unreasonably interferes with the plaintiff employee's work performance. The inquiry "is particularly unsuited for summary judgment because it is quintessentially a question of fact." [citation omitted].

Here, Mr. Tademy has alleged a series of acts of harassment, "culminating in the life-sized lynching noose[,]" an incident that affected him so profoundly that he did not return to work at Union Pacific. Considering the evidence in the light most favorable to Mr. Tademy, we conclude that a reasonable jury could find the harassment alleged by Mr. Tademy was "sufficiently severe ... to alter the conditions of [his] employment and create an abusive working environment."

In addition, a jury could easily find that the noose was an egregious act of discrimination calculated to intimidate African-Americans. *See Williams v. N.Y.C. Housing Auth.*, 154 F. Supp. 2d 820, 825 (S.D. N.Y. 2001) ("The ... noose remains a potent and threatening symbol for African-Americans, in part because the grim specter of racially motivated violence continues to manifest itself in present day hate crimes."). While it is associated with vigilante justice in the American West, and even state-sanctioned capital punishment, Judge Robert Carter, a judge in the Southern District of New York and a leading figure in civil rights law, has observed that

> [i]t is impossible to appreciate the impact of the display of a noose without understanding this nation's opprobrious legacy of violence against African-Americans. One study notes that from 1882, the earliest date for reliable statistics, to 1968, 3,446 African-Americans died at the hands of lynch mobs. *See* Robert L. Zangrado, the NAACP Crusade Against Lynching, 1909–1950 4 (1980). Obviously, these figures underestimate the actual number of blacks who were the victims of lynchings because such atrocities were underreported.

> The effect of such violence on the psyche of African-Americans cannot be exaggerated.

[citation omitted].

In the instant case, Mr. Tademy was so disturbed by the sight of the noose that he became physically ill. The noose incident must also be viewed in light of the fact that Mr. Tademy was aware of the "hang all N*****s and jews" graffiti, a fact that understandably intensified his reaction. We acknowledge that the placement of the noose may have involved no racist intent at all, as Mr. Erickson maintained. In any event, while there may be legitimate arguments on both sides, these arguments should take place before a jury that will have the opportunity to evaluate the evidence, demeanor, and candor of witnesses.

... While it is possible that a jury might believe that the slaves e-mail and Mr. Bleckert's remark were not racially motivated, the question of whether they were and, if so, how they would have affected Mr. Tademy's work environment are "particularly unsuited for summary judgment because [they are] quintessentially question[s] of fact."

We also note that "evidence of a general work atmosphere, including evidence of harassment of other [racial minorities], may be considered in evaluating a claim," as long as Mr. Tademy presents evidence that he knew about the offending behavior.

[The court reversed summary judgment and remanded for trial of Tademy's harassment claim.]

---

## Exercise 5.8

Recall that, as an employment discrimination attorney, your role is often to provide advice to clients before a lawsuit has been filed. In many ways, lawyers for employers play an important role in advising their clients about preventing discrimination and discrimination claims.

You are in house counsel for the J and L Railroad. The J and L human resource office has been receiving anonymous complaints about racial hostility in the workplace. Following up on one such complaint, the human resources director finds racial epithets written on the walls of two different men's rooms. In addition, an African American woman employee complains to the human resources office that someone slashed her tires in the parking lot at work. What advice will you give J and L's management?

## ✦ Core Concept: Motive vs. Content of Harassment

Sometimes courts fail to recognize sex-motivated hostile environment harassment because the content of the harassment is sex-neutral. The term "sexual harassment" has generally been used to describe sex-based harassment, whether sexual in content or not. Harassing conduct need not be motivated by sexual *desire* to support an inference of discrimination on the basis of sex.

Here is an example: *because of the target's sex*, the harasser screams hateful words at the target, calls her "stupid and incompetent," puts dirt in her lunch box, excludes her from important meetings, sends her hate mail and flattens the tires of her car. There is nothing sexual in the content of the harassment, but the harasser's motive (what animates the harasser) is, indeed, the target's sex. The conduct qualifies as actionable sex-based harassment, even though it is not sexual. This instance of sex-based harassment is similar to race-based harassment, which is discussed in the *Tademy* case. Because sexual harassment has sometimes overshadowed other types of discriminatory harassment, courts and others have occasionally failed to recognize such content-neutral harassment as sex-based. This confusion probably dates back to 1980, when the Equal Employment Opportunity Commission adopted a single guideline ostensibly pertaining to all harassment based on sex, titling it "Sexual Harassment." That Guideline limited the prohibitions to sexualized conduct:

> Unwelcome sexual advances, requests for sexual favors, and other verbal or physical conduct of a sexual nature constitute sexual harassment when this conduct explicitly or implicitly affects an individual's employment, unreasonably interferes with an individual's work performance, or creates an intimidating, hostile, or offensive work environment.

The EEOC webpage now corrects any misimpression by additionally defining discriminatory harassment more broadly, to include sex-motivated harassment.

> Harassment is a form of employment discrimination that violates Title VII of the Civil Rights Act of 1964, the Age Discrimination in Employment Act of 1967, and the Americans with Disabilities Act of 1990.

> Harassment is unwelcome conduct that is based on race, color, religion, sex, national origin, age (40 or older), disability, or genetic information. Harassment becomes unlawful where 1) enduring the offensive conduct becomes a condition of continued employment, or 2) the conduct is severe or pervasive enough to create a work environment that a reasonable person would consider intimidating, hostile, or abusive.

EEOC Prohibited Practices: Harassment, http://www.eeoc.gov/laws/practices/harassment.cfm (last visited Sept. 17, 2013).

For some graphic examples of sex-based hostile environment harassment (both sexual and non-sexual in content), *see* NORTH COUNTRY (Indus. Ent'mt. 2005), a narrative film based loosely on the case of *Jenson v. Eveleth Taconite Co.,* 130 F.3d 1287 (8th Cir. 1997), a harassment class action lawsuit.

## ✦ Core Concept: Employer Liability for Harassment

Once the plaintiff has proven that workplace harassment occurred, the question becomes whether the employer should be held liable for that harassment. Courts generally agree that Title VII and the other federal employment discrimination statutes do not allow recovery against the discriminating wrongdoer in an individual capacity. Thus, a plaintiff will recover only if the harasser is one for whose actions the employer will be held liable.

For most types of discrimination, there is little question of whether the employer should be held responsible for the acts of those it entrusts to conduct its business. If a supervisor sets pay or hires or fires in a discriminatory manner, the supervisor clearly is exercising powers delegated by the employer, and the employer is thus liable for wrongdoing in that exercise. Liability for workplace harassment is different because, although the supervisor may abuse delegated authority in harassing an employee, the employer usually does not delegate authority to harass. "Harassing employees" is not typically in anyone's job description. Rules governing when the employer should be held liable for workplace harassment have evolved over decades.

Prior to 1998, there was confusion among the courts on the standard(s) of employer liability that should apply to hostile environment discriminatory harassment cases. Liability in the quid pro quo cases had always been imputed to the employer under agency principles because the supervisor was arguably using power granted by the employer to extract sexual favors. The hostile environment situation was different because environmental harassment does not necessarily involve delegated authority. The Supreme Court's *Meritor* decision left the issue open, although it acknowledged that the question ultimately would be resolved under agency principles.

## Meritor Savings Bank, FSB v. Vinson
### 477 U.S. 57 (1986)

Justice Rehnquist delivered the opinion of the Court.

... This debate over the appropriate standard for employer liability has a rather abstract quality about it given the state of the record in this case. We do not know at this stage whether Taylor made any sexual advances toward plaintiff at all, let alone whether those advances were unwelcome, whether they were sufficiently pervasive to constitute a condition of employment, or whether they were "so pervasive and so long continuing ... that the employer must have become conscious of [them]," *Taylor v. Jones,* 653 F.2d 1193, 1197–99 (8th Cir. 1981) (holding employer liable for racially hostile working environment based on constructive knowledge).

We therefore decline the parties' invitation to issue a definitive rule on employer liability, but we do agree with the EEOC that Congress wanted courts to look to agency principles for guidance in this area. While such common-law principles may not be transferable in all their particulars to Title VII, Congress' decision to define "employer" to include any "agent" of an employer, 42 U. S. C. § 2000e(b), surely evinces an intent to place some limits on the acts of employees for which employers under Title VII are to be held responsible. For this reason, we hold that the Court of Appeals erred in concluding that employers are always automatically liable for sexual harassment by their supervisors. *See generally* Restatement (Second) of Agency §§ 219–237 (1958). For the same reason, absence of notice to an employer does not necessarily insulate that employer from liability. *Ibid.*

Finally, we reject defendant's view that the mere existence of a grievance procedure and a policy against discrimination, coupled with plaintiff's failure to invoke that procedure, must insulate defendant from liability. While those facts are plainly relevant, the situation before us demonstrates why they are not necessarily dispositive. Defendant's general nondiscrimination policy did not address sexual harassment in particular, and thus did not alert employees to their employer's interest in correcting that form of discrimination. Moreover, the bank's grievance procedure apparently required an employee to complain first to her supervisor, in this case Taylor. Since Taylor was the alleged perpetrator, it is not altogether surprising that plaintiff failed to invoke the procedure and report her grievance to him. Defendant's contention that plaintiff's failure should insulate it from liability might be substantially stronger if its procedures were better calculated to encourage victims of harassment to come forward.

---

## Subsequent Developments

The Supreme Court did not seek to resolve the question left open in *Meritor* until the two 1998 cases of *Faragher v. City of Boca Raton* and *Burlington Industries, Inc. v. Ellerth*. In both opinions, the Court engaged in lengthy discussions about traditional agency principles. In the end, though, the Court arguably jettisoned those principles and devised an entirely new framework out of whole cloth.

---

### Focus Question: *Faragher v. City of Boca Raton*

*Describe the employer's affirmative defense to liability and state the condition(s) under which an employer may validly assert the defense.*

---

# Faragher v. City of Boca Raton
### 524 U.S. 775 (1998)

Justice Souter delivered the opinion of the Court.

This case calls for identification of the circumstances under which an employer may be held liable under Title VII for the acts of a supervisory employee whose sexual harassment of subordinates has created a hostile work environment amounting to employment discrimination. We hold that an employer is vicariously liable for actionable discrimination caused by a supervisor, but subject to an affirmative defense looking to the reasonableness of the employer's conduct as well as that of a plaintiff victim.

I

Between 1985 and 1990, ... petitioner Beth Ann Faragher worked ... as an ocean lifeguard for ... the City of Boca Raton, Florida (City). During this period, Faragher's immediate supervisors were Bill Terry, David Silverman, and Robert Gordon. In June 1990, Faragher resigned.

In 1992, Faragher brought an action against Terry, Silverman, and the City, asserting claims under Title VII ... and Florida law. So far as it concerns the Title VII claim, the complaint alleged that Terry and Silverman created a "sexually hostile atmosphere" at the beach by repeatedly subjecting Faragher and other female lifeguards to "uninvited and offensive touching," by making lewd remarks, and by speaking of women in offensive terms. The complaint contained specific allegations that Terry once said that he would never promote a woman to the rank of lieutenant, and that Silverman had said to Faragher, "Date me or clean the toilets for a year." ...

...

The lifeguards and supervisors were stationed at the city beach and worked out of the Marine Safety Headquarters, a small one-story building containing an office, a meeting room, and a single, unisex locker room with a shower. Their work routine was structured in a "paramilitary configuration," with a clear chain of command. Lifeguards reported to lieutenants and captains, who reported to Terry. He was supervised by the Recreation Superintendent, who in turn reported to a Director of Parks and Recreation, answerable to the City Manager. The lifeguards had no significant contact with higher city officials like the Recreation Superintendent.

In February 1986, the City adopted a sexual harassment policy, which it stated in a memorandum from the City Manager addressed to all employees. In May 1990, the City revised the policy and reissued a statement of it. Although the City may actually have circulated the memos and statements to some employees, it completely failed to disseminate its policy among employees of the Marine Safety Section, with the result that Terry, Silverman, Gordon, and many lifeguards were unaware of it.

... During [the period that Faragher worked for the city], Terry repeatedly touched the bodies of female employees without invitation, would put his arm around Faragher, with his hand on her buttocks, and once made contact with another female lifeguard in a motion of sexual simulation. He made crudely demeaning references to women generally, and once commented disparagingly on Faragher's shape. During a job interview with a woman he hired as a lifeguard, Terry said that the female lifeguards had sex with their male counterparts and asked whether she would do the same.

Silverman behaved in similar ways. He once tackled Faragher and remarked that, but for a physical characteristic he found unattractive, he would readily have had sexual relations with her. Another time, he pantomimed an act of oral sex. Within earshot of the female lifeguards, Silverman made frequent, vulgar references to women and sexual matters, commented on the bodies of female lifeguards and beachgoers, and at least twice told female lifeguards that he would like to engage in sex with them.

Faragher did not complain to higher management about Terry or Silverman. Although she spoke of their behavior to Gordon, she did not regard these discussions as formal complaints to a supervisor but as conversations with a person she held in high esteem. Other female lifeguards had similarly informal talks with Gordon, but because Gordon did not feel that it was his place to do so, he did not report these complaints to Terry, his own supervisor, or to any other city official. Gordon responded to the complaints of one lifeguard by saying that "the City just [doesn't] care."

In April 1990, however, two months before Faragher's resignation, Nancy Ewanchew, a former lifeguard, wrote to Richard Bender, the City's Personnel Director, complaining that Terry and Silverman had harassed her and other female lifeguards. Following investigation of this complaint, the City found that Terry and Silverman had behaved improperly, reprimanded them, and required them to choose between a suspension without pay or the forfeiture of annual leave.

[After a bench trial, the trial court found that harassment had occurred and concluded that the employer should be liable for the harassment under three agency theories: (1) the supervisors were acting as agents of the employer when they harassed Faragher, (2) the supervisors were aided by the agency relationship in harassing her; and (3) Gordon's knowledge combined with his inaction were enough to impute liability to the city. The appellate court disagreed with the trial court on all three of these bases. As to the harassers' acting as the employer's agents in perpetrating the harassment, the court concluded that the harassment constituted a "frolic," unrelated to authorized tasks. The appellate court also concluded that the supervisors were not aided by the agency relationship when they harassed Faragher, because they did not invoke their supervisory power to fire or demote Faragher in perpetrating the harassment. Finally, the appellate court found in the record no ground to conclude that the harassment was so pervasive that management should have known that is was happening or that the city should be liable through Gordon's imputed knowledge. In this regard, the appellate court thus concluded that harassment may be pervasive enough to qualify as harassment under the "severe or pervasive" standard and still not be so pervasive that management may be assumed to know about it.]

Since our decision in *Meritor,* Courts of Appeals have struggled to derive manageable standards to govern employer liability for hostile environment harassment perpetrated by supervisory employees. While following our admonition to find guidance in the common law of agency, as embodied in the Restatement, the Courts of Appeals have adopted different approaches. We granted certiorari to address the divergence, and now reverse the judgment of the Eleventh Circuit and remand for entry of judgment in Faragher's favor.

II

A

Under Title VII of the Civil Rights Act of 1964, "[i]t shall be an unlawful employment practice for an employer ... to fail or refuse to hire or to discharge any individual, or otherwise to discriminate against any individual with respect to his compensation, terms, conditions, or privileges of employment, because of such individual's race, color, religion, sex, or national origin." We have repeatedly made clear that although the statute mentions specific employment decisions with immediate consequences, the scope of the prohibition "is not limited to 'economic' or 'tangible' discrimination," and that it covers more than " 'terms' and 'conditions' in the narrow contractual sense." Thus, in *Meritor* we held that sexual harassment so "severe or pervasive" as to " 'alter the conditions of [the victim's] employment and create an abusive working environment' " violates Title VII.

[The Court noted that agency issues had not been an issue in many prior cases because those cases involved employer liability for harassment where the employer had actual knowledge of the harassment and failed to correct it, where the harasser was a member of top management, thus effectively a proxy for the organization, and where the harassment culminated in tangible results, such as firing or changes in work assignment.]

B

... The Court of Appeals identified, and rejected, three possible grounds drawn from agency law for holding the City vicariously liable for the hostile environment created by the supervisors. It considered whether the two supervisors were acting within the scope of their employment, ... and whether they were significantly aided by the agency relationship and also ... considered the possibility of imputing knowledge of the harassment to the City [because Faragher had told a supervisor of the harassment] and finding the employer negligent for failing to prevent the harassment. Faragher relies principally on the latter three theories of liability.

1

A "master is subject to liability for the torts of his servants committed while acting in the scope of their employment." Restatement § 219(1). This doctrine has traditionally defined the "scope of employment" as including conduct "of the kind [a servant] is employed to perform," occurring "substantially within the authorized time and space limits," and "actuated, at least in part, by a purpose to serve the master," but as excluding an intentional use of force "unexpectable by the master." *Id.*, § 228(1).

Courts of Appeals have typically held, or assumed, that conduct similar to the subject of this complaint falls outside the scope of employment.... In so doing, the courts have emphasized that harassment consisting of unwelcome remarks and touching is motivated solely by individual desires and serves no purpose of the employer. For this reason, courts have likened hostile environment sexual harassment to the classic "frolic and detour" for which an employer has no vicarious liability.

These cases ostensibly stand in some tension with others arising outside Title VII, where the scope of employment has been defined broadly enough to hold employers vicariously liable for intentional torts that were in no sense inspired by any purpose to serve the employer. In *Ira S. Bushey & Sons, Inc. v. United States*, 398 F.2d 167 (2d Cir. 1968), for example the Second Circuit charged the Government with vicarious liability for the depredation of a drunken sailor returning to his ship after a night's carouse, who inexplicably opened valves that flooded a drydock, damaging both the drydock and the ship. Judge Friendly acknowledged that the sailor's conduct was not remotely motivated by a purpose to serve his employer, but relied on the "deeply rooted sentiment that a business enterprise cannot justly disclaim responsibility for accidents which may fairly be said to be characteristic of its activities," and imposed vicarious liability on the ground that the sailor's conduct "was not so 'unforeseeable' as to make it unfair to charge the Government with responsibility." Other examples of an expansive sense of scope of employment are readily found.... The rationales for these decisions have varied, with some courts ... explaining that the employee's acts were foreseeable and that the employer should in fairness bear the resulting costs of doing business, and others finding that the employee's sexual misconduct arose from or was in some way related to the employee's essential duties. *See e.g.*, *Samuels v. Southern Baptist Hospital*, 594 So.2d 571, 574 (La. App. 1992) (nursing assistant raped patient — tortious conduct was "reasonably incidental" to the performance of the nursing assistant's duties in caring for a "helpless" patient in a "locked environment").

[The term, "within the scope of employment,"] is "devoid of meaning in itself" and is "obviously no more than a bare formula to cover the unordered and unauthorized acts of the servant for which it is found to be expedient to charge the master with liability, as well as to exclude other acts for which it is not." *W. Keeton, D. Dobbs, R. Keeton, & D. Owen*, Prosser and Keaton on Law of Torts 502 (5th ed.1984)....

The proper analysis here, then, calls not for a mechanical application of indefinite and malleable factors set forth in the Restatement, but rather an inquiry into the reasons that would support a conclusion that harassing behavior ought to be held within the scope of a supervisor's employment, and the reasons for the opposite view.... *See generally Taber v. Maine,* 67 F.3d 1029, 1037 (2d Cir. 1995) ("As the leading Torts treatise has put it, 'the integrating principle' of *respondeat superior* is 'that the employer should be liable for those faults that may be fairly regarded as risks of his business, whether they are committed in furthering it or not'" (quoting 5 *F. Harper, F. James, & O. Gray,* Law of Torts § 26.8, pp. 40–41 (2d ed.1986)).

In the case before us, a justification for holding the offensive behavior within the scope of [the supervisors'] employment was well put in Judge Barkett's dissent: "[A] pervasively hostile work environment of sexual harassment is never (one would hope) authorized, but the supervisor is clearly charged with maintaining a productive, safe work environment. The supervisor directs and controls the conduct of the employees, and the manner of doing so may inure to the employer's benefit or detriment, including subjecting the employer to Title VII liability." It is by now well recognized that hostile environment sexual harassment by supervisors (and, for that matter, co-employees) is a persistent problem in the workplace. An employer can, in a general sense, reasonably anticipate the possibility of such conduct occurring in its workplace, and one might justify the assignment of the burden of the untoward behavior to the employer as one of the costs of doing business, to be charged to the enterprise rather than the victim. [D]evelopments like this occur from time to time in the law of agency.

Two things counsel us to draw the contrary conclusion. First, there is no reason to suppose that Congress wished courts to ignore the traditional distinction between acts falling within the scope and acts amounting to what the older law called frolics or detours from the course of employment. Such a distinction can readily be applied to the spectrum of possible harassing conduct by supervisors, as the following examples show. First, a supervisor might discriminate racially in job assignments in order to placate the prejudice pervasive in the labor force. Instances of this variety of the heckler's veto would be consciously intended to further the employer's interests by preserving peace in the workplace. Next, supervisors might reprimand male employees for workplace failings with banter, but respond to women's shortcomings in harsh or vulgar terms. A third example might be the supervisor who, as here, expresses his sexual interests in ways having no apparent object whatever of serving an interest of the employer. If a line is to be drawn between scope and frolic, it would lie between the first two examples and the third, and it thus makes sense in terms of traditional agency law to analyze the scope issue, in cases like the third example, just as most federal courts addressing that issue have done, classifying the harassment as beyond the scope of employment.

The second reason goes to an even broader unanimity of views among the holdings of District Courts and Courts of Appeals thus far. Those courts have ... uniformly judg[ed] employer liability for co-worker harassment under a negligence standard, ... implicitly treat[ing it] as outside the scope of common employees' duties as well.... The rationale for placing harassment within the scope of supervisory authority would be the fairness of requiring the employer to bear the burden of foreseeable social behavior, and the same rationale would apply when the behavior was that of co-employees.... As between an innocent employer and an innocent employee, if we use scope-of-employment reasoning to require the employer to bear the cost of an actionably hostile workplace created by one class of employees (*i.e.,* supervisors), it could appear just as appropriate to do the same when the environment was created by another class (*i.e.,* co-workers).

...

2

The Court of Appeals also rejected vicarious liability on the part of the City insofar as it might rest on the concluding principle set forth in § 219(2)(d) of the Restatement, that an employer "is not subject to liability for the torts of his servants acting outside the scope of their employment unless ... the servant purported to act or speak on behalf of the principal and there was reliance on apparent authority, or he was aided in accomplishing the tort by the existence of the agency relation." Faragher points to several ways in which the agency relationship aided Terry and Silverman in carrying out their harassment. She argues that in general offending supervisors can abuse their authority to keep subordinates in their presence while they make offensive statements, and that they implicitly threaten to misuse their supervisory powers to deter any resistance or complaint. Thus, she maintains that power conferred on Terry and Silverman by the City enabled them to act for so long without provoking defiance or complaint.

The illustrations accompanying [Restatement § 219(2)(d)] make clear that it covers ... cases involving the abuse of apparent authority, [and] also cases in which tortious conduct is made possible or facilitated by the existence of the actual agency relationship. *See* Restatement § 219, cmt. *e* (noting employer liability where "the servant may be able to cause harm because of his position as agent, as where a telegraph operator sends false messages purporting to come from third persons" and where the manager who operates a store "for an undisclosed principal is enabled to cheat the customers because of his position"); *id.,* § 247, Illustration 1 (noting a newspaper's liability for a libelous editorial published by an editor acting for his own purposes).

We therefore agree with Faragher that in implementing Title VII it makes sense to hold an employer vicariously liable for some tortious conduct of a supervisor made possible by abuse of his supervisory authority, and that the aided-by-agency-relation principle embodied in § 219(2)(d) of the Restatement provides an appropriate starting point for determining liability for the kind of harassment presented here.[1] ... The agency relationship affords contact with an employee subjected to a supervisor's sexual harassment, and the victim may well be reluctant to accept the risks of blowing the whistle on a superior. When a person with supervisory authority discriminates in the terms and conditions of subordinates' employment, his actions necessarily draw upon his superior position over the people who report to him, or those under them, whereas an employee generally cannot check a supervisor's abusive conduct the same way that she might deal with abuse from a co-worker. When a fellow employee harasses, the victim can walk away or tell the offender where to go, but it may be difficult to offer such responses to a supervisor, whose "power to supervise—[which may be] to hire and fire, and to set work schedules and pay rates— does not disappear ... when he chooses to harass through insults and offensive gestures rather than directly with threats of firing or promises of promotion." Recognition of employer liability when discriminatory misuse of supervisory authority alters the terms and conditions of a victim's employment is underscored by the fact that the employer has a greater opportunity to guard against misconduct by supervisors than by common workers. ...

---

1. We say "starting point" because our obligation here is not to make a pronouncement of agency law in general or to transplant § 219(2)(d) into Title VII. Rather, it is to adapt agency concepts to the practical objectives of Title VII. As we said in *Meritor Savings Bank, FSB v. Vinson,* 477 U.S. 57, 72 (1986), "common-law principles may not be transferable in all their particulars to Title VII."

... We are not entitled to recognize this theory [of vicarious liability] under Title VII unless we can square it with *Meritor*'s holding that an employer is not "automatically" liable for harassment by a supervisor who creates the requisite degree of discrimination. [W]e think there are two basic alternatives, one being to require proof of some affirmative invocation of that authority by the harassing supervisor, the other to recognize an affirmative defense to liability in some circumstances, even when a supervisor has created the actionable environment.

[N]eat examples illustrating the line between the affirmative and merely implicit uses of power are not easy to come by in considering management behavior.... We think plaintiffs and defendants alike would be poorly served by a ... rule [requiring affirmative invocation of authority].

The other basic alternative to automatic liability would ... allow an employer to show as an affirmative defense to liability that the employer had exercised reasonable care to avoid harassment and to eliminate it when it might occur, and that the complaining employee had failed to act with like reasonable care to take advantage of the employer's safeguards and otherwise to prevent harm that could have been avoided. This composite defense would, we think, implement the statute sensibly, for reasons that are not hard to fathom.

Although Title VII seeks "to make persons whole for injuries suffered on account of unlawful employment discrimination," its "primary objective," like that of any statute meant to influence primary conduct, is not to provide redress but to avoid harm. As long ago as 1980, the EEOC, charged with the enforcement of Title VII, adopted regulations advising employers to "take all steps necessary to prevent sexual harassment from occurring, such as ... informing employees of their right to raise and how to raise the issue of harassment," 29 C.F.R. § 1604.11(f) (1997), and in 1990 the EEOC issued a policy statement enjoining employers to establish a complaint procedure "designed to encourage victims of harassment to come forward [without requiring] a victim to complain first to the offending supervisor." EEOC Policy Guidance on Sexual Harassment, 8 FEP Manual 405:6699 (Mar. 19, 1990). It would therefore implement clear statutory policy and complement the Government's Title VII enforcement efforts to recognize the employer's affirmative obligation to prevent violations and give credit here to employers who make reasonable efforts to discharge their duty. Indeed, a theory of vicarious liability for misuse of supervisory power would be at odds with the statutory policy if it failed to provide employers with some such incentive.

The requirement to show that the employee has failed in a coordinate duty to avoid or mitigate harm reflects an equally obvious policy imported from the general theory of damages, that a victim has a duty "to use such means as are reasonable under the circumstances to avoid or minimize the damages" that result from violations of the statute. [citation omitted]. An employer may, for example, have provided a proven, effective mechanism for reporting and resolving complaints of sexual harassment, available to the employee without undue risk or expense. If the plaintiff unreasonably failed to avail herself of the employer's preventive or remedial apparatus, she should not recover damages that could have been avoided if she had done so. If the victim could have avoided harm, no liability should be found against the employer who had taken reasonable care, and if damages could reasonably have been mitigated no award against a liable employer should reward a plaintiff for what her own efforts could have avoided.

In order to accommodate the principle of vicarious liability for harm caused by misuse of supervisory authority, as well as Title VII's equally basic policies of encouraging forethought by employers and saving action by objecting employees, we adopt the following holding in this case and in *Burlington Industries, Inc. v. Ellerth*, 524 U.S. 742 (1998), also decided today. An employer is subject to vicarious liability to a victimized employee for an actionable hostile environment created by a supervisor with immediate (or successively higher) authority over the employee. When no tangible employment action is taken, a defending employer may raise an affirmative defense to liability or damages, subject to proof by a preponderance of the evidence. The defense comprises two necessary elements: (a) that the employer exercised reasonable care to prevent and correct promptly any sexually harassing behavior, and (b) that the plaintiff employee unreasonably failed to take advantage of any preventive or corrective opportunities provided by the employer or to avoid harm otherwise. While proof that an employer had promulgated an antiharassment policy with complaint procedure is not necessary in every instance as a matter of law, the need for a stated policy suitable to the employment circumstances may appropriately be addressed in any case when litigating the first element of the defense. And while proof that an employee failed to fulfill the corresponding obligation of reasonable care to avoid harm is not limited to showing an unreasonable failure to use any complaint procedure provided by the employer, a demonstration of such failure will normally suffice to satisfy the employer's burden under the second element of the defense. No affirmative defense is available, however, when the supervisor's harassment culminates in a tangible employment action, such as discharge, demotion, or undesirable reassignment.

Applying these rules here, we believe that the judgment of the Court of Appeals must be reversed. The District Court found that the degree of hostility in the work environment rose to the actionable level and was attributable to Silverman and Terry. It is undisputed that these supervisors "were granted virtually unchecked authority" over their subordinates, "directly controll[ing] and supervis[ing] all aspects of [Faragher's] day-to-day activities." It is also clear that Faragher and her colleagues were "completely isolated from the City's higher management." The City did not seek review of these findings.

While the City would have an opportunity to raise an affirmative defense if there were any serious prospect of its presenting one, it appears from the record that any such avenue is closed. The District Court found that the City had entirely failed to disseminate its policy against sexual harassment among the beach employees and that its officials made no attempt to keep track of the conduct of supervisors like Terry and Silverman. The record also makes clear that the City's policy did not include any assurance that the harassing supervisors could be bypassed in registering complaints. Under such circumstances, we hold as a matter of law that the City could not be found to have exercised reasonable care to prevent the supervisors' harassing conduct. Unlike the employer of a small work force, who might expect that sufficient care to prevent tortious behavior could be exercised informally, those responsible for city operations could not reasonably have thought that precautions against hostile environments in any one of many departments in far-flung locations could be effective without communicating some formal policy against harassment, with a sensible complaint procedure.

The City points to nothing that might justify a conclusion by the District Court on remand that the City had exercised reasonable care. Nor is there any reason to remand for consideration of Faragher's efforts to mitigate her own damages, since the award to her was solely nominal.

III

The judgment of the Court of Appeals for the Eleventh Circuit is reversed, and the case is remanded for reinstatement of the judgment of the District Court.

It is so ordered.

## Notes

1. Keep distinct in your mind the questions of (a) whether harassment is proven to have occurred; (b) whether the harasser is someone for whose acts the employer/institution may be held legally responsible; and, if so, (c) whether a defense is available to get the employer/institution off the hook.

2. *Faragher* and *Ellerth* indicate that, if the harasser is a co-worker or customer, the employer is held to a negligence standard. Thus, if the employer (management) knows or should know of the harassment and fails to take reasonable action to correct it, then the employer may be held liable. If the harasser is an alter ego of the company, such as the sole proprietor of a business, the employer is presumptively liable for the harassment. If the harasser is the target's supervisor, the employer is presumptively liable for the harassment, though it may have an affirmative defense in certain circumstances. When is an employer entitled to the affirmative defense?

3. After the Supreme Court decisions in *Ellerth* and *Faragher*, it is clear that the standard for holding the employer liable depends on whether the harasser is the target's supervisor or merely a co-worker or other third party, such as a customer. In the case of *Vance v. Ball State University*, an excerpt of which appears below, the Supreme Court refined the definition of "supervisor" for purposes of the *Faragher/Ellerth* test.

### Focus Questions: *Vance v. Ball State University*

1. *As you read* Vance, *consider whether it is appropriate to treat cases of racial harassment by the same standards that apply to sex-based harassment.*

2. *What is the difference between a "vicarious liability" standard and a negligence standard in the context of discriminatory harassment? Why do the parties care so much about this issue?*

3. *Are there any differences between the position of Vance and the position of Ball State University on the issue of whether those with responsibility for day-to-day work assignments should be deemed supervisors?*

## Vance v. Ball State University

### 133 S. Ct. 2434 (2013)

Justice Alito delivered the opinion of the Court.

In this case, we decide a question left open in *Burlington Industries, Inc. v. Ellerth* and *Faragher v. Boca Raton*, namely, who qualifies as a "supervisor" in a case in which an employee asserts a Title VII claim for workplace harassment?

Under Title VII, an employer's liability for such harassment may depend on the status of the harasser. If the harassing employee is the victim's co-worker, the employer is liable only if it was negligent in controlling working conditions. In cases in which the harasser is a "supervisor," however, different rules apply. If the supervisor's harassment culminates in a tangible employment action, the employer is strictly liable. But if no tangible employment action is taken, the employer may escape liability by establishing, as an affirmative defense, that (1) the employer exercised reasonable care to prevent and correct any harassing behavior and (2) that the plaintiff unreasonably failed to take advantage of the preventive or corrective opportunities that the employer provided. Under this framework, therefore, it matters whether a harasser is a "supervisor" or simply a co-worker.

We hold that an employee is a "supervisor" for purposes of vicarious liability under Title VII if he or she is empowered by the employer to take tangible employment actions against the victim, and we therefore affirm the judgment of the Seventh Circuit.

I

Maetta Vance, an African-American woman, began working for Ball State University (BSU) in 1989 as a substitute server in the University Banquet and Catering division of Dining Services. In 1991, BSU promoted Vance to a part-time catering assistant position, and in 2007 she applied and was selected for a position as a full-time catering assistant.

Over the course of her employment with BSU, Vance lodged numerous complaints of racial discrimination and retaliation, but most of those incidents are not at issue here. For present purposes, the only relevant incidents concern Vance's interactions with a fellow BSU employee, Saundra Davis.

During the time in question, Davis, a white woman, was employed as a catering specialist in the Banquet and Catering division. The parties vigorously dispute the precise nature and scope of Davis' duties, but they agree that Davis did not have the power to hire, fire, demote, promote, transfer, or discipline Vance.

In late 2005 and early 2006, Vance filed internal complaints with BSU and charges with the Equal Employment Opportunity Commission (EEOC), alleging racial harassment and discrimination, and many of these complaints and charges pertained to Davis. Vance complained that Davis "gave her a hard time at work by glaring at her, slamming pots and pans around her, and intimidating her." She alleged that she was "left alone in the kitchen with Davis, who smiled at her"; that Davis "blocked" her on an elevator and "stood there with her cart smiling;" and that Davis often gave her "weird" looks.

Vance's workplace strife persisted despite BSU's attempts to address the problem. As a result, Vance filed this lawsuit..., claiming, among other things, that she had been subjected to a racially hostile work environment in violation of Title VII. In her complaint, she alleged that Davis was her supervisor and that BSU was liable for Davis' creation of a racially hostile work environment.

Both parties moved for summary judgment, and the District Court entered summary judgment in favor of BSU. The court explained that BSU could not be held vicariously liable for Davis' alleged racial harassment because Davis could not "hire, fire, demote, promote, transfer, or discipline" Vance and, as a result, was not Vance's supervisor under the Seventh Circuit's interpretation of that concept. The court further held that BSU could not be liable in negligence because it responded reasonably to the incidents of which it was aware.

The Seventh Circuit affirmed. It explained that, under its settled precedent, supervisor status requires "the power to hire, fire, demote, promote, transfer, or discipline an employee." The court concluded that Davis was not Vance's supervisor and thus that Vance could not recover from BSU unless she could prove negligence. Finding that BSU was not negligent with respect to Davis' conduct, the court affirmed.

## II

### A

Title VII [prohibits] the creation or perpetuation of a discriminatory work environment. In the leading case of *Rogers v. EEOC*, the Fifth Circuit ... reasoned that "the phrase 'terms, conditions, or privileges of employment' in [Title VII] is an expansive concept which sweeps within its protective ambit the practice of creating a working environment heavily charged with ethnic or racial discrimination." ... Following this decision, the lower courts generally held that an employer was liable for a racially hostile work environment if the employer was negligent, *i.e.*, if the employer knew or reasonably should have known about the harassment but failed to take remedial action.

When the issue eventually reached this Court, we agreed that Title VII prohibits the creation of a hostile work environment. In such cases, we have held, the plaintiff must show that the work environment was so pervaded by discrimination that the terms and conditions of employment were altered.

### B

Consistent with *Rogers*, we have held that an employer is directly liable for an employee's unlawful harassment if the employer was negligent with respect to the offensive behavior. Courts have generally applied this rule to evaluate employer liability when a co-worker harasses the plaintiff.

In *Ellerth* and *Faragher*, however, we held that different rules apply where the harassing employee is the plaintiff's "supervisor." In those instances, an employer may be *vicariously* liable for its employees' creation of a hostile work environment....

### C

Under *Ellerth* and *Faragher*, it is obviously important whether an alleged harasser is a "supervisor" or merely a co-worker, and the lower courts have disagreed about the meaning of the concept of a supervisor in this context. Some courts, including the Seventh Circuit below, have held that an employee is not a supervisor unless he or she has the power to hire, fire, demote, promote, transfer, or discipline the victim. Other courts have substantially followed the more open-ended approach advocated by the EEOC's Enforcement Guidance, which ties supervisor status to the ability to exercise significant direction over another's daily work.

## III

We hold that an employer may be vicariously liable for an employee's unlawful harassment only when the employer has empowered that employee to take tangible employment actions against the victim, *i.e.*, to effect a "significant change in employment status, such as hiring, firing, failing to promote, reassignment with significantly different responsibilities, or a decision causing a significant change in benefits." We reject the nebulous definition of a "supervisor" advocated in the EEOC Guidance and substantially adopted by several courts of appeals. Petitioner's reliance on colloquial uses of the term "supervisor" is misplaced, and her contention that our cases require the EEOC's abstract definition is simply wrong.

As we will explain, the framework set out in *Ellerth* and *Faragher* presupposes a clear distinction between supervisors and co-workers. Those decisions contemplate a unitary category of supervisors, *i.e.*, those employees with the authority to make tangible employment decisions. There is no hint in either decision that the Court had in mind two categories of supervisors: first, those who have such authority and, second, those who, although lacking this power, nevertheless have the ability to direct a co-worker's labor to some ill-defined degree. On the contrary, the *Ellerth/Faragher* framework is one under which supervisory status can usually be readily determined, generally by written documentation. The approach recommended by the EEOC Guidance, by contrast, would make the determination of supervisor status depend on a highly case-specific evaluation of numerous factors.

The *Ellerth/Faragher* framework represents what the Court saw as a workable compromise....; it can be applied without undue difficulty at both the summary judgment stage and at trial....

## A

Petitioner contends that her expansive understanding of the concept of a "supervisor" is supported by the meaning of the word in general usage and in other legal contexts, but this argument is both incorrect on its own terms and, in any event, misguided. In general usage, the term "supervisor" lacks a sufficiently specific meaning to be helpful for present purposes....

If we look beyond general usage to the meaning of the term in other legal contexts, we find much the same situation. Sometimes the term is reserved for those in the upper echelons of the management hierarchy. But sometimes the term is used to refer to lower ranking individuals....

In sum, the term "supervisor" has varying meanings both in colloquial usage and in the law. And for this reason, petitioner's argument, taken on its own terms, is unsuccessful. [T]he way to understand the meaning of the term "supervisor" for present purposes is to consider the interpretation that best fits within the highly structured framework that [*Faragher* and *Ellerth*] adopted.

## B

[Contrary to petitioner's contention, the alleged harassers in *Faragher* and *Ellerth* did possess the power to take tangible employment actions against the victims.]

[W]e have no difficulty rejecting petitioner's argument that the question before us in the present case was effectively settled in her favor by our treatment of the alleged harassers in *Ellerth* and *Faragher*.

The dissent acknowledges that our prior cases do "not squarely resolve whether an employee without power to take tangible employment actions may nonetheless qualify as a supervisor," but accuses us of ignoring the "all-too-plain reality" that employees with authority to control their subordinates' daily work are aided by that authority in perpetuating a discriminatory work environment. As *Ellerth* recognized, however, "most workplace tortfeasors are aided in accomplishing their tortious objective by the existence of the agency relation," and consequently "something more" is required in order to warrant vicarious liability. The ability to direct another employee's tasks is simply not sufficient. Employees with such powers are certainly capable of creating intolerable work environments, but so are many other co-workers. Negligence provides the better framework for evaluating an employer's liability when a harassing employee lacks the power to take tangible employment actions.

## C

Although our holdings in *Faragher* and *Ellerth* do not resolve the question now before us, we believe that the answer to that question is implicit in the characteristics of the framework that we adopted.

[The *Ellerth/Faragher* Court consistently defined the role of "supervisors" by reference to supervisors' ability to take tangible employment actions against the worker. Under the *Faragher/Ellerth* rationale, it] is because a supervisor has that authority—and its potential use hangs as a threat over the victim—that vicarious liability (subject to the affirmative defense) is justified....

[T]he EEOC's definition of a supervisor, which both petitioner and the United States defend, is a study in ambiguity.... [The EEOC construes its own Enforcement Guidance to limit supervisors to those who] wield authority "of sufficient magnitude so as to assist the harasser explicitly or implicitly in carrying out the harassment." But *any* authority over the work of another employee provides at least some assistance, and that is not what the United States interprets the Guidance to mean. Rather, it informs us, the authority must exceed both an ill-defined temporal requirement (it must be more than "occasiona[l]") and an ill-defined substantive requirement ("an employee who directs 'only a limited number of tasks or assignments' for another employee ... would not have sufficient authority to qualify as a supervisor."

We read the EEOC Guidance as saying that the number (and perhaps the importance) of the tasks [that a purported supervisor directs] is a factor to be considered in determining whether an employee qualifies as a supervisor. And if this is a correct interpretation of the EEOC's position, what we are left with is a proposed standard of remarkable ambiguity.

The vagueness of this standard was highlighted at oral argument when the attorney representing the United States was asked to apply that standard to the situation in *Faragher*, where the alleged harasser supposedly threatened to assign the plaintiff to clean the toilets in the lifeguard station for a year if she did not date him. Since cleaning the toilets is just one task, albeit an unpleasant one, the authority to assign that job would not seem to meet the more-than-a-limited-number-of-tasks requirement in the EEOC Guidance. Nevertheless, the Government attorney's first response was that the authority to make this assignment would be enough. He later qualified that answer by saying that it would be necessary to "know how much of the day's work [was] encompassed by cleaning the toilets." He did not explain what percentage of the day's work (50%, 25%, 10%?) would suffice.

The Government attorney's inability to provide a definitive answer to this question was the inevitable consequence of the vague standard that the Government asks us to adopt. Key components of that standard—"sufficient" authority, authority to assign more than a "limited number of tasks," and authority that is exercised more than "occasionally"—have no clear meaning. Applying these standards would present daunting problems for the lower federal courts and for juries.

Under the definition of "supervisor" that we adopt today, the question of supervisor status, when contested, can very often be resolved as a matter of law before trial.... And even where the issue of supervisor status cannot be eliminated from the trial (because there are genuine factual disputes about an alleged harasser's authority to take tangible employment actions), this preliminary question is relatively straightforward....

Contrary to the dissent's suggestions, this approach will not leave employees unprotected against harassment by co-workers who possess the authority to inflict psychological injury by assigning unpleasant tasks or by altering the work environment in objectionable ways. In such cases, the victims will be able to prevail simply by showing that the employer was negligent in permitting this harassment to occur, and the jury should be instructed that the nature and degree of authority wielded by the harasser is an important factor to be considered in determining whether the employer was negligent....

## D

The dissent argues that the definition of a supervisor that we now adopt is out of touch with the realities of the workplace, where individuals with the power to assign daily tasks are often regarded by other employees as supervisors. But in ... modern organizations that have abandoned a highly hierarchical management structure, it is common for employees to have overlapping authority with respect to the assignment of work tasks. Members of a team may each have the responsibility for taking the lead with respect to a particular aspect of the work and thus may have the responsibility to direct each other in that area of responsibility.

Finally, petitioner argues that tying supervisor status to the authority to take tangible employment actions will encourage employers to attempt to insulate themselves from liability for workplace harassment by empowering only a handful of individuals to take tangible employment actions. But a broad definition of "supervisor" is not necessary to guard against this concern.... If an employer does attempt to confine decisionmaking power to a small number of individuals, those individuals will ... likely rely on other workers who actually interact with the affected employee.... Under those circumstances, the employer may be held to have effectively delegated the power to take tangible employment actions to the employees on whose recommendations it relies.

## IV

Importuning Congress, the dissent suggests that the standard we adopt today would cause the plaintiffs to lose in a handful of cases involving shocking allegations of harassment. However, the dissent does not mention *why* the plaintiffs would lose in those cases....

In any event, the dissent is wrong in claiming that our holding would preclude employer liability in other cases with facts similar to these. Assuming that a harasser is not a supervisor, a plaintiff could still prevail by showing that his or her employer was negligent in failing to prevent harassment from taking place. Evidence that an employer did not monitor the workplace, failed to respond to complaints, failed to provide a system for registering complaints, or effectively discouraged complaints from being filed would be relevant. Thus, it is not true, as the dissent asserts, that our holding "relieves scores of employers of responsibility" for the behavior of workers they employ....

Despite its rhetoric, the dissent acknowledges that Davis, the alleged harasser in this case, would probably not qualify as a supervisor even under the dissent's preferred approach. On that point, we agree.... [U]nder the dissent's preferred approach, supervisor status hinges not on formal job titles or "paper descriptions" but on "specific facts about the working relationship." Turning to the "specific facts" of petitioner's and Davis' working relationship, there is simply no evidence that Davis directed petitioner's day-to-day activities. The record indicates that Bill Kimes (the general manager of the Catering Division) and the chef assigned petitioner's daily tasks, which were given to her on "prep lists." The fact that Davis sometimes may have handed prep lists to petitioner, is insufficient to confer supervisor status. And Kimes — *not* Davis — set petitioner's work schedule.

[The dissent critiques the Court's approach based on unfortunate outcomes it would hypothetically yield in scenarios other than that before the Court.] We are skeptical that there are a great number of such cases. However, we are confident that, in every case, the approach we take today will be more easily administrable than the approach advocated by the dissent.

We hold that an employee is a "supervisor" for purposes of vicarious liability under Title VII if he or she is empowered by the employer to take tangible employment actions against the victim. Because there is no evidence that BSU empowered Davis to take any tangible employment actions against Vance, the judgment of the Seventh Circuit is affirmed.

[Ed. note: Justice Thomas wrote a concurring opinion, noting his view that *Ellerth* and *Faragher* were wrongly decided but that the Court's opinion in the instant case provides the narrowest and most workable rule for when an employer may be held vicariously liable for an employee's harassment.]

Justice Ginsburg, with whom Justice Breyer, Justice Sotomayor, and Justice Kagan join, dissenting.

In *Faragher* and *Ellerth*, this Court held that an employer can be vicariously liable under Title VII for harassment by an employee given supervisory authority over subordinates. In line with those decisions, in 1999, the Equal Employment Opportunity Commission (EEOC) provided enforcement guidance "regarding employer liability for harassment by supervisors based on sex, race, color, religion, national origin, age, disability, or protected activity." Addressing who qualifies as a supervisor, the EEOC answered: (1) an individual authorized "to undertake or recommend tangible employment decisions affecting the employee," including "hiring, firing, promoting, demoting, and reassigning the employee"; *or* (2) an individual authorized "to direct the employee's daily work activities."

The Court today strikes from the supervisory category employees who control the day-to-day schedules and assignments of others, confining the category to those formally empowered to take tangible employment actions. The limitation the Court decrees diminishes the force of *Faragher* and *Ellerth*, ignores the conditions under which members of the work force labor, and disserves the objective of Title VII to prevent discrimination from infecting the Nation's workplaces. I would follow the EEOC's Guidance and hold that the authority to direct an employee's daily activities establishes supervisory status under Title VII.

I

A

. . .

B

The distinction *Faragher* and *Ellerth* drew between supervisors and co-workers corresponds to the realities of the workplace. Exposed to a fellow employee's harassment, one can walk away or tell the offender to "buzz off." A supervisor's slings and arrows, however, are not so easily avoided. An employee who confronts her harassing supervisor risks, for example, receiving an undesirable or unsafe work assignment or an unwanted transfer. She may be saddled with an excessive workload or with placement on a shift spanning hours disruptive of her family life. And she may be demoted or fired. Facing such dangers, she may be reluctant to blow the whistle on her superior, whose "power and authority invests his or her harassing conduct with a particular threatening character." In short, as *Faragher* and *Ellerth* recognized, harassment by supervisors is more likely to cause palpable harm and to persist unabated than similar conduct by fellow employees.

II

While *Faragher* and *Ellerth* differentiated harassment by supervisors from harassment by co-workers, neither decision gave a definitive answer to the question: Who qualifies as a supervisor? Two views have emerged. One view, in line with the EEOC's Guidance, counts as a supervisor anyone with authority to take tangible employment actions or to direct an employee's daily work activities, [and the] other view ranks as supervisors only those authorized to take tangible employment actions.

Notably, respondent Ball State University agreed with petitioner Vance and the United States, as *amicus curiae,* that the tangible-employment-action-only test "does not necessarily capture all employees who may qualify as supervisors." "[V]icarious liability," Ball State acknowledged, "also may be triggered when the harassing employee has the authority to control the victim's daily work activities in a way that materially enables the harassment."

The different view taken by the Court today is . . . blind to the realities of the workplace, and it discounts the guidance of the EEOC, the agency Congress established to interpret, and superintend the enforcement of, Title VII. . . .

### A

Until today, our decisions have assumed that employees who direct subordinates' daily work are supervisors. In *Faragher,* the city of Boca Raton, Florida, employed Bill Terry and David Silverman to oversee the city's corps of ocean lifeguards. Terry and Silverman "repeatedly subject[ed] Faragher and other female lifeguards to uninvited and offensive touching," and they regularly "ma[de] lewd remarks, and [spoke] of women in offensive terms." Terry told a job applicant that "female lifeguards had sex with their male counterparts," and then "asked whether she would do the same." Silverman threatened to assign Faragher to toilet-cleaning duties for a year if she refused to date him. In words and conduct, Silverman and Terry made the beach a hostile place for women to work.

As Chief of Boca Raton's Marine Safety Division, Terry had authority to "hire new lifeguards (subject to the approval of higher management), to supervise all aspects of the lifeguards' work assignments, to engage in counseling, to deliver oral reprimands, and to make a record of any such discipline." Silverman's duties as a Marine Safety lieutenant included "making the lifeguards' daily assignments, and . . . supervising their work and fitness training." Both men "were granted virtually unchecked authority over their subordinates, directly controlling and supervising all aspects of Faragher's day-to-day activities."

We may assume that Terry would fall within the definition of supervisor the Court adopts today. But nothing in the *Faragher* record shows that Silverman would. Silverman had oversight and assignment responsibilities—he could punish lifeguards who would not date him with full-time toilet-cleaning duty—but there was no evidence that he had authority to take tangible employment actions. Holding that Boca Raton was vicariously liable for Silverman's harassment, the Court characterized him as Faragher's supervisor, and there was no dissent on that point.

Subsequent decisions reinforced *Faragher*'s use of the term "supervisor" to encompass employees with authority to direct the daily work of their victims. In *Pennsylvania State Police v. Suders,* the Court considered whether a constructive discharge occasioned by supervisor harassment ranks as a tangible employment action. The harassing employees lacked authority to discharge or demote the complainant, but they were "responsible for the day-to-day supervision" of the workplace and for overseeing employee shifts. Describing the harassing employees as the complainant's "supervisors," the Court proceeded to evaluate the complainant's constructive discharge claim under the *Ellerth* and *Faragher* framework.

It is true, as the Court says, that *Faragher* and later cases did not squarely resolve whether an employee without power to take tangible employment actions may nonetheless qualify as a supervisor. But in laboring to establish that Silverman's supervisor status, undisputed in *Faragher,* is not dispositive here, the Court misses the forest for the trees. *Faragher* illustrates an all-too-plain reality: A supervisor with authority to control subordinates' daily work is no less aided in his harassment than is a supervisor with authority to fire, demote, or transfer. That Silverman could threaten Faragher with toilet-cleaning duties while Terry could orally reprimand her was inconsequential in *Faragher,* and properly so. What mattered was that both men took advantage of the power vested in them as agents of Boca Raton to facilitate their abuse. And when, assisted by an agency relationship, in-charge superiors like Silverman perpetuate a discriminatory work environment, our decisions have appropriately held the employer vicariously liable, subject to the above-described affirmative defense.

### B

[The dissent continues with a discussion of harassment scenarios in which harassers would be deemed not supervisors under the Court's definition.]

### C

Within a year after the Court's decisions in *Faragher* and *Ellerth,* the EEOC defined "supervisor" to include any employee with "authority to undertake or recommend tangible employment decisions," *or* with "authority to direct [another] employee's daily work activities." That definition should garner "respect proportional to its 'power to persuade.'"[4]

The EEOC's definition of supervisor reflects the agency's "informed judgment" and "body of experience" in enforcing Title VII. For 14 years, in enforcement actions and litigation, the EEOC has firmly adhered to its definition.

In developing its definition of supervisor, the EEOC paid close attention to the *Faragher* and *Ellerth* framework. An employer is vicariously liable only when the authority it has delegated enables actionable harassment, the EEOC recognized. For that reason, a supervisor's authority must be "of a sufficient magnitude so as to assist the harasser ... in carrying out the harassment." Determining whether an employee wields sufficient authority is not a mechanical inquiry, the EEOC explained; instead, specific facts about the employee's job function are critical. Thus, an employee with authority to increase another's workload or assign undesirable tasks may rank as a supervisor, for those powers can enable harassment. On the other hand, an employee "who directs only a limited number of tasks or assignments" ordinarily would not qualify as a supervisor, for her harassing conduct is not likely to be aided materially by the agency relationship....

### III

Exhibiting remarkable resistance to the thrust of our prior decisions, workplace realities, and the EEOC's Guidance, the Court embraces a position that relieves scores of employers of responsibility for the behavior of the supervisors they employ. Trumpeting the virtues of simplicity and administrability, the Court restricts supervisor status to those with power to take tangible employment actions. In so restricting the definition of supervisor,

---

4. Respondent's *amici* maintain that the EEOC Guidance is ineligible for deference under *Skidmore v. Swift & Co.,* because it interprets *Faragher* and *Ellerth,* not the text of Title VII. They are mistaken. The EEOC Guidance rests on the employer liability framework set forth in *Faragher* and *Ellerth,* but both the framework and EEOC Guidance construe the term "agent" in 42 U.S.C. § 2000e(b).

the Court once again shuts from sight the "robust protection against workplace discrimination Congress intended Title VII to secure." [citation omitted].

## A

The Court purports to rely on the *Ellerth* and *Faragher* framework to limit supervisor status to those capable of taking tangible employment actions. That framework, we are told, presupposes "a sharp line between co-workers and supervisors." The definition of supervisor decreed today, the Court insists, is "clear," "readily applied," and "easily workable," when compared to the EEOC's vague standard.

There is reason to doubt just how "clear" and "workable" the Court's definition is. A supervisor, the Court holds, is someone empowered to "take tangible employment actions against the victim, *i.e.*, to effect a 'significant change in employment status, such as hiring, firing, failing to promote, reassignment with significantly different responsibilities, or a decision causing a significant change in benefits.'" (quoting *Ellerth*). Whether reassignment authority makes someone a supervisor might depend on whether the reassignment carries economic consequences. The power to discipline other employees, when the discipline has economic consequences, might count, too. *Ibid.* So might the power to initiate or make recommendations about tangible employment actions. And when an employer "concentrates all decisionmaking authority in a few individuals" who rely on information from "other workers who actually interact with the affected employee," the other workers may rank as supervisors (or maybe not; the Court does not commit one way or the other).

Someone in search of a bright line might well ask, what counts as "significantly different responsibilities"? Can *any* economic consequence make a reassignment or disciplinary action "significant," or is there a minimum threshold? How concentrated must the decisionmaking authority be to deem those not formally endowed with that authority nevertheless "supervisors"? The Court leaves these questions unanswered, and its liberal use of "mights" and "mays," dims the light it casts.

That the Court has adopted a standard, rather than a clear rule, is not surprising, for no crisp definition of supervisor could supply the unwavering line the Court desires. Supervisors, like the workplaces they manage, come in all shapes and sizes. Whether a pitching coach supervises his pitchers (can he demote them?), or an artistic director supervises her opera star (can she impose significantly different responsibilities?), or a law firm associate supervises the firm's paralegals (can she fire them?) are matters not susceptible to mechanical rules and on-off switches. One cannot know whether an employer has vested supervisory authority in an employee, and whether harassment is aided by that authority, without looking to the particular working relationship between the harasser and the victim. That is why *Faragher* and *Ellerth* crafted an employer liability standard embracive of all whose authority significantly aids in the creation and perpetuation of harassment.

The Court's focus on finding a definition of supervisor capable of instant application is at odds with the Court's ordinary emphasis on the importance of particular circumstances in Title VII cases. The question of supervisory status, no less than the question whether retaliation or harassment has occurred, "depends on a constellation of surrounding circumstances, expectations, and relationships." [citation omitted]. The EEOC's Guidance so perceives.

## B

As a consequence of the Court's truncated conception of supervisory authority, the *Faragher* and *Ellerth* framework has shifted in a decidedly employer-friendly direction.

This realignment will leave many harassment victims without an effective remedy and undermine Title VII's capacity to prevent workplace harassment.

[The negligence standard that the Court allows for cases where the harasser is someone who supervises the victim's day-to-day work results in employer liability only if the employer] knew or should have known of the conduct but failed to take appropriate corrective action. It is not uncommon for employers to lack actual or constructive notice of a harassing employee's conduct. An employee may have a reputation as a harasser among those in his vicinity, but if no complaint makes its way up to management, the employer will escape liability under a negligence standard.

*Faragher* is illustrative. After enduring unrelenting harassment, Faragher reported Terry's and Silverman's conduct informally to Robert Gordon, another immediate supervisor. But the lifeguards were "completely isolated from the City's higher management," and it did not occur to Faragher to pursue the matter with higher ranking city officials distant from the beach. Applying a negligence standard, the Eleventh Circuit held that, despite the pervasiveness of the harassment, and despite Gordon's awareness of it, Boca Raton lacked constructive notice and therefore escaped liability. Under the vicarious liability standard, however, Boca Raton could not make out the affirmative defense, for it had failed to disseminate a policy against sexual harassment.

On top of the substantive differences in the negligence and vicarious liability standards, harassment victims, under today's decision, are saddled with the burden of proving the employer's negligence whenever the harasser lacks the power to take tangible employment actions. *Faragher* and *Ellerth,* by contrast, placed the burden squarely on the employer to make out the affirmative defense. This allocation of the burden was both sensible and deliberate: An employer has superior access to evidence bearing on whether it acted reasonably to prevent or correct harassing behavior, and superior resources to marshal that evidence.

… We can expect that, as a consequence of restricting the supervisor category to those formally empowered to take tangible employment actions, victims of workplace harassment with meritorious Title VII claims will find suit a hazardous endeavor.

Inevitably, the Court's definition of supervisor will hinder efforts to stamp out discrimination in the workplace…. "[T]he employer has a greater opportunity to guard against misconduct by supervisors than by common workers," and a greater incentive to "screen [supervisors], train them, and monitor their performance."… When employers know they will be answerable for the injuries a harassing jobsite boss inflicts, their incentive to provide preventative instruction is heightened….

## IV

I turn now to the case before us…. Because I would hold that the Seventh Circuit erred in restricting supervisor status to employees formally empowered to take tangible employment actions, I would remand for application of the proper standard to Vance's claim. On this record, however, there is cause to anticipate that Davis would not qualify as Vance's supervisor….

## V

Regrettably, the Court has seized upon Vance's thin case to narrow the definition of supervisor, and thereby manifestly limit Title VII's protections against workplace harassment. Not even Ball State, the defendant-employer in this case, has advanced the restrictive definition the Court adopts. Yet the Court, insistent on constructing artificial categories where context should be key, proceeds on an immoderate and unrestrained course to corral Title VII.

Congress has, in the recent past, intervened to correct this Court's wayward interpretations of Title VII. *See* Lilly Ledbetter Fair Pay Act of 2009; *see also* Civil Rights Act of 1991. The ball is once again in Congress' court to correct the error into which this Court has fallen, and to restore the robust protections against workplace harassment the Court weakens today.

## Note

Do you agree with the Court that *Ellerth* and *Faragher* contemplate "a unitary category of supervisors," limited to "those with the authority to make tangible employment actions"?

The next case, *Lauderdale*, is an example of a lower court's application of the *Faragher/ Ellerth* ruling.

---

### Focus Questions: *Lauderdale v. Texas Dept. of Criminal Justice*

1. Lauderdale *is an appellate court decision applying the 1998 Supreme Court decisions in* Faragher *and* Ellerth. *The employer is strictly (without a showing of negligence) liable for the supervisor's harassment of a subordinate employee, but the employer may assert an affirmative defense if the harassment does not involve a tangible employment action.*

2. *Do you agree with the court's decision that defendant satisfied both prongs of the affirmative defense—that the defendant responded adequately and that plaintiff did not? How would you argue for a contrary result on these facts?*

3. *The* Lauderdale *court states that a plaintiff may, in some cases, be deemed to satisfy the harm avoidance prong of the Ellerth/Faragher defense where she fails to make a second request for action when the first request is ineffective. In what circumstances would the* Lauderdale *court forgive a plaintiff's failure to make further reports after the first report is ignored?*

4. *Why did Ms. Lauderdale fear retaliation, and what role should such fear play in the court's consideration of whether the plaintiff was reasonable in avoiding harm?*

---

## Lauderdale v. Texas Dept. of Criminal Justice
### 512 F.3d 157 (5th Cir. 2007)

Judge Smith.

Debra Lauderdale alleges she was sexually harassed by her ultimate supervisor, Rodrick Arthur, over the period of almost four months during which she worked as a correctional officer for the Texas Department of Criminal Justice ("TDCJ"). Lauderdale sued the TDCJ under Title VII of the Civil Rights Act of 1964.... The district court granted summary judgment.... We affirm in part, reverse in part, and remand.

I

Lauderdale began her employment with the TDCJ on June 3, 2004.... Her first two weeks consisted of on-the-job training ... during which time she met Arthur. Upon completion of Lauderdale's training, Arthur, as acting warden on the night shift, became her ultimate supervisor.

In late July, shortly after Lauderdale completed her on-the-job training, Arthur began to pursue a relationship with her. According to Lauderdale, Arthur would call her multiple times at her duty station during the night shift. During one of the first phone conversations, he asked her to get coffee with him after the shift ended. After this first evening of phone calls, Lauderdale told Sergeant Kroll, her immediate supervisor, that Arthur had been telephoning her. Kroll told Lauderdale she could speak to the warden about the calls but that she should not mention Kroll's name.

The calls and requests to go out after the night shift continued and, though they varied in frequency, eventually reached an average of ten to fifteen calls during a shift. During one call, Arthur asked Lauderdale whether she was married; she lied and told him she was, to which Arthur responded that his heart was broken and he might hang himself. At other times, Arthur told Lauderdale she was beautiful and that he loved her.

On another occasion, Arthur called Lauderdale and, during the course of the discussion, asked her what she enjoyed doing. She told him she enjoyed gambling. Arthur suggested that the two of them could go to Las Vegas and "snuggle;" Lauderdale said "No." Other topics of conversation during the phone calls included Arthur's family and horses. On one occasion, he called and Lauderdale explained that she was upset that, for some reason, she was not going to rotate according to the schedule.

In August, after Lauderdale began working in another building at the unit, Arthur called and told her he missed her, then showed up at the building in which she was working. He would also invite her to sit with him in the warden's office during her breaks; she refused those invitations. After a break one evening in mid-October, as she returned to her duty station, Lauderdale passed Arthur in the hall by the "searcher's desk." Arthur grabbed her handcuff case, which she wore in the middle of her back on her belt, and pulled her to himself. Her lower back touched his stomach before she jerked away from him.

Finally, on October 25, Arthur sent for Lauderdale, presumably ordering her to report to him. She believed he had no legitimate reason to see her, and she refused to report to him. After this incident, she did not return to work. Before her next shift she telephoned a supervisor and indicated she would not be at work that day; she did not, however, indicate that she no longer intended to work for the TDCJ. After receiving a letter from Human Resources indicating that she would not receive her last pay check until she turned in her uniforms, Lauderdale returned to the unit on December 3 and officially resigned and indicated "Dissatisfaction with supervisors or coworkers" as the reason. She then spoke with Assistant Warden Sizemore and filed a formal EEO complaint against Arthur for sexual harassment.

The TDCJ investigated Lauderdale's allegations and found sufficient evidence to deem Arthur guilty of "Discourteous Conduct of a Sexual Nature." This determination resulted in a four-day suspension without pay and a nine-month probation. Arthur ultimately resigned at some point following the investigation.

Lauderdale does not allege that any adverse employment actions were taken against her; she concedes that she was able to perform her duties fully despite Arthur's harassment. She also acknowledges she received and read a copy of the various policies covering sexual harassment and watched a training video on the subject. Save for her discussion with Kroll in late July, Lauderdale admits that she never complained to anyone else who was in her chain of command or was identified in the TDCJ sexual harassment policy. She contends that she did not complain to anyone other than Kroll because she feared retaliation.

## II

"This Court reviews grants of summary judgment *de novo*, applying the same standard as does a district court, viewing the evidence in a light most favorable to the non-movant." ...

## A

The district court granted the TDCJ's motion for summary judgment because it held that, as a matter of law, Arthur's behavior was neither severe nor pervasive and, therefore, did not create a hostile work environment. We disagree.

...

The only issue is whether Arthur's behavior created a hostile or abusive working environment.... [T]he harassment "must be sufficiently severe or pervasive to alter the conditions of [the victim's] employment and create an abusive working environment." [citation omitted]. The environment must be deemed "both objectively and subjectively offensive, one that a reasonable person would find hostile or abusive, and one that the victim in fact did perceive to be so." [citation omitted].

...

Viewing Lauderdale's allegations in the most favorable light, as we must, Arthur's behavior was pervasive. Lauderdale alleges that he called her ten to fifteen times a night for almost four months. Though Lauderdale does not assert that each phone call carried sexual overtones, the frequency of unwanted attention, over a four-month time period, amounts to pervasive harassment. Given this pervasiveness, the level of severity necessary to establish an altered work environment is diminished and Arthur's invitation to Lauderdale to "snuggle" in Las Vegas, the physical act of pulling her to himself, and the repeated requests to get coffee after work all satisfy the requirement. Thus, Lauderdale has a viable hostile work environment claim under Title VII.

## B

Because there is a genuine issue of material fact regarding the creation of a hostile work environment, we must consider the TDCJ's assertion of the *Ellerth/Faragher* affirmative defense. In *Burlington Industries v. Ellerth* and *Faragher*, the Court recognized one affirmative defense that employers may raise against a Title VII claim alleging a hostile work environment created by a supervisor's sexual harassment. So long as the supervisor's actions did not result in a "tangible employment action" against the employee, employers may assert the *Ellerth/Faragher* defense, which requires the employer to prove by a preponderance of the evidence "(a) that the employer exercised reasonable care to prevent and correct promptly any sexually harassing behavior, and (b) that the plaintiff employee unreasonably failed to take advantage of any preventive or corrective opportunities provided by the employer or to avoid harm otherwise."

It is undisputed that no tangible employment action resulted from Arthur's behavior; Lauderdale was never demoted, reassigned, or had her hours changed because of his actions. Thus, the TDCJ is entitled to raise the *Ellerth/Faragher* defense. The TDCJ has satisfied the requirements of the first prong by virtue of its institutional policies and educational programs regarding sexual harassment. It is undisputed that Lauderdale received the requisite training and copies of the TDCJ's sexual-harassment policy statements. There is no allegation that the TDCJ's program, designed to avoid, report, and correct instances of sexual harassment, is insufficient or unreasonable.

The contested issue is whether the second prong of the affirmative defense is satisfied. Lauderdale claims the *Ellerth/Faragher* defense is unavailable to the TDCJ because she took advantage of the TDCJ's sexual-harassment prevention and remediation policies by reporting Arthur's harassment to Kroll, her immediate supervisor, as dictated by TDCJ policy. The TDCJ's policy offers numerous avenues for reporting sexual harassment, including any supervisor, the Employee Relations Office of the Human Resources Department, the TDCJ Executive Director, the United States Equal Employment Opportunity Commission, and the Texas Commission on Human Rights. It was therefore unreasonable for Lauderdale not to pursue any other avenue available under the TDCJ policy after Kroll explicitly indicated his unwillingness to act on her complaint.

We have confronted a similar circumstance before. In *Wyatt v. Hunt Plywood Co.*, the plaintiff reported her supervisor's harassment to his supervisor, who dealt ineffectively with the harassment and subsequently began harassing the plaintiff himself. 297 F.3d 405 (5th Cir. 2002). We held that it was unreasonable for the plaintiff not to report the harassment to another person listed in the defendant's reporting policy once her initial complaint was obviously ineffective. *Id.* at 413. Thus, *Wyatt* counsels that Lauderdale's failure to use one of the other reporting avenues provided by the TDCJ was unreasonable.

In most cases, as here, once an employee knows his initial complaint is ineffective, it is unreasonable for him not to file a second complaint, so long as the employer has provided multiple avenues for such a complaint. This conclusion is consistent with Title VII's intent to encourage "saving action by objecting employees." Although it is conceivable that under certain circumstances an employee's failure to file a subsequent complaint would not be unreasonable, even where there are multiple reporting avenues, Lauderdale's circumstances do not render her failure reasonable.

Likewise, Lauderdale's formal complaint on December 3, 2004, the date of her resignation, does not defeat the second prong of the *Ellerth/Faragher* defense. Filing a complaint upon, or after, resigning does not mitigate any of the damage, because it does not allow the employer to remediate the situation. A complaint filed at such a late date is no longer a saving action contemplated and encouraged by Title VII.... [H]ence it is not sufficient to defeat the *Ellerth/Faragher* affirmative defense. "[I]f damages could reasonably have been mitigated no award against a liable employer should reward a plaintiff for what her own efforts could have avoided." [citation omitted]. Thus, Lauderdale's complaint, filed on the day she resigned, does not defeat the affirmative defense.

Furthermore, the TDCJ conducted an investigation after Lauderdale formally complained. That investigation resulted in disciplinary action against Arthur. The TDCJ's prompt remedial action upon receiving Lauderdale's complaint confirms that the first prong of the *Ellerth/Faragher* defense has been satisfied and that Lauderdale could have mitigated the harm had she tried to make a second complaint after Kroll had refused to intervene.

In light of the TDCJ's standing policies on sexual harassment, its training program, and its prompt action following Lauderdale's formal complaint, the TDCJ has satisfied the first prong of the *Ellerth/Faragher* defense. Lauderdale's failure to complain after her initial conversation with Kroll is a failure to take advantage of the TDCJ's prevention program, thereby satisfying the second prong. Thus, the TDCJ avoids vicarious liability.

### III

... [B]ecause the TDCJ has successfully asserted the *Ellerth/Faragher* defense, the summary judgment in favor of the TDCJ is affirmed....

## ✦ Core Concept: Tangible Employment Action

As *Vance v. Ball State* suggests, the concept of "tangible employment action" can be pivotal because a finding that action qualified as a tangible employment action cuts off the possibility that the defendant can avoid liability through the *Ellerth/Faragher* defense. The Court in *Ellerth* and *Faragher* defined "tangible employment action" as "a significant change in employment status, such as hiring, firing, failing to promote, reassignment with significantly different responsibilities, or a decision causing a significant change in benefits." In a subsequent Supreme Court decision, *Pennsylvania State Police v. Suders*, 542 U.S. 129, 148 (2004), the Court clarified that only official company acts qualify as tangible employment actions.

This qualification had significant ramifications for the issue in *Suders*: whether or when a constructive discharge qualifies as a tangible employment action, so as to cut off the defendant's access to the affirmative defense. In employment law, a constructive discharge occurs when a plaintiff experiences work conditions so intolerable that a reasonable person would resign, rather than continue to submit to them. In *Suders*, the plaintiff, Nancy Drew Suders, alleged sexually harassing conduct by her supervisors—officers of the Pennsylvania State Police—of such severity that she was forced to resign. The Court held that constructive discharges do not qualify as tangible employment actions unless they involve "an employer-sanctioned adverse action officially changing her employment status or situation, for example, a humiliating demotion, extreme cut in pay, or transfer to a position in which she would face unbearable working conditions." In essence, then, a hostile environment harassment constructive discharge is likely to qualify as a tangible employment action only if the harassment leading to the resignation entails an independent tangible employment action.

---

### Exercise 5.9

You are a lawyer in private practice. Pamela Pine has been terminated from her position at Acme Asbestos and comes to you to find out whether she was wrongfully terminated under the federal employment discrimination laws. She wants to know whether she might successfully sue. She is a white, thirty-six year old mother of two. Just prior to her termination, Pamela was involved in an incident that she believes may have caused her employer to terminate her. On the day before she was fired, Pamela was called into the office of Jack Russell, the office supervisor. Jack told Pamela that she had better straighten up and fly right if she wanted to continue with Acme. When Pamela inquired what on earth Jack was talking about, Jack explained, "Every other good looking woman on the staff has already paid a visit to the No-Tell Motel with me. It's your turn!" Pamela responded, "In your dreams," and concluded the meeting by walking out of the office. What questions do you have for Ms. Pine? How will you counsel her?

---

### Exercise 5.10

Unrelated to Ms. Pine's case, two other Acme employees come to you to see whether you will represent them in a discriminatory harassment suit. Jane and

Tom are warehouse workers at Acme. They tell you that the truck drivers whose trucks they are required to load and unload at the dock harass them mercilessly. In addition to talking daily relentlessly about Jane's and Tom's physiques (in particular, their private parts), the drivers make lewd remarks about sexual encounters they envision Jane and Tom have when Jane and Tom are alone in the warehouse. One of the drivers, Mary, physically caresses Jane's and Tom's necks and shoulders whenever she can get close enough. The drivers also ridicule Jane and Tom for their status as mere warehouse workers, rather than members of the "elite" corps of drivers. In addition, the drivers ridicule Jane and Tom for their weight, for the way they dress (jeans and flannel shirts), and for their general appearances. Several times Jane and Tom ask the dock manager to insist that the behavior stop, and the dock manager hangs anti-harassment signs up on the loading dock bulletin board, but nothing changes. Life is miserable for Jane and Tom, but they "grin and bear it," until they finally cannot take any more, at which time they file a charge with the EEOC. The EEOC issues a right to sue letter, which Jane and Tom bring with them when they come to your office. What questions do you have for Jane and Tom? How will you counsel them?

---

## ➤ Beyond the Basics: Harassment

1. In *Reeves v. C.H. Robinson Worldwide, Inc.*, the Eleventh Circuit held that hostility not directed at plaintiff, but directed at her "target group" (the group sharing her protected trait) may nevertheless support the plaintiff's hostile environment claim. 594 F.3d 798, 811 (11th Cir. 2010) (en banc).

2. Can a target consent to "harassment"? In *Lyle v. Warner Brothers Television Productions*, 132 P.3d 211 (Cal. 2006), the California Supreme Court considered a claim by Lyle who had accepted a position as a note-taker for the writers of the television show, "Friends." The court rejected Lyle's harassment claim even though the writers "made masturbatory hand gestures and drew crude figures of female genitalia." The defense contended that sexual speech was necessary to generate ideas. The court rejected the plaintiff's claim, stating that the defendant had forewarned Lyle of the sexual nature of the show, the writers did not make any sexual comments toward her, and, in light of the studio's creative environment, the conduct at issue was not severe or pervasive enough to constitute harassment.

3. Some scholars and defendants have argued that the First Amendment should serve as a defense in discriminatory harassment cases. The argument is that the First Amendment protects the right to speak out against other people and that this protected speech may overlap with speech that is legally defined as harassment. As a federal statute, Title VII constitutes government action and thus may be subjected to scrutiny under the First Amendment. One court looked at this issue in *Robinson v. Jacksonville Shipyards*, 760 F. Supp. 1486 (D. Fla. 1991). There, the plaintiff, a female welder, argued that the employer created and encouraged a sexually hostile, intimidating work environment. Her claim was based on sexually suggestive pictures of women and remarks made by male employees and supervisors demeaning to women. The court rejected the First Amendment defense: "verbal harassment [is] not protected speech because [it] act[s] as discriminatory conduct in the form of a hostile work environment." *Robinson*, 760 F. Supp. at 1535 (citing *Roberts v. United States Jaycees*, 468 U.S. 609, 628 (1984) & *Hishon v. King & Spalding*, 467 U.S. 69, 78 (1984)). The court reasoned that the speech was not just speech, but more akin

to a crime, which the state has power to punish. It viewed the regulation of discriminatory speech at work as simply a time, place, and manner regulation, noting that the workers are a captive audience and that Title VII is narrowly drawn to serve a compelling state interest. *See* J.M. Balkin, *Free Speech and Hostile Environments*, 99 Colum. L. Rev. 2295 (1998) (explaining circumstances in which collateral censorship—where one private party limits another's speech to avoid liability—may violate the First Amendment); Marie Joy Mendoza, Note, *Making Friends: Sexual Harassment in the Workplace Free Speech and* Lyle v. Warner Bros., 40 U.C. Davis L. Rev. 1965, 1968 (2007).

## Exercise 5.11

In your role as an advisor about employment discrimination issues, you may be asked to draft policies for employers. In undertaking such a task, you will often draw upon policies that are publicly available or that you or your law firm have drafted in the past. While it is a good idea to consider other available policies, recall that an employment discrimination policy should be tailored for the particular employer.

In creating such a policy, it is important to consider the size of the employer, its structure, the reporting hierarchy for employees, the resources available for training, the turnover rate for employees and whether the employer has a human resources department or officer.

ACME Company has 1,000 employees spread across three campuses in the same state. ACME is a paint manufacturer. Most of its employees work in the paint manufacturing facility. ACME has retained your services to create an anti-harassment policy and procedure for the company. Think about the questions you might ask your contact at ACME before drafting the policy.

Create an outline of the policy and procedure that you will propose. Be prepared to explain to the company's managers the reasons why the particular proposals are legally necessary. Also think about the ways that the policy will be communicated to management and to employees. Remember the role that a policy can play in defending discrimination claims. Having evidence that a plaintiff or an alleged discriminator was aware of the company's policy may be important.

Think about how your advice might change if ACME has 20 employees who are all managed by the same supervisor.

## Exercise 5.12

As a lawyer trained in employment discrimination law, you may be called on by clients to provide training to employees. In some states, state law mandates that training be provided to certain individuals. *See, e.g.,* Me. Rev. Stat. Ann. tit. 26, §807(3).

Such training can educate employees about legal prohibitions against discrimination, teach employees how to recognize discriminatory actions, communicate the employer's policies regarding discrimination, and communicate how to respond if discrimination is occurring. Note also that providing training can help support a defense if a subsequent suit is filed. Employers should be encouraged to offer regular training to employees and to document when employees receive such training.

The ACME Company has decided to retain your firm to provide training to all its employees on the legal prohibitions against discriminatory workplace harassment.

Consider the following questions:

1. What information do you view as essential to be conveyed?

2. What, other than conveying information, will you hope to accomplish in the training?

3. Consider the techniques that are likely to be effective to convey the information, and those that are not likely to be effective. Will this vary depending on whether the audience consists of managers, office staff, dock workers, factory workers? You actually are an expert on the subject of effective training techniques because you have spent so many years in formal education. Thus, to answer this question, you might consider what kinds of classroom instruction you have found to be useful in your own educational experience and what kinds you believe were not helpful.

# Chapter 6

# Retaliation

In addition to prohibiting differential treatment based on protected traits, the employment discrimination statutes prohibit retaliation against employees for invoking the protections of those statutes. Why do you suppose Congress thought it was important to include protection against retaliation? What is achieved by prohibiting retaliation? How is a claim for retaliation different from one for discrimination? Keep your answers to these questions in mind as you read this Chapter and consider whether the statutes and court decisions advance the interests that underlie the prohibitions against retaliation.

Before you consider the law, however, consider the practical dynamics of retaliation. Imagine that a co-worker has accused you or a close work friend of discriminating against him based on a protected trait. How would you feel about such an accusation? How might you respond? Could your response be considered retaliation?

Consider the applicable statutory language. Section 704(a) of Title VII provides:

Discrimination for making charges, testifying, assisting, or participating in enforcement proceedings

It shall be an unlawful employment practice for an employer to discriminate against any of his employees or applicants for employment ... because he has opposed any practice made an unlawful employment practice by this subchapter, or because he has made a charge, testified, assisted, or participated in any manner in an investigation, proceeding, or hearing under this subchapter.

42 U.S.C. § 2000e-3(a).

The ADEA, the ADA, and the Equal Pay Act (EPA) contain retaliation provisions. *See* 29 U.S.C. § 623(d) (ADEA); 42 U.S.C. § 12203(a) (ADA); 29 U.S.C. § 215(a)(3) (EPA). In many instances, the statutory language of the retaliation provisions in the ADEA, the ADA, and the EPA tracks that of section 704. The ADA has additional language that makes it unlawful "to coerce, intimidate, threaten, or interfere with any individual in the exercise or enjoyment of, or on account of his or her having exercised or enjoyed, or on account of his or her having aided or encouraged any other individual in the exercise or enjoyment of, any right granted or protected by this chapter." 42 U.S.C. § 12203(b).

The case law construing the Title VII retaliation provision is generally transferrable to the other statutes. As the First Circuit stated in *Fennell v. First Step Designs Ltd.*, "the analytical framework for ADEA discrimination and retaliation cases was patterned after the framework for Title VII cases, and ... precedents [for the two] are largely interchangeable." 83 F.3d 526, 535 n.9 (1st Cir. 1996). Although the statutory language is silent on the issue, section 1981 has also been construed by case law to permit a retaliation action comparable to that under section 704.

When the retaliation provisions refer to an employee, this term has been interpreted to include applicants for employment and former employees. Although the statutory language does not expressly protect former employees from retaliation, the Supreme Court has held that former employees are protected. *Robinson v Shell Oil*, 519 U.S. 337, 346 (1997).

## ✦ Core Concept: Elements of the Statutory Claim for Retaliation

Courts vary in how they define the necessary elements of a plaintiff's retaliation case. Even though the exact articulation of the elements may vary by circuit, a retaliation analysis typically involves the following three concepts:

1) Whether the employee engaged in **protected activity** under Title VII;

2) Whether the employee suffered a **materially adverse employment action**; and

3) Whether a **causal link** existed between the protected activity and the adverse employment action, which is to say that the protected activity motivated the adverse employment action.

Some courts use a modified *McDonnell-Douglas* test when evaluating retaliation claims based on circumstantial evidence. Although not consistently articulated, many courts treat the three elements listed above as the prima facie case. *See, e.g., Bryant v. Jones*, 575 F.3d 1281, 1307 (11th Cir. 2009). Once these are established, such courts require the employer to articulate a legitimate, non-discriminatory reason for its actions, and the plaintiff may prevail by rebutting the employer's reason.

The Supreme Court cases below explain the elements likely to form part of the plaintiff's case. The first two cases, *Clark County School District v. Breeden* (Breeden I) and *Crawford v. Nashville*, help to explain what qualifies as **protected activity**. The third case, *Burlington Northern v. White*, focuses on what qualifies as a **materially adverse employment action**. After *Burlington*, a second segment of *Clark County School District v. Breeden* (Breeden II) is included because it discusses the **causal link** element of the statutory claim. The required causal standard is then explored in *University of Texas Southwestern Medical Center v. Nassar*. Following these cases dealing with the elements, you will find a section titled "Beyond the Basics," which includes some of the more complex retaliation issues. This section includes excerpts from the case of *Gomez-Perez v. Potter*, pertaining to expanding protection against retaliation under the ADEA to include employees in the federal government and *CBOCS West, Inc. v. Humphries*, recognizing a retaliation claim under section 1981.

## ✦ Core Concept: Protected Activity

To ask whether an activity is "protected," is to ask whether employees who engage in that activity will be safeguarded from employer retaliation. If an activity is not protected, that means that the employer may, without fear of sanction, take action against employees who engage in that activity.

Notice that the statute recognizes two types of protected activity: "participation" and "opposition." Employees *participate* when they file a discrimination charge or complaint or are involved in the processing of such claims whether with the EEOC, a parallel state agency or a court. *Opposition* encompasses objecting to employer behavior in a less formal manner.

*Participation Clause.* The participation or "free access" clause tends to be straightforward. Usually, it is clear that an employee either is or is not participating in a covered process. Examples of participation include filing a charge with the EEOC or comparable state agency, testifying or otherwise cooperating in an EEOC or parallel state proceeding, and filing or testifying in a discrimination law suit in federal or state court. Once conduct is identified as "participation," the courts give it almost unqualified protection from employer retaliation. This is so even where the participation activity is in a proceeding that is ultimately resolved in the employer's favor—where the underlying employer action being challenged turns out not to have violated the statute. Some courts protect employees who file fraudulent or malicious charges in bad faith. *Johnson v. University of Cincinnati*, 215 F.3d 561, 582 (6th Cir. 2000); *Pettaway v. American Case Iron Pipe Co.*, 411 F.2d 998, 1008 (5th Cir. 1969). Others require good faith. *Mattson v. Caterpillar, Inc.*, 359 F.3d 885, 890 (7th Cir. 2004) (baseless charge filed in bad faith not protected from retaliation).

What might be the rationale for protecting participation that is malicious and fraudulent?

*Opposition Clause.* Because opposition clause cases are less clear cut, most protected activity issues are litigated under this clause. What qualifies as protected activity is not as straightforward an issue under the opposition clause as it is under the participation clause. In addition, the degree of protection afforded to opposition behavior is less absolute than that afforded to participation activity.

A broad range of activities potentially qualifies as informal opposition. For example, courts have found protected opposition behavior where employees refused to facilitate allegedly unlawful retaliatory treatment of co-workers in the hiring/promotion process. *Thomas v. City of Beaverton*, 379 F.3d 802, 805 (9th Cir. 2004) (voicing informal complaints to superiors about sexual harassment); *Fye v. Oklahoma Corp. Com'n*, 516 F.3d 1217, 1228 (10th Cir. 2008) (refusing to implement an ostensibly discriminatory policy). The *Crawford* case explores the issue of whether an employee's testimony in an internal employer investigation should qualify as *protected opposition activity*.

---

## Focus Questions: *Crawford v. Nashville*

1. How does Crawford *answer the question of whether testifying in an internal investigation qualifies as protected activity?*

2. *Distinguish between the claim that could have been asserted based on the underlying Title VII violation and the retaliation claim that is the subject of this litigation.*

3. In Crawford, *the lower courts rejected both the participation clause claim and the opposition clause claim. As to each, what were the lower courts' grounds for concluding that the plaintiff's conduct did not qualify?*

4. *The Supreme Court uses the dictionary to define "oppose." Do the dictionary definitions resolve the issue to your satisfaction? Do you think the dictionary is necessary to the resolution of the issue? After the* Crawford *decision, what is the test for assessing whether an employee communication to the employer constitutes protected opposition activity?*

5. *Notice the irony: the person who is charged with harassing is the person responsible for controlling harassment.*

---

# Crawford v. Nashville

### 555 U.S. 271 (2009)

Justice Souter delivered the opinion of the Court.

Title VII of the Civil Rights Act of 1964 forbids retaliation by employers against employees who report workplace ... discrimination. The question here is whether this protection extends to an employee who speaks out about discrimination not on her own initiative, but in answering questions during an employer's internal investigation. We hold that it does.

## I

In 2002, respondent Nashville, Tennessee (Metro), began looking into rumors of sexual harassment by the Metro School District's employee relations director, Gene Hughes.[1] When Veronica Frazier, a Metro human resources officer, asked petitioner Vicky Crawford, a 30-year Metro employee, whether she had witnessed "inappropriate behavior" on the part of Hughes, Crawford described several instances of sexually harassing behavior: once, Hughes had answered her greeting, "Hey Dr. Hughes, what's up?," by grabbing his crotch and saying "[Y]ou know what's up"; he had repeatedly "put his crotch up to [her] window"; and on one occasion he had entered her office and "grabbed her head and pulled it to his crotch." Two other employees also reported being sexually harassed by Hughes. Although Metro took no action against Hughes, it did fire Crawford and the two other accusers soon after finishing the investigation, saying in Crawford's case that it was for embezzlement. Crawford claimed Metro was retaliating for her report of Hughes's behavior and filed a charge of a Title VII violation with the Equal Employment Opportunity Commission (EEOC), followed by this suit in the United States District Court for the Middle District of Tennessee.

The Title VII antiretaliation provision has two clauses, making it "an unlawful employment practice for an employer to discriminate against any of his employees ... [1] because he has opposed any practice made an unlawful employment practice by this subchapter, or [2] because he has made a charge, testified, assisted, or participated in any manner in an investigation, proceeding, or hearing under this subchapter. The one is known as the "opposition clause," the other as the "participation clause," and Crawford accused Metro of violating both.

The District Court granted summary judgment for Metro. It held that Crawford could not satisfy the opposition clause because she had not "instigated or initiated any complaint," but had "merely answered questions by investigators in an already-pending internal investigation, initiated by someone else." It concluded that her claim also failed under the participation clause, which Sixth Circuit precedent confined to protecting "an employee's participation in an employer's internal investigation ... where that investigation occurs pursuant to a pending EEOC charge" (not the case here). The Court of Appeals affirmed on the same grounds, holding that the opposition clause "demands active, consistent opposing activities to warrant ... protection against retaliation," whereas Crawford did "not claim to have instigated or initiated any complaint prior to her participation in the investigation, nor did she take any further action following the investigation and prior to her firing." Again like the trial judge, the Court of Appeals understood that Crawford could show no violation of the participation clause because her "employer's internal investigation" was not conducted "pursuant to a pending EEOC charge."

## II

The opposition clause makes it "unlawful ... for an employer to discriminate against any ... employe[e] ... because he has opposed any practice made ... unlawful ... by this subchapter." The term "oppose," being left undefined by the statute, carries its ordinary

---

1. Because this case arises out of the District Court's grant of summary judgment for Metro, "we are required to view all facts and draw all reasonable inferences in favor of the nonmoving party, [Crawford]."

meaning: "to resist or antagonize …; to contend against; to confront; resist; withstand," Webster's New International Dictionary 1710 (2d ed. 1958). Although these actions entail varying expenditures of energy, "RESIST frequently implies more active striving than OPPOSE." *Ibid.*; *see also* Random House Dictionary of the English Language 1359 (2d ed. 1987) (defining "oppose" as "to be hostile or adverse to, as in opinion").

The statement Crawford says she gave to Frazier is thus covered by the opposition clause, as an ostensibly disapproving account of sexually obnoxious behavior toward her by a fellow employee…. Crawford's description of the louche goings-on would certainly qualify in the minds of reasonable jurors as "resist[ant]" or "antagoni[stic]" to Hughes's treatment….

"Oppose" goes beyond "active, consistent" behavior in ordinary discourse, where we would naturally use the word to speak of someone who has taken no action at all to advance a position beyond disclosing it. Countless people were known to "oppose" slavery before Emancipation, or are said to "oppose" capital punishment today, without writing public letters, taking to the streets, or resisting the government…. There is, then, no reason to doubt that a person can "oppose" by responding to someone else's question just as surely as by provoking the discussion, and nothing in the statute requires a freakish rule protecting an employee who reports discrimination on her own initiative but not one who reports the same discrimination in the same words when her boss asks a question.

Metro and its *amici* support the Circuit panel's insistence on "active" and "consistent" opposition by arguing that the lower the bar for retaliation claims, the less likely it is that employers will look into what may be happening outside the executive suite. As they see it, if retaliation is an easy charge when things go bad for an employee who responded to enquiries, employers will avoid the headache by refusing to raise questions about possible discrimination.

The argument is unconvincing, for we think it underestimates the incentive to enquire that follows from our decisions in *Burlington Industries, Inc. v. Ellerth*, 524 U.S. 742 (1998), and *Faragher v. Boca Raton*, 524 U.S. 775 (1998). *Ellerth* and *Faragher* hold "[a]n employer … subject to vicarious liability to a victimized employee for an actionable hostile environment created by a supervisor with … authority over the employee." Although there is no affirmative defense if the hostile environment "culminates in a tangible employment action" against the employee, an employer does have a defense "[w]hen no tangible employment action is taken" if it "exercised reasonable care to prevent and correct promptly any" discriminatory conduct and "the plaintiff employee unreasonably failed to take advantage of any preventive or corrective opportunities provided by the employer or to avoid harm otherwise." [citation omitted]. Employers are thus subject to a strong inducement to ferret out and put a stop to any discriminatory activity in their operations as a way to break the circuit of imputed liability. The possibility that an employer might someday want to fire someone who might charge discrimination traceable to an internal investigation does not strike us as likely to diminish the attraction of an *Ellerth-Faragher* affirmative defense.

That aside, we find it hard to see why the Sixth Circuit's rule would not itself largely undermine the *Ellerth-Faragher* scheme, along with the statute's "primary objective" of "avoid[ing] harm" to employees. [citation omitted]. If it were clear law that an employee who reported discrimination in answering an employer's questions could be penalized with no remedy, prudent employees would have a good reason to keep quiet about Title VII offenses against themselves or against others. This is no imaginary horrible given the documented indications that "[f]ear of retaliation is the leading reason why people stay silent instead of voicing their concerns about bias and discrimination." [citation omitted]. The appeals court's rule would thus create a real dilemma for any knowledgeable employee in a hostile work environment if the boss took steps to assure a defense under our cases. If the employee reported discrimination in response to the enquiries, the employer might well be free to penalize her for speaking up. But if she kept quiet about the discrimination and later filed a Title VII claim, the employer might well escape liability, arguing that it "exercised reasonable care to prevent and correct [any discrimination] promptly" but "the plaintiff employee unreasonably failed to take advantage of … preventive or corrective opportunities provided by the employer." [citation omitted]. Nothing in the statute's text or our precedent supports this catch-22.

Because Crawford's conduct is covered by the opposition clause, we do not reach her argument that the Sixth Circuit misread the participation clause as well. But that does not mean the end of this case, for Metro's motion for summary judgment raised several defenses to the retaliation charge besides the scope of the two clauses; the District Court never reached these others owing to its ruling on the elements of retaliation, and they remain open on remand.

## III

The judgment of the Court of Appeals for the Sixth Circuit is reversed, and the case is remanded for further proceedings consistent with this opinion.

It is so ordered.

Justice Alito, with whom Justice Thomas joins, concurring in the judgment.

The question in this case is whether Title VII of the Civil Rights Act of 1964 prohibits retaliation against an employee who testifies in an internal investigation of alleged sexual harassment. I agree with the Court that the "opposition clause" prohibits retaliation for such conduct. I also agree with the Court's primary reasoning, which is based on "the point argued by the Government and explained by an EEOC guideline: 'When an employee communicates to her employer a belief that the employer has engaged in … a form of employment discrimination, that communication' virtually always 'constitutes the employee's *opposition* to the activity.'" [citation omitted]. I write separately to emphasize my understanding that the Court's holding does not and should not extend beyond employees who testify in internal investigations or engage in analogous purposive conduct….

In order to decide the question that is before us, we have no need to adopt a definition of the term "oppose" that is broader than the definition that petitioner advances. But in dicta, the Court notes that the fourth listed definition in the Random House Dictionary of the English Language goes further, defining "oppose" to mean "to be hostile or adverse to, *as in opinion.*" (emphasis added). Thus, this definition embraces silent opposition.

While this is certainly *an* accepted usage of the term "oppose," the term is not always used in this sense, and it is questionable whether silent opposition is covered by the opposition clause….

The number of retaliation claims filed with the EEOC has proliferated in recent years. An expansive interpretation of protected opposition conduct would likely cause this trend to accelerate.

The question whether the opposition clause shields employees who do not communicate their views to their employers through purposive conduct is not before us in this case; the answer to that question is far from clear; and I do not understand the Court's holding to reach that issue here. For present purposes, it is enough to hold that the opposition clause does protect an employee, like petitioner, who testifies about unlawful conduct in an internal investigation.

## Notes

1. In a portion of the concurrence not reproduced here, Justice Alito states that employees' complaining at the water cooler about an unlawful employer practice should not receive protection under the opposition clause. If such complaints do not receive protection, that means that the employer may retaliate for them with impunity. Should employer retaliation in such cases be acceptable?

2. In concurrence, Justice Alito justifies limiting the scope of protected opposition activity on the ground that an expanded role for that protection would likely accelerate the proliferation of retaliation claims being filed. In your opinion, what role should a potential proliferation of retaliation cases play in deciding what the statute means?

3. To prove a case of retaliation, the plaintiff has the burden of proving that (1) the plaintiff engaged in protected activity; (2) the defendant took adverse action against the plaintiff; and (3) the protected activity caused the adverse action. If that is so, is there really a need to make the plaintiff show that the opposition was publicly expressed? Shouldn't it suffice for the plaintiff simply to show that the defendant knew about the protected activity?

4. The *Crawford* Court determines that the plaintiff's conduct qualifies as opposition and therefore does not reach the question of whether it would qualify as participation. Recall that participation activity is more absolutely protected from retaliation than opposition activity. For example, some courts protect opposition only if the plaintiff's belief that the statute was violated is reasonable, whereas participation is protected even where the employee is unreasonable in her belief. Why do you suppose that the courts protect participation more than they protect opposition? Can you devise arguments for why it should be the other way around?

## ✦ Core Concept: Reasonableness of Opposition Conduct

The employment discrimination statutes do not insulate employees from the consequences of certain misbehavior, even if the conduct is sincerely undertaken to protest discriminatory conduct. A clear example of behavior that is not reasonable conduct and that does not qualify for protection is criminal activity. *Green v. McDonnell Douglas*, 463 F.2d 337, 341 (8th Cir. 1972). In *Green*, the employees who protested McDonnell Douglas' race discrimination engaged in illegal methods of protest, such as stall-outs. Taking malicious actions that grossly violate company policy also are not protected opposition, at least when legal or non-disruptive alternatives exist. *Niswander v. Cincinnati Ins. Co.*, 529 F.3d 714, 727 (6th Cir. 2008).

Conduct that is disloyal or excessively disruptive has been held not to be protected opposition. *Hochstadt v. Worcester Foundation for Experimental Biology*, 545 F.2d 222, 232–33 (1st Cir. 1976). Likewise, courts have refused to protect employee conduct that "so interferes with the performance of his job that it renders him ineffective in the position for which he was employed." *Hardy v. City of Tupelo, Miss.*, No. 1:08-CV-28-SA-JAD, 2009 WL 1854271, at *8 (N.D. Miss. June 26, 2009).

Outside the criminal context, it may be difficult to determine in advance whether a court will consider certain kinds of opposition conduct to be reasonable. As one court noted: "It is less clear to what extent militant self-help activity…, such as particular types of on-the-job opposition to alleged discrimination, vociferousness, expressions of hostility to an employer or superior and the like, are protected." *Hochstadt*, 545 F.2d at 230–231. Some courts have adopted a balancing test to determine whether conduct is reasonable, "requiring the employee's conduct to be reasonable in light of the circumstances and balancing the employer's right to run his business against the right of the employee to express grievances and promote her own welfare." *Smith v. Texas Dept. of Water Resources*, 818 F.2d 363, 366 (5th Cir. 1987).

## ✦ Core Concept: Reasonable Belief That the Act Has Been Violated

The *Crawford* case discusses whether various *employee* behaviors are protected from retaliation. Retaliation cases sometimes also raise questions about the underlying *employer* behavior that the employee has challenged. Thus, an employee may engage in proper opposition activity—such as by reporting harassment to management—but be mistaken about whether the challenged conduct (the harassment) violated the statute. Whether such errors thwart the subsequent retaliation claim often turns on whether the retaliation claim is asserted under the opposition clause or the participation clause.

Participation activity receives blanket protection, even where the underlying employer conduct did not actually violate the statute or even occur at all. In participation cases, the employee is protected as long as the employee "filed a charge, testified, assisted, or participated in any manner in an investigation, proceeding, or hearing" under the act. Although courts may impose a good faith or fraud limit on this protection, the employee is absolutely protected if the employee mistakenly believes the act was violated.

Opposition activity receives less absolute protection. Courts generally protect opposition activity only if the plaintiff **reasonably believed** that the challenged employer conduct violated the statute. As you will see, the *Breeden* case did not decide whether this approach is correct, but simply assumed the standard's correctness for the sake of argument and concluded that the plaintiff in *Breeden* had not met the reasonableness standard and thus was not protected from retaliation.

---

### Focus Questions: *Clark County School District v. Breeden*

1.  *What, exactly, does Shirley Breeden oppose?*

2.  *What level of understanding does the* Breeden *Court expect lay people to have on legal issues? Is the Supreme Court realistic in its expectations of lay people?*

3.  *Is* Breeden *a special case that should be limited to its unique facts?*

4.  *Think again about the* Faragher/Ellerth *affirmative defense. Does an individual who is subjected to harassment face a dilemma regarding when to complain? If you were an attorney advising a plaintiff facing harassment, when would you instruct the employee to complain to the employer?*

---

# Clark County School District v. Breeden
### 532 U.S. 268 (2001)
### (Breeden I)

Per Curiam.

Under Title VII it is unlawful "for an employer to discriminate against any of his employees ... because [the employee] has opposed any practice made an unlawful employment practice by [Title VII], or because [the employee] has made a charge, testified, assisted, or participated in any manner in an investigation, proceeding, or hearing under [Title VII]." [citation omitted]. In 1997, respondent [Breeden] filed a retaliation claim against petitioner Clark County School District. The claim as eventually amended alleged that petitioner had taken two separate adverse employment actions against her in response to two different protected activities in which she had engaged. The District Court granted summary judgment to [the employer], but a panel of the Court of Appeals for the Ninth Circuit reversed over the dissent of Judge Fernandez. We grant the writ of certiorari and reverse.

On October 21, 1994, respondent's male supervisor met with respondent and another male employee to review the psychological evaluation reports of four job applicants. The report for one of the applicants disclosed that the applicant had once commented to a co-worker, "I hear making love to you is like making love to the Grand Canyon." At the meeting respondent's supervisor read the comment aloud, looked at respondent and stated, "I don't know what that means." The other employee then said, "Well, I'll tell you later," and both men chuckled. Respondent later complained about the comment to the offending employee, to Assistant Superintendent George Ann Rice, the employee's supervisor, and to another assistant superintendent of petitioner. Her first claim of retaliation asserts that she was punished for these complaints.

The Court of Appeals for the Ninth Circuit has applied [Title VII's retaliation provision] to protect employee "oppos[ition]" not just to practices that are actually "made ... unlawful" by Title VII, but also to practices that the employee could reasonably believe were unlawful. We have no occasion to rule on the propriety of this interpretation, because even assuming it is correct, no one could reasonably believe that the incident recounted above violated Title VII.

Title VII forbids actions taken on the basis of sex that "discriminate against any individual with respect to his compensation, terms, conditions, or privileges of employment." 42 U.S.C. § 2000e-2(a)(1). Just three Terms ago, we reiterated, what was plain from our previous decisions, that sexual harassment is actionable under Title VII only if it is "so 'severe or pervasive' as to 'alter the conditions of [the victim's] employment and create an abusive working environment.'" [citation omitted]. Workplace conduct is not measured in isolation; instead, "whether an environment is sufficiently hostile or abusive" must be judged "by 'looking at all the circumstances,' including the 'frequency of the discriminatory conduct; its severity; whether it is physically threatening or humiliating, or a mere offensive utterance; and whether it unreasonably interferes with an employee's work performance.'" [citation omitted]. Hence, "[a] recurring point in [our] opinions is that simple teasing, offhand comments, and isolated incidents (unless extremely serious) will not amount to discriminatory changes in the 'terms and conditions of employment.'" [citation omitted]. No reasonable person could have believed that the single incident recounted above violated Title VII's standard. The ordinary terms and conditions of respondent's job required her to review the sexually explicit statement in the course of screening job applicants. Her co-workers who participated in the hiring process were subject to the same requirement, and indeed, in the District Court respondent "conceded that it did not bother or upset her" to read the statement in the file. Her supervisor's comment, made at a meeting to review the application, that he did not know what the statement meant; her co-worker's responding comment; and the chuckling of both are at worst an "isolated inciden[t]" that cannot remotely be considered "extremely serious," as our cases require. The holding of the Court of Appeals to the contrary must be reversed.

## Note

When Breeden complained, she was complaining, not about the original vulgar statement, but about her supervisor's and co-worker's response to it in her presence. Would Breeden's prospects of winning have been better if she had witnessed and objected to the original statement?

## ✦ Core Concept: Materially Adverse Employment Action

Up until now, this Chapter has focused primarily on the first statutory element: the plaintiff engaged in protected activity, whether opposition or participation. The second of the three elements in the retaliation claim is that the "employee suffered an **adverse employment action**." In *Burlington Northern*, the Supreme Court explains the range of employer actions that qualify as "adverse employment actions." Note that distinctions between opposition cases and participation cases are irrelevant to analysis of the adverse employment action element. All retaliation cases—both opposition and participation—require a showing of adverse employment action.

It is helpful to try to keep separate two concepts that use similar terminology. In *Faragher/Ellerth*, the courts use the term "tangible employment action" to describe the dividing line between harassment cases in which an employer will have an affirmative defense to claims and those where no affirmative defense is available. In contrast, the term "adverse employment action" in the retaliation context refers to whether the conduct taken against the employee is serious enough to merit statutory protection.

---

### Focus Questions: *Burlington Northern & Santa Fe Railway Co. v. White*

1. *Before* Burlington Northern, *the circuit courts disagreed about what constitutes a sufficient "adverse employment action" for purposes of proving retaliation. The Sixth Circuit required the plaintiff to show "a materially adverse change in the terms and conditions of employment." The Fifth and Eighth Circuits demanded a showing of "ultimate employment action." In* Burlington Northern, *the Supreme Court adopts the position of the Seventh and District of Columbia Circuits. What is that position?*

2. *Do you see a difference between the standard adopted by the Supreme Court and the standard espoused by the Ninth Circuit and EEOC (requiring "adverse treatment that is based on a retaliatory motive and is reasonably likely to deter the charging party or others from engaging in protected activity")?*

---

## Burlington Northern & Santa Fe Railway Co. v. White

### 548 U.S. 53 (2006)

Justice Breyer delivered the opinion of the Court.

Title VII of the Civil Rights Act of 1964 forbids employment discrimination against "any individual" based on that individual's "race, color, religion, sex, or national origin." A separate section of the Act—its anti-retaliation provision—forbids an employer from "discriminat[ing] against" an employee or job applicant because that individual "opposed any practice" made unlawful by Title VII or "made a charge, testified, assisted, or participated in" a Title VII proceeding or investigation. [citation omitted].

The Courts of Appeals have come to different conclusions about the scope of the Act's anti-retaliation provision, particularly the reach of its phrase "discriminate against." Does that provision confine actionable retaliation to activity that affects the terms and conditions of employment? And how harmful must the adverse actions be to fall within its scope?

We conclude that the anti-retaliation provision does not confine the actions and harms it forbids to those that are related to employment or occur at the workplace. We also conclude that the provision covers those (and only those) employer actions that would have been materially adverse to a reasonable employee or job applicant. In the present context that means that the employer's actions must be harmful to the point that they could well dissuade a reasonable worker from making or supporting a charge of discrimination.

I

A

This case arises out of actions that supervisors at petitioner Burlington Northern & Santa Fe Railway Company took against respondent Sheila White, the only woman working in the Maintenance of Way department at Burlington's Tennessee Yard. In June 1997, Burlington's roadmaster, Marvin Brown, interviewed White and expressed interest in her previous experience operating forklifts. Burlington hired White as a "track laborer," a job that involves removing and replacing track components, transporting track material, cutting brush, and clearing litter and cargo spillage from the right-of-way. Soon after White arrived on the job, a co-worker who had previously operated the forklift chose to assume other responsibilities. Brown immediately assigned White to operate the forklift. While she also performed some of the other track laborer tasks, operating the forklift was White's primary responsibility.

In September 1997, White complained to Burlington officials that her immediate supervisor, Bill Joiner, had repeatedly told her that women should not be working in the Maintenance of Way department. Joiner, White said, had also made insulting and inappropriate remarks to her in front of her male colleagues. After an internal investigation, Burlington suspended Joiner for 10 days and ordered him to attend a sexual-harassment training session.

On September 26, Brown told White about Joiner's discipline. At the same time, he told White that he was removing her from forklift duty and assigning her to perform only standard track laborer tasks. Brown explained that the reassignment reflected co-worker's complaints that, in fairness, a "more senior man" should have the "less arduous and cleaner job" of forklift operator.

On October 10, White filed a complaint with the Equal Employment Opportunity Commission (EEOC or Commission). She claimed that the reassignment of her duties amounted to unlawful gender-based discrimination and retaliation for her having earlier complained about Joiner. In early December, White filed a second retaliation charge with the Commission, claiming that Brown had placed her under surveillance and was monitoring her daily activities. That charge was mailed to Brown on December 8.

A few days later, White and her immediate supervisor, Percy Sharkey, disagreed about which truck should transport White from one location to another. The specific facts of the disagreement are in dispute, but the upshot is that Sharkey told Brown later that afternoon that White had been insubordinate. Brown immediately suspended White without pay. White invoked internal grievance procedures. Those procedures led Burlington to conclude that White had *not* been insubordinate. Burlington reinstated White to her position and awarded her backpay for the 37 days she was suspended. White filed an additional retaliation charge with the EEOC based on the suspension.

## B

After exhausting administrative remedies, White filed this Title VII action against Burlington in federal court. As relevant here, she claimed that Burlington's actions — (1) changing her job responsibilities, and (2) suspending her for 37 days without pay — amounted to unlawful retaliation in violation of Title VII. A jury found in White's favor on both of these claims. It awarded her $43,500 in compensatory damages, including $3,250 in medical expenses. The District Court denied Burlington's post-trial motion for judgment as a matter of law.

Initially, a divided Sixth Circuit panel reversed the judgment and found in Burlington's favor on the retaliation claims. The full Court of Appeals vacated the panel's decision, however, and heard the matter en banc. The court then affirmed the District Court's judgment in White's favor on both retaliation claims. While all members of the en banc court voted to uphold the District Court's judgment, they differed as to the proper standard to apply.

## II

Title VII's anti-retaliation provision forbids employer actions that "discriminate against" an employee (or job applicant) because he has "opposed" a practice that Title VII forbids or has "made a charge, testified, assisted, or participated in" a Title VII "investigation, proceeding, or hearing." No one doubts that the term "discriminate against" refers to distinctions or differences in treatment that injure protected individuals. But different Circuits have come to different conclusions about ... how harmful that action must be to constitute retaliation.

... The Sixth Circuit majority in this case, for example, said that a plaintiff must show an "adverse employment action," which it defined as a "materially adverse change in the terms and conditions" of employment.... The Fifth and the Eighth Circuits ... employ an "ultimate employment decisio[n]" standard, which limits actionable retaliatory conduct to acts "such as hiring, granting leave, discharging, promoting, and compensating."

Other Circuits have not so limited the scope of the provision. The Seventh and the District of Columbia Circuits have said that the plaintiff must show that the "employer's challenged action would have been material to a reasonable employee," which in contexts like the present one means that it would likely have "dissuaded a reasonable worker from making or supporting a charge of discrimination." And the Ninth Circuit, following EEOC guidance, has said that the plaintiff must simply establish "adverse treatment that is based on a retaliatory motive and is reasonably likely to deter the charging party or others from engaging in protected activity." The concurring judges below would have applied this last mentioned standard.

We granted certiorari to resolve this disagreement. To do so requires us to ... characterize how harmful an act of retaliatory discrimination must be in order to fall within the provision's scope.

## A

[The first part of the opinion addressed an issue not before the Court: whether section 704 governing retaliation reaches employer actions above and beyond those that affect the employee's compensation, terms, conditions, or privileges of employment. The Court concluded that Title VII prohibits retaliation that takes place outside the workplace. Although this part of the Court's opinion is dicta, some lower courts rely upon it. *See, e.g., Kuntzman v. Wal-Mart*, 673 F. Supp. 2d 690, 714 (N.D. Ind. 2009) (holding that Wal-Mart's filing of criminal charges against plaintiff after she resigned is the "type of adverse action that could deter an employee from making a charge of discrimination").]

… Interpreting the antiretaliation provision to provide broad protection from retaliation helps ensure the cooperation upon which accomplishment of the Act's primary objective depends.… The scope of the antiretaliation provision extends beyond workplace-related or employment-related retaliatory acts and harm.…

## B

The anti-retaliation provision protects an individual not from all retaliation, but from retaliation that produces an injury or harm. As we have explained, the Courts of Appeals have used differing language to describe the level of seriousness to which this harm must rise before it becomes actionable retaliation. We agree with the formulation set forth by the Seventh and the District of Columbia Circuits. In our view, a plaintiff must show that a reasonable employee would have found the challenged action materially adverse, "which in this context means it well might have 'dissuaded a reasonable worker from making or supporting a charge of discrimination.'"

We speak of *material* adversity because we believe it is important to separate significant from trivial harms. Title VII, we have said, does not set forth "a general civility code for the American workplace." An employee's decision to report discriminatory behavior cannot immunize that employee from those petty slights or minor annoyances that often take place at work and that all employees experience. The anti-retaliation provision seeks to prevent employer interference with "unfettered access" to Title VII's remedial mechanisms. It does so by prohibiting employer actions that are likely "to deter victims of discrimination from complaining to the EEOC," the courts, and their employers. [citation omitted]. And normally petty slights, minor annoyances, and simple lack of good manners will not create such deterrence.

We refer to reactions of a *reasonable* employee because we believe that the provision's standard for judging harm must be objective. An objective standard is judicially administrable. It avoids the uncertainties and unfair discrepancies that can plague a judicial effort to determine a plaintiff's unusual subjective feelings.…

We phrase the standard in general terms because the significance of any given act of retaliation will often depend upon the particular circumstances. Context matters. "The real social impact of workplace behavior often depends on a constellation of surrounding circumstances, expectations, and relationships which are not fully captured by a simple recitation of the words used or the physical acts performed." [citation omitted]. A schedule change in an employee's work schedule may make little difference to many workers, but may matter enormously to a young mother with school-age children.… A supervisor's refusal to invite an employee to lunch is normally trivial, a nonactionable petty slight. But to retaliate by excluding an employee from a weekly training lunch that contributes significantly to the employee's professional advancement might well deter a reasonable employee from complaining about discrimination.…

## III

Applying this standard to the facts of this case, we believe that there was a sufficient evidentiary basis to support the jury's verdict on White's retaliation claim. The jury found that two of Burlington's actions amounted to retaliation: the reassignment of White from forklift duty to standard track laborer tasks and the 37-day suspension without pay.

Burlington does not question the jury's determination that the motivation for these acts was retaliatory. But it does question the statutory significance of the harm these acts caused. The District Court instructed the jury to determine whether respondent "suffered a materially adverse change in the terms or conditions of her employment," and the Sixth Circuit upheld the jury's finding based on that same stringent interpretation of the anti-retaliation provision....

First, Burlington argues that a reassignment of duties cannot constitute retaliatory discrimination where, as here, both the former and present duties fall within the same job description. We do not see why that is so. Almost every job category involves some responsibilities and duties that are less desirable than others. Common sense suggests that one good way to discourage an employee such as White from bringing discrimination charges would be to insist that she spend more time performing the more arduous duties and less time performing those that are easier or more agreeable....

To be sure, reassignment of job duties is not automatically actionable. Whether a particular reassignment is materially adverse depends upon the circumstances of the particular case, and "should be judged from the perspective of a reasonable person in the plaintiff's position, considering 'all the circumstances.'" [citation omitted]....

Second, Burlington argues that the 37-day suspension without pay lacked statutory significance because Burlington ultimately reinstated White with backpay. Burlington says that "it defies reason to believe that Congress would have considered a rescinded investigatory suspension with full back pay" to be unlawful.... White did receive backpay. But White and her family had to live for 37 days without income. They did not know during that time whether or when White could return to work. Many reasonable employees would find a month without a paycheck to be a serious hardship....

IV

For these reasons, the judgment of the Court of Appeals is affirmed.

[Justice Alito concurred in the judgment, but disagreed with the test adopted by the majority. Justice Alito would require a materially adverse employment action, which he defines to include both that the employer's action relate to the job and that it cause material harm.]

---

## Notes

1. Note the strong emphasis this 2006 Supreme Court decision places on employee deterrence. If the adverse employment action is sufficiently severe that fear of it would deter a reasonable employee from engaging in a protected activity, then the employment action qualifies for purposes of section 704. Note, also, that the Supreme Court's 2009 opinion in *Crawford* includes a similar reference: "If it were clear law that an employee who reported discrimination in answering an employer's questions could be penalized with no remedy, prudent employees would have a good reason to keep quiet about Title VII offenses against themselves or against others." Is deterrence now a mainstay of retaliation jurisprudence? Should it be?

2. *Harassment as an adverse employment action.* Often, retaliation takes the form of supervisor or coworker harassment. In a parallel state law context, an employee named

Wigley blew the whistle on the employer for violations of the law. Several weeks later, Wigley's supervisor began calling him "old son of a bitch" and "old bastard," and telling him that he was too old to do the job and should "get gone." *Wigley v. R&D Maintenance Services, Inc*, No. 2:08-cv-00535, 2009 U.S. Dist. LEXIS 63495 at *7 (S.D. Ala. July 22, 2009). Ultimately, Wigley's employment was terminated. It is unclear whether he was dismissed or resigned. Under the "materially adverse" standard of *Burlington Northern*, how bad must the harassment be in order to qualify as an adverse employment action for purposes of retaliation? Must it rise to the level of being actionable in its own right?

3. In *Cole v. Illinois*, the Seventh Circuit applied *Burlington Northern* to a Family Medical Leave Act (FMLA) case. The court in *Cole* discussed the "adverse action" requirement in the FMLA context:

> [W]e have consistently required that the adverse action giving rise to an FMLA retaliation claim be "materially adverse." ... The Supreme Court has noted in the similar context of Title VII claims that "it is important to separate significant from trivial harms." *Burlington*, 548 U.S. at 68. The decision to take FMLA leave "cannot immunize that employee from those petty slights or minor annoyances that often take place at work and that all employees experience." *Id.*

562 F.3d 812, 816 (2009).

4. In the wake of *Burlington Northern*, courts and commentators have continued to use the term "adverse employment action," to define the harm required by Title VII's section 704. "Adverse employment action" has traditionally been used to describe changes in compensation, terms, conditions, or privileges of employment as prohibited by section 703. It remains unclear how *Burlington Northern* affects the definition of "adverse employment action" in the discrimination context, although the Court in *Burlington Northern* noted that the discrimination and retaliation provisions should be interpreted differently. Should a new term be coined for the section 704 context?

## ✦ Core Concept: Causal Link

The third statutory element in the retaliation claim is that a **causal link** exists between the protected activity and the adverse employment action, which is to say that the employer took the adverse action because of the protected activity. This section contains two cases pertaining to causal link. The first, *Clark County School District v. Breeden*, considers what evidence is probative on the issue of causation. The second focuses on the availability of mixed-motive analysis in the retaliation context under Title VII.

The plaintiff may prove the causal link in several ways. The plaintiff may use direct evidence, such as a statement of the supervisor acknowledging that the adverse employment action was, indeed, motivated by the plaintiff's protected activity. In the absence of direct evidence, the plaintiff may prove causation by showing temporal proximity (closeness in time) between the supervisor's learning that the plaintiff engaged in protected activity and the superior's taking adverse action against the plaintiff. This temporal proximity allows a factfinder to infer that retaliation was the reason for the action. Courts differ on how close in time protected activity and an adverse action must be to justify an inference of retaliation based on temporal proximity alone; however, many courts hold that causation may be inferred if three or fewer months have passed. *See, e.g., Singfield v. Akron Metro. Hous. Auth.*, 389 F.3d 555, 556 (6th Cir. 2004). It is also possible for the plaintiff to prove causation simply by showing that another identically situated employee who had not engaged in protected activity was NOT subjected to the adverse treatment to which plaintiff was subjected.

---

### Focus Questions: *Clark County School District v. Breeden*

1. *Create a timeline of plaintiff's and her supervisor's acts to keep track of the events underlying the District Court's decision that plaintiff did not establish causation based on the supervisor's knowledge of plaintiff's April 1 complaint.*

2. *Why does the Supreme Court reject the appellate court's reliance on the right to sue letter in support of a finding of causation?*

---

# Clark County School District v. Breeden

### 532 U.S. 268 (2001)
### (Breeden II)

... Besides claiming that she was punished for complaining to petitioner's personnel about the alleged sexual harassment, respondent also claimed that she was punished for filing charges against petitioner with the Nevada Equal Rights Commission and the Equal Employment Opportunity Commission (EEOC) and for filing the present suit. Respondent filed her lawsuit on April 1, 1997; on April 10, 1997, respondent's supervisor, Assistant Superintendent Rice, "mentioned to [the] Executive Director of plaintiff's union, that she was contemplating transferring plaintiff to the position of Director of Professional Development Education"; and this transfer was "carried through" in May. In order to show, as her defense against summary judgment required, the existence of a causal connection between her protected activities and the transfer, respondent "relie[d] wholly on the temporal proximity of the filing of her complaint on April 1, 1997 and Rice's statement to plaintiff's union representative on April 10, 1997...." The District Court, however, found that respondent did not serve petitioner with the summons and complaint until April 11, 1997, one day *after* Rice had made the statement, and Rice filed an affidavit stating that she did not become aware of the lawsuit until after April 11, a claim that respondent did not challenge. Hence, the court concluded, respondent "ha[d] not shown that any causal connection exists between her protected activities and the adverse employment decision."

The Court of Appeals reversed, relying on two facts: The EEOC had issued a right-to-sue letter to respondent three months before Rice announced she was contemplating the transfer, and the actual transfer occurred one month after Rice learned of respondent's suit. The latter fact is immaterial in light of the fact that petitioner concededly was contemplating the transfer before it learned of the suit. Employers need not suspend previously planned transfers upon discovering that a Title VII suit has been filed, and their proceeding along lines previously contemplated, though not yet definitively determined, is no evidence whatever of causality.

As for the right-to-sue letter: Respondent did not rely on that letter in the District Court and did not mention it in her opening brief on appeal. Her demonstration of causality all along had rested upon the connection between the transfer and the filing of her lawsuit — to which connection the letter was irrelevant. When, however, petitioner's answering brief in the Court of Appeals demonstrated conclusively the lack of causation between the filing of respondent's lawsuit and Rice's decision, respondent mentioned the letter for the first time in her reply brief. The Ninth Circuit's opinion did not adopt respondent's utterly implausible suggestion that the EEOC's issuance of a right-to-sue letter — an action in which the employee takes no part—is a protected activity of the employee. Rather, the opinion suggests that the letter provided petitioner with its first notice of respondent's charge before the EEOC, and hence allowed the inference that the transfer proposal made three months later was petitioner's reaction to the charge. This will not do.

First, there is no indication that Rice even knew about the right-to-sue letter when she proposed transferring respondent. And second, if one presumes she knew about it, one must also presume that she (or her predecessor) knew *almost two years earlier* about the protected action (filing of the EEOC complaint) that the letter supposedly disclosed. The complaint had been filed on August 23, 1995, and both Title VII and its implementing regulations require that an employer be given notice within 10 days of filing. The cases that accept mere temporal proximity between an employer's knowledge of protected activity and an adverse employment action as sufficient evidence of causality to establish a prima facie case uniformly hold that the temporal proximity must be "very close." Action taken (as here) 20 months later suggests, by itself, no causality at all.

In short, neither the grounds that respondent presented to the District Court, nor the ground she added on appeal, nor even the ground the Court of Appeals developed on its own, sufficed to establish a dispute substantial enough to withstand the motion for summary judgment. The District Court's granting of that motion was correct. The judgment of the Court of Appeals is reversed.

––––––––––

Although courts often applied mixed-motive analysis in retaliation cases following *Price Waterhouse v. Hopkins*, the case of *Gross v. FBL Financial Services*, 557 U.S. 167 (2009), called that practice into question. The *Gross* decision, which you studied in Chapter 3, concluded that plaintiffs must establish "but for" cause in ADEA disparate treatment cases. The *Gross* Court held *Price Waterhouse v. Hopkins*, 490 U.S. 228 (1989), and the subsequent 1991 amendment to Title VII did not apply to the ADEA. The 2013 case of *University of Texas Southwestern Medical Center v. Nassar* addressed this question in the Title VII retaliation context and concluded plaintiffs must establish "but for" cause in those cases.

––––––––––

## Focus Questions:
### *University of Texas Southwestern Medical Center v. Nassar*

1. *The majority and the dissent present different accounts of the development of the motivating-factor standard under Title VII. Which account is correct?*

2. *Is it appropriate for the Court to borrow the "but for" standard from tort law? Does tort law require the use of a "but for" standard? Should employment discrimination cases necessarily be decided in accordance with tort principles?*

3. *Should Dr. Nassar prevail on remand under the new causation standard?*

4. *Does the new causation standard make it harder or easier for plaintiffs to establish retaliation claims?*

5. *The majority asserts that it chooses the "but for" standard to guard against fake claims. Is this an appropriate policy to use? Are there other policies that lean in another direction?*

––––––––––

# University of Texas Southwestern Medical Center v. Nassar

## 133 S.Ct. 2517 (2013)

Justice Kennedy delivered the opinion of the Court.

When the law grants persons the right to compensation for injury from wrongful conduct, there must be some demonstrated connection, some link, between the injury sustained and the wrong alleged. The requisite relation between prohibited conduct and compensable injury is governed by the principles of causation, a subject most often arising in elaborating the law of torts. This case requires the Court to define those rules in the context of Title VII of the Civil Rights Act of 1964, 42 U.S.C. § 2000e *et seq.*, which provides remedies to employees for injuries related to discriminatory conduct and associated wrongs by employers.

Title VII is central to the federal policy of prohibiting wrongful discrimination in the Nation's workplaces and in all sectors of economic endeavor. This opinion discusses the causation rules for two categories of wrongful employer conduct prohibited by Title VII. The first type is called, for purposes of this opinion, status-based discrimination. The term is used here to refer to basic workplace protection such as prohibitions against employer discrimination on the basis of race, color, religion, sex, or national origin, in hiring, firing, salary structure, promotion and the like. *See* § 2000e-2(a). The second type of conduct is employer retaliation on account of an employee's having opposed, complained of, or sought remedies for, unlawful workplace discrimination. *See* § 2000e-3(a).

An employee who alleges status-based discrimination under Title VII need not show that the causal link between injury and wrong is so close that the injury would not have occurred but for the act. So-called but-for causation is not the test. It suffices instead to show that the motive to discriminate was one of the employer's motives, even if the employer also had other, lawful motives that were causative in the employer's decision. This principle is the result of an earlier case from this Court, *Price Waterhouse v. Hopkins,* 490 U.S. 228 (1989), and an ensuing statutory amendment by Congress that codified in part and abrogated in part the holding in *Price Waterhouse, see* §§ 2000e-2(m), 2000e-5(g)(2)(B). The question the Court must answer here is whether that lessened causation standard is applicable to claims of unlawful employer retaliation under § 2000e-3(a).

Although the Court has not addressed the question of the causation showing required to establish liability for a Title VII retaliation claim, it has addressed the issue of causation in general in a case involving employer discrimination under a separate but related statute, the Age Discrimination in Employment Act of 1967 (ADEA), 29 U.S.C. § 623. *See Gross v. FBL Financial Services, Inc.,* 557 U.S. 167 (2009). In *Gross,* the Court concluded that the ADEA requires proof that the prohibited criterion was the but-for cause of the prohibited conduct. The holding and analysis of that decision are instructive here.

I

Petitioner, the University of Texas Southwestern Medical Center (University), is an academic institution within the University of Texas system. The University specializes in medical education for aspiring physicians, health professionals, and scientists. Over the years, the University has affiliated itself with a number of healthcare facilities including, as relevant in this case, Parkland Memorial Hospital (Hospital). As provided in its affiliation agreement with the University, the Hospital permits the University's students to gain clinical experience working in its facilities. The agreement also requires the Hospital to offer empty staff physician posts to the University's faculty members, and, accordingly, most of the staff physician positions at the Hospital are filled by those faculty members.

Respondent is a medical doctor of Middle Eastern descent who specializes in internal medicine and infectious diseases. In 1995, he was hired to work both as a member of the University's faculty and a staff physician at the Hospital. He left both positions in 1998 for additional medical education and then returned in 2001 as an assistant professor at the University and, once again, as a physician at the Hospital.

In 2004, Dr. Beth Levine was hired as the University's Chief of Infectious Disease Medicine. In that position Levine became respondent's ultimate (though not direct) superior. Respondent alleged that Levine was biased against him on account of his religion and ethnic heritage, a bias manifested by undeserved scrutiny of his billing practices and productivity, as well as comments that "Middle Easterners are lazy." On different occasions during his employment, respondent met with Dr. Gregory Fitz, the University's Chair of Internal Medicine and Levine's supervisor, to complain about Levine's alleged harassment. Despite obtaining a promotion with Levine's assistance in 2006, respondent continued to believe that she was biased against him. So he tried to arrange to continue working at the Hospital without also being on the University's faculty. After preliminary negotiations with the Hospital suggested this might be possible, respondent resigned his teaching post in July 2006 and sent a letter to Dr. Fitz (among others), in which he stated that the reason for his departure was harassment by Levine. That harassment, he asserted, "stems from ... religious, racial and cultural bias against Arabs and Muslims." After reading that letter, Dr. Fitz expressed consternation at respondent's accusations, saying that Levine had been "publicly humiliated by th[e] letter" and that it was "very important that she be publicly exonerated."

Meanwhile, the Hospital had offered respondent a job as a staff physician, as it had indicated it would. On learning of that offer, Dr. Fitz protested to the Hospital, asserting that the offer was inconsistent with the affiliation agreement's requirement that all staff physicians also be members of the University faculty. The Hospital then withdrew its offer.

After exhausting his administrative remedies, respondent filed this Title VII suit.... He alleged two discrete violations of Title VII. The first was a status-based discrimination claim under § 2000e-2(a). Respondent alleged that Dr. Levine's racially and religiously motivated harassment had resulted in his constructive discharge from the University. Respondent's second claim was that Dr. Fitz's efforts to prevent the Hospital from hiring him were in retaliation for complaining about Dr. Levine's harassment, in violation of § 2000e-3(a). The jury found for respondent on both claims. It awarded him over $400,000 in backpay and more than $3 million in compensatory damages. The District Court later reduced the compensatory damages award to $300,000.

[On appeal, the Court of Appeals for the Fifth Circuit vacated the constructive discharge portion of the jury's verdict and affirmed the retaliation finding.]

## II

### A

This case requires the Court to define the proper standard of causation for Title VII retaliation claims. Causation in fact—*i.e.*, proof that the defendant's conduct did in fact cause the plaintiff's injury—is a standard requirement of any tort claim, see Restatement of Torts § 9 (1934) (definition of "legal cause"); § 431, Comment *a* (same); § 279, and Comment *c* (intentional infliction of physical harm); § 280 (other intentional torts); § 281(c) (negligence). This includes federal statutory claims of workplace discrimination.

*Hazen Paper Co. v. Biggins,* 507 U.S. 604, 610 (1993) (In intentional-discrimination cases, "liability depends on whether the protected trait" "actually motivated the employer's decision" and "had a determinative influence on the outcome"); *Los Angeles Dept. of Water and Power v. Manhart,* 435 U.S. 702, 711 (1978)....

In the usual course, this standard requires the plaintiff to show "that the harm would not have occurred" in the absence of—that is, but for—the defendant's conduct. Restatement of Torts § 431, Comment *a* (negligence); § 432(1), and Comment *a* (same); see § 279, and Comment *c* (intentional infliction of bodily harm); § 280 (other intentional torts); Restatement (Third) of Torts: Liability for Physical and Emotional Harm § 27, and Comment *b* (2010) (noting the existence of an exception for cases where an injured party can prove the existence of multiple, independently sufficient factual causes, but observing that "cases invoking the concept are rare"). *See also* Restatement (Second) of Torts § 432(1) (1963 and 1964) (negligence claims); § 870, Comment *l* (intentional injury to another); cf. § 435a, and Comment *a* (legal cause for intentional harm). It is thus textbook tort law that an action "is not regarded as a cause of an event if the particular event would have occurred without it." W. Keeton, D. Dobbs, R. Keeton, & D. Owen, Prosser and Keeton on Law of Torts 265 (5th ed. 1984). This, then, is the background against which Congress legislated in enacting Title VII, and these are the default rules it is presumed to have incorporated, absent an indication to the contrary in the statute itself. [citations omitted.]

B

Since the statute's passage in 1964, it has prohibited employers from discriminating against their employees on any of seven specified criteria. Five of them—race, color, religion, sex, and national origin—are personal characteristics and are set forth in § 2000e-2. (As noted at the outset, discrimination based on these five characteristics is called status-based discrimination in this opinion.) And then there is a point of great import for this case: The two remaining categories of wrongful employer conduct—the employee's opposition to employment discrimination, and the employee's submission of or support for a complaint that alleges employment discrimination—are not wrongs based on personal traits but rather types of protected employee conduct. These latter two categories are covered by a separate, subsequent section of Title VII, § 2000e-3(a).

Under the status-based discrimination provision, it is an "unlawful employment practice" for an employer "to discriminate against any individual ... because of such individual's race, color, religion, sex, or national origin." § 2000e-2(a). [In the Court's 1989 *Price Waterhouse* decision, six justices agreed that a plaintiff could prevail on a claim of status-based discrimination by showing that one of the prohibited traits was a "motivating" or "substantial" factor in the employer's decision, even though other motives were also present.] If the plaintiff made that showing, the burden of persuasion would shift to the employer, which could escape liability if it could prove that it would have taken the same employment action in the absence of all discriminatory animus.... In other words, the employer had to show that a discriminatory motive was not the but-for cause of the adverse employment action.

Two years later, Congress passed the Civil Rights Act of 1991 (1991 Act), 105 Stat. 1071. This statute (which had many other provisions) codified the burden-shifting and lessened-causation framework of *Price Waterhouse* in part but also rejected it to a substantial degree. The legislation first added a new subsection to the end of § 2000e-2, *i.e.,* Title VII's principal ban on status-based discrimination. The new provision, § 2000e-2(m), states:

[A]n unlawful employment practice is established when the complaining party demonstrates that race, color, religion, sex, or national origin was a motivating factor for any employment practice, even though other factors also motivated the practice.

This, of course, is a lessened causation standard.

The 1991 Act also abrogated a portion of *Price Waterhouse*'s framework by removing the employer's ability to defeat liability once a plaintiff proved the existence of an impermissible motivating factor....

So, in short, the 1991 Act substituted a new burden-shifting framework for the one endorsed by *Price Waterhouse*. Under that new regime, a plaintiff could obtain declaratory relief, attorney's fees and costs, and some forms of injunctive relief based solely on proof that race, color, religion, sex, or nationality was a motivating factor in the employment action; but the employer's proof that it would still have taken the same employment action would save it from monetary damages and a reinstatement order.

[The Court describes its holding in *Gross* that plaintiffs must establish "but for" cause to prevail on an ADEA disparate treatment claim.]

In *Gross*, the Court was careful to restrict its analysis to the statute before it and withhold judgment on the proper resolution of a case, such as this, which arose under Title VII rather than the ADEA. But the particular confines of *Gross* do not deprive it of all persuasive force. Indeed, that opinion holds two insights for the present case. The first is textual and concerns the proper interpretation of the term "because" as it relates to the principles of causation underlying both §623(a) and §2000e-3(a). The second is the significance of Congress' structural choices in both Title VII itself and the law's 1991 amendments. These principles do not decide the present case but do inform its analysis, for the issues possess significant parallels.

### III
### A

As noted, Title VII's antiretaliation provision ... appears in a different section from Title VII's ban on status-based discrimination. The antiretaliation provision states, in relevant part:

It shall be an unlawful employment practice for an employer to discriminate against any of his employees ... because he has opposed any practice made an unlawful employment practice by this subchapter, or because he has made a charge, testified, assisted, or participated in any manner in an investigation, proceeding, or hearing under this subchapter.

This enactment, like the statute at issue in *Gross*, makes it unlawful for an employer to take adverse employment action against an employee "because" of certain criteria. Given the lack of any meaningful textual difference between the text in this statute and the one in *Gross*, the proper conclusion here, as in *Gross*, is that Title VII retaliation claims require proof that the desire to retaliate was the but-for cause of the challenged employment action.

...

[In contrast,] the text of the motivating-factor provision, while it begins by referring to "unlawful employment practices," then proceeds to address only five of the seven prohibited discriminatory actions—actions based on the employee's status, *i.e.*, race, color, religion, sex, and national origin. This indicates Congress' intent to confine that provision's coverage to only those types of employment practices. The text of §2000e-

2(m) says nothing about retaliation claims. Given this clear language, it would be improper to conclude that what Congress omitted from the statute is nevertheless within its scope....

What is more, a different portion of the 1991 Act contains an express reference to all unlawful employment actions, thereby reinforcing the conclusion that Congress acted deliberately when it omitted retaliation claims from § 2000e-2(m). The relevant portion of the 1991 Act, § 109(b), allowed certain overseas operations by U.S. employers to engage in "any practice prohibited by section 703 or 704," *i.e.*, § 2000e-2 or § 2000e-3, "if compliance with such section would cause such employer ... to violate the law of the foreign country in which such workplace is located."

If Congress had desired to make the motivating-factor standard applicable to all Title VII claims, it could have used language similar to that which it invoked in § 109....

[The Court describes a series of decisions in which it had held that the concept of discrimination included the idea of retaliation.]

These decisions are not controlling here. It is true these cases do state the general proposition that Congress' enactment of a broadly phrased antidiscrimination statute may signal a concomitant intent to ban retaliation against individuals who oppose that discrimination, even where the statute does not refer to retaliation in so many words. What those cases do not support, however, is the quite different rule that every reference to race, color, creed, sex, or nationality in an antidiscrimination statute is to be treated as a synonym for "retaliation." For one thing, § 2000e-2(m) is not itself a substantive bar on discrimination. Rather, it is a rule that establishes the causation standard for proving a violation defined elsewhere in Title VII....

B

The proper interpretation and implementation of § 2000e-3(a) and its causation standard have central importance to the fair and responsible allocation of resources in the judicial and litigation systems. This is of particular significance because claims of retaliation are being made with ever-increasing frequency. The number of these claims filed with the Equal Employment Opportunity Commission (EEOC) has nearly doubled in the past 15 years—from just over 16,000 in 1997 to over 31,000 in 2012. Indeed, the number of retaliation claims filed with the EEOC has now outstripped those for every type of status-based discrimination except race.

In addition lessening the causation standard could also contribute to the filing of frivolous claims, which would siphon resources from efforts by employers, administrative agencies, and courts to combat workplace harassment. Consider in this regard the case of an employee who knows that he or she is about to be fired for poor performance, given a lower pay grade, or even just transferred to a different assignment or location. To forestall that lawful action, he or she might be tempted to make an unfounded charge of racial, sexual, or religious discrimination; then, when the unrelated employment action comes, the employee could allege that it is retaliation. If respondent were to prevail in his argument here, that claim could be established by a lessened causation standard, all in order to prevent the undesired change in employment circumstances. Even if the employer could escape judgment after trial, the lessened causation standard would make it far more difficult to dismiss dubious claims at the summary judgment stage. It would be inconsistent with the structure and operation of Title VII to so raise the costs, both financial and reputational, on an employer whose actions were not in fact the result of any discriminatory or retaliatory intent. Yet there would be a significant risk of that consequence if respondent's position were adopted here.

If it were proper to apply the motivating-factor standard to respondent's retaliation claim, the University might well be subject to liability on account of Dr. Fitz's alleged desire to exonerate Dr. Levine, even if it could also be shown that the terms of the affiliation agreement precluded the Hospital's hiring of respondent and that the University would have sought to prevent respondent's hiring in order to honor that agreement in any event. That result would be inconsistent with both the text and purpose of Title VII.

In sum, Title VII defines the term "unlawful employment practice" as discrimination on the basis of any of seven prohibited criteria: race, color, religion, sex, national origin, opposition to employment discrimination, and submitting or supporting a complaint about employment discrimination. The text of §2000e-2(m) mentions just the first five of these factors, the status-based ones; and it omits the final two, which deal with retaliation. When it added §2000e-2(m) to Title VII in 1991, Congress inserted it within the section of the statute that deals only with those same five criteria, not the section that deals with retaliation claims or one of the sections that apply to all claims of unlawful employment practices. And while the Court has inferred a congressional intent to prohibit retaliation when confronted with broadly worded antidiscrimination statutes, Title VII's detailed structure makes that inference inappropriate here. Based on these textual and structural indications, the Court now concludes as follows: Title VII retaliation claims must be proved according to traditional principles of but-for causation, not the lessened causation test stated in §2000e-2(m). This requires proof that the unlawful retaliation would not have occurred in the absence of the alleged wrongful action or actions of the employer.

[In Section IV of the opinion, the Court declined to defer to EEOC guidance.]

### V

The text, structure, and history of Title VII demonstrate that a plaintiff making a retaliation claim under §2000e-3(a) must establish that his or her protected activity was a but-for cause of the alleged adverse action by the employer. The University claims that a fair application of this standard, which is more demanding than the motivating-factor standard adopted by the Court of Appeals, entitles it to judgment as a matter of law. It asks the Court to so hold. That question, however, is better suited to resolution by courts closer to the facts of this case. The judgment of the Court of Appeals for the Fifth Circuit is vacated, and the case is remanded for further proceedings consistent with this opinion.

*It is so ordered.*

Justice Ginsburg, with whom Justice Breyer, Justice Sotomayor, and Justice Kagan join, dissenting.

...

### II

This Court has long acknowledged the symbiotic relationship between proscriptions on discrimination and proscriptions on retaliation. Antidiscrimination provisions, the Court has reasoned, endeavor to create a workplace where individuals are not treated differently on account of race, ethnicity, religion, or sex.... As the Court has comprehended, "Title VII depends for its enforcement upon the cooperation of employees who are willing to file complaints and act as witnesses." ...

Adverting to the close connection between discrimination and retaliation for complaining about discrimination, this Court has held, in a line of decisions unbroken until today, that a ban on discrimination encompasses retaliation....

III

A

The Title VII provision key here, § 2000e-2(m), states that "an unlawful employment practice is established when the complaining party demonstrates that race, color, religion, sex, or national origin was a motivating factor for any employment practice, even though other factors also motivated the practice." Section 2000e-2(m) was enacted as part of the Civil Rights Act of 1991, which amended Title VII, along with other federal antidiscrimination statutes. The amendments were intended to provide "additional protections against unlawful discrimination in employment," and to "respon[d] to a number of ... decisions by [this Court] that sharply cut back on the scope and effectiveness" of antidiscrimination laws, H.R.Rep. No. 102-40, pt. II, pp. 2–4 (1991) (hereinafter House Report Part II).

Among the decisions found inadequately protective was *Price Waterhouse v. Hopkins,* 490 U.S. 228 (1989).... Congress endorsed the plurality's conclusion that, to be actionable under Title VII, discrimination must be a motivating factor in, but need not be the but-for cause of, an adverse employment action. Congress disagreed with the Court, however, insofar as the *Price Waterhouse* decision allowed an employer to escape liability by showing that the same action would have been taken regardless of improper motive. House Report Part II, at 18. "If Title VII's ban on discrimination in employment is to be meaningful," the House Report explained, "victims of intentional discrimination must be able to obtain relief, and perpetrators of discrimination must be held liable for their actions."

Superseding *Price Waterhouse* in part, Congress sought to "restore" the rule of decision followed by several Circuits that any discrimination "actually shown to play a role in a contested employment decision may be the subject of liability." House Report Part II, at 18.... Critically, the rule Congress intended to "restore" was not limited to substantive discrimination. As the House Report explained, "the Committee endors[ed] ... the decisional law" in *Bibbs v. Block,* 778 F.2d 1318 (C.A.8 1985) (en banc), which held that a violation of Title VII is established when the trier of fact determines that "an unlawful motive played some part in the employment decision or decisional process." *Id.,* at 1323; *see* House Report Part I, at 48. Prior to the 1991 Civil Rights Act, *Bibbs* had been applied to retaliation claims. *See, e.g., Johnson v. Legal Servs. of Arkansas, Inc.,* 813 F.2d 893, 900 (C.A.8 1987) ("Should the court find that retaliation played some invidious part in the [plaintiff's] termination, a violation of Title VII will be established under *Bibbs*."). *See also EEOC v. General Lines, Inc.,* 865 F.2d 1555, 1560 (C.A.10 1989).

B

There is scant reason to think that, despite Congress' aim to "restore and strengthen ... laws that ban discrimination in employment," House Report Part II, at 2, Congress meant to exclude retaliation claims from the newly enacted "motivating factor" provision. Section 2000e-2(m) provides that an "unlawful employment practice is established" when the plaintiff shows that a protected characteristic was a factor driving "any employment practice." Title VII, in § 2000e-3(a), explicitly denominates retaliation, like status-based discrimination, an "unlawful employment practice." Because "any employment practice" necessarily encompasses practices prohibited under § 2000e-3(a), § 2000e-2(m), by its plain terms, covers retaliation.

Notably, when it enacted § 2000e-2(m), Congress did not tie the new provision specifically to §§ 2000e-2(a)–(d), which proscribe discrimination "because of" race, color, religion, gender, or national origin. Rather, Congress added an entirely new provision to codify the causation standard, one encompassing "any employment practice." § 2000e-2(m)....

## C

[The EEOC, whose position merits respect, has construed § 2000e-2(m) to apply to retaliation cases.]

## IV

The Court draws the opposite conclusion, ruling that retaliation falls outside the scope of § 2000e-2(m). In so holding, the Court ascribes to Congress the unlikely purpose of separating retaliation claims from discrimination claims, thereby undermining the Legislature's effort to fortify the protections of Title VII. None of the reasons the Court offers in support of its restrictive interpretation of § 2000e-2(m) survives inspection.

## A

The Court first asserts that reading § 2000e-2(m) to encompass claims for retaliation "is inconsistent with the provision's plain language." The Court thus sees retaliation as a protected activity entirely discrete from status-based discrimination.

This vision of retaliation as a separate concept runs up against precedent. Until today, the Court has been clear eyed on just what retaliation is: a manifestation of status-based discrimination. As *Jackson* explained in the context of sex discrimination, "retaliation is discrimination 'on the basis of sex' because it is an intentional response to the nature of the complaint: an allegation of sex discrimination." 544 U.S., at 174.

...

## V
## A

Having narrowed § 2000e-2(m) to exclude retaliation claims, the Court turns to *Gross v. FBL Financial Services, Inc.*, 557 U.S. 167 (2009), to answer the question presented: Whether a plaintiff must demonstrate but-for causation to establish liability under § 2000e-3(a).... Yet *Gross,* which took pains to distinguish ADEA claims from Title VII claims, is invoked by the Court today as pathmarking.

The word "because" in Title VII's retaliation provision, § 2000e-3(a), the Court tells us, should be interpreted not to accord with the interpretation of that same word in the companion status-based discrimination provision of Title VII, § 2000e-2(a). Instead, statutory lines should be crossed: The meaning of "because" in Title VII's retaliation provision should be read to mean just what the Court held "because" means for ADEA-liability purposes. *But see Gross,* 557 U.S., at 174, ("When conducting statutory interpretation, we 'must be careful not to apply rules applicable under one statute to a different statute without careful and critical examination.'" (quoting *Holowecki,* 552 U.S., at 393)). In other words, the employer prevailed in *Gross* because, according to the Court, the ADEA's antidiscrimination prescription is not like Title VII's. But the employer prevails again in Nassar's case, for there is no "meaningful textual difference," between the ADEA's use of "because" and the use of the same word in Title VII's retaliation provision. What sense can one make of this other than "heads the employer wins, tails the employee loses"?

It is a standard principle of statutory interpretation that identical phrases appearing in the same statute—here, Title VII—ordinarily bear a consistent meaning. Following that principle, Title VII's retaliation provision, like its status-based discrimination provision, would permit mixed-motive claims, and the same causation standard would apply to both provisions.

## B

The Court's decision to construe § 2000e-3(a) to require but-for causation in line with *Gross* is even more confounding in light of *Price Waterhouse*. Recall that *Price Waterhouse* interpreted "because of" in § 2000e-2(a) to permit mixed-motive claims. The Court today rejects the proposition that, if § 2000e-2(m) does not cover retaliation, such claims are governed by *Price Waterhouse*'s burden-shifting framework, *i.e.*, if the plaintiff shows that discrimination was *a* motivating factor in an adverse employment action, the defendant may escape liability only by showing it would have taken the same action had there been no illegitimate motive. It is wrong to revert to *Price Waterhouse*, the Court says, because the 1991 Civil Rights Act's amendments to Title VII abrogated that decision.

This conclusion defies logic. Before the 1991 amendments, several courts had applied *Price Waterhouse*'s burden-shifting framework to retaliation claims. In the Court's view, Congress designed § 2000e-2(m)'s motivating-factor standard not only to exclude retaliation claims, but also to override, *sub silentio*, Circuit precedent applying the *Price Waterhouse* framework to such claims. And with what did the 1991 Congress replace the *Price Waterhouse* burden-shifting framework? With a but-for causation requirement *Gross* applied to the ADEA 17 years after the 1991 amendments to Title VII. Shut from the Court's sight is a legislative record replete with statements evincing Congress' intent to strengthen antidiscrimination laws and thereby hold employers accountable for prohibited discrimination. It is an odd mode of statutory interpretation that divines Congress' aim in 1991 by looking to a decision of this Court, *Gross*, made under a different statute in 2008, while ignoring the overarching purpose of the Congress that enacted the 1991 Civil Rights Act.

## C

… Asking jurors to determine liability based on different standards in a single case is virtually certain to sow confusion. That would be tolerable if the governing statute required double standards, but here, for the reasons already stated, it does not.

## VI
## A

The Court's assertion that the but-for cause requirement it adopts necessarily follows from § 2000e-3(a)'s use of the word "because" fails to convince. Contrary to the Court's suggestion, the word "because" does not inevitably demand but-for causation to the exclusion of all other causation formulations. When more than one factor contributes to a plaintiff's injury, but-for causation is problematic. *See, e.g.,* 1 Restatement (Third) of Torts § 27, Comment *a*, p. 385 (2005) (noting near universal agreement that the but-for standard is inappropriate when multiple sufficient causes exist) (hereinafter Restatement Third); Restatement of Torts § 9, Comment *b*, p. 18 (1934) (legal cause is a cause that is a "substantial factor in bringing about the harm").

When an event is "overdetermined," *i.e.*, when two forces create an injury each alone would be sufficient to cause, modern tort law permits the plaintiff to prevail upon showing that either sufficient condition created the harm. In contrast, under the Court's approach (which it erroneously calls "textbook tort law,") a Title VII plaintiff alleging retaliation *cannot* establish liability if her firing was prompted by both legitimate and illegitimate factors.

Today's opinion rehashes arguments rightly rejected in *Price Waterhouse*. Concurring in the judgment in that case, Justice O'Connor recognized the disconnect between the standard the dissent advocated, which would have imposed on the plaintiff the burden of showing but-for causation, and the common-law doctrines on which the dissent relied. As Justice O'Connor explained:

> [I]n the area of tort liability, from whence the dissent's "but-for" standard of causation is derived, ... the law has long recognized that in certain "civil cases" leaving the burden of persuasion on the plaintiff to prove "but-for" causation would be both unfair and destructive of the deterrent purposes embodied in the concept of duty of care. Thus, in multiple causation cases, where a breach of duty has been established, the common law of torts has long shifted the burden of proof to ... defendants to prove that their negligent actions were not the "but-for" cause of the plaintiff's injury.

Justice Brennan's plurality opinion was even less solicitous of the dissent's approach. Noting that, under the standard embraced by the dissent in *Price Waterhouse*, neither of two sufficient forces would constitute cause even if either one alone would have led to the injury, the plurality remarked: "We need not leave our common sense at the doorstep when we interpret a statute." 490 U.S., at 241.

### B

As the plurality and concurring opinions in *Price Waterhouse* indicate, a strict but-for test is particularly ill suited to employment discrimination cases. Even if the test is appropriate in some tort contexts, "it is an entirely different matter to determine a 'but-for' relation when ... consider[ing], not physical forces, but the mind-related characteristics that constitute motive." *Gross*, 557 U.S., at 190 (Breyer, J., dissenting). When assessing an employer's multiple motives, "to apply 'but-for' causation is to engage in a hypothetical inquiry about what would have happened if the employer's thoughts and other circumstances had been different." *Id.*, at 191.

This point, lost on the Court, was not lost on Congress. When Title VII was enacted, Congress considered and rejected an amendment that would have placed the word "solely" before "because of [the complainant's] race, color, religion, sex, or national origin." *See* 110 Cong. Rec. 2728, 13837–13838 (1964). Senator Case, a prime sponsor of Title VII, commented that a "sole cause" standard would render the Act "totally nugatory." *Id.*, at 13837. Life does not shape up that way, the Senator suggested, commenting "[i]f anyone ever had an action that was motivated by a single cause, he is a different kind of animal from any I know of." *Ibid.*

... Today's misguided judgment, along with the judgment in *Vance v. Ball State Univ.* should prompt yet another Civil Rights Restoration Act.

---

## Notes

1. Justice Kennedy explains the negative repercussions that would ensue if the standard by which Dr. Nassar were required to prove causation were the "motivating-factor"

standard. One of those negatives, he writes, is that the employer could be held liable even if, in fact, it would have sought to prevent the hospital's hiring of Dr. Nassar in order to honor the agreement in the absence of retaliatory motive. Justice Kennedy describes this result as "inconsistent with both the text and purpose of Title VII." Do you agree?

2. In your own world view, which is more morally culpable, status discrimination or retaliation? Does your view on comparative moral culpability color your view on what should be the relative ease or difficulty of proving either type of wrong?

## ➤ Beyond the Basics: Third-Party Retaliation

Sometimes more than one employee is involved in a retaliation scenario. If one employee engages in protected conduct, and the employer retaliates against a *second* employee who is in a close relationship with the first, does the second employee have a retaliation claim? Before the Supreme Court's decision in *Thompson v. North American Stainless, LP*, four federal circuits concluded the second employee is not protected from retaliation. *See generally* Alex B. Long, *The Troublemaker's Friend: Retaliation against Third Parties and the Right of Association in the Workplace*, 59 FLA. L. REV. 931 (2007). In *Thompson*, the Supreme Court concluded that the employee who does not engage in protected activity but is closely related to that employee and subjected to reprisal for the protected activity may have a right to sue under Title VII. Note that the Supreme Court grapples with two issues in *Thompson*: whether NAS's firing of Thompson violated Title VII, and whether Thompson fell within the "zone of interest" necessary to give him the right to sue for any such violation.

---

### Focus Questions: *Thompson v. North American Stainless, LP.*

1. *Who filed the first complaint, and do we know why?*

2. *Why does the Court think that Regalado should be upset if Thompson is fired? If Thompson and Regalado had terminated their relationship prior to the charge, do you think the Court would have reached the same conclusion?*

---

# Thompson v. North American Stainless, LP.

### 131 S.Ct. 863 (2011)

Justice Scalia delivered the opinion of the Court

Until 2003, both petitioner Eric Thompson and his fiancée, Miriam Regalado, were employees of respondent North American Stainless (NAS). In February 2003, the Equal Employment Opportunity Commission (EEOC) notified NAS that Regalado had filed a charge alleging sex discrimination. Three weeks later, NAS fired Thompson.

Thompson then filed a charge with the EEOC [and ultimately sued in federal district court], claiming that NAS had fired him in order to retaliate against Regalado for filing her charge with the EEOC. The [trial and appellate courts] concluded that Title VII "does not permit third party retaliation claims." The [appellate] court reasoned that because

Thompson did not "engag[e] in any statutorily protected activity, either on his own behalf or on behalf of Miriam Regalado," he "is not included in the class of persons for whom Congress created a retaliation cause of action."

[The Supreme Court reversed.]

## I

Title VII provides that "[i]t shall be an unlawful employment practice for an employer to discriminate against any of his employees ... because he has made a charge" under Title VII. [citations omitted throughout]. The statute permits "a person claiming to be aggrieved" to file a charge with the EEOC alleging that the employer committed an unlawful employment practice, and, if the EEOC declines to sue the employer, it permits a civil action to "be brought ... by the person claiming to be aggrieved ... by the alleged unlawful employment practice." It is undisputed that Regalado's filing of a charge with the EEOC was protected conduct under Title VII. In the procedural posture of this case [appeal from grant of summary judgment for the defendant], we are also required to assume that NAS fired Thompson in order to retaliate against Regalado for filing a charge of discrimination. This case therefore presents two questions: First, did NAS's firing of Thompson constitute unlawful retaliation? And second, if it did, does Title VII grant Thompson a cause of action?

## II

With regard to the first question, we have little difficulty concluding that if the facts alleged by Thompson are true, then NAS's firing of Thompson violated Title VII. In *Burlington N. & S.F.R. Co. v. White*, we held that Title VII's antiretaliation provision ... "unlike the substantive provision, is not limited to discriminatory actions that affect the terms and conditions of employment." Rather, Title VII's antiretaliation provision prohibits any employer action that "well might have dissuaded a reasonable worker from making or supporting a charge of discrimination."

We think it obvious that a reasonable worker might be dissuaded from engaging in protected activity if she knew that her fiance would be fired. Indeed, NAS does not dispute that Thompson's firing meets the standard set forth in *Burlington*. NAS raises the concern, however, that prohibiting reprisals against third parties will lead to difficult line-drawing problems concerning the types of relationships entitled to protection. Perhaps retaliating against an employee by firing his fiancée would dissuade the employee from engaging in protected activity, but what about firing an employee's girlfriend, close friend, or trusted co-worker? Applying the *Burlington* standard to third-party reprisals, NAS argues, will place the employer at risk any time it fires any employee who happens to have a connection to a different employee who filed a charge with the EEOC.

Although we acknowledge the force of this point, we do not think it justifies a categorical rule that third-party reprisals do not violate Title VII. As explained above, we adopted a broad standard in *Burlington* because Title VII's antiretaliation provision is worded broadly. We think there is no textual basis for making an exception to it for third-party reprisals, and a preference for clear rules cannot justify departing from statutory text.

We must also decline to identify a fixed class of relationships for which third-party reprisals are unlawful. We expect that firing a close family member will almost always meet the *Burlington* standard, and inflicting a milder reprisal on a mere acquaintance will almost never do so, but beyond that we are reluctant to generalize. As we explained in

*Burlington,* "the significance of any given act of retaliation will often depend upon the particular circumstances." Given the broad statutory text and the variety of workplace contexts in which retaliation may occur, Title VII's antiretaliation provision is simply not reducible to a comprehensive set of clear rules. We emphasize, however, that "the provision's standard for judging harm must be objective," so as to "avoi[d] the uncertainties and unfair discrepancies that can plague a judicial effort to determine a plaintiff's unusual subjective feelings."

III

The more difficult question in this case is whether Thompson may sue NAS for its alleged violation of Title VII. The statute provides that "a civil action may be brought ... by the person claiming to be aggrieved."

We have suggested in dictum that the Title VII aggrievement requirement conferred a right to sue on all who satisfied Article III standing. *Trafficante v. Metropolitan Life Ins. Co.* involved the "person aggrieved" provision of Title VIII (the Fair Housing Act) rather than Title VII. In deciding the case, however, we relied upon, and cited with approval, a Third Circuit opinion involving Title VII, which, we said, "concluded that the words used showed 'a congressional intention to define standing as broadly as is permitted by Article III of the Constitution.'"

We now find that this dictum was ill-considered, and we decline to follow it. If any person injured in the Article III sense by a Title VII violation could sue, absurd consequences would follow. For example, a shareholder would be able to sue a company for firing a valuable employee for racially discriminatory reasons, so long as he could show that the value of his stock decreased as a consequence. At oral argument Thompson acknowledged that such a suit would not lie. We agree, and therefore conclude that the term "aggrieved" must be construed more narrowly than the outer boundaries of Article III.

At the other extreme from the position that "person aggrieved" means anyone with Article III standing, NAS argues that it is a term of art that refers only to the employee who engaged in the protected activity. We know of no other context in which the words carry this artificially narrow meaning, and if that is what Congress intended it would more naturally have said "person claiming to have been discriminated against" rather than "person claiming to be aggrieved." We see no basis in text or prior practice for limiting the latter phrase to the person who was the subject of unlawful retaliation [i.e., the employee whose protected action resulted in the reprisal, here Regalado].

In our view there is a common usage of the term "person aggrieved" that avoids the extremity of equating it with Article III and yet is fully consistent with our application of the term in *Trafficante.* The Administrative Procedure Act, authorizes suit to challenge a federal agency by any "person ... adversely affected or aggrieved ... within the meaning of a relevant statute." We have held that this language establishes a regime under which a plaintiff may not sue unless he "falls within the 'zone of interests' sought to be protected by the statutory provision whose violation forms the legal basis for his complaint." We have described the "zone of interests" test as denying a right of review "if the plaintiff's interests are so marginally related to or inconsistent with the purposes implicit in the statute that it cannot reasonably be assumed that Congress intended to permit the suit." We hold that the term "aggrieved" in Title VII incorporates this test, enabling suit by any plaintiff with an interest "arguably [sought] to be protected by the statutes," while excluding plaintiffs who might technically be injured in an Article III sense but whose interests are unrelated to the statutory prohibitions in Title VII.

Applying that test here, we conclude that Thompson falls within the zone of interests protected by Title VII. Thompson was an employee of NAS, and the purpose of Title VII is to protect employees from their employers' unlawful actions. Moreover, accepting the facts as alleged, Thompson is not an accidental victim of the retaliation—collateral damage, so to speak, of the employer's unlawful act. To the contrary, injuring him was the employer's intended means of harming Regalado. Hurting him was the unlawful act by which the employer punished her. In those circumstances, we think Thompson well within the zone of interests sought to be protected by Title VII. He is a person aggrieved with standing to sue.

Justice Ginsburg, concurring.

I join the Court's opinion, and add a fortifying observation: Today's decision accords with the longstanding views of the Equal Employment Opportunity Commission (EEOC), the federal agency that administers Title VII. In its Compliance Manual, the EEOC counsels that Title VII "prohibit[s] retaliation against someone so closely related to or associated with the person exercising his or her statutory rights that it would discourage or prevent the person from pursuing those rights." Such retaliation "can be challenged," the Manual affirms, "by both the individual who engaged in protected activity and the relative, where both are employees." The EEOC's statements in the Manual merit deference under *Skidmore v. Swift & Co.*

---

## Notes

1. Why does the Court decline to identify a fixed class of relationships for which third-party reprisals are unlawful, rather than establishing a bright line rule? How are lower courts to determine whether a particular third-party reprisal is unlawful?

2. Once the Court concludes that Thompson's Title VII rights have been violated, the Court goes on to decide that Thompson has standing to sue for that violation. Construing the Title VII language allowing suit by an "aggrieved" employee, the Court considers two extremes for Title VII retaliation standing: (1) that everyone with Article III standing may sue for violation of Title VII, and, at the opposite extreme, (2) that only the individual whose protected acts motivated the retaliation may sue for a violation. Rejecting these two extremes, the Court steers a middle course. It borrows from the Administrative Procedure Act, adopting a "zone of interest" test, which permits suit by plaintiffs with interests "arguably [sought] to be protected by the statutes," but not those who, though technically injured for purposes of Article III standing, possess interests not closely enough related to the statute's purpose.

3. How exactly are lower courts to determine whether a given plaintiff falls within the "zone of interest"?

---

## ▶ Beyond the Basics: Retaliation Protection under Section 1981

### Focus Question: *CBOCS West, Inc. v. Humphries*

*Based on the Court's discussion of* Sullivan, *would you say that policy considerations require permitting retaliation claims by any third-party who is punished for defending another's right to be free of discrimination?*

# CBOCS West, Inc. v. Humphries

## 553 U.S. 442 (2008)

Justice Breyer delivered the opinion of the Court.

A longstanding civil rights law, first enacted just after the Civil War, provides that "[a]ll persons within the jurisdiction of the United States shall have the same right in every State and Territory to make and enforce contracts ... as is enjoyed by white citizens." 42 U.S.C. § 1981(a). The basic question before us is whether the provision encompasses a complaint of retaliation against a person who has complained about a violation of another person's contract-related "right." We conclude that it does.

### I

The case before us arises out of a claim by respondent, Hedrick G. Humphries, a former assistant manager of a Cracker Barrel restaurant, that CBOCS West, Inc. (Cracker Barrel's owner) dismissed him (1) because of racial bias (Humphries is a black man) and (2) because he had complained to managers that a fellow assistant manager had dismissed another black employee, Venus Green, for race-based reasons. Humphries timely filed a charge with the Equal Employment Opportunity Commission (EEOC), pursuant to 42 U.S.C. § 2000e-5, and received a "right to sue" letter. He then filed a complaint in Federal District Court charging that CBOCS' actions violated both Title VII and the older "equal contract rights" provision here at issue, § 1981. The District Court dismissed Humphries' Title VII claims for failure to pay necessary filing fees on a timely basis. It then granted CBOCS' motion for summary judgment on Humphries' two § 1981 claims. Humphries appealed.

The U.S. Court of Appeals for the Seventh Circuit ruled against Humphries and upheld the District Court's grant of summary judgment in respect to his direct discrimination claim. But it ruled in Humphries' favor and remanded for a trial in respect to his § 1981 retaliation claim. In doing so, the Court of Appeals rejected CBOCS' argument that § 1981 did not encompass a claim of retaliation. CBOCS sought certiorari, asking us to consider this last-mentioned legal question. And we agreed to do so.

### II

The question before us is whether § 1981 encompasses retaliation claims. We conclude that it does. And because our conclusion rests in significant part upon principles of *stare decisis*, we begin by examining the pertinent interpretive history.

### A

The Court first considered a comparable question in 1969, in *Sullivan v. Little Hunting Park, Inc.* The case arose under 42 U.S.C. § 1982, a statutory provision that Congress enacted just after the Civil War, along with § 1981, to protect the rights of black citizens. The provision was similar to § 1981 except that it focused, not upon rights to make and to enforce contracts, but rights related to the ownership of property. The statute provides that "[a]ll citizens of the United States shall have the same right, in every State and Territory, as is enjoyed by white citizens thereof to inherit, purchase, lease, sell, hold, and convey real and personal property." § 1982.

Paul E. Sullivan, a white man, had rented his house to T.R. Freeman, Jr., a black man. He had also assigned Freeman a membership share in a corporation, which permitted the owner to use a private park that the corporation controlled. Because of Freeman's race, the corporation, Little Hunting Park, Inc., refused to approve the share assignment. And, when Sullivan protested, the association expelled Sullivan and took away his membership shares.

Sullivan sued Little Hunting Park, claiming that its actions violated § 1982. The Court upheld Sullivan's claim. It found that the corporation's refusal "to approve the assignment of the membership share ... was clearly an interference with Freeman's [the black lessee's] right to 'lease.'" It added that Sullivan, the white lessor, "has standing to maintain this action," because, as the Court had previously said, "the white owner is at times 'the only effective adversary' of the unlawful restrictive covenant." The Court noted that to permit the corporation to punish Sullivan "for trying to vindicate the rights of minorities protected by § 1982" would give "impetus to the perpetuation of racial restrictions on property." And this Court has made clear that *Sullivan* stands for the proposition that § 1982 encompasses retaliation claims. [citations omitted].

While the *Sullivan* decision interpreted § 1982, our precedents have long construed §§ 1981 and 1982 similarly. In *Runyon v. McCrary*, 427 U.S. 160, 173 (1976), the Court considered whether § 1981 prohibits private acts of discrimination. Citing *Sullivan*, along with *Jones v. Alfred H. Mayer Co.*, and *Tillman v. Wheaton-Haven Recreation Assn., Inc.*, the Court reasoned that this case law "necessarily requires the conclusion that § 1981, like § 1982, reaches private conduct." [citations omitted].

As indicated in *Runyon*, the Court has construed §§ 1981 and 1982 alike because it has recognized the sister statutes' common language, origin, and purposes. Like § 1981, § 1982 traces its origin to § 1 of the Civil Rights Act of 1866. Like § 1981, § 1982 represents an immediately post-Civil War legislative effort to guarantee the then newly freed slaves the same legal rights that other citizens enjoy. Like § 1981, § 1982 uses broad language that says "[a]ll citizens of the United States shall have the same right, in every State and Territory, as is enjoyed by white citizens...." Indeed, § 1982 differs from § 1981 only in that it refers, not to the "right ... to make and enforce contracts," but to the "right ... to inherit, purchase, lease, sell, hold, and convey real and personal property."

In light of these precedents, it is not surprising that following *Sullivan*, federal appeals courts concluded, on the basis of *Sullivan* or its reasoning, that § 1981 encompassed retaliation claims.

B

In 1989, 20 years after *Sullivan*, this Court in *Patterson v. McLean Credit Union*, significantly limited the scope of § 1981. The Court focused upon § 1981's words "to make and enforce contracts" and interpreted the phrase narrowly. It wrote that the statutory phrase did not apply to "conduct by the employer *after the contract relation has been established*, including breach of the terms of the contract or imposition of discriminatory working conditions." The Court added that the word "enforce" does not apply to post-contract-formation conduct unless the discrimination at issue "*infects the legal process* in ways that prevent one from enforcing contract rights." Thus § 1981 did not encompass the claim of a black employee who charged that her employer had violated her employment contract by harassing her and failing to promote her, all because of her race.

Since victims of an employer's retaliation will often have opposed discriminatory conduct taking place *after* the formation of the employment contract, *Patterson*'s holding, for a brief time, seems in practice to have foreclosed retaliation claims. With one exception, we have found no federal court of appeals decision between the time we decided *Patterson* and 1991 that permitted a § 1981 retaliation claim to proceed.

In 1991, however, Congress weighed in on the matter. Congress passed the Civil Rights Act of 1991, § 101 with the design to supersede *Patterson*. Insofar as is relevant here, the new law changed 42 U.S.C. § 1981 by reenacting the former provision, designating it as § 1981(a), and adding a new subsection, (b), which, says:

> "Make and enforce contracts" defined
>
> For purposes of this section, the term "make and enforce contracts" includes the making, performance, modification, and termination of contracts, and the enjoyment of all benefits, privileges, terms, and conditions of the contractual relationship.

An accompanying Senate Report pointed out that the amendment superseded *Patterson* by adding a new subsection (b) that would "reaffirm that the right 'to make and enforce contracts' includes the enjoyment of all benefits, privileges, terms and conditions of the contractual relationship." Among other things, it would "ensure that Americans may not be harassed, *fired* or otherwise discriminated against in contracts because of their race." An accompanying House Report said that in "cutting back the scope of the rights to 'make' and 'enforce' contracts[,] *Patterson* ... has been interpreted to eliminate retaliation claims that the courts had previously recognized under section 1981." It added that the protections that subsection (b) provided, in "the context of employment discrimination ... would include, but not be limited to, claims of harassment, discharge, demotion, promotion, transfer, *retaliation,* and hiring." It also said that the new law "would restore rights to sue for such retaliatory conduct." [citations omitted].

After enactment of the new law, the Federal Courts of Appeals again reached a broad consensus that § 1981, as amended, encompasses retaliation claims.

The upshot is this: (1) in 1969, *Sullivan,* as interpreted by *Jackson,* recognized that § 1982 encompasses a retaliation action; (2) this Court has long interpreted §§ 1981 and 1982 alike; (3) in 1989, *Patterson,* without mention of retaliation, narrowed § 1981 by excluding from its scope conduct, namely post-contract-formation conduct, where retaliation would most likely be found; but in 1991, Congress enacted legislation that superseded *Patterson* and explicitly defined the scope of § 1981 to include post-contract-formation conduct; and (4) since 1991, the lower courts have uniformly interpreted § 1981 as encompassing retaliation actions.

### C

*Sullivan,* as interpreted and relied upon by *Jackson,* as well as the long line of related cases where we construe §§ 1981 and 1982 similarly, lead us to conclude that the view that § 1981 encompasses retaliation claims is indeed well embedded in the law. That being so, considerations of *stare decisis* strongly support our adherence to that view. And those considerations impose a considerable burden upon those who would seek a different interpretation that would necessarily unsettle many Court precedents.

### III

In our view, CBOCS' several arguments, taken separately or together, cannot justify a departure from what we have just described as the well-embedded interpretation of § 1981....

### IV

We conclude that considerations of *stare decisis* strongly support our adherence to *Sullivan* and the long line of related cases where we interpret §§ 1981 and 1982 similarly.

CBOCS' arguments do not convince us to the contrary. We consequently hold that 42 U.S.C. § 1981 encompasses claims of retaliation. The judgment of the Court of Appeals is affirmed.

It is so ordered.

[The dissenting opinion of Justice Thomas, joined by Justice Scalia, is omitted.]

---

## ➤ Beyond the Basics: Federal Employee Protections

Both the ADEA and Title VII protect federal employees from discrimination, but neither expressly protects federal employees from retaliation. The ADEA contains no such language, but the Supreme Court has now recognized such a cause of action in the decision of *Gomez-Perez v. Potter*, which is excerpted below. Likewise, courts have interpreted Title VII as providing retaliation protections for federal employees. In *Caldwell v. Johnson*, the Fourth Circuit extended the *Burlington Northern* standard to federal government employees bringing retaliation claims under § 2000e-16(a). 289 Fed. App'x 579, 592 (4th Cir. 2008).

During the same term it decided *CBOCS West*, the Supreme Court also decided *Gomez-Perez v. Potter*, construing the federal employment provisions of the ADEA to allow a retaliation claim. The Court wrote:

> The federal-sector provision of the ADEA provides that "[a]ll personnel actions affecting employees or applicants for employment who are at least 40 years of age ... shall be made free from any discrimination based on age." The key question in this case is whether the statutory phrase "discrimination based on age" includes retaliation based on the filing of an age discrimination complaint. We hold that it does.
>
> In reaching this conclusion, we are guided by our prior decisions interpreting similar language in other antidiscrimination statutes. In *Sullivan v. Little Hunting Park, Inc.*, 396 U.S. 229 (1969), we considered whether a claim of retaliation could be brought under 42 U.S.C. § 1982, which provides that "[a]ll citizens of the United States shall have the same right ... as is enjoyed by white citizens ... to inherit, purchase, lease, sell, hold, and convey real and personal property."
>
> In *Sullivan*, a white man (Sullivan) held membership shares in a nonstock corporation that operated a park and playground for residents of the area in which he owned a home. Under the bylaws of the corporation, a member who leased a home in the area could assign a membership share in the corporation. But when Sullivan rented his house and attempted to assign a membership share to an African-American (Freeman), the corporation disallowed the assignment because of Freeman's race and subsequently expelled Sullivan from the corporation for protesting that decision. Sullivan sued the corporation, and we held that his claim that he had been expelled "for the advocacy of Freeman's cause" was cognizable under § 1982. A contrary holding, we reasoned, would have allowed Sullivan to be "punished for trying to vindicate the rights of minorities" and would have given "impetus to the perpetuation of racial restrictions on property."
>
> More recently, in *Jackson v. Birmingham Bd. of Ed.*, 544 U.S. 167 (2005), we relied on *Sullivan* in interpreting Title IX of the Education Amendments of 1972. Jackson, a public school teacher, sued his school board under Title IX, "alleging that the Board retaliated against him because he had complained about sex dis-

crimination in the high school's athletic program." Title IX provides in relevant part that "[n]o person in the United States shall, *on the basis of sex*, … be subjected to *discrimination* under any education program or activity receiving Federal financial assistance." Holding that this provision prohibits retaliation, we wrote:

> Retaliation against a person because that person has complained of sex discrimination is another form of intentional sex discrimination…. Retaliation is, by definition, an intentional act. It is a form of "discrimination" because the complainant is being subjected to differential treatment. Moreover, retaliation is discrimination "on the basis of sex" because it is an intentional response to the nature of the complaint: an allegation of sex discrimination. We conclude that when a funding recipient retaliates against a person *because* he complains of sex discrimination, this constitutes intentional "discrimination" "on the basis of sex," in violation of Title IX.

This interpretation, we found, flowed naturally from *Sullivan:* "Retaliation for Jackson's advocacy of the rights of the girls' basketball team in this case is 'discrimination' 'on the basis of sex,' just as retaliation for advocacy on behalf of a black lessee in *Sullivan* was discrimination on the basis of race."

Following the reasoning of *Sullivan* and *Jackson*, we interpret the ADEA federal-sector provision's prohibition of "discrimination based on age" as likewise proscribing retaliation. The statutory language at issue here ("discrimination based on age") is not materially different from the language at issue in *Jackson* ("discrimination on the basis of sex") and is the functional equivalent of the language at issue in *Sullivan*. And the context in which the statutory language appears is the same in all three cases; that is, all three cases involve remedial provisions aimed at prohibiting discrimination.

553 U.S. 474 (2008).

## Exercise 6.1

Bob works at a law firm as a paralegal. One day, he saw a young female associate run out of a partner's office in tears. As she passed Bob, she said, "I cannot believe this happened to me." Shortly thereafter, the young female associate left the law firm to work for another employer. Bob never talked to her about the incident.

The partner involved in the incident was John Tucker. From office gossip, Bob knew that John had a reputation for dating female secretaries, even though John was married. Bob thinks that John is not a very moral person.

It turns out that the associate left the firm because she failed the bar exam, and John Tucker was the partner tasked with delivering the news to the associate. Bob does not know this piece of information.

Based on what he saw, Bob tells his friend at the law firm, Tanya, that he thinks John Tucker sexually harassed the young associate and that she quit in response. Bob tells Tanya that he thinks this conduct is illegal. Tanya tells her supervisor about Bob's comments during a casual work lunch.

Two months later, Bob is turned down for a pay raise. You are a plaintiff's lawyer, and Bob comes to your office seeking advice. Does Bob have a good retaliation claim? Focus your response on the elements discussed in this Chapter.

## Exercise 6.2

Ben Brattle is the director of marketing at Markheed Corporation. Ben supports his employees in all their endeavors and rewards them for all accomplishments in a fair and generous manner. Cindy Calliope, the least productive member of Ben's team, is ungrateful. She files a claim at the EEOC asserting that Ben doles out benefits according to people's sex, rather than merit. When Ben receives notice of the charge, he calls Cindy in to his office to ask her about her charge. She then files a second charge at the EEOC contending that Ben called her in to his office to reprimand her for the first charge, thus violating the section 704 prohibition against retaliation. Cindy then tries to organize a group of other women, encouraging them to complain to the EEOC about Ben, suggesting that he is condescending toward women and treats men more generously. Ben would like to fire or transfer Cindy to resolve these problems. If you are Ben's lawyer, how will you counsel him?

## Exercise 6.3

Because of the events described in Exercise 6.2, the Markheed Office of General Counsel will hold a training session for managers on permissible and impermissible responses to employee complaints of discrimination. You are the Assistant General Counsel who is asked to present this material. Consider the training techniques that were discussed in the Discriminatory Harassment Chapter, and develop some concrete examples and, perhaps role-plays, to help the managers understand what they will need to know to avoid legal liability for retaliation. Make it interesting!

Preliminary Questions

1. What information do you view as essential to be conveyed?

2. What, other than conveying information, will you hope to accomplish in the training?

3. Create a list of techniques that are likely to be effective to convey the information, and techniques that are not likely to be effective. You actually are an expert on the subject of effective training techniques because you have spent so many years in formal education. Thus, to answer this question, you might consider what kinds of classroom teaching you have found to be useful in your own educational experience and what you have found to be ineffective.

4. Create an outline of the presentation, including in logical order:

   • Introductory overview of what the presentation will include;

   • Information to be conveyed—work on developing the most concise, clear articulation you can;

   • Hands-on, experiential activities to be used with the audience;

   • Interactive question and answer periods scheduled at those points in the presentation when you think questions are most likely to arise;

   • Concluding synopsis.

## Exercise 6.4

Recall that you should be constantly testing your understanding of the material. Think about the concepts of tangible employment action used in the *Faragher/ Ellerth* context and the concepts of adverse action or materially adverse action used in the context of discrimination and retaliation cases. The words used are similar, but are they the same? If not, in what ways are they different? In what types of cases would these differences matter?

# Chapter 7

# Religion and Accommodation

Title VII, as originally enacted in 1964, prohibited discrimination in employment because of an individual's religion but imposed no obligation on the employer to accommodate an employee's religious beliefs. 42 U.S.C. § 2000e-2(a). In 1972, Congress amended Title VII to add an accommodation requirement. The statute thus provides that the term "religion" includes "all aspects of religious observance and practice, as well as belief, *unless an employer demonstrates that he is unable to reasonably accommodate an employee's or prospective employee's religious observance or practice without undue hardship on the conduct of the employer's business.*" 42 U.S.C. § 2000e-(j) (emphasis added). The prohibition against religious discrimination applies to both private and public employers covered by Title VII.

The materials in this Chapter begin with a theoretical discussion of why religious discrimination is prohibited by Title VII and why an accommodation obligation is a part of Title VII religious discrimination law. The materials then cover several core concepts: the definition of religion; proof structures in religious discrimination cases; reasonable accommodation and undue hardship; and exemptions and exceptions to religious discrimination.

## ✦ Core Concept: The Differences of Religious Discrimination

The treatment of religion as a protected category under Title VII and the accommodation requirement imposed on employers under the Act provide an opportunity to consider the theoretical underpinnings of employment discrimination law.

Race, color, sex, national origin, and age are linked by the fact that they generally are immutable characteristics or status. In most circumstances, one does not choose to be African-American, or choose to be a woman, or choose to be 55 years old, etc. This may seem an obvious point, but it is worth noting because religion departs from this conceptual link. Religious beliefs and practices *are* often a matter of personal choice. Consequently, the protection of religious beliefs appears to mean that employment discrimination protections need not be limited to a person's immutable characteristics. A federal statute may give protection from employment discrimination to individuals based on personal choices and their expression of those choices. But where does one draw that proverbial line? Why is religion, which involves a certain personal choice and means of personal expression, protected by federal law and other forms of choice and expression are not protected by the Act?

For example, assume an employee named Fred loves baseball. In fact, baseball is the most important thing in the world to Fred and, in particular, Fred loves the New York Mets. Fred's employer hates baseball and knows that Fred is a huge baseball fan. The employer fires Fred because Fred is a baseball fan. To push the point further, why does the employer not have an obligation to accommodate Fred's baseball fandom by letting him off work for a day to go watch the Mets play a baseball game at Citi Field? Why is Fred's baseball infatuation not protected and accommodated under Title VII?

The legislative history of Title VII provides scant information as to why Congress decided to prohibit religious discrimination in employment. But there are a variety of possibilities as to why religious belief is protected. First, perhaps religion is protected because a person's religious belief does not have anything to do with his technical ability to do a job. For example, whether a person is Christian, Jewish, Muslim, or Atheist has no bearing on whether a pipefitter has the technical ability to cut and lay pipe. One could also say that religion makes sense as a protected category because generally speaking the other protected traits like race, sex, national origin are irrelevant to a person's qualifications and ability to do the job as well. Of course, the same thing could be said for Fred's baseball fanaticism. Fred's love of baseball is irrelevant to his ability to do the job but he is not entitled to protection from *baseball* discrimination in employment. Moreover, recall that the at-will rule holds that an employer should have the right to refuse to hire or fire an employee for a good reason, *a bad reason*, or no reason at all. Under American employment law, it is certainly legal in many instances for an employer to refuse to hire or fire a person for a reason that has no relevance to the person's ability to do the job. This argument thus seems to break down upon further inquiry.

Second, perhaps religion is protected like the other protected categories in part because they share a history of inspiring persecution. History proves that human beings tend to discriminate against and persecute other persons with such characteristics on a *large scale,* which causes substantial damage to societal tranquility and, for a lack of a better phrase, the ability of people to just get along. Human history is filled with a glaring number of instances in which racial minorities and religious minority groups have been discriminated against in terrible ways. From a macroeconomic employment perspective, this type of discrimination against people with certain characteristics on a large scale impacts not only individuals and groups of individuals but also the productive capacity of the American workforce as a whole. Discrimination against baseball fans does not appear to fit the religion-sex-race-national origin-age discrimination mold.

Ultimately, one could argue that Title VII protects against religious discrimination because religious tolerance is a societal value of the highest order. In the religiously pluralistic society that we live in, people have to tolerate the religious beliefs and practices of others even though they may strongly disagree with those beliefs. Of course, one need look no further then the First Amendment to the United States Constitution to understand that religious tolerance and religious freedom are fundamental components of American society. Title VII reflects those values imbued in the First Amendment.

## Exercise 7.1

In your view, what are the theoretical justifications for including religion as a protected category under the federal antidiscrimination laws? What is your test for determining whether other characteristics should be included as protected categories under federal employment discrimination laws?

Another theoretical question related to religious discrimination is why Title VII requires accommodation of religious practices and beliefs. Religious tolerance is a value of the highest order. Title VII transports this value into the law of the American workplace. To promote this value, Title VII could go no further than to say that employers must treat their employees the same regardless of their religious beliefs. This formal equal treatment principle is one that you should be very familiar with at this point. The idea is that the protected characteristic has no part in an employment decision. For example, an employer cannot refuse or decide to hire an individual for a position because the individual is Mormon and the employer dislikes the Mormon religion. Of course, Title VII incorporates this equal treatment principle into its prohibition against religious discrimination, but it goes further.

Title VII includes a limited accommodation obligation on employers to accommodate the religious beliefs and practices of their employees. Accommodation is a strain that runs through religious discrimination law and, as you will learn in the subsequent Chapter, disability discrimination law. The principle of accommodation presents a paradigm shift in employment discrimination law. Instead of merely saying employers must treat all employees the same regardless of the protected characteristic, the accommodation principle says the employer *must* give different treatment to an employee because of his or her *protected characteristic* in order to promote equality. Thus, a Sabbatarian employee is allowed to take off work on Sunday to accommodate his religious beliefs and practices but a similarly-situated employee who does not have such a religious belief must work on Sunday.

Why does Title VII require employers in some circumstances to accommodate their employees' religious beliefs and practices? It must be because Congress has deemed that facilitating the employees' observance and practice of their religion is a societal value of the highest order and this value is appropriately advanced by imposing some limited accommodation obligation on employers when the employees' religious beliefs and practices conflict with neutrally-applicable workplace demands. Drawing the line between accommodation of religious practices that are required by Title VII and those that are not is discussed later on in the part on Reasonable Accommodation and Undue Hardship.

## ✦ Core Concept: Defining Religion

Chapter 2 provided an overview of how religion is defined under Title VII. Recall that the text of Title VII does not otherwise define the term "religion," and in many cases, further definition is not required, especially where the religion is widely accepted as such. The Supreme Court in a non-Title VII case defined religious belief as a sincere belief that occupies in the life of the believer a parallel place to that of God in traditional religions. *See U.S. v. Seeger*, 380 U.S. 163, 165–66 (1965).

The EEOC has provided further guidance on the definition of religious practice. The EEOC defines religious practices to include "moral or ethical beliefs as to what is right and wrong which are sincerely held with the strength of traditional religious views." *See* 29 C.F.R. § 1605.1. No specific religious organization is required to espouse the beliefs held by a protected individual. *See id.* The fact that the religious group to which an individual professes belonging does not espouse a particular belief or practice does not prohibit that belief or practice from being considered a religious one. *See id.*

## Exercise 7.2

If you need a refresher regarding the definition of "religion," review the scenarios in Exercise 2.2 of the casebook.

## ✦ Core Concept: Proof Structures in Religion Cases

Employees may use the same theories — disparate treatment and disparate impact — in asserting religious discrimination claims, as they can for other protected traits under Title VII. For example, a plaintiff could bring an individual disparate treatment claim, alleging she was discriminated against based on her religion. Disparate treatment cases based on religion proceed along the same lines as disparate treatment cases based on race or sex. The familiar *McDonnell-Douglas* framework often takes center stage at least in some modified form. A key distinction is that some courts alter the *McDonnell-Douglas* framework to require the plaintiff to prove that the employer had knowledge of the plaintiff's religion or religious practices when knowledge is disputed. This is because a person's religion, as opposed to a person's race or sex, is often neither readily identifiable nor obvious. *See Reed v. Great Lakes Cos.*, 330 F.3d 931 (7th Cir. 2003) ("It is difficult to see how an employer can be charged with discrimination on the basis of the employee's religion when he doesn't know the employee's religion."); *Lubetsky v. Applied Card Sys.*, 296 F.3d 1301 (11th Cir. 2002) (plaintiff required to produce evidence that decision-maker had knowledge of his religion to establish a prima facie case). Disparate impact cases based on religion are rare but may be factually possible.

The accommodation obligation makes religious discrimination different from other protected characteristics. In many cases, a particular claim of religious discrimination is best viewed as raising either a disparate treatment claim or an accommodation claim. However, some disparate treatment cases may also be accommodation cases. For example, the employer who allows its Jewish employees to wear religious symbols, but not its Catholic employees, is discriminating against the Catholic employee because of his religious beliefs and is also refusing to accommodate the Catholic employee's religious beliefs.

Failure-to-accommodate cases have their own unique proof structure.

---

### Focus Question: *Chalmers v. Tulon Company of Richmond*

*What are the basic elements of the plaintiff's prima facie case in a religious accommodation claim?*

---

# Chalmers v. Tulon Company of Richmond
## 101 F.3d 1012 (4th Cir. 1996)

Circuit Judge Motz.

. . .

Although Title VII similarly classifies religion, sex, and race as illegal considerations, the definition of "religion" in the statute places it in a special category. "Religion" is defined to include "all aspects of religious observance and practice, as well as belief, unless an employer demonstrates that he is unable to reasonably accommodate an employee's ... religious observance or practice without undue hardship on the conduct of the employer's business." 42 U.S.C. § 2000e(j). Because this definition includes a requirement that an employer "accommodate" an employee's religious expression, an employee is not limited to the disparate treatment theory to establish a discrimination claim. An employee can also bring suit based on the theory that the employer discriminated against her by failing to *accommodate* her religious conduct. *See Trans World Airlines, Inc. v. Hardison*, 432 U.S. 63 (1977).

In a religious accommodation case, an employee can establish a claim even though she cannot show that other (unprotected) employees were treated more favorably or cannot rebut an employer's legitimate, non-discriminatory reason for her discharge. This is because an employer must, to an extent, actively attempt to accommodate an employee's religious expression or conduct even if, absent the religious motivation, the employee's conduct would supply a legitimate ground for discharge.

. . .

To establish a prima facie religious accommodation claim, a plaintiff must establish that: (1) he or she has a bona fide religious belief that conflicts with an employment requirement; (2) he or she informed the employer of this belief; (3) he or she was disciplined for failure to comply with the conflicting employment requirement. If the employee establishes a prima facie case, the burden then shifts to the employer to show that it could not accommodate the plaintiff's religious needs without undue hardship.

---

### ✦ Core Concept: Reasonable Accommodation and Undue Hardship

The burden is on the employer to try and accommodate the employee's religious needs once the employer is made aware of the employee's conflict. *See EEOC v. Ithaca Indus., Inc.*, 849 F.2d 116 (4th Cir. 1988) (en banc) (holding that if the employee refuses to work on his Sabbath day, the burden is on the employer to attempt to accommodate the employee's religious beliefs by proposing alternatives). The employee and employer should engage in an interactive communication process that tries to resolve the conflict if possible. As evidenced by the following case, a fundamental question is whether the proposed accommodation requires the employer to bear an undue hardship in that the accommodation would impose on it more than a *de minimis* cost.

---

### Focus Questions: *Trans World Airlines, Inc. v. Hardison*

1. *Why is anything more than a de minimis burden on the employer an undue hardship?*

2. *Why isn't the Sabbatarian entitled to an accommodation that would allow him not to work on his Sabbath day?*

3. *Should one of the key purposes of the religious accommodation obligation be to accommodate Sabbatarians?*

---

# Trans World Airlines, Inc. v. Hardison

## 432 U.S. 63 (1977)

Justice White delivered the opinion of the Court.

... The issue in this case is the extent of the employer's obligation under Title VII to accommodate an employee whose religious beliefs prohibit him from working on Saturdays.

Petitioner Trans World Airlines (TWA) operates a large maintenance and overhaul base in Kansas City, Mo. On June 5, 1967, respondent Larry G. Hardison was hired by TWA to work as a clerk in the Stores Department at its Kansas City base. Because of its essential role in the Kansas City operation, the Stores Department must operate 24 hours per day, 365 days per year, and whenever an employee's job in that department is not filled, an employee must be shifted from another department, or a supervisor must cover the job, even if the work in other areas may suffer.

Hardison, like other employees at the Kansas City base, was subject to a seniority system contained in a collective-bargaining agreement that TWA maintains with petitioner International Association of Machinists and Aerospace Workers (IAM). The seniority system is implemented by the union steward through a system of bidding by employees for particular shift assignments as they become available. The most senior employees have first choice for job and shift assignments, and the most junior employees are required to work when the union steward is unable to find enough people willing to work at a particular time or in a particular job to fill TWA's needs.

In the spring of 1968 Hardison began to study the religion known as the Worldwide Church of God. One of the tenets of that religion is that one must observe the Sabbath by refraining from performing any work from sunset on Friday until sunset on Saturday. The religion also proscribes work on certain specified religious holidays.

When Hardison informed Everett Kussman, the manager of the Stores Department, of his religious conviction regarding observance of the Sabbath, Kussman agreed that the union steward should seek a job swap for Hardison or a change of days off; that Hardison would have his religious holidays off whenever possible if Hardison agreed to work the traditional holidays when asked; and that Kussman would try to find Hardison another job that would be more compatible with his religious beliefs. The problem was temporarily solved when Hardison transferred to the 11 p.m.–7 a.m. shift. Working this shift permitted Hardison to observe his Sabbath.

The problem soon reappeared when Hardison bid for and received a transfer from Building 1, where he had been employed, to Building 2, where he would work the day shift. The two buildings had entirely separate seniority lists; and while in Building 1 Hardison had sufficient seniority to observe the Sabbath regularly, he was second from the bottom on the Building 2 seniority list.

In Building 2 Hardison was asked to work Saturdays when a fellow employee went on vacation. TWA agreed to permit the union to seek a change of work assignments for Hardison, but the union was not willing to violate the seniority provisions set out in the collective-bargaining contract, and Hardison had insufficient seniority to bid for a shift. A proposal that Hardison work only four days a week was rejected by the company. Hardison's job was essential, and on weekends he was the only available person on his shift to perform it. To leave the position empty would have impaired supply shop functions, which were critical to airline operations; to fill Hardison's position with a supervisor or an employee from another area would simply have undermanned another operation; and to employ someone not regularly assigned to work Saturdays would have required TWA to pay premium wages.

When an accommodation was not reached, Hardison refused to report for work on Saturdays. A transfer to the twilight shift proved unavailing since that schedule still required Hardison to work past sundown on Fridays. After a hearing, Hardison was discharged on grounds of insubordination for refusing to work during his designated shift.

[Hardison sued TWA and the union claiming that the discharge violated Title VII's prohibition against religious discrimination. The parties tried the case to the district judge. After the bench trial, the district court ruled in favor of TWA and the union. The Eighth Circuit affirmed the judgment for the union, but reversed the judgment for TWA.]

...

### III

The Court of Appeals held that TWA had not made reasonable efforts to accommodate Hardison's religious needs under the 1967 EEOC guidelines in effect at the time the relevant events occurred. In its view, TWA had rejected three reasonable alternatives, any one of which would have satisfied its obligation without undue hardship. First, within the framework of the seniority system, TWA could have permitted Hardison to work a four-day week, utilizing in his place a supervisor or another worker on duty elsewhere. That this would have caused other shop functions to suffer was insufficient to amount to undue hardship in the opinion of the Court of Appeals. Second—according to the Court of Appeals, also within the bounds of the collective-bargaining contract—the company could have filled Hardison's Saturday shift from other available personnel competent to do the job, of which the court said there were at least 200. That this would have involved premium overtime pay was not deemed an undue hardship. Third, TWA could have arranged a "swap between Hardison and another employee either for another shift or for the Sabbath days." In response to the assertion that this would have involved a breach of the seniority provisions of the contract, the court noted that it had not been settled in the courts whether the required statutory accommodation to religious needs stopped short of transgressing seniority rules, but found it unnecessary to decide the issue because, as the Court of Appeals saw the record, TWA had not sought, and the union had therefore not declined to entertain, a possible variance from the seniority provisions of the collective-bargaining agreement. The company had simply left the entire matter to the union steward who the Court of Appeals said "likewise did nothing."

We disagree with the Court of Appeals in all relevant respects. It is our view that TWA made reasonable efforts to accommodate and that each of the Court of Appeals' suggested alternatives would have been an undue hardship within the meaning of the statute as construed by the EEOC guidelines.

### A

It might be inferred from the Court of Appeals' opinion and from the brief of the EEOC in this Court that TWA's efforts to accommodate were no more than negligible. The findings of the District Court, supported by the record, are to the contrary. In summarizing its more detailed findings, the District Court observed:

> TWA established as a matter of fact that it did take appropriate action to accommodate as required by Title VII. It held several meetings with plaintiff at which it attempted to find a solution to plaintiff's problems. It did accommodate plaintiff's observance of his special religious holidays. It authorized the union

steward to search for someone who would swap shifts, which apparently was normal procedure.

It is also true that TWA itself attempted without success to find Hardison another job. The District Court's view was that TWA had done all that could reasonably be expected within the bounds of the seniority system.

. . .

We shall say more about the seniority system, but at this juncture it appears to us that the system itself represented a significant accommodation to the needs, both religious and secular, of all of TWA's employees. As will become apparent, the seniority system represents a neutral way of minimizing the number of occasions when an employee must work on a day that he would prefer to have off. Additionally, recognizing that weekend work schedules are the least popular, the company made further accommodation by reducing its work force to a bare minimum on those days.

## B

We are also convinced, contrary to the Court of Appeals, that TWA itself cannot be faulted for having failed to work out a shift or job swap for Hardison. Both the union and TWA had agreed to the seniority system; the union was unwilling to entertain a variance over the objections of men senior to Hardison; and for TWA to have arranged unilaterally for a swap would have amounted to a breach of the collective-bargaining agreement.

## (1)

Hardison and the EEOC insist that the statutory obligation to accommodate religious needs takes precedence over both the collective-bargaining contract and the seniority rights of TWA's other employees. We agree that neither a collective-bargaining contract nor a seniority system may be employed to violate the statute, but we do not believe that the duty to accommodate requires TWA to take steps inconsistent with the otherwise valid agreement. Collective bargaining, aimed at effecting workable and enforceable agreements between management and labor, lies at the core of our national labor policy, and seniority provisions are universally included in these contracts. Without a clear and express indication from Congress, we cannot agree with Hardison and the EEOC that an agreed-upon seniority system must give way when necessary to accommodate religious observances. The issue is important and warrants some discussion.

Any employer who, like TWA, conducts an around-the-clock operation is presented with the choice of allocating work schedules either in accordance with the preferences of its employees or by involuntary assignment. Insofar as the varying shift preferences of its employees complement each other, TWA could meet its manpower needs through voluntary work scheduling. In the present case, for example, Hardison's supervisor foresaw little difficulty in giving Hardison his religious holidays off since they fell on days that most other employees preferred to work, while Hardison was willing to work on the traditional holidays that most other employees preferred to have off.

Whenever there are not enough employees who choose to work a particular shift, however, some employees must be assigned to that shift even though it is not their first choice. Such was evidently the case with regard to Saturday work; even though TWA cut back its weekend work force to a skeleton crew, not enough employees chose those days off to staff the Stores Department through voluntary scheduling. In these circumstances, TWA and IAM agreed to give first preference to employees who had worked in a particular department the longest.

Had TWA nevertheless circumvented the seniority system by relieving Hardison of Saturday work and ordering a senior employee to replace him, it would have denied the latter his shift preference so that Hardison could be given his. The senior employee would also have been deprived of his contractual rights under the collective-bargaining agreement.

It was essential to TWA's business to require Saturday and Sunday work from at least a few employees even though most employees preferred those days off. Allocating the burdens of weekend work was a matter for collective bargaining. In considering criteria to govern this allocation, TWA and the union had two alternatives: adopt a neutral system, such as seniority, a lottery, or rotating shifts; or allocate days off in accordance with the religious needs of its employees. TWA would have had to adopt the latter in order to assure Hardison and others like him of getting the days off necessary for strict observance of their religion, but it could have done so only at the expense of others who had strong, but perhaps nonreligious, reasons for not working on weekends. There were no volunteers to relieve Hardison on Saturdays, and to give Hardison Saturdays off, TWA would have had to deprive another employee of his shift preference at least in part because he did not adhere to a religion that observed the Saturday Sabbath.

Title VII does not contemplate such unequal treatment. The repeated, unequivocal emphasis of both the language and the legislative history of Title VII is on eliminating discrimination in employment, and such discrimination is proscribed when it is directed against majorities as well as minorities. Indeed, the foundation of Hardison's claim is that TWA and IAM engaged in religious discrimination in violation of 703(a)(1) when they failed to arrange for him to have Saturdays off. It would be anomalous to conclude that by "reasonable accommodation" Congress meant that an employer must deny the shift and job preference of some employees, as well as deprive them of their contractual rights, in order to accommodate or prefer the religious needs of others, and we conclude that Title VII does not require an employer to go that far.

(2)

Our conclusion is supported by the fact that seniority systems are afforded special treatment under Title VII itself. Section 703(h) provides in pertinent part:

> Notwithstanding any other provision of this subchapter, it shall not be an unlawful employment practice for an employer to apply different standards of compensation, or different terms, conditions, or privileges of employment pursuant to a bona fide seniority or merit system ... provided that such differences are not the result of an intention to discriminate because of race, color, religion, sex, or national origin.

"[T]he unmistakable purpose of §703(h) was to make clear that the routine application of a bona fide seniority system would not be unlawful under Title VII." *Teamsters v. United States*, 431 U.S. 324, 352 (1977). Section 703(h) is "a definitional provision; as with the other provisions of §703, subsection (h) delineates which employment practices are illegal and thereby prohibited and which are not." *Franks v. Bowman Transportation Co.*, 424 U.S. 747, 758 (1976). Thus, absent a discriminatory purpose, the operation of a seniority system cannot be an unlawful employment practice even if the system has some discriminatory consequences.

There has been no suggestion of discriminatory intent in this case. "The seniority system was not designed with the intention to discriminate against religion nor did it act to lock members of any religion into a pattern wherein their freedom to exercise their religion was limited. It was coincidental that in plaintiff's case the seniority system acted to compound his problems in exercising his religion." The Court of Appeals' conclusion that TWA was not limited by the terms of its seniority system was in substance nothing more than a ruling that operation of the seniority system was itself an unlawful employment practice even though no discriminatory purpose had been shown. That ruling is plainly inconsistent with the dictates of § 703(h), both on its face and as interpreted in the recent decisions of this Court.

As we have said, TWA was not required by Title VII to carve out a special exception to its seniority system in order to help Hardison to meet his religious obligations.

C

The Court of Appeals also suggested that TWA could have permitted Hardison to work a four-day week if necessary in order to avoid working on his Sabbath. Recognizing that this might have left TWA short-handed on the one shift each week that Hardison did not work, the court still concluded that TWA would suffer no undue hardship if it were required to replace Hardison either with supervisory personnel or with qualified personnel from other departments. Alternatively, the Court of Appeals suggested that TWA could have replaced Hardison on his Saturday shift with other available employees through the payment of premium wages. Both of these alternatives would involve costs to TWA, either in the form of lost efficiency in other jobs or higher wages.

To require TWA to bear more than a de minimis cost in order to give Hardison Saturdays off is an undue hardship. Like abandonment of the seniority system, to require TWA to bear additional costs when no such costs are incurred to give other employees the days off that they want would involve unequal treatment of employees on the basis of their religion. By suggesting that TWA should incur certain costs in order to give Hardison Saturdays off the Court of Appeals would in effect require TWA to finance an additional Saturday off and then to choose the employee who will enjoy it on the basis of his religious beliefs. While incurring extra costs to secure a replacement for Hardison might remove the necessity of compelling another employee to work involuntarily in Hardison's place, it would not change the fact that the privilege of having Saturdays off would be allocated according to religious beliefs.

As we have seen, the paramount concern of Congress in enacting Title VII was the elimination of discrimination in employment. In the absence of clear statutory language or legislative history to the contrary, we will not readily construe the statute to require an employer to discriminate against some employees in order to enable others to observe their Sabbath.

Justice Marshall, with whom Justice Brennan joins, dissenting.

. . .

Today's decision deals a fatal blow to all efforts under Title VII to accommodate work requirements to religious practices. The Court holds, in essence, that although the EEOC regulations and the Act state that an employer must make reasonable adjustments in his work demands to take account of religious observances, the regulation and Act do not really mean what they say. An employer, the Court concludes, need not grant even the most minor special privilege to religious observers to enable them to follow their faith. As a question of social policy, this result is deeply troubling, for a society that truly values religious pluralism cannot compel adherents of minority religions to make the cruel choice of surrendering their religion or their job. And as a matter of law today's result is intolerable, for the Court adopts the very position that Congress expressly rejected in 1972, as if we were free to disregard congressional choices that a majority of this Court thinks unwise. I therefore dissent.

With respect to each of the proposed accommodations to respondent Hardison's religious observances that the Court discusses, it ultimately notes that the accommodation would have required "unequal treatment," in favor of the religious observer. That is quite true. But if an accommodation can be rejected simply because it involves preferential treatment, then the regulation and the statute, while brimming with "sound and fury," ultimately "signif[y] nothing."

The accommodation issue by definition arises only when a neutral rule of general applicability conflicts with the religious practices of a particular employee. In some of the reported cases, the rule in question has governed work attire; in other cases it has required attendance at some religious function; in still other instances, it has compelled membership in a union; and in the largest class of cases, it has concerned work schedules. What all these cases have in common is an employee who could comply with the rule only by violating what the employee views as a religious commandment. In each instance, the question is whether the employee is to be exempt from the rule's demands. To do so will always result in a privilege being "allocated according to religious beliefs," unless the employer gratuitously decides to repeal the rule in toto. What the statute says, in plain words, is that such allocations are required unless "undue hardship" would result.

. . .

What makes today's decision most tragic, however, is not that respondent Hardison has been needlessly deprived of his livelihood simply because he chose to follow the dictates of his conscience. Nor is the tragedy exhausted by the impact it will have on thousands of Americans like Hardison who could be forced to live on welfare as the price they must pay for worshiping their God. The ultimate tragedy is that despite Congress' best efforts, one of this Nation's pillars of strength—our hospitality to religious diversity—has been seriously eroded. All Americans will be a little poorer until today's decision is erased.

---

## Further Discussion

Assume that three proposed alternatives are on the table between the employee and the employer regarding a conflict between the employee's religious practices and the employer's workplace requirements. Alternative 1 is a reasonable accommodation and is most beneficial to the employee. It will satisfy the employee in the way he desires. Alternative 2 is not really an accommodation at all. Alternative 3 is not the most beneficial accommodation to the employee but is a *reasonable* accommodation to the employee's conflict. The employer chooses to go with Alternative 3. Does the statute require the employer to accept Alternative 1 unless it can prove that Alternative 1 is an undue hardship? The Supreme Court addressed the scenario outlined above in the next case.

---

### Focus Question: *Ansonia Board of Education v. Philbrook*

*Putting* Hardison *and* Philbrook *together, how would you describe the analysis of the employer's defense of inability to reasonably accommodate without undue hardship?*

---

# Ansonia Board of Education v. Philbrook

## 479 U.S. 60 (1986)

Chief Justice Rehnquist delivered the opinion of the Court.

[Under collective-bargaining agreements, teachers were granted three days' annual leave for observance of religious holidays. Teachers also accumulated annual sick leave, three days of which could be used for "necessary personal business." However, teachers could not use the three personal days for religious observance. Pursuant to the collective-bargaining agreements, high school teacher Ronald Philbrook used the three days granted for religious holidays each year, and then either took unauthorized unpaid leave, scheduled required hospital visits on church holy days, or worked on those days. Respondent repeatedly asked the School Board either to adopt the policy of allowing use of the three days of personal business leave for religious observance or, in the alternative, to allow him to pay the cost of a substitute and receive full pay for additional days off for religious observances. The School Board refused Philbrook's requests, but allowed him to take unpaid leave for religious observance.]

... The Court of Appeals assumed that the employer had offered a reasonable accommodation of Philbrook's religious beliefs. This alone, however, was insufficient in that court's view to allow resolution of the dispute. The court observed that the duty to accommodate "cannot be defined without reference to undue hardship." It accordingly determined that the accommodation obligation includes a duty to accept "the proposal the employee prefers unless that accommodation causes undue hardship on the employer's conduct of his business." Because the District Court had not considered whether Philbrook's proposals would impose undue hardship, the Court of Appeals remanded for further consideration of those proposals.

We find no basis in either the statute or its legislative history for requiring an employer to choose any particular reasonable accommodation. By its very terms the statute directs that any reasonable accommodation by the employer is sufficient to meet its accommodation obligation. The employer violates the statute unless it "demonstrates that [it] is unable to reasonably accommodate ... an employee's ... religious observance or practice without undue hardship on the conduct of the employer's business." 42 U.S.C. § 2000e(j). Thus, where the employer has already reasonably accommodated the employee's religious needs, the statutory inquiry is at an end. The employer need not further show that each of the employee's alternative accommodations would result in undue hardship. As *Hardison* illustrates, the extent of undue hardship on the employer's business is at issue only where the employer claims that it is unable to offer any reasonable accommodation without such hardship. Once the Court of Appeals assumed that the school board had offered to Philbrook a reasonable alternative, it erred by requiring the Board to nonetheless demonstrate the hardship of Philbrook's alternatives.

The legislative history of § 701(j), as we noted in *Hardison*, is of little help in defining the employer's accommodation obligation. To the extent it provides any indication of congressional intent, however, we think that the history supports our conclusion. Senator Randolph, the sponsor of the amendment that became § 701(j), expressed his hope that accommodation would be made with "flexibility" and "a desire to achieve an adjustment." 118 Cong. Rec. 706 (1972). Consistent with these goals, courts have noted that "bilateral cooperation is appropriate in the search for an acceptable reconciliation of the needs of the employee's religion and the exigencies of the employer's business." [citation omitted]. Under the approach articulated by the Court of Appeals, however, the employee is given every incentive to hold out for the most beneficial accommodation, despite the fact that an employer offers a reasonable resolution of the conflict. This approach, we think, conflicts with both the language of the statute and the views that led to its enactment. We accordingly hold that an employer has met its obligation under § 701(j) when it demonstrates that it has offered a reasonable accommodation to the employee.

---

## Further Discussion

Where the rubber meets the road in many religious accommodation cases is deciding whether, and how much, Title VII requires the employer to pay financially to satisfy its accommodation obligation and whether, and how much, the law permits co-workers to be inconvenienced or harmed by permitting the accommodation. For example, in *Hardison* the court was concerned that permitting the Sabbatarian to avoid work on Saturdays meant the employer would have to hire a worker at premium rates to cover the Sabbatarian's Saturday shift or force another co-worker with greater seniority to work on Saturday, which the co-worker would not have had to do but for the religious accommodation obligation. *See also Weber v. Roadway Exp. Inc.*, 199 F.3d 270 (5th Cir. 2000) (undue hardship to accommodate driver's religious objections to being partnered with a female driver because accommodation would burden other employees). Does the very nature of an accommodation law mean that some workers might be burdened by the fellow employee's religious practices? Why should the Sabbatarian's religious practice not trump the rights or preferences of other non-religious workers?

If the employer is not financially affected or otherwise tangibly impacted by the proposed accommodation and fellow co-workers are not impacted in any meaningful way, the proposed accommodation is very likely reasonable. Cases in which an employee simply wants to wear his or her religious dress are often fairly easy to accommodate because the impact on the employer and co-workers is de minimis. However, employers who refuse to permit the wearing of religious dress sometimes do so for safety reasons or because the legal liability of the employer would be increased. *See Kalsi v. New York City Transit Authority*, 62 F. Supp. 2d 745 (E.D. N.Y. 1998) (transit authority not required to accommodate plaintiff's request to wear turban during work because company policy required car inspectors to wear hard hat at all times and policy was justified for safety reasons).

The impact of a proposed accommodation on fellow co-workers is a real sticking point in some accommodation cases. If accommodation is allowed in a case like *Hardison*, a co-worker might have to work a shift he or she might not otherwise be required to work. The accommodation impacts the co-worker in *work* terms but the worker is not directly confronted with the religious employee's personal religious views. In other cases, the religious employee wants an accommodation that would allow her to express her religious views on the job in a way that directly imposes those religious views on others in the workplace. These scenarios are among the most difficult for employers to handle because the employer must reasonably accommodate its employees' religious beliefs and practices, but it must also ensure that its employees are not *religiously* harassed.

---

### Focus Questions: *Chalmers v. Tulon Company of Richmond*

1.  *Is this case a failure-to-accommodate case or a disparate treatment case? Explain.*

2.  *Why is the plaintiff required to notify her employer of her religious practice before she may receive an accommodation?*

3.  *Is there any way that the employer could have accommodated the plaintiff in this situation? How?*

4.  *Why are the co-employees' reactions to the plaintiff's letters relevant to the question of whether religious discrimination occurred?*

5.  *How would you handle this situation if you were in charge of the personnel decision?*

---

# Chalmers v. Tulon Company of Richmond

## 101 F.3d 1012 (4th Cir. 1996)

Circuit Judge Motz.

Charita Chalmers contends that the district court erred in granting summary judgment to her employer, Tulon Co., on her claim that Tulon failed to accommodate her religious conduct. Because Chalmers provided Tulon with no notice of her need to engage in this conduct and because, in any event, this conduct was not susceptible to accommodation, we affirm.

Chalmers worked for Tulon from October 1988 until September 21, 1993. Tulon's business involves the manufacturing of drill bits and routers used in the printed circuit board industry. Tulon maintains a number of service centers throughout the United States, including a center in Richmond, Virginia where Chalmers worked. During Chalmers' years at Tulon, the Richmond center employed from six to fifteen employees.

Chalmers began her employment as a repoint operator, and, after three years, was promoted to supervisor. During her employment with Tulon, although Chalmers had some issues with her job training, she believed Tulon treated her fairly with respect to compensation, benefits, and job assignments. Prior to her discharge, Chalmers never felt anyone at the company discriminated against her, or harassed her because of her religious beliefs or practices.

As repoint supervisor, Chalmers was the only management-level employee working regularly at the Richmond center. Chalmers' immediate supervisor, Richard C. LaMantia, was in charge of sales throughout the eastern part of the United States but, according to Chalmers, visited Richmond only a few days every few months. At all other times, Chalmers was responsible for the operation of the Richmond center. Chalmers recognized that it was part of her supervisory responsibility to promote harmony in the workplace and set an example for her subordinates.

Chalmers has been a Baptist all of her life, and in June 1984 became an evangelical Christian. At that time, she accepted Christ as her personal savior and determined to go forth and do work for him. As an evangelical Christian, Chalmers believes she should share the gospel and looks for opportunities to do so.

Chalmers felt that LaMantia respected her, generally refraining from using profanity around her, while around other employees who did not care, "he would say whatever he wanted to say." LaMantia had taken Chalmers and her husband to dinner once and she felt that she and LaMantia had a "personal relationship" and that she could talk to him. Chalmers stated that "in the past we have talked about God." Chalmers further testified that "starting off" she and LaMantia had discussed religion about "everytime he came to the service center ... maybe every three months" but "then, towards the end maybe not as frequently." LaMantia never discouraged these conversations, expressed discomfort with them, or indicated that they were improper. In one of these conversations, LaMantia told Chalmers that three people had approached him about accepting Christ.

Two or three years after this conversation, Chalmers "knew it was time for [LaMantia] to accept God." She believed LaMantia had told customers information about the turnaround time for a job when he knew that information was not true. Chalmers testified that she was "led by the Lord" to write LaMantia and tell him "there were things he needed to get right with God, and that was one thing that ... he needed to get right with him."

Accordingly, on Labor Day, September 6, 1993, Chalmers mailed the following letter to LaMantia at his home:

Dear Rich,

The reason I'm writing you is because the Lord wanted me to share somethings [sic] with you. After reading this letter you do not have to give me a call, but talk to God about everything.

One thing the Lord wants you to do is get your life right with him. The bible says in Roman 10:9 vs that if you confess with your mouth the Lord *Jesus* and believe in your heart that God hath raised him from the dead, thou shalt be saved. vs 10—For with the heart man believeth unto righteousness, and with the mouth confession is made unto salvation. The two verse are [sic] saying for you to get right with God *now*.

The last thing is, you are doing somethings [sic] in your life that God is not please [sic] with and He wants you to stop. All you have to do is go to God and ask for forgiveness before it's too late.

I wrote this letter at home so if you have a problem with it you can't relate it to work.

I have to answer to God just like you do, so that's why I wrote you this letter. Please take heed before it's too late.

In his name,

Charita Chalmers

Chalmers was unaware of any other Tulon employees who sent to co-workers at their homes letters regarding religious beliefs, or, indeed, any mail, other than Christmas, birthday, or congratulatory cards. Chalmers acknowledged that LaMantia had never said or done anything that signaled to her that he consented to a letter like this. When asked whether she knew "what Rich LaMantia's religious beliefs are," Chalmers responded that she knew "he believed in God, that's about it." She did not know his religious affiliation or whether he attended church regularly. Nevertheless, Chalmers felt that she could write the above letter to LaMantia at his home because of their "personal relationship" and their conversation two or three years earlier concerning people approaching LaMantia about accepting Christ.

On September 10, 1993 when Chalmers' letter arrived at LaMantia's home, he was out of town on Tulon business and his wife opened and read the letter in his absence. Mrs. LaMantia became distraught, interpreting the references to her husband's improper conduct as indicating that he was committing adultery. In tears, she called Chalmers and asked her if LaMantia was having an affair with someone in the New Hampshire area where LaMantia supervised another Tulon facility. Mrs. LaMantia explained that three years before she and LaMantia had separated because of his infidelity. Chalmers told Mrs. LaMantia that she did not know about any affair because she was in the Richmond area. When Mrs. LaMantia asked her what she had meant by writing that there was something in LaMantia's life that "he needed to get right with God," Chalmers explained about the turnaround time problem. Mrs. LaMantia responded that she would take the letter and rip it up so LaMantia could not read it. Chalmers answered, "Please don't do that, the Lord led me to send this to Rich, so let him read it." The telephone conversation then ended.

Mrs. LaMantia promptly telephoned her husband, interrupting a Tulon business presentation, to accuse him of infidelity. LaMantia, in turn, called the Richmond office and asked to speak with Chalmers; she was in back and by the time she reached the telephone, LaMantia had hung up. Chalmers then telephoned the LaMantias' home and, when she failed to reach anyone, left a message on the answering machine that she was sorry "if the letter offended" LaMantia or his wife and that she "did not mean to offend him or make him upset about the letter."

LaMantia also telephoned Craig A. Faber, Vice President of Administration at Tulon. LaMantia told Faber that the letter had caused him personal anguish and placed a serious strain on his marriage. LaMantia informed Faber that he felt he could no longer work with Chalmers. LaMantia recommended that Tulon management terminate Chalmers' employment. At her deposition, Chalmers was asked what reaction she would have if one of the employees who worked for her telephoned her husband and told him she was committing adultery. Chalmers pointed out that she had not telephoned anyone and had not written a letter stating that LaMantia was committing adultery, but she acknowledged that if another employee did telephone her husband with this information, it probably would affect her relationship with that co-worker.

While investigating LaMantia's complaint, Faber discovered that Chalmers had sent a second letter, on the same day as she had sent the letter to LaMantia, to another Tulon employee. That employee, Brenda Combs, worked as a repoint operator in the Richmond office and Chalmers was her direct supervisor. Chalmers knew that Combs was convalescing at her home, suffering from an undiagnosed illness after giving birth out of wedlock. Chalmers sent Combs the following letter:

> Brenda,
>
> You probably do not want to hear this at this time, but you need the Lord *Jesus* in your life right now.
>
> One thing about God, He doesn't like when people commit adultery. You know what you did is wrong, so now you need to go to God and ask for forgiveness.
>
> Let me explain something about *God*. He's a God of Love and a God of Wrath. When people sin against Him, He will allow things to happen to them or their family until they open their eyes and except [sic] Him. God can put a sickness on you that no doctor could ever find out what it is. I'm not saying this is what happened to you, all I'm saying is get right with God right now. Romans 10:9;10vs says that is [sic] you confess with your mouth the Lord Jesus and believe in your heart that God has raised him from the dead thou shalt be saved. For with the

heart man believeth unto righteousness; and with the mouth confession is made unto salvation. All I'm saying you need to invite God into your heart and live a life for him and things in your life will get better.

That's not saying you are not going to have problems but it's saying you have someone to go to.

Please take this letter in love and be obedient to God.

In his name,

Charita Chalmers

Upon receiving the letter Combs wept. Faber discussed the letter with Combs who told him that she had been "crushed by the tone of the letter." Combs believed that Chalmers implied that "an immoral lifestyle" had caused her illness and found Chalmers' letter "cruel." Combs, in a later, unsworn statement, asserted that although the letter "upset her" it did not "offend" her or "damage her working relationship" with Chalmers.

Faber consulted with other members of upper management and concluded that the letters caused a negative impact on working relationships, disrupted the workplace, and inappropriately invaded employee privacy. On behalf of Tulon, Faber then sent Chalmers a memorandum, informing her that she was terminated from her position. The memorandum stated in relevant part:

We have decided to terminate your employment with Tulon Co. effective today, September 21, 1993. Our decision is based on a serious error in judgment you made in sending letters to Rich LaMantia and Brenda Combs, which criticized their personal lives and beliefs. The letters offended them, invaded their privacy, and damaged your work relationships, making it too difficult for you to continue to work here.

We expect all of our employees to show good judgment, especially those in supervisory positions, such as yours. We would hope you can learn from this experience and avoid similar mistakes in the future.

Chalmers had apologized to LaMantia for any distress the letter caused. Chalmers believed that except for the fact that LaMantia did not want to discuss the letter with her, neither he nor Combs changed their conduct toward her after receipt of the letters. Richmond center employees blamed Combs for Chalmers' termination. Although Combs disclaimed any damage to her working relationship with Chalmers as a result of the letter, Tulon's termination decision remained firm.

As a result of the preceding events, Chalmers filed suit, alleging that Tulon discriminated against her based on her religion, in violation of Title VII. She contended that her letter writing constituted protected religious activity that Tulon, by law, should have accommodated with a lesser punishment than discharge.

. . .

III

To establish a prima facie religious accommodation claim, a plaintiff must establish that: (1) he or she has a bona fide religious belief that conflicts with an employment requirement; (2) he or she informed the employer of this belief; (3) he or she was disciplined for failure to comply with the conflicting employment requirement. If the employee establishes a prima facie case, the burden then shifts to the employer to show that it could not accommodate the plaintiff's religious needs without undue hardship.

Chalmers has alleged that she holds bona fide religious beliefs that caused her to write the letters. Tulon offers no evidence to the contrary. The parties agree that Tulon fired Chalmers because she wrote the letters. Accordingly, Chalmers has satisfied the first and third elements of the prima facie test. However, in other equally important respects, Chalmers' accommodation claim fails.

### A

Chalmers cannot satisfy the second element of the prima facie test. She has forecast no evidence that she notified Tulon that her religious beliefs required her to send personal, disturbing letters to her co-workers. Therefore she did not allow the company any sort of opportunity to attempt reasonable accommodation of her beliefs.

As Chalmers recognizes, a prima facie case under the accommodation theory requires evidence that she informed her employer that her religious needs conflicted with an employment requirement and asked the employer to accommodate her religious needs. *See Redmond v. GAF Corp.*, 574 F.2d 897, 901 (7th Cir. 1978) (prima facie standard includes a "requirement that plaintiff inform his employer of both his religious needs and his need for an accommodation").

Chalmers concedes that she did not expressly notify Tulon that her religion required her to write letters like those at issue here to her co-workers, or request that Tulon accommodate her conduct. Nonetheless, for several reasons, she contends that such notice was unnecessary in this case.

Initially, Chalmers asserts that Tulon never explicitly informed her of a company policy against writing religious letters to fellow employees at their homes and so she had "no reason to request an accommodation." However, companies cannot be expected to notify employees explicitly of all types of conduct that might annoy co-workers, damage working relationships, and thereby provide grounds for discharge. As noted previously, Chalmers implicitly acknowledged in the letters themselves that they might distress her co-workers. Moreover, she conceded that, as a supervisor, she had a responsibility to "promote harmony in the workplace."

Although a rule justifying discharge of an employee because she has disturbed co-workers requires careful application in the religious discrimination context (many religious practices might be perceived as "disturbing" to others), Chalmers, particularly as a supervisor, is expected to know that sending personal, distressing letters to co-workers' homes, criticizing them for assertedly ungodly, shameful conduct, would violate employment policy. Accordingly, the failure of the company to expressly forbid supervisors from disturbing other employees in this way, provides Chalmers with no basis for failing to notify Tulon that her religious beliefs required her to write such letters.

Alternatively, Chalmers contends that the notoriety of her religious beliefs within the company put it on notice of her need to send these letters. In her view, Chalmers satisfied the notice requirement because Tulon required "only enough information about an employee's religious needs to permit the employer to understand the existence of a conflict between the employee's religious practices and the employer's job requirements." *Brown v. Polk County*, 61 F.3d 650, 654 (8th Cir. 1995) (*en banc*).

Knowledge that an employee has strong religious beliefs does not place an employer on notice that she might engage in any religious activity, no matter how unusual. Chalmers concedes that she did not know of any other employee who had ever written distressing or judgmental letters to co-workers before, and that nothing her co-workers had said or done indicated that such letters were acceptable. Accordingly, any knowledge Tulon may have possessed regarding Chalmers' beliefs could not reasonably have put it on notice that she would write and send accusatory letters to co-workers' homes.

Chalmers also contends that the letters themselves provided notice that her religious beliefs compelled her to write them. But giving notice to co-workers at the same time as an employee violates employment requirements is insufficient to provide adequate notice to the employer and to shield the employee's conduct. *See Johnson v. Angelica Uniform Group, Inc.*, 762 F.2d 671 (8th Cir. 1985) (plaintiff failed to provide adequate notice to establish prima facie case where she left a note to her employer immediately before she went away for several days, informing the employer that she would need to exceed her allotted leave time for religious reasons).

In a similar vein, Chalmers appears to contend that because Tulon was necessarily aware of the religious nature of the letters after her co-workers received them and before her discharge, Tulon should have attempted to accommodate her by giving her a sanction less than a discharge, such as a warning. This raises a false issue. There is nothing in Title VII that requires employers to give lesser punishments to employees who claim, after they violate company rules (or at the same time), that their religion caused them to transgress the rules.

Part of the reason for the advance notice requirement is to allow the company to avoid or limit any "injury" an employee's religious conduct may cause. Additionally, the refusal even to attempt to accommodate an employee's religious requests, prior to the employee's violation of employment rules and sanction, provides some indication, however slight, of improper motive on the employer's part. The proper issue, therefore, is whether Chalmers made Tulon aware, *prior* to her letter writing, that her religious beliefs would cause her to send the letters. Since it is clear that she did not, her claims fail.

In sum, Chalmers has not pointed to any evidence that she gave Tulon—either directly or indirectly—advance notice of her need for accommodation. For this reason, Chalmers has failed to establish a prima facie case of discrimination under the religious accommodation theory.

### B

If we had concluded that Chalmers had established a prima facie case, Chalmers' religious accommodation claim would nonetheless fail. This is so because Chalmers' conduct is not the type that an employer can possibly accommodate, even with notice.

Chalmers concedes in the letters themselves that she knew the letters to her co-workers, accusing them of immoral conduct (in the letter to Combs, suggesting that Combs' immoral conduct caused her illness), might cause them distress. Even if Chalmers had notified Tulon expressly that her religious beliefs required her to write such letters, *i.e.*, that she was "led by the Lord" to write them, Tulon was without power under any circumstance to accommodate Chalmers' need.

Typically, religious accommodation suits involve religious conduct, such as observing the Sabbath, wearing religious garb, etc., that result in indirect and minimal burdens, if any, on other employees. An employer can often accommodate such needs without inconveniencing or unduly burdening other employees.

In a case like the one at hand, however, where an employee contends that she has a religious need to impose personally and directly on fellow employees, invading their privacy and criticizing their personal lives, the employer is placed between a rock and a hard place. If Tulon had the power to authorize Chalmers to write such letters, and if

Tulon had granted Chalmers' request to write the letters, the company would subject itself to possible suits from Combs and LaMantia claiming that Chalmers' conduct violated *their* religious freedoms or constituted religious harassment. Chalmers' supervisory position at the Richmond office heightens the possibility that Tulon (through Chalmers) would appear to be imposing religious beliefs on employees.

Thus, even if Chalmers had notified Tulon that her religion required her to send the letters at issue here to her co-workers, Tulon would have been unable to accommodate that conduct.

### IV

We do not in any way question the sincerity of Chalmers' religious beliefs or practices. However, it is undisputed that Chalmers failed to notify Tulon that her religious beliefs led her to send personal, disturbing letters to her fellow employees accusing them of immorality. It is also undisputed that the effect of a letter on one of the recipients, LaMantia's wife, whether intended or not, caused a co-worker, LaMantia, great stress and caused him to complain that he could no longer work with Chalmers. Finally, it is undisputed that another employee, Combs, told a company officer that Chalmers' letter upset her (although she later claimed that her working relationship with Chalmers was unaffected). Under these facts, Chalmers cannot establish a religious accommodation claim. Accordingly, the district court's order granting summary judgment to Tulon is affirmed.

Circuit Judge Niemeyer, dissenting.

Charita Chalmers was a star employee of Tulon Company, and Tulon had rapidly promoted her to the top management position in its Richmond office. There is no suggestion in the record that she did not perform her job well, that she was ever disciplined before the incident in this case, or that Tulon's Richmond office did not function successfully. Nevertheless, Chalmers was fired without warning after she sent a proselytizing letter to her supervisor as a continuation of their earlier religious discussions. The letter, written because of Chalmers' unease with her supervisor's business practices, urged her supervisor "to get right with God" by repenting. While the letter stated that the supervisor was doing "some things" that were not pleasing to God, it made no specific accusations. Chalmers sent the letter to her supervisor's home, explaining, "I wrote this letter at home so if you have a problem with it you can't relate it to work." She also wrote that she expected no response and that any response should be made to God.

. . .

### II

The legal analysis for a claim under those provisions must therefore address two burdens: Chalmers' burden of showing that she was fired because of a religious practice and Tulon's burden of demonstrating that it could not accommodate the practice without undue hardship.

To satisfy her burden and establish a *prima facie* case of religious discrimination under Title VII, Chalmers must prove (1) that she engaged in a religious practice, (2) that the employer discharged her or took other adverse employment action against her, and (3) that the employer's action was motivated at least in part by her religious practice. In short, she must show she was discharged "because of" the religious practice. Because Chalmers' conduct in sending proselytizing letters was unquestionably a religious practice and she was discharged, she has indisputably established the first two elements of her case. As for the third element, a factfinder could reasonably conclude that her discharge was motivated by the religious practice of sending proselytizing letters. Tulon advised Chalmers she was being terminated because she sent the two letters, and indeed, the majority appropriately notes that "the parties agree that Tulon fired Chalmers because she wrote the letters." In providing evidence to establish these three statutorily required elements, Chalmers has made out a *prima facie* case of religious discrimination. Yet the majority would impose a significantly greater burden on Chalmers without explaining how its views are either required or warranted by the statute.

## A

It is legal error to construe Title VII to impose a burden on the employee of informing her employer in advance about each practice the employee will follow in furtherance of religious beliefs. It is undoubtedly true that an employer cannot be held liable for religious discrimination by, for example, assigning an employee to work on Sunday when the employer has no knowledge that work on Sunday violates the employee's religious beliefs. But that does not impose an additional religious disclosure burden on Title VII plaintiffs. Instead, it is merely a recognition that Title VII's "because of" requirement cannot be satisfied where the employer has no knowledge that the conduct warranting discharge was religious in nature.

The majority has grafted a claim-defeating notice requirement onto the statutory requirements for establishing a *prima facie* case, concluding as a matter of law, "any knowledge Tulon may have possessed regarding Chalmers' beliefs could not reasonably have put it on notice that she would write and send accusatory letters to co-workers' homes." This notice requirement would preclude liability for every adverse employment action taken because of a religious practice if the employer did not know *in advance* that the practice would take place, even though the employer recognized the practice as religious in nature. Under that rule an employer would automatically be exonerated from liability when, *e.g.*, it fired an employee who arrived at work on Ash Wednesday with a cross of ashes marked on her forehead, because the employee violated a work rule against face paint. The irrationality of such a rule is readily apparent.

...

The majority's rule would mean that *as a matter of law* a Jew could not make out a *prima facie* case under Title VII if, on the first day of work, he was fired for wearing a yarmulke that, unknown to him, violated his company's dress code. Similarly, a Muslim would have no case for being fired the first time mandatory company meetings conflicted with his prayer schedule; a Jehovah's Witness would have none upon being fired for her disrespect in refusing to attend a company-wide celebration of the CEO's birthday; a Mormon would have none for being fired the first time he refused to work late on church-wide family nights. And, of course, as the majority concludes, an evangelical Baptist's case would fail as a matter of law if she is fired the first time she puts in writing the religious ideas that she has been permitted and encouraged to speak. This is not the law of Title VII. If the employer knows that conduct is religious when it makes the discharge decision "because of" that conduct, the *prima facie* elements of a religious discrimination claim have been satisfied.

## B

Even assuming that the law requires Chalmers to inform Tulon about the practices she might take in furtherance of her beliefs, the majority impermissibly finds facts when it says "any knowledge Tulon may have possessed regarding Chalmers' beliefs *could not reasonably have put it on notice* that she would write and send accusatory letters to co-workers' homes." (emphasis added). While one might be able to conclude that Tulon had no notice that the LaMantias would experience stress from Chalmers' letter—a fact irrelevant for assessing Chalmers' *prima facie* case—a factfinder would certainly be entitled to view the record and conclude (1) that LaMantia was aware that Chalmers believed she should urge co-workers to accept Jesus Christ and (2) that the letters were a religious practice in furtherance of that belief. Indeed, when viewed in a light most favorable to Chalmers, Chalmers' assertions that she discussed religion repeatedly with LaMantia, that LaMantia talked about his own religious encounters, that he showed Chalmers particular respect in the workplace, and that he never objected or took exception to any religious discussion with Chalmers could support the conclusion that he was encouraging her to continue her practices. The majority seems to conclude, however, that religious conversations are so dissimilar from written letters of identical content that a reasonable factfinder could never find sufficient employer notice of the employee's religious practices. But, if Tulon denies the sufficiency of notice based on LaMantia's experience with Chalmers, then the issue is in dispute and can only be resolved by factfinding.

### III

Once a plaintiff establishes a *prima facie* case under Title VII, the burden shifts to the employer to demonstrate that it is "unable to reasonably accommodate to the ... [religious] practice without undue hardship on the conduct of the employer's business." 42 U.S.C. § 2000e(j).

To meet its burden, Tulon must at a minimum demonstrate that Chalmers' practice was inconsistent with the needs of its workplace. Absent some inconsistency, Tulon cannot rely on the practice as a reason for discharging Chalmers. That is, if a religious practice is not in some way inconsistent with a company policy, custom, or requirement (whether explicit or not), permitting the practice cannot unduly burden the conduct of business. Yet Tulon has failed to demonstrate that the letters violated any company policy, custom, or requirement. Indeed, in briefing this case Tulon has pointedly conceded that it "had [no] policy prohibiting ... the sending of letters (religious or not) to the homes of Tulon employees." Nor has it established beyond dispute that sending the letters in fact disrupted the workplace. Despite the statements of Combs and Chalmers that the workplace was not disrupted, the majority finds the opposite. To conclude, as the majority has, that the employee disrupted the workplace requires several factual findings that are impermissible on review of a summary judgment.

Without Tulon even taking a position that it could not accommodate Chalmers' religious practice, the majority rules also that "Chalmers' conduct is not the type that an employer can possibly accommodate, even with notice." Even if it were within the majority's province to make such a finding, it could not do so on the present record, drawing all legitimate inferences in favor of Chalmers.

The majority assumes that Chalmers' "need" to write evangelical letters is absolute and that she would not stop writing them if asked to do so. This conclusion is drawn from the unsupported belief that Chalmers' "religious beliefs *required* her to send personal, disturbing letters to her co-workers," or that they "compelled her to write them," and that "she has a religious *need* to impose personally and directly on fellow employees." These conclusions, however, are not supported by the record. Chalmers stated that she was "*led* by the Lord" and "*inspired*" to write LaMantia. To conclude that these statements mean that she could not, consistent with her religious beliefs, accept requests to stop writing may not even be a legitimate inference, much less the only legitimate inference. Certainly, it requires factfinding, which we are not free to do.

The majority's holding that Chalmers' conduct was beyond accommodation is even more remarkable in light of the fact that the statute imposes the burden on the *employer* to demonstrate that a religious practice *cannot* be accommodated without undue hardship. The parties have not even been given an opportunity to explore that issue at trial. By ruling that as a matter of law Chalmers' conduct was not susceptible to accommodation, the majority in effect shifts to Title VII plaintiffs the burden of refuting a defense that the defendant neither asserted nor demonstrated.

### IV

Whatever we or the district court think about Chalmers' religious practices, it is not our place to preempt a trial of her claim by assuming that all factual disputes will be resolved against her. And we err legally by imposing a statutorily ungrounded prior notice requirement in circumstances where the employer fully appreciates the religious nature of a practice. Finally, we compound that error by shifting to the plaintiff a burden that the statute places on the defendant.

The judgment should be vacated and the case remanded for trial.

## Exercise 7.3

Shelly Sides, a Roman Catholic, made a vow after being inspired by God that she would be a "living witness" against abortion and that she would wear an anti-abortion button on her person at all times "until there was an end to abortion or until she could no longer fight the fight." The button shows a color photograph of an 18-week old fetus with the phrase "Stop Abortion." She wears the button at all times unless sleeping or bathing. She believes that taking off the button except during the aforementioned times would compromise her vow and lose her soul. Consistent with her vow, Sides wears her button to work every day at her job as a computer systems analyst at Data East Communications. Sides works in an office cubicle. During her interactions with co-workers, the button is clearly visible to fellow employees. Several co-workers complain to Data East management that the button is disturbing and offensive. The button causes substantial disruption in the workplace. Several employees threaten to walk off their jobs because of the button. However, some employees have no problem with the button. Data East has no company dress code policy.

Are there any reasonable accommodation(s) that Data East can offer Sides? Explain. Would permitting Sides to continue to wear the button cause Data East an undue hardship? Explain.

## Exercise 7.4

Jane has a religious belief that homosexuality is immoral and a religious belief that she is required to protest homosexuality. Jane's company adopts a policy that prohibits sexual orientation discrimination. Jane believes that such a policy offends her moral beliefs and that she has a duty to protest it. She does so by hanging signs outside her cubicle stating that homosexuality is wrong, all who practice it are going to hell, and that the company policy is immoral. The company comes to you seeking your advice on how to proceed. What should you tell the employer?

---

## ➤ Beyond the Basics: The Religious Employer Exemption

It should come as no surprise to you that religious entities are exempted from Title VII's prohibition against religious discrimination. For example, it is not a violation of Title VII for a Catholic church to refuse to hire a person for a position at the church because that person is not Catholic and instead hire a person who is a practicing Catholic. Section 702(a), 42 U.S.C. § 2000e-1(a) states:

> [Title VII] shall not apply … to a religious corporation, association, educational institution, or society with respect to the employment of individuals of a particular religion to perform work connected with the carrying on by such corporation, association, educational institution, or society of its activities.

Title VII also contains a separate provision directed to religious educational institutions. Section 703(e)(2); 42 U.S.C. § 2000e-2(e)(2) provides:

> [I]t shall not be an unlawful employment practice for a school, college, university, or educational institution or institution of learning to hire and employ employees of a particular religion if such school, college, university, or other educational institution or institution of learning is, in whole or in substantial part, owned, supported, controlled, or managed by a particular religion or by a particular religious corporation, association, or society, or if the curriculum of such school, college, university, or other educational institution or institution of learning is directed toward the propagation of a particular religion.

The policy underlying these exemptions is self-evident: a religious employer must have the freedom to make personnel decisions based on the institution's own religious tenets and beliefs so that the institution can promote and achieve its own religious purposes and missions. The Section 702 exemption extends to permit religious employers to discriminate in *non*-religious jobs as well as religious jobs in order for the institution to try and achieve its mission. *See Corporation of the Presiding Bishop v. Amos*, 483 U.S. 327 (1987). The Establishment Clause of the First Amendment is not violated when religious employers discriminate in hiring for *non*-religious jobs because "there is ample room [under the Clause] for benevolent neutrality which will permit religious exercise to exist without sponsorship and without interference." *Id.* at 334.

The Section 702 religious employer exemption applies only to those institutions whose purpose and character are primarily religious. The determination is to be made based on all significant religious and secular characteristics. Although no one factor is dispositive, significant factors to consider that would indicate whether a particular entity is religious include:

- Do its articles of incorporation state a religious purpose?
- Are its day-to-day operations religious (*e.g.*, are the services the entity performs, the products it produces, or the educational curriculum it provides directed toward propagation of the religion)?
- Is it not-for-profit?
- Is it affiliated with or supported by a church or other religious organization?

*See* EEOC Compliance Manual on Religious Discrimination No. 915.003 (July 22, 2008).

## Exercise 7.5

A religious corporation owned by The Church of Jesus Christ of Latter-Day Saints, the Mormon Church, discharges a building engineer from employment at the corporation because the engineer failed to qualify for a temple recommend. A temple recommend is a certificate that a person is a member of the Church and eligible to attend its temples. The building engineer job requirements are limited to designing, building, and maintaining the corporation's buildings. If the engineer sues the corporation for discriminating against him because he is non-Mormon in violation of Title VII, does §702 shield the corporation from liability? Should it shield the corporation from liability? Explain.

## ➤ Beyond the Basics: The Ministerial Exception to Federal Anti-Discrimination Statutes

The text of the federal employment discrimination statutes does not exempt religious institutions from discrimination because of other protected characteristics such as race, sex, national origin, age, or disability. Consequently, in theory, a church that discriminates against an employee on the basis of sex violates Title VII. But the Free Exercise rights of the church may trump Title VII and shield the church from liability in such a case because of what is called the ministerial exception to the anti-discrimination statutes. The ministerial exception is a judicially-created exception that is rooted in the First Amendment and based on the notion that religious institutions should be protected from governmental interference in selecting their ministers and religious leaders. Over the last 40 years, the federal circuits have recognized the ministerial exception in some form or fashion. *See, e.g., EEOC v. Roman Catholic Diocese of Raleigh*, 213 F.3d 795 (4th Cir. 2000); *Young v. Northern Illinois Conference of United Methodist Church*, 21 F.3d 184 (7th Cir. 1994); *EEOC v. Catholic Univ. of America*, 83 F.3d 455 (D.C. Cir. 1996). In 2012, the U.S. Supreme Court recognized the ministerial exception for the first time.

### Focus Questions: *Hosanna-Tabor Evangelical Lutheran Church and School v. EEOC*

1. *Which Constitutional amendment grounds the recognition of the ministerial exception to federal and state employment discrimination laws?*

2. *What is the policy underlying the exception?*

3. *What is the test for determining whether an employee of a religious institution fits within the ministerial exception? How does the Court define a "minister"?*

4. *Why did the plaintiff's employment fit within the ministerial exception?*

5. *How does the ministerial exception operate from a civil procedure perspective?*

6. *If you represented a religious organization, what steps would you advise the religious organization to take to ensure that its "ministers" fall within this exception?*

# Hosanna-Tabor Evangelical
# Lutheran Church and School v. EEOC

## 132 S. Ct. 694 (2012)

Chief Justice Roberts delivered the opinion of the Court.

Certain employment discrimination laws authorize employees who have been wrongfully terminated to sue their employers for reinstatement and damages. The question presented is whether the Establishment and Free Exercise Clauses of the First Amendment bar such an action when the employer is a religious group and the employee is one of the group's ministers.

### I
### A

Petitioner Hosanna-Tabor Evangelical Lutheran Church and School is a member congregation of the Lutheran Church-Missouri Synod, the second largest Lutheran denomination in America. Hosanna-Tabor operated a small school in Redford, Michigan, offering a "Christ-centered education" to students in kindergarten through eighth grade.

The Synod classifies teachers into two categories: "called" and "lay." "Called" teachers are regarded as having been called to their vocation by God through a congregation. To be eligible to receive a call from a congregation, a teacher must satisfy certain academic requirements. One way of doing so is by completing a "colloquy" program at a Lutheran college or university. The program requires candidates to take eight courses of theological study, obtain the endorsement of their local Synod district, and pass an oral examination by a faculty committee. A teacher who meets these requirements may be called by a congregation. Once called, a teacher receives the formal title "Minister of Religion, Commissioned." A commissioned minister serves for an open-ended term; at Hosanna-Tabor, a call could be rescinded only for cause and by a supermajority vote of the congregation.

"Lay" or "contract" teachers, by contrast, are not required to be trained by the Synod or even to be Lutheran. At Hosanna-Tabor, they were appointed by the school board, without a vote of the congregation, to one-year renewable terms. Although teachers at the school generally performed the same duties regardless of whether they were lay or called, lay teachers were hired only when called teachers were unavailable.

Respondent Cheryl Perich was first employed by Hosanna-Tabor as a lay teacher in 1999. After Perich completed her colloquy later that school year, Hosanna-Tabor asked her to become a called teacher. Perich accepted the call and received a "diploma of vocation" designating her a commissioned minister.

Perich taught kindergarten during her first four years at Hosanna-Tabor and fourth grade during the 2003–2004 school year. She taught math, language arts, social studies, science, gym, art, and music. She also taught a religion class four days a week, led the students in prayer and devotional exercises each day, and attended a weekly school-wide chapel service. Perich led the chapel service herself about twice a year.

Perich became ill in June 2004 with what was eventually diagnosed as narcolepsy. Symptoms included sudden and deep sleeps from which she could not be roused. Because of her illness, Perich began the 2004–2005 school year on disability leave. On January 27, 2005, however, Perich notified the school principal, Stacey Hoeft, that she would be able to report to work the following month. Hoeft responded that the school had already contracted with a lay teacher to fill Perich's position for the remainder of the school year. Hoeft also expressed concern that Perich was not yet ready to return to the classroom.

On January 30, Hosanna-Tabor held a meeting of its congregation at which school administrators stated that Perich was unlikely to be physically capable of returning to work that school year or the next. The congregation voted to offer Perich a "peaceful release" from her call, whereby the congregation would pay a portion of her health insurance premiums in exchange for her resignation as a called teacher. Perich refused to resign and produced a note from her doctor stating that she would be able to return to work on February 22. The school board urged Perich to reconsider, informing her that the school no longer had a position for her, but Perich stood by her decision not to resign.

On the morning of February 22 — the first day she was medically cleared to return to work — Perich presented herself at the school. Hoeft asked her to leave but she would not do so until she obtained written documentation that she had reported to work. Later that afternoon, Hoeft called Perich at home and told her that she would likely be fired. Perich responded that she had spoken with an attorney and intended to assert her legal rights.

Following a school board meeting that evening, board chairman Scott Salo sent Perich a letter stating that Hosanna-Tabor was reviewing the process for rescinding her call in light of her "regrettable" actions. Salo subsequently followed up with a letter advising Perich that the congregation would consider whether to rescind her call at its next meeting. As grounds for termination, the letter cited Perich's "insubordination and disruptive behavior" on February 22, as well as the damage she had done to her "working relationship" with the school by "threatening to take legal action." The congregation voted to rescind Perich's call on April 10, and Hosanna-Tabor sent her a letter of termination the next day.

### B

Perich filed a charge with the Equal Employment Opportunity Commission, alleging that her employment had been terminated in violation of the Americans with Disabilities Act, 42 U.S.C. § 12101 et seq. (1990)....

The EEOC brought suit against Hosanna-Tabor, alleging that Perich had been fired in retaliation for threatening to file an ADA lawsuit. Perich intervened in the litigation, claiming unlawful retaliation under both the ADA and the Michigan Persons with Disabilities Civil Rights Act. [citation omitted]. The EEOC and Perich sought Perich's reinstatement to her former position (or frontpay in lieu thereof), along with backpay, compensatory and punitive damages, attorney's fees, and other injunctive relief.

Hosanna-Tabor moved for summary judgment. Invoking what is known as the "ministerial exception," the Church argued that the suit was barred by the First Amendment because the claims at issue concerned the employment relationship between a religious institution and one of its ministers. According to the Church, Perich was a minister, and she had been fired for a religious reason — namely, that her threat to sue the Church violated the Synod's belief that Christians should resolve their disputes internally.

[The district court determined that the suit was barred by the ministerial exception and granted summary judgment in Hosanna-Tabor's favor. The Sixth Circuit Court of Appeals vacated and remanded back to the district court. The U.S. Supreme Court granted certiorari.]

### II

The First Amendment provides, in part, that "Congress shall make no law respecting an establishment of religion, or prohibiting the free exercise thereof." We have said that these two Clauses "often exert conflicting pressures," [citation omitted], and that there can be "internal tension ... between the Establishment Clause and the Free Exercise Clause," [citation omitted]. Not so here. Both Religion Clauses bar the government from interfering with the decision of a religious group to fire one of its ministers.

## A

[A discussion of the historical background that shaped the adoption of the Religion Clauses of the First Amendment and subsequent interpretations of the Religion Clauses by government officials is omitted. The Supreme Court pointed out through historical illustrations the importance of a religious institution's right to determine its religious leaders without any interference from the State.]

## B

Given this understanding of the Religion Clauses — and the absence of government employment regulation generally — it was some time before questions about government interference with a church's ability to select its own ministers came before the courts. This Court touched upon the issue indirectly, however, in the context of disputes over church property. Our decisions in that area confirm that it is impermissible for the government to contradict a church's determination of who can act as its ministers.

In *Watson v. Jones*, 80 U.S. 679 (1872), the Court considered a dispute between antislavery and proslavery factions over who controlled the property of the Walnut Street Presbyterian Church in Louisville, Kentucky. The General Assembly of the Presbyterian Church had recognized the antislavery faction, and this Court — applying not the Constitution but a "broad and sound view of the relations of church and state under our system of laws" — declined to question that determination. [citation omitted]. We explained that "whenever the questions of discipline, or of faith, or ecclesiastical rule, custom, or law have been decided by the highest of [the] church judicatories to which the matter has been carried, the legal tribunals must accept such decisions as final, and as binding on them." [citation omitted]. As we would put it later, our opinion in *Watson* "radiates ... a spirit of freedom for religious organizations, an independence from secular control or manipulation — in short, power to decide for themselves, free from state interference, matters of church government as well as those of faith and doctrine." [citation omitted].

... This Court reaffirmed these First Amendment principles in *Serbian Eastern Orthodox Diocese for United States and Canada v. Milivojevich*, 426 U. S. 696 (1976), a case involving a dispute over control of the American-Canadian Diocese of the Serbian Orthodox Church, including its property and assets. The Church had removed Dionisije Milivojevich as bishop of the American-Canadian Diocese because of his defiance of the church hierarchy. Following his removal, Dionisije brought a civil action in state court challenging the Church's decision, and the Illinois Supreme Court "purported in effect to reinstate Dionisije as Diocesan Bishop," on the ground that the proceedings resulting in his removal failed to comply with church laws and regulations.

Reversing that judgment, this Court explained that the First Amendment "permit[s] hierarchical religious organizations to establish their own rules and regulations for internal discipline and government, and to create tribunals for adjudicating disputes over these matters." When ecclesiastical tribunals decide such disputes, we further explained, "the Constitution requires that civil courts accept their decisions as binding upon them." [citation omitted]. We thus held that by inquiring into whether the Church had followed its own procedures, the State Supreme Court had "unconstitutionally undertaken the resolution of quintessentially religious controversies whose resolution the First Amendment commits exclusively to the highest ecclesiastical tribunals" of the Church.

C

Until today, we have not had occasion to consider whether this freedom of a religious organization to select its ministers is implicated by a suit alleging discrimination in employment. The Courts of Appeals, in contrast, have had extensive experience with this issue. Since the passage of Title VII of the Civil Rights Act of 1964, 42 U.S.C. § 2000e et seq., and other employment discrimination laws, the Courts of Appeals have uniformly recognized the existence of a "ministerial exception," grounded in the First Amendment, that precludes application of such legislation to claims concerning the employment relationship between a religious institution and its ministers.

We agree that there is such a ministerial exception. The members of a religious group put their faith in the hands of their ministers. Requiring a church to accept or retain an unwanted minister, or punishing a church for failing to do so, intrudes upon more than a mere employment decision. Such action interferes with the internal governance of the church, depriving the church of control over the selection of those who will personify its beliefs. By imposing an unwanted minister, the state infringes the Free Exercise Clause, which protects a religious group's right to shape its own faith and mission through its appointments. According the state the power to determine which individuals will minister to the faithful also violates the Establishment Clause, which prohibits government involvement in such ecclesiastical decisions.

The EEOC and Perich acknowledge that employment discrimination laws would be unconstitutional as applied to religious groups in certain circumstances. They grant, for example, that it would violate the First Amendment for courts to apply such laws to compel the ordination of women by the Catholic Church or by an Orthodox Jewish seminary. According to the EEOC and Perich, religious organizations could successfully defend against employment discrimination claims in those circumstances by invoking the constitutional right to freedom of association—a right "implicit" in the First Amendment. *Roberts v. United States Jaycees*, 468 U.S. 609, 622 (1984). The EEOC and Perich thus see no need—and no basis—for a special rule for ministers grounded in the Religion Clauses themselves.

We find this position untenable. The right to freedom of association is a right enjoyed by religious and secular groups alike. It follows under the EEOC's and Perich's view that the First Amendment analysis should be the same, whether the association in question is the Lutheran Church, a labor union, or a social club. That result is hard to square with the text of the First Amendment itself, which gives special solicitude to the rights of religious organizations. We cannot accept the remarkable view that the Religion Clauses have nothing to say about a religious organization's freedom to select its own ministers.

The EEOC and Perich also contend that our decision in *Employment Div., Dept. of Human Resources of Ore. v. Smith*, 494 U.S. 872 (1990), precludes recognition of a ministerial exception. In *Smith*, two members of the Native American Church were denied state unemployment benefits after it was determined that they had been fired from their jobs for ingesting peyote, a crime under Oregon law. We held that this did not violate the Free Exercise Clause, even though the peyote had been ingested for sacramental purposes, because the "right of free exercise does not relieve an individual of the obligation to comply with a valid and neutral law of general applicability on the ground that the law proscribes (or prescribes) conduct that his religion prescribes (or proscribes)." [citations omitted].

It is true that the ADA's prohibition on retaliation, like Oregon's prohibition on peyote use, is a valid and neutral law of general applicability. But a church's selection of its ministers is unlike an individual's ingestion of peyote. Smith involved government regulation of only outward physical acts. The present case, in contrast, concerns government interference with an internal church decision that affects the faith and mission of the church itself. [citation omitted]. The contention that *Smith* forecloses recognition of a ministerial exception rooted in the Religion Clauses has no merit.

## III

Having concluded that there is a ministerial exception grounded in the Religion Clauses of the First Amendment, we consider whether the exception applies in this case. We hold that it does. Every Court of Appeals to have considered the question has concluded that the ministerial exception is not limited to the head of a religious congregation, and we agree. We are reluctant, however, to adopt a rigid formula for deciding when an employee qualifies as a minister. It is enough for us to conclude, in this our first case involving the ministerial exception, that the exception covers Perich, given all the circumstances of her employment.

To begin with, Hosanna-Tabor held Perich out as a minister, with a role distinct from that of most of its members. When Hosanna-Tabor extended her a call, it issued her a "diploma of vocation" according her the title "Minister of Religion, Commissioned." She was tasked with performing that office "according to the Word of God and the confessional standards of the Evangelical Lutheran Church as drawn from the Sacred Scriptures." The congregation prayed that God "bless [her] ministrations to the glory of His holy name, [and] the building of His church." In a supplement to the diploma, the congregation undertook to periodically review Perich's "skills of ministry" and "ministerial responsibilities," and to provide for her "continuing education as a professional person in the ministry of the Gospel."

Perich's title as a minister reflected a significant degree of religious training followed by a formal process of commissioning. To be eligible to become a commissioned minister, Perich had to complete eight college-level courses in subjects including biblical interpretation, church doctrine, and the ministry of the Lutheran teacher. She also had to obtain the endorsement of her local Synod district by submitting a petition that contained her academic transcripts, letters of recommendation, personal statement, and written answers to various ministry-related questions. Finally, she had to pass an oral examination by a faculty committee at a Lutheran college. It took Perich six years to fulfill these requirements. And when she eventually did, she was commissioned as a minister only upon election by the congregation, which recognized God's call to her to teach. At that point, her call could be rescinded only upon a supermajority vote of the congregation—a protection designed to allow her to "preach the Word of God boldly."

Perich held herself out as a minister of the Church by accepting the formal call to religious service, according to its terms. She did so in other ways as well. For example, she claimed a special housing allowance on her taxes that was available only to employees earning their compensation "in the exercise of the ministry." In a form she submitted to the Synod following her termination, Perich again indicated that she regarded herself as a minister at Hosanna-Tabor, stating: "I feel that God is leading me to serve in the teaching ministry.... I am anxious to be in the teaching ministry again soon."

Perich's job duties reflected a role in conveying the Church's message and carrying out its mission. Hosanna-Tabor expressly charged her with "lead[ing] others toward Christian maturity" and "teach[ing] faithfully the Word of God, the Sacred Scriptures, in its truth and purity and as set forth in all the symbolical books of the Evangelical Lutheran Church." In fulfilling these responsibilities, Perich taught her students religion four days a week, and led them in prayer three times a day. Once a week, she took her students to a school-wide chapel service, and—about twice a year—she took her turn leading it, choosing the liturgy, selecting the hymns, and delivering a short message based on verses from the Bible. During her last year of teaching, Perich also led her fourth graders in a brief devotional exercise each morning. As a source of religious instruction, Perich performed an important role in transmitting the Lutheran faith to the next generation.

In light of these considerations—the formal title given Perich by the Church, the substance reflected in that title, her own use of that title, and the important religious functions she performed for the Church—we conclude that Perich was a minister covered by the ministerial exception. In reaching a contrary conclusion, the Court of Appeals committed three errors. First, the Sixth Circuit failed to see any relevance in the fact that Perich was a commissioned minister. Although such a title, by itself, does not automatically ensure coverage, the fact that an employee has been ordained or commissioned as a minister is surely relevant, as is the fact that significant religious training and a recognized religious mission underlie the description of the employee's position. It was wrong for the Court of Appeals—and Perich, who has adopted the court's view, to say that an employee's title does not matter.

Second, the Sixth Circuit gave too much weight to the fact that lay teachers at the school performed the same religious duties as Perich. We express no view on whether someone with Perich's duties would be covered by the ministerial exception in the absence of the other considerations we have discussed. But though relevant, it cannot be dispositive that others not formally recognized as ministers by the church perform the same functions—particularly when, as here, they did so only because commissioned ministers were unavailable.

Third, the Sixth Circuit placed too much emphasis on Perich's performance of secular duties. It is true that her religious duties consumed only 45 minutes of each work-day, and that the rest of her day was devoted to teaching secular subjects. The EEOC regards that as conclusive, contending that any ministerial exception "should be limited to those employees who perform exclusively religious functions." We cannot accept that view. Indeed, we are unsure whether any such employees exist. The heads of congregations themselves often have a mix of duties, including secular ones such as helping to manage the congregation's finances, supervising purely secular personnel, and overseeing the upkeep of facilities.

Although the Sixth Circuit did not adopt the extreme position pressed here by the EEOC, it did regard the relative amount of time Perich spent performing religious functions as largely determinative. The issue before us, however, is not one that can be resolved by a stopwatch. The amount of time an employee spends on particular activities is relevant in assessing that employee's status, but that factor cannot be considered in isolation, without regard to the nature of the religious functions performed and the other considerations discussed above.

Because Perich was a minister within the meaning of the exception, the First Amendment requires dismissal of this employment discrimination suit against her religious employer. The EEOC and Perich originally sought an order reinstating Perich to her former position as a called teacher. By requiring the Church to accept a minister it did not want, such an order would have plainly violated the Church's freedom under the Religion Clauses to select its own ministers.

Perich no longer seeks reinstatement, having abandoned that relief before this Court. But that is immaterial. Perich continues to seek frontpay in lieu of reinstatement, backpay, compensatory and punitive damages, and attorney's fees. An award of such relief would operate as a penalty on the Church for terminating an unwanted minister, and would be no less prohibited by the First Amendment than an order overturning the termination. Such relief would depend on a determination that Hosanna-Tabor was wrong to have relieved Perich of her position, and it is precisely such a ruling that is barred by the ministerial exception.

The EEOC and Perich suggest that Hosanna-Tabor's asserted religious reason for firing Perich—that she violated the Synod's commitment to internal dispute resolution—was pretextual. That suggestion misses the point of the ministerial exception. The purpose of the exception is not to safeguard a church's decision to fire a minister only when it is made for a religious reason. The exception instead ensures that the authority to select and control who will minister to the faithful—a matter "strictly ecclesiastical,"—is the church's alone.[1]

## IV

The EEOC and Perich foresee a parade of horribles that will follow our recognition of a ministerial exception to employment discrimination suits. According to the EEOC and Perich, such an exception could protect religious organizations from liability for retaliating against employees for reporting criminal misconduct or for testifying before a grand jury or in a criminal trial. What is more, the EEOC contends, the logic of the exception would confer on religious employers "unfettered discretion" to violate employment laws by, for example, hiring children or aliens not authorized to work in the United States.

Hosanna-Tabor responds that the ministerial exception would not in any way bar criminal prosecutions for interfering with law enforcement investigations or other proceedings. Nor, according to the Church, would the exception bar government enforcement of general laws restricting eligibility for employment, because the exception applies only to suits by or on behalf of ministers themselves. Hosanna-Tabor also notes that the ministerial exception has been around in the lower courts for 40 years, see *McClure v. Salvation Army*, 460 F.2d 553, 558 (CA5 1972), and has not given rise to the dire consequences predicted by the EEOC and Perich.

The case before us is an employment discrimination suit brought on behalf of a minister, challenging her church's decision to fire her. Today we hold only that the ministerial exception bars such a suit. We express no view on whether the exception bars other types of suits, including actions by employees alleging breach of contract or tortious conduct by their religious employers. There will be time enough to address the applicability of the exception to other circumstances if and when they arise.

The interest of society in the enforcement of employment discrimination statutes is undoubtedly important. But so too is the interest of religious groups in choosing who

---

1. A conflict has arisen in the Courts of Appeals over whether the ministerial exception is a jurisdictional bar or a defense on the merits. Compare *Hollins*, 474 F. 3d, at 225 (treating the exception as jurisdictional); and *Tomic v. Catholic Diocese of Peoria*, 442 F.3d 1036, 1038–1039 (CA7 2006) (same), with *Petruska*, 462 F. 3d, at 302 (treating the exception as an affirmative defense); *Bryce*, 289 F. 3d, at 654 (same); *Bollard v. California Province of Soc. of Jesus*, 196 F.3d 940, 951 (CA9 1999) (same); and *Natal*, 878 F. 2d, at 1576 (same). We conclude that the exception operates as an affirmative defense to an otherwise cognizable claim, not a jurisdictional bar. That is because the issue presented by the exception is "whether the allegations the plaintiff makes entitle him to relief," not whether the court has "power to hear [the] case." *Morrison v. National Australia Bank Ltd.*, 130 S. Ct. 2869 (2010), (internal quotation marks omitted). District courts have power to consider ADA claims in cases of this sort, and to decide whether the claim can proceed or is instead barred by the ministerial exception.

will preach their beliefs, teach their faith, and carry out their mission. When a minister who has been fired sues her church alleging that her termination was discriminatory, the First Amendment has struck the balance for us. The church must be free to choose those who will guide it on its way.

[The concurring opinions of Justices Thomas and Alito are omitted].

---

### Exercise 7.6

Pastor Lisa Perry served as the Associate Pastor of Calvin Presbyterian Church from December 2013 to December 2014. Shortly after she took the position, the Church's Senior Pastor, Steve Schmidt, made repeated gender-specific comments to her stating things like "this isn't a place for little women pastors" and "what do women know about running a church." He also made repeated comments to her about her "big boobs" and "hot body." On several occasions, he slapped her bottom. Pastor Perry formally complained to several church elders about Schmidt's behavior, but nothing was done by the Church to investigate her allegations.

On October 5, 2014, Pastor Perry filed a charge with the EEOC against the Church alleging sexual harassment. The Church placed her on leave on December 4, 2014, and the Church voted later that month to terminate its employment relationship with her. The Church subsequently notified Pastor Perry that its Committee on Ministry had decided against permitting her to circulate her church resume, or "personal information form," effectively preventing her from acquiring other pastoral employment in any Presbyterian church in the United States. Pastor Perry then filed a second charge with the EEOC alleging unlawful retaliation and subsequently filed a complaint in federal district court. The complaint asserted federal causes of action based on sexual harassment and the termination of employment, all in violation of Title VII.

The Church claims that Pastor Perry's Title VII claims are barred by the ministerial exception to Title VII. Do you agree? Why or why not? What information should Pastor Perry seek to discover from the Church regarding the applicability of the ministerial exception? How should Pastor Perry discover information in this case regarding the application of the ministerial exception?

---

### ➤ Beyond the Basics: Religious Discrimination and Public Employers

Public employers must consider the First Amendment as well as Title VII in situations where a public employee's religious beliefs and expression conflict with workplace requirements. *See Cruz v. Beto*, 405 U.S. 319, 322 (1972) (noting that the First Amendment is applicable to state-created governmental units by virtue of the Fourteenth Amendment); *Connick v. Myers*, 461 U.S. 138, 142 (1983) (holding that public employees do not relinquish the First Amendment rights they have as citizens). The catch-22 in these cases is that the government must respect its employees' Free Exercise of religion rights under the First Amendment while not violating the Establishment Clause by appearing to endorse its employees' religious expression. First Amendment jurisprudence under the Free Exercise clause requires that a public employer not substantially burden the employee's religious activities without a compelling governmental interest. This means that:

[T]he first amendment protects at least as much religious activity as Title VII does. Another way of framing that holding is to say that any religious activities of employees that can be accommodated without undue hardship to the employer [under Title VII], are also protected by the first amendment. In other words, if a governmental employer has violated Title VII, it has also violated the guarantees of the first amendment.

*Brown v. Polk County, Iowa*, 61 F.3d 650, 654 (8th Cir. 1995).

The Eighth Circuit's explanation of the law begs the question whether in some situations the First Amendment protects *more* religious activity than Title VII does. The answer is not clear. In *Pickering v. Board of Education*, 391 U.S. 563 (1968), the U.S. Supreme Court articulated a balancing test for resolving free speech cases brought by public employees against a governmental employer. Under this test, courts must balance the public employee's interest in commenting upon matters of public concern with the government's interest, as employer, in efficiently performing the public services it performs through its employees. The Ninth and Second Circuits have held that the *Pickering* balancing test applies to free exercise claims brought by public employees against their public employers where the employees allege that their religious activity connected to the job is constitutionally protected. *See Berry v. Dep't of Soc. Servs.*, 447 F.3d 642, 650 (9th Cir. 2006); *Knight v. State Dep't of Public Health*, 275 F.3d 156, 164 (2d Cir. 2001). Perhaps the *Pickering* balancing test is malleable enough that in the hands of some courts more religious activity could be constitutionally protected than would be the case under Title VII, but many cases exist where a public employer lawfully restricted its employees' religious expression under this test. *Berry*, 447 F.3d at 652 (concluding that "under the [*Pickering*] balancing test, the Department's need to avoid an appearance of endorsement of religion outweighs the curtailment on [the employee's] ability to display religious items in his cubicle, which is frequented by the Department's clients.").

## Exercise 7.7

Reconsider the "abortion button" case from one of the earlier exercises in this section. If the employer had been a public employer, would the employee be entitled to more protection under the First Amendment than Title VII provides? Should the outcome of the case be different because the employer is public instead of private? Why or why not?

# Chapter 8

# Disability Discrimination

The Americans with Disabilities Act ("ADA") was enacted in 1990 and signed into law by President George H.W. Bush. The ADA addresses disability discrimination with regards to employment, public services, and public accommodations provided by both public and private entities. The ADA is not the first federal disability discrimination statute. The Rehabilitation Act of 1973 created protections for disabled individuals in programs receiving federal financial assistance and for disabled individuals working for federal agencies or federal contractors. But the ADA was the first comprehensive federal effort to prohibit disability discrimination in both the private and public sectors in regards to both accommodations and employment. The focus of this Chapter is on the ADA and how it prohibits disability discrimination in employment.

Because the ADA deals with disability discrimination in various contexts, it is structurally different than the other statutes you have encountered. The ADA begins with a findings and purpose section and continues with a section that defines important terms that are used throughout the statute. 42 U.S.C. §§ 12101–12102. Five titles come after these beginning sections. Title I of the ADA deals with disability discrimination in employment. 42 U.S.C. §§ 12111–12117. The focus of this Chapter is on Title I. Title II covers disability discrimination by public entities. *Id.* §§ 12131–12181. Title III covers disability discrimination in public accommodations and services provided by private entities. *Id.* §§ 12181–12189. Title IV is a "Communications" section. *See* Pub. L. No. 101-336, 104 Stat. 366 (1990). Title V is titled "Miscellaneous Provisions." 42 U.S.C. §§ 12202–12213. Several of the miscellaneous provisions are relevant to disability discrimination in employment.

Over the years, the Supreme Court has interpreted terms of art under the ADA rather restrictively. On September 25, 2008, President George W. Bush signed into law the ADA Amendments Act of 2008 (ADAAA). The ADAAA became effective on January 1, 2009. One of the main purposes of the ADAAA is to reject the courts' restrictive interpretation of what "disability" means under the ADA and to establish a standard of broad coverage for individuals under the Act.

In enacting the ADA, Congress made the following findings:

Physical or mental disabilities in no way diminish a person's right to fully participate in all aspects of society, yet many people with physical or mental disabilities have been precluded from doing so because of discrimination; others who have a record of a disability or are regarded as having a disability also have been subjected to discrimination;

historically, society has tended to isolate and segregate individuals with disabilities, and, despite some improvements, such forms of discrimination against individuals with disabilities continue to be a serious and pervasive social problem;

discrimination against individuals with disabilities persists in such critical areas as employment, housing, public accommodations, education, transportation, communication, recreation, institutionalization, health services, voting, and access to public services; …

individuals with disabilities continually encounter various forms of discrimination, including outright intentional exclusion, the discriminatory effects of architectural, transportation, and communication barriers, overprotective rules and policies, failure to make modifications to existing facilities and practices, exclusionary qualification standards and criteria, segregation, and relegation to lesser services, programs, activities, benefits, jobs, or other opportunities; …

the Nation's proper goals regarding individuals with disabilities are to assure equality of opportunity, full participation, independent living, and economic self-sufficiency for such individuals; and

the continuing existence of unfair and unnecessary discrimination and prejudice denies people with disabilities the opportunity to compete on an equal basis and to pursue those opportunities for which our free society is justifiably famous, and costs the United States billions of dollars in unnecessary expenses resulting from dependency and nonproductivity.

42 U.S.C. § 12101(a).

The ADA prohibits discrimination and retaliation, just like the other statutes studied so far. Thus, it would be illegal for an employer to have a blanket policy prohibiting individuals with disabilities from working for the employer. Furthermore, it would constitute prohibited retaliation for an employer to terminate an individual for reasonably claiming protections under the ADA. Likewise, it would be inappropriate for the employer to harass individuals because of their disabilities. Like Title VII, the ADA also has a requirement that coverage under the Act requires that the employer must employ a certain number of employees—15.

However, unlike the other protected traits studied so far except religious discrimination, the ADA also requires that the employer accommodate disabilities in certain contexts. 42 U.S.C. § 12112(b)(5)(A). Further, it prohibits the employer from making medical inquiries in certain instances. 42 U.S.C. § 12112(d). The ADA also prohibits "excluding or otherwise denying equal jobs or benefits to a qualified individual because of the known disability of an individual with whom the qualified individual is known to have a relationship or association." 42 U.S.C. § 12112(b)(4).

Re-read the operative provisions of the ADA listed in Chapter 2. Notice that the ADA provides, among other things, that:

No covered entity shall discriminate against a qualified individual on the basis of disability in regard to job application procedures, the hiring, advancement, or discharge of employees, employee compensation, job training and other terms, conditions, and privileges of employment.

42 U.S.C. § 12111(a). From this operative provision, you can pick out several important terms: disability, qualified individual, and discriminate (which under the ADA is defined to include the failure to provide a reasonable accommodation, unless doing so would constitute an undue hardship). These terms will be described in the Chapter.

## ✦ Core Concept: Disability, Individuals, and Social Policy

The ADA provides important protections for individuals with disabilities; however, some would argue that it does not go far enough in providing individuals with disabilities realistic opportunities to work. Consider an individual who, because of a disability, uses a wheelchair and is not able to drive a car.

Think about the difficulties this individual might face in getting to and from job interviews and work. In a city without a reliable public transportation system, it may be difficult for the individual to get to work. Even in cities with public transportation systems, these systems may not be completely accessible to individuals with disabilities. Even with reliable, accessible public transportation, the individual may have difficulties getting from the public transportation system to the employer and these difficulties may be exacerbated by inclement weather or construction. If you do not use a wheelchair, the next time you travel from home to school, think about the route from the perspective of an individual who uses a wheelchair. What difficulties would you face?

This is just one example of the difficulties an individual with a disability might face that are not fully remedied by the ADA. Because of these deficiencies, some argue that the ADA should be supplemented with a social welfare model that attempts to assist the individual in all areas of living, not just the narrow areas protected by the ADA.

All people, disabled or not, should think deeply about how the law should assist disabled persons in employment and all other aspects of society. Vulnerability theory posits the idea that humans in general are vulnerable to impairment and that impairment (or the possibility of it) is a part of the common human experience. Think about how this conception of a person is different than the traditional model of an independent, fully functioning adult. Does vulnerability theory provide you a different way of thinking about the costs of accommodation or what kinds of accommodations should be offered? If you are not a person with a disability, think about ways in which you might become disabled in the future. Does thinking about this change the way you think about disability law? Does it help you think of the ADA as providing protections for all individuals, rather than just protections for individuals with disabilities? For more about vulnerability theory, see Ani Satz, *Disability, Vulnerability, and the Limits of Anti-Discrimination Law*, 83 WASH. L. REV. 513 (2008).

## ✦ Core Concept: Definition of Disability

For many ADA claims, to get protection under the statute, a person has to show that he or she has a "disability," as that term is defined by the ADA. There are three ways that this can be accomplished. The three-pronged definition of disability is maintained and is not changed by the ADAAA. The ADA defines a "disability" as:

(A) A physical or mental impairment that substantially limits one or more of the major life activities of such individual;

(B) A record of such an impairment; or

(C) Being regarded as having such an impairment.

42 U.S.C. § 12102(1)(A)-(1)(C).

Prior to the ADAAA, a plaintiff typically proceeded under the actual disability route. The "record of" route was not well-developed through case law. The "regarded as" route was very difficult to satisfy. And as a practical matter, the first route was difficult to satisfy because of case law interpretations of disability. The ADAAA clarifies that the courts should broadly construe the definition of disability under the ADA in favor of coverage. 42 U.S.C. § 12102(4).

If a person has a disability and satisfies the definition of being a "qualified individual," then the employer cannot discriminate against that person with respect to employment decisions because of the disability. Thus, if the person can do the job without any accommodation, the person's disability cannot be used against him or her in making an employment decision. Also if the person can do the job in spite of his or her disability but just needs a "reasonable accommodation" to do that, then the employer must provide that accommodation.

The thing to understand at the outset is that "disability" status is the first hurdle that one must pass through in order to get most of the benefits and protections of the statute. Note that a plaintiff need not have a disability, if he or she is trying to claim associational discrimination or retaliation under the ADA. An individual is not required to have a disability in order to claim that an employer is making improper medical inquiries under the statute. However, in most cases, the plaintiff must have a disability to fall within the statute's coverage. In other words, if an individual does not have a disability — as defined by the statute — the employer can use a medical condition against the individual in making an employment decision, whether or not that seems justifiably fair or not.

Disability status is based on satisfying the ADA's definition of disability and not on whether an individual is "disabled," as that term is defined under other federal statutes that may have different purposes. However, an individual who claims, for example, that she is totally disabled under the Social Security Act may have to explain any apparent inconsistency between claiming SSA disability status and later filing an ADA suit. In *Cleveland v. Policy Management Systems Corp.*, the Supreme Court declined to apply any legal presumption that would prohibit a person who has applied for, or received, Social Security Disability Insurance benefits from bringing an ADA suit. 526 U.S. 795 (1999). But, the Court stated that an earlier SSDI claim may pose a genuine conflict with an ADA claim, in some cases. If an apparent conflicts exists, the ADA plaintiff must proffer a sufficient explanation as to why the claims are not inconsistent.

## ✦ Core Concept: Actual Disability

The first way for a plaintiff to meet the definition of disability is to show a "physical or mental impairment that substantially limits one or more of the major life activities of such individual." 42 U.S.C. § 12102(1). This portion of the disability definition has been referred to as the actual disability prong.

Notice that this definition involves three separate concepts: (1) a physical or mental impairment that (2) substantially limits (3) one or more major life activities.

The first prong of the statute's definition of disability asks whether the person has a physical or mental impairment. The ADA did not define the term. But the EEOC, which is given the authority to promulgate regulations that interpret the statute, has set forth the following definition:

> Physical or mental impairment — any physiological disorder, or condition, cosmetic disfigurement, or anatomical loss affecting one or more of the following body systems: neurological, musculoskeletal, special sense organs, respiratory (including speech organs), cardiovascular, reproductive, digestive, genitorurinary, hemic and lymphatic, skin, and endocrine; or any mental or psychological disorder, such as mental retardation, organic brain syndrome, emotional or mental illness, and specific learning disabilities.

29 C.F.R. § 1630.2(h).

Cases interpreting the concept of physical or mental impairment have held that the following conditions constitute an impairment under the ADA.

- *Bragdon v. Abbott*, 524 U.S. 624 (1998) — HIV infection
- *Toyota Motor Manufacturing v. Williams*, 534 U.S. 184 (2002) — carpal tunnel syndrome
- *Sutton v. United Air Lines*, 527 U.S. 471 (1999) — severe myopia (nearsightedness)
- *Murphy v. UPS*, 527 U.S. 516 (1999) — hypertension (high blood pressure)

Neither the case law nor the regulation provides an exhaustive list of all the conditions that constitute impairments. The impairment question was found to be fairly easy to resolve in most cases prior to the ADAAA.

Although the impairment question was often easy to determine, the question of whether one's impairment "substantially limited a major life activity" became a more difficult question. A series of U.S. Supreme Court cases interpreted this language in such a restrictive manner that many people who one would think were disabled were actually not disabled under the statute. Most importantly, the Supreme Court, in *Sutton v. United Air Lines, Inc.*, held that in considering whether a person was substantially limited, courts were required to look at any mitigating measures that helped alleviate the disability.

---

## Focus Questions: *Sutton v. United Air Lines, Inc.*

1. Did the ADA, as originally enacted, specifically state whether disability status is determined by looking to corrective measures?

2. Are there persuasive policy reasons that would justify looking to mitigating measures in judging whether a person is truly disabled?

3. Please carefully consider Justice Stevens's point of view in the dissenting opinion. Is the majority unnecessarily keeping individuals from ADA protection?

---

# Sutton v. United Air Lines, Inc.

### 527 U.S. 471 (1999)

Justice O'Connor delivered the opinion of the Court.

. . .

### I

Petitioners are twin sisters, both of whom have severe myopia. Each petitioner's uncorrected visual acuity is 20/200 or worse in her right eye and 20/400 or worse in her left eye, but "with the use of corrective lenses, each ... has vision that is 20/20 or better." Consequently, without corrective lenses, each "effectively cannot see to conduct numerous activities such as driving a vehicle, watching television or shopping in public stores," but with corrective measures, such as glasses or contact lenses, both "function identically to individuals without a similar impairment."

In 1992, petitioners applied to respondent for employment as commercial airline pilots. They met respondent's basic age, education, experience, and FAA certification qualifications.

After submitting their applications for employment, both petitioners were invited by respondent to an interview and to flight simulator tests. Both were told during their interviews, however, that a mistake had been made in inviting them to interview because petitioners did not meet respondent's minimum vision requirement, which was uncorrected visual acuity of 20/100 or better. Due to their failure to meet this requirement, petitioners' interviews were terminated, and neither was offered a pilot position.

In light of respondent's proffered reason for rejecting them, petitioners filed a charge of disability discrimination under the ADA with the Equal Employment Opportunity Commission (EEOC). After receiving a right to sue letter, petitioners filed suit in the United States District Court for the District of Colorado, alleging that respondent had discriminated against them "on the basis of their disability, or because [respondent] regarded [petitioners] as having a disability" in violation of the ADA. Specifically, petitioners alleged that due to their severe myopia they actually have a substantially limiting impairment or are regarded as having such an impairment, and are thus disabled under the Act....

### III

... We turn first to the question whether petitioners have stated a claim under subsection (A) of the disability definition, that is, whether they have alleged that they possess a physical impairment that substantially limits them in one or more major life activities. *See* 42 U.S.C. § 12102(2)(A). Because petitioners allege that with corrective measures their vision "is 20/20 or better," they are not actually disabled within the meaning of the Act if the "disability" determination is made with reference to these measures. Consequently, with respect to subsection (A) of the disability definition, our decision turns on whether disability is to be determined with or without reference to corrective measures.

Petitioners maintain that whether an impairment is substantially limiting should be determined without regard to corrective measures. They argue that, because the ADA does not directly address the question at hand, the Court should defer to the agency interpretations of the statute, which are embodied in the agency guidelines issued by the EEOC and the Department of Justice. These guidelines specifically direct that the determination of whether an individual is substantially limited in a major life activity be made without regard to mitigating measures. *See* 29 C.F.R. pt. 1630, App. § 1630.2(j)....

Respondent, in turn, maintains that an impairment does not substantially limit a major life activity if it is corrected. It argues that the Court should not defer to the agency guidelines cited by petitioners because the guidelines conflict with the plain meaning of the ADA. The phrase "substantially limits one or more major life activities," it explains, requires that the substantial limitations actually and presently exist. Moreover, respondent argues, disregarding mitigating measures taken by an individual defies the statutory command to examine the effect of the impairment on the major life activities "of such individual." And even if the statute is ambiguous, respondent claims, the guidelines' directive to ignore mitigating measures is not reasonable, and thus this Court should not defer to it.

We conclude that respondent is correct that the approach adopted by the agency guidelines—that persons are to be evaluated in their hypothetical uncorrected state—is an impermissible interpretation of the ADA. Looking at the Act as a whole, it is apparent that if a person is taking measures to correct for, or mitigate, a physical or mental impairment, the effects of those measures—both positive and negative—must be taken into account when judging whether that person is "substantially limited" in a major life activity and thus "disabled" under the Act. The dissent relies on the legislative history of the ADA for the contrary proposition that individuals should be examined in their uncorrected state. Because we decide that, by its terms, the ADA cannot be read in this manner, we have no reason to consider the ADA's legislative history.

Three separate provisions of the ADA, read in concert, lead us to this conclusion. The Act defines a "disability" as "a physical or mental impairment that *substantially limits* one or more of the major life activities" of an individual. §12102(2)(A) (emphasis added). Because the phrase "substantially limits" appears in the Act in the present indicative verb form, we think the language is properly read as requiring that a person be presently— not potentially or hypothetically—substantially limited in order to demonstrate a disability. A "disability" exists only where an impairment "substantially limits" a major life activity, not where it "might," "could," or "would" be substantially limiting if mitigating measures were not taken. A person whose physical or mental impairment is corrected by medication or other measures does not have an impairment that presently "substantially limits" a major life activity. To be sure, a person whose physical or mental impairment is corrected by mitigating measures still has an impairment, but if the impairment is corrected it does not "substantially limit" a major life activity.

The definition of disability also requires that disabilities be evaluated "with respect to an individual" and be determined based on whether an impairment substantially limits the "major life activities of such individual." §12102(2). Thus, whether a person has a disability under the ADA is an individualized inquiry. *See Bragdon* v. *Abbott*, 524 U.S. 624 (1998) (declining to consider whether HIV infection is a *per se* disability under the ADA); 29 C.F.R. pt. 1630, App. §1630.2(j) ("The determination of whether an individual has a disability is not necessarily based on the name or diagnosis of the impairment the person has, but rather on the effect of that impairment on the life of the individual").

The agency guidelines' directive that persons be judged in their uncorrected or unmitigated state runs directly counter to the individualized inquiry mandated by the ADA. The agency approach would often require courts and employers to speculate about a person's condition and would, in many cases, force them to make a disability determination based on general information about how an uncorrected impairment usually affects individuals, rather than on the individual's actual condition. For instance, under this view, courts would almost certainly find all diabetics to be disabled, because if they failed to monitor their blood sugar levels and administer insulin, they would almost certainly be substantially limited in one or more major life activities. A diabetic whose illness does not impair his or her daily activities would therefore be considered disabled simply because he or she has diabetes. Thus, the guidelines approach would create a system in which persons often must be treated as members of a group of people with similar impairments, rather than as individuals. This is contrary to both the letter and the spirit of the ADA.

The guidelines approach could also lead to the anomalous result that in determining whether an individual is disabled, courts and employers could not consider any negative side effects suffered by an individual resulting from the use of mitigating measures, even when those side effects are very severe. This result is also inconsistent with the individualized approach of the ADA.

Finally, and critically, findings enacted as part of the ADA require the conclusion that Congress did not intend to bring under the statute's protection all those whose uncorrected conditions amount to disabilities. Congress found that "some 43,000,000 Americans have one or more physical or mental disabilities, and this number is increasing as the population as a whole is growing older." §12101(a)(1). This figure is inconsistent with the definition of disability pressed by petitioners.

... Because it is included in the ADA's text, the finding that 43 million individuals are disabled gives content to the ADA's terms, specifically the term "disability." Had Congress intended to include all persons with corrected physical limitations among those covered by the Act, it undoubtedly would have cited a much higher number of disabled persons in the findings. That it did not is evidence that the ADA's coverage is restricted to only those whose impairments are not mitigated by corrective measures.

The dissents suggest that viewing individuals in their corrected state will exclude from the definition of "disabled" those who use prosthetic limbs, or take medicine for epilepsy or high blood pressure. This suggestion is incorrect. The use of a corrective device does not, by itself, relieve one's disability. Rather, one has a disability under subsection A if, notwithstanding the use of a corrective device, that individual is substantially limited in a major life activity. For example, individuals who use prosthetic limbs or wheelchairs may be mobile and capable of functioning in society but still be disabled because of a substantial limitation on their ability to walk or run. The same may be true of individuals who take medicine to lessen the symptoms of an impairment so that they can function but nevertheless remain substantially limited. Alternatively, one whose high blood pressure is "cured" by medication may be regarded as disabled by a covered entity, and thus disabled under subsection C of the definition. The use or nonuse of a corrective device does not determine whether an individual is disabled; that determination depends on whether the limitations an individual with an impairment *actually* faces are in fact substantially limiting.

Applying this reading of the Act to the case at hand, we conclude that the Court of Appeals correctly resolved the issue of disability in respondent's favor. As noted above, petitioners allege that with corrective measures, their visual acuity is 20/20, and that they "function identically to individuals without a similar impairment." In addition, petitioners concede that they "do not argue that the use of corrective lenses in itself demonstrates a substantially limiting impairment." Accordingly, because we decide that disability under the Act is to be determined with reference to corrective measures, we agree with the courts below that petitioners have not stated a claim that they are substantially limited in any major life activity.

Justice Stevens, with whom Justice Breyer joins, dissenting.

When it enacted the Americans with Disabilities Act in 1990, Congress certainly did not intend to require United Airlines to hire unsafe or unqualified pilots. Nor, in all likelihood, did it view every person who wears glasses as a member of a "discrete and insular minority." Indeed, by reason of legislative myopia it may not have foreseen that its definition of "disability" might theoretically encompass, not just "some 43,000,000 Americans," 42 U.S.C. § 12101(a)(1), but perhaps two or three times that number. Nevertheless, if we apply customary tools of statutory construction, it is quite clear that the threshold question whether an individual is "disabled" within the meaning of the Act— and, therefore, is entitled to the basic assurances that the Act affords—focuses on her past or present physical condition without regard to mitigation that has resulted from re-habilitation, self-improvement, prosthetic devices, or medication. One might reasonably argue that the general rule should not apply to an impairment that merely requires a near-sighted person to wear glasses. But I believe that, in order to be faithful to the remedial purpose of the Act, we should give it a generous, rather than a miserly, construction.

I

... The three parts (of the definition of disability) do not identify mutually exclusive, discrete categories. On the contrary, they furnish three overlapping formulas aimed at ensuring that individuals who now have, or ever had, a substantially limiting impairment are covered by the Act.

An example of a rather common condition illustrates this point: There are many individuals who have lost one or more limbs in industrial accidents, or perhaps in the service of their country in places like Iwo Jima. With the aid of prostheses, coupled with courageous determination and physical therapy, many of these hardy individuals can perform all of their major life activities just as efficiently as an average couch potato. If the Act were just concerned with their present ability to participate in society, many of these individuals' physical impairments would not be viewed as disabilities. Similarly, if the statute were solely concerned with whether these individuals viewed themselves as disabled—or with whether a majority of employers regarded them as unable to perform most jobs—many of these individuals would lack statutory protection from discrimination based on their prostheses.

The sweep of the statute's three-pronged definition, however, makes it pellucidly clear that Congress intended the Act to cover such persons. The fact that a prosthetic device, such as an artificial leg, has restored one's ability to perform major life activities surely cannot mean that subsection (A) of the definition is inapplicable. Nor should the fact that the individual considers himself (or actually is) "cured," or that a prospective employer considers him generally employable, mean that subsections (B) or (C) are inapplicable. But under the Court's emphasis on "the present indicative verb form" used in subsection (A), that subsection presumably would not apply. And under the Court's focus on the individual's "present—not potential or hypothetical"—condition, and on whether a person is "precluded from a broad range of jobs," subsections (B) and (C) presumably would not apply.

In my view, when an employer refuses to hire the individual "because of" his prosthesis, and the prosthesis in no way affects his ability to do the job, that employer has unquestionably discriminated against the individual in violation of the Act. Subsection (B) of the definition, in fact, sheds a revelatory light on the question whether Congress was concerned only about the corrected or mitigated status of a person's impairment. If the Court is correct that "[a] 'disability' exists only where" a person's "present" or "actual" condition is substantially impaired, there would be no reason to include in the protected class those who were once disabled but who are now fully recovered. Subsection (B) of the Act's definition, however, plainly covers a person who previously had a serious hearing impairment that has since been completely cured. *See School Bd. of Nassau Cty.* v. *Arline,* 480 U.S. 273, 281 (1987). Still, if I correctly understand the Court's opinion, it holds that one who *continues to wear* a hearing aid that she has worn all her life might not be covered—fully cured impairments are covered, but merely treatable ones are not. The text of the Act surely does not require such a bizarre result.

The three prongs of the statute, rather, are most plausibly read together not to inquire into whether a person is currently "functionally" limited in a major life activity, but only into the existence of an impairment—present or past—that substantially limits, or did so limit, the individual before amelioration. This reading avoids the counterintuitive conclusion that the ADA's safeguards vanish when individuals make themselves more employable by ascertaining ways to overcome their physical or mental limitations. To the extent that there may be doubt concerning the meaning of the statutory text, ambiguity is easily removed by looking at the legislative history....

In my judgment, the Committee Reports and the uniform agency regulations merely confirm the message conveyed by the text of the Act—at least insofar as it applies to impairments such as the loss of a limb, the inability to hear, or any condition such as diabetes that is substantially limiting without medication. The Act generally protects individuals who have "correctable" substantially limiting impairments from unjustified employment discrimination on the basis of those impairments. The question, then, is whether the fact that Congress was specifically concerned about protecting a class that included persons characterized as a "discrete and insular minority" and that it estimated that class to include "some 43,000,000 Americans" means that we should construe the term "disability" to exclude individuals with impairments that Congress probably did not have in mind....

## II

... If a narrow reading of the term "disability" were necessary in order to avoid the danger that the Act might otherwise force United to hire pilots who might endanger the lives of their passengers, it would make good sense to use the "43,000,000 Americans" finding to confine its coverage. There is, however, no such danger in this case. If a person is "disabled" within the meaning of the Act, she still cannot prevail on a claim of discrimination unless she can prove that the employer took action "because of" that impairment, 42 U.S.C. § 12112(a), and that she can, "with or without reasonable accommodation, ... perform the essential functions" of the job of a commercial airline pilot. *See* § 12111(8). Even then, an employer may avoid liability if it shows that the criteria of having uncorrected visual acuity of at least 20/100 is "job-related and consistent with business necessity" or if such vision (even if correctable to 20/20) would pose a health or safety hazard. §§ 12113(a) and (b).

This case, in other words, is not about whether petitioners are genuinely qualified or whether they can perform the job of an airline pilot without posing an undue safety risk. The case just raises the threshold question whether petitioners are members of the ADA's protected class. It simply asks whether the ADA lets petitioners in the door in the same way as the Age Discrimination in Employment Act of 1967 does for every person who is at least 40 years old, *see* 29 U.S.C. § 631(a), and as Title VII of the Civil Rights Act of 1964 does for every single individual in the work force. Inside that door lies nothing more than basic protection from irrational and unjustified discrimination because of a characteristic that is beyond a person's control. Hence, this particular case, at its core, is about whether, assuming that petitioners can prove that they are "qualified," the airline has any duty to come forward with some legitimate explanation for refusing to hire them because of their uncorrected eyesight, or whether the ADA leaves the airline free to decline to hire petitioners on this basis even if it is acting purely on the basis of irrational fear and stereotype.

I think it quite wrong for the Court to confine the coverage of the Act simply because an interpretation of "disability" that adheres to Congress' method of defining the class it intended to benefit may also provide protection for "significantly larger numbers" of individuals, than estimated in the Act's findings....

Accordingly, although I express no opinion on the ultimate merits of petitioners' claim, I am persuaded that they have a disability covered by the ADA. I therefore respectfully dissent.

---

## Further Discussion

The *Sutton* Court's decision and its application to people who just need glasses or contacts to see "normally" might not seem that bad a result. The problem was that the holding penalized many individuals who most people would think are disabled simply because such individuals were able to successfully function despite their medical condition due to their own special efforts and dedication. For example, a person with severe diabetes might not be considered to be substantially limited if his or her condition was well-controlled by medication. A person who did not have a right leg might not be considered to be substantially limited if he was able to walk with the aid of a prosthetic limb.

The U.S. Supreme Court subsequently issued another decision that interpreted the ADA in a restrictive manner. In *Toyota Motor Manufacturing, Kentucky, Inc. v. Williams*, the Court held that to be limited in the major activity of working, the individual had to be limited in a broad class of jobs, not just the particular job in question. 534 U.S. 184 (2002). For example, an individual whose disability prohibited him from doing certain manual tasks associated with working on an automobile assembly line would not be considered to be substantially limited in the life activity of working, if the individual could perform other jobs. The Court also reiterated that the definition of disability must be interpreted strictly to create a demanding standard for qualifying as disabled. The Court held that to be substantially limited in performing a major life activity like manual tasks an individual must have an impairment that "prevents or *severely restricts* the individual from doing activities that are of central importance to most people's daily lives." *Id.* at 198.

The ADAAA provides for a broad reading of the definition of "disability" and the term "substantially limits" and specifically rejects the restrictive interpretations of those terms in the *Sutton* and *Williams* decisions. The ADAAA specifically provides that, in most circumstances, mitigating measures should not be considered in determining whether an impairment substantially limits a major life activity. However, there are special rules regarding mitigation and the effects of eye glasses and contact lenses. In making a determination about disability, the mitigating effects of normal eye glasses and contact lenses may be considered. The following contains pertinent ADAAA language that broadens the scope of coverage.

### ADA Amendments Act of 2008

Sec. 2. Findings and Purposes

(a) *Findings.*—Congress finds that—

(1) in enacting the Americans with Disabilities Act of 1990 (ADA), Congress intended that the Act "provide a clear and comprehensive national mandate for the elimination of discrimination against individuals with disabilities" and provide broad coverage; ...

(4) the holdings of the Supreme Court in *Sutton v. United Airlines, Inc.* and its companion cases have narrowed the broad scope of protection intended to be afforded by the ADA, thus eliminating protection for many individuals whom Congress intended to protect; ...

(7) in particular, the Supreme Court, in the case of *Toyota Motor Manufacturing, Kentucky, Inc. v. Williams*, interpreted the term "substantially limits" to require a greater degree of limitation than was intended by Congress; ...

(b) *Purposes.*—The purposes of this Act are—

(1) to carry out the ADA's objectives of providing "a clear and comprehensive national mandate for the elimination of discrimination" and "clear, strong, consistent, enforceable standards addressing discrimination" by reinstating a broad scope of protection to be available under the ADA;

(2) to reject the requirement enunciated by the Supreme Court in *Sutton v. United Air Lines, Inc.*, and its companion cases that whether an impairment substantially limits a major life activity is to be determined with reference to the ameliorative effects of mitigating measures; ...

(4) to reject the standards enunciated by the Supreme Court in *Toyota Motor Manufacturing, Kentucky, Inc. v. Williams,* that the terms "substantially" and "major" in the definition of disability under the ADA "need to be interpreted strictly to create a demanding standard for qualifying as disabled," and that to be substantially limited in performing a major life activity under the ADA "an individual must have an impairment that prevents or severely restricts the individual from doing activities that are of central importance to most people's daily lives";

(5) to convey congressional intent that the standard created by the Supreme Court in the case of *Toyota Motor Manufacturing, Kentucky, Inc. v. Williams* for "substantially limits", and applied by lower courts in numerous decisions, has created an inappropriately high level of limitation necessary to obtain coverage under the ADA, to convey that it is the intent of Congress that the primary object of attention in cases brought under the ADA should be whether entities covered under the ADA have complied with their obligations, and to convey that the question of whether an individual's impairment is a disability under the ADA should not demand extensive analysis; ...

### Americans with Disabilities Act as amended by the ADAAA

(4) Rules of construction regarding the definition of disability. — The definition of "disability" in paragraph (1) shall be construed in accordance with the following:

(B) The term "substantially limits" shall be interpreted consistently with the findings and purposes of the ADA Amendments Act of 2008.

(C) An impairment that substantially limits one major life activity need not limit other major life activities in order to be considered a disability.

(D) An impairment that is episodic or in remission is a disability if it would substantially limit a major life activity when active.

(E)(i) The determination of whether an impairment substantially limits a major life activity shall be made without regard to the ameliorative effects of mitigating measures such as—

(I) medication, medical supplies, equipment, or appliances, low-vision devices (which do not include ordinary eyeglasses or contact lenses), prosthetics including limbs and devices, hearing aids and cochlear implants or other implantable hearing devices, mobility devices, or oxygen therapy equipment and supplies;

(II) use of assistive technology;

(III) reasonable accommodations or auxiliary aids or services; or

(IV) learned behavioral or adaptive neurological modifications.

(ii) The ameliorative effects of the mitigating measures of ordinary eyeglasses or contact lenses shall be considered in determining whether an impairment substantially limits a major life activity....

42 U.S.C. § 12102(4).

The third part of the definition of actual disability requires that an impairment substantially affect a *major life activity*. The ADAAA broadly defines "major life activities" to include the following:

(A) In general

For purposes of paragraph (1), major life activities include, but are not limited to, caring for oneself, performing manual tasks, seeing, hearing, eating, sleeping, walking, standing, lifting, bending, speaking, breathing, learning, reading, concentrating, thinking, communicating, and working.

(B) Major bodily functions

For purposes of paragraph (1), a major life activity also includes the operation of a major bodily function, including but not limited to, functions of the immune system, normal cell growth, digestive, bowel, bladder, neurological, brain, respiratory, circulatory, endocrine, and reproductive functions.

42 U.S.C. § 12102(2).

The ADAAA clarifies that a condition that is episodic or in remission can constitute a disability, if it would substantially limit a major life activity when active. 42 U.S.C. § 12102 (4)(D).

## Exercise 8.1

Eric cannot read. Can Eric proceed under the "actual disability" prong of the ADA?

## Exercise 8.2

Sally has multiple sclerosis. She believes that she has been terminated after her employer found out about her condition. In determining whether Sally meets the definition of having an actual disability, what kinds of questions do you need to ask Sally?

## Exercise 8.3

Tom has severe hearing loss in both ears. Tom wears hearing aids that mitigate the effects of his hearing loss so that his hearing loss is mild. Under the pre-ADAAA interpretation of disability, would Tom be considered to be a person with a disability? What about under the current definition?

## ✦ Core Concept: Record of Disability

Prior to the ADAAA, courts required plaintiffs to meet an almost impossible set of facts to establish a "record of" disability claim. Not only did the employer have to have a record of the employee's impairment, but the record also had to reflect that the impairment substantially limited a major life activity. Thus, if an employer had a record showing that it knew an employee might have cancer, a court might deny a "record of" claim by reasoning that the simple notation of cancer did not establish that the employer thought the cancer substantially limited a major life activity.

Given the broad reading to be given to the definition of disability under the ADAAA, it is believed that the prior restrictions on "record of" claims are no longer appropriate. However, the precise contours of "record of" claims under the ADAAA remain to be developed through case law interpreting the Act.

### ✦ Core Concept: Regarded as Disabled

Under the original definition of "regarded as" under the ADA, an individual who had no impairment at all but was treated as having a substantially limiting impairment would be protected under the ADA. Similarly, an individual who had an impairment, but one that was not substantially limiting, would be covered if the defendant incorrectly believed the impairment was substantially limiting. This prong of the definition was designed to deal with employers acting against a person because of fears, myths, or stereotypes about the person's disability and/or disease.

Prior to the ADAAA, courts interpreted the "regarded as" prong to require that the employee prove that the employer regarded the individual as having an impairment that substantially limited a major life activity. From a practical perspective, it was very difficult for plaintiffs to make this showing.

The ADAAA made a big change in the "regarded as" prong. An individual meets the requirement of being "regarded as having such an impairment" if the individual establishes that "he or she has been subjected to an action prohibited under this Act because of an actual or perceived physical or mental impairment whether or not the impairment limits or is perceived to limit a major life activity." 42 U.S.C. § 12102(3).

In other words, an ADA plaintiff no longer must prove that the defendant's misperception of his or her condition was *so severe* as to amount to a belief that the condition substantially limited a major life activity. If the impairment motivated the employer's adverse employment action, the plaintiff is protected no matter how limiting the impairment actually is or is perceived to be by the employer. In short, the plaintiff is protected from discrimination because of his impairment whether real or perceived. However, the ADAAA does not prohibit an employer from taking an action if it regards an individual as having an impairment that is transitory and minor in nature, which the statute defines as having a duration of six months or less. 42 U.S.C. § 12102(3). For example, an employer might be able to take action against an employee who suffers a (normally) broken leg.

The amendments clarify that "regarded as" plaintiffs are not entitled to reasonable accommodation. 42 U.S.C. § 12201(h). In order to be entitled to a reasonable accommodation, an individual must have an actual disability. Accordingly, the ADAAA overturned the line of prior cases which held that "regarded as" plaintiffs are entitled to reasonable accommodation. *See D'Angelo v. Conagra Foods*, 422 F.3d 1220 (11th Cir. 2005); *Kelly v. Metallics West, Inc.*, 410 F.3d 670 (10th Cir. 2005); *Williams v. Phila. Hous. Author. Police Dep't*, 380 F.3d 751 (3d Cir. 2004).

### ➤ Beyond the Basics: The Three-Pronged Definition of Disability and the ADAAA

The ADA Amendments Act became effective on January 1, 2009. As of the date of publication of this textbook, few reported circuit court cases exist applying the ADAAA.

The following case is one of the first reported cases to consider the amendments and their impact on the definition of disability.

---

### Focus Questions: *Horgan v. Morgan Services, Inc.*

1.  *Actual Disability. Does HIV positive status itself substantially limit a major life activity under the ADAAA? If so, is this result different from the result that would have existed prior to the amendments?*

2.  *Regarded as Disabled. What allegations suggested that the employer terminated the Plaintiff's employment because it regarded his HIV positive status as an impairment?*

3.  *Pleadings. Is it relevant that the district court addresses the disability question at the 12(b)(6) stage of litigation? How should the case turn out on summary judgment?*

---

# Horgan v. Morgan Services, Inc.

No. 09-C-6796, 2010 U.S. Dist. LEXIS 36915 (N.D. Ill. April 12, 2010)

District Judge Castillo.

### *Memorandum Opinion and Order*

Kenneth Horgan ("Plaintiff") brings this action alleging employment discrimination and invasion of privacy against Timothy Simmons and Morgan Services, Inc. Plaintiff claims that Defendants unlawfully terminated him because of his disability and impermissibly inquired as to his disability under the Americans with Disabilities Act ("ADA").... Currently before the Court is Defendants' motion to dismiss pursuant to Federal Rule of Civil Procedure 12(b)(6).

### *Relevant Facts*

Plaintiff has been diagnosed as HIV positive for the past ten years, but kept his status confidential, disclosing his medical condition only to his close friends. In February 2001, he began working for Morgan, a linen and uniform rental services company, as a sales manager in Los Angeles. In January 2008, Defendants promoted him to General Manager of the Chicago facility. Plaintiff claims that his HIV positive status never interfered with his ability to perform the essential functions of his job and that he "has always met or exceeded Morgan's legitimate expectations." Specifically, in 2009, Plaintiff claims he brought in a lucrative account with the company's "biggest customer in the country."

Simmons is Morgan's president and was Plaintiff's supervisor in Chicago. On July 15, 2009, Plaintiff alleges that Simmons asked to meet with him for what Simmons termed a "social visit." During their visit, Plaintiff alleges that Simmons "told plaintiff that he was really worried about him." When Plaintiff responded by discussing his work performance, Plaintiff claims that Simmons cut him off saying "this is not about results." Plaintiff alleges that Simmons then "demanded" to know what was going on with him, telling Plaintiff that "if there was something medical going on, [he] needed to know." Plaintiff insisted that there was nothing that affected his ability to work. However, Plaintiff claims that

Simmons "continued to insist there was something physical or mental that was affecting [Plaintiff]." Plaintiff claims he was "compelled to tell Simmons that he was HIV positive," but he assured Simmons that his status did not affect his ability to do his job.

Plaintiff alleges that Simmons then asked him about his prognosis. Plaintiff responded that "he had been HIV positive for a long time and that the condition was under control and that his T-cell count was over 300." Next, Plaintiff alleges that Simmons asked "what would happen if his T-cell count went below 200," and Plaintiff replied that he would then have AIDS. After urging Plaintiff to inform his family about his condition, Plaintiff alleges that Simmons asked him "how he could ever perform his job with his HIV positive condition and how he could continue to work with a terminal illness." Additionally, Plaintiff claims that Simmons told him "that a General Manager needs to be respected by the employees and have the ability to lead," and indicated that he "did not know how [Plaintiff] could lead if the employees knew about his condition."

Simmons allegedly ended the meeting by telling Plaintiff that he needed "to recover" and that he should "go on vacation" and "leave the plant immediately." Simmons then told Plaintiff that he would discuss the situation with Morgan's owner. The next day, Plaintiff alleges that he received a copy of an email sent to all general managers and corporate staff indicating that "effective immediately" Plaintiff was "no longer a member of Morgan."

### 12(b)(6) Standard

A motion under Rule 12(b)(6) challenges the sufficiency of the complaint. In ruling on a motion to dismiss brought pursuant to Rule 12(b)(6), the court construes the complaint "in the light most favorable to the nonmoving party, accept[ing] well-pleaded facts as true, and draw[ing] all inferences in her favor." [citation omitted]. To survive a motion to dismiss, the complaint must overcome "two easy-to-clear hurdles": (1) "the complaint must describe the claim in sufficient detail to give the defendant fair notice of what the claim is and the grounds on which it rests"; and (2) "its allegations must actually *suggest* that the plaintiff has a right to relief, by providing allegations that raise a right to relief above the 'speculative level.'" [citation omitted].

### Analysis

The ADA makes it unlawful for an employer to "discriminate against a qualified individual on the basis of disability in regard to ... terms, conditions, and privileges of employment." 42 U.S.C. § 12112(a). "To prevail on an ADA claim, the plaintiff must show (1) he is disabled; (2) he is qualified to perform the essential function of the job with or without accommodation; and (3) he suffered an adverse employment action because of his disability." [citation omitted]. The ADA defines "disability," with respect to an individual, as: (1) "a physical or mental impairment that substantially limits one or more major life activities of such individual"; (2) "a record of such an impairment"; or (3) "being regarded as having such an impairment." 42 U.S.C. § 12102(1). Plaintiff alleges that he was terminated on the basis of his disability: being HIV positive. Although Defendants acknowledge that being HIV positive is a physical impairment, they argue that Plaintiff has not pled "a limitation of a major life activity," and thus fails to state a claim of disability under the ADA.

[Actual Disability]

Effective January 1, 2009, Congress amended the ADA to "[reinstate] a broad scope of protection." *See* ADA Amendments Act of 2008 ("ADAAA"), Pub. L. No. 110-325, 122 Stat. 3553 (2008). Specifically, Congress found that the Supreme Court had "narrowed" the protection intended to be afforded by the ADA, and through the ADAAA rejected the holdings of *Sutton v. United Air Lines, Inc.*, 527 U.S. 471 (1999) and *Toyota Motor Manufacturing, Kentucky, Inc., v. Williams*, 534 U.S. 184 (2002).... Although the ADAAA left the ADA's three-category definition of "disability" intact, significant changes were made to how these categories were interpreted.

As relevant to this case, the ADAAA clarified that the operation of "major bodily functions," including "functions of the immune system," constitute major life activities under the ADA's first definition of disability. In addition, "an impairment that is episodic or in remission is a disability if it would substantially limit a major life activity when active." Congress also instructed that "[t]he term 'substantially limits' shall be interpreted consistently with the findings and purposes of the [ADAAA]." Noting that courts had "created an inappropriately high level of limitation," the ADAAA states that "it is the intent of Congress that the primary object of attention in cases brought under the ADA should be whether entities covered under the ADA have complied with their obligations...." Therefore, the "question of whether an individual's impairment is a disability under the ADA should not demand extensive analysis."

Defendants claim that even with the additional language of the ADAAA, Plaintiff fails to plead a disability sufficient to state an actionable ADA claim. This Court disagrees. Drawing all inferences in Plaintiffs favor, it is certainly plausible — particularly, under the amended ADA — that Plaintiff's HIV positive status substantially limits a major life activity: the function of his immune system. Such a conclusion is consistent with the EEOC's proposed regulations to implement the ADAAA which lists HIV as an impairment that will consistently meet the definition of disability. [citation omitted].

Relying primarily on the decision in *Lee's Log Cabin*, Defendants argue that a substantial limitation of an identifiable major life activity is "an essential basis" to establish a claim for relief under the ADA. In that case, the Seventh Circuit "decline[d] to adopt" a rule that HIV is a *per se* disability under the ADA. However, the court explicitly stated that its decision, which was decided at the summary judgment stage, should not "be read to suggest that the EEOC's complaint failed to state a claim." The Court finds that the level of pleading which Defendants argue is not required at this stage. *See* Fed. R. Civ. P. 8(a)(2).

[Regarded as Disabled]

Further, although Plaintiff does not argue it in his brief, the complaint also establishes a disability under the third definition set forth by the ADA because he was regarded as having any impairment. "An individual meets the requirement of 'being regarded as having such an impairment' if the individual establishes that he or she has been subjected to an action prohibited under [the ADA] because of an actual or perceived physical or mental impairment whether or not the impairment limits or is perceived to limit a major life activity." 42 U.S.C. § 12102(3)(A). Here, Plaintiff alleges that when he told Simmons that he was HIV positive, Simmons allegedly told Plaintiff that "a General Manager needs to be respected by the employees and have the ability to lead" and that Simmons "did not know how [Plaintiff] could lead if the employees knew about his condition." The next day, Plaintiff alleges that he was terminated. This Court finds that such allegations are sufficient to plausibly suggest that Plaintiff was terminated because Defendants regarded his HIV positive status as an impairment.

Accordingly, this Court finds that Plaintiff has overcome the "two easy-to-clear hurdles" necessary to survive a motion to dismiss: (1) Defendants have notice of the claims and the grounds on which they rest; and (2) the allegations suggest that Plaintiff has a right to relief. Defendants' motion to dismiss Plaintiff's first claim is therefore denied.

## Exercise 8.4

Juan has an auto-immune condition called Reiter's syndrome, which causes pain in the joints and makes it difficult to walk during "flare-ups." Juan works as a mechanic and his job involves bending and squatting. Juan's employer fires him immediately after learning that Juan has an immune system abnormality, stating that "I don't see how you can work here if you have pain in your joints due to this immune disorder." Did Juan's employer terminate his employment because it regarded him as disabled? If Juan proves that the employer acted on the basis of his auto-immune condition, does Juan's "regarded as" claim depend on how limiting Juan's condition actually is?

## ✦ Core Concept: Qualified Individual

The ADA prohibits a covered entity from discriminating against a "qualified individual on the basis of disability." 42 U.S.C. § 12112. After considering whether an individual has a disability, as that term is defined by the statute, it must be determined whether the individual is a qualified individual under the statute. This limitation is important because the ADA is not a welfare program and does not require the employment of all individuals who have disabilities.

The statute defines the term "qualified individual" as follows:

> an individual who, with or without reasonable accommodation, can perform the essential functions of the employment position that such individual holds or desires. For the purposes of this subchapter, consideration shall be given to the employer's judgment as to what functions of a job are essential, and if an employer has prepared a written description before advertising or interviewing applicants for the job, this description shall be considered evidence of the essential functions of the job.

42 U.S.C. § 12111(8).

This definition provides several important pieces of information. First, an individual is qualified if he or she can perform the essential functions of a job without an accommodation. Thus, it would be illegal for a covered entity to terminate an individual because of a disability if the individual could perform his or her job functions, unless the employer could assert another defense to liability.

Note, that the definition only requires the employee be able to perform the essential functions of his or her job. This means that an employer may not take action against an employee, if the employee is unable to perform non-essential functions of the job. In determining whether a function is essential, courts may consider the functions listed in any written job descriptions issued by the employer. 42 U.S.C. § 12111(8). However, the job description is not given complete deference.

In considering whether a job function is essential, courts will often consider (1) whether individuals in the plaintiff's position are actually required to perform a certain job function and (2) if individuals are required to perform the job function, whether removal of the job function would fundamentally alter the job. In other words, the ADA may require an employer to eliminate a non-essential function of an employee's job, if the employee cannot perform the function because of a disability.

In determining whether a job function is essential, the amount of time spent on the job performing the function is relevant. But, in some cases, a particular job function will be essential even if rarely required. Consider the following Tenth Circuit opinion.

---

**Focus Question:** *Hennagir v. Utah Department of Corrections*

*Why is the rarely required job function in this case—emergency response reaction—an essential function for the position of physician's assistant at a prison?*

---

# Hennagir v. Utah Department of Corrections
## 587 F.3d 1255 (10th Cir. 2009)

Circuit Judge Lucero.

… This case requires us to determine whether a job function that is rarely required in the normal course of an employee's duties may nonetheless be an essential job function under the Americans with Disabilities Act, 42 U.S.C. § 12101 *et seq.* ("ADA"). We conclude that when the potential consequences of employing an individual who is unable to perform the function are sufficiently severe, such a function may be deemed essential. We further conclude that it is unreasonable for an employee to demand identical job duties less the disputed essential job requirement, regardless of the label given to the proposed accommodation.

Plaintiff Barbara Hennagir was employed as a physician's assistant ("PA") by the Utah Department of Corrections ("DOC"). Following several years of successful work by Hennagir, DOC added a physical safety training requirement to medical and clinical positions that required inmate contact, including Hennagir's position. Unable to complete the training because of a number of physical impairments, Hennagir complained of disability discrimination and requested that she be able to continue in her position without fulfilling the new requirement. DOC refused, leading to this lawsuit.

I

From April 1997 until August 2005, Hennagir was employed as a PA at DOC's Central Utah Correctional Facility in Gunnison, Utah ("Gunnison"). When she was hired, DOC did not require Peace Officer Standards and Training ("POST") certification for medical and clinical staff at Gunnison. In 2001, however, DOC sought to enter such staff into Utah's Public Safety Retirement system ("PSR"). To enroll in PSR, all covered positions in the agency must be POST certified. POST certification includes an assessment of physical strength, flexibility, and endurance.

DOC considered the POST certification requirement for medical staff for several years. As early as September 1998, a DOC division director recommended POST certification to the executive director. In 1999, a medical technician was attacked by a Gunnison inmate, and the victim sued DOC and a number of its employees, leading the State Risk Management Division to echo the POST certification recommendation. The following year, DOC clinical services administrators met to discuss POST certification. At that meeting, questions were raised as to whether incumbent employees could be "grandfathered" in—that is, exempted from the POST requirement based on their status as current employees.

In 2001, DOC contacted Utah Retirement Systems ("URS") regarding its plan to enroll medical and clinical personnel in PSR. URS advised that workers could be eligible for PSR only if every employee in a given position was POST certified. In 2002, DOC applied for PSR for all its clinical personnel whose job duties required contact with inmates. Because Hennagir's PA position at Gunnison included inmate contact, it was approved for PSR, and thus POST certification was mandated.

Gunnison medical staff began attending a POST "academy" in October of 2002. Hennagir attended, but was given permission not to participate in the physical activities because of her medical conditions. Hennagir complains of a number of impairments, including lupus, osteoarthritis, rheumatism, avascular necrosis, Sjogren's syndrome, and fibromyalgia. She has had both hips replaced and undergone surgery on her left shoulder. As a result of these maladies, Hennagir is limited in activities such as sitting, bathing, sleeping, lifting, bending and flexing, climbing stairs, running, and biking.

DOC eventually opted to require POST certification for incumbent employees. In October 2003, Hennagir was notified that she would be unable to continue working as a PA at Gunnison because she was unable to meet the POST certification requirement.

[The court describes how Hennagir filed an administrative grievance, EEOC charge, and a lawsuit claiming that DOC violated the ADA when it required her to meet the POST certification requirement and took an adverse employment action against her, ultimately terminating her employment, because she did not satisfy the POST certification requirement.]

I

A

Hennagir first argues that DOC discriminated against her in violation of the ADA. To succeed on an ADA claim, a plaintiff must show: (1) she is disabled as defined by the ADA; (2) she is qualified to perform the essential functions of the job with or without reasonable accommodation; and (3) she suffered discrimination on the basis of her disability. [citation omitted]. Because each of these elements is essential to an ADA claim, and we conclude that Hennagir cannot satisfy the "qualified individual" prong, we need not address remaining elements. [citation omitted].

Hennagir bears the burden of showing that she is able to perform the essential functions of her job, with or without reasonable accommodation. To determine whether POST certification is an essential job function, we begin by deciding "whether [DOC] actually requires all employees in the particular position to satisfy the alleged job-related requirement." [citation omitted]. If it does, we look to whether POST certification is fundamental to the Gunnison PA position. Among the factors we consider in this inquiry are:

    (i) The employer's judgment as to which functions are essential;

    (ii) Written job descriptions prepared before advertising or interviewing applicants for the job;

    (iii) The amount of time spent on the job performing the function;

    (iv) The consequences of not requiring the incumbent to perform the function;

    (v) The terms of a collective bargaining agreement;

    (vi) The work experience of past incumbents in the job; and/or

    (vii) The current work experience of incumbents in similar jobs.

29 C.F.R. § 1630.2(n)(3). However, this analysis "is not intended to second guess the employer or to require him to lower company standards.... Provided that any necessary job specification is job-related, uniformly enforced, and consistent with business necessity, the employer has a right to establish what a job is and what is required to perform it." [citation omitted].

The undisputed evidence shows that all PAs at Gunnison must become POST certified. Under URS rules, all employees in a position must achieve POST certification once that position is approved for PSR enrollment. Further, Medical Director Garden testified that every medical doctor, registered nurse, and PA at Gunnison had become POST certified. Hennagir does not attempt to controvert this evidence. Instead, she argues that POST certification was not required when she was hired, that she successfully performed her job duties for years without being POST certified, and that the POST certification requirement was added to the PA position in order to qualify for PSR, not because it is essential.

We begin by noting that the essential function inquiry is not conducted as of an individual's hire date. "The ADA does not limit an employer's ability to establish or change the content, nature, or functions of a job." [citation omitted]. We must look instead to whether a job function was essential at the time it was imposed on Hennagir. We conclude it was.

We weigh heavily the employer's judgment regarding whether a job function is essential. *See* 29 C.F.R. § 1630.2(n)(3)(I) (listing "[t]he employer's judgment as to which functions are essential" as a factor to be considered). DOC decision-makers are unanimous regarding the importance of POST certification. As early as 1998, a DOC division director sought to implement POST certification for medical staff because "[t]he institutional setting requires, first and foremost, that all employees have a security mission," and the lack of certification "tends to create a conflict amongst our staff as to who's [sic] responsibility it is to ensure safety and control." Michael Chabries, DOC's Executive Director when the POST certification requirement was implemented, explained that, "like certified corrections officers, the medical staff often had daily, direct inmate contact and thus daily exposure to the myriad risks of working with an inmate population." By enrolling these employees in PSR, Chabries stated, "the Department could require these employees to become fully trained and certified as peace officers and thus better able to handle, directly, the risks and dangers found at the prison's facilities." Garden opined that "POST certification is important in terms of training, insuring that the staff are not injured, [and] that the staff understand the danger of working in that environment."

Further, the risks involved in direct inmate contact strike at the heart of another factor used to determine whether a job function is essential: the consequences of not requiring an employee to perform the function. *See* 29 C.F.R. § 1630.2(n)(3)(iv). Sadly, DOC's fears regarding the physical safety of its medical and clinical staff were realized in 1999, when a medical technician was attacked by an inmate during the course of her duties. That incident led the State Risk Management Division to recommend a POST certification requirement. The common sense nature of this recommendation is patent: Because the potential consequences of an inmate attack are severe, it is reasonable to require employees who have direct contact with inmates to undergo training on responding to these dangerous scenarios. *Cf. Liebson v. N.M. Corr. Dep't*, 73 F.3d 274, 275 (10th Cir. 1996) (describing the kidnapping and sexual assault of a prison librarian by an inmate).

Hennagir acknowledges that she spent much of her time meeting with prison inmates, taking their medical histories, and physically examining them. She contends, however, that she never had to employ emergency training during her eight years at Gunnison, and that other employees have had similar experiences. This argument goes to a number of properly weighed factors: the amount of time spent on the job performing the function, the work experience of past incumbents, and the current work experience of incumbents in similar jobs. *See* 29 C.F.R. § 1630.2(n)(3)(iii), (vi), (vii). In light of the undisputed evidence described in the preceding paragraphs, however, we find this argument insufficient to create a material issue of fact.

The Sixth Circuit faced a similar set of circumstances when it addressed whether the ability to restrain an inmate was an essential job function of a sheriff's deputy. *Hoskins v. Oakland County Sheriff's Dep't*, 227 F.3d 719, 727 (6th Cir. 2000). As our sibling circuit explained, "Although a deputy [sheriff] may be required physically to restrain inmates only infrequently, the potential for physical confrontation with inmates exists on a daily basis, and the consequence of failing to require a deputy to perform this function when the occasion arises could be a serious threat to security." *Id.*; 29 C.F.R. pt. 1630, app. ("[A]lthough a firefighter may not regularly have to carry an unconscious adult out of a burning building, the consequence of failing to require the firefighter to be able to perform this function would be serious."). Like the sheriff's deputy in *Hoskins*, Hennagir came face to face with inmates on a daily basis. We agree with the Sixth Circuit that, in such circumstances, completion of emergency response training is an essential job function.

---

### Exercise 8.5

Demi is a receptionist whose main job function is to answer telephones. One of the workers who works in the office also thinks it is the receptionist's job to get him coffee during the day. The job description for the receptionist position states that the primary function of the job is to answer the telephone. However, the job description indicates that the receptionist may also be assigned other tasks as needed.

Demi has a disability that makes it difficult for her to walk and balance a coffee cup in her hand. In considering whether Demi is a qualified individual, can the employer or the court consider her inability to get the coffee?

---

### ✦ Core Concept: Reasonable Accommodation

Many disability discrimination cases involve questions about whether an employer is required to accommodate a disability. Under the ADA, the term "discriminate" is defined to include:

> (5) (A) not making reasonable accommodations to the known physical or mental limitations of an otherwise qualified individual with a disability who is an applicant or employee, unless such covered entity can demonstrate that the accommodation would impose an undue hardship on the operation of the business of such covered entity.

42 U.S.C. § 12112(b)(5)(A).

In most instances, an employee who needs an accommodation is required to ask for one. The employee is not required to use the word "accommodation" or officially invoke the ADA in order to be considered to have made such a request. According to EEOC Guidance, an accommodation request is made when the employer is notified that because of a medical condition, an individual needs a change in his or her working environment. In some instances, a request is not necessary because of the obviousness of the medical condition and of the need for accommodation. The ADA does allow an employer to ask for information regarding the medical condition to allow the employer to determine whether it constitutes a disability.

The accommodation must be reasonable. The concept of reasonableness encompasses several concepts. First, an accommodation is reasonable if it is effective. The employer is not required to provide the exact accommodation an employee requests; however, any accommodation provided must allow the employee to perform his or her essential job functions. An accommodation that is not effective for the employee is not reasonable.

Once an employee requests an accommodation, the ADA contemplates that the employee and employer will engage in an interactive process, whereby each side communicates its concerns and reaches a mutually agreeable accommodation. Again, the employer is not required to provide the requested accommodation; however, in some circuits, an employee can maintain a claim for the employer's failure to engage in the interactive process. As a practical matter, if litigation arises, it is helpful to the employer's case if it can argue that it engaged in the interactive process in good faith, especially because "good faith" in attempting to make a reasonable accommodation is an affirmative defense to the plaintiff's recovery of punitive damages under the ADA. *See* 42 U.S.C. § 1981a(a)(3).

A second concept inherent in the idea of reasonableness is that the accommodation is one that would not pose an inordinate burden on the employer in normal circumstances. In making out a failure to accommodate case, some courts require the plaintiff to establish that a reasonable accommodation was available. The plaintiff would meet this burden by showing that an accommodation existed that would allow the employee to perform his essential job functions and that would be reasonable in the normal set of circumstances. *U.S. Airways v. Barnett*, 535 U.S. 391 (2002).

An example may be helpful. Consider a plaintiff who has diabetes and needs a 15-minute break every four hours to take insulin shots. The break would allow the plaintiff to perform all of his job functions. Under a normal set of circumstances, such a break would not cause an undue hardship to the employer. The plaintiff would thus be able to establish that a reasonable accommodation was available.

However, such an analysis does not cover all cases. There are instances in which a plaintiff may be requesting a unique accommodation or one that would not be reasonable in run of the mill circumstances. It is not clear how courts would structure the analysis in such cases, but arguments can be made that the ADA requires accommodation as long as the accommodation is not an undue hardship.

Another example may be helpful. Consider an employee who is blind and needs an expensive software program to help her perform her job. To a company with a small number of employees, the expense may not be reasonable. But if the employee works for a large company, it is more likely that the accommodation is reasonable and not an undue hardship.

The ADA provides examples of accommodations that might be reasonable.

Reasonable accommodation. — The term "reasonable accommodation" may include —

(A) making existing facilities used by employees readily accessible to and usable by individuals with disabilities; and

(B) job restructuring, part-time or modified work schedules, reassignment to a vacant position, acquisition or modification of equipment or devices, appropriate adjustment or modifications of examinations, training materials or policies, the provision of qualified readers or interpreters, and other similar accommodations for individuals with disabilities.

42 U.S.C. § 12111(9).

The EEOC Guidance provides examples of requests that would be unreasonable. An employer would not be required to promote an individual or to eliminate an essential job function. In the *Hennagir* case, for example, the plaintiff argued that the POST certification requirement be waived, grandfathered into her current job title, or that her job title be altered as a reasonable accommodation. In essence, she requested elimination of an essential job function, the POST certification requirement, as her reasonable accommodation. The Tenth Circuit held that elimination of an essential job function is not a reasonable accommodation and thus rejected her proposals. *Hennagir*, 587 F.3d at 1264–65. Remember that an employer may always exceed its obligations under the ADA, if it so chooses.

The ADA requires an employer to provide an accommodation unless doing so would pose an undue hardship. Note that unlike the accommodation obligation under Title VII for religion, the ADA imposes substantial obligations on an employer. The term "undue hardship" means the following:

(A) In general.—The term "undue hardship" means an action requiring significant difficulty or expense, when considered in light of the factors set forth in subparagraph (B).

(B) Factors to be considered.—In determining whether an accommodation would impose an undue hardship on a covered entity, factors to be considered include—

(i) the nature and cost of the accommodation needed under this chapter;

(ii) the overall financial resources of the facility or facilities involved in the provision of the reasonable accommodation; the number of persons employed at such facility; the effect on expenses and resources, or the impact otherwise of such accommodation upon the operation of the facility;

(iii) the overall financial resources of the covered entity; the overall size of the business of a covered entity with respect to the number of its employees; the number, type, and location of its facilities; and

(iv) the type of operation or operations of the covered entity, including the composition, structure, and functions of the workforce of such entity; the geographic separateness, administrative, or fiscal relationship of the facility or facilities in question to the covered entity.

42 U.S.C. § 12111(10).

As you can see, whether an accommodation constitutes an undue hardship will vary depending on the facts and circumstances of the case and the particular employer. An accommodation that might be reasonable for a large employer may pose an undue hardship for a smaller one.

Frankly, many courts conflate the reasonable accommodation and undue hardship concepts. Regardless, some commentators argue that cost-benefit analysis should be utilized to determine whether the proposed accommodation must be provided, whether the analysis takes place as part of reasonable accommodation or undue hardship. In other words, just because the employee's proposed accommodation effectively solves the employee's issue does not necessarily mean that the accommodation is reasonable if the costs of providing that benefit far outweigh the benefits. Do you agree that some type of economic cost-benefit analysis is a key part of disability discrimination accommodation law? Consider Judge Posner's opinion in the following case.

---

### Focus Questions: *Vande Zande v. State of Wisconsin Department of Administration*

1.  *Is cost relevant to whether an employer must accommodate an employee's disability?*

2.  *Is cost part of the reasonable accommodation analysis, undue hardship analysis, or both? Does it matter at what point cost comes into play? Why or why not?*

3.  *How much money, if any, should the Wisconsin Department of Administration have been required to spend to lower the kitchenette sink for Ms. Vande Zande?*

4.  *Does an employer have a duty to expend even modest amounts of money to bring about an exact identity in working conditions between disabled and nondisabled workers?*

5.  *Did the Wisconsin Department of Administration go far enough in trying to accommodate Ms. Vande Zande's disability? What more, if anything, should the Department have done to satisfy its obligations under the ADA?*

---

# Vande Zande v. State of Wisconsin Department of Administration

### 44 F.3d 538 (7th Cir. 1995)

Chief Judge Posner.

In 1990, Congress passed the Americans with Disabilities Act, 42 U.S.C. §§ 12101 *et seq.* The stated purpose is "to provide a clear and comprehensive national mandate for the elimination of discrimination against individuals with disabilities," said by Congress to be 43 million in number and growing. §§ 12101(a), (b)(1). "Disability" is broadly defined. It includes not only "a physical or mental impairment that substantially limits one or more of the major life activities of [the disabled] individual," but also the state of "being regarded as having such an impairment." §§ 12102(2)(A), (C). The latter definition, although at first glance peculiar, actually makes a better fit with the elaborate preamble to the Act, in which people who have physical or mental impairments are compared to victims of racial and other invidious discrimination. Many such impairments are not in fact disabling but are believed to be so, and the people having them may be denied employment or otherwise shunned as a consequence. Such people, objectively capable of performing as well as the unimpaired, are analogous to capable workers discriminated against because of their skin color or some other vocationally irrelevant characteristic....

The more problematic case is that of an individual who has a vocationally relevant disability—an impairment such as blindness or paralysis that limits a major human capability, such as seeing or walking. In the common case in which such an impairment interferes with the individual's ability to perform up to the standards of the workplace, or increases the cost of employing him, hiring and firing decisions based on the impairment are not "discriminatory" in a sense closely analogous to employment discrimination on racial grounds. The draftsmen of the Act knew this. But they were unwilling to confine the concept of disability discrimination to cases in which the disability is irrelevant to the performance of the disabled person's job. Instead, they defined "discrimination" to include an employer's "not making reasonable accommodations to the known physical or mental limitations of an otherwise qualified individual with a disability who is an applicant or employee, unless … [the employer] can demonstrate that the accommodation would impose an undue hardship on the operation of the … [employer's] business." § 12112(b)(5)(A).

The term "reasonable accommodations" is not a legal novelty, even if we ignore its use in the provision of Title VII forbidding religious discrimination in employment. 42 U.S.C. § 2000e(j); *see Trans World Airlines, Inc. v. Hardison*, 432 U.S. 63, 84–85 (1977). It is one of a number of provisions in the employment subchapter that were borrowed from regulations issued by the Equal Employment Opportunity Commission in implementation of the Rehabilitation Act of 1973. [citation omitted]. Indeed, to a great extent the employment provisions of the new Act merely generalize to the economy as a whole the duties, including that of reasonable accommodation, that the regulations under the Rehabilitation Act imposed on federal agencies and federal contractors. We can therefore look to the decisions interpreting those regulations for clues to the meaning of the same terms in the new law.

It is plain enough what "accommodation" means. The employer must be willing to consider making changes in its ordinary work rules, facilities, terms, and conditions in order to enable a disabled individual to work. The difficult term is "reasonable." The plaintiff in our case, a paraplegic, argues in effect that the term just means apt or efficacious. An accommodation is reasonable, she believes, when it is tailored to the particular individual's disability. A ramp or lift is thus a reasonable accommodation for a person who like this plaintiff is confined to a wheelchair. Considerations of cost do not enter into the term as the plaintiff would have us construe it. Cost is, she argues, the domain of "undue hardship"—a safe harbor for an employer that can show that it would go broke or suffer other excruciating financial distress were it compelled to make a reasonable accommodation in the sense of one effective in enabling the disabled person to overcome the vocational effects of the disability.

These are questionable interpretations both of "reasonable" and of "undue hardship." To "accommodate" a disability is to make some change that will enable the disabled person to work. An unrelated, inefficacious change would not be an accommodation of the disability at all. So "reasonable" may be intended to qualify (in the sense of weaken) "accommodation," in just the same way that if one requires a "reasonable effort" of someone this means less than the maximum possible effort, or in law that the duty of "reasonable care," the cornerstone of the law of negligence, requires something less than the maximum possible care. It is understood in that law that in deciding what care is reasonable the court considers the cost of increased care. Similar reasoning could be used to flesh out the meaning of the word "reasonable" in the term "reasonable accommodations." It would not follow that the costs and benefits of altering a workplace to enable a disabled person to work would always have to be quantified, or even that an accommodation would have to be deemed unreasonable if the cost exceeded the benefit however slightly. But, at the very least, the cost could not be disproportionate to the benefit. Even if an employer is so large or wealthy—or, like the principal defendant in this case, is a state, which can raise taxes in order to finance any accommodations that it must make to disabled employees—that it may not be able to plead "undue *hardship*," it would not be required to expend enormous sums in order to bring about a trivial improvement in the life of a disabled employee. If the nation's employers have potentially unlimited financial obligations to 43 million disabled persons, the Americans with Disabilities Act will have imposed an indirect tax potentially greater than the national debt. We do not find an intention to bring about such a radical result in either the language of the Act or its history. The preamble actually "markets" the Act as a cost saver, pointing to "billions of dollars in unnecessary expenses resulting from dependency and nonproductivity." § 12101(a)(9). The savings will be illusory if employers are required to expend many more billions in accommodation than will be saved by enabling disabled people to work.

The concept of reasonable accommodation is at the heart of this case. The plaintiff sought a number of accommodations to her paraplegia that were turned down. The principal defendant as we have said is a state, which does not argue that the plaintiff's proposals were rejected because accepting them would have imposed undue hardship on the state or because they would not have done her any good. The district judge nevertheless granted summary judgment for the defendants on the ground that the evidence obtained in discovery, construed as favorably to the plaintiff as the record permitted, showed that they had gone as far to accommodate the plaintiff's demands as reasonableness, in a sense distinct from either aptness or hardship—a sense based, rather, on considerations of cost and proportionality—required. On this analysis, the function of the "undue hardship" safe harbor ... is to excuse compliance by a firm that is financially distressed, even though the cost of the accommodation to the firm might be less than the benefit to disabled employees.

This interpretation of "undue hardship" is not inevitable—in fact probably is incorrect. It is a defined term in the Americans with Disabilities Act, and the definition is "an action requiring significant difficulty or expense," 42 U.S.C. § 12111(10)(A). The financial condition of the employer is only one consideration in determining whether an accommodation otherwise reasonable would impose an undue hardship. *See* 42 U.S.C. §§ 12111(1)(B)(ii), (iii). The legislative history equates "undue hardship" to "unduly costly." These are terms of relation. We must ask, "undue" in relation to what? Presumably (given the statutory definition and the legislative history) in relation to the benefits of the accommodation to the disabled worker as well as to the employer's resources.

So it seems that costs enter at two points in the analysis of claims to an accommodation to a disability. The employee must show that the accommodation is reasonable in the sense both of efficacious and of proportional to costs. Even if this prima facie showing is made, the employer has an opportunity to prove that upon more careful consideration the costs are excessive in relation either to the benefits of the accommodation or to the employer's financial survival or health....

Lori Vande Zande, aged 35, is paralyzed from the waist down as a result of a tumor of the spinal cord. Her paralysis makes her prone to develop pressure ulcers, treatment of which often requires that she stay at home for several weeks.... We hold that Vande Zande's pressure ulcers are a part of her disability, and therefore a part of what the State of Wisconsin had a duty to accommodate—reasonably.

Vande Zande worked for the housing division of the state's department of administration for three years, beginning in January 1990. The housing division supervises the state's public housing programs. Her job was that of a program assistant, and involved preparing public information materials, planning meetings, interpreting regulations, typing, mailing, filing, and copying. In short, her tasks were of a clerical, secretarial, and administrative assistant character. In order to enable her to do this work, the defendants, as she acknowledges, "made numerous accommodations relating to the plaintiff's disability." As examples, in her words, "they paid the landlord to have bathrooms modified and to have a step ramped; they bought special adjustable furniture for the plaintiff; they ordered and paid for one-half of the cost of a cot that the plaintiff needed for daily personal care at work; they sometimes adjusted the plaintiff's schedule to perform backup telephone duties to accommodate the plaintiff's medical appointments; they made changes to the plans for a locker room in the new state office building; and they agreed to provide some of the specific accommodations the plaintiff requested in her October 5, 1992 Reasonable Accommodation Request."

But she complains that the defendants did not go far enough in two principal respects. One concerns a period of eight weeks when a bout of pressure ulcers forced her to stay home. She wanted to work full time at home and believed that she would be able to do so if the division would provide her with a desktop computer at home (though she already had a laptop). Her supervisor refused, and told her that he probably would have only 15 to 20 hours of work for her to do at home per week and that she would have to make up the difference between that and a full work week out of her sick leave or vacation leave. In the event, she was able to work all but 16.5 hours in the eight-week period. She took 16.5 hours of sick leave to make up the difference. As a result, she incurred no loss of income, but did lose sick leave that she could have carried forward indefinitely. She now works for another agency of the State of Wisconsin, but any unused sick leave in her employment by the housing division would have accompanied her to her new job. Restoration of the 16.5 hours of lost sick leave is one form of relief that she seeks in this suit.

She argues that a jury might have found that a reasonable accommodation required the housing division either to give her the desktop computer or to excuse her from having to dig into her sick leave to get paid for the hours in which, in the absence of the computer, she was unable to do her work at home. No jury, however, could in our view be permitted to stretch the concept of "reasonable accommodation" so far. Most jobs in organizations public or private involve team work under supervision rather than solitary unsupervised work, and team work under supervision generally cannot be performed at home without a substantial reduction in the quality of the employee's performance. This will no doubt change as communications technology advances, but is the situation today. Generally, therefore, an employer is not required to accommodate a disability by allowing the disabled worker to work, by himself, without supervision, at home. This is the majority view....

And if the employer, because it is a government agency and therefore is not under intense competitive pressure to minimize its labor costs or maximize the value of its output, or for some other reason, bends over backwards to accommodate a disabled worker— goes further than the law requires—by allowing the worker to work at home, it must not be punished for its generosity by being deemed to have conceded the reasonableness of so far-reaching an accommodation. That would hurt rather than help disabled workers. Wisconsin's housing division was not required by the Americans with Disabilities Act to allow Vande Zande to work at home; even more clearly it was not required to install a computer in her home so that she could avoid using up 16.5 hours of sick leave. It is conjectural that she will ever need those 16.5 hours; the expected cost of the loss must, therefore, surely be slight. An accommodation that allows a disabled worker to work at home, at full pay, subject only to a slight loss of sick leave that may never be needed, hence never missed, is, we hold, reasonable as a matter of law. *See* 29 C.F.R. pt. 1630 app., § 1630.2(o).

Vande Zande complains that she was reclassified as a part-time worker while she was at home, and that this was gratuitous. She was not reclassified. She received her full pay (albeit with a little help from her entitlement to sick leave), and full benefits, throughout the period. It is true that at first her supervisor did not think he would have full-time work for her to do at home. Had that turned out to be true, we do not see on what basis she could complain about being reclassified; she would be working on a part-time basis. It did not turn out to be true, so she was not reclassified, and we therefore do not understand what she is complaining about.

Her second complaint has to do with the kitchenettes in the housing division's building, which are for the use of employees during lunch and coffee breaks. Both the sink and the counter in each of the kitchenettes were 36 inches high, which is too high for a person in a wheelchair. The building was under construction, and the kitchenettes not yet built, when the plaintiff complained about this feature of the design. But the defendants refused to alter the design to lower the sink and counter to 34 inches, the height convenient for a person in a wheelchair. Construction of the building had begun before the effective date of the Americans with Disabilities Act, and Vande Zande does not argue that the failure to include 34-inch sinks and counters in the design of the building violated the Act. She could not argue that; the Act is not retroactive. But she argues that once she brought the problem to the attention of her supervisors, they were obliged to lower the sink and counter, at least on the floor on which her office was located but possibly on the other floors in the building as well, since she might be moved to another floor. All that the defendants were willing to do was to install a shelf 34 inches high in the kitchenette area on Vande Zande's floor. That took care of the counter problem. As for the sink, the defendants took the position that since the plumbing was already in place it would be too costly to lower the sink and that the plaintiff could use the bathroom sink, which is 34 inches high.

Apparently it would have cost only about $150 to lower the sink on Vande Zande's floor; to lower it on all the floors might have cost as much as $2,000, though possibly less. Given the proximity of the bathroom sink, Vande Zande can hardly complain that the inaccessibility of the kitchenette sink interfered with her ability to work or with her physical comfort. Her argument rather is that forcing her to use the bathroom sink for activities (such as washing out her coffee cup) for which the other employees could use the kitchenette sink stigmatized her as different and inferior; she seeks an award of compensatory damages for the resulting emotional distress. We may assume without having to decide that emotional as well as physical barriers to the integration of disabled persons into the workforce are relevant in determining the reasonableness of an accommodation. But we do not think an employer has a duty to expend even modest amounts of money to bring about an absolute identity in working conditions between disabled and nondisabled workers. The creation of such a duty would be the inevitable consequence of deeming a failure to achieve identical conditions "stigmatizing." That is merely an epithet. We conclude that access to a particular sink, when access to an equivalent sink, conveniently located, is provided, is not a legal duty of an employer. The duty of reasonable accommodation is satisfied when the employer does what is necessary to enable the disabled worker to work in reasonable comfort.

## Exercise 8.6

Jim is blind. Jim wants to apply for the position of ID-checker for a company. An ID-checker looks at employee's IDs to determine whether the employees are entitled to access to a particular wing of the building. The only way that Jim could perform this task is to have the company hire an individual to assist him in looking at the identification cards. Would the company be required to provide the accommodation?

Change the facts. Assume that Jim is an attorney. Jim would need a reader to help him with some of his work assignments. Would the company be required to provide the accommodation? Do you need additional facts to make this determination? If so, what are they?

## ✦ Core Concept: Proof Structures

So far, this Chapter has explored individual topics relating to disability discrimination claims. It is important to understand how these individual topics come together in a framework for evaluating claims. As discussed earlier, the ADA recognizes discrimination, harassment, and retaliations claims and often uses frameworks similar to those used under Title VII and the ADEA.

For example, assume that a person claims that she was not being compensated enough because of her disability, and the evidence that the plaintiff has to support her claim is that similarly situated co-workers without a disability were treated differently. The plaintiff in this case might proceed under the *McDonnell-Douglas* framework. In the first prong, where the plaintiff proves that she is a member of a protected class, it would have to be established that the plaintiff was a qualified individual with a disability.

Where the courts have distinguished the ADEA and Title VII, it is important to remember that litigants and courts may need to determine whether the ADA follows the Title VII model, the ADEA model, or perhaps that the ADA requires a different model than either of the other statutes.

To prevail on a failure to accommodate claim, circuits use the following analytical framework in some form or fashion. The exact form of the analytical framework varies by circuit. A plaintiff establishes a prima facie case of failure to accommodate an employee's disability by showing: (1) that he is an individual who has a disability within the meaning of the statute; (2) that the employer had notice of his disability; (3) that with reasonable accommodation he could perform the essential functions of the position; and (4) that the employer refused to make such accommodations. An employer can defeat a prima facie claim if it shows (1) that making a reasonable accommodation would cause it hardship, and (2) that the hardship would be undue. *See Mitchell v. Washingtonville Cent. Sch. Dist.*, 190 F.3d 1, 6 (2d Cir. 1999).

In establishing whether a person is a qualified individual with a disability and whether an accommodation is reasonable or an undue burden, difficult questions remain about which party bears the burdens of productions and persuasion; however, in many instances, these questions are not dispositive of the case. An in-depth discussion of these complexities is contained in a Beyond the Basics section at the end of the Chapter.

## ✦ Core Concept: Direct Threat Defense

The ADA does provide employers with an affirmative defense to liability under some circumstances. The ADA provides:

> It may be a defense to a charge of discrimination under this Act that an alleged application of qualification standards, tests, or selection criteria that screen out

or tend to screen out or otherwise deny a job or benefit to an individual with a disability has been shown to be *job-related and consistent with business necessity,* and such performance cannot be accomplished by *reasonable accommodation,* as required under this title.

The term "qualification standards" may include a requirement that an individual shall not pose a *direct threat* to the *health or safety* of *other individuals in the workplace.*

42 U.S.C. § 12113(a) & (b) (emphasis added).

Under this provision, an employer may take action against an employee if the employee is a "direct threat" to others in the workplace. For example, if an employee had typhoid fever, the employer could refuse to let the employee work on the premises while the disease was contagious. Under the statute, the term "direct threat" means a *significant risk* to the health or safety of others that cannot be eliminated by *reasonable accommodation.* 42 U.S.C. § 12111(3).

The EEOC provides the following additional interpretation of the term.

Direct Threat means a significant risk of *substantial harm* to the health or safety *of the individual or others* that cannot be eliminated or reduced by *reasonable accommodation.* The determination that an individual poses a "direct threat" shall be based on an *individualized assessment* of the individual's present ability to safely perform the essential functions of the job. The assessment shall be based on a reasonable medical judgment that relies on the *most current medical knowledge and/or on the best available objective evidence.* In determining whether an individual would pose a direct threat, the *factors* to be considered include: (1) the nature of the risk; (2) the nature and severity of the potential harm; (3) the likelihood that the potential harm will occur; and (4) the imminence of the potential harm.

29 C.F.R. § 1630.2(r) (emphasis added).

Consider the following direct threat case decided by the U.S. Supreme Court in 2002.

---

## Focus Questions: *Chevron v. Echazabal*

1. *Why does Chevron want to prohibit Echazabal from working in the refinery? Are the employer's concerns here legitimate?*

2. *Why shouldn't the employee have the right to choose whether he or she wants to take the risks of the job? Isn't the employer being paternalistic here? Why did the court in* Johnson Controls *prohibit the employer from being paternalistic of the health of the woman and her fetus, but would not take the same action here?*

3. *If Chevron is concerned about litigation, could it condition a job on the signing of a release of all future claims arising out of exposure to toxins?*

4. *Does this case have to be defended on the "direct threat" ground? Could it be argued that being able to perform a job without posing a danger to one's self is an essential job function?*

---

# Chevron v. Echazabal

## 536 U.S. 73 (2002)

Justice Souter delivered the opinion of the Court.

A regulation of the Equal Employment Opportunity Commission authorizes refusal to hire an individual because his performance on the job would endanger his own health, owing to a disability. The question in this case is whether the Americans with Disabilities Act of 1990, 42 U.S.C. § 12101 *et seq.*, permits the regulation. We hold that it does.

### I

Beginning in 1972, respondent Mario Echazabal worked for independent contractors at an oil refinery owned by petitioner Chevron U.S.A. Inc. Twice he applied for a job directly with Chevron, which offered to hire him if he could pass the company's physical examination. *See* 42 U.S.C. § 12112(d)(3) (1994 ed.). Each time, the exam showed liver abnormality or damage, the cause eventually being identified as Hepatitis C, which Chevron's doctors said would be aggravated by continued exposure to toxins at Chevron's refinery. In each instance, the company withdrew the offer, and the second time it asked the contractor employing Echazabal either to reassign him to a job without exposure to harmful chemicals or to remove him from the refinery altogether. The contractor laid him off in early 1996.

Echazabal filed suit, ultimately removed to federal court, claiming, among other things, that Chevron violated the Americans with Disabilities Act (ADA or Act) in refusing to hire him, or even to let him continue working in the plant, because of a disability, his liver condition. Chevron defended under a regulation of the Equal Employment Opportunity Commission (EEOC) permitting the defense that a worker's disability on the job would pose a "direct threat" to his health, *see* 29 C.F.R. § 1630.15(b)(2) (2001). Although two medical witnesses disputed Chevron's judgment that Echazabal's liver function was impaired and subject to further damage under the job conditions in the refinery, the District Court granted summary judgment for Chevron. It held that Echazabal raised no genuine issue of material fact as to whether the company acted reasonably in relying on its own doctors' medical advice, regardless of its accuracy.

On appeal, the Ninth Circuit asked for briefs on a threshold question not raised before, whether the EEOC's regulation recognizing a threat-to-self defense, exceeded the scope of permissible rulemaking under the ADA. The Circuit held that it did and reversed the summary judgment. The court rested its position on the text of the ADA itself in explicitly recognizing an employer's right to adopt an employment qualification barring anyone whose disability would place others in the workplace at risk, while saying nothing about threats to the disabled employee himself. The majority opinion reasoned that "by specifying only threats to 'other individuals in the workplace,' the statute makes it clear that threats to other persons—including the disabled individual himself—are not included within the scope of the [direct threat] defense," and it indicated that any such regulation would unreasonably conflict with congressional policy against paternalism in the workplace. The court went on to reject Chevron's further argument that Echazabal was not "otherwise qualified" to perform the job, holding that the ability to perform a job without risk to one's health or safety is not an "essential function" of the job.

The decision conflicted with one from the Eleventh Circuit, and raised tension with the Seventh Circuit case.... We granted certiorari, and now reverse.

## II

Section 102 of the ADA prohibits "discriminat[ion] against a qualified individual with a disability because of the disability ... in regard to" a number of actions by an employer, including "hiring." 42 U.S.C. § 12112(a). The statutory definition of "discriminat[ion]" covers a number of things an employer might do to block a disabled person from advancing in the workplace, such as "using qualification standards ... that screen out or tend to screen out an individual with a disability." § 12112(b)(6). By that same definition, as well as by separate provision, § 12113(a), the Act creates an affirmative defense for action under a qualification standard "shown to be job-related for the position in question and ... consistent with business necessity." Such a standard may include "a requirement that an individual shall not pose a direct threat to the health or safety of other individuals in the workplace," § 12113(b), if the individual cannot perform the job safely with reasonable accommodation, § 12113(a). By regulation, the EEOC carries the defense one step further, in allowing an employer to screen out a potential worker with a disability not only for risks that he would pose to others in the workplace but for risks on the job to his own health or safety as well: "The term 'qualification standard' may include a requirement that an individual shall not pose a direct threat to the health or safety of the individual or others in the workplace." 29 C.F.R. § 1630.15(b)(2) (2001).

Chevron relies on the regulation here, since it says a job in the refinery would pose a "direct threat" to Echazabal's health. In seeking deference to the agency, it argues that nothing in the statute unambiguously precludes such a defense, while the regulation was adopted under authority explicitly delegated by Congress, 42 U.S.C. § 12116, and after notice-and-comment rulemaking. *See Chevron U.S.A. Inc. v. Natural Resources Defense Council, Inc.,* 467 U.S. 837, 842–844 (1984). Echazabal, on the contrary, argues that as a matter of law the statute precludes the regulation, which he claims would be an unreasonable interpretation even if the agency had leeway to go beyond the literal text.

## A

As for the textual bar to any agency action as a matter of law, Echazabal says that Chevron loses on the threshold question whether the statute leaves a gap for the EEOC to fill. Echazabal recognizes the generality of the language providing for a defense when a plaintiff is screened out by "qualification standards" that are "job-related and consistent with business necessity" (and reasonable accommodation would not cure the difficulty posed by employment). 42 U.S.C. § 12113(a). Without more, those provisions would allow an employer to turn away someone whose work would pose a serious risk to himself. That possibility is said to be eliminated, however, by the further specification that " 'qualification standards' may include a requirement that an individual shall not pose a direct threat to the health or safety of other individuals in the workplace." § 12113(b); *see also* § 12111(3) (defining "direct threat" in terms of risk to others). Echazabal contrasts this provision with an EEOC regulation under the Rehabilitation Act of 1973, as amended, 29 U.S.C. § 701 *et seq.,* antedating the ADA, which recognized an employer's right to consider threats both to other workers and to the threatening employee himself. Because the ADA defense provision recognizes threats only if they extend to another, Echazabal reads the statute to imply as a matter of law that threats to the worker himself cannot count.

The argument follows the reliance of the Ninth Circuit majority on the interpretive canon, *expressio unius est exclusio alterius,* "expressing one item of [an] associated group or series excludes another left unmentioned." [citation omitted]. The rule is fine when it applies, but this case joins some others in showing when it does not.

The first strike against the expression-exclusion rule here is right in the text that Echazabal quotes. Congress included the harm-to-others provision as an example of legitimate qualifications that are "job-related and consistent with business necessity." These are spacious defensive categories, which seem to give an agency (or in the absence of agency action, a court) a good deal of discretion in setting the limits of permissible qualification standards. That discretion is confirmed, if not magnified, by the provision that "qualification standards" falling within the limits of job relation and business necessity "may include" a veto on those who would directly threaten others in the workplace. Far from supporting Echazabal's position, the expansive phrasing of "may include" points directly away from the sort of exclusive specification he claims.

Just as statutory language suggesting exclusiveness is missing, so is that essential extrastatutory ingredient of an expression-exclusion demonstration, the series of terms from which an omission bespeaks a negative implication. The canon depends on identifying a series of two or more terms or things that should be understood to go hand in hand, which is abridged in circumstances supporting a sensible inference that the term left out must have been meant to be excluded.

Strike two in this case is the failure to identify any such established series, including both threats to others and threats to self, from which Congress appears to have made a deliberate choice to omit the latter item as a signal of the affirmative defense's scope. The closest Echazabal comes is the EEOC's rule interpreting the Rehabilitation Act of 1973, a precursor of the ADA. That statute excepts from the definition of a protected "qualified individual with a handicap" anyone who would pose a "direct threat to the health or safety of other individuals," but, like the later ADA, the Rehabilitation Act says nothing about threats to self that particular employment might pose. 42 U.S.C. § 12113(b). The EEOC nonetheless extended the exception to cover threat-to-self employment, 29 C.F.R. § 1613.702(f) (1990), and Echazabal argues that Congress's adoption only of the threat-to-others exception in the ADA must have been a deliberate omission of the Rehabilitation Act regulation's tandem term of threat-to-self, with intent to exclude it.

But two reasons stand in the way of treating the omission as an unequivocal implication of congressional intent. The first is that the EEOC was not the only agency interpreting the Rehabilitation Act, with the consequence that its regulation did not establish a clear, standard pairing of threats to self and others. While the EEOC did amplify upon the text of the Rehabilitation Act exclusion by recognizing threats to self along with threats to others, three other agencies adopting regulations under the Rehabilitation Act did not. See 28 C.F.R. § 42.540(l)(1) (1990) (Department of Justice), 29 C.F.R. § 32.3 (1990) (Department of Labor), and 45 C.F.R. § 84.3(k)(1) (1990) (Department of Health and Human Services). It would be a stretch, then, to say that there was a standard usage, with its source in agency practice or elsewhere, that connected threats to others so closely to threats to self that leaving out one was like ignoring a twin.

Even if we put aside this variety of administrative experience, however, and look no further than the EEOC's Rehabilitation Act regulation pairing self and others, the congressional choice to speak only of threats to others would still be equivocal. Consider what the ADA reference to threats to others might have meant on somewhat different facts. If the Rehabilitation Act had spoken only of "threats to health" and the EEOC regulation had read that to mean threats to self or others, a congressional choice to be more specific in the ADA by listing threats to others but not threats to self would have carried a message. The most probable reading would have been that Congress understood what a failure to specify could lead to and had made a choice to limit the possibilities. The statutory basis for any agency rulemaking under the ADA would have been different from its basis under the Rehabilitation Act and would have indicated a difference in the agency's rulemaking discretion. But these are not the circumstances here. Instead of making the ADA different from the Rehabilitation Act on the point at issue, Congress used identical language, knowing full well what the EEOC had made of that language under the earlier statute. Did Congress mean to imply that the agency had been wrong in reading the earlier language to allow it to recognize threats to self, or did Congress just assume that the agency was free to do under the ADA what it had already done under the earlier Act's identical language? There is no way to tell. Omitting the EEOC's reference to self-harm while using the very language that the EEOC had read as consistent with recognizing self-harm is equivocal at best. No negative inference is possible.

There is even a third strike against applying the expression-exclusion rule here. It is simply that there is no apparent stopping point to the argument that by specifying a threat-to-others defense Congress intended a negative implication about those whose safety could be considered. When Congress specified threats to others in the workplace, for example, could it possibly have meant that an employer could not defend a refusal to hire when a worker's disability would threaten others outside the workplace? If Typhoid Mary had come under the ADA, would a meat packer have been defenseless if Mary had sued after being turned away? *See* 42 U.S.C. § 12113(d). *Expressio unius* just fails to work here.

B

Since Congress has not spoken exhaustively on threats to a worker's own health, the agency regulation can claim adherence under the rule in *Chevron*, so long as it makes sense of the statutory defense for qualification standards that are "job-related and consistent with business necessity." 42 U.S.C. § 12113(a). Chevron's reasons for calling the regulation reasonable are unsurprising: moral concerns aside, it wishes to avoid time lost to sickness, excessive turnover from medical retirement or death, litigation under state tort law, and the risk of violating the national Occupational Safety and Health Act of 1970, as amended, 29 U.S.C. § 651 *et seq*. Although Echazabal claims that none of these reasons is legitimate, focusing on the concern with OSHA will be enough to show that the regulation is entitled to survive.

Echazabal points out that there is no known instance of OSHA enforcement, or even threatened enforcement, against an employer who relied on the ADA to hire a worker willing to accept a risk to himself from his disability on the job. In Echazabal's mind, this shows that invoking OSHA policy and possible OSHA liability is just a red herring to excuse covert discrimination. But there is another side to this. The text of OSHA itself says its point is "to assure so far as possible every working man and woman in the Nation safe and healthful working conditions," § 651(b), and Congress specifically obligated an employer to "furnish to each of his employees employment and a place of employment which are free from recognized hazards that are causing or are likely to cause death or serious physical harm to his employees," § 654(a)(1). Although there may be an open question whether an employer would actually be liable under OSHA for hiring an individual who knowingly consented to the particular dangers the job would pose to him, there is no denying that the employer would be asking for trouble: his decision to hire would put Congress's policy in the ADA, a disabled individual's right to operate on equal terms within the workplace, at loggerheads with the competing policy of OSHA, to ensure the safety of "each" and "every" worker. Courts would, of course, resolve the tension if there were no agency action, but the EEOC's resolution exemplifies the substantive choices that agencies are expected to make when Congress leaves the intersection of competing objectives both imprecisely marked but subject to the administrative leeway found in 42 U.S.C. § 12113(a).

Nor can the EEOC's resolution be fairly called unreasonable as allowing the kind of workplace paternalism the ADA was meant to outlaw. It is true that Congress had paternalism in its sights when it passed the ADA, *see* § 12101(a)(5) (recognizing "overprotective rules and policies" as a form of discrimination). But the EEOC has taken this to mean that Congress was not aiming at an employer's refusal to place disabled workers at a specifically demonstrated risk, but was trying to get at refusals to give an even break to classes of disabled people, while claiming to act for their own good in reliance on untested and pretextual stereotypes. Its regulation disallows just this sort of sham protection, through demands for a particularized enquiry into the harms the employee would probably face. The direct threat defense must be "based on a reasonable medical judgment that relies on the most current medical knowledge and/or the best available objective evidence," and upon an expressly "individualized assessment of the individual's present ability to safely perform the essential functions of the job," reached after considering, among other things, the imminence of the risk and the severity of the harm portended. 29 C.F.R. § 1630.2(r) (2001). The EEOC was certainly acting within the reasonable zone when it saw a difference between rejecting workplace paternalism and ignoring specific and documented risks to the employee himself, even if the employee would take his chances for the sake of getting a job.

Similarly, Echazabal points to several of our decisions expressing concern under Title VII, which like the ADA allows employers to defend otherwise discriminatory practices that are "consistent with business necessity," 42 U.S.C. § 2000e-2(k), with employers adopting rules that exclude women from jobs that are seen as too risky. *See, e.g., Dothard v. Rawlinson,* 433 U.S. 321 (1977); *Automobile Workers v. Johnson Controls, Inc.,* 499 U.S. 187 (1991). Those cases, however, are beside the point, as they, like Title VII generally, were concerned with paternalistic judgments based on the broad category of gender, while the EEOC has required that judgments based on the direct threat provision be made on the basis of individualized risk assessments.

Finally, our conclusions that some regulation is permissible and this one is reasonable are not open to Echazabal's objection that they reduce the direct threat provision to "surplusage." The mere fact that a threat-to-self defense reasonably falls within the general "job related" and "business necessity" standard does not mean that Congress accomplished nothing with its explicit provision for a defense based on threats to others. The provision made a conclusion clear that might otherwise have been fought over in litigation or administrative rulemaking. It did not lack a job to do merely because the EEOC might have adopted the same rule later in applying the general defense provisions, nor was its job any less responsible simply because the agency was left with the option to go a step further. A provision can be useful even without congressional attention being indispensable.

Accordingly, we reverse the judgment of the Court of Appeals and remand the case for proceedings consistent with this opinion.

---

## Exercise 8.7

Angelica is a recovering heroin addict. She was a hard-core heroin user for many years but has been clean for 3 years. Angelica is a pharmacist by trade. Assume that the State of Nevada has licensed her as a pharmacist in spite of her drug problems and that Angelica's addiction is protected by the ADA as a disability. Angelica applies for a pharmacy position at Dean's Drugs Pharmacy in Las Vegas. Does Dean's have a "direct threat" defense that would allow it to refuse to hire her because of her addiction?

## Exercise 8.8

Frederick is HIV-positive. He is a physician's assistant by trade. He applies for a position with a physicians' group in which his job duties will include assisting physicians during surgical procedures. On occasion, he will be expected to reach into the surgical patient's body cavity. Does the employer have a "direct threat" defense to refusing to hire Frederick because of his HIV-status?

## ➤ Beyond the Basics: Drug and Alcohol Use

The term "qualified individual with a disability" does not include any employee or applicant who is *currently* engaging in the illegal use of drugs. 42 U.S.C. § 12114(a). The statutory exclusion does not apply to individuals who have successfully completed a supervised drug rehabilitation program and are no longer engaging in the illegal use of drugs or who are participating in a rehabilitation program and are no longer engaging in such use. 42 U.S.C. § 12114(b). *See Zenor v. El Paso Health Care*, 176 F.3d 847 (5th Cir. 1999) (finding that a cocaine addict pharmacist was not entitled to ADA protection because the pharmacist used cocaine one month prior to the time that the employer decided to terminate the pharmacist's employment).

Alcoholism, even current alcoholism, is a protected disability under the ADA. However, the ADA has special rules related to alcohol on the job. An employer certainly has the right to take adverse employment action against an alcoholic for being drunk on the job, for misconduct related to being drunk on the job, or for poor work performance related to being an alcoholic. 42 U.S.C. § 12114(c).

## ➤ Beyond the Basics: Medical Examinations and Inquiries

The ADA also contains limits on the types of medical exams and inquiries that can be made. There are two main issues regarding medical exams and inquiries: when they can be given and what constitutes a medical exam or inquiry. Given the introductory nature of this class, only the broad outlines of these issues will be provided. If you practice in this area, you will need to read through the EEOC's Enforcement Guidance on Disability-Related Inquiries and Medical Examinations. *See EEOC Enforcement Guidance on Disability-Related Inquiries and Medical Examinations of Employees under the Americans with Disabilities Act* (July 2000), available at http://www.eeoc.gov/policy/docs/guidance-inquiries.html (last visited Sept. 26, 2013) (hereinafter EEOC Enforcement Guidance on Medical Examinations); *ADA Enforcement Guidance: Preemployment Disability-Related Questions and Medical Examinations* (October 1995), available at http://www.eeoc.gov/policy/docs/preemp.html (last visited Sept. 26, 2013).

The ADA provides:

(d) Medical examinations and inquiries.

(1) In general. The prohibition against discrimination as referred to in subsection (a) of this section shall include medical examinations and inquiries.

(2) *Pre-employment.*

(A) Prohibited examination or inquiry. Except as provided in paragraph (3), a covered entity shall not conduct a medical examination or make inquiries of a job applicant as to whether such applicant is an individual with a disability or as to the nature or severity of such disability.

(B) Acceptable inquiry. A covered entity may make pre-employment inquiries into the ability of an applicant to perform job-related functions.

(3) *Employment entrance examination.* A covered entity may require a medical examination after an offer of employment has been made to a job applicant and prior to the commencement of the employment duties of such applicant, and may condition an offer of employment on the results of such examination, if

(A) all entering employees are subjected to such an examination regardless of disability;

(B) information obtained regarding the medical condition or history of the applicant is collected and maintained on separate forms and in separate medical files and is treated as a confidential medical record, except that

(i) supervisors and managers may be informed regarding necessary restrictions on the work or duties of the employee and necessary accommodations;

(ii) first aid and safety personnel may be informed, when appropriate, if the disability might require emergency treatment; and

(iii) government officials investigating compliance with this chapter shall be provided relevant information on request; and

(C) the results of such examination are used only in accordance with this subchapter.

(4) *Examination and inquiry.*

(A) Prohibited examinations and inquiries. A covered entity shall not require a medical examination and shall not make inquiries of an employee as to whether such employee is an individual with a disability or as to the nature or severity of the disability, unless such examination or inquiry is shown to be job-related and consistent with business necessity.

(B) Acceptable examinations and inquiries. A covered entity may conduct voluntary medical examinations, including voluntary medical histories, which are part of an employee health program available to employees at that work site. A covered entity may make inquiries into the ability of an employee to perform job-related functions.

(C) Requirement. Information obtained under subparagraph (B) regarding the medical condition or history of any employee are subject to the requirements of subparagraphs (B) and (C) of paragraph (3).

42 U.S.C. § 12112(d).

Different standards govern medical examinations and inquiries depending upon where the applicant or employee is in the employment process: (1) pre-offer; (2) post-offer, but pre-employment; and (3) post-employment. Prior to an offer being given, there is a near-complete prohibition on medical exams and inquiries. 42 U.S.C. § 12112(d)(2)(A). However, it is not considered to be a medical inquiry to ask an individual whether he or she can perform the essential functions of a job with or without accommodation. 42 U.S.C. § 12112(d)(2)(B).

After a job offer has been extended, an employer can make that job offer contingent on the passage of a medical examination, as long as the medical examination is given to all employees in a particular job classification. 42 U.S.C. § 12112(d)(3).

After employment, an employer can require an employee to submit to medical examinations, as long as the medical exams are "job-related and consistent with business necessity." 42 U.S.C. § 12112(d)(4)(A). The EEOC's enforcement guidance provides further assistance regarding when medical exams of current employees are "job-related and consistent with business necessity." The guidance suggests that in order to require a medical examination the employer must have an individualized reasonable belief that an employee's medical condition impairs his or her ability to perform essential functions or poses a direct threat. Typically, this reasonable belief will be based on evidence of current performance problems or observable evidence suggesting that an employee will pose a direct threat. *See* EEOC Enforcement Guidance on Medical Examinations, Job-Related and Consistent with Business Necessity.

There are a several exceptions to this individualized reasonable belief requirement. First, employers do not run afoul of the ADA when they require employees to submit to mandatory periodic medical examinations even when there is no individualized reasonable belief of a health problem if such periodic medical examinations are required by state or federal law. For example, certain categories of employees, such as commercial truck drivers, commercial airline pilots, marine pilots, and hoist operators in open pit mines, are required by federal law to submit to mandatory periodic medical examinations as part of their fitness-for-duty certification process. *See* EEOC Enforcement Guidance on Medical Examinations at Question 21.

Second, employers may require employees in positions affecting public safety to submit to mandatory periodic medical examinations that are narrowly tailored to address specific job-related concerns even if federal or state law does not require such exams. *Id.* at Question 18. For more a more detailed explanation regarding the EEOC's Enforcement Guidance on medical examinations of employees *see* Jarod S. Gonzalez, *A Matter of Life and Death—Why the ADA Permits Mandatory Periodic Medical Examinations of "Remote-Location" Employees*, 66 LA. L. REV. 681, 694–696 (2006).

Notice that the ADA also requires the employer to treat information about medical examinations and inquiries confidential and kept in a separate file from the employee's normal personnel file. *See* 42 U.S.C. § 12112(d)(3)(B).

The EEOC gives guidance on the types of examinations and inquiries that do and do not constitute medical examinations and inquiries under the statute. If a certain examination or question does not fall within the definition of a medical examination or inquiry, it does not fall within the ADA's limitations. The following is excerpted from the EEOC Guidance on Medical Examinations. *See* EEOC Enforcement Guidance on Medical Examinations.

### *EEOC Guidance on Medical Examinations*

A "medical examination" is a procedure or test that seeks information about an individual's physical or mental impairments or health. The guidance on Preemployment Questions and Medical Examinations lists the following factors that should be considered to determine whether a test (or procedure) is a medical examination: (1) whether the test is administered by a health care professional; (2) whether the test is interpreted by a health care professional; (3) whether the test is designed to reveal an impairment of physical or mental health; (4) whether the test is invasive; (5) whether the test measures an employee's performance of a task or measures his/her physiological responses to performing the task; (6) whether the test normally is given in a medical setting; and, (7) whether medical equipment is used.

In many cases, a combination of factors will be relevant in determining whether a test or procedure is a medical examination. In other cases, one factor may be enough to determine that a test or procedure is medical.

Medical examinations include, but are not limited to, the following:

- vision tests conducted and analyzed by an ophthalmologist or optometrist;
- blood, urine, and breath analyses to check for alcohol use;
- blood, urine, saliva, and hair analyses to detect disease or genetic markers (*e.g.*, for conditions such as sickle cell trait, breast cancer, Huntington's disease);
- blood pressure screening and cholesterol testing;
- nerve conduction tests (*i.e.*, tests that screen for possible nerve damage and susceptibility to injury, such as carpal tunnel syndrome);
- range-of-motion tests that measure muscle strength and motor function;
- pulmonary function tests (*i.e.*, tests that measure the capacity of the lungs to hold air and to move air in and out);
- psychological tests that are designed to identify a mental disorder or impairment; and,
- diagnostic procedures such as x-rays, computerized axial tomography (CAT) scans, and magnetic resonance imaging (MRI).

There are a number of procedures and tests employers may require that generally are not considered medical examinations, including:

- tests to determine the current illegal use of drugs;
- physical agility tests, which measure an employee's ability to perform actual or simulated job tasks, and physical fitness tests, which measure an employee's performance of physical tasks, such as running or lifting, as long as these tests do not include examinations that could be considered medical (*i.e.*, measuring heart rate or blood pressure);
- tests that evaluate an employee's ability to read labels or distinguish objects as part of a demonstration of the ability to perform actual job functions;
- psychological tests that measure personality traits such as honesty, preferences, and habits; and
- polygraph examinations.

### Other Sources of Obligations Related to Exams and Inquiries

When determining whether an examination is legal, an attorney must necessarily consider sources of law other than the ADA. For example, the Employee Polygraph Protection Act (EPPA), 29 U.S.C. §§ 2001–2009, makes the use of polygraph examinations by employers illegal in most situations.

The Genetic Information Non-Discrimination Act of 2008 (GINA), Pub. L. No. 110-233, 122 Stat. 881, codified at 42 U.S.C. § 2000ff *et seq.*, which became effective on November 21, 2009, provides further limitations on an employer's right to gather certain medical information about employees. In other words, some inquiries that are permissible under the ADA would violate GINA.

Genetic technology has progressed to the point that medical science can now identify a variety of current or possible future medical conditions based on one's genetics. This technology will continue to advance in the future. Employers might want access to an applicant or employee's genetic information on the ground that such information could shed light on their current or future ability to perform a job. Employers may also want to use genetic screening to cut down on health insurance costs. Genetic screening may identify individuals with a predisposition to costly medical conditions. Employers may use this information against individuals as a way of eliminating employment opportunities for such individuals because of the substantial negative impact they may have on the company's health insurance costs. While such use of genetic information by employers may or may not be rational, Congress has made a policy judgment that it is clearly off limits to employers. Workers are protected from discrimination based on their genetic information.

Title II of GINA makes it illegal for employers to acquire genetic information about employees and to discriminate against employees in any way with respect to their terms and conditions of employment because of the employee's "genetic information." GINA § 202(a). The Act defines "genetic information" to include, with respect to an individual, "information about such individual's genetic tests, the genetic tests of family members of such individual, and the manifestation of a disease or disorder in family members of such individual." GINA § 201(4)(A). A "genetic test" is "an analysis of human DNA, RNA, chromosomes, proteins, or metabolites, that detects genotypes, mutations, or chromosomal changes." GINA § 201(7)(A). GINA does not cover manifestation of a disease in an employee.

There are several narrow exceptions to the rule prohibiting an employer from acquiring genetic information about its employees. Inadvertent acquisitions of genetic information do not violate GINA, such as when a manager overhears an employee discussing a family member's illness at the "water cooler." Genetic information may be obtained as part of a voluntary wellness program offered by the employer if certain requirements are satisfied. Genetic information may be acquired as part of the FMLA certification process, where an employee is asking for leave to care for a family member with a serious health condition. An employer who discovers genetic information about an employee through commercially available sources like a newspaper is not in violation of GINA so long as the employer was not looking for such information. Genetic information may be lawfully acquired in unique circumstances where a worker is required by law to be monitored for biological exposure to toxic substances in the workplace. Finally, there is an exception for employers who engage in DNA testing for law enforcement purposes. GINA § 202(b)(1)-(6). *See also* http://www.eeoc.gov/laws/statutes/gina.cfm (last visited Sept. 26, 2013).

## Exercise 8.9

The Smithsburgh Fire Department requires employees for whom firefighting is an essential job function to have a comprehensive visual examination every two years and to have an annual electrocardiogram because it is concerned that certain visual disorders and heart problems will affect their ability to do their job without posing a direct threat. Are these mandatory periodic medical examinations legal under the ADA?

## Exercise 8.10

Global Oil Company conducts offshore drilling operations in the Gulf of Mexico. There are limited medical facilities on the offshore oil rigs. The nearest medical facilities on the mainland are located 300 miles away from the rigs. Roustabout Roy suffers a heart attack while working on the rig one day. He is flown by airplane to the nearest medical hospital in Mexico but the doctors are unable to save him. Global Oil Company subsequently introduces a policy that requires all company employees that work on the company's offshore oil rigs to submit to mandatory annual electrocardiogram exams because it is concerned that certain heart problems will affect the employees' ability to do their job without posing a direct threat and that the remote location makes it difficult to get employees who suffer heart attacks to medical facilities. Does the policy violate the ADA?

## Exercise 8.11

Jill works as an account manager for a nation-wide retailer of household appliances, Appliances, Inc., and applies for a promotion with the company. In order to secure a promotion, the company requires Jill to submit to a variety of tests designed to measure math and language skills, as well as interests and personality traits, and to satisfy a certain scoring range. As one part of this overall testing process, Appliances required that Jill take the Minnesota Multiphasic Personality Inventory (MMPI) test. The MMPI test measures personality traits like whether someone works well in groups. It also considers where an applicant falls on scales measuring traits such as depression, hysteria, paranoia, and mania. Jill scores low on the MMPI test and in combination with her scores on the other tests does not score well enough to secure a promotion. Is the MMPI test a "medical examination" under the ADA?

## Exercise 8.12

Valorie works for SFRA Railroad Company. SFRA learns that Valorie has an inherited condition called Factor V Leiden. Factor V Leiden is not a disease. It is an inherited blood clotting disorder that is passed along to a person through his or her parents. This hypercoaguability disorder is detected through the presence of a particular gene. A person with Factor V Leiden is more likely than the average person in the general population to develop blood clots in the legs, heart, and lungs. Valorie has never had any blood clots but she has been told by doctors that she does have Factor V Leiden. SFRA terminates Valorie's employment because she has Factor V Leiden. Does SFRA's action violate GINA?

## ➤ Beyond the Basics: Burdens of Production and Persuasion in Disability Cases

In an ADA reasonable accommodation case, it is not always entirely clear where the burden of proof lies. In general, the plaintiff has the burden to establish a reasonable accommodation. The employer has the burden to prove undue hardship. But specific factual scenarios demonstrate that the appropriate proof structure in accommodation cases is open to some interpretation. Consider the fact pattern from *U.S. Airways v. Barnett.* 535 U.S. 391 (2002). In *U.S Airways*, an employee worked in a cargo handler position and requested the airline-employer to accommodate his disability by re-assigning him to a mailroom position. The employer refused to honor the disabled employee's reassignment request because the mailroom position was the subject of a seniority-based bidding system and other employees were entitled to the mailroom positions under the terms of the system. The question in the case concerned whether the requested reassignment was a "reasonable accommodation." The plaintiff argued that the seniority system had no bearing on whether the requested reassignment was a *reasonable* accommodation. At most, the seniority system was a factor to consider in determining whether the employer could not accommodate the disabled employee on undue hardship grounds. According to the plaintiff, the employer had the burden to make this specialized showing of "undue hardship." Any other interpretation would create a burden of proof dilemma. The employer argued that the presence of the seniority system alone meant that the disabled employee's request was not reasonable. In other words, the employer claimed that a disability-neutral seniority rule always trumps a conflicting accommodation request regardless of the nature of the request and seniority rule. Think about how the majority of the Court resolved the alleged "burden of proof dilemma" and whether you agree with the majority's decision.

## U.S. Airways v. Barnett

### 535 U.S. 391 (2002)

Justice Breyer delivered the opinion of the Court.

. . .

### II

... In answering the question presented, we must consider the following statutory provisions. First, the ADA says that an employer may not "discriminate against a qualified individual with a disability." 42 U.S.C. § 12112(a). Second, the ADA says that a "qualified" individual includes "an individual with a disability who, *with* or without *reasonable accommodation*, can perform the essential functions of" the relevant "employment position." § 12111(8) (emphasis added). Third, the ADA says that "discrimination" includes an employer's "*not making reasonable accommodations* to the known physical or mental limitations of an otherwise qualified ... employee, *unless* [the employer] can demonstrate that the accommodation would impose an *undue hardship* on the operation of [its] business." § 12112(b)(5)(A) (emphasis added). Fourth, the ADA says that the term "'reasonable accommodation' may include ... reassignment to a vacant position." § 12111(9)(B).

The parties interpret this statutory language as applied to seniority systems in radically different ways. In US Airways' view, the fact that an accommodation would violate the rules of a seniority system always shows that the accommodation is not a "reasonable" one. In Barnett's polar opposite view, a seniority system violation never shows that an accommodation sought is not a "reasonable" one. Barnett concedes that a violation of seniority rules might help to show that the accommodation will work "undue" employer "hardship," but that is a matter for an employer to demonstrate case by case. We shall initially consider the parties' main legal arguments in support of these conflicting positions.

US Airways' claim that a seniority system virtually always trumps a conflicting accommodation demand rests primarily upon its view of how the Act treats workplace "preferences." Insofar as a requested accommodation violates a disability-neutral workplace rule, such as a seniority rule, it grants the employee with a disability treatment that other workers could not receive. Yet the Act US Airways says, seeks only "equal" treatment for those with disabilities. *See, e.g.,* 42 U.S.C. § 12101(a)(9). It does not, it contends, require an employer to grant preferential treatment. Hence it does not require the employer to grant a request that, in violating a disability-neutral rule, would provide a preference.

While linguistically logical, this argument fails to recognize what the Act specifies, namely, that preferences will sometimes prove necessary to achieve the Act's basic equal opportunity goal. The Act requires preferences in the form of "reasonable accommodations" that are needed for those with disabilities to obtain the *same* workplace opportunities that those without disabilities automatically enjoy. By definition any special "accommodation" requires the employer to treat an employee with a disability differently, *i.e.,* preferentially. And the fact that the difference in treatment violates an employer's disability-neutral rule cannot by itself place the accommodation beyond the Act's potential reach.

Were that not so, the "reasonable accommodation" provision could not accomplish its intended objective. Neutral office assignment rules would automatically prevent the accommodation of an employee whose disability-imposed limitations require him to work on the ground floor. Neutral "break-from-work" rules would automatically prevent the accommodation of an individual who needs additional breaks from work, perhaps to permit medical visits. Neutral furniture budget rules would automatically prevent the accommodation of an individual who needs a different kind of chair or desk. Many employers will have neutral rules governing the kinds of actions most needed to reasonably accommodate a worker with a disability. *See* 42 U.S.C. § 12111(9)(b) (setting forth examples such as "job restructuring," "part-time or modified work schedules," "acquisition or modification of equipment or devices," "and other similar accommodations"). Yet Congress, while providing such examples, said nothing suggesting that the presence of such neutral rules would create an automatic exemption. Nor have the lower courts made any such suggestion....

In sum, the nature of the "reasonable accommodation" requirement, the statutory examples, and the Act's silence about the exempting effect of neutral rules together convince us that the Act does not create any such automatic exemption. The simple fact that an accommodation would provide a "preference"—in the sense that it would permit the worker with a disability to violate a rule that others must obey—cannot, *in and of itself,* automatically show that the accommodation is not "reasonable." As a result, we reject the position taken by US Airways and Justice Scalia to the contrary.

US Airways also points to the ADA provisions stating that a "'reasonable accommodation' may include ... reassignment to a *vacant* position." § 12111(9)(B) (emphasis added). And it claims that the fact that an established seniority system would assign that position to another worker automatically and always means that the position is not a "vacant" one. Nothing in the Act, however, suggests that Congress intended the word "vacant" to have a specialized meaning. And in ordinary English, a seniority system can give employees seniority rights allowing them to bid for a "vacant" position. The position in this case was held, at the time of suit, by Barnett, not by some other worker; and that position, under the US Airways seniority system, became an "open" one. Moreover, US Airways has said that it "reserves the right to change any and all" portions of the seniority system at will. Consequently, we cannot agree with US Airways about the position's vacancy; nor do we agree that the Act would automatically deny Barnett's accommodation request for that reason.

Barnett argues that the statutory words "reasonable accommodation" mean only "effective accommodation," authorizing a court to consider the requested accommodation's ability to meet an individual's disability-related needs, and nothing more. On this view, a seniority rule violation, having nothing to do with the accommodation's effectiveness, has nothing to do with its "reasonableness." It might, at most, help to prove an "undue hardship on the operation of the business." But, he adds, that is a matter that the statute requires the employer to demonstrate, case by case.

In support of this interpretation Barnett points to Equal Employment Opportunity Commission (EEOC) regulations stating that "reasonable accommodation means ... modifications or adjustments ... that *enable* a qualified individual with a disability to perform the essential functions of [a] position." 29 C.F.R. § 1630(o)(ii) (2001) (emphasis added).... Barnett adds that any other view would make the words "reasonable accommodation" and "undue hardship" virtual mirror images—creating redundancy in the statute. And he says that any such other view would create a practical burden of proof dilemma.

The practical burden of proof dilemma arises, Barnett argues, because the statute imposes the burden of demonstrating an "undue hardship" upon the employer, while the burden of proving "reasonable accommodation" remains with the plaintiff, here the employee. This allocation seems sensible in that an employer can more frequently and easily prove the presence of business hardship than an employee can prove its absence. But suppose that an employee must counter a claim of "seniority rule violation" in order to prove that an "accommodation" request is "reasonable." Would that not force the employee to prove what is in effect an absence, *i.e.*, an absence of hardship, despite the statute's insistence that the employer "demonstrate" hardship's presence?

These arguments do not persuade us that Barnett's legal interpretation of "reasonable" is correct. For one thing, in ordinary English the word "reasonable" does not mean "effective." It is the word "accommodation," not the word "reasonable," that conveys the need for effectiveness. An *ineffective* "modification" or "adjustment" will not *accommodate* a disabled individual's limitations. Nor does an ordinary English meaning of the term "reasonable accommodation" make of it a simple, redundant mirror image of the term "undue hardship." The statute refers to an "undue hardship on the operation of the business." 42 U.S.C. § 12112 (b)(5)(A). Yet a demand for an effective accommodation could prove unreasonable because of its impact, not on business operations, but on fellow employees—say because it will lead to dismissals, relocations, or modification of employee benefits to which an employer, looking at the matter from the perspective of the business itself, may be relatively indifferent.

Neither does the statute's primary purpose require Barnett's special reading. The statute seeks to diminish or to eliminate the stereotypical thought processes, the thoughtless actions, and the hostile reactions that far too often bar those with disabilities from participating fully in the Nation's life, including the workplace. *See generally* §§ 12101(a) and (b). These objectives demand unprejudiced thought and reasonable responsive reaction on the part of employers and fellow workers alike. They will sometimes require affirmative conduct to promote entry of disabled people into the workforce. They do not, however, demand action beyond the realm of the reasonable.

Neither has Congress indicated in the statute, or elsewhere, that the word "reasonable" means no more than "effective." The EEOC regulations do say that reasonable accommodations "enable" a person with a disability to perform the essential functions of a task. But that phrasing simply emphasizes the statutory provision's basic objective. The regulations do not say that "enable" and "reasonable" mean the same thing. And as discussed below, no circuit court has so read them....

Finally, an ordinary language interpretation of the word "reasonable" does not create the "burden of proof" dilemma to which Barnett points. Many of the lower courts, while rejecting both US Airways and Barnett's more absolute views, have reconciled the phrases "reasonable accommodation" and "undue hardship" in a practical way.

They have held that a plaintiff/employee (to defeat a defendant/employer's motion for summary judgment) need only show that an "accommodation" seems reasonable on its face, *i.e.*, ordinarily or in the run of cases....

Once the plaintiff has made this showing, the defendant/employer then must show special (typically case-specific) circumstances that demonstrate undue hardship in the particular circumstances....

Not every court has used the same language, but their results are functionally similar. In our opinion, that practical view of the statute, applied consistently with ordinary summary judgment principles, *see* Fed. Rule Civ. Proc. 56, avoids Barnett's burden of proof dilemma, while reconciling the two statutory phrases ("reasonable accommodation" and "undue hardship").

### III

The question in the present case focuses on the relationship between seniority systems and the plaintiff's need to show that an "accommodation" seems reasonable on its face, *i.e.*, ordinarily or in the run of cases. We must assume that the plaintiff, an employee, is an "individual with a disability." He has requested assignment to a mailroom position as a "reasonable accommodation." We also assume that normally such a request would be reasonable within the meaning of the statute, were it not for one circumstance, namely, that the assignment would violate the rules of a seniority system. *See* § 12111(9) ("reasonable accommodation" may include "reassignment to a vacant position"). Does that circumstance mean that the proposed accommodation is not a "reasonable" one?

In our view, the answer to this question ordinarily is "yes." The statute does not require proof on a case-by-case basis that a seniority system should prevail. That is because it would not be reasonable in the run of cases that the assignment in question trump the rules of a seniority system. To the contrary, it will ordinarily be unreasonable for the assignment to prevail.

Several factors support our conclusion that a proposed accommodation will not be reasonable in the run of cases. Analogous case law supports this conclusion, for it has recognized the importance of seniority to employee-management relations. This Court has held that, in the context of a Title VII religious discrimination case, an employer need not adapt to an employee's special worship schedule as a "reasonable accommodation" where doing so would conflict with the seniority rights of other employees. *Trans World Airlines, Inc.* v. *Hardison*, 432 U.S. 63, 79–80 (1977). The lower courts have unanimously found that collectively bargained seniority trumps the need for reasonable accommodation in the context of the linguistically similar Rehabilitation Act. And several Circuits, though differing in their reasoning, have reached a similar conclusion in the context of seniority and the ADA. All these cases discuss *collectively bargained* seniority systems, not systems (like the present system) which are unilaterally imposed by management. But the relevant seniority system advantages, and related difficulties that result from violations of seniority rules, are not limited to collectively bargained systems.

For one thing, the typical seniority system provides important employee benefits by creating, and fulfilling, employee expectations of fair, uniform treatment. These benefits include "job security and an opportunity for steady and predictable advancement based on objective standards." [citation omitted]....

Most important for present purposes, to require the typical employer to show more than the existence of a seniority system might well undermine the employees' expectations of consistent, uniform treatment—expectations upon which the seniority system's benefits depend. That is because such a rule would substitute a complex case-specific "accommodation" decision made by management for the more uniform, impersonal operation of seniority rules. Such management decision making, with its inevitable discretionary elements, would involve a matter of the greatest importance to employees, namely, layoffs; it would take place outside, as well as inside, the confines of a court case; and it might well take place fairly often. We can find nothing in the statute that suggests Congress intended to undermine seniority systems in this way. And we consequently conclude that the employer's showing of violation of the rules of a seniority system is by itself ordinarily sufficient.

The plaintiff (here the employee) nonetheless remains free to show that special circumstances warrant a finding that, despite the presence of a seniority system (which the ADA may not trump in the run of cases), the requested "accommodation" is "reasonable" on the particular facts. That is because special circumstances might alter the important expectations described above. The plaintiff might show, for example, that the employer, having retained the right to change the seniority system unilaterally, exercises that right fairly frequently, reducing employee expectations that the system will be followed—to the point where one more departure, needed to accommodate an individual with a disability, will not likely make a difference. The plaintiff might show that the system already contains exceptions such that, in the circumstances, one further exception is unlikely to matter. We do not mean these examples to exhaust the kinds of showings that a plaintiff might make. But we do mean to say that the plaintiff must bear the burden of showing special circumstances that make an exception from the seniority system reasonable in the particular case. And to do so, the plaintiff must explain why, in the particular case, an exception to the employer's seniority policy can constitute a "reasonable accommodation" even though in the ordinary case it cannot.

Justice Scalia, with whom Justice Thomas joins, dissenting.

The question presented asks whether the "reasonable accommodation" mandate of the Americans with Disabilities Act of 1990 (ADA or Act) requires reassignment of a disabled employee to a position that "another employee is entitled to hold ... under the employer's bona fide and established seniority system." Indulging its penchant for eschewing clear rules that might avoid litigation, the Court answers "maybe." It creates a presumption that an exception to a seniority rule is an "unreasonable" accommodation, but allows that presumption to be rebutted by showing that the exception "will not likely make a difference."

The principal defect of today's opinion, however, goes well beyond the uncertainty it produces regarding the relationship between the ADA and the infinite variety of seniority systems. The conclusion that any seniority system can ever be overridden is merely one consequence of a mistaken interpretation of the ADA that makes all employment rules and practices—even those which (like a seniority system) pose no *distinctive* obstacle to the disabled—subject to suspension when that is (in a court's view) a "reasonable" means of enabling a disabled employee to keep his job. That is a far cry from what I believe the accommodation provision of the ADA requires: the suspension (within reason) of those employment rules and practices *that the employee's disability prevents him from observing....*

---

## Notes

1. *Making sense of Barnett.* The *Barnett* opinion indicates that in reasonable accommodation cases the plaintiff generally has the burden to demonstrate that an accommodation "is reasonable on its face, *i.e.*, ordinarily or in the run of cases." Once the plaintiff satisfies that burden, the burden shifts to the employer to prove that, even though the accommodation is generally of the type that is reasonable, the employer's own specific circumstances prove the accommodation would place an undue hardship on the employer.

In the specific fact pattern in which the proposed accommodation conflicts with a seniority system rule, the *employer* need only prove the presence of the seniority system rule and its applicability to the personnel decision. The rebuttable presumption is that the seniority system rule trumps the proposed accommodation. The *employee* "must bear the burden of showing special circumstances that make an exception from the seniority system reasonable in the particular case. And to do so, the [employee] must explain why, in the particular case, an exception to the employer's seniority policy can constitute a 'reasonable accommodation' even though in the ordinary case it cannot." *Barnett*, 535 U.S. at 405–406.

2. *Burden of Proof and Essential Job Functions.* In a case that turns on whether a particular job function is an *essential* job function—because the parties dispute whether the job function is in fact essential or merely marginal—the question may arise as to which party has the burden to demonstrate or define what the essential job functions of a particular job actually are. Does the employee as part of its case have the burden of persuasion to demonstrate that a particular function is non-essential or must the employer demonstrate by a preponderance of the evidence that a particular function is essential? This issue is not clear-cut.

The ADA's statutory language, *see* 42 U.S.C. § 12112 and 12111(8), indicates that the plaintiff has the burden to prove that it can perform the essential functions of the job with or without a reasonable accommodation. *Barnett*, 535 U.S. at 400. In other words, "essential functions" is an element of the plaintiff's case that it must prove. The First Circuit follows this view to a large degree. In that Circuit, the employer has the burden of production to come forward with "some evidence" that a particular function is essential, but the plaintiff always has the ultimate burden of persuasion to demonstrate that she is a qualified individual with a disability who can perform the essential functions of the job in question. The plaintiff bears the burden of persuasion on the "essential function" element. *See Richardson v. Friendly Ice Cream Corp.*, 594 F.3d 69, 76 (1st Cir. 2010). But this is not the law in all of the circuits. *See Hamlin v. Charter Twp. of Flint*, 165 F.3d 426, 439 (6th Cir. 1999) ("If one were simply to read what the statute says, one might suppose that a person claiming to have been discriminated against in violation of the ADA would have the burden of proving his ability to perform the 'essential functions' of the position in question. One might further suppose that in the event of a disagreement as to whether a given job function is or is not 'essential,' the plaintiff would have the burden of proving it is not. In this circuit, however, one would be wrong.").

For a variety of reasons, some courts have stated that the employer has the burden of persuasion to show that a particular function is an essential function of the job. In *Monette v. Electronic Data Sys. Corp.*, 90 F.3d 1173, 1184 (6th Cir. 1996), the Sixth Circuit held that if a disabled individual challenges a particular job requirement as "unessential," the burden of proving by a preponderance of the evidence that the job function is essential is on the employer. The *Monette* Court articulated a textual basis for its decision. The Court noted that under 42 U.S.C. § 12112(b)(6) employers must prove that their qualification standards are "job-related and consistent with business necessity" and analogized an essential job function as roughly equivalent to a qualification standard. The Eight Circuit also takes the position that the employer has the burden of persuasion to show a particular job function is an essential function of the job. *See Rehrs v. The Iams Co.*, 486 F.3d 353, 356 (8th Cir. 2007).

One possible policy justification for placing the burden on the employer is that the information typically needed to make such a showing lies in the hands of the employer. For example, the employer may have evidence of written job descriptions that list particular functions of a job and/or records that detail the amount of time spent by an employee working on a particular function. Indeed, one factor that a court may look to in determining whether a job function is essential is the employer's *own* judgment as to whether the function is essential. *See, e.g., Benson v. Northwest Airlines, Inc.*, 62 F.3d 1108, 1113 (8th Cir. 1995) (noting that much of the information which determines essential job functions lies uniquely with the employer).

## Exercise 8.13

The standards for religious accommodation and disability accommodation use similar language. How are these obligations different? How are they the same?

# Chapter 9

# Protected Traits and Special Issues

Chapter 2 provided an introductory discussion of traits protected by the federal employment discrimination statutes. This Chapter presents a more in-depth discussion of the protected traits and addresses other special issues that arise in the discrimination context. You will see that other than Affirmative Action, which was identified as a Core Concept in Chapter 3, this Chapter is not organized using that terminology. Rather, each of these topics is designed to enhance your understanding of topics covered elsewhere in the book.

The topics covered in this Chapter include the following:

1. Affirmative Action

2. Sex, Pregnancy and Maternal Wall

3. Sex-Based Pay Discrimination

4. Family and Medical Leave Act (FMLA)

5. Race/Color

6. Age

7. Lesbian, Gay, Bisexual and Transgender (LGBT) Individuals

8. Grooming Codes

9. National Origin

## ✦ Core Concept: Affirmative Action

Definitions of "affirmative action" tend to vary depending on who is defining the term. In general, affirmative action encompasses a range of efforts by employers, governments, and educational institutions to accomplish equal opportunity goals. Scholars describe a continuum of such efforts, ranging from "hard" affirmative action (including race- or sex-based quotas and preferences) to "soft" affirmative action (including self studies and counseling). *See, e.g.,* Michelle Adams, *The Last Wave of Affirmative Action,* 1998 Wis. L. Rev. 1395, 1402 (1998).

Several federal laws affirmatively permit or require "affirmative" action in employment. On March 6, 1961, President John F. Kennedy signed Executive Order 10,925, requiring federal contractors to take *affirmative action* with regard to the employment of minorities. *See* 26 Fed. Reg. 1977 (1961). This requirement is now embodied in Executive Order 11,246. Executive Order 11,246 requires covered federal contractors to "take *affirmative action* to ensure that applicants are employed and that employees are treated during employment, without regard to their *race, color, religion, sex, or national origin.*" (emphasis added). *See* 30 Fed. Reg. 12,320 (1965); 41 C.F.R. § 60-1.4(a). Federal law also imposes on federal contractors affirmative action obligations related to qualified individuals with disabilities in certain circumstances. *See, e.g.,* 29 U.S.C. § 793 (providing requirements for certain government contractors). The Office of Federal Contract Compliance Programs (OFCCP) within the Department of Labor oversees many of the federally required affirmative action requirements, including the ones mentioned in this paragraph.

What does it mean for a covered federal contractor to "take affirmative action"? OFCCP regulations require a covered contractor with 50 or more employees and a federal contract of $50,000 or more to develop and maintain a written affirmative action program for each of its establishments. 41 C.F.R. § 60-1.40. Affirmative action programs include qualitative analyses, action-oriented items, auditing steps, and documentation requirements designed to address the "underutilization" of minorities and women in the contractor's workforce. The pertinent regulation provides in part:

> An affirmative action program is a management tool designed to ensure equal employment opportunity. A central premise underlying affirmative action is that, absent discrimination, over time a contractor's workforce, generally, will reflect the gender, racial and ethnic profile of the labor pools from which the contractor recruits and selects. Affirmative action programs contain a diagnostic component which includes a number of quantitative analyses designed to evaluate the composition of the workforce of the contractor and compare it to the composition of the relevant labor pools. Affirmative action programs also include action-oriented programs. If women and minorities are not being employed at a rate to be expected given their availability in the relevant labor pool, the contractor's affirmative action program includes specific practical steps designed to address this underutilization. Effective affirmative action programs also include internal auditing and reporting systems as a means of measuring the contractor's progress toward achieving the workforce that would be expected in the absence of discrimination.

41 C.F.R. § 60-2.10(a)(1).

Covered contractors are expected to engage in "good faith" efforts to correct the underutilization of minorities and women, if it exists, through goals and objectives. *See* 41 C.F.R. §§ 60-2.17, -2.35. A covered contractor's substantial or material violation of its affirmative action obligations under Executive Order 11,246 and OFCCP regulations could lead the Department of Justice to initiate enforcement proceedings to ensure compliance. *See* Exec. Order No. 11,246, § 209(a)(2); 30 Fed. Reg. 12,322 (1965). The Department of Labor has the power to cancel, suspend, or terminate the contractor's federal contract or to debar a contractor from future federal government contracts if the contractor does not comply with its affirmative action obligations. *Id.* at § 209(a)(5)-(6); 30 Fed. Reg. 12,323 (1965). But cancellation or debarment is not common. The government prefers to work with the contractor through conference, conciliation, and mediation until it is in compliance. *Id.* at § 209(b); 30 Fed. Reg. 12,323 (1965).

Support for affirmative action also is found in Title VII. As discussed in the Remedies Chapter, Title VII allows affirmative action to be granted as a remedy in employment discrimination cases. Additionally, the EEOC has construed Title VII to allow employers and others covered to take voluntary affirmative action to avoid liability for disparate impact discrimination, and to "correct the effects of prior discriminatory practices," as measured by "comparison between the employer's work force ... and an appropriate segment of the labor force." 29 C.F.R. § 1608.3. Similarly, courts have sometimes upheld employer affirmative action plans, as variously defined, in the face of constitutional and Title VII challenges by the majority employees who feel disadvantaged by such plans.

The legality and fairness of affirmative action are hotly debated. Much is at stake. Exercise 9.1 asks you to consider the emotional effects on both sides of the dispute.

## Exercise 9.1

Imagine the town of Cuthbert, where the only large employer is the Cuthbert Industrial Supplies Company (CISC). CISC has a history of reserving the better factory positions for white workers and hiring African Americans only for more menial labor. Thus, although the population in Cuthbert and the surrounding area is split evenly between white and African-American people, and although none of the positions in question require any prior training or experience, CISC's assembly line is composed entirely of white workers, and its cleaning staff and menial laborers are all African American. The average white worker at CISC earns exactly twice what the average African-American worker earns.

Imagine that you are Frank Meyers, an 18-year-old African American in the town of Cuthbert. Members of your family have never succeeded in obtaining full employment with benefits, and have often had to work at part-time menial labor, including at Cuthbert. Because work has been so scarce, you have grown up in poverty. Your mother, who has worked as a daily laborer cleaning homes all her life, has become ill and can no longer work. You want to support the family. Presently, you are mowing lawns at CISC. When a job vacancy occurs on the assembly line, you apply for it, even though no African American has ever before been hired for the assembly line. Instead of you, CISC hires a white classmate of yours, Roy Raymond, a young man who comes from an economically middle class family and who, you happen to know, gets in trouble with the police for vandalism almost every weekend. Considering this situation from your perspective as Frank Meyers, what is your reaction to the news that Roy got the job?

Now imagine that, shortly after CISC prefers the white applicant to Frank Meyers, lawyers inform CISC that the absence of any African-American workers on the assembly line could subject CISC to liability for race discrimination. Accordingly, on advice of counsel, CISC adopts an affirmative action plan that requires hiring managers choosing between two equally qualified applicants to prefer the African American.

Change your role-play identity. You are now Jack Brandiff, a white male, with a stay-at-home spouse and four children. Your family has always been poor. You want to move from working at the local gas station, where you earn minimum wage and no benefits, to working at CISC, where you would earn 50% more and receive benefits. When a vacancy occurs at CISC, you apply for it and are told that you are qualified. In the end, however, the position goes to Janice Hauser, an African-American female, because of the newly adopted affirmative action plan. Although you are told that Janice and you are equally qualified, you happen to know that her attendance record from her last job was deficient, and you think that the hiring manager at CISC must be aware of that. You also know that Janice comes from a wealthy family and has no children to support. From your role-play perspective as Jack Brandiff, how do you react to this?

## Exercise 9.2

Using any sources, web-based or otherwise, identify arguments for and against affirmative action. How do the proponents and opponents define the term "affirmative action"? Reflect on which side is more consistent with your own views. Then make a list of the most persuasive arguments you can offer on behalf of the opposing view.

### Legal Challenges to Affirmative Action

Affirmative action litigation in employment usually involves claims brought by majority workers, who contend they lost an employment opportunity because minority members were favored under an affirmative action plan. In some cases, the employer may assert as a defense that the decision was properly made pursuant to a valid affirmative action plan. The legal standards governing such disputes vary depending on the type of employer and the nature of the affirmative action. In general, affirmative action cases may be divided into those challenging affirmative action under the constitutional equal protection principle and those challenging affirmative action under Title VII.

When government action is involved, the challenger is likely to invoke equal protection under the Fourteenth (state action) or Fifth Amendment (federal action), in addition to Title VII, as grounds for the challenge. Government action may take several forms:

- A federal, state or municipal employer may voluntarily adopt the affirmative action plan.

- The affirmative action may be ordered by a government entity, whether a court or an agency. In this connection, Congress, itself, could be deemed the government entity if a statute (Title VII or other) is deemed to require affirmative action. Executive Order 11,246 constitutes government action.

- Two parties to a legal dispute agree to affirmative action measures to settle the dispute and ask the court to put its imprimatur on that agreement in the form of a consent decree. That imprimatur renders the plan, in a sense, governmental.

On the other hand, if a private employer engages in voluntary affirmative action, there is no government action. In the absence of government action, constitutional equal protection principles do not apply. Thus, the only federal law limitation on voluntary private employer affirmative action is Title VII. In fact, the defendant in *Johnson v. Transportation Agency* (reproduced below) was a government entity, but the plaintiff limited his claim to Title VII, and no equal protection analysis took place.

This section gives an overview of both types of challenges to affirmative action: constitutional and statutory. It first discusses the law governing constitutional challenges to government affirmative action. It then provides an excerpt from the case of *Johnson v. Transportation Agency*, 480 U.S. 616 (1987), about a Title VII challenge to voluntary private employer affirmative action.

### Constitutional Challenges to Affirmative Action

Government employers' affirmative action may be challenged under the Constitution. The Fifth Amendment Due Process Clause has been interpreted as providing an equal protection requirement that applies when the challenge is to federal government action. The Fourteenth Amendment Equal Protection Clause governs such challenges when they are made to a state or local government's affirmative action plan. Supreme Court precedent applying these clauses to affirmative action have all been in the context of race, not sex. Those precedents allow courts to uphold race-based affirmative action under these clauses only if the affirmative action meets the strict scrutiny standard. Strict scrutiny requires that the racial classifications provided for in the plan be "narrowly tailored" and further "compelling government interests." *Adarand Constructors v. Pena*, 515 U.S. 200, 227 (1995); *Richmond v. J.A. Croson Co.*, 488 U.S. 469, 471 (1989). The primary questions in these types of affirmative cases are often: (1) what constitutes a compelling governmental interest; and (2) when is the government's plan narrowly tailored.

There is some Supreme Court precedent on the question of what qualifies as a compelling government interest in the contexts of government employment and government-run education. In the 1986 case of *Wygant v. Jackson Board of Education*, the Supreme Court held that a public school employer could not take race into account merely to correct societal discrimination or to provide same-race role models for minority students. The Court suggested that public employers might take race into account to provide a remedy to individuals who personally had been victims of that employer's own past discrimination. 476 U.S. 267 (1986). In a concurring opinion, Justice O'Connor suggested that the strict scrutiny standard might allow recognition of compelling interests other than the employer's own past discrimination. In the context of higher education admissions, the Supreme Court has more recently found the interest in diversifying public higher education to be compelling. *Grutter v. Bollinger*, 539 U.S. 306, 328 (2003). Some lower courts have extended this aspect of *Grutter* to the context of government employers. *See, e.g., Petit v. City of Chicago*, 352 F. 3d 1111, 1114 (7th Cir. 2003) (diversity a compelling need for police force in a racially diverse city).

On the narrowly tailored requirement, the Supreme Court has spoken, also in the context of education. In *Grutter v. Bollinger*, the Court held that plans are not narrowly enough tailored if race is the decisive factor in making a decision, but are sufficiently narrow if race is one of many factors considered. 539 U.S. at 334. The Supreme Court has not addressed how and to what extent its decisions about affirmative action in the education context apply in employment cases.

### Voluntary Affirmative Action under Title VII

In 1979, the Supreme Court decided *United Steelworkers v. Weber*, 443 U.S. 193 (1979). The *Weber* Court held that Title VII's nondiscrimination provisions do not prohibit race-conscious decision-making pursuant to a valid affirmative action plan. The Court reasoned that a statute designed to remedy the effects of past discrimination against racial minorities should not be construed to prohibit employers' race-conscious actions intended to accomplish the same remedial purpose. The Court also found in Title VII's language and history evidence that Congress intended employers to undertake voluntary affirmative action. As you will see in the dispute between the majority and the dissents in the *Johnson* case, the *Weber* decision is a controversial one. Nevertheless, *Weber* remains the law, and subsequent cases have focused, not on the permissibility of affirmative action, but on the scope of permissible affirmative action under Title VII.

In *Johnson v. Transportation Agency*, the Supreme Court applied *Weber* to sex-based affirmative action. A male employee challenged the Transportation Agency's promotion of a female over the male, arguing that the Transportation Agency's reliance on an affirmative action plan violated Title VII.

---

## Focus Questions: *Johnson v. Transportation Agency*

1. *What exactly are the differences between the credentials of Johnson, who challenged the promotion, and Joyce, who was promoted?*

2. *What are the criteria that the* Weber *case (discussed in* Johnson*) established for upholding an employer affirmative action plan that is challenged under Title VII?*

3. *What evidence demonstrates a "manifest imbalance" in a "traditionally segregated job category"?*

---

# Johnson v. Transportation Agency

### 480 U.S 616 (1987)

Justice Brennan delivered the opinion of the Court.

Respondent, Transportation Agency of Santa Clara County, California, unilaterally promulgated an Affirmative Action Plan applicable to promotions of employees. In selecting applicants for the promotional position of road dispatcher, the Agency, pursuant to the Plan, passed over petitioner Paul Johnson, a male employee, and promoted a female employee applicant, Diane Joyce. The question for decision is whether in making the promotion the Agency impermissibly took into account the sex of the applicants in violation of Title VII. [The appellate court held that respondent had not violated Title VII.] We affirm.[2]

### I

### A

In December 1978, the Santa Clara County Transit District Board of Supervisors adopted an Affirmative Action Plan (Plan) for the County Transportation Agency. The Plan implemented a County Affirmative Action Plan, which had been adopted, declared the County, because "mere prohibition of discriminatory practices is not enough to remedy the effects of past practices and to permit attainment of an equitable representation of minorities, women and handicapped persons." Relevant to this case, the Agency Plan provides that, in making promotions to positions within a traditionally segregated job classification in which women have been significantly underrepresented, the Agency is authorized to consider as one factor the sex of a qualified applicant.

In reviewing the composition of its work force, the Agency noted in its Plan that women were represented in numbers far less than their proportion of the County labor force in both the Agency as a whole and in five of seven job categories. Specifically, while women constituted 36.4% of the area labor market, they composed only 22.4% of Agency employees. Furthermore, women working at the Agency were concentrated largely in

---

2. No constitutional issue was either raised or addressed in the litigation below. We therefore decide in this case only the issue of the prohibitory scope of Title VII. Of course, where the issue is properly raised, public employers must justify the adoption and implementation of a voluntary affirmative action plan under the Equal Protection Clause. *See Wygant v. Jackson Board of Education,* 476 U.S. 267 (1986).

EEOC job categories traditionally held by women. [N]one of the 238 Skilled Craft Worker positions was held by a woman. The Plan noted that this underrepresentation of women in part reflected the fact that women had not traditionally been employed in these positions, and that they had not been strongly motivated to seek training or employment in them "because of the limited opportunities that have existed in the past for them to work in such classifications." ...

The Plan acknowledged that a number of factors might make it unrealistic to rely on the Agency's long-term goals in evaluating the Agency's progress in expanding job opportunities for minorities and women.... As a result, the Plan counseled that short-range goals be established and annually adjusted to serve as the most realistic guide for actual employment decisions....

The Agency's Plan ... set aside no specific number of positions for minorities or women, but authorized the consideration of ethnicity or sex as a factor when evaluating qualified candidates for jobs in which members of such groups were poorly represented. One such job was the road dispatcher position that is the subject of the dispute in this case.

B

On December 12, 1979, the Agency announced a vacancy for the promotional position of road dispatcher in the Agency's Roads Division. Dispatchers assign road crews, equipment, and materials, and maintain records pertaining to road maintenance jobs. The position requires at minimum four years of dispatch or road maintenance work experience for Santa Clara County. The EEOC job classification scheme designates a road dispatcher as a Skilled Craft Worker.

Twelve County employees applied for the promotion, including Joyce and Johnson. Joyce had worked for the County since 1970, serving as an account clerk until 1975. She had applied for a road dispatcher position in 1974, but was deemed ineligible because she had not served as a road maintenance worker. In 1975, Joyce transferred from a senior account clerk position to a road maintenance worker position, becoming the first woman to fill such a job. During her four years in that position, she occasionally worked out of class as a road dispatcher.

Petitioner Johnson began with the County in 1967 as a road yard clerk, after private employment that included working as a supervisor and dispatcher. He had also unsuccessfully applied for the road dispatcher opening in 1974. In 1977, his clerical position was downgraded, and he sought and received a transfer to the position of road maintenance worker. He also occasionally worked out of class as a dispatcher while performing that job.

... The scores awarded [on a preliminary interview] ranged from 70 to 80. Johnson was tied for second with a score of 75, while Joyce ranked next with a score of 73. A second interview was conducted by three Agency supervisors, who ultimately recommended that Johnson be promoted. Prior to the second interview, Joyce had contacted the County's Affirmative Action Office because [her past experience of the two interviewers gave her concerns about fairness.] The Office in turn contacted the Agency's Affirmative Action Coordinator, whom the Agency's Plan makes responsible for keeping the Director informed of opportunities for the Agency to accomplish its objectives under the Plan. At the time, the Agency employed no women in any Skilled Craft position, and had never employed a woman as a road dispatcher. The Coordinator recommended to the Director of the Agency, James Graebner, that Joyce be promoted.

... Graebner concluded that the promotion should be given to Joyce. As he testified: "I tried to look at the whole picture, the combination of her qualifications and Mr.

Johnson's qualifications, their test scores, their expertise, their background, affirmative action matters, things like that.... I believe it was a combination of all those." ... Graebner testified that he did not regard as significant the fact that Johnson scored 75 and Joyce 73 when interviewed by the two-person board.

Petitioner Johnson ... sued, alleging that he had been denied promotion on the basis of sex in violation of Title VII ... The District Court found that Johnson was more qualified for the dispatcher position than Joyce, and that the sex of Joyce was the "determining factor *in her selection*." ...

## II

As a preliminary matter, we note that petitioner bears the burden of establishing the invalidity of the Agency's Plan.... This case also fits readily within the analytical framework set forth in *McDonnell Douglas Corp. v. Green*. Once a plaintiff establishes a prima facie case that race or sex has been taken into account in an employer's employment decision, the burden shifts to the employer to articulate a nondiscriminatory rationale for its decision. The existence of an affirmative action plan provides such a rationale. If such a plan is articulated as the basis for the employer's decision, the burden shifts to the plaintiff to prove that the employer's justification is pretextual and the plan is invalid. As a practical matter, of course, an employer will generally seek to avoid a charge of pretext by presenting evidence in support of its plan....

The assessment of the legality of the Agency Plan must be guided by our decision in *Weber*, 443 U.S. 193 (1979)....

The first issue is therefore whether consideration of the sex of applicants for Skilled Craft jobs was justified by the existence of a "manifest imbalance" that reflected underrepresentation of women in "traditionally segregated job categories." [I]n determining whether an imbalance exists that would justify taking sex or race into account, a comparison of the percentage of minorities or women in the employer's work force with the percentage in the area labor market or general population is appropriate in analyzing jobs that require no special expertise. Where a job requires special training, however, the comparison should be with those in the labor force who possess the relevant qualifications. The requirement that the "manifest imbalance" relate to a "traditionally segregated job category" provides assurance both that sex or race will be taken into account in a manner consistent with Title VII's purpose of eliminating the effects of employment discrimination, and that the interests of those employees not benefiting from the plan will not be unduly infringed.

A manifest imbalance need not be such that it would support a prima facie case against the employer, as suggested in Justice O'Connor's concurrence, since we do not regard as identical the constraints of Title VII and the Federal Constitution on voluntarily adopted affirmative action plans. Application of the "prima facie" standard in Title VII cases would be inconsistent with *Weber*'s focus on statistical imbalance, and could inappropriately create a significant disincentive for employers to adopt an affirmative action plan. *See Weber*, 443 U.S. at 204 (Title VII intended as a "catalyst" for employer efforts to eliminate vestiges of discrimination). A corporation concerned with maximizing return on investment, for instance, is hardly likely to adopt a plan if in order to do so it must compile evidence that could be used to subject it to a colorable Title VII suit.

It is clear that the decision to hire Joyce was made pursuant to an Agency plan that directed that sex or race be taken into account for the purpose of remedying underrepresentation. The Agency Plan acknowledged the "limited opportunities that have existed in the past," for women to find employment in certain job classifications "where women have not been traditionally employed in significant numbers." As a result, observed the Plan, women were concentrated in traditionally female jobs in the Agency, and represented a lower percentage in other job classifications than would be expected if such traditional segregation had not occurred.... The Plan sought to remedy these imbalances through "hiring, training and promotion of ... women throughout the Agency in all major job classifications where they are underrepresented."

As an initial matter, the Agency adopted as a benchmark for measuring progress in eliminating underrepresentation the long-term goal of a work force that mirrored in its major job classifications the percentage of women in the area labor market.... The Plan ... directed that annual short-term goals be formulated that would provide a more realistic indication of the degree to which sex should be taken into account in filling particular positions. The Plan stressed that such goals "should not be construed as 'quotas' that must be met," but as reasonable aspirations in correcting the imbalance in the Agency's work force.... The Plan specifically directed that, in establishing such goals, the Agency work with the County Planning Department and other sources ... to compile data on the percentage of minorities and women in the local labor force that were actually working in the [relevant] job classifications. From the outset, therefore, the Plan sought annually to develop even more refined measures of the underrepresentation in each job category that required attention....

As the Agency Plan recognized, women were most egregiously underrepresented in the Skilled Craft job category, since *none* of the 238 positions was occupied by a woman. In mid-1980, when Joyce was selected for the road dispatcher position, the Agency was still in the process of refining its short-term goals for Skilled Craft Workers in accordance with the directive of the Plan. This process did not reach fruition until 1982, when the Agency established a short-term goal for that year of 3 women for the 55 expected openings in that job category — a modest goal of about 6% for that category.

We reject petitioner's argument that, since only the long-term goal was in place for Skilled Craft positions at the time of Joyce's promotion, it was inappropriate for the Director to take into account affirmative action considerations in filling the road dispatcher position. The Agency's Plan emphasized that the long-term goals were not to be taken as guides for actual hiring decisions, but that supervisors were to consider a host of practical factors in seeking to meet affirmative action objectives, including the fact that in some job categories women were not qualified in numbers comparable to their representation in the labor force.

By contrast, had the Plan simply calculated imbalances in all categories according to the proportion of women in the area labor pool, and then directed that hiring be governed solely by those figures, its validity fairly could be called into question. This is because analysis of a more specialized labor pool normally is necessary in determining underrepresentation in some positions....

The Agency's Plan emphatically did *not* authorize such blind hiring. It expressly directed that numerous factors be taken into account in making hiring decisions, including specifically the qualifications of female applicants for particular jobs. Thus, despite the fact that no precise short-term goal was yet in place for the Skilled Craft category in mid-1980, the Agency's management nevertheless had been clearly instructed that they were not to hire solely by reference to statistics. The fact that only the long-term goal had been established for this category posed no danger that personnel decisions would be made by reflexive adherence to a numerical standard.

... Given the obvious imbalance in the Skilled Craft category, and given the Agency's commitment to eliminating such imbalances, it was plainly not unreasonable for the Agency to determine that it was appropriate to consider as one factor the sex of Ms. Joyce in making its decision. The promotion of Joyce thus satisfies the first requirement enunciated in *Weber,* since it was undertaken to further an affirmative action plan designed to eliminate Agency work force imbalances in traditionally segregated job categories.

We next consider whether the Agency Plan unnecessarily trammeled the rights of male employees or created an absolute bar to their advancement.... The Plan expressly states that "[t]he 'goals' established for each Division should not be construed as 'quotas' that must be met." Rather, the Plan merely authorizes that consideration be given to affirmative action concerns when evaluating qualified applicants.... Similarly, the Agency Plan requires women to compete with all other qualified applicants. *No* persons are automatically excluded from consideration; *all* are able to have their qualifications weighed against those of other applicants.

In addition, petitioner had no absolute entitlement to the road dispatcher position. Seven of the applicants were classified as qualified and eligible, and the Agency Director was authorized to promote any of the seven. Thus, denial of the promotion unsettled no legitimate, firmly rooted expectation on the part of petitioner. Furthermore, while petitioner in this case was denied a promotion, he retained his employment with the Agency, at the same salary and with the same seniority, and remained eligible for other promotions....

Finally, the Agency's Plan was intended to *attain* a balanced work force, not to maintain one. The Plan contains 10 references to the Agency's desire to "attain" such a balance, but no reference whatsoever to a goal of maintaining it....

The Agency acknowledged the difficulties that it would confront in remedying the imbalance in its work force, and it anticipated only gradual increases in the representation of minorities and women. It is thus unsurprising that the Plan contains no explicit end date, for the Agency's flexible, case-by-case approach was not expected to yield success in a brief period of time. Express assurance that a program is only temporary may be necessary if the program actually sets aside positions according to specific numbers.... In this case, however, substantial evidence shows that the Agency has sought to take a moderate, gradual approach to eliminating the imbalance in its work force, one which establishes realistic guidance for employment decisions, and which visits minimal intrusion on the legitimate expectations of other employees. Given this fact, as well as the Agency's express commitment to "attain" a balanced work force, there is ample assurance that the Agency does not seek to use its Plan to maintain a permanent racial and sexual balance.

## III

In evaluating the compliance of an affirmative action plan with Title VII's prohibition on discrimination, we must be mindful of "this Court's and Congress' consistent emphasis on 'the value of voluntary efforts to further the objectives of the law.'" The Agency in the case before us has undertaken such a voluntary effort, and has done so in full recognition of both the difficulties and the potential for intrusion on males and nonminorities. The Agency has identified a conspicuous imbalance in job categories traditionally segregated by race and sex. It has made clear from the outset, however, that employment decisions may not be justified solely by reference to this imbalance, but must rest on a multitude of practical, realistic factors. It has therefore committed itself to annual adjustment of goals so as to provide a reasonable guide for actual hiring and promotion decisions. The Agency earmarks no positions for anyone; sex is but one of several factors that may be taken into account in evaluating qualified applicants for a position. As both the Plan's language and its manner of operation attest, the Agency has no intention of establishing a work force whose permanent composition is dictated by rigid numerical standards.

We therefore hold that the Agency appropriately took into account as one factor the sex of Diane Joyce in determining that she should be promoted to the road dispatcher position. The decision to do so was made pursuant to an affirmative action plan that represents a moderate, flexible, case-by-case approach to effecting a gradual improvement in the representation of minorities and women in the Agency's work force. Such a plan is fully consistent with Title VII, for it embodies the contribution that voluntary employer action can make in eliminating the vestiges of discrimination in the workplace. Accordingly, the judgment of the Court of Appeals is [affirmed].

[Justice Stevens wrote a concurring opinion in which he expressed disagreement with the Court's earlier cases approving voluntary affirmative action under Title VII, but found himself bound by those precedents.]

[Justice O'Connor wrote a concurring opinion in which she argued that the applicable standard should be identical for cases challenging affirmative action under Title VII and those challenging affirmative action under the Constitution. That standard, in Justice O'Connor's view, requires statistics sufficient to support a prima facie pattern and practice claim by the beneficiaries of the affirmative action plan. Justice O'Connor believed that the interests of the employer's nonminority employees would be insufficiently protected if affirmative action were upheld on a lesser statistical showing. Although no finding of discrimination had been made in the *Johnson* case, Justice O'Connor wrote, "at the time the affirmative action plan was adopted, there were *no* women in its skilled craft positions. Petitioner concedes that women constituted approximately 5% of the local labor pool of skilled craft workers in 1970. Thus, when compared to the percentage of women in the qualified work force, the statistical disparity would have been sufficient for a prima facie Title VII case brought by unsuccessful women job applicants."]

[The dissenting opinion of Justice White is omitted.]

Justice Scalia, with whom Chief Justice Rehnquist joins, and with whom Justice White joins in Parts I and II, dissenting.

… The most significant proposition of law established by today's decision is that racial or sexual discrimination is permitted under Title VII when it is intended to overcome the effect, not of the employer's own discrimination, but of societal attitudes that have limited the entry of certain races, or of a particular sex, into certain jobs. Even if the societal attitudes in question consisted exclusively of conscious discrimination by other employers, this holding would contradict a decision of this Court rendered only last Term. *Wygant v. Jackson Board of Education*, 476 U.S. 267 (1986), held that the objective of remedying societal discrimination cannot prevent remedial affirmative action from violating the Equal Protection Clause....

In fact, however, today's decision goes well beyond merely allowing racial or sexual discrimination in order to eliminate the effects of prior societal *discrimination*. The majority opinion often uses the phrase "traditionally segregated job category" to describe the evil against which the plan is legitimately (according to the majority) directed. As originally used in *Steelworkers* v. *Weber*, 443 U.S. 193 (1979), that phrase described skilled jobs from which employers and unions had systematically and intentionally excluded black workers — traditionally segregated jobs, that is, in the sense of conscious, exclusionary discrimination. But that is assuredly not the sense in which the phrase is used here. It is absurd to think that the nationwide failure of road maintenance crews, for example, to achieve the Agency's ambition of 36.4% female representation is attributable primarily, if even substantially, to systematic exclusion of women eager to shoulder pick and shovel. It is a "traditionally segregated job category" *not* in the *Weber* sense, but in the sense that, because of longstanding social attitudes, it has not been regarded *by women themselves* as desirable work.... Given this meaning of the phrase, it is patently false to say that "[the] requirement that the 'manifest imbalance' relate to a 'traditionally segregated job category' provides assurance ... that sex or race will be taken into account in a manner consistent with Title VII's purpose of eliminating the effects of employment discrimination." There are, of course, those who believe that the social attitudes which cause women themselves to avoid certain jobs and to favor others are as nefarious as conscious, exclusionary discrimination. Whether or not that is so (and there is assuredly no consensus on the point equivalent to our national consensus against intentional discrimination), the two phenomena are certainly distinct. And it is the alteration of social attitudes, rather than the elimination of discrimination, which today's decision approves as justification for state-enforced discrimination. This is an enormous expansion, undertaken without the slightest justification or analysis....

It is unlikely that today's result will be displeasing to politically elected officials, to whom it provides the means of quickly accommodating the demands of organized groups to achieve concrete, numerical improvement in the economic status of particular constituencies. Nor will it displease the world of corporate and governmental employers (many of whom have filed briefs as *amici* in the present case, all on the side of Santa Clara) for whom the cost of hiring less qualified workers is often substantially less — and infinitely more predictable — than the cost of litigating Title VII cases and of seeking to convince federal agencies by nonnumerical means that no discrimination exists. In fact, the only losers in the process are the Johnsons of the country, for whom Title VII has been not merely repealed but actually inverted. The irony is that these individuals — predominantly unknown, unaffluent, unorganized — suffer this injustice at the hands of a Court fond of thinking itself the champion of the politically impotent. I dissent.

---

## Notes

1. The *Weber* and *Johnson* Courts required that, to be upheld, a voluntary affirmative action plan be designed to "eliminate manifest racial imbalances in traditionally segregated job categories" within the employer's own workforce.

   a.   What goal of Title VII is this requirement intended to serve?

   b.   Notice that the Agency's affirmative action plan seeks to achieve a workforce that reflects the 36.4% of women in the area labor market. Why would this standard, if it were applied as the goal in the case of the skilled craft position in question, be problematic?

   c.   Does this standard require a finding that the employer's own past discrimination contributed to those imbalances? In the alternative, is societal discrimination enough?

   d.   In your own view, should the manifest imbalance suffice to uphold a voluntary affirmative action plan under Title VII, or should the employer be required to show statistics sufficient to establish a prima facie pattern and practice case?

   e.   To determine whether a manifest imbalance exists, courts compare the "relevant labor pool" with the employer's workforce. What groups within and outside the defendant's workforce were compared to determine whether there was a manifest imbalance in *Johnson*?

   f.   In a situation where societal discrimination causes a group not to aspire to a particular type of skilled work, the relevant labor pool can be expected to be very small. Should the Court permit a comparison with the general population to compensate for this?

2. In addition to the manifest imbalance, the Court required that the plan not "unnecessarily trammel the interests of the white employees." What were the factors at work in *Johnson* that caused the Court to conclude that the Agency's plan did not unnecessarily trammel majority rights?

Because *Johnson* involved promotions, as to which no particular one of several qualified applicants could legitimately have settled expectations, it was fairly easy to find the majority's rights not trammeled. What would have happened if the case had involved layoffs instead? In *Taxman v. Piscataway*, the Third Circuit struck down an affirmative action plan, in part, for trammeling majority employee's expectations. 91 F.3d 1547, 1564 (3d Cir. 1996) (en banc), *cert. granted*, 521 U.S. 1117 (1997), *cert. dismissed*, 522 U.S. 1010 (1997). There the two workers who were candidates for layoff were deemed equivalent, and the employer broke the tie by using race as a plus factor. The Third Circuit struck down this affirmative action as interfering with the laid-off employee's expectations. A coin toss, by contrast, would have been an acceptable ground for deciding. The *Taxman* facts could be distinguished from *Johnson* in that the employer in *Taxman* had already achieved racial balance.

3. Note that the existence of a formal plan itself is also an essential element in the plan's validity. Ad hoc affirmative action decisions do not withstand scrutiny under Title VII. *Lehman v. Yellow Freight System, Inc.*, 651 F.2d 520, 526–527 (7th Cir. 1981).

4. The *Johnson v. Transportation Agency* majority argues that, if Congress had not agreed with the Court's *Weber* decision allowing affirmative action under Title VII, Congress would have amended the statute to reverse *Weber* as it had done in other contexts. Subsequent to *Johnson*, Congress enacted the 1991 Civil Rights Act, which included language in Section 116 of the Act tending to preserve the permissibility of affirmative action: "Nothing in the amendments made by this title shall be construed to affect court-ordered remedies, affirmative action, or conciliation agreements, that are in accordance with the law." 42 U.S.C. § 1981 note (1991).

5. Recall that in *Ricci v. DeStefano* the Supreme Court concluded that the City of New Haven could justify setting aside some test results that favored whites only if the city had a strong basis in evidence that its failure to do so would result in disparate impact liability. New Haven's decision to throw away the test results was not affirmative action, but it resembled it. It was not affirmative action because there was no affirmative action plan in place that required the city to take the action it took. It resembled affirmative action in that the city took action that harmed whites because there might otherwise have been a harmful effect on blacks and Hispanics. Compare the result in *Ricci* with the discussion in *Johnson* about whether the statistical disparity necessary to support affirmative action would need to be sufficiently severe to support a prima facie pattern and practice case.

## Sex, Pregnancy and Maternal Wall

In 1978, Congress amended Title VII to include a ban on pregnancy discrimination. The Pregnancy Discrimination Act of 1978 (PDA) was passed to reverse the Supreme Court decision in *General Electric Company v. Gilbert*, which held that the Title VII ban on "sex" discrimination did not reach pregnancy discrimination. 429 U.S. 125 (1976). *Gilbert* pertained to an employer exclusion of pregnancy from disability compensation coverage. The PDA went well beyond the specific facts presented in *Gilbert*, providing broad anti-discrimination protections to pregnant women.

The PDA amended section 701 of Title VII by adding the following:

> (k) The terms "because of sex" or "on the basis of sex" include, but are not limited to, because of or on the basis of pregnancy, childbirth, or related medical conditions; and women affected by pregnancy, childbirth, or related medical conditions shall be treated the same for all employment-related purposes, including receipt of benefits under fringe benefit programs, as other persons not so affected but similar in their ability or inability to work, and nothing in section 703(h) of this title shall be interpreted to permit otherwise. This subsection shall not require an employer to pay for health insurance benefits for abortion, except where the life of the mother would be endangered if the fetus were carried to term, or except where medical complications have arisen from an abortion: Provided, That nothing herein shall preclude an employer from providing abortion benefits or otherwise affect bargaining agreements in regard to abortion.

42 U.S.C. § 2000e(k) (2009).

Notice that the PDA contains three mandates: (1) it plainly prohibits discrimination on the basis of pregnancy; (2) it requires equal treatment of pregnant workers and non-pregnant workers whose ability to work is similar; and (3) it specifies the ramifications of the PDA on abortion funding. Do you see a difference between requiring nondiscrimination and requiring equal treatment? The Supreme Court has rejected the argument that the second clause (requiring equal treatment) forbids employers to give more *favorable* treatment to pregnant workers than to nonpregnant workers. *In California Federal Savings & Loan Assoc. v. Guerra*, the Court stated that the second clause of the PDA imposes a "floor beneath which pregnancy benefits may not drop—not a ceiling above which they may not rise." 479 U.S. 272 (1987).

Several circuits have used the *McDonnell-Douglas* framework to analyze pregnancy discrimination claims based on circumstantial evidence. In doing so, these circuits have articulated the prima facie case as having the following factors: (1) the plaintiff was pregnant; (2) she was qualified for her job or meeting the employer's legitimate expectations; (3) she was subjected to an adverse employment decision; and (4) there is a nexus (causation) between her pregnancy and the adverse employment decision. *Cline v. Catholic Diocese of Toledo*, 206 F.3d 651, 658 (6th Cir. 2000); *Pickworth v. Entrepreneurs' Organization*, 261 Fed.Appx. 491 (4th Cir. 2008).

Some of the legal disputes arising under the PDA center on exactly what is encompassed in the first prong, beyond the simple fact of being pregnant. The statute prohibits discrimination based on "pregnancy, childbirth, or related medical conditions." The case of *Union Pacific* considers whether the PDA reaches an employer insurance policy that fails to provide coverage for contraception.

# In re Union Pacific Railroad Employment Practices Litigation

479 F.3d 936 (8th Cir. 2007)

Circuit Judge Gruender.

## I. BACKGROUND

Union Pacific, a freight company headquartered in Omaha, Nebraska, provides health care benefits to those of its employees who are covered by collective bargaining agreements ... through one of five plans. [T]he plans ... exclude both male and female contraceptive methods, prescription and non-prescription, when used for the sole purpose of contraception....

Standridge and Phillips are two ... female ... employees [who] brought individual suits against Union Pacific alleging that Union Pacific discriminated against its female employees by not providing coverage of prescription contraception in violation of Title VII, as amended by the PDA. The Judicial Panel on Multidistrict Litigation consolidated [several actions and] [t]he district court granted class certification....

The district court held that Union Pacific ... violated the PDA, because "it treats medical care women need to prevent pregnancy less favorably than it treats medical care needed to prevent other medical conditions that are no greater threat to employees' health than is pregnancy." ...

## II. DISCUSSION

### A. PDA Analysis

As an initial matter, the district court incorrectly characterized Union Pacific's policy as the denial of prescription contraception coverage for women. Union Pacific excludes all types of contraception, whether prescription, non-prescription or surgical and whether for men or women, unless an employee has a non-contraception medical necessity for the contraception. While prescription contraception is currently only available for women, non-prescription contraception is available for men and women. Therefore, the issue is whether Union Pacific's policy of denying coverage for all contraception violates ... the PDA.

Title VII provides that "[i]t shall be an unlawful employment practice for an employer ... to discriminate against any individual with respect to his compensation, terms, conditions, or privileges of employment, because of such individual's ... sex." Congress [enacted] the PDA to amend this provision in response to the Supreme Court's holding that the exclusion of pregnancy benefits did not violate Title VII. *See Gen. Elec. Co. v. Gilbert*, 429 U.S. 125 (1976). The PDA provides:

> The terms "because of sex" or "on the basis of sex" include, but are not limited to, because of or on the basis of pregnancy, childbirth, or related medical conditions; and women affected by pregnancy, childbirth, or related medical conditions shall be treated the same for all employment-related purposes, including receipt of benefits under fringe benefit programs, as other persons not so affected but similar in their ability or inability to work.... This subsection shall not require an employer to pay for health insurance benefits for abortion, except where the life of the mother would be endangered if the fetus were carried to term, or except where medical complications have arisen from an abortion.

42 U.S.C. § 2000e(k).

Neither the circuit courts nor the Supreme Court has considered whether the PDA applies to contraception.[3] ...

In *Krauel v. Iowa Methodist Medical Center*, 95 F.3d 674, 679 (8th Cir. 1996), we applied ... Supreme Court precedents and held that the PDA does not extend to *infertility treatments*.... Infertility is "strikingly different" from pregnancy and childbirth because infertility prevents conception, while pregnancy, childbirth and medical conditions related to them can occur

---

3. District court decisions are split as to whether the PDA requires companies to provide coverage of contraception....

only after conception. Therefore, *Krauel* holds that infertility is "outside of the PDA's protection because it is not pregnancy, childbirth, or a related medical condition."

In concluding that the PDA does not extend to infertility, we also distinguished the Supreme Court's holding in *Johnson Controls*. [W]e held that *Johnson Controls* does not support an expansion of the PDA to cover fertility matters prior to conception because "[p]otential pregnancy, unlike infertility, is a medical condition that is sex-related because only women can become pregnant.... [B]ecause the policy of denying insurance benefits for treatment of fertility problems applies to both female and male workers ... [it] is gender-neutral[.]"

With the guidance of these decisions, we now determine whether contraception is "related to" pregnancy for PDA purposes. While contraception may certainly affect the causal chain that leads to pregnancy, we have specifically rejected the argument that a causal connection, by itself, results in a medical condition being "related to" pregnancy for PDA purposes. Union Pacific argues that contraception, analogous to infertility, is gender-neutral. Standridge and Phillips argue that the district court correctly found that contraception implicates potential pregnancy and that the PDA covers contraception because it prevents a gender-specific condition.

Following *Krauel,* we hold that contraception is not "related to" pregnancy for PDA purposes because, like infertility treatments, contraception is a treatment that is only indicated prior to pregnancy. Contraception is not a medical treatment that occurs when or if a woman becomes pregnant; instead, contraception prevents pregnancy from even occurring. *See* Merriam-Webster's Collegiate Dictionary 271 (11th ed. 2005) (defining contraception as the "deliberate prevention of conception or impregnation"). As in *Krauel,* the result in *Johnson Controls* does not require coverage of contraception because contraception is not a gender-specific term like "potential pregnancy," but rather applies to both men and women like "infertility." In conclusion, the PDA does not require coverage of contraception because contraception is not "related to" pregnancy for PDA purposes and is gender-neutral.

We are not persuaded by the contention of Standridge and Phillips and the amici members of Congress that Congress intended to address the coverage of prescription contraception in the PDA. In their views, the PDA was a "broad response" to the *Gilbert* decision, and Congress wanted to protect women in all areas concerning pregnancy, including the prevention of it. However, the plain language of the PDA makes no reference to contraception. Additionally, the House and Senate legislative histories do not mention contraception.[4]

We also do not agree with Standridge and Phillips's argument that the PDA's express exclusion of coverage of abortion, without an accompanying express exclusion of coverage for contraception, implies an intent to include coverage of contraception. Abortion is "the termination of a pregnancy," Merriam-Webster's Collegiate Dictionary 3, while contraception prevents pregnancy from even occurring. While we do not need to decide whether the PDA would cover abortion without this exclusion, abortion arguably would be "related to" pregnancy in a manner that contraception is not because abortion can only occur when a woman is pregnant. In contrast, there would be no reason for Congress to expressly exclude a treatment that is not "related to" pregnancy for PDA purposes, such as contraception.

Finally, we are not persuaded by the EEOC decision that interpreted the PDA as requiring employers to cover prescription contraception for women if they cover "other

---

4. Amici members of Congress emphasize their intent that the PDA cover contraception. However, in our constrained role of interpreting a statute, we cannot assume that these amici members represent the viewpoints of a majority of both houses of Congress in 1978.

prescription drugs and devices, or other types of services, that are used to prevent the occurrences of other medical conditions."

In conclusion, based on the language of the PDA and our previous holding in *Krauel*, we hold that the PDA does not encompass contraception. Contraception, like infertility treatments, is a treatment that is only indicated prior to pregnancy because contraception actually prevents pregnancy from occurring. Furthermore, like infertility, contraception is a gender-neutral term. Therefore, Union Pacific's denial of coverage for contraception for both sexes did not discriminate against its female employees in violation of Title VII, as amended by the PDA.

B. Title VII Analysis

... Standridge and Phillips brought a claim of disparate treatment based on gender discrimination.... The district court compared the "medicines or medical services [that] prevent employees from developing diseases or conditions that pose an equal or lesser threat to employees' health than does pregnancy." It found that the health plans treated men more favorably because the plans covered preventive medicines and services such as medication for male-pattern baldness, routine physical exams, tetanus shots, and drug and alcohol treatments. Union Pacific argues that the district court's comparator was too broad because it treated pregnancy as a disease that needed to be prevented instead of focusing on the narrow issue of contraception.

We decline to address whether pregnancy is a "disease." Instead, we simply hold that the district court erred in using the comparator "medicines or medical services [that] prevent employees from developing diseases or conditions that pose an equal or lesser threat to employees' health than does pregnancy." As previously discussed, this case concerns Union Pacific's coverage of contraception for men and women. The proper comparator is the provision of the medical benefit in question, contraception. Union Pacific's health plans do not cover any contraception used by women such as birth control, sponges, diaphragms, intrauterine devices or tubal ligations or any contraception used by men such as condoms and vasectomies. Therefore, the coverage provided to women is not less favorable than that provided to men. Thus, there is no violation of Title VII.

### III. CONCLUSION

Accordingly, we reverse the district court's judgment and remand the case for further proceedings consistent with this opinion.

Judge Bye, dissenting.

... The Court ends with the following pronouncement in footnote five: "Union Pacific provides an equal policy for its female and male employees." This is a good place to begin. When one looks at the medical effect of Union Pacific's failure to provide insurance coverage for prescription contraception, the inequality of coverage is clear. This failure only medically affects females, as they bear all of the health consequences of unplanned pregnancies. An insurance policy providing comprehensive coverage for preventative medical care, including coverage for preventative prescription drugs used exclusively by males, but fails to cover prescription contraception used exclusively by females, can hardly be called equal. It just isn't so.

The Court begins its analysis by finding the district court erred in confining its inquiry to Union Pacific's exclusion of coverage for prescription contraception used by women because its policy also excludes coverage for non-prescription contraception coverage (condoms) and surgical procedures to prevent male fertility (vasectomies). The district court did not err in limiting its inquiry to prescription contraception. That its policy does not provide coverage for condoms is unsurprising—Union Pacific has not identified any health insurance policy which would provide coverage for non-prescription, contraceptive devices available in drug stores and gas stations nationwide. As for vasectomies, even if we were to look at its exclusion of coverage for vasectomies, the policy nonetheless discriminates against females. When a policy excludes coverage for vasectomies, the medical effect of this exclusion is born entirely by women, as the record demonstrates women are the only gender which can become pregnant.

The Court holds Union Pacific's failure to cover prescription contraception is not covered by the PDA because prescription contraception use occurs prior to pregnancy....

While the plain language of the PDA does not specifically include pre-pregnancy conditions, there is some indication Congress intended the act to cover pre-pregnancy discrimination. Congress used the phrase "related medical conditions." The word "related" indicates the PDA covers more than mere pregnancy. In this case, the district court relied on the second clause of the PDA which is drafted even more broadly than the first, covering "women *affected by* pregnancy, childbirth, or related medical conditions." *In re Union Pac. R.R. Employment Practices Litig.*, 378 F. Supp. 2d 1139, 1143 (D. Neb. 2005) (emphasis added) ("Because the PDA plainly states that its protection from discrimination, including discrimination in 'receipt of benefits under fringe benefit programs,' applies to 'women affected by pregnancy' and not merely to pregnant women, the clear language of the statute requires that [Union Pacific's] Plans treat the risk of pregnancy no less favorably than the Plans treat other similar health risks."). Finally, as noted by certain members of Congress, writing as *amici* on behalf of Standridge and Phillips, the first clause of the PDA specifically states: "The terms 'because of sex' or 'on the basis of sex' *include, but are not limited to,* because of or on the basis of pregnancy, childbirth, or related medical conditions." The use of the phrase "include, but are not limited to" mandates a broad reading of the PDA because it suggests Congress was being illustrative rather than exclusive with the list following the phrase....

Even if Congress did not intend the PDA to cover pre-pregnancy discrimination, the Supreme Court ostensibly broadened the scope of the PDA to include pre-pregnancy discrimination in *International Union, United Automobile, Aerospace & Agricultural Implement Workers, UAW v. Johnson Controls, Inc.,* 499 U.S. 187 (1991). The Court found classifying employees on the basis of childbearing capacity, whether or not they were already pregnant, "must be regarded, for Title VII purposes, in the same light as explicit sex discrimination." In *Johnson Controls,* a battery manufacturer enforced a gender-based, fetal-protection policy excluding fertile women (women who were pregnant or capable of becoming pregnant) from working in jobs where they would be exposed to lead. The bias was clear, as the policy at issue excluded only women. The Court used the PDA to bolster its holding the policy discriminated on its face as it "explicitly classifies on the basis of potential for pregnancy."

This court addressed the scope of the first clause of the PDA in *Krauel v. Iowa Methodist Medical Center.* In *Krauel,* we held an insurance policy excluding coverage for *infertility treatments* did not violate the PDA, as *treatment for infertility* is not treatment of a medical condition related to pregnancy or childbirth. Because "[p]regnancy and childbirth, which occur after conception, are strikingly different from infertility, which prevents conception," we [concluded] that infertility is outside of the PDA's protection because it is not pregnancy, childbirth, or a related medical condition." We explicitly acknowledged however, under *Johnson Controls,* "[p]otential pregnancy, unlike infertility, is a medical condition that is sex-related because only women can become pregnant." Because infertility, unlike potential pregnancy, is gender-neutral, it could not form the basis of a PDA claim.

Potential pregnancy, like infertility, by its definition occurs prior to conception. The same can be said for the use of prescription contraception. The reason *Krauel* determined the PDA did not apply to an employer's failure to cover *infertility treatments*, even in light of *Johnson Controls*, was because infertility, unlike potential pregnancy, is a gender-neutral affliction. After *Krauel*, denial of coverage for *infertility treatments* does not implicate the PDA because infertility affects both men and women. The Court suggests *infertility treatments* and contraception are both pre-pregnancy and this fact makes the difference. Although both are used prior to conception, when one looks at the medical effect of the denial of insurance coverage, prescription contraception is easily distinguishable from *infertility treatments....* More importantly, the Court's holding here—"that contraception is not 'related to' pregnancy for PDA purposes because, like *infertility treatments*, contraception is a treatment that is only indicated prior to pregnancy,"—is inconsistent with *Johnson Controls.*

In addition to holding the PDA does not apply under *Krauel*, the Court also holds Union Pacific's policy does not discriminate against women under Title VII, because the policy excludes contraception coverage for both men and women.... What is comparable coverage? The district court determined the proper comparison is between prescription contraception coverage and other preventative coverage. In contrast, the Court concludes the proper comparison is between coverage for female contraception (prescription contraception) and male contraception (condoms and *vasectomies*). As noted above, I agree with the district court about contraception being a gender-specific, female issue because of the adverse health consequences of an unplanned pregnancy (or even the general health consequences of any pregnancy). As such, I agree the proper comparison is between the preventative health coverage provided to each gender.

The history of the PDA supports the district court's choice of comparators. The PDA was enacted specifically to overrule the reasoning employed by the majority in *General Electric Co. v. Gilbert*, and to adopt the reasoning of the *Gilbert* dissenters. In *Gilbert*, the Court refused to require employers to cover pregnancy in their short-term disability plans, noting that without the pregnancy coverage, plans for men and women were equal and covered the same risks. In his dissent, Justice Stevens argued this was discriminatory because the employer treated absenteeism based on pregnancy differently than all other types of absenteeism. Likewise, Justice Brennan explained it was discriminatory for a company to devise "a policy that, but for pregnancy, offers protection for all risks, even those that are 'unique to' men or heavily male dominated." Put another way, the *Gilbert* dissenters recognized, to be equal, a plan would have to cover for the uniquely female risk of pregnancy, although this required giving women additional benefits men would not receive. Under this reasoning, as prescription contraception is a treatment for (or a method to control the occurrence and timing of) the uniquely female condition of potential pregnancy, the exclusion of this coverage in a plan providing other preventative coverage is discriminatory. Union Pacific provides coverage for a wide range of preventative medicines and procedures, including coverage for prescription drugs used exclusively by males to prevent *benign prostatic hypertrophy*. Union Pacific specifically excludes coverage for prescription contraception when used for a preventative purpose. Under the reasoning of the *Gilbert* dissenters, as adopted by Congress with the PDA, this is discriminatory.

Women are uniquely and specifically disadvantaged by Union Pacific's failure to cover prescription contraception. Because I believe such a policy is violative of Title VII, as amended by the PDA, I respectfully dissent. Although the district court's decision might appear to grant women benefits above and beyond those of men, the PDA requires such benefits be included in an otherwise comprehensive health care plan.

## Notes

1. The Court's opinion states both that non-coverage of contraceptives is "gender-neutral" because the plan excluded contraception for both males and females and that contraception is not sufficiently "related to" pregnancy because it is indicated only prior to pregnancy. Judge Bye's dissent states that the failure to provide contraception insurance coverage "only medically affects females, as they bear all of the health consequences of unplanned pregnancies." With which position do you agree? Do you think Congress intended coverage of contraception to be included in the PDA?

2. The *Union Pacific* decision relied upon *Krauel v. Iowa Methodist Medical Center*, which held that healthcare coverage of infertility treatments is "outside of the PDA's protection because it is not pregnancy, childbirth, or a related medical condition." 95 F.3d 674, 679 (8th Cir. 1996). Compare these cases with *Hall v. Nalco Co.*, where the Seventh Circuit found that the PDA prohibits firing a worker for taking time off to undergo in vitro fertilization treatments because IVF is performed only on women of childbearing capacity. 534 F.3d 644 (7th Cir. 2008).

The next case considers the PDA as it relates to abortion.

---

## Focus Questions: *Doe v. C.A.R.S. Protection Plus, Inc.*

1. *Think about the employer's leave policy. Some may consider it to be cruel. Can you think of reasons why an employer would not offer paid leave to its employees?*

2. *If you disagree with the employer's leave policies, consider whether the anti-discrimination statutes are the best way to address them.*

---

# Doe v. C.A.R.S. Protection Plus, Inc.

## 527 F.3d 358 (3rd Cir. 2008)

Jane Doe sued her former employer, C.A.R.S. Protection Plus, Inc. (CARS), alleging employment discrimination based on gender, in violation of Title VII. The District Court granted the employer's motion for summary judgment, finding that Doe had failed to establish a prima facie case of discrimination. We will reverse.

### I

We exercise plenary review over the District Court's grant of summary judgment and apply the same standard, *i.e.*, whether there are any genuine issues of material fact such that a reasonable jury could return a verdict for the plaintiff. We view the facts of this case in the light most favorable to the nonmoving party and draw all inferences in that party's favor.... The employer must persuade us that even if all of the inferences which could reasonably be drawn from the evidentiary materials of record were viewed in the light most favorable to the plaintiff, no reasonable jury could find in the plaintiff's favor.

## A

CARS does business in several states insuring used cars. CARS hired Jane Doe as a graphic artist in June 1999. Doe's sister-in-law, Leona Dunnett, was the CARS office manager. Fred Kohl, Vice-President and part-owner of the company, was Doe's supervisor. In May of 2000, Doe learned that she was pregnant. When she told Kohl she was pregnant, she asked Kohl about making up any time missed for doctor's appointments. Kohl told Doe they would "play it by ear."

On Monday, August 7, 2000, Doe's doctor telephoned her at work to inform her that problems were detected in her recent blood test and that further tests were necessary. An amniocentesis test was scheduled for the next day. Kohl was not in the office on August 7, 2000, so Doe told Leona Dunnett and Alivia Babich (who was Kohl's personal secretary), that she needed to be off work on Tuesday, August 8, 2000. Babich notified Kohl that Doe would be absent.

The amniocentesis test was not performed on the 8th, but a sonogram was, and additional tests were scheduled for the following day. Doe's husband telephoned Kohl and informed him that there were problems with the pregnancy and that the test would be performed on August 9th. Kohl approved the absence and said to contact him the next day.

On Wednesday, August 9th, Doe learned that her baby had severe deformities and her physician recommended that her pregnancy be terminated. That afternoon, Doe's husband again telephoned Kohl and told him that Doe would not be at work the next day. Kohl approved the absence and asked that Doe's husband call him the following day.

Doe had an additional doctor's appointment on Thursday, August 10th. Doe's husband testified that he called CARS again on that Thursday, and first spoke to Leona Dunnett. Then, he spoke with Kohl and told him that the pregnancy would be terminated the following day. Doe's husband requested that she be permitted to take one week of vacation the following week. According to Doe's husband's testimony, Kohl approved the request for a one-week vacation. Her pregnancy was terminated on Friday, August 11, 2000. Neither Doe nor her husband called Kohl over the weekend of August 12th.

A funeral was arranged for Doe's baby on Wednesday, August 16th. Kohl gave Leona Dunnett (the baby's aunt) permission to take one hour off work to attend the funeral. As she was leaving for the funeral, Leona noticed Babich packing up Doe's personal belongings from her desk. After the funeral, Leona told Doe what she had seen. Doe called Kohl who told her that she had been discharged. [Subsequently, Kohl stated that the reason for Doe's termination was her failure to call in each day of her absence to notify Kohl or another supervisor that she would be absent.]

[Doe filed an EEOC charge, was issued a right-to-sue letter and filed this action,] alleging employment discrimination based on gender, a violation of Title VII, as amended by the Pregnancy Discrimination Act (PDA). Doe maintained that CARS terminated her employment because she underwent a surgical abortion.... Whether the protections generally afforded pregnant women under the PDA also extend to women who have elected to terminate their pregnancies is a question of first impression in this Circuit.

## II
### A

... We note that the Sixth Circuit Court of Appeals has held that "an employer may not discriminate against a woman employee because 'she has exercised her right to have an abortion.'" ... Likewise, the Equal Employment Opportunity Commission (EEOC) has taken the position that it is an unlawful employment practice to fire a woman "because she is pregnant or has had an abortion." ... Similarly, the legislative history of section 2000e(k) provides [that] "no employer may ... fire or refuse to hire a woman simply because she has exercised her right to have an abortion."

Clearly, the plain language of the statute, together with the legislative history and the EEOC guidelines, support a conclusion that an employer may not discriminate against a woman employee because she has exercised her right to have an abortion. We now hold that the term "related medical conditions" includes an abortion.

### B

... Disparate treatment discrimination is proven by either using direct evidence of intent to discriminate or using indirect evidence from which a court could infer intent to discriminate. Doe supports her claim with evidence from which discrimination may be inferred. We therefore use the familiar *McDonnell Douglas* burden-shifting framework to analyze her Title VII pregnancy discrimination claims. Under this analysis, the employee must first establish a prima facie case. If the employee is able to present such a case, then the burden shifts to the employer to provide a legitimate, nondiscriminatory reason for its adverse employment decision. If the employer is able to do so, the burden shifts back to the employee, who, to defeat a motion for summary judgment, must show that the employer's articulated reason was a pretext for intentional discrimination.

... Neither party disputes that Doe has met her burden on the first three elements of a prima facie pregnancy discrimination case: (1) she is or was pregnant and that her employer knew she was pregnant; (2) she was qualified for her job; and (3) she suffered an adverse employment decision. It is the fourth element that is in dispute, namely whether there is some nexus between her pregnancy and her employment termination that would permit a fact-finder to infer unlawful discrimination.

The evidence most often used to establish this nexus is ... a plaintiff['s] show[ing] that she was treated less favorably than similarly situated employees who are not in plaintiff's protected class. Although we have held that "the PDA does not require that employers treat pregnant employees better than other temporarily disabled employees" the PDA does require that employers treat pregnant employees no worse. Comparing Doe to other non-pregnant workers who were temporarily disabled, we conclude that Doe has provided sufficient evidence to satisfy the fourth element of the prima facie case and has thus raised an inference of discrimination sufficient to defeat summary judgment.

Our factual analysis starts with CARS' somewhat less than compassionate leave policies. A memorandum authored by Kohl reveals that CARS employees were given no personal or sick leave. After one year on the job, employees were given five days' paid vacation. After five years' employment, they were given ten days. Any time taken off during a work day was to be deducted from the employee's vacation time or be unpaid.

Kohl testified that when an employee is so ill that he or she cannot work, CARS required the employee or spouse to call him or another designated supervisor on a daily basis....

[T]estimony indicates that although other employees were not [in actuality] expected to call the office every day, Doe's employment was terminated for precisely this reason. This testimony alone satisfies Doe's burden of establishing that other employees who were similarly situated were treated differently than her.... Babich's testimony as well as Kohl's own testimony establishes that the treatment given other employees differed from that given to Doe. This raises an inference of discrimination sufficient to satisfy her minimal burden of establishing a prima facie case.

The District Court also indicated that these employees had all made arrangements before missing work. There is evidence, however, that Doe did exactly that. Her husband testified that he called Kohl to request a week of vacation for his wife to recover from her surgical procedure and that Kohl agreed to the request. Doe's husband testified that all of the phone calls to Kohl were made from his father's house. Doe's husband further testified that he talked to Kohl on Thursday, August 10th and got Kohl's permission for his wife to take a vacation the following week. The District Court discounted this testimony because telephone records do not show a phone call from Doe's father-in-law's number to CARS telephone number. Doe's husband's testimony on this point, however, at least raises an issue of material fact. Doe testified that the call from her father-in-law's house may have originated from a cell phone as "there was a lot going on at that time."

Additionally, Doe points to testimony of Leona Dunnett to re-enforce the point. Leona Dunnett testified that on August 10th, Kohl asked her about coverage of the reception desk for the following week:

Q: What was the substance of the conversation [with Kohl]?

A: About coverage for the reception desk for the following week. He asked me if I had everything covered.

Q: Did [Doe] regularly cover the reception desk?

A: Yes.

Q: All day long?

A: No. Just for the lunch hour.

Q: What was said?

A: There was specific personnel that he did not want answering the phones, so I needed to rearrange lunch schedules so that it was covered without having those persons answering the phones for the following week.

Q: Did [Kohl] say that [Doe] would not be in work for the next week?

A: He said we needed to arrange coverage for the next week.

Doe points to this as confirmation that the August 10th phone call did take place— Kohl wanted to make sure that the telephones were covered because he knew Doe would be off the following week. . . .

Finally, Doe argues that her discharge only three working days after having an abortion raises an inference of discrimination because the temporal proximity between her abortion and the adverse employment action is "unusually suggestive." We have held temporal proximity sufficient to create an inference of causality to defeat summary judgment. In assessing causation, we are mindful of the procedural posture of the case. ["There is . . . a difference between a plaintiff relying upon temporal proximity to satisfy her prima facie case for the purpose of summary judgment, and to reverse a verdict."]

Here, Doe was fired on the day her baby was buried, just three working days after she notified Kohl that she would have to undergo an abortion. Because the District Court found Doe's discharge to coincide with her failure to "make further phone calls to Kohl as he had asked her to do," it reasoned that the timing was not unusually suggestive of discrimination. The temporal proximity, however, is sufficient here to meet Doe's minimal prima facie case burden as to the causal connection element.

Summary judgment is to be used sparingly in employment discrimination cases.... Mindful that the plaintiff's burden at this first stage is not particularly onerous, we conclude that Doe has established a prima facie case.

### C

The District Court held that even if Doe had established a prima facie case, she failed to show that the nondiscriminatory reasons for her employment discharge were pretextual. The record refutes the holding. Once the plaintiff establishes a prima facie case, the burden of production shifts to the employer to articulate some legitimate nondiscriminatory reason for the adverse employment action. When the defendant meets this burden, the court's "factual inquiry then proceeds to a new level of specificity." The presumption of discrimination established by the prima facie showing "simply drops out of the picture." *St. Mary's Honor Ctr. v. Hicks*, 509 U.S. 502 (1993).

If the defendant meets this burden, the plaintiff must then show that the legitimate reasons offered by the defendant are merely a pretext for discrimination. In order to show pretext, a plaintiff must submit evidence which (1) casts doubt upon the legitimate reason proffered by the employer such that a fact-finder could reasonably conclude that the reason was a fabrication; or (2) would allow the fact-finder to infer that discrimination was more likely than not a motivating or determinative cause of the employee's termination.

Lastly, it is important to remember that the prima facie case and pretext inquiries often overlap. As our jurisprudence recognizes, evidence supporting the prima facie case is often helpful in the pretext stage, and nothing about the *McDonnell Douglas* formula requires us to ration the evidence between one stage or the other.

CARS maintains that it fired Doe because she abandoned her job (the week she thought she was "on vacation" following the abortion and the funeral). Specifically, CARS asserts that Doe was fired because neither she nor her husband called to request Friday, August 11th or the week of August 14th off from work. Unexcused absence from work is a legitimate, nondiscriminatory reason for terminating employment.

Before the District Court and again before us on appeal, Kohl asserts that he never received a telephone call from Doe's husband informing him that Doe would be off work on Friday the 11th and would need vacation time for the week of the 14th. As we noted earlier, that fact is subject to dispute from contradictory evidence. Doe pointed to her husband's testimony to the contrary. The District Court discounted Doe's husband's testimony, finding it "belied by the telephone records of calls from [Doe's husband's] father's telephone number." Here, the District Court inappropriately narrowed Doe's husband's testimony, who indicated that he may have called from a borrowed cell phone. This testimony is also backed-up by Doe's own testimony that the call "had to be from a cell phone" and that "there was a lot going on at that time."

Additionally, the testimony of Leona Dunnett could be viewed by a fact-finder as substantiating Doe's claim that the call was made and that she received a week of vacation from Kohl. Leona Dunnett testified that Doe's husband called her on Friday, August 11th and asked what he would need to do for Doe to use vacation time for the week of August 14th. Dunnett also testified that she explained to Doe's husband that he would need to request it from Kohl, and that she then transferred the call to Kohl. She further testified that, after that call, Kohl asked her to make sure she had the receptionist station covered by other employees during the lunch hour for the week in question (a task for which Doe was usually responsible). Kohl's awareness of a receptionist-coverage issue permits an inference that he knew Doe would be on vacation that week.

... This testimony creates a genuine issue of material fact as to whether CARS' proffered reasons for terminating Doe's employment were a pretext....

### IV

Doe has established a prima facie case. Furthermore, she has pointed to sufficient evidence from which a fact-finder could infer that the CARS' non-discriminatory reason for firing Doe was a pretext. The District Court's order will be reversed and the cause remanded for further proceedings not inconsistent with this opinion.

---

## Notes

1. The court offers its opinion that the CARS leave policies are "somewhat less than compassionate." What do you think of courts' offering such negative commentary on an employer's policies? Is this relevant to the issue of discrimination or is it gratuitous? When should the court's opinion that an employer is miserly be permitted to affect the court's decision on whether the employer discriminated?

2. The Court relied on the language of the statute and the EEOC Guidelines to find that an employer may not discriminate against an employee who exercises a right to have an abortion. How does this reconcile with the explicit language of the PDA? That language expressly disclaims any requirement that the employer provide benefits for abortions:

> This subsection shall not require an employer to pay for health insurance benefits for abortion, except where the life of the mother would be endangered if the fetus were carried to term, or except where medical complications have arisen from an abortion: Provided, That nothing herein shall preclude an employer from providing abortion benefits or otherwise affect bargaining agreements in regard to abortion.

42 U.S.C. § 2000e(k) (2009).

The EEOC Guidelines state:

> Health insurance benefits for abortion, except where the life of the mother would be endangered if the fetus were carried to term or where medical complications have arisen from an abortion, are not required to be paid by an employer; nothing herein, however, precludes an employer from providing abortion benefits or otherwise affects bargaining agreements in regard to abortion.

29 C.F.R. § 1604.10 (2007).

### Equal Treatment of Pregnant Employees

The next case considers the second clause of the PDA, the requirement that the employer treat pregnant workers the same as non-pregnant workers who are similar in their ability to work.

---

**Focus Questions: *Tysinger v. Zanesville***

1.  *Does the PDA require accommodation? Should it?*

2.  *Place yourself in the position of the plaintiff. What would you have done in these circumstances?*

---

# Tysinger v. Zanesville
### 463 F.3d 569 (6th Cir. 2006)

Judge McKeague.

Plaintiff-appellant Teresa Tysinger, a patrol officer and eight-year member of the City of Zanesville Police Department, brought suit against her employer alleging that she was subject to pregnancy discrimination, a form of sex discrimination, in violation of federal and Ohio law. After completion of discovery, the police department moved for and was granted summary judgment. The district court found that plaintiff had failed to make out a *prima facie* case. On due consideration, we affirm for the reasons that follow.

## I. BACKGROUND

Teresa Tysinger was hired by the City of Zanesville Police Department on September 8, 1992. She worked as a patrol officer. In August 2000, she became aware that she was pregnant. Although she and her husband had one child prior to her employment with the Zanesville Police Department, this was her first pregnancy since becoming a police officer. Concerned that some of her duties, like "pushing vehicles and fighting with suspects," might endanger her unborn child, Tysinger raised her concern with her superiors almost immediately. Various alternative temporary assignments were discussed (*i.e.*, detective bureau processing of vehicles in impound lots, and assignment to a desk job answering phone calls), but no action was taken. In September 2000, after Tysinger had been in a physical altercation with a suspect, her doctor prescribed a work restriction, providing that "Teresa is to be on light duty during her pregnancy." When she presented this to Police Chief Eric Lambes, he advised her that there was no light duty position within the department and that she would have to be off work until she was able to return to full active duty.

Tysinger's leave of absence commenced on September 27, 2000....

Tysinger gave birth on March 26, 2001, and returned to work in June 2001. On April 30, 2001, she filed a charge of discrimination with the Equal Employment Opportunity Commission and the Ohio Civil Rights Commission. Her EEOC right to sue letter was issued on September 18, 2001. Tysinger timely commenced this action by filing a two-count complaint. Count I asserts a claim for pregnancy discrimination under Title VII. Count II sets forth a parallel pregnancy discrimination claim under Ohio law. Essentially, Tysinger alleges that the Zanesville Police Department engaged in sex discrimination when it denied her accommodation of her pregnancy, despite having suitable positions available, and despite having granted accommodations to other similarly situated non-pregnant workers in the past.

The Zanesville Police Department moved for summary judgment on both federal and state pregnancy discrimination claims. The district court concluded that Tysinger had failed to make out a *prima facie* case because she had failed to adduce evidence demonstrating that she had been subjected to disparate treatment because of her pregnancy.... The court thus awarded summary judgment to the police department on Tysinger's pregnancy discrimination claims....

On appeal, Tysinger ... contends the district court erred ... by failing to properly consider her evidence of similarly situated non-pregnant employees who received more favorable treatment....

## II. ANALYSIS

### A. Standard of Review

The court of appeals reviews *de novo* an order granting summary judgment. Summary judgment is proper "if the pleadings, depositions, answers to interrogatories, and admissions on file, together with the affidavits, if any, show that there is no genuine issue as to any material fact and that the moving party is entitled to a judgment as a matter of law." Fed. R. Civ. P. 56(c). The court must view the evidence in the light most favorable to the non-moving party and draw all reasonable inferences in its favor. Not just any alleged factual dispute between the parties will defeat an otherwise properly supported motion for summary judgment; the dispute must present a *genuine* issue of *material* fact.... A factual dispute concerns a "material" fact only if its resolution might affect the outcome of the suit under the governing substantive law.

[Section B., discussing the proper defendant, is omitted.]

### C. Pregnancy Discrimination

#### 1. *Prima Facie Case*

The federal and state pregnancy discrimination claims are evaluated generally under the same substantive standards. Under the Pregnancy Discrimination Act provisions of Title VII, discrimination because of or on the basis of pregnancy, childbirth, or related medical conditions is defined as a kind of sex discrimination and is prohibited. Women who are affected by pregnancy, childbirth or related medical conditions are required to be treated the same, for all employment purposes, as other persons not so affected but who are similar in their ability or inability to work.

Plaintiff Teresa Tysinger's claims are not premised on direct evidence of pregnancy-based discriminatory animus. Therefore, her claims are subject to analysis under the evidentiary framework established in *McDonnell Douglas v. Green*. To sustain her claims, as a threshold matter, she must satisfy the elements of a *prima facie* case by showing that "(1) she was pregnant, (2) she was qualified for her job, (3) she was subjected to an adverse employment decision, and (4) there is a nexus between her pregnancy and the adverse employment decision." [citation omitted].

[D]efendant City of Zanesville questions whether Tysinger was in fact "qualified" for her patrol officer position after she became pregnant. Although Tysinger had competently performed as a patrol officer for some eight years, defendant contends that she had ceased to be qualified to perform all the duties of the position, pursuant to her own physician's prescribed work restrictions, when she became pregnant. The question posed is whether a plaintiff's qualifications are assessed before or after the events or circumstances precipitating the complained of adverse action. For purposes of the *prima facie* case analysis, a plaintiff's qualifications are to be assessed in terms of whether he or she was meeting the employer's expectations prior to and independent of the events that led to the adverse action. Prior to becoming pregnant, there is no dispute that Tysinger was meeting her employer's expectations. The second element of her *prima facie* case was therefore properly deemed satisfied.

[T]he district court correctly determined, for purposes of summary judgment analysis, that defendant, by denying Tysinger accommodating work within her restrictions and requiring her to take an extended leave of absence, partly without pay, subjected her to an adverse employment decision.

In order to satisfy the fourth element of her *prima facie* case, showing a causal nexus between her pregnancy and the denial of accommodation, Tysinger relies primarily on evidence of similarly situated non-pregnant employees who were granted more favorable treatment by defendant. Indeed, such "comparables" evidence may give rise to an inference that the pregnancy was the reason for the less favorable treatment — but only if the comparable employees were similarly situated "in all *relevant* respects." [citation omitted]. In relation specifically to a pregnancy discrimination claim, the "relevant respects" in which comparables must be similarly situated are their "ability or inability to work." *Ensley-Gaines v. Runyon,* 100 F.3d 1220, 1226 (6th Cir. 1996). Hence, to satisfy the fourth element, Tysinger is required to "demonstrate that another employee who was similar in her or his ability or inability to work received the benefits denied to her." *Id.*

Tysinger relies on the experiences of two male employees who sustained non-work related injuries that affected their ability to work. Officer Tom Landerman was a warrant officer, whose duties included those of a patrol officer, when he injured his quadriceps muscle in a non-work related accident. His physician ordered him not to work during the recovery period, but he continued working, even though he was not able to run and would not have been able to apprehend a suspect if required to. Though Chief Lambes was aware of the injury, Landerman did not advise him that his physician had ordered him off work and Lambes did not require him to take a leave of absence. A second comparable employee was Officer Jeff Madden. Madden was assigned to the detective bureau when he fractured a toe on his right foot while off-duty. He was off work for a couple of days, but returned to work before he was fully recovered, when his ability to run and use physical force would have been limited, without advising Chief Lambes of any need for a restricted duty assignment. Plaintiff Tysinger contends that both officers were similarly situated to her in that both were temporarily unable to perform all the duties of their positions; yet neither of them was required to take a leave of absence.

Both Landerman and Madden were similarly situated to Tysinger in that they were temporarily unable to perform all the duties of their positions. In this respect, they satisfy the first half of the "comparables" requirement. But did they receive more favorable treatment than Tysinger? It is undisputed that they were not granted an accommodation in the form of light or restricted duties. This is the more favorable treatment that Tysinger requested and was denied. In this respect, Landerman and Madden did not receive more favorable treatment than Tysinger. There is no evidence that either officer received the accommodation that Tysinger claims to have been wrongfully denied.

In fact, there is no evidence that either officer sought an accommodation of any kind or even advised Chief Lambes that his physician had ordered him off work or prescribed restrictions. Despite their temporary inability to perform all the duties of their positions, they continued working in their usual assigned capacities. It is in this crucial respect that Landerman and Madden were *not* similarly situated to Tysinger. Despite their temporary infirmities, they presented themselves to their employer as willing and able to continue working in their ordinary capacities. Tysinger, on the other hand, distinguished herself by asserting the need for and requesting a temporary alteration in her job duties. In this respect, she sought from her employer not the same or equal treatment received by Landerman and Madden, but *more favorable* treatment. Chief Lambes affirmatively stated that Tysinger would have received the same treatment as Landerman and Madden, if she had elected to continue working as a patrol officer despite her pregnancy: "Had she been willing to perform full duty work, she would not have been removed from the active duty roster."

On this record, the district court correctly concluded that "plaintiff has not proved that any other of defendant's non-pregnant employees similarly situated in their ability to work received any more favorable treatment so as to create a genuine issue of material fact." In the absence of such evidence, Tysinger was and is unable to satisfy the fourth element of her *prima facie* case of pregnancy discrimination. She failed to demonstrate a causal nexus between the adverse action she was subjected to and the fact that her infirmity was the result of pregnancy. Rather, the record demonstrates that she was required to take a leave of absence because she, in contrast to her non-pregnant colleagues, did not present herself to her employer as ready and able to perform all the duties of her position. She was in this crucial respect, in terms of "ability or inability to work," as viewed from the employer's perspective, not similarly situated to the asserted comparables. This difference undermines the asserted inference that her adverse treatment was the product of unlawful pregnancy discrimination.[5]

As the district court was careful to observe, the Pregnancy Discrimination Act does not require preferential treatment for pregnant employees. Rather, it mandates that employers treat pregnant employees *the same* as nonpregnant employees who are similarly situated with respect to their ability to work. The Landerman and Madden evidence, rather than showing that Tysinger was subjected to less favorable treatment than they, instead shows that she received the same treatment—just what the Pregnancy Discrimination Act mandates.[6]

Accordingly, we conclude that the district court correctly determined that plaintiff Tysinger failed to make out a *prima facie* case of pregnancy discrimination....

---

5. The dissent views the record differently. In the name of viewing the evidence in the light most favorable to the nonmovant, the dissent conceives a factually unsupported scenario. The dissent correctly observes that Tysinger started a dialogue about alternative work assignments, but she did not continue it as the dissent imagines. When she presented doctor-prescribed work restrictions requiring a light duty assignment, Chief Lambes responded, consistent with City-wide policy, that no light duty assignment was available. There being no work available within the prescribed restrictions, he further advised that she would have to be off work until able to resume full duties.

In this, the Police Department is said to have "forced" Tysinger to take a leave of absence by denying her the choice to continue working, as had Landerman and Madden. Yet, Lambes's explanation that Tysinger would have been allowed to continue working if she had been willing to perform full duties—as had Landerman and Madden—stands unrefuted. There is no evidence that Tysinger wished or requested to continue working in her patrol officer position. If she had been willing and had communicated this to Lambes, this would have been a simple matter for her to substantiate by affidavit. And, if she had made this request and been denied, then, yes, her pregnancy discrimination claim would have been stronger. On this critical point, however, the record is silent.

The conclusion is thus inescapable that Tysinger chose not to continue working as a patrol officer. The notion that the Police Department denied her the choice and forced her to take a leave of absence simply finds no support in the record.

6. Tysinger is not to be faulted for asserting her physician-prescribed need for restricted duty. In contrast to her colleagues, who, rightly or wrongly, "assumed the risk" that they would be able to handle the demands of their jobs despite their temporary leg infirmities, Tysinger had to exercise due regard for the health and well-being of another human being, her unborn child. This interest undeniably deserved and arguably even demanded *her* preferential treatment. However, the law, rightly or wrongly, does not extend this preferential obligation to the employer. A pregnant employee's employer is required only to afford equal treatment, not preferential treatment.

Judge Boyce Martin, Jr., dissenting.

The majority holds that Tysinger, by requesting light work, "did not present herself to her employer as ready and able to perform all the duties of her position" and was, therefore, different from Madden and Landerman. However, this is no different than the condition in which the City found those two men. The superiors of both men knew, either implicitly or explicitly, that because of their injuries, they were not "ready and able to perform all the duties" of their respective positions. Officer Landerman walked around his workplace with a metal brace for six weeks and a limp for four weeks after that. In addition, Chief Lambes was made explicitly aware of the injury within two weeks after Landerman was injured, when the two men discussed the injury and how it would affect Landerman's job performance. As for Officer Madden, Captain Miller knew he was injured because Madden was taking time off due to his broken toe, at which point Miller called Madden and asked him to come back to work despite the physically-limiting injury. Just because Madden and Landerman failed explicitly to request light duty does not change the fact that their superiors were aware of their limitations and silently agreed with the two employees to ignore those limitations and have them "bear with it." ...

-------

## Further Discussion

Although the Supreme Court concluded in *California Federal Savings & Loan Assoc. v. Guerra* that the PDA imposes a "floor not a ceiling," allowing employers to give pregnant workers better benefits than they give to nonpregnant workers, 479 U.S. 272, 286–87 (1987), courts generally agree that the PDA does not require employers to accommodate pregnant workers more than they would accommodate other similarly situated workers. In the words of one appellate court, "[e]mployers can treat pregnant women as badly as they treat similarly affected but nonpregnant employees, even to the point of conditioning the availability of an employment benefit on an employee's decision to return to work after the end of the medical disability that pregnancy causes." *Troupe v. May Dep't Stores Co.*, 20 F.3d 734, 738 (7th Cir. 1994). Another court concluded that "Congress sought to limit the burden on employers by making clear that the amendment was intended only to prevent the exclusion of pregnancy coverage, not to require that employers who had no disability or medical benefits at all provide them to pregnant women." *Carney v. Martin Luther Home, Inc.*, 824 F.2d 643, 646 (8th Cir. 1987).

Some scholars have argued that the PDA should be construed to require employers to accommodate pregnant workers, even where the employer would not accommodate similarly situated nonpregnant workers. *See* Herma Hill Kay, *Equality and Difference: The Case of Pregnancy*, 1 BERKELEY WOMEN'S L.J. 1, 30–31 (1985). Can you think of supportable policy arguments to support that argument?

The next case considers discrimination after the baby is born. The plaintiff seeks to prove sex discrimination with evidence that the employer based her termination on stereotypes about the role of mothers. The case arises under Title 42 U.S.C. § 1983, which provides, in part:

> Every person who, under color of any statute, ordinance, regulation, custom, or usage, of any State or Territory or the District of Columbia, subjects, or causes to be subjected, any citizen of the United States or other person within the jurisdiction thereof to the deprivation of any rights, privileges, or immunities

secured by the Constitution and laws, shall be liable to the party injured in an action at law, suit in equity, or other proper proceeding for redress....

---

## Focus Question: *Back v. Hastings on Hudson Union Free School District*

*Notice that the individuals who criticized the plaintiff's performance did not do so by reference to her pregnancy. If this is the case, think about how a plaintiff would prove that the evaluations were because of her pregnancy.*

---

# Back v. Hastings on Hudson Union Free School District
### 365 F.3d 107 (2d Cir. 2004)

Judge Calabresi.

In 1998, Plaintiff-Appellant Elana Back was hired as a school psychologist at the Hillside Elementary School ("Hillside") on a three-year tenure track. At the end of that period, when Back came up for review, she was denied tenure and her probationary period was terminated. Back subsequently brought this lawsuit, seeking damages and injunctive relief under 42 U.S.C. § 1983. She alleged that the termination violated her constitutional right to equal protection of the laws. Defendants-Appellees contend that Back was fired because she lacked organizational and interpersonal skills. Back asserts that the real reason she was let go was that the defendants presumed that she, as a young mother, would not continue to demonstrate the necessary devotion to her job, and indeed that she could not maintain such devotion while at the same time being a good mother....

*A. Background*

... Defendant-Appellee Marilyn Wishnie, the Principal of Hillside, and defendant-appellee Ann Brennan, the Director of Pupil Personnel Services for the District, were Back's supervisors.... In the plaintiff's first two years at Hillside, Brennan and Wishnie consistently gave her excellent evaluations.... In her second year at Hillside, Back took approximately three months of maternity leave. After she returned, she [twice] garnered ... "outstanding evaluation[s]." Defendant-Appellant John Russell, the Superintendent of the School District, also rated ... her performance "superior." ... In addition, according to Back, all three individual defendants repeatedly assured her throughout this time that she would receive tenure.

...

*ii. Alleged Stereotyping*

Back asserts that things changed dramatically as her tenure review approached. The first allegedly discriminatory comments came in spring 2000, when Back's written evaluations still indicated that she was a very strong candidate for tenure. At that time, shortly after Back had returned from maternity leave, the plaintiff claims that Brennan, (a) inquired about how she was "planning on spacing [her] offspring," (b) said "'[p]lease do not get pregnant until I retire,'" and (c) suggested that Back "wait until [her son] was in kindergarten to have another child."

[The plaintiff testified that Brennan and Wishnie repeatedly told her that she would not be able to do her job as a school psychologist because she was a mother, that they believed she was putting on an act of working hard to get tenure and would work less hard upon receiving tenure and, finally, that they would recommend that she be denied tenure.]

Brennan and Wishnie both testified in depositions that they never questioned Back's ability to combine work and motherhood, and did not insinuate that they thought the commitment that Back had previously demonstrated was an "act." They contended, instead, that Back was told ... that both had concerns about her performance.

### iii. Denial of Tenure

... On May 29, 2001, Brennan and Wishnie sent a formal memo to Russell informing him that they could not recommend Back for tenure. Their reasons included (a) that although their formal reports had been positive, their informal interactions with her had been less positive, (b) that there were "far too many" parents and teachers who had "serious issues" with the plaintiff and did not wish to work with her, and (c) that she had persistent difficulties with the planning and organization of her work, and with in-accuracies in her reports, and that she had not shown improvement in this area, despite warnings.

[An attorney retained by Back] informed Russell that Back believed that Brennan and Wishnie were retaliating against her, citing, *inter alia*, that Brennan was "openly hostile" towards Back, that she falsely accused Back of mishandling cases and giving false information, that she increased Back's workload, and that positive letters were removed from Back's file.

On or around June 13, 2001, Wishnie and Brennan filed the first negative evaluation of Back, which gave her several "below average" marks and charged her with being inconsistent, defensive, difficult to supervise, the source of parental complaints, and inaccurate in her reports. Their evaluation, which was submitted to Russell, concluded that Back should not be granted tenure....

On June 18, 2001, Russell informed Back by letter that he had received Wishnie and Brennan's annual evaluation, and was recommending to the Board of Education that her probationary appointment be terminated.... [Following an unsuccessful grievance, the Plaintiff's employment was terminated.]

### iv. Proceedings in the District Court

In October 2001, Back brought this claim in the United States District Court for the Southern District of New York under 42 U.S.C. § 1983, alleging gender discrimination in violation of the Equal Protection Clause.... The district court granted summary judgment for the defendants, on the grounds (a) that this Circuit had not held that a "sex plus" claim can be brought under § 1983, (b) that defendants' comments were "stray remarks" which did not show sex discrimination, [and] (c) that Back had failed to prove that the reasons given for not granting her tenure were pretextual....

### Discussion

Plaintiff ... contends that an adverse employment consequence imposed because of stereotypes about motherhood is a form of gender discrimination which contravenes the Equal Protection Clause....

### A. Theory of Discrimination

Individuals have a clear right, protected by the Fourteenth Amendment, to be free from discrimination on the basis of sex in public employment.... To make out such a claim, the plaintiff must prove that she suffered purposeful or intentional discrimination on the basis of gender. Discrimination based on gender, once proven, can only be tolerated if the state provides an "exceedingly persuasive justification" for the rule or practice. [citation omitted] ...

In deciding whether Back has alleged facts that could support a finding of discrimination, we must first address the district court's suggestion, and the defendants' argument, that Back's claim is a "gender-plus" claim, and as such, not actionable under § 1983. This contention is without merit. The term "sex plus" or "gender plus" is simply a ... judicial convenience developed in the context of Title VII to affirm that plaintiffs can, under certain circumstances, survive summary judgment even when not all members of a disfavored class are discriminated against....

To show sex discrimination, Back relies upon a *Price Waterhouse* "stereotyping" theory. Accordingly, she argues that comments made about a woman's inability to combine work and motherhood are direct evidence of such discrimination.... "[S]tereotyped remarks can certainly be evidence that gender played a part" in an adverse employment decision. [citation omitted]. Just as "[i]t takes no special training to discern sex stereotyping in a description of an aggressive female employee as requiring 'a course at charm school,'" so it takes no special training to discern stereotyping in the view that a woman cannot "be a good mother" and have a job that requires long hours, or in the statement that a mother who received tenure "would not show the same level of commitment [she] had shown because [she] had little ones at home." ...

The defendants argue that stereotypes about pregnant women or mothers are not based upon gender, but rather, "gender plus parenthood," thereby implying that such stereotypes cannot, without comparative evidence of what was said about fathers, be presumed to be "on the basis of sex." [A]t least where stereotypes are considered, the notions that mothers are insufficiently devoted to work, and that work and motherhood are incompatible, are properly considered to be, themselves, gender-based.... Defendants are thus wrong in their contention that Back cannot make out a claim that survives summary judgment unless she demonstrates that the defendants treated similarly situated men differently. Back has admittedly proffered no evidence about the treatment of male administrators with young children. Although her case would be stronger had she provided or alleged the existence of such evidence, there is no requirement that such evidence be adduced....

*B. Was Summary Judgment Appropriate?*

... We must also determine whether the plaintiff has adduced enough evidence to defeat summary judgment as regards her discrimination claim, and has done so with respect to each of the defendants sued. We review a district court's grant of summary judgment *de novo*. To justify summary judgment, the defendants must show that "there is no genuine issue as to any material fact" and that they are "entitled to a judgment as a matter of law." Fed. R. Civ. P. 56(c). We resolve all ambiguities, and credit all rational factual inferences, in favor of the plaintiff.

*i. Section 1983 Claim Against Brennan and Wishnie ...*

*a. Deprivation of Federal Right*

Applying [the *McDonnell Douglas* proof structure] to the facts before us, we hold that Back has clearly produced sufficient evidence to defeat summary judgment as to Brennan and Wishnie. She has made out her prima facie case by offering evidence of discriminatory comments, which can constitute "direct evidence," and are adequate to make out a prima facie case, even where uncorroborated. The nondiscriminatory reasons proffered by

Brennan and Wishnie for their negative evaluations—namely, Back's poor organizational skills and her negative interactions with parents—are in no way dispositive.[7]

[The court found that plaintiff had introduced sufficient evidence to permit a jury to find that the defendants' proffered reasons were pretext, that there was a causal relationship between the sex discrimination and the decision to terminate her.]

. . .

*Conclusion*

We find that the plaintiff adduced facts sufficient to allow a jury to determine that defendants Brennan and Wishnie discriminated against Back on the basis of gender. . . .

---

## Notes

1. The EEOC has issued guidance specifically addressing discrimination against individuals because of their caregiving responsibilities. The concept of "maternal wall" is often used to describe discrimination against women based on their role as mothers. The EEOC addresses discrimination based on caregiving more broadly, recognizing that people are sometimes discriminated against because they care for sick or elderly relatives. *See* http://www.eeoc.gov/policy/docs/caregiving.pdf (last visited Oct. 3, 2013).

2. Other than what was mentioned in the court's opinion, what kinds of evidence would be helpful to the factfinder in *Back v. Hastings*?

3. In 2010, Congress added new protections for nursing mothers. The Patient Protection and Affordable Care Act ("PPACA") of 2010 (P.L. 111-148) amended Section 7 of the Fair Labor Standards Act to require employers to provide breaks for nursing mothers to express breast milk for the first year of the child's life. Employers must provide a private location for this purpose other than a bathroom. The employer is not required to provide compensated break time and is not required to provide breaks for individuals who are exempt from the overtime pay requirements of the FLSA. The protections provided in the FLSA do not preempt state law that provides greater protection for mothers. Fact Sheet #73, Break Time for Nursing Mothers Under the FLSA, http://www.dol.gov/whd/regs/compliance/whdfs73.htm (last visited Oct. 3, 2013).

## Sex-Based Pay Discrimination

Federal law provides two statutory protections against sex-based pay discrimination. You are already familiar with Title VII's prohibition against sex discrimination, which, of course, prohibits discrimination in pay, as well as other terms of employment. The

---

7. The district court inaccurately characterized Brennan and Wishnie's purported statements about Back's inability to combine work and motherhood as "stray remarks." The comments alleged were (1) made repeatedly, (2) drew a direct link between gender stereotypes and the conclusion that Back should not be tenured, and (3) were made by supervisors who played a substantial role in the decision to terminate. As such, they are sufficient to support a finding of discriminatory motive.

federal Equal Pay Act (EPA) is an entirely separate federal statute that also prohibits sex (but not other) discrimination in pay. Congress enacted the EPA in 1963, one year before it passed Title VII.

Enacted as a section of the Fair Labor Standards Act, the EPA provides:

> No employer having employees subject to any provisions of this section shall discriminate, within any establishment in which such employees are employed, between employees on the basis of sex by paying wages to employees in such establishment at a rate less than the rate at which he pays wages to employees of the opposite sex in such establishment for equal work on jobs the performance of which requires equal skill, effort, and responsibility, and which are performed under similar working conditions, except where such payment is made pursuant to (i) a seniority system; (ii) a merit system; (iii) a system which measures earnings by quantity or quality of production; or (iv) a differential based on any other factor other than sex: *Provided,* That an employer who is paying a wage rate differential in violation of this subsection shall not, in order to comply with the provisions of this subsection, reduce the wage rate of any employee.

29 U.S.C. §206(d)(1).

The redundancy between Title VII and the EPA is not complete. The EPA statute of limitations is two years (three for willful violations), so there are situations where it may be too late to file a charge or sue under Title VII, but a claim under the EPA is still timely. In addition, the EPA provides as remedies unpaid wages, which are doubled as liquidated damages. These remedies are different from the Title VII remedies, which you will read about in Chapter 11. Also, unlike Title VII, the EPA does not require an exhaustion of administrative remedies. As you can see in the statutory language quoted above, moreover, the EPA imposes limits on claims not contained in Title VII. The EPA applies only where a male and female being compared work in the same establishment doing equal work.

### Comparable Worth

Congress added the Bennett Amendment to Title VII to synchronize the coverage of the two statutes. That amendment states:

> It shall not be an unlawful employment practice under this title for any employer to differentiate upon the basis of sex in determining the amount of wages or compensation paid to employees of such employer if such differentiation is authorized by the EPA.

42 U.S.C. 2000e-2(h). Although it was argued that the Bennett Amendment meant that the absence of a comparator doing equal work should be fatal to a Title VII claim for sex-based pay discrimination, the Supreme Court rejected this construction. In *County of Washington v. Gunther*, the Court held that the Bennett Amendment is intended simply to incorporate into Title VII the EPA's four exceptions, available where the unequal pay is pursuant to (1) a seniority system; (2) a merit system; (3) a system measuring earnings by quantity or quality of production; or (4) a differential based on any other factor other than sex. 452 U.S. 161 (1981). Thus the absence of a male comparator was not fatal where the plaintiffs had direct evidence of pay discrimination.

Because the *Gunther* plaintiffs had direct evidence of pay discrimination, the Court did not reach the question of whether "comparable worth" is a viable claim under Title

VII. Nevertheless, the *Gunther* Court acknowledged that comparable worth had been the subject of much scholarly debate, noting that the theory would allow a plaintiff to "claim increased compensation on the basis of a comparison of the intrinsic worth or difficulty of their job with that of other jobs in the same organization or community." 452 U.S. at 166. Thus, the essential argument in comparable worth cases is that the employer pays employees in positions traditionally held by women less than it pays individuals in positions traditionally held by men, even though the work performed might be of comparable worth to the employer.

The comparable worth theory arose again in the 1985 case of *American Federation of State, County and Municipal Employees v. Washington*, 770 F.2d 1401 (9th Cir. 1985). There, plaintiffs argued that a State of Washington study that demonstrated that women were paid inequitably, compared to men whose work was of comparable worth, though not identical, should be entitled to a legal remedy. The Ninth Circuit reversed a trial court decision for the plaintiff, accepting the State's defense that the reason for the differential was market factors.

Recently, the comparable worth argument was revived in the form of the Fair Pay Act of 2009, which was introduced in both houses of Congress, but did not become law. That bill provided the following:

> no employer having employees ... shall discriminate, within any establishment in which such employees are employed, between employees on the basis of sex, race, or national origin by paying wages to employees in such establishment in a job that is dominated by employees of a particular sex, race, or national origin at a rate less than the rate at which the employer pays wages to employees in such establishment in another job that is dominated by employees of the opposite sex or of a different race or national origin, respectively, for work on equivalent jobs.

Fair Pay Act, H.R. 2151, 111th Cong. § 3(a) (2009), S. 904, 111th Cong. § 3(a) (2009).

## Family and Medical Leave Act (FMLA)

### Bases for FMLA Leave

As originally enacted, the Family and Medical Leave Act (FMLA) entitles covered employees to up to 12 weeks unpaid leave for four different reasons: (1) the birth and care of a newborn child; (2) the placement of a child for adoption or foster care; (3) the care of a child, spouse, or parent with a serious health condition; or (4) the employee's own serious health condition. 29 U.S.C. § 2612(a)(1). When Congress enacted the FMLA in 1993, it expressly found that existing employment policies did not adequately respond to an increase in "single-parent households and two-parent households in which ... both parents work." 29 U.S.C. § 2601(a)(1). Congress also recognized that the primary responsibility for caretaking falls upon women, with resulting negative effects on the employment opportunities of women. 29 U.S.C. § 2601(a)(5). The express purposes of the statute were "to minimize ... employment discrimination on the basis of sex and ... to promote the goal of equal employment opportunity for women and men." 29 U.S.C. § 2601(b).

In two subsequent amendments, Congress provided additional FMLA leave entitlements. An employee who is the spouse, son, daughter, parent, or next of kin of a covered service member may take up to 26 work weeks of leave to care for a member of the Armed Forces undergoing medical treatment for certain reasons. 29 U.S.C. §2612(a)(3). Additionally, the Act provides for "qualifying exigency leave," which entitles a spouse, son, daughter, or parent of certain members of the Armed Forces up to 12 weeks of leave to take care of "qualifying exigencies" that arise because the member of the Armed Forces is on active duty or called to active duty. 29 U.S.C. §2612(a)(1)(E).

The FMLA limits coverage to specific employees and employers. To be eligible for leave, an employee must:

(1)  have worked for the employer for a total of 12 months;

(2)  have worked at least 1,250 hours over the previous 12 months; and

(3)  work for a covered employer.

Covered employers include private sector employers that employ 50 or more employees, *as well as* state, local and federal employers.

Employees who take leave under the Act are entitled to a maximum of twelve work weeks of unpaid leave during a 12-month period. All 12 weeks of leave do not need to be taken at the same time. In certain circumstances, an employee may request that such leave be taken intermittently (in separate blocks of time) or that it be granted through a reduced work schedule. During the leave period, employers are required to keep paying any portion of an employee's health benefits that the employer previously paid; however, under certain circumstances, the employer may recover the premiums paid if the employee fails to return to work after FMLA leave.

Notice that the leave provided under the FMLA is unpaid. Some states require paid leave.

Upon the conclusion of the leave, employees who are well enough to return to work generally are entitled to be restored to the position held prior to leave or an equivalent position.

### FMLA Interference and Retaliation Claims

Violations of the FMLA can give rise to two different types of claims: interference/entitlement and retaliation/discrimination. An interference/entitlement claim arises when the employer interferes with an employee's exercise of FMLA rights to which the employee is entitled. For example, the employer denies an employee's proper request for FMLA leave. A retaliation claim arises when the employer retaliates against an employee for exercising FMLA rights. For example, the employer terminates the employee because the employee took FMLA leave. In many factual circumstances, an employee may invoke both kinds of claims.

---

### Focus Questions: *Lawson v. Plantation General Hosp.*

1.  *Why does the plaintiff base her claim on a retaliation theory, rather than interference?*

2.  *Based on the facts, do you think the employer retaliated against plaintiff for taking FMLA leave? Do you think the employer thought it was retaliating against plaintiff for taking FMLA leave?*

---

# Lawson v. Plantation General Hosp.

704 F. Supp. 2d 1254 (S.D. Fla. 2010)

Magistrate Judge Rosenbaum.

This matter is before the Court upon Defendant's Motion for Summary Judgment.... After a full review, the Court finds that Defendant's Motion for Summary Judgment should be granted in part and denied in part.

## BACKGROUND

... Plaintiff is a ... female who suffers from sickle cell disease and who was formerly employed by Defendant as an executive secretary in the Administrative Offices of the Hospital. Plaintiff claims that following a sickle cell crisis that required hospitalization and then bed rest, Defendant involuntarily transferred Plaintiff to another position in the Hospital—as Medical Staff Administrative Assistant. Plaintiff contends that the transfer constituted a demotion and asserts that a less qualified, younger Hispanic male, Miguel Cruz, was promoted to her former executive secretary position. Following this transfer and an allegedly unfair evaluation of Plaintiff, Defendant terminated Plaintiff's employment. Plaintiff contends that Defendant's actions ... were made in retaliation for Plaintiff's taking of FMLA leave....

## MATERIAL FACTS

The Court notes that it must take the facts in the light most favorable to Plaintiff, but sets forth the events from each party's perspective so that it may establish a complete picture of the parties' positions.... In September of 1995, Defendant hired Plaintiff to work as an executive secretary.... In her role as Executive Secretary in Administration, Plaintiff performed administrative duties.... Plaintiff received consistently good performance reviews as well as pay raises each year that she performed her duties as Executive Secretary in Administration.

As noted previously, Plaintiff suffers from sickle cell disease, a permanent condition with which she was first diagnosed in 1972.... During Plaintiff's twelve years of employment at the Hospital, Plaintiff suffered at least five major sickle cell crises—in 1998, 2002, 2003, 2004, and 2006. All of the crises required hospitalization, during which Plaintiff received oxygen and pain medication, followed by bed rest. In addition to these crises, Plaintiff experienced non-major crises that required bed rest and prescription medication.

Plaintiff states that she receives ongoing treatment for her sickle cell disease....

[Plaintiff's doctor's records reflect] that Plaintiff suffers weakness, weight loss, and shortness of breath. Plaintiff indicates that she experiences joint/muscle weakness and fatigue on a daily basis. Plaintiff also states that she suffers from chronic anemia, her gall bladder has been removed, and she has a heart murmur, gout, an enlarged spleen, and elevated bilirubin, which she asserts are all complications of sickle cell disease. Plaintiff also notes that she had a stroke and continues to suffer from hypertension. In connection with her sickle cell disease, Plaintiff indicates that she must avoid stress, cannot engage in extreme physical activity such as running, and is not able to care for herself when she has a major crisis....

Plaintiff's last major sickle cell crisis occurred in December of 2006.... During this major crisis, Plaintiff was hospitalized for ten days and then ordered to bed rest for an additional period of time before returning to work on January 15, 2007. As a result of the major crisis, Plaintiff requested and was granted FMLA leave. Plaintiff claims that this is the only time that she officially applied for FMLA leave, but Defendant asserts that Plaintiff has never been denied request for time off as a result of her illness. Both parties agree that Plaintiff has been able to work since her return to work on January 15, 2007, through April 2, 2009 (the date of her deposition).

Following Plaintiff's FMLA leave in December of 2006, she returned to her position as Executive Secretary in Administration on January 15, 2007. According to Plaintiff, within days of returning to work, [her supervisor] transferred Plaintiff to another unit in the Hospital. Hospital documents reflect that effective February 4, 2007, Plaintiff was transferred from Executive Secretary in Administration to a new position as Administrative Assistant in the Hospital's Medical Staff Office. At the same time, Miguel Cruz ("Cruz"), a younger Hispanic male, was transferred from Administrative Assistant in the Medical Staff Office to Executive Secretary in Administration. Defendant claims, however, that Plaintiff's Executive Secretary position was eliminated and when Cruz transferred into Administration, a new position was created which included Plaintiff's former job responsibilities and the additional responsibility of handling physician contracts.

Defendant asserts that Plaintiff's transfer was based on legitimate business reasons, [essentially arguing that it made more sense administratively for the positions to be reorganized.]

... Upon her transfer, Plaintiff retained the same pay, benefits, and schedule as when she was an Executive Secretary, but her title changed to Administrative Assistant.... Plaintiff worked in her new role ... from early February of 2007 until she was terminated nine months later on October 19, 2007....

In early July of 2007, [Plaintiff received an evaluation that] indicated that Plaintiff met expectations in many areas, but also rated Plaintiff as inconsistent in other areas. For example, one of the criticisms listed in the Evaluation stated that Plaintiff showed an unwillingness to assist [her former supervisor] in completing meeting minutes for the Ethics and Compliance Committee.... At this time, [plaintiff was] provided with a Performance Improvement Plan ("PIP") that set forth the areas in which Plaintiff needed to improve and asked Plaintiff to prepare a response that would map out Plaintiff's plan to address each area of perceived deficiency. Plaintiff felt that the evaluation and PIP were unfair, not reflective of her job performance, and completely contrary to all other evaluations she had received while employed at the Hospital. Plaintiff also emphasizes that during this same time frame, [another employee] told Plaintiff that [the employee] was asked to "find stuff to write about [Plaintiff]."

Plaintiff drafted and submitted various versions of her response to the PIP, with the first two responses being deemed insufficient. Indeed, after Plaintiff submitted her first response, the Vice President of Human Resources, Ben Bittner ("Bittner"), met with Plaintiff to discuss the PIP and Plaintiff's response. During the meeting, ... Bittner asked Plaintiff to go back and attempt to further develop her response. Sensing Plaintiff's frustration with her new position and performance evaluation, as an alternative to continuing her employment in the Medical Staff unit, Bittner offered Plaintiff a severance package. Plaintiff, however, responded that she did not wish to accept a severance package. Subsequently, Plaintiff drafted a revision to her response, which was also deemed unsatisfactory, but then provided a final response to the PIP dated August 23, 2007, which Bittner deemed to be sufficient. After Plaintiff submitted her final response, her supervisors noted that Plaintiff's performance had improved.

Less than two months later, on October 19, 2007, Defendant terminated Plaintiff's employment, at which time Bittner explained to Plaintiff that her position had been eliminated as a result of a reduction in force ("RIF"). Defendant set Plaintiff's effective date of termination as November 2, 2007, which allowed Plaintiff to enjoy the continuation of benefits through the end of November. Plaintiff also received twelve weeks of severance pay.

Although the parties agree that Plaintiff's employment was terminated, they dispute the reasons for the termination. Defendant claims that in the fall of 2007, the Hospital's East Florida Division Office directed the CEO, CFO, and COO to reduce its workforce by either five or six full-time employees. [Defendant] stated that this reduction was necessitated by budgetary concerns and a drop in patient census.... Defendant asserts that [other employees] were capable of carrying out the clerical duties of Plaintiff's position, but that Plaintiff had not been trained in the job functions of [others]; hence, her position could be eliminated. Defendant contends that Plaintiff's position was eliminated, that no one replaced her, and that no other positions in the office were available at the time of her elimination.

Plaintiff disputes that her termination resulted from a RIF.... Plaintiff points to the fact that four other individuals were terminated along with Plaintiff [and that these individuals] had taken FMLA leave more than once within the prior two years....

### ANALYSIS

...

### C. Plaintiff's FMLA Retaliation Claim

The FMLA provides an eligible employee up to a total of twelve weeks of unpaid leave in any one-year period "[b]ecause of a serious health condition that makes the employee unable to perform the functions of the position of such employee." 29 U.S.C. § 2612(a). The FMLA creates two types of claims: interference claims, in which the employee asserts that his employer denied or otherwise interfered with his substantive rights, and retaliation claims, in which the employee contends that her employer discriminated against her because she engaged in a protected activity. 29 U.S.C. § 2615(a)(1) and (2).

In her Complaint, Plaintiff asserts only a claim for FMLA retaliation. To successfully make a claim for FMLA retaliation, Plaintiff must demonstrate the following: (1) she engaged in statutorily protected conduct; (2) she suffered an adverse employment action; and (3) a causal connection exists between the protected activity and the adverse employment action. Where Plaintiff establishes a retaliation case without direct evidence of the employer's retaliatory intent, the burden-shifting framework set forth in *McDonnell Douglas* applies.

In this case, no dispute exists that Plaintiff engaged in statutorily protected activity by taking medical leave pursuant to the FMLA. Hence, Defendant concedes for purposes of its Motion for Summary Judgment that the first prong of Plaintiff's *prima facie* case is met. Defendant claims that Plaintiff's retaliation claim fails, however, because Plaintiff cannot show that she suffered an adverse employment action and cannot demonstrate a causal connection between any alleged adverse employment action and her medical leave.

[After a lengthy discussion, the Court found] that a genuine issue of material fact exists as to whether Plaintiff's transfer from Administration to Medical Staff constitutes an adverse action.... Moreover, although the parties do not emphasize it in their briefs, the Hospital ultimately terminated Plaintiff's employment. Obviously, this constitutes an adverse employment action.

... Defendant next contends that Plaintiff's retaliation claim must fail because, even assuming that an adverse employment action took place, no causal connection exists between the protected activity (*i.e.*, the FMLA leave) and the adverse action. In this regard, Defendant points out that Plaintiff's termination occurred nine months after her FMLA leave ended.... Defendant asserts that this lapse of time is too great to allow an inference of unlawful retaliation. Consequently, Defendant seeks for the Court to enter summary judgment against Plaintiff on her retaliation claim because she cannot show a close temporal proximity between the protected activity and the adverse action.

Plaintiff, on the other hand, argues that close temporal proximity is not the only way to prove causation in a retaliation case. In this matter, Plaintiff points to additional evidence such as the fact that other employees who had taken FMLA leave were terminated at the same time as Plaintiff. Additionally, Plaintiff asserts that her FMLA leave and termination are temporally connected by a chain of intervening retaliatory acts such that a causal connection is established. For instance, Plaintiff emphasizes that she returned from FMLA leave on January 15, 2007, and her transfer to Medical Staff became effective on February 4, 2007 — a mere two weeks later. Next, at her three-month performance review, Plaintiff received unfavorable comments in several areas of her new position. Plaintiff's supervisors then sought for Plaintiff to file a response to the PIP, requiring Plaintiff to compose several drafts indicating how Plaintiff intended to correct her allegedly insufficient job performance. These drafts were submitted over time until a final draft was accepted. Moreover, Plaintiff indicated that during this same time frame, [another employee] confided in Plaintiff that [the other employee] was asked to "find stuff to write about Plaintiff." ... According to Plaintiff, all of these events provide sufficient indicia of a causal connection.

Despite the fact that a jury may ultimately agree with Defendant, the Court concludes that there is a genuine issue of material fact regarding whether a causal connection exists between Plaintiff's FMLA leave and her transfer and then termination.

... With respect to Plaintiff's selection for transfer to Medical Staff, the temporal proximity to her protected activity is significant. Indeed, Plaintiff's transfer to the unit occurred only two weeks after she returned to the Hospital from her FMLA leave. Eleventh Circuit case law has made it clear that close temporal proximity between the protected activity and the adverse action may suffice to establish a causal connection.... Here, the temporal proximity is extremely close.

Likewise, the decision to terminate Plaintiff's employment at the Hospital presents similar questions of fact that must be resolved by a jury, particularly when those facts are viewed in the light most favorable to Plaintiff. As noted by Plaintiff, other events occurred between the transfer and the termination that could be construed as evidence of a causal link. During Plaintiff's three-month review, Plaintiff received numerous negative remarks on her performance evaluation, whereas in her prior twelve-year tenure with the Hospital, Plaintiff had received positive evaluations. Additionally, after Plaintiff received the negative performance evaluation, Bittner told Plaintiff that if she was unhappy with the transfer, she could simply accept a severance package and leave the Hospital. Both of these actions could be seen as an attempt by the Hospital to force Plaintiff out. This is true particularly in light of [the other employee's] alleged comment that she was asked to "find stuff to write about Plaintiff."

... Finally, it is undisputed that other employees terminated at the same time as Plaintiff had taken FMLA leave on more than one occasion during the two years prior to their termination. Although the Hospital has come forth with other reasons for these employees' termination, the Court must take these facts in the light most favorable to Plaintiff. For all of the reasons set forth herein, the Court declines to find that no genuine issue of fact exists as to whether Plaintiff can show a causal connection between her FMLA leave and her termination....

In sum, because the Court finds that material issues of fact exist as to whether there is a causal connection between Plaintiff's FMLA leave, her selection for transfer to Medical Staff and her ultimate termination, Defendant's Motion for Summary Judgment must be denied....

---

### Focus Question: *Mitchell v. County of Wayne*

*As you read the court's discussion, consider your understanding of the difference between interference/entitlement claims and retaliation claims. Does the appellate court distinguish between the two types of claims?*

---

# Mitchell v. County of Wayne

### 337 Fed. Appx. 526 (6th Cir. 2009)

Circuit Judge Clay.

Plaintiff Robert Mitchell ("Mitchell") appeals the district court's order denying his motion for judgment as a matter of law or for a new trial, following a jury verdict in favor of Defendant County of Wayne (the "County") with respect to Mitchell's claim under the Family Medical Leave Act ("FMLA"). On appeal, Mitchell contends that he presented sufficient evidence that the County interfered with his FMLA rights, and retaliated against him for exercising those rights, when it terminated him upon his return from approved FMLA leave. For the following reasons, we affirm the district court's order.

## BACKGROUND

### I. Procedural History

On September 27, 2005, Mitchell filed a complaint against the County, retired County Undersheriff Harold Cureton ("Cureton"), and County Sheriff Department Commander Karen Kreyger ("Commander Kreyger"), alleging violations of the FMLA. In the complaint, Mitchell alleged that Commander Kreyger terminated his employment at the County Sheriff's Department because Mitchell failed to appear for a scheduled drug test on February 23, 2005, the day he began a period of sick leave pursuant to the FMLA. The complaint alleged that Commander Kreyger's actions constituted interference with, and retaliation for, Mitchell's exercise of his FMLA rights....

### II. Trial Testimony

Mitchell began working for the Sheriff's Department in 1993, and subsequently held a variety of posts, most recently performing floor security at jails and hospitals. During the time at issue in this case, Mitchell was working a daytime shift from 7:00 a.m. to 3:00 p.m. Mitchell testified that during his twelve years of employment, he was subjected to three to five drug tests, and tested negative each time. Mitchell testified that on February 22, 2005, one of his supervisors, Sergeant Khalib Sabbough ("Sergeant Sabbough"), informed him that he would need to appear for a random drug test the following day at a local hospital. Sergeant Sabbough handed Mitchell a formal notice of the scheduled test.

Mitchell testified that at approximately 7:00 p.m. on February 22, he fell on some ice while off duty and injured his lower back. The next morning, Mitchell called the Sheriff's Department at approximately 5:20 a.m., when the night shift was still on duty; Mitchell could not recall the person with whom he spoke, other than that it was a "midnight shift sergeant or whoever." Mitchell called the midnight shift because he was aware of the Sheriff's Department's policy requiring employees calling in sick to do so at least one hour before their shift begins. He informed the person on the phone that he had a test scheduled for that day, but that he would not be able to appear for it; although it is unclear from Mitchell's testimony whether he specifically identified "the test" as a drug test, he acknowledged that he had said in his deposition that he was not sure whether he had referred to it as a drug test. The person took Mitchell's name and the call ended. Mitchell's parents arrived at his house shortly thereafter and drove him to a chiropractor, who treated him and advised him to stay off his feet for at least "the first couple weeks." Mitchell testified that he did not see a medical doctor or go to an emergency room for his injury, and he did not take any prescription medication.

While at the chiropractor's office, Mitchell filled out the required FMLA leave notification forms and his mother faxed the forms to the Sheriff's Department for him. In the forms, Mitchell requested leave from February 23, 2005 through March 14, 2005. Mitchell recalled that later that day, he called John Asquini ("Asquini"), the Sheriff Department's senior personnel officer, to confirm that Asquini had received the FMLA forms, but did not mention to Asquini that he had been scheduled to take a drug test that day. Mitchell testified that this was the third period of FMLA leave that he took because of injuries to his lower back since July 2004, each time receiving approval from the Sheriff's Department personnel office.

Mitchell testified that he called the Sheriff's Department every morning for approximately six days to advise that he was still on leave. Around March 1, when Mitchell made his morning call, he spoke with Sergeant David Boisvert ("Sergeant Boisvert"), and asked him if it would be necessary to continue calling every day; he also told Sergeant Boisvert about his missed drug test. Sergeant Boisvert called Asquini, then got back on the phone with Mitchell and told him that "John Asquini says you're on leave." On March 7, 2005, while Mitchell was still on leave, he received a phone call from Commander Kreyger, informing him that she was revoking his police powers and writing up a Conduct Incident Report because Mitchell failed to appear for his scheduled drug test on February 23, 2005. On March 14, 2005, Mitchell submitted another set of FMLA forms, including a note from his chiropractor, stating that he needed to extend his leave until March 23, 2005.

Mitchell testified that on March 24, 2005, he went to the Sheriff's Department personnel office to provide notice that he was ready to return to work, but was informed that Commander Kreyger did not approve of him returning to work, and that Commander Kreyger would call him shortly to discuss his situation. On March 25, 2005, Commander Kreyger called him into the office and issued him a Conduct Incident Report, which informed him that she was suspending him because of his failure to appear for his drug test on February 23, 2005. As part of the standard procedure for issuing a Conduct Incident Report, Commander Kreyger informed Mitchell that he had twenty-four hours to respond to its allegation. Mitchell wrote a short memo stating that he missed the drug test because he had injured his back the previous evening.

Mitchell testified that at an administrative review hearing on April 1, 2005 with Commander Kreyger and his union representative, he again explained his reason for missing the drug test, but Commander Kreyger told him that "it just looks suspicious." At the end of the administrative review, the union representative conferred with Commander Kreyger, and then informed Mitchell that he could return to work as long as he agreed to receiving random drug testing for the next year. Mitchell testified that although he did not have a problem with that condition, Commander Kreyger also told him that if he returned to work, she could place him on any shift she wanted to, regardless of his seniority rights; Mitchell asserted that when Mitchell refused to agree to that additional condition, Commander Kreyger terminated his employment.

During cross-examination, Mitchell acknowledged he had taken FMLA leave of four weeks in 1994, four weeks in 1995, almost a full year in 1996, "a couple of months" in 1998, and one month in 2000 for various injuries, before taking leave three times in 2004 and 2005 for his bad back. Mitchell testified that the County had never denied a request for medical leave during his twelve years of employment. Mitchell acknowledged that pursuant to his union's collective bargaining agreement with the County, employees may be terminated for refusing to take a drug test.

Asquini, the senior personnel officer, confirmed that Mitchell faxed the FMLA forms requesting leave from February 23 to March 14, 2005. Asquini could not recall whether Mitchell had also called him on February 23, 2005 to confirm his receipt of the fax, but testified that if Mitchell had called him, he did not mention that his drug test was scheduled for that day. Asquini stated that he first learned that a drug test had been scheduled when Sergeant Boisvert called him around March 1, 2005 to relay Mitchell's message that he had missed the test.

Commander Kreyger testified that she first learned of Mitchell's failure to appear for his drug test on March 1, 2005, when she received a memorandum from the County's central personnel office that Mitchell had failed to appear for his drug test. Commander Kreyger testified that when she terminated Mitchell, she understood that he had begun an approved FMLA leave on the day of his scheduled drug test, but still issued the Conduct Incident Report because she considered Mitchell's failure to appear for his drug test or notify a supervisor that he would not be able to appear to be "refusing to follow an order." She testified that Mitchell did not provide a reason why he was unable to follow the order to appear for a drug test, and "[t]here's nothing in his rebuttal that excused him from that order." Commander Kreyger later elaborated, "the issue with ... Mr. Mitchell at the time was that he was given an order to report for a drug screen. He signed for the order. He didn't report for the order and he did not call anybody to ask, What do you want me to do now?" Commander Kreyger stated that she did not factor Mitchell's FMLA leave into her decision to discipline him, and while she believed that Mitchell was "manipulating the system" and that the timing of his FMLA leave was "suspicious, my suspicion was not a factor in the case." However, she stated that "I did take [into account] the fact that he did not make a call to anybody to get the [drug test] order changed when I knew that he did make a call that he wasn't coming to work. He did make calls to Sheriff's personnel about his FMLA paperwork, he did make calls to his parents to go to the chiropractor, but the only call that he never made was in regards to his drug testing order." Commander Kreyger confirmed that, following the April 1, 2005 administrative hearing, she offered Mitchell a settlement, pursuant to which Mitchell would have returned to work and would have been subject to random drug testing for the next twelve months. Commander Kreyger denied that the settlement would have otherwise altered the conditions of Mitchell's employment. Commander Kreyger further testified that, when she informed Mitchell that under the agreement she would personally schedule his random tests, Mitchell "kind of laughed and said, [n]o way."

Commander Kreyger's testimony was consistent with that of Cureton, who at the time of Mitchell's termination was the undersheriff of the Sheriff's Department. Cureton testified that he and Commander Kreyger agreed to offer Mitchell his job back under the condition that he submit to random drug testing for twelve months, and without any loss of seniority rights.

Sergeant Sabbough, the supervisor who had served the drug test order on Mitchell, testified that the County did not have a written policy instructing employees what to do in the event that they had to miss a drug test. Although Sergeant Sabbough initially stated that he would not have believed that the failure to appear for a drug test due to injury would have constituted "a refusal" to take the test, he also stated that, when an employee is physically able to notify the Sheriff's Department that he cannot appear for the test but fails to do so, the failure to notify could constitute a refusal.

Sergeant Boisvert's testimony confirmed that when Mitchell called him around March 1, Mitchell told him that he had missed a drug test on February 23, 2005. Sergeant Boisvert testified that under Sheriff's Department rules, it is the employee's duty to inform a supervising sergeant or commander if the employee needs to miss a drug test, and that supervisor is then responsible for reporting the missed drug test to the personnel department. Sergeant Boisvert stated his belief that Mitchell's failure to appear for his drug test did not constitute a refusal to take the test because he "was incapable of carrying [the order] out." However, Sergeant Boisvert added that if Mitchell had been capable of notifying the Sheriff's Department that he was incapable of taking the test but failed to do so, such a failure "would not be in accordance with the order he was given."

At the close of evidence, the district court granted a stipulated order dismissing the claims against Commander Kreyger and Cureton with prejudice, because under the FMLA they could not be held liable as Mitchell's employer. Before the court submitted the case to the jury, Mitchell moved for judgment as a matter of law, and the court denied the motion. On March 22, 2007, the jury returned a verdict in favor of the County, finding in its verdict sheet that the County did not interfere with, or retaliate against, Mitchell's exercise of his FMLA rights. On April 4, 2007, Mitchell renewed his motion for judgment as a matter of law or for a new trial. The court again denied Mitchell's motion. Mitchell timely appealed.

## DISCUSSION

### I. Standard of Review

This Court reviews de novo the district court's denial of a renewed motion for a judgment as a matter of law. Judgment as a matter of law is proper if the nonmoving party "has been fully heard on an issue and there is no legally sufficient evidentiary basis for a reasonable jury to find for that party on that issue."

This Court reviews the district court's denial of Mitchell's motion for a new trial pursuant to Rule 59 for abuse of discretion. Reversal is warranted only if there is "a definite and firm conviction that the trial court committed a clear error of judgment." [citation omitted].

### II. Sufficiency of the Evidence

The FMLA entitles qualifying employees to up to twelve weeks of unpaid leave each year if, among other things, an employee has a "serious health condition that makes the employee unable to perform the functions of the position of such employee." Upon return from FMLA leave, an employee is entitled "(A) to be restored by the employer to the position of employment held by the employee when the leave commenced; or (B) to be restored to an equivalent position with equivalent employment benefits, pay, and other terms and conditions of employment." The parties agree that Mitchell validly exercised protected FMLA rights when he took a leave of absence from February 23, 2005 to March 14, 2005.

The FMLA recognizes two theories of civil liability: that an employer interferes with an employee's exercise of his or her FMLA rights, and that an employer retaliates against an employee for exercising his or her FMLA rights. Mitchell claims the County violated the FMLA when it disciplined him and terminated his employment upon return from FMLA leave, because those acts constituted interference with his FMLA rights and retaliation for exercising those rights. On the jury verdict form, the jury separately answered "no" with respect to both of the theories.

## A. Interference

An employer may not "interfere with, restrain, or deny the exercise of or the attempt to exercise, any right provided under [the FMLA]." Under the interference (or entitlement) theory of recovery, "[t]he issue is simply whether the employer provided its employee the entitlements set forth in the FMLA—for example, a twelve-week leave or reinstatement after taking a medical leave." [citation omitted]. "To prevail on an entitlement claim, an employee must prove that: (1) she was an eligible employee, (2) the defendant was an employer as defined under the FMLA, (3) she was entitled to leave under the FMLA, (4) she gave the employer notice of her intention to take leave, and (5) the employer denied the employee FMLA benefits to which she was entitled." The parties agree that Mitchell satisfied the first four elements. Thus, the dispute focuses on whether the County's disciplining Mitchell upon his return and his subsequent termination constituted the denial of an FMLA benefit.

If an employer denies an employee the right to return to work from FMLA leave, such an act constitutes interference, regardless of whether the employer intended to interfere with the employee's FMLA rights. However, "an employer who interferes with an employee's FMLA rights will not be liable if the employer can prove it would have made the same decision had the employee not exercised the employee's FMLA rights." [citation omitted]. Thus, "interference with an employee's FMLA rights does not constitute a violation if the employer has a legitimate reason unrelated to the exercise of FMLA rights for engaging in the challenged conduct." [citation omitted]. "If the employee cannot show that he was discharged because he took leave—or at least that his taking of leave was a negative factor in the employer's decision to discharge him—he cannot show a violation of the FMLA." [citations omitted].

In the instant case, there was sufficient evidence adduced at trial for a reasonable jury to conclude that the County's decision to terminate Mitchell was based on a legitimate reason unrelated to his FMLA leave—*i.e.* that he had disobeyed an order.

First, the evidence supported the conclusion that Mitchell defied an order by failing to appear for the drug test or properly notify the Sheriff's Department that he would not be able to appear. Although Mitchell said that he told someone at the Sheriff's Department on February 23, 2005 that he had a "test" scheduled, he could not recall whether he even specified that the test was a drug test. As Mitchell could not identify the person to whom he had spoken when he called on his first day of FMLA leave, the jury was entitled to discredit Mitchell's testimony that he even called the Sheriff's Department in the first place. More importantly, Sergeant Boisvert's testimony indicated that such notification, without more, would have been insufficient anyway, because Mitchell was required to notify a supervising sergeant or commander about his inability to appear for the test. Asquini testified that Mitchell did not mention the missed drug test when he called on February 23 to confirm Asquini's receipt of the FMLA forms, and by all accounts, no sergeant or supervisor learned of the missed drug test for several days. Both Sergeant Sabbough and Sergeant Boisvert testified that if Mitchell had been capable of calling in to report that he could not take the test but failed to do so, such a failure could be viewed within the Sheriff's Department as refusing to take the test. Thus, the jury could have concluded Mitchell's failure to notify constituted a violation of a rule of the Sheriff's Department.

Second, the jury could have reasonably concluded that Commander Kreyger's decision to terminate Mitchell was based upon his failure to obey the order to call regarding the drug test. Commander Kreyger testified that she terminated Mitchell because he failed to appear for a drug test, and failed to notify the Sheriff's Department that he would be unable to appear. Although Commander Kreyger admitted that she found the timing of Mitchell's FMLA leave "suspicious" and that she thought Mitchell might have been "manipulating the system[,]" she also testified that she did not take that suspicion into account when she terminated Mitchell's employment. The jury was entitled to believe her. Cureton corroborated Commander Kreyger's account when he testified that the decision to terminate Mitchell was based solely upon his failure to follow the drug test order. The numerous times Mitchell previously took FMLA leave and was promptly reinstated upon his return also supported a finding that the County's reason for disciplining and then terminating Mitchell's employment was unrelated to his FMLA leave.

Mitchell argues that the County's explanation that it disciplined Mitchell because of his missed drug test constituted an admission that it interfered with his FMLA rights, because the County effectively admitted that it imposed an additional notification requirement beyond the requirements of the statute. To be sure, this Court has held that "the FMLA does not permit an employer to limit his employee's FMLA rights by denying them whenever an employee fails to comply with internal procedural requirements that are more strict than those contemplated by the FMLA." In *Cavin*, the defendant terminated the plaintiff's employment specifically because he did not obey a call-in requirement for FMLA absences that was more stringent than required by the FMLA. However, neither *Cavin* nor any other precedent of this Court has held that employees on FMLA leave need not comply with notification requirements unrelated to the employee's absence from the workplace.... Nothing in the evidence suggests that Mitchell was physically incapable of making the required phone call to alert a supervisor that he would be unable to appear for his test, and the jury could have found that Mitchell's failure to obey an order was not related to his absence from the workplace.

In sum, because there is a "legally sufficient evidentiary basis" for the jury to have concluded that Mitchell violated an order and that he was terminated for that reason, the district court properly denied Mitchell's motion for a judgment as a matter of law with respect to his interference theory.

## B. Retaliation

"It shall be unlawful for any employer to discharge or in any other manner discriminate against any individual for opposing any practice made unlawful by [the FMLA]." 29 U.S.C. § 2615(a)(2). "This prohibition includes retaliatory discharge for taking leave." [citation omitted]. A retaliation theory of recovery under the FMLA is different from an interference theory because under a retaliation theory, the intent of the employer matters. "The employer's motive is relevant because retaliation claims impose liability on employers that act against employees specifically because those employees invoked their FMLA rights." [citation omitted.] Thus, employers may not " 'discriminat[e] against employees ... who have used FMLA leave,' nor can they 'use the taking of FMLA leave as a negative factor in employment actions.' " [citations omitted].

Mitchell's motion for a judgment as a matter of law fails for the same reason under the retaliation theory that it failed under the interference theory: the evidence was sufficient for the jury to conclude that the County did not terminate Mitchell's employment because of his exercise of FMLA rights, but because he failed to follow an order and either appear for his drug test or be granted permission to miss it. The jury was entitled to find that Mitchell's decision to take FMLA leave did not factor into the County's decision at all, a finding that would be largely based upon an assessment of the credibility of the County's witnesses.

Accordingly, the district court properly denied Mitchell's motion for judgment as a matter of law. Finally, because the jury did not commit a clear error in judgment and there was no allegation of unfairness or bias in the conduct of the trial, the district court did not abuse its discretion in denying Mitchell's motion for a new trial.

## CONCLUSION

For the foregoing reasons, the judgment of the district court is affirmed.

---

## Notes

1. Mitchell's contention is that his superiors penalized him for taking leave. Do you find credible the superiors' contention that they terminated Mitchell because he failed to report to a supervisor that he had to miss the drug test? What do you suppose caused the jury to believe the employer's witnesses?

2. The Tenth Circuit Court of Appeals, in *Smith v. Diffee Ford-Lincoln Mercury, Inc.*, clarified the difference between interference and retaliation claims, stating that each claim arises out of a separate theory. The Court found that an employee could therefore pursue a claim regarding an alleged wrongful dismissal under either theory:

> Courts have recognized two theories for recovery on FMLA claims under § 2615, the retaliation or discrimination theory and the entitlement or interference theory. The retaliation or discrimination theory arises from § 2615(a)(2), which provides that "[i]t shall be unlawful for any employer to discharge or in any other manner discriminate against any individual for opposing any practice made unlawful by this subchapter." The entitlement or interference theory arises from § 2615(a)(1): "[i]t shall be unlawful for any employer to interfere with, restrain, or deny the exercise of or the attempt to exercise, any right provided in this subchapter."
>
> We have not explored the entire range of reasons for dismissal that would support recovery under the interference/entitlement theory. The fact that the interference/entitlement theory and the retaliation/discrimination theory are recognized as separate theories makes it evident, however, that retaliation is not the only impermissible reason for dismissal. A plaintiff can prevail under an entitlement theory if she was denied her substantive rights under the FMLA for a reason connected with her FMLA leave. Such a reason need not be retaliation. Smith's decision not to pursue her claim under the retaliation theory is thus not fatal to her case.

298 F.3d 955, 960–61 (2002).

3. In *Mitchell v. Wayne*, if, instead of hurting his back on the night before the scheduled drug test, Mitchell had been in a serious car accident and was hospitalized for a period

of several days, do you think that would have altered the outcome? Under these alternative facts or the actual facts, are there additional arguments that Mitchell could have made that might have altered the outcome?

## Race/Color

An entire course could be dedicated to how race and color affect employment. The cases throughout this book have focused largely on issues of race discrimination. You saw allegations of disparate treatment on the basis of race in the *McDonnell-Douglas* case, among others. Similarly, you encountered racially discriminatory harassment in the *Tademy* case. This section aims to help you think more critically about race generally and race-based employment discrimination specifically. The first case, *Rogers v. American Airlines, Inc.*, raises issues about whether Title VII protects only immutable expressions of race and about intersectionality, where both race and sex motivate employment decisions. The second case, *Salas v. Wisconsin Dept. of Corrections*, considers Title VII's protections against color discrimination. This section concludes by considering the disparate impact that can result when employers base employment decisions on arrest records.

---

### Exercise 9.3

Should Title VII protect only immutable expressions of race or should it also be interpreted to include other expressions of race? Should Title VII protect employees who dress or present themselves in ways that have racial significance, even if a majority of people within the race do not make the same choices?

How race is conceived by the courts is important to how the courts interpret discrimination cases. Consider the court's conception of Title VII's definition of race in the following case.

---

### *What Constitutes Race?*

### Focus Questions: *Rogers v. American Airlines, Inc.*

1. *Does the defendant's hair policy demonstrate an inherent racial bias? Why do you think the employer considered corn rows to be an unprofessional hairstyle?*

2. *Is requiring the plaintiff to comply with the grooming policy a demand that she assimilate to a "white" appearance norm? Why or why not?*

# Rogers v. American Airlines, Inc.

527 F. Supp. 229 (D.C.N.Y. 1981)

District Judge Soafer.

Plaintiff is a black woman who seeks $10,000 in damages, injunctive, and declaratory relief against enforcement of a grooming policy of the defendant American Airlines that prohibits employees in certain employment categories from wearing an all-braided hairstyle. Plaintiff has been an American Airlines employee for approximately eleven years, and has been an airport operations agent for over one year. Her duties involve extensive passenger contact, including greeting passengers, issuing boarding passes, and checking luggage. She alleges that the policy violates her rights under ... Title VII of the Civil Rights Act and under 42 U.S.C. § 1981, in that it discriminates against her as a woman, and more specifically as a black woman. She claims that denial of the right to wear her hair in the "corn row" style intrudes upon her rights and discriminates against her. Plaintiff has exhausted her administrative remedies and has been issued a right to sue letter by the Equal Employment Opportunity Commission ("EEOC").

. . .

The [Defendant's motion to dismiss is] meritorious with respect to the statutory claims insofar as they challenge the policy on its face. The statutory bases alleged, Title VII and section 1981, are indistinguishable in the circumstances of this case, and will be considered together. The policy is addressed to both men and women, black and white. Plaintiff's assertion that the policy has practical effect only with respect to women is not supported by any factual allegations. Many men have hair longer than many women. Some men have hair long enough to wear in braids if they choose to do so. Even if the grooming policy imposed different standards for men and women, however, it would not violate Title VII. It follows, therefore, that an even-handed policy that prohibits to both sexes a style more often adopted by members of one sex does not constitute prohibited sex discrimination. This is because this type of regulation has at most a negligible effect on employment opportunity. It does not regulate on the basis of any immutable characteristic of the employees involved.... The complaint does not state a claim for sex discrimination.

The considerations with respect to plaintiff's race discrimination claim would clearly be the same, except for plaintiff's assertion that the "corn row" style has a special significance for black women. She contends that it "has been, historically, a fashion and style adopted by Black American women, reflective of the cultural, historical essence of the Black women in American society. The style was 'popularized' so to speak, within the larger society, when Cicely Tyson adopted the same for an appearance on a nationally viewed Academy Awards presentation several years ago.... It was and is analogous to the public statement by the late Malcolm X regarding the Afro hair style.... At the bottom line, the completely braided hair style, sometimes referred to as corn rows, has been and continues to be part of the cultural and historical essence of Black American women. There can be little doubt that, if American adopted a policy which foreclosed Black women/all women from wearing hair styled as an 'Afro/bush,' that policy would have very pointedly racial dynamics and consequences reflecting a vestige of slavery unwilling to die (that is, a master mandate that one wear hair divorced from ones historical and cultural perspective and otherwise consistent with the 'white master' dominated society and preference thereof)."

Plaintiff is entitled to a presumption that her arguments, largely repeated in her affidavit, are true. But the grooming policy applies equally to members of all races, and plaintiff does not allege that an all-braided hair style is worn exclusively or even predominantly by black people. Moreover, it is proper to note that defendants have alleged without contravention that plaintiff first appeared at work in the all-braided hairstyle on or about September 25, 1980, soon after the style had been popularized by a white actress in the film "10." Plaintiff may be correct that an employer's policy prohibiting the "Afro/bush" style might offend Title VII and section 1981. But if so, this chiefly would be because banning a natural hairstyle would implicate the policies underlying the prohibition of discrimination on the basis of immutable characteristics. In any event, an all-braided hairstyle is a different matter. It is not the product of natural hair growth but of artifice. An all-braided hair style is an "easily changed characteristic," and, even if socioculturally associated with a particular race or nationality, is not an impermissible basis for distinctions in the application of employment practices by an employer.

Save for religion, the discriminations on which the Act focuses its laser of prohibition are those that are either beyond the victim's power to alter, or that impose a burden on an employee on one of the prohibited bases.... "(A) hiring policy that distinguishes on some other ground, such as grooming codes or length of hair, is related more closely to the employer's choice of how to run his business than to equality of employment opportunity." [citation omitted].

. . .

Moreover, the airline did not require plaintiff to restyle her hair. It suggested that she could wear her hair as she liked while off duty, and permitted her to pull her hair into a bun and wrap a hairpiece around the bun during working hours. Plaintiff has done this, but alleges that the hairpiece has caused her severe headaches. A larger hairpiece would seem in order. But even if any hairpiece would cause such discomfort, the policy does not offend a substantial interest.

Plaintiff also asserts in her complaint that the regulation has been applied in an uneven and discriminatory manner. She claims that white women in particular have been permitted to wear pony tails and shag cuts. She goes on to claim, in fact, that some black women are permitted to wear the same hairstyle that she has been prohibited from wearing. These claims seriously undercut her assertion that the policy discriminates against women, and her claim that it discriminates against black women in particular. Conceivably, however, the complaint could be construed as alleging that the policy has been applied in a discriminatory manner against plaintiff because she is black by some representative of the defendant. On its face, this allegation is sufficient, although it might be subject to dismissal on a summary judgment motion if it is not supplemented with some factual claims.

. . .

This action is dismissed, except for plaintiff's claim of discriminatory treatment in the application of the grooming policy....

---

## Note

The EEOC interprets race more broadly than some courts have. In the EEOC Compliance Manual, it provides the following explanation of race discrimination:

Title VII's prohibition of race discrimination generally encompasses:

**Ancestry:** Employment discrimination because of racial or ethnic ancestry. Discrimination against a person because of his or her ancestry can violate Title VII's prohibition against race discrimination. Note that there can be considerable overlap between "race" and "national origin," but they are not identical....

**Physical Characteristics:** Employment discrimination based on a person's physical characteristics associated with race, such as a person's color, hair, facial features, height and weight.

**Race-linked Illness:** Discrimination based on race-linked illnesses. For example, sickle cell anemia is a genetically-transmitted disease that affects primarily persons of African descent. Other diseases, while not linked directly to race or ethnicity, may nevertheless have a disproportionate impact. For example, Native Hawaiians have a disproportionately high incidence of diabetes. If the employer applies facially neutral standards to exclude treatment for conditions or risks that disproportionately affect employees on the basis of race or ethnicity, the employer must show that the standards are based on generally accepted medical criteria.

**Culture:** Employment discrimination because of cultural characteristics related to race or ethnicity. Title VII prohibits employment discrimination against a person because of cultural characteristics often linked to race or ethnicity, such as a person's name, cultural dress and grooming practices, or accent or manner of speech. For example, an employment decision based on a person having a so-called "Black accent," or "sounding White," violates Title VII if the accent or manner of speech does not materially interfere with the ability to perform job duties.

**Perception:** Employment discrimination against an individual based on a belief that the individual is a member of a particular racial group, regardless of how the individual identifies himself. Discrimination against an individual based on a perception of his or her race violates Title VII even if that perception is wrong.

...

**Subgroup or "Race Plus":** Title VII prohibits discrimination against a subgroup of persons in a racial group because they have certain attributes in addition to their race. Thus, for example, it would violate Title VII for an employer to reject Black women with preschool age children, while not rejecting other women with preschool age children.

Section 15, II.

## *Color Discrimination*

# Salas v. Wisconsin Dept. of Corrections

No. 05-C-399-C, 2006 U.S. Dist. LEXIS 21140 (W.D. Wis. April 17, 2006)

Judge Crabb.

In this civil action for monetary relief, plaintiff Francisco Salas contends that defendant ... discriminated ... against him because of his ... race and national origin [in violation of Title VII].

Before the court is defendants' motion to dismiss plaintiff's ... Title VII claims.... Defendants' motion to dismiss will be denied with respect to plaintiff's Title VII claims against the Wisconsin Department of Corrections because plaintiff has stated a claim against the department for discriminatory firing based upon his national origin and color.

I draw the following facts from the allegations of plaintiff's complaint.

## ALLEGATIONS OF FACT

A. *Parties*

... From January 27, 1986 to June 1989, plaintiff was employed by defendant Wisconsin Department of Corrections Division of Adult Institutions as a correctional officer. He was promoted to the position of Social Worker in June 1989, Social Worker 2 in June 1991 and Social Worker 3 in June 1993. In August 1993, plaintiff became a Licensed Social Worker, certified by the Wisconsin Board of Social Workers, Marriage and Family Therapists and Professional Counselors. Plaintiff trained all newly-hired prison social workers and was the team leader for the Emergency Response Unit's hostage negotiation team.

In October 1995, plaintiff was transferred to the Division of Community Corrections as a Senior Probation/Parole Agent. In that position, plaintiff co-facilitated sex offender, anger management and cognitive intervention treatment groups.

...

[Defendant] terminated plaintiff's employment because of plaintiff's alleged violation of Wisconsin Department of Corrections Work Rules 2, 4 and 6. Work Rule 2 requires employees to follow policies and procedures, including the fraternization policy and arrest and conviction policy. Work Rule 4 prohibits negligence in the performance of assigned duties. Work Rule 6 prohibits employees from falsifying records, knowingly giving false information or knowingly permitting, encouraging or directing others to do so.

[Plaintiff alleges that the reasons given for his termination were false.] It was defendant Wisconsin Department of Corrections's policy not to terminate employment on the ground that an employee had made the errors attributed to plaintiff. No one else plaintiff's age or of non-Hispanic origin had been fired by the department for the same reason plaintiff was fired.

[Plaintiff alleged that his supervisors tried to] "build a false case in support of the termination of plaintiff's employment." One or more defendants altered, destroyed or removed evidence in order to build a false case against plaintiff.

At the time plaintiff was fired, he worked at the Division of Community Corrections office located in Madison, Wisconsin. The office employed 33 people. Plaintiff was the only Hispanic male and one of only two Hispanic employees in the office....

## OPINION

When a federal court reviews the sufficiency of a complaint, "its task is necessarily a limited one." *Swierkiewicz v. Sorema N. A.*, 534 U.S. 506, 511 (2002). To decide whether a plaintiff has stated a claim under Fed. R. Civ. P. 12(b)(6), the court must "accept as true all well-pleaded allegations in the complaint and draw all reasonable inferences in the plaintiff's favor." [citation omitted]. A claim may not be dismissed unless "it is clear that no relief could be granted under any set of facts that could be proved consistent with the allegations." *Hishon v. King & Spalding*, 467 U.S. 69, 73 (1984). The question is not whether a plaintiff will ultimately prevail but whether he is entitled to offer evidence in support of his claims. *Swierkiewicz*, 534 U.S. at 511.

In his complaint, plaintiff alleges that he was one of two Hispanic workers employed by the Wisconsin Department of Corrections Division of Community Corrections at its Madison, Wisconsin office. Moreover, he alleges that defendants terminated his employment because of his "national origin, color [and] ancestry." ...

Defendants contend that plaintiff has failed to state a claim against the Wisconsin Department of Corrections because his complaint does not indicate the "hue of his skin" or "the country from which his forebear[er]s came." Defendants contend that the term "Hispanic" is a racial description only, and is insufficient to establish either plaintiff's national origin or his color. Consequently, defendants contend, plaintiff's Title VII claims should be dismissed in their entirety under Fed. R. Civ. P. 12(b)(6) for failure to state a claim.

Before deciding whether plaintiff's allegation that he is Hispanic is relevant to his race, national origin or color, it is worth noting that to state an actionable claim under Title VII all plaintiff must do is allege that his status as a "Hispanic" man was a motivating factor in his termination.

Defendants contend that the plaintiff's national origin discrimination claim should be dismissed because plaintiff did not identify in his complaint the country from which he or his ancestors originated in his complaint. According to defendants, plaintiff's self-identification as "Hispanic" is a statement of his "race" but not of his national origin.

Laying aside the contentious debate regarding social and anthropological constructions of "race" and how it should be defined, the meaning and use of the term "Hispanic" contradicts defendants' assertion. The *New Oxford American Dictionary* 806 (2001) defines the word Hispanic as "of or related to Spanish-speaking countries, especially those of Latin America." The *American Heritage Dictionary* 832 (4th ed. 2000) defines the word similarly and explains its usage as follows:

> Though often used interchangeably in American English, Hispanic and Latino are not identical terms, and in certain contexts the choice between them can be significant. Hispanic, from the Latin word for "Spain," has the broader reference, potentially encompassing all Spanish-speaking peoples in both hemispheres and emphasizing the common denominator of language among communities that sometimes have little else in common ... In practice, however, this distinction is of little significance when referring to residents of the United States, most of whom are of Latin American origin and can theoretically be called by either word.... Hispanic, the term used by the U.S. Census Bureau and other government agencies, is said to bear the stamp of an Anglo establishment far removed from the concerns of the Spanish-speaking community.

Because the term Hispanic relates to language and culture, it is an ethnic designation more than a racial classification, used to refer to individuals of Spanish-speaking descent, whether from Spain itself or from Spanish-speaking Latin-American countries.

... Because I find that plaintiff has designated his national origin adequately by alleging that he is Hispanic, defendant's motion to dismiss plaintiff's national origin discrimination claim will be denied.

...

Technically speaking, "color discrimination" is distinct from racial discrimination. Cynthia Nance, *Colorable Claims: The Continuing Significance of Color under Title VII Forty Years After Its Passage*, 26 Berkeley J. Emp. & Lab. L. 435, 462 (2005). Despite the legal distinction between the concepts, many courts conflate claims of racial and color discrimination. *Id.* at 464. The reason for this is clear:

> People often confuse skin color and race because skin color is used to assign people to racial categories. Indeed, color is commonly used to describe the difference between racial categories (*i.e.*, Black is used to describe African-

Americans and White is used to describe Caucasians). In addition, people are misled because of the positive correlation between the values associated with being a member of the White race and the values attributed to a lighter skin tone.

Trina Jones, *Shades of Brown, The Law of Skin Color,* 49 DUKE L.J. 1487, 1498 (2000). Although color may be a factor in racial discrimination (for example, when an employer prefers a white job candidate over an equally qualified black candidate), color discrimination refers specifically to preferring an individual because of the *hue* of his skin (for example, treating a light-skinned African woman more favorably than a dark-skinned African woman).

In this case, plaintiff does not allege that he was treated differently from the other Hispanic employee in his office because of the hue of his skin. Nevertheless, he clearly believes that the way he looked (that is, his "color") caused defendants to treat him differently from other similarly-situated employees. Just as racial and national origin classifications can often blur, *Saint Francis College,* 481 U.S. at 614 (Brennan, J., concurring), so too can designations relating to skin color. *E.g., Oranika v. City of Chicago,* 2005 WL 2663562, *3 (N.D. Ill. 2005) (finding race, national origin and color discrimination claims under Title VII based upon allegation that plaintiff was "Nigerian"). Although individuals of Hispanic origin may have skin tones that range from dark to fair, the term Hispanic is often associated with color as well as ethnicity. To pretend otherwise would be patently disingenuous.

To survive dismissal, plaintiff's complaint must do no more than put defendants on notice of the allegations against them. Although plaintiff's allegations could have been made with greater precision, there is no question that defendants understand the nature of his charges. Plaintiff's allegation that he is Hispanic, combined with his contention that defendants discriminated against him because of the color of his skin, is sufficient to state a claim under Title VII. Therefore, defendants' motion to dismiss will be denied with respect to plaintiff's claim that defendants terminated his employment because of his color.

---

## Note

Think again about the "same protected class inference"—an assumption that discrimination does not occur if the alleged discriminator and the victim are of the same protected class. In a color discrimination case, a plaintiff may need to educate the Court about discrimination that might occur based on differences in the color of a person's skin. Some judges may erroneously assume that because a plaintiff and an alleged discriminator are the same race, that no discrimination has occurred.

### Race and Arrest Records

The following case considers whether an employer may use a potential employee's arrest record as a consideration in its hiring decision.

---

### Focus Question: *Gregory v. Litton Systems, Inc.*

*Why might the use of arrest records create a disparate impact based on race?*

---

# Gregory v. Litton Systems, Inc.

472 F.2d 631 (9th Cir. 1972)

Circuit Judge Goodwin.

Litton appeals from an injunction, damages, and attorney fees, awarded pursuant to Title VII, following a finding by the district court that Litton's employment questionnaire discriminated against black job-seekers by requiring each applicant to reveal his arrest record.

. . .

It is stipulated that Litton's decision not to hire Gregory as a sheet-metal worker was predicated upon his statement that he had been arrested fourteen times, and not upon any consideration of convictions, or of national security, the latter a point relevant to certain of Litton's government contracts but not pertinent here.

The district court found, upon a record which contains substantial evidence to support the finding, that the apparently racially-neutral questionnaire actually operated to bar employment to black applicants in far greater proportion than to white applicants. Litton showed no reasonable business purpose for continuing to ask prospective employees about their arrest records. The district court accordingly found the practice to be in violation of the remedial legislation under which the action was brought.

In deciding that statistics demonstrated the racially discriminatory character of Litton's questionnaire, without first finding a discriminatory purpose, Judge Hill correctly anticipated the subsequent decision in *Griggs v. Duke Power Co.*, 401 U.S. 424 (1971).

---

## Note

On April 25, 2012, the EEOC issued new enforcement guidance on the Consideration of Arrest and Conviction Records in Employment Decisions, http://www.eeoc.gov/laws/guidance/arrest_conviction.cfm (last visited June 16, 2013). With respect to arrest records, the Guidance states:

> The fact of an arrest does not establish that criminal conduct has occurred. Arrests are not proof of criminal conduct. Many arrests do not result in criminal charges, or the charges are dismissed. Even if an individual is charged and subsequently prosecuted, he is presumed innocent unless proven guilty.

> An arrest, however, may in some circumstances trigger an inquiry into whether the conduct underlying the arrest justifies an adverse employment action. Title VII calls for a fact-based analysis to determine if an exclusionary policy or practice is job related and consistent with business necessity. Therefore, an exclusion based on an arrest, in itself, is not job related and consistent with business necessity.

> Another reason for employers not to rely on arrest records is that they may not report the final disposition of the arrest (e.g., not prosecuted, convicted, or acquitted).... [M]any arrest records in the FBI's III database and state criminal record repositories are not associated with final dispositions. Arrest records also may include inaccuracies or may continue to be reported even if expunged or sealed.

### Example: Arrest Record Is Not Grounds for Exclusion.

Mervin and Karen, a middle-aged African American couple, are driving to church in a predominantly white town. An officer stops them and interrogates them about their destination. When Mervin becomes annoyed and comments that his offense is simply "driving while Black," the officer arrests him for disorderly conduct. The prosecutor decides not to file charges against Mervin, but the arrest remains in the police department's database and is reported in a background check when Mervin applies with his employer of fifteen years for a promotion to an executive position. The employer's practice is to deny such promotions to individuals with arrest records, even without a conviction, because it views an arrest record as an indicator of untrustworthiness and irresponsibility. If Mervin filed a Title VII charge based on these facts, and disparate impact based on race were established, the EEOC would find reasonable cause to believe that his employer violated Title VII.

Although an arrest record standing alone may not be used to deny an employment opportunity, an employer may make an employment decision based on the conduct underlying the arrest if the conduct makes the individual unfit for the position in question. The conduct, not the arrest, is relevant for employment purposes.

### Example: Employer's Inquiry into Conduct Underlying Arrest.

Andrew, a Latino man, worked as an assistant principal in Elementary School for several years. After several ten and eleven-year-old girls attending the school accused him of touching them inappropriately on the chest, Andrew was arrested and charged with several counts of endangering the welfare of children and sexual abuse. Elementary School has a policy that requires suspension or termination of any employee who the school believes engaged in conduct that impacts the health or safety of the students. After learning of the accusations, the school immediately places Andrew on unpaid administrative leave pending an investigation. In the course of its investigation, the school provides Andrew a chance to explain the events and circumstances that led to his arrest. Andrew denies the allegations, saying that he may have brushed up against the girls in the crowded hallways or lunchroom, but that he doesn't really remember the incidents and does not have regular contact with any of the girls. The school also talks with the girls, and several of them recount touching in crowded situations. The school does not find Andrew's explanation credible. Based on Andrew's conduct, the school terminates his employment pursuant to its policy.

Andrew challenges the policy as discriminatory under Title VII. He asserts that it has a disparate impact based on national origin and that his employer may not suspend or terminate him based solely on an arrest without a conviction because he is innocent until proven guilty. After confirming that an arrest policy would have a disparate impact based on national origin, the EEOC concludes that no discrimination occurred. The school's policy is linked to conduct that is relevant to the particular jobs at issue, and the exclusion is made based on descriptions of the underlying conduct, not the fact of the arrest. The Commission finds no reasonable cause to believe Title VII was violated.

## Age

This section explains in detail the statutory meaning of employment discrimination because of an individual's age under the ADEA.

The ADEA prohibits discrimination in employment because of an individual's age, 29 U.S.C. §623(a), but only protects those employees who are at least 40 years old. 29 U.S.C. §631(a). Accordingly, the starting point for an ADEA claim is that the plaintiff be at least 40 years of age. Individuals who are under 40 years of age are outside the protected class and not protected by the Act. For example, it is not a violation of the statute for an employer to hire a 22-year old worker over a 38-year old worker because the 22-year old is younger. The 38-year old is not protected by the Act even though he experienced discrimination because of his relatively *older* age. Even though discrimination against *relatively* older people could begin before a person is 40 years old in some lines of work—the television and film industry, for example—Congress decided that this problem is not worthy of statutory protection. Nor did Congress determine that *youth* discrimination for those under 40 is worthy of protection even though an employer could certainly stereotype a 25-year old because of his young age as too inexperienced and undependable to hire despite impeccable abilities and qualifications. Recall that state statutes or municipal or county ordinances may provide age discrimination protections for those under the age of 40.

Remember there is no requirement that the ADEA plaintiff prove that he was discriminated against in favor of someone outside the protected class, *i.e.*, under 40 years of age. In *O'Connor v. Consolidated Coin Caterers Corp.*, 517 U.S. 308 (1996), the Court decided that an ADEA plaintiff alleging individual disparate treatment is not required to demonstrate as part of the *McDonnell-Douglas* prima facie case that the plaintiff was replaced by someone outside the protected class (a person under 40). The Court explained that the ADEA prohibits discrimination on the basis of age and not class membership. The "more reliable indicator of age discrimination" is the fact that a replacement is *substantially younger* than the plaintiff. Thus, a 58-year old could establish that he was discriminated against in favor of a 43-year old even though both of them fell within the protected class. In light of *O'Connor*, the circuit courts require that the plaintiff demonstrate as part of the prima facie case that the employer filled the job with a person *significantly* younger than the plaintiff. The plaintiff should point to some evidence that the employer acted with knowledge as to the significant age discrepancy. *Woodman v. WWOR-TV, Inc.*, 411 F.3d 69, 80 (2d Cir. 2005). The circuits vary regarding how much of an age differential or gap is sufficient to establish a prima facie case. Age differences of ten or more years have generally been held to be sufficiently substantial to satisfy the last part of the age discrimination prima facie case. *Grosjean v. First Energy Corp.*, 349 F.3d 332, 336 (6th Cir. 2003) (collecting cases). There is conflicting authority over whether age differences of ten years or less are sufficient. *See Carter v. City of Miami*, 870 F.2d 578, 583 (11th Cir. 1989) (age gap of three years sufficient); *Rachid v. Jack-in-the-Box, Inc.*, 376 F.3d 305, 313 (5th Cir. 2004) (stating that an age difference of five years is a "close question"); *Grosjean v. First Energy Corp.*, 349 F.3d 332, 340 (6th Cir. 2003) (age difference of six years or less between an employee and a replacement is not significant unless there is direct evidence that the employer considered age to be significant).

---

### Focus Questions: *General Dynamics Land Systems, Inc. v. Cline*

1. *Assume that two people apply for the same position, and one is 42 years of age and the other 52 years of age. If the employer chooses to hire the 42-year-old*

*instead of the 52-year-old because the 52-year-old is "too old," the ADEA is clearly violated. But is the Act violated if the employer chooses the 52-year-old over the 42-year-old because of the 42-year-old's age? Is it lawful for the employer to favor older workers over younger workers when both are protected by the Act, i.e., are 40 years of age or older? Consider the following U.S. Supreme Court decision.*

2. *If you could write an age discrimination statute on a clean slate, would you prohibit discrimination in favor of older workers over younger workers? Why or why not?*

3. *Why is age discrimination against younger workers any different from race discrimination against Caucasians or male-on-male sexual harassment, both of which violate Title VII? Why is Justice Thomas so adamant that the majority has departed from settled principles of statutory interpretation?*

---

# General Dynamics Land Systems, Inc. v. Cline

## 540 U.S. 581 (2004)

Justice Souter delivered the opinion of the Court.

The Age Discrimination in Employment Act of 1967 forbids discriminatory preference for the young over the old. The question in this case is whether it also prohibits favoring the old over the young. We hold it does not.

### I

In 1997, a collective-bargaining agreement between petitioner General Dynamics and the United Auto Workers eliminated the company's obligation to provide health benefits to subsequently retired employees, except as to then-current workers at least 50 years old. Respondents (collectively, Cline) were then at least 40 and thus protected by the Act, but under 50 and so without promise of the benefits. All of them objected to the new terms, although some had retired before the change in order to get the prior advantage, some retired afterwards with no benefit, and some worked on, knowing the new contract would give them no health coverage when they were through.

Before the Equal Employment Opportunity Commission (EEOC or Commission) they claimed that the agreement violated the ADEA, because it "discriminate[d against them] ... with respect to ... compensation, terms, conditions, or privileges of employment, because of [their] age," §623(a)(1). The EEOC agreed, and invited General Dynamics and the union to settle informally with Cline.

When they failed, Cline brought this action against General Dynamics combining claims under the ADEA and state law....

### II

The common ground in this case is the generalization that the ADEA's prohibition covers "discriminat[ion] ... because of [an] individual's age," 29 U.S.C. §623(a)(1), that helps the younger by hurting the older. In the abstract, the phrase is open to an argument for a broader construction, since reference to "age" carries no express modifier and the word could be read to look two ways. This more expansive possible understanding does not, however, square with the natural reading of the whole provision prohibiting discrimination, and in fact Congress's interpretive clues speak almost unanimously to an understanding of discrimination as directed against workers who are older than the ones getting treated better.

Congress chose not to include age within discrimination forbidden by Title VII of the Civil Rights Act of 1964 being aware that there were legitimate reasons as well as invidious ones for making employment decisions on age. Instead it called for a study of the issue by the Secretary of Labor, who concluded that age discrimination was a serious problem, but one different in kind from discrimination on account of race. The Secretary spoke of disadvantage to older individuals from arbitrary and stereotypical employment distinctions (including then-common policies of age ceilings on hiring), but he examined the problem in light of rational considerations of increased pension cost and, in some cases, legitimate concerns about an older person's ability to do the job. When the Secretary ultimately took the position that arbitrary discrimination against older workers was widespread and persistent enough to call for a federal legislative remedy, he placed his recommendation against the background of common experience that the potential cost of employing someone rises with age, so that the older an employee is, the greater the inducement to prefer a younger substitute. The report contains no suggestion that reactions to age level off at some point, and it was devoid of any indication that the Secretary had noticed unfair advantages accruing to older employees at the expense of their juniors.

Congress then asked for a specific proposal, which the Secretary provided in January 1967. Extensive House and Senate hearings ensued.

The testimony at both hearings dwelled on unjustified assumptions about the effect of age on ability to work.... The record thus reflects the common facts that an individual's chances to find and keep a job get worse over time; as between any two people, the younger is in the stronger position, the older more apt to be tagged with demeaning stereotype. Not surprisingly, from the voluminous records of the hearings, we have found (and Cline has cited) nothing suggesting that any workers were registering complaints about discrimination in favor of their seniors.

[The Court noted that the introductory provisions of the ADEA mirrored the findings of the Wirtz report and the House and Senate committee transcripts.]

In sum, except on one point, all the findings and statements of objectives are either cast in terms of the effects of age as intensifying over time, or are couched in terms that refer to "older" workers, explicitly or implicitly relative to "younger" ones. The single subject on which the statute speaks less specifically is that of "arbitrary limits" or "arbitrary age discrimination." But these are unmistakable references to the Wirtz Report's finding that "[a]lmost three out of every five employers covered by [a] 1965 survey have in effect age limitations (most frequently between 45 and 55) on new hires which they apply without consideration of an applicant's other qualifications." The ADEA's ban on "arbitrary limits" thus applies to age caps that exclude older applicants, necessarily to the advantage of younger ones.

Such is the setting of the ADEA's core substantive provision, § 4 (as amended, 29 USC § 623), prohibiting employers and certain others from "discriminat[ion] ... because of [an] individual's age." ... The prefatory provisions and their legislative history make a case that we think is beyond reasonable doubt, that the ADEA was concerned to protect a relatively old worker from discrimination that works to the advantage of the relatively young.

Nor is it remarkable that the record is devoid of any evidence that younger workers were suffering at the expense of their elders, let alone that a social problem required a federal statute to place a younger worker in parity with an older one. Common experience is to the contrary, and the testimony, reports, and congressional findings simply confirm that Congress used the phrase "discriminat[ion] ... because of [an] individual's age" the same way that ordinary people in common usage might speak of age discrimination any day of the week. One commonplace conception of American society in recent decades is its character as a "youth culture," and in a world where younger is better, talk about discrimination because of age is naturally understood to refer to discrimination against the older.

This same, idiomatic sense of the statutory phrase is confirmed by the statute's restriction of the protected class to those 40 and above. If Congress had been worrying about protecting the younger against the older, it would not likely have ignored everyone under 40. The youthful deficiencies of inexperience and unsteadiness invite stereotypical and discriminatory thinking about those a lot younger than 40, and prejudice suffered by a 40-year-old is not typically owing to youth, as 40-year-olds sadly tend to find out. The enemy of 40 is 30, not 50.... Even so, the 40-year threshold was adopted over the objection that some discrimination against older people begins at an even younger age; female flight attendants were not fired at 32 because they were too young.... Thus, the 40-year threshold makes sense as identifying a class requiring protection against preference for their juniors, not as defining a class that might be threatened by favoritism toward seniors.

## III

Cline and *amicus* EEOC proffer three rejoinders in favor of their competing view that the prohibition works both ways. First, they say (as does Justice Thomas), that the statute's meaning is plain when the word "age" receives its natural and ordinary meaning and the statute is read as a whole giving "age" the same meaning throughout. And even if the text does not plainly mean what they say it means, they argue that the soundness of their version is shown by a colloquy on the floor of the Senate involving Senator Yarborough, a sponsor of the bill that became the ADEA. Finally, they fall back to the position (fortified by Justice Scalia's dissent) that we should defer to the EEOC's reading of the statute. On each point, however, we think the argument falls short of unsettling our view of the natural meaning of the phrase speaking of discrimination, read in light of the statute's manifest purpose.

## A

The first response to our reading is the dictionary argument that "age" means the length of a person's life, with the phrase "because of such individual's age" stating a simple test of causation: "discriminat[ion] ... because of [an] individual's age" is treatment that would not have occurred if the individual's span of years had been longer or shorter. The case for this reading calls attention to the other instances of "age" in the ADEA that are not limited to old age, such as 29 U.S.C. §623(f), which gives an employer a defense to charges of age discrimination when "age is a bona fide occupational qualification." Cline and the EEOC argue that if "age" meant old age, §623(f) would then provide a defense (old age is a bona fide qualification) only for an employer's action that on our reading would never clash with the statute (because preferring the older is not forbidden).

The argument rests on two mistakes. First, it assumes that the word "age" has the same meaning wherever the ADEA uses it. But this is not so, and Cline simply misemploys the "presumption that identical words used in different parts of the same act are intended to have the same meaning." *Atlantic Cleaners & Dyers, Inc.* v. *United States*, 286 U.S. 427, 433 (1932). Cline forgets that "the presumption is not rigid and readily yields whenever there is such variation in the connection in which the words are used as reasonably to warrant the conclusion that they were employed in different parts of the act with different intent." *Id.* The presumption of uniform usage thus relents when a word used has several commonly understood meanings among which a speaker can alternate in the course of an ordinary conversation, without being confused or getting confusing.

"Age" is that kind of word. As Justice Thomas agrees, the word "age" standing alone can be readily understood either as pointing to any number of years lived, or as common shorthand for the longer span and concurrent aches that make youth look good. Which alternative was probably intended is a matter of context; we understand the different choices of meaning that lie behind a sentence like "Age can be shown by a driver's license," and the statement, "Age has left him a shut-in." So it is easy to understand that Congress chose different meanings at different places in the ADEA, as the different settings readily show. Hence the second flaw in Cline's argument for uniform usage: it ignores the cardinal rule that "[s]tatutory language must be read in context [since] a phrase 'gathers meaning from the words around it.'" [citation omitted]. The point here is that we are not asking an abstract question about the meaning of "age"; we are seeking the meaning of the whole phrase "discriminate ... because of such individual's age," where it occurs in the ADEA. As we have said, social history emphatically reveals an understanding of age discrimination as aimed against the old, and the statutory reference to age discrimination in this idiomatic sense is confirmed by legislative history. For the very reason that reference to context shows that "age" means "old age" when teamed with "discrimination," the provision of an affirmative defense when age is a bona fide occupational qualification readily shows that "age" as a qualification means comparative youth. As context tells us that "age" means one thing in §623(a)(1) and another in §623(f), so it also tells us that the presumption of uniformity cannot sensibly operate here.

The comparisons Justice Thomas urges to *McDonald* v. *Santa Fe Trail Transp. Co.,* 427 U.S. 273 (1976), and *Oncale* v. *Sundowner Offshore Services, Inc.,* 523 U.S. 75 (1998), serve to clarify our position. Both cases involved Title VII and its prohibition on employment discrimination "because of [an] individual's *race* ... [or] *sex*," §2000e-2(a)(1) (emphasis added). The term "age" employed by the ADEA is not, however, comparable to the terms "race" or "sex" employed by Title VII. "Race" and "sex" are general terms that in every day usage require modifiers to indicate any relatively narrow application. We do not commonly understand "race" to refer only to the black race, or "sex" to refer only to the female. But the prohibition of age discrimination is readily read more narrowly than analogous provisions dealing with race and sex. That narrower reading is the more natural one in the textual setting, and it makes perfect sense because of Congress's demonstrated concern with distinctions that hurt older people....

[The Court explained away Senator Yarborough's comment on the floor of the Senate that appeared to contradict the Court's interpretation of the meaning of "age." Finally, the Court explained why deference to EEOC's position, which was in line with Senator Yarborough's comment, was not warranted.]

## IV

We see the text, structure, purpose, and history of the ADEA, along with its relationship to other federal statutes, as showing that the statute does not mean to stop an employer from favoring an older employee over a younger one. The judgment of the Court of Appeals is reversed.

[The dissenting opinion of Justice Scalia is omitted.]

Justice Thomas, with whom Justice Kennedy joins, dissenting.

This should have been an easy case. The plain language of 29 U.S.C. §623(a)(1) mandates a particular outcome: that the respondents are able to sue for discrimination against them in favor of older workers. The agency charged with enforcing the statute has adopted a regulation and issued an opinion as an adjudicator, both of which adopt this natural interpretation of the provision. And the only portion of legislative history relevant to the question before us is consistent with this outcome. Despite the fact that these traditional tools of statutory interpretation lead inexorably to the conclusion that respondents can state a claim for discrimination against the relatively young, the Court, apparently disappointed by this result, today adopts a different interpretation. In doing so, the Court, of necessity, creates a new tool of statutory interpretation, and then proceeds to give this newly created "social history" analysis dispositive weight. Because I cannot agree with the Court's new approach to interpreting anti-discrimination statutes, I respectfully dissent.

I

...

The plain language of the ADEA clearly allows for suits brought by the relatively young when discriminated against in favor of the relatively old. The phrase "discriminate ... because of such individual's age," 29 U.S.C. § 623(a)(1), is not restricted to discrimination because of relatively *older* age. If an employer fired a worker for the sole reason that the worker was under 45, it would be entirely natural to say that the worker had been discriminated against because of his age. I struggle to think of what other phrase I would use to describe such behavior. I wonder how the Court would describe such incidents, because the Court apparently considers such usage to be unusual, atypical, or aberrant.

The parties do identify a possible ambiguity, centering on the multiple meanings of the word "age." As the parties note, "age," does have an alternative meaning, namely "[t]he state of being old; old age." American Heritage Dictionary 33 (3d ed. 1992); *see also* Oxford American Dictionary 18 (1999); Webster's Third New International Dictionary 40 (1993). First, this secondary meaning is, of course, less commonly used than the primary meaning, and appears restricted to those few instances where it is clear in the immediate context of the phrase that it could have no other meaning. The phrases "hair white with age," American Heritage Dictionary, or *"eyes ... dim with age,"* Random House Dictionary of the English Language 37 (2d ed. 1987), cannot possibly be using "age" to include "young age," unlike a phrase such as "he fired her because of her age." Second, the use of the word "age" in other portions of the statute effectively destroys any doubt. The ADEA's advertising prohibition, 29 U.S.C. § 623(e), and the bona fide occupational qualification defense, § 623(f)(1), would both be rendered incoherent if the term "age" in those provisions were read to mean only "older age." Although it is true that the "presumption that identical words used in different parts of the same act are intended to have the same meaning" is not "rigid" and can be overcome when the context is clear, the presumption is not rebutted here. As noted, the plain and common reading of the phrase "such individual's age" refers to the individual's chronological age. At the very least, it is manifestly unclear that it bars *only* discrimination against the relatively older. Only by incorrectly concluding that § 623(a)(1) clearly and unequivocally bars only discrimination as "against the older," can the Court then conclude that the "context" of §§ 623(f)(1) and 623(e) allows for an alternative meaning of the term "age."

The one structural argument raised by the Court in defense of its interpretation of "discriminates ... because of such individual's age" is the provision limiting the ADEA's protections to those over 40 years of age. *See* 29 U.S.C. § 631(a). At first glance, this might look odd when paired with the conclusion that § 623(a)(1) bars discrimination against the relatively young as well as the relatively old, but there is a perfectly rational explanation.

Congress could easily conclude that age discrimination directed against those under 40 is not as damaging, since a young worker unjustly fired is likely to find a new job or otherwise recover from the discrimination. A person over 40 fired due to irrational age discrimination (whether because the worker is too young or too old) might have a more difficult time recovering from the discharge and finding new employment. Such an interpretation also comports with the many findings of the Wirtz report, ... and the parallel findings in the ADEA itself. *See, e.g.*, 29 U.S.C. §621(a)(1) (finding that "older workers find themselves disadvantaged in their efforts to retain employment, and especially to regain employment when displaced from jobs"); §621(a)(3) (finding that "the incidence of unemployment, especially long-term unemployment with resultant deterioration of skill, morale, and employer acceptability is, relative to the younger ages, high among older workers").

[The dissent explained how the plain meaning of the ADEA is bolstered by the EEOC's interpretation of the Act.]

...

Finally, the only relevant piece of legislative history addressing the question before the Court—whether it would be possible for a younger individual to sue based on discrimination against him in favor of an older individual—comports with the plain reading of the text. Senator Yarborough, in the only exchange that the parties identified from the legislative history discussing this particular question, confirmed that the text really meant what it said. *See* 113 Cong. Rec. 31255 (1967). Although the statute is clear, and hence there is no need to delve into the legislative history, this history merely confirms that the plain reading of the text is correct.

## II

Strangely, the Court does not explain why it departs from accepted methods of interpreting statutes. It does, however, clearly set forth its principal reason for adopting its particular reading of the phrase "discriminate ... based on [an] individual's age" in Part III-A of its opinion. "The point here," the Court states, "is that we are not asking in the abstract how the ADEA uses the word 'age,' but seeking the meaning of the whole phrase 'discriminate ... because of [an] individual's age.' As we have said, *social history* emphatically points to the sense of age discrimination as aimed against the old, and the statutory reference to age discrimination in this idiomatic sense is confirmed by legislative history." The Court does not define "social history," although it is apparently something different from legislative history, because the Court refers to legislative history as a separate interpretive tool in the very same sentence. Indeed, the Court has never defined "social history" in any previous opinion, probably because it has never sanctioned looking to "social history" as a method of statutory interpretation. Today, the Court takes this unprecedented step, and then places dispositive weight on the new concept.

It appears that the Court considers the "social history" of the phrase "discriminate ... because of [an] individual's age" to be the principal evil that Congress targeted when it passed the ADEA. In each section of its analysis, the Court pointedly notes that there was no evidence of widespread problems of antiyouth discrimination, and that the primary concerns of Executive Branch officials and Members of Congress pertained to problems that workers generally faced as they increased in age. The Court reaches its final, legal conclusion as to the meaning of the phrase (that "ordinary people employing the common usage of language" would "talk about discrimination because of age [as] naturally [referring to] discrimination against the older") only after concluding both that "the ADEA was concerned to protect a relatively old worker from discrimination that works to the advantage of the relatively young" and that "the record is devoid of any evidence that younger workers were suffering at the expense of their elders, let alone that a social problem required a federal statute to place a younger worker in parity with an older one." Hence, the Court apparently concludes that if Congress has in mind a particular, principal, or primary form of discrimination when it passes an antidiscrimination provision prohibiting persons from "discriminating because of [some personal quality]," then the phrase "discriminate because of [some personal quality]" only covers the principal or most common form of discrimination relating to this personal quality.

The Court, however, has not typically interpreted nondiscrimination statutes in this odd manner. "[S]tatutory prohibitions often go beyond the principal evil to cover reasonably comparable evils, and it is ultimately the provisions of our laws rather than the principal concerns of our legislators by which we are governed." *Oncale v. Sundowner Offshore Services, Inc.*, 523 U.S. 75, 79 (1998). The oddity of the Court's new technique of statutory interpretation is highlighted by this Court's contrary approach to the racial-discrimination prohibition of Title VII.

[The dissent delves into the legislative history of Title VII and concludes that there is no record evidence to suggest that Congress enacted the Title VII provision prohibiting discrimination "because of race" to prevent discrimination against white persons.]

It is abundantly clear, then, that the Court's new approach to antidiscrimination statutes would lead us far astray from well-settled principles of statutory interpretation. The Court's examination of "social history" is in serious tension (if not outright conflict) with our prior cases in such matters. Under the Court's current approach, for instance, *McDonald* and *Oncale* are wrongly decided. One can only hope that this new technique of statutory interpretation does not catch on, and that its errors are limited to only this case.

As the ADEA clearly prohibits discrimination because of an individual's age, whether the individual is too old or too young, I would affirm the Court of Appeals. Because the Court resorts to interpretive sleight of hand to avoid addressing the plain language of the ADEA, I respectfully dissent.

## Lesbian, Gay, Bisexual and Transgender (LGBT) Individuals

The federal antidiscrimination laws do not include any express protection for LGBT individuals, although some have argued that Title VII's prohibition against sex discrimination should apply to protect against certain instances of LGBT discrimination. Bills to create a federal protection against some forms of LGBT discrimination have been introduced in every Congress since 1975. There are already many state and local protections against such discrimination. Though courts do not recognize a Title VII claim for discrimination based on sexual orientation, they have held that sex-motivated harassment directed towards someone of the same sex constitutes sex-based discrimination under Title VII. *See Oncale v. Sundowner Offshore Services, Inc.* 523 U.S. 75 (1998).

LGBT individuals include lesbians (females who are attracted to females), gay men (males who are attracted to males), bisexuals (individuals who are attracted to both males and females), and transgender individuals. The term, "transgender," is often used as an umbrella term for people who experience or display their gender in ways not socially typical. The term transgender may be used to encompass anyone from occasional cross-dressers to transsexuals who live and identify as a gender different from their birth sex. Some laws designed to protect transgender individuals protect against "gender identity or expression" discrimination. Gender identity is defined as the gender an individual claims for herself, regardless of sex at birth; gender expression connotes the way a person behaves, appears or presents herself, regardless of her birth sex. *DeJohn v. Temple University*, 537 F.3d 301, 319 n.20 (3d Cir. 2008).

The Supreme Court has declined to extend heightened scrutiny to homosexuals under the Equal Protection Clause of the Fourteenth Amendment of the federal Constitution. In a dissent, however, Justice Brennan disagreed, arguing that

> homosexuals constitute a significant and insular minority of this country's population. Because of immediate and severe opprobrium often manifested against homosexuals once so identified publicly, members of this group are particularly powerless to pursue their rights openly in the political arena. Moreover, homosexuals have historically been the object of pernicious and sustained hostility, and it is fair to say that discrimination against homosexuals is "likely ... to reflect deep-seated prejudice rather than ... rationality." ... State action taken against members of such groups based simply on status as members of the group traditionally has been subjected to strict, or at least heightened, scrutiny.

*Rowland v. Mad River School Dist.*, 470 U.S. 1009 (1985) (Brennan, J., dissenting from denial of certiorari). Some lower courts have found that discrimination against LGBT individuals violates rational basis review.

In the 2013 case of *United States v. Windsor*, the Supreme Court declined an opportunity to determine what level of scrutiny applies to distinctions based on sexual orientation. *See* 133 S. Ct. 2675. In *Windsor*, the Court struck down section 3 of the federal Defense of Marriage Act (DOMA), which had prohibited the federal government from recognizing same-sex marriages performed in the states. By a vote of five to four, the Court held section 3 unconstitutional, finding no legitimate purpose to overcome the illegitimate purpose of disparaging those whom the state marriage laws sought to protect. Rather than reach the level of scrutiny issue, the Court based its decision on the liberty interests protected by the Fifth Amendment of the Constitution.

---

### Focus Questions: *Weaver v. Nebo School District*

1. *As a matter of social policy, should schools be able to discriminate based on sexual orientation? Why or why not?*

2. *In thinking about question 1, think about how courts have often drawn a line between immutable characteristics and choices. Does it make a difference whether sexual orientation is perceived to be immutable or a choice?*

---

## Weaver v. Nebo School District

### 29 F. Supp. 2d 1279 (D. Utah 1998)

Senior District Judge Jenkins.

For the past nineteen years, plaintiff Wendy Weaver has been a teacher at Spanish Fork High School in the Nebo School District. Ms. Weaver, a tenured faculty member since 1982, teaches psychology and physical education. Her reputation as an educator at Spanish Fork is unblemished: she has always been considered an effective and capable teacher, her evaluations range from good to excellent, and she has never been the subject of any disciplinary action.

In addition to her teaching responsibilities, Ms. Weaver has served as the girl's volleyball coach since 1979. She has been effective in this endeavor, leading the team to four state championships.

Unlike her teaching position, however, Ms. Weaver's position as coach was not tenured. Instead, as is the case with all coaching positions at Spanish Fork High School, Ms. Weaver was hired as volleyball coach on a year-to-year basis.... During the 1995 and 1996 school years, Ms. Weaver did not coach the volleyball team. With the consent of Principal Wadley, she took a break from her coaching duties to pursue a master's degree at the University of Utah. She did, however, anticipate a return to coaching in 1997, an anticipation she shared with Principal Wadley. In the spring of 1997, after completing her graduate work, Ms. Weaver again met with Principal Wadley and told him that she was prepared to return to coaching.

In the late spring and early summer of 1997, Ms. Weaver began preparing for the upcoming school volleyball season—as she did in the past—by organizing two summer volleyball camps for prospective team players.... Ms. Weaver telephoned prospective volleyball team members to inform them of the camp schedules. One of the calls went to a senior team member. During the conversation, the team member asked Ms. Weaver. "Are you gay"?[8] Ms. Weaver truthfully responded, "Yes." The team member then told Ms. Weaver that she would not play on the volleyball team in the fall. On July 14, 1997, the team member and her parents met with defendants Almon Mosher, Director of Human Resources for the Nebo School District, and Larry Kimball, Director of Secondary Education for the Nebo School District, and told them that Ms. Weaver told them that she is gay and that the team member decided she would not play volleyball.... In May of 1997, [the school administration had numerous discussions of Ms. Weaver's sexual orientation and received a call from the team member and her mother to tell them the student would not be playing volleyball because she was uncomfortable with Ms. Weaver's sexual orientation.]

In response to these reports, and after meeting again with the team member's family on July 14, 1997, defendants Mosher and Kimball discussed taking some action against Ms. Weaver because they felt Ms. Weaver's comments about her sexual orientation were in "violation of district policy." Several days later, on July 21, 1997, Ms. Weaver met with Principal Wadley, who informed her that she would not be assigned to coach volleyball for the 1997–98 school year.

The following day, Ms. Weaver was called to a meeting at the School District office and presented a letter, printed on the School District letterhead, which reads in part:

> The District has received reports that you have made public and expressed to students your homosexual orientation and lifestyle. If these reports are true, we are concerned about the potential disruption in the school community and advise you of the following:
>
> —You are not to make any comments, announcements or statements to students, staff members, or parents of students regarding your homosexual orientation or lifestyle.

---

8. The word "gay" is used in the vernacular of this age. A similar inquiry put in the Nineteenth Century would reflect an entirely different status or characteristic. In those days synonyms were, among others, lighthearted, blithe, airy, sprightly, vivacious, frolicsome, jolly, jovial, joyful, and glad.

—If students, staff members, or parents of students ask about your sexual orientation or anything concerning the subject, you shall tell them that the subject is private and personal and inappropriate to discuss with them.

This memo is to place you on notice of the expectations the school district has for you concerning this matter. A violation of these requirements may jeopardize your job and be cause for termination.

... On October 20, 1997, Ms. Weaver commenced an action in this court under 42 U.S.C. § 1983 challenging the restraints on her speech contained in the July 22 letter as well as her removal as volleyball coach. Nine days after the action was filed, the School District delivered another letter to Ms. Weaver, to "clarify" the July 22 letter. In part, the October 29, 1997 letter reads:

The District's intent with the July 22 letter was that the foregoing restrictions [contained in the July 22 letter] on your communications apply only while you are acting within the course and scope of your duties as a teacher for the District. Our main areas of concern are situations such as classroom teaching, extracurricular school-sponsored activities and parent-teacher conferences where, we believe, discussion of one's sexual orientation would be inappropriate. We believed that this intent was apparent in the July 22 letter from the fact that it was written on District stationary and addressed the issue of "disruption in the school community."

As further clarification of the July 22 letter, we strongly encourage you to avoid discussions of the foregoing matters at any time with students because we believe that in virtually any interaction you have with a student, including off-campus contacts, you are always perceived by the student as a teacher, authority figure and role model.

The letter, printed on the School District's letterhead, was signed by defendants Mosher and Kimball, and like the July 22 letter, placed in Ms. Weaver's personnel file.

*Discussion*

Ms. Weaver makes the following claims:

1.  The letters dated July 22 and October 29 directed to her, and particularly the restrictions on speech contained therein, are vague and overbroad and restrain constitutionally protected speech.

2.  Her removal as volleyball coach was based on an impermissible reason—namely sexual orientation—and thus violates the Fourteenth Amendment of the United States Constitution.

Ms. Weaver has moved for summary judgment on these claims. The defendants have cross-moved for summary judgment. [B]ecause there is no genuine issue of material fact, the court is in a position to apply the law to the facts as presented in the motions. *See* Fed. R. Civ. P. 56(c).

[The court discussed plaintiff's First Amendment claim and determined the letters violated plaintiff's rights.]

## II

Despite mounting evidence that gay males and lesbians suffer from employment discrimination and, as recent events in Wyoming remind us, other more life-threatening expressions of bias,[9] courts, including the Supreme Court, have not yet recognized a person's sexual orientation as a status that deserves heightened protection. To date, Congress has expressly prohibited employment discrimination on the basis of race, religion, national origin, gender, age, and disability, but not sexual orientation. As of this year, eleven states and the District of Columbia offer statutory protection against discrimination on the basis of sexual orientation; thirty-nine states, including Utah, do not.

Nevertheless, the Fourteenth Amendment of the United States Constitution entitles all persons to equal protection under the law. It appears that the plain language of the Fourteenth Amendment's Equal Protection Clause prohibits a state government or agency from engaging in intentional discrimination — even on the basis of sexual orientation — absent some rational basis for so doing.

The Supreme Court has recognized that an "irrational prejudice" cannot provide the rational basis to support a state action against an equal protection challenge. In *City of Cleburne, Texas v. Cleburne Living Center, Inc.*, 473 U.S. 432 (1985), the Court reviewed whether a local ordinance that required a special use permit for homes for the mentally retarded, but not for nursing homes, apartment houses, dormitories, hospitals, and similar multiple occupant dwellings, violated the Equal Protection Clause. Even under rational basis review, the Court had no trouble concluding that the ordinance did indeed violate the Equal Protection Clause. The Court began its rational basis review by stating that "a bare ... desire to harm a politically unpopular group" is not a legitimate state interest. [T]he Court concluded that the permit requirement rested on an "irrational prejudice against the mentally retarded" and therefore violated the Fourteenth Amendment.

Other Supreme Court precedents have similarly recognized that when state action reflects an animus directed at a defined minority, it cannot be supported under the Equal Protection Clause....

More recently, in *Romer v. Evans*, 517 U.S. 620 (1996), the Court was called upon to examine whether an amendment to Colorado's state constitution, prohibiting any legislation or judicial action designed to protect the status of a person based on sexual orientation violated the Fourteenth Amendment. It had no trouble finding that it did. In *Romer*, the Court noted that under the ordinary deferential equal protection standard — that is, rational basis — the Court would "insist on knowing the relation between the classification adopted and the object to be obtained." It is this search for a "link" between classification and objective, noted the Court, that "gives substance to the Equal Protection Clause." In *Romer*, such a "link" was noticeably absent. Noting that the "inevitable inference" that arises from a law of this sort is that it is "born of animosity toward the class of persons affected," the Court described the amendment as "a status-based enactment divorced from any factual context from which we could discern a relationship to legitimate state interests."

Several courts of appeal have recently considered the question of equal protection and sexual orientation and applied the same rational basis test the Supreme Court announced in *Romer*. These cases, which dealt with the constitutionality of the military's current "Don't Ask, Don't Tell" policy, examined whether the forced separation from service of a person who engages in a homosexual act or who states that he or she is a homosexual violates the Equal Protection Clause. In holding that the policy did not violate the Equal

---

9. The deep-seated prejudice on the part of some persons against the gay and lesbian community can be summed up in a single quote from ardent anti-gay activist and former entertainer Anita Bryant: "I'd rather my child be dead than be a homosexual." [citation omitted].

Protection Clause, these courts relied on the uniqueness of the military setting and the deference accorded military decisions. Nevertheless, like the Supreme Court in City of Cleburne and Romer, these courts also recognized that government action in a civil rather than a military setting cannot survive a rational basis review when it is motivated by irrational fear and prejudice towards homosexuals.

When faced with equal protection challenges on the basis of sexual orientation in other contexts, the lower courts have also reviewed the challenged state action under a rational basis standard. [citations omitted].

The question then is whether bias concerning Ms. Weaver's sexual orientation furnishes a rational basis for the defendants' decision not to assign her as volleyball coach. The "negative reaction" some members of the community may have to homosexuals is not a proper basis for discriminating against them. So reasoned the Supreme Court in the context of race. See, e.g., Brown v. Board of Educ., 347 U.S. 483, 495 (1954) (declaring that racial school segregation is unconstitutional despite the widespread acceptance of the practice in the community and in the country). If the community's perception is based on nothing more than unsupported assumptions, outdated stereotypes, and animosity, it is necessarily irrational and under Romer and other Supreme Court precedent, it provides no legitimate support for the School District's decisions.

The record now before the court contains no job-related justification for not assigning Ms. Weaver as volleyball coach. Nor have the defendants demonstrated how Ms. Weaver's sexual orientation bears any rational relationship to her competency as teacher or coach, or her job performance as coach—a position she has held for many years with distinction. As mentioned earlier, it is undisputed that she was an excellent coach and apparently, up until the time her sexual orientation was revealed, the likely candidate for the position. Principal Wadley's decision not to assign Ms. Weaver (a decision reached after consulting with the other defendants) was based solely on her sexual orientation. Absent some rational relationship to job performance, a decision not to assign Ms. Weaver as coach because of her sexual orientation runs afoul of the Fourteenth Amendment's equal protection guarantee.

Although the Constitution cannot control prejudices, neither this court nor any other court should, directly or indirectly, legitimize them.... Indeed, as the Supreme Court has recently admonished, "[i]f the constitutional conception of 'equal protection of the laws' means anything, it must at the very least mean that a bare ... desire to harm a politically unpopular group cannot constitute a legitimate governmental interest." Romer, 517 U.S. at 634. Nor can public officials avoid their constitutional duty by "bowing to the hypothetical effects of private ... prejudice that they assume to be both widely and deeply held." [citation omitted]. Simply put, the private antipathy of some members of a community cannot validate state discrimination. Because a community's animus towards homosexuals can never serve as a legitimate basis for state action, the defendants' actions based on that animus violate the Equal Protection Clause.

It is ordered that plaintiff's Motion for Summary Judgment is granted and defendants' motion is denied.

---

## Further Discussion

Although LGBT claims have not generally succeeded under the Constitution, they have sometimes met with success under Title VII, even though Title VII does not explicitly provide protection. Some LGBT individuals have successfully pursued Title VII sex discrimination claims based upon *Price Waterhouse v. Hopkins*, 490 U.S. 228 (1989), holding that sex stereotyping is a form of sex discrimination. *See Smith v. City of Salem*, 378 F.3d 566, 575 (6th Cir. 2004); *Lopez v. River Oaks Imaging & Diagnostic Group, Inc.*, 542 F. Supp. 2d 653 (S.D. Tex. 2008) (discussing court's disagreement about recognizing a transgender individual's Title VII claim based on gender stereotyping).

The case of *Oncale v. Sundowner Offshore Services*, 523 U.S. 75 (1998), excerpted in Chapter 5, set forth guidelines for courts deciding whether occurrences of same-sex harassment qualify as sex discrimination for purposes of Title VII. *Bibby v. Coca Cola*, excerpted below, is a lower court decision applying the *Oncale* ruling.

---

### Focus Questions: *Bibby v. Coca Cola Bottling Co.*

1. *Can you formulate an argument that the treatment of Bibby actually was because of his sex?*

2. *Would the harassment in this case have met the severe or pervasive requirement of* Harris v. Forklift, *discussed in Chapter 5?*

---

# Bibby v. Coca Cola Bottling Co.

260 F.3d 257 (3d Cir. 2001)

Circuit Judge Barry.

John J. Bibby claimed to have been subjected to same-sex sexual harassment at the hands of his employer, the Philadelphia Coca-Cola Bottling Company, in violation of Title VII. The District Court granted summary judgment to the employer, and Bibby appealed. Because we conclude that Bibby did not present sufficient evidence to demonstrate that he suffered discrimination "because of sex," we will affirm the judgment of the District Court.

### BACKGROUND

John Bibby has been an employee of the Philadelphia Coca-Cola Bottling Company since June 1978....

On December 23, 1993 ... Bibby was assaulted in a locker room by a co-worker, Frank Berthcsi. Berthcsi told Bibby to get out of the locker room, shook his fist in Bibby's face, grabbed Bibby by the shirt collar, and threw him up against the lockers. On January 22, 1995, Berthcsi again came after Bibby. On that day, Bibby was at the top of a set of steps working at a machine that puts cases of soda on wooden or plastic pallets. Berthcsi was driving a forklift loaded with pallets, and he "slammed" the load of pallets under the stairs, blocking Bibby's exit from the platform on which he was standing. Bibby paged a supervisor, and Berthcsi was ordered to remove the pallets. He refused. Berthcsi and Bibby then exchanged some angry words, and Berthcsi repeatedly yelled at Bibby that "everybody knows you're gay as a three dollar bill," "everybody knows you're a faggot," and "everybody knows you take it up the ass." Later that day, Berthcsi called Bibby a "sissy." Bibby filed a complaint with the union and with the employer, and Berthcsi was suspended pending an investigation. Bibby refused the union's request that he withdraw the complaint, and Berthcsi's employment was terminated. The union filed a grievance on behalf of Berthcsi, and he was reinstated subject to the employer's condition that he undergo anger management training.

Bibby claims that supervisors also harassed him by yelling at him, ignoring his reports of problems with machinery, and arbitrarily enforcing rules against him in situations where infractions by other employees would be ignored. He does not assert that there was any sexual component to any of this alleged harassment. Finally, Bibby claims that graffiti of a sexual nature, some bearing his name, was written in the bathrooms and allowed to remain on the walls for much longer than some other graffiti. The record does not disclose the contents of any graffiti that allegedly mentioned Bibby's name.

Shortly after the January 1995 incident with Berthcsi, Bibby filed a complaint with the Philadelphia Human Rights Commission (PHRC) alleging that he was being discriminated against on the basis of his sexual orientation. In late 1997, after completing an investigation, the PHRC notified Bibby that it was closing the case and issuing him a 90-day right to sue letter.

On January 20, 1998, Bibby filed a pro se complaint in the Eastern District of Pennsylvania. He subsequently retained counsel, however, and an amended complaint was filed on June 30, 1998. The amended complaint named as defendants the employer and nine individual officers or employees of the employer. In the amended complaint, Bibby alleged that he had been sexually harassed in violation of Title VII, and sought compensatory and punitive damages. The complaint also included two supplemental state law claims, one for intentional infliction of emotional distress and one for assault and battery.

On November 20, 1998, the District Court granted in part defendants' motion to dismiss, dismissing all individual defendants and dismissing Bibby's assault and battery claim. Following a period of discovery, the employer filed a motion for summary judgment on the remaining counts. On March 2, 2000, the District Court granted this motion. In its twenty-page memorandum and order, the Court determined that the evidence indicated that Bibby was harassed because of his sexual orientation and not because of his sex. Because Title VII provides no protection from discrimination on the basis of sexual orientation, summary judgment was granted on Bibby's Title VII claim. Having dismissed the only federal claim, the Court chose not to exercise supplemental jurisdiction over the remaining state law claim and dismissed that claim without prejudice.

It is from the grant of summary judgment to the employer that Bibby appeals....

This appeal presents a single issue: did Bibby present evidence sufficient to support a claim of same-sex sexual harassment under Title VII? The District Court found that Bibby was harassed because of his sexual orientation, not because of his sex, and therefore rejected his sexual harassment claim. Bibby argues that the District Court erred and further argues that its finding, if upheld, would place a special burden on gay and lesbian plaintiffs alleging same-sex sexual harassment because they will be required to prove that harassment was not motivated by their sexual orientation. We disagree on both scores.

1

Title VII provides that "[i]t shall be an unlawful employment practice ... to discriminate against any individual ... because of ... sex." [Most citations deleted throughout]. It is clear, however, that Title VII does not prohibit discrimination based on sexual orientation. Congress has repeatedly rejected legislation that would have extended Title VII to cover sexual orientation. Thus, Bibby can seek relief under Title VII only for discrimination because of sex.

Until 1998, it was unclear whether and under what circumstances Title VII would apply in a case of sexual harassment where both the harasser and the victim were of the same sex.... In *Oncale v. Sundowner Offshore Services, Inc.*, the Supreme Court unanimously held that Title VII does provide a cause of action for same-sex sexual harassment. In *Oncale*, the Court reviewed a Fifth Circuit decision which held that, as a matter of law, Title VII categorically barred any claim for same-sex sexual harassment. The Court reversed. Title VII, it observed, protects men as well as women and just as there can be no absolute presumption that a person of one race would not discriminate against another person of the same race, there can be no absolute presumption that a person of one gender would not discriminate against another person of the same gender. The Court reasoned that it is not the sex of the harasser or the victim that is important to a sexual harassment claim, but, rather, what is important is that the victim "prove that the conduct at issue was not merely tinged with offensive sexual connotations, but actually constituted 'discriminat[ion] ... because of ... sex.' "

The question of how to prove that same-sex harassment is because of sex is not an easy one to answer. As the Supreme Court noted in *Oncale*, when the harasser and victim are of the opposite sex, there is a reasonable inference that the harasser is acting because of the victim's sex. Thus, when a heterosexual man makes implicit or explicit proposals of sexual activity to a woman co-worker or subordinate, it is easy to conclude or at least infer that the behavior is motivated by her sex. Similarly, if a man is aggressively rude to a woman, disparaging her or sabotaging her work, it is possible to infer that he is acting out of a general hostility to the presence of women in the workplace. These inferences are not always so clear when the harasser and victim are of the same sex.

There are several situations in which same-sex harassment can be seen as discrimination because of sex. The first is where there is evidence that the harasser sexually desires the victim. Thus, when a gay or lesbian supervisor treats a same-sex subordinate in a way that is sexually charged, it is reasonable to infer that the harasser acts as he or she does because of the victim's sex.

Same-sex harassment might also be found where there is no sexual attraction but where the harasser displays hostility to the presence of a particular sex in the workplace. For example, a woman chief executive officer of an airline might believe that women should not be pilots and might treat women pilots with hostility amounting to harassment. Similarly, a male doctor might believe that men should not be employed as nurses, leading him to make harassing statements to a male nurse with whom he works. In each of these hypothetical situations, it would be easy to conclude that the harassment was caused by a general hostility to the presence of one sex in the workplace or in a particular work function, and, therefore, amounted to discrimination because of sex.

Further, although it is less clear, a plaintiff may be able to prove that same-sex harassment was discrimination because of sex by presenting evidence that the harasser's conduct was motivated by a belief that the victim did not conform to the stereotypes of his or her gender.

The gender stereotypes method for proving same-sex sexual harassment is based on *Price Waterhouse v. Hopkins*.... A plurality of the Court agreed that "[i]n the specific context of sex stereotyping, an employer who acts on the basis of a belief that a woman cannot be aggressive, or that she must not be, has acted on the basis of gender." The Court noted that "we are beyond the day when an employer could evaluate employees by assuming or insisting that they matched the stereotype associated with their group, for '[i]n forbidding employers to discriminate against individuals because of their sex, Congress intended to strike at the entire spectrum of disparate treatment of men and women resulting from sex stereotypes.'" Neither of the two concurring opinions in *Price Waterhouse* disagreed.

Relying on *Price Waterhouse*, and as we noted above, the Seventh Circuit held that where evidence indicated that the harassment of a sixteen-year old young man was motivated by his co-workers' belief that because he wore an earring he was not sufficiently masculine, there was sufficient evidence to support a finding that the harassment amounted to discrimination because of sex.

Thus, there are at least three ways by which a plaintiff alleging same-sex sexual harassment might demonstrate that the harassment amounted to discrimination because of sex—the harasser was motivated by sexual desire, the harasser was expressing a general hostility to the presence of one sex in the workplace, or the harasser was acting to punish the victim's noncompliance with gender stereotypes. Based on the facts of a particular case and the creativity of the parties, other ways in which to prove that harassment occurred because of sex may be available.

That having been said, however, it is clear that "[w]hatever evidentiary route the plaintiff chooses to follow, he or she must always prove that the conduct at issue was not merely tinged with offensive sexual connotations, but actually constituted '*discrimina[tion]* ... because of ... sex.'" Bibby simply failed in this respect; indeed, he did not even argue that he was being harassed because he was a man and offered nothing that would support such a conclusion. There was no allegation that his alleged harassers were motivated by sexual desire, or that they possessed any hostility to the presence of men in the workplace or in Bibby's particular job. Moreover, he did not claim that he was harassed because he failed to comply with societal stereotypes of how men ought to appear or behave or that as a man he was treated differently than female co-workers. His claim was, pure and simple, that he was discriminated against because of his sexual orientation. No reasonable finder of fact could reach the conclusion that he was discriminated against because he was a man.

As noted earlier, Bibby argues that in reaching this conclusion, we will be placing an extra burden on gay and lesbian plaintiffs bringing an action for same-sex sexual harassment by requiring that such plaintiffs prove that their harassers were not motivated by anti-gay animus. Bibby is wrong. Whatever the sexual orientation of a plaintiff bringing a same-sex sexual harassment claim, that plaintiff is required to demonstrate that the harassment was directed at him or her because of his or her sex. Once such a showing has been made, the sexual orientation of the plaintiff is irrelevant. In addition, once it has been shown that the harassment was motivated by the victim's sex, it is no defense that the harassment may have also been partially motivated by anti-gay or anti-lesbian animus. For example, had the plaintiff in *Price Waterhouse* been a lesbian, that fact would have provided the employer with no excuse for its decision to discriminate against her because she failed to conform to traditional feminine stereotypes.

Harassment on the basis of sexual orientation has no place in our society.... Congress has not yet seen fit, however, to provide protection against such harassment. Because the evidence produced by Bibby—and, indeed, his very claim—indicated only that he was being harassed on the basis of his sexual orientation, rather than because of his sex, the District Court properly determined that there was no cause of action under Title VII.

---

### Focus Question: *Etsitty v. Utah Transit Authority*

*Is the reason offered by the defendant a legitimate, non-discriminatory reason?*

---

# Etsitty v. Utah Transit Authority

502 F.3d 1215 (10th Cir. 2007)

Circuit Judge Murphy.

## I. Introduction

Krystal Etsitty, a transsexual and former employee of Utah Transit Authority ("UTA"), sued UTA and Betty Shirley, her former supervisor, pursuant to Title VII and 42 U.S.C. § 1983. In her complaint, she alleged the defendants terminated her because she was a transsexual and because she failed to conform to their expectations of stereotypical male behavior. She alleged that terminating her on this basis constituted gender discrimination in violation of both Title VII and the Equal Protection Clause of the Fourteenth Amendment. The defendants filed a motion for summary judgment and the district court granted the motion. In doing so, it determined transsexuals are not a protected class for purposes of Title VII and the prohibition against sex stereotyping recognized by some courts should not be applied to transsexuals. It also concluded that even if a transsexual could state a Title VII claim under a sex stereotyping theory, there was no evidence in this case that Etsitty was terminated for failing to conform to a particular gender stereotype. Etsitty appeals the district court's order granting summary judgment to the defendants. Exercising jurisdiction pursuant to 28 U.S.C. § 1291, this court affirms the district court's grant of summary judgment.

## II. Background

Etsitty is a transsexual who has been diagnosed with Adult Gender Identity Disorder. Although Etsitty was born as a biological male and given the name "Michael," she identifies herself as a woman and has always believed she was born with the wrong anatomical sex organs. Even before she was diagnosed with a gender identity disorder, Etsitty lived and dressed as a woman outside of work and used the female name of "Krystal." Eventually, Etsitty began to see an endocrinologist who prescribed her female hormones to prepare for a sex reassignment surgery in the future. Etsitty made the decision at that time to live full time as a woman. While she has begun the transition from male to female by taking female hormones, she has not yet completed the sex reassignment surgery. Thus, Etsitty describes herself as a "pre-operative transgendered individual."

Nearly four years after Etsitty had begun taking female hormones, she applied for a position as a bus operator with UTA. She was hired and, after successfully completing a six-week training course, was assigned to a position as an extra-board operator. As an operator on the extra board, Etsitty was not assigned to a permanent route or shift. Instead, she would fill in for regular operators who were on vacation or called in sick. As a result, Etsitty drove many of UTA's 115 to 130 routes in the Salt Lake City area over approximately ten weeks as an extra-board operator. While on their routes, UTA employees use public restrooms.

Throughout her training period at UTA, Etsitty presented herself as a man and used male restrooms. Soon after being hired, however, she met with her supervisor, Pat Chatterton, and informed him that she was a transsexual. She explained that she would begin to appear more as a female at work and that she would eventually change her sex. Chatterton expressed support for Etsitty and stated he did not see any problem with her being a transsexual. After this meeting, Etsitty began wearing makeup, jewelry, and acrylic nails to work. She also began using female restrooms while on her route. Shirley, the operations manager of the UTA division where Etsitty worked, heard a rumor that there was a male operator who was wearing makeup. She spoke with Chatterton and he informed her Etsitty was a transsexual and would be going through a sex change. When Chatterton told her this, Shirley expressed concern about whether Etsitty would be using a male or female restroom. Shirley told Chatterton she would speak with Human Resources about whether Etsitty's restroom usage would raise any concerns for UTA.

Shirley then called Bruce Cardon, the human resources generalist for Shirley's division, and they decided to set up a meeting with Etsitty. At the meeting, Shirley and Cardon asked Etsitty where she was in the sex change process and whether she still had male genitalia. Etsitty explained she still had male genitalia because she did not have the money to complete the sex change operation. Shirley expressed concern about the possibility of liability for UTA if a UTA employee with male genitalia was observed using the female restroom. Shirley and Cardon also expressed concern that Etsitty would switch back and forth between using male and female restrooms.

Following their meeting with Etsitty, Shirley and Cardon placed Etsitty on administrative leave and ultimately terminated her employment. Shirley explained the reason Etsitty was terminated was the possibility of liability for UTA arising from Etsitty's restroom usage. Cardon similarly explained to Etsitty that the reason for her termination was UTA's inability to accommodate her restroom needs. Shirley felt it was not possible to accommodate Etsitty's restroom usage because she typically used public restrooms along her routes rather than restrooms at the UTA facility. Shirley also testified she did not believe it was appropriate to inquire into whether people along UTA routes would be offended if a transsexual with male genitalia were to use the female restrooms. On the record of termination, Shirley indicated Etsitty would be eligible for rehire after completing sex re-assignment surgery. At the time of the termination, UTA had received no complaints about Etsitty's performance, appearance, or restroom usage.

Etsitty filed suit against UTA and Shirley, alleging they had engaged in unlawful gender discrimination, in violation of Title VII and the Equal Protection Clause of the Fourteenth Amendment. She claimed she was terminated because she was a transsexual and because she failed to conform to UTA's expectations of stereotypical male behavior. The defendants filed a motion for summary judgment, arguing transsexuals are not a protected class under Title VII or the Equal Protection Clause and that Etsitty was not terminated for failing to conform to male stereotypes. The district court granted the motion. In doing so, it agreed transsexuals are not a protected class and concluded there was no evidence that Etsitty was terminated for any reason other than Shirley's stated concern about Etsitty's restroom usage.

## III. Analysis

This court reviews a district court's decision to grant summary judgment de novo.

...

### A. Title VII

In the Title VII context, this court applies the three-part burden-shifting framework established in *McDonnell Douglas Corp. v. Green*, 411 U.S. 792, 802–05 (1973). Under this framework, the plaintiff must first establish a prima facie case of prohibited employment action. If the plaintiff does so, the burden shifts to the employer to articulate a "legitimate, nondiscriminatory reason for its adverse employment action." *Id.* (quotations omitted). If the employer satisfies this burden, "summary judgment is warranted unless the employee can show there is a genuine issue of material fact as to whether the proffered reasons are pretextual." *Id.* Because this court concludes transsexuals are not a protected class under

Title VII and because Etsitty has failed to raise a genuine issue of material fact as to whether UTA's asserted non-discriminatory reason for her termination is pretextual, this court concludes the district court properly granted summary judgment on Etsitty's Title VII claims.

### 1. Prima Facie Claim

Title VII provides that "[i]t shall be an unlawful employment practice for an employer ... to discharge any individual, or otherwise to discriminate against any individual ... because of such individual's ... sex." 42 U.S.C. § 2000e-2(a)(1).... Thus, the threshold question in this case is whether Etsitty's claim can properly be construed as a claim that she was terminated or discriminated against "because of sex." If it cannot, as UTA argues and the district court held, Etsitty has not presented an actionable legal claim under Title VII and summary judgment was properly granted. The question of whether, and to what extent, a transsexual may claim protection from discrimination under Title VII is a question this court has not previously addressed.

On appeal, Etsitty presents two separate legal theories in support of her contention that she was discriminated against because of sex in violation of Title VII. First, she argues discrimination based on an individual's identity as a transsexual is literally discrimination because of sex and that transsexuals are therefore a protected class under Title VII as transsexuals. Alternatively, she argues that even if Title VII does not prohibit discrimination on the basis of a person's transsexuality, she is nevertheless entitled to protection under Title VII because she was discriminated against for failing to conform to sex stereotypes....

### a. Transsexuals as a Protected Class

Etsitty first argues she is protected under Title VII from discrimination based on her status as a transsexual. She argues that because a person's identity as a transsexual is directly connected to the sex organs she possesses, discrimination on this basis must constitute discrimination because of sex.

Although this court has not previously considered whether transsexuals are a protected class under Title VII, other circuits to specifically address the issue have consistently held they are not. [citations omitted]....

While Etsitty argues for a more expansive interpretation of sex that would include transsexuals as a protected class, she acknowledges that few courts have been willing to adopt such an interpretation. Even the Sixth Circuit, which extended protection to transsexuals under the *Price Waterhouse* theory discussed below, explained that an individual's status as a transsexual should be irrelevant to the availability of Title VII protection. *Smith v. City of Salem*, 378 F.3d 566, 574 (6th Cir. 2004). Further, this court has explicitly declined to extend Title VII protections to discrimination based on a person's sexual orientation. Although there is certainly a distinction between a class delineated by sexual orientation and a class delineated by sexual identity, ... [this court is reluctant] to expand the traditional definition of sex in the Title VII context.

... At this point in time and with the record and arguments before this court, however, we conclude discrimination against a transsexual because she is a transsexual is not "discrimination because of sex." Therefore, transsexuals are not a protected class under Title VII and Etsitty cannot satisfy her prima facie burden on the basis of her status as a transsexual.[10]

---

10. This court is aware of the difficulties and marginalization transsexuals may be subject to in the workplace. The conclusion that transsexuals are not protected under Title VII as transsexuals should not be read to allow employers to deny transsexual employees the legal protection other

### b. *Price Waterhouse* Theory

Etsitty next argues that even if transsexuals are not entitled to protection under Title VII as transsexuals, she is nevertheless entitled to protection as a biological male who was discriminated against for failing to conform to social stereotypes about how a man should act and appear.[11]

She argues that although courts have previously declined to extend Title VII protection to transsexuals based on a narrow interpretation of "sex," this approach has been supplanted by the more recent rationale of *Price Waterhouse*. Etsitty contends that after *Price Waterhouse*, an employer's discrimination against an employee based on the employee's failure to conform to stereotypical gender norms is discrimination "because of sex" and may provide a basis for an actionable Title VII claim....

A number of courts have relied on *Price Waterhouse* to expressly recognize a Title VII cause of action for discrimination based on an employee's failure to conform to stereotypical gender norms.... In fact, the Sixth Circuit recently relied on *Price Waterhouse* to recognize a cause of action for a transsexual claiming protection under Title VII.... In so holding, the court explained that just as an employer who discriminates against women for not wearing dresses or makeup is engaging in sex discrimination under the rationale of *Price Waterhouse*, "employers who discriminate against men because they do wear dresses and makeup, or otherwise act femininely, are also engaging in sex discrimination, because the discrimination would not occur but for the victim's sex." [citations omitted].

This court need not decide whether discrimination based on an employee's failure to conform to sex stereotypes always constitutes discrimination "because of sex" and we need not decide whether such a claim may extend Title VII protection to transsexuals who act and appear as a member of the opposite sex. Instead, because we conclude Etsitty has not presented a genuine issue of material fact as to whether UTA's stated motivation for her termination is pretextual, we assume, without deciding, that such a claim is available and that Etsitty has satisfied her prima facie burden.

### 2. Legitimate Nondiscriminatory Reason

Assuming Etsitty has established a prima facie case under the *Price Waterhouse* theory of gender stereotyping, the burden then shifts to UTA to articulate a legitimate, nondiscriminatory reason for Etsitty's termination. At this stage of the *McDonnell Douglas* framework, UTA does not "need to litigate the merits of the reasoning, nor does it need to prove that the reason relied upon was bona fide, nor does it need to prove that the reasoning was applied in a nondiscriminatory fashion." *EEOC v. Flasher Co.*, 986 F.2d 1312, 1316 (10th Cir. 1992). Rather, UTA need only "explain its actions against the plaintiff in terms that are not facially prohibited by Title VII." *Jones v. Denver Post Corp.*, 203 F.3d 748, 753 (10th Cir. 2000) (quotation omitted).

UTA has explained its decision to discharge Etsitty was based solely on her intent to use women's public restrooms while wearing a UTA uniform, despite the fact she still had

---

employees enjoy merely by labeling them as transsexuals. *See Smith v. City of Salem*, 378 F.3d 566, 575 (6th Cir. 2004) ("Sex stereotyping based on a person's gender non-conforming behavior is impermissible discrimination, irrespective of the cause of that behavior; a label, such as 'transsexual,' is not fatal to a sex discrimination claim where the victim has suffered discrimination because of his or her gender nonconformity."). If transsexuals are to receive legal protection apart from their status as male or female, however, such protection must come from Congress and not the courts....

11. Although Etsitty identifies herself as a woman, her *Price Waterhouse* claim is based solely on her status as a biological male. Etsitty does not claim protection under Title VII as a woman who fails to conform to social stereotypes about how a woman should act and appear.

male genitalia. The record also reveals UTA believed, and Etsitty has not demonstrated otherwise, that it was not possible to accommodate her bathroom usage because UTA drivers typically use public restrooms along their routes rather than restrooms at the UTA facility. UTA states it was concerned the use of women's public restrooms by a biological male could result in liability for UTA. This court agrees with the district court that such a motivation constitutes a legitimate, nondiscriminatory reason for Etsitty's termination under Title VII.

Etsitty argues UTA's concern regarding which restroom she would use cannot qualify as a facially non-discriminatory reason because the use of women's restrooms is an inherent part of Etsitty's status as a transsexual and, thus, an inherent part of her non-conforming gender behavior. Therefore, she argues, terminating her because she intended to use women's restrooms is essentially another way of stating that she was terminated for failing to conform to sex stereotypes.

Title VII's prohibition on sex discrimination, however, does not extend so far. It may be that use of the women's restroom is an inherent part of one's identity as a male-to-female transsexual and that a prohibition on such use discriminates on the basis of one's status as a transsexual. As discussed above, however, Etsitty may not claim protection under Title VII based upon her transsexuality per se. Rather, Etsitty's claim must rest entirely on the *Price Waterhouse* theory of protection as a man who fails to conform to sex stereotypes. However far *Price Waterhouse* reaches, this court cannot conclude it requires employers to allow biological males to use women's restrooms. Use of a restroom designated for the opposite sex does not constitute a mere failure to conform to sex stereotypes....

The critical issue under Title VII "is whether members of one sex are exposed to disadvantageous terms or conditions of employment to which members of the other sex are not exposed." *Oncale*, 523 U.S. at 80 (quotation omitted). Because an employer's requirement that employees use restrooms matching their biological sex does not expose biological males to disadvantageous terms and does not discriminate against employees who fail to conform to gender stereotypes, UTA's proffered reason of concern over restroom usage is not discriminatory on the basis of sex. Thus, it is not "facially prohibited by Title VII" and may satisfy UTA's burden on the second part of the *McDonnell Douglas* framework.

3. Pretext

Once UTA has advanced a legitimate, nondiscriminatory reason for Etsitty's termination, the burden shifts back to Etsitty to "show there is a genuine issue of material fact as to whether the proffered reason [is] pretextual." [citation omitted]. "A plaintiff demonstrates pretext by showing either that a discriminatory reason more likely motivated the employer or that the employer's proffered explanation is unworthy of credence." [citation omitted]. Such a showing may be made by revealing "such weaknesses, implausibilities, inconsistencies, incoherence, or contradictions, in the employer's proffered legitimate reasons for its action that a reasonable factfinder could ... infer that the employer did not act for the asserted non-discriminatory reasons." [citation omitted]. Although this court must resolve all doubts in Etsitty's favor, "[m]ere conjecture that the employer's explanation is pretext is insufficient to defeat summary judgment." [citation omitted].

In support of Etsitty's contention that she was terminated for failing to conform to gender stereotypes and not because of UTA's concern regarding her restroom usage, she relies primarily on the testimony of Shirley and Cardon. Specifically, she points to Shirley's deposition testimony in which she stated, "We both felt that there was an image issue out there for us, that we could have a problem with having someone who, even though his appearance may look female, he's still a male because he still had a penis." Additionally, Cardon testified, "We have expectations of operators and how they appear to the public.... [I]f we see something that is considered radical or could be interpreted by the public as being inappropriate, we talk to the operators about that and expect them to have a professional appearance." Etsitty argues these statements provide sufficient evidence to allow a rational jury to conclude she was terminated because she was a biological male who did not act and appear as UTA believed a man should.

If these statements stood alone, they may constitute sufficient evidence of pretext to preclude summary judgment. A complete review of the deposition testimony, however, indicates otherwise. Although the specific statements cited by Etsitty address Etsitty's appearance, they fall within the larger context of an explanation of UTA's concerns regarding Etsitty's restroom usage. Immediately after Shirley mentions Etsitty's appearance, she explains the problem with this appearance is that she may not be able to find a unisex bathroom on the route and that liability may arise if Etsitty was using female restrooms. When Cardon was asked what he found unprofessional about Etsitty's appearance, he similarly responded with concerns about her restroom usage. Thus, the isolated and tangential comments about Etsitty's appearance are insufficient to alone permit an inference of pretext. Instead, the testimony of Shirley and Cardon, viewed in its entirety and in context, provides further support for UTA's assertion that Etsitty was terminated not because she failed to conform to stereotypes about how a man should act and appear, but because she was a biological male who intended to use women's public restrooms.

In addition to the statements made by Shirley and Cardon, Etsitty argues UTA's asserted reason for her termination must be pretextual because UTA had no reason to be concerned regarding her use of women's restrooms. In support of this claim, Etsitty makes the following arguments: (1) UTA could not be subject to liability, as a matter of law, for allowing a male-to-female transsexual employee to use women's restrooms; (2) UTA had received no complaints regarding Etsitty's restroom usage; (3) UTA made no attempt to investigate whether there were unisex restrooms available; and (4) because Etsitty looked and acted like a woman, no one would know she was not biologically female and therefore could not take offense to her use of women's restrooms.

None of the arguments raised by Etsitty is sufficient to raise a genuine issue as to whether UTA's asserted concern regarding her use of the women's restrooms is pretext. Although Etsitty states in her brief that there is no evidence she intended to use female restrooms, she admitted at oral argument that she was required to use female restrooms and that she informed Shirley of this at their meeting prior to her termination. Thus, UTA's belief that Etsitty intended to use female restrooms was well-grounded. While Etsitty contends this fact should not have given rise to her termination, her argument is more akin to a challenge to UTA's business judgment than a challenge to its actual motivation. Nevertheless, "[t]he relevant inquiry is not whether [the defendant's] proffered reasons were wise, fair or correct, but whether [it] honestly believed those reasons and acted in good faith upon those beliefs." [citation omitted].

While this court may disagree with UTA that a male-to-female transsexual's intent to use women's restrooms should be grounds for termination before complaints have arisen, there is insufficient evidence to permit an inference that UTA did not actually terminate Etsitty for this reason. To the contrary, all of the evidence suggests UTA did in fact terminate Etsitty because of its concerns about her restroom usage. Both at the time of Etsitty's termination and in subsequent deposition testimony, Shirley consistently explained the termination decision in terms of her concerns regarding liability for UTA and the inability of UTA to accommodate Etsitty's restroom needs. Although Shirley and Cardon specifically asked Etsitty whether she possessed male genitalia, such an inquiry is not the "smoking gun" Etsitty suggests. Rather, the record is clear that this inquiry was only relevant to UTA's evaluation of whether Etsitty's restroom usage could become a problem.

UTA's legitimate explanation is not made implausible by any of the circumstantial evidence relied on by Etsitty in her brief. The fact UTA had not yet received complaints about Etsitty's restroom usage at the time of the termination does not mean UTA could not have been concerned about such complaints arising in the future, especially where Etsitty had only recently begun using the women's restroom. Similarly, Etsitty has pointed to nothing in the record to indicate the feasibility of an investigation into the availability of unisex restrooms along each of UTA's routes or the likelihood complaints would arise. Therefore, in this case, Shirley's failure to conduct such an investigation has little, if any, bearing on the veracity of her stated concern.

Etsitty's reliance on *Cruzan v. Special School District # 1* to call into question UTA's asserted motivation is also misplaced. 294 F.3d 981 (8th Cir. 2002). In *Cruzan*, the Eighth Circuit held that a male-to-female transsexual's use of the women's employee restroom does not create a hostile work environment for purposes of a Title VII sexual harassment claim. *Id.* at 984. Even if such a rule were to be adopted in this circuit and applied to actions arising outside the employment context, however, it would say nothing about whether UTA was nevertheless genuinely concerned about the possibility of liability and public complaints. The question of whether UTA was legally correct about the merits of such potential lawsuits is irrelevant. [citation omitted].

Finally, Etsitty argues that because UTA typically resolves complaints about its employees' restroom usage simply by requiring the employees to stop using the restroom for which the complaint was received, Etsitty was treated differently than similarly situated employees. [citation omitted]. The prior complaints received by UTA, however, involved problems with the cleanliness of the restrooms and with UTA employees congregating around a hotel swimming pool. An employee's use of bathrooms designated for the opposite sex is sufficiently different from these prior problems as to make UTA's treatment of restroom complaints in the past of little significance to the question of pretext in the case at bar.

... Etsitty has therefore failed to raise a genuine issue as to whether UTA's proffered reason is pretextual and the district court properly granted summary judgment on Etsitty's Title VII claim.

### IV. Conclusion

For the foregoing reasons, this court affirms the district court's grant of summary judgment to the defendants.

---

## Further Discussion

As suggested above, some individuals in Etsitty's situation have succeeded under Title VII by invoking the *Price Waterhouse* stereotyping doctrine. The EEOC decision in *Macy v. Holder*, which is excerpted below, relied on many of these decisions in concluding that Title VII's prohibition against sex discrimination prohibits discrimination on the basis of transgender status. This issue remains the subject of hot debate, with some arguing that *Price Waterhouse* is being misread and applied in more situations than the Supreme

Court intended. One example is the following excerpt from Judge Posner's concurrence in *Hamm v. Weyuwega Milk Products, Inc.*:

> The origin of this curious distinction, which would be very difficult to explain to a lay person (an indication, often and I think here, that the law is indeed awry), is the Supreme Court's decision in *Price Waterhouse v. Hopkins*, 490 U.S. 228 (1989). Part of the evidence that the plaintiff in that case had been denied promotion because she was a woman was that her male superiors hadn't liked her failure to conform to their expectations regarding feminine dress and deportment. That was indeed a reason to suspect that the firm discriminated against women. But there is a difference that subsequent cases have ignored between, on the one hand, using evidence of the plaintiff's failure to wear nail polish (or, if the plaintiff is a man, his using nail polish) to show that her sex played a role in the adverse employment action of which she complains, and, on the other hand, creating a subtype of sexual discrimination called "sex stereotyping," as if there were a federally protected right for male workers to wear nail polish and dresses and speak in falsetto and mince about in high heels, or for female ditchdiggers to strip to the waist in hot weather. If a court of appeals requires lawyers presenting oral argument to wear conservative business dress, should a male lawyer have a legal right to argue in drag provided that the court does not believe that he is a homosexual, against whom it is free to discriminate? That seems to me a very strange extension of the *Hopkins* case.

332 F.3d 1058, 1066 (7th Cir. 2003).

---

### Focus Questions: *Macy v. Holder*

1. *What is the procedural posture of this case?*

2. *Is transgender status the same as sex?*

3. *Is changing from Christianity to Judaism the same, for purposes of discrimination law, as changing from female to male?*

---

# Macy v. Holder

### EEOC Appeal No. 0120120821 (April 20, 2012)

Bernadette B. Wilson, Acting Executive Officer, Executive Secretariat.

On December 9, 2011, Complainant filed an appeal concerning her equal employment opportunity (EEO) complaint alleging employment discrimination in violation of Title VII. [Most citations and footnotes omitted throughout]. For the following reasons, the Commission finds that the Complainant's complaint of discrimination based on gender identity, change of sex, and/or transgender status is cognizable under Title VII and remands the complaint to the Agency for further processing.

## BACKGROUND

Complainant, a transgender woman, was a police detective in Phoenix, Arizona. In December 2010 she decided to relocate to San Francisco for family reasons. According to her formal complaint, Complainant was still known as a male at that time, having not yet made the transition to being a female.

Complainant [applied for a position at] the Bureau of Alcohol, Tobacco, Firearms and Explosives (Agency) ... Walnut Creek crime laboratory for which the Complainant was qualified. Complainant is trained and certified as a National Integrated Ballistic Information Network (NIBIN) operator and a BrassTrax ballistics investigator.

Complainant discussed the position with the Director of the Walnut Creek lab by telephone, in either December 2010 or January 2011, while still presenting as a man. According to Complainant, the telephone conversation covered her experience, credentials, salary and benefits. Complainant further asserts that, following the conversation, the Director told her she would be able to have the position assuming no problems arose during her background check. The Director also told her that the position would be filled as a civilian contractor through an outside company.

Complainant states that she talked again with the Director in January 2011 and asked that he check on the status of the position. According to Complainant in her formal complaint, the Director did so and reasserted that the job was hers pending completion of the background check. Complainant asserts, as evidence of her impending hire, that Aspen of DC ("Aspen"), the contractor responsible for filling the position, contacted her to begin the necessary paperwork and that an investigator from the Agency was assigned to do her background check.

On March 29, 2011, Complainant informed Aspen via email that she was in the process of transitioning from male to female and she requested that Aspen inform the Director of the Walnut Creek lab of this change. According to Complainant, on April 3, 2011, Aspen informed Complainant that the Agency had been informed of her change in name and gender. Five days later, on April 8, 2011, Complainant received an email from the contractor's Director of Operations stating that, due to federal budget reductions, the position at Walnut Creek was no longer available.

According to Complainant, she was concerned about this quick change in events and on May 10, 2011, she contacted an agency EEO counselor to discuss her concerns. She states that the counselor told her that the position at Walnut Creek had not been cut but, rather, that someone else had been hired for the position. Complainant further states that the counselor told her that the Agency had decided to take the other individual because that person was farthest along in the background investigation. Complainant claims that this was a pretextual explanation because the background investigation had been proceeding on her as well. Complainant believes she was incorrectly informed that the position had been cut because the Agency did not want to hire her because she is transgender....

On June 13, 2011, Complainant filed her formal EEO complaint with the Agency. On her formal complaint form, Complainant checked off "sex" and the box "female," and then typed in "gender identity" and "sex stereotyping" as the basis of her complaint. In the narrative accompanying her complaint, Complainant stated that she was discriminated against on the basis of "my sex, gender identity (transgender woman) and on the basis of sex stereotyping."

[Rules applicable to the Agency require complainants to pursue claims of sexual orientation or gender identity discrimination under an internal procedure, but permit complainants to take sex discrimination claims to the EEOC. Under those rules, the question of whether the transgender claim would qualify as sex discrimination would determine whether the Complainant could receive consideration at the EEOC or would be limited to the agency process, which allowed for fewer remedies and no right to a hearing. The Complainant was concerned that, if the Agency retained the transgender discrimination claim, that claim would not be treated as a sex discrimination claim cognizable under Title VII. This appeal to the EEOC challenged the Agency's decision that transgender discrimination should be retained for agency adjudication, rather than proceed to the EEOC.]

. . . .

ANALYSIS AND FINDINGS

The narrative accompanying Complainant's complaint makes clear that she believes she was not hired for the position as a result of making her transgender status known. . . . Although it is possible that the Agency would have fully addressed her claims under that portion of her complaint . . . , the Agency's communications prompted in Complainant a reasonable belief that the Agency viewed the gender identity discrimination she alleged as outside the scope of Title VII's sex discrimination prohibitions. Based on these communications, Complainant believed that her complaint would not be investigated effectively by the Agency, and she filed the instant appeal. . . .

We find that the Agency mistakenly separated Complainant's complaint into separate claims: one described as discrimination based on "sex" (which the Agency accepted for processing under Title VII) and others that were . . . described . . . as "sex stereotyping," "gender transition/change of sex," "gender identity," "gender identity stereotyping," and . . . "gender identity, change of sex and/or transgender status." . . . Each of the formulations of Complainant's claims are simply different ways of stating the same claim of discrimination "based on . . . sex," a claim cognizable under Title VII.

Title VII states that, except as otherwise specifically provided, "[a]ll personnel actions affecting [federal] employees or applicants for employment . . . shall be made free from any discrimination based on . . . sex[.]" As used in Title VII, the term "sex" "encompasses both sex — that is, the biological differences between men and women — and gender." *See Schwenk v. Hartford*, 204 F.3d 1187, 1202 (9th Cir. 2000); *see also Smith v. City of Salem*, 378 F.3d 566, 572 (6th Cir. 2004) ("The Supreme Court made clear that in the context of Title VII, discrimination because of 'sex' includes gender discrimination."). As the Eleventh Circuit noted in *Glenn v. Brumby*, six members of the Supreme Court in *Price Waterhouse* agreed that Title VII barred "not just discrimination because of biological sex, but also gender stereotyping — failing to act and appear according to expectations defined by gender." As such, the terms "gender" and "sex" are often used interchangeably to describe the discrimination prohibited by Title VII.

That Title VII's prohibition on sex discrimination proscribes gender discrimination, and not just discrimination on the basis of biological sex, is important. If Title VII proscribed only discrimination on the basis of biological sex, the only prohibited gender-based disparate treatment would be when an employer prefers a man over a woman, or vice versa. But the statute's protections sweep far broader than that, in part because the term "gender" encompasses not only a person's biological sex but also the cultural and social aspects associated with masculinity and femininity.

In *Price Waterhouse*, the employer refused to make a female senior manager, Hopkins, a partner at least in part because she did not act as some of the partners thought a woman should act. She was informed, for example, that to improve her chances for partnership she should "walk more femininely, talk more femininely, dress more femininely, wear make-up, have her hair styled, and wear jewelry." The Court concluded that discrimination for failing to conform with gender-based expectations violates Title VII, holding that "[i]n the specific context of sex stereotyping, an employer who acts on the basis of a belief that a woman cannot be aggressive, or that she must not be, has acted on the basis of gender."

Although the partners at Price Waterhouse discriminated against Ms. Hopkins for failing to conform to stereotypical gender norms, gender discrimination occurs any time an employer treats an employee differently for failing to conform to any gender-based expectations or norms. "What matters, for purposes of ... the *Price Waterhouse* analysis, is that in the mind of the perpetrator the discrimination is related to the sex of the victim." *Schwenk; see also Price Waterhouse* (noting the illegitimacy of allowing "sex-linked evaluations to play a part in the [employer's] decision-making process")....

When an employer discriminates against someone because the person is transgender, the employer has engaged in disparate treatment "related to the sex of the victim." *See Schwenk.* This is true regardless of whether an employer discriminates against an employee because the individual has expressed his or her gender in a non-stereotypical fashion, because the employer is uncomfortable with the fact that the person has transitioned or is in the process of transitioning from one gender to another, or because the employer simply does not like that the person is identifying as a transgender person. In each of these circumstances, the employer is making a gender-based evaluation, thus violating the Supreme Court's admonition that "an employer may not take gender into account in making an employment decision."

Since *Price Waterhouse*, courts have widely recognized the availability of the sex stereotyping theory as a valid method of establishing discrimination "on the basis of sex" in many scenarios involving individuals who act or appear in gender-nonconforming ways. And since *Price Waterhouse*, courts also have widely recognized the availability of the sex stereotyping theory as a valid method of establishing discrimination "on the basis of sex" in scenarios involving transgender individuals.

For example, in *Schwenk*, a prison guard had sexually assaulted a pre-operative male-to-female transgender prisoner, and the prisoner sued, alleging that the guard had violated the Gender Motivated Violence Act (GMVA). The U.S. Court of Appeals for the Ninth Circuit found that the guard had known that the prisoner "considered herself a transsexual and that she planned to seek sex reassignment surgery in the future." According to the court, the guard had targeted the transgender prisoner "only after he discovered that she considered herself female[,]" and the guard was "motivated, at least in part, by [her] gender" — that is, "by her assumption of a feminine rather than a typically masculine appearance or demeanor." On these facts, the Ninth Circuit readily concluded that the guard's attack constituted discrimination because of gender within the meaning of both the GMVA and Title VII.

The court relied on *Price Waterhouse*, reasoning that it stood for the proposition that discrimination based on sex includes discrimination based on a failure "to conform to socially-constructed gender expectations." Accordingly, the Ninth Circuit concluded, discrimination against transgender females — i.e., "as anatomical males whose outward behavior and inward identity [do] not meet social definitions of masculinity" — is actionable discrimination "because of sex."

[The Officer here discussed federal circuit and district court decisions recognizing that discrimination because of a person's gender non-conformity is actionable as sex discrimination.]

Thus, a transgender person who has experienced discrimination based on his or her gender identity may establish a prima facie case of sex discrimination through any number of different formulations. These different formulations are not, however, different claims of discrimination that can be separated out and investigated within different systems. Rather, they are simply different ways of describing sex discrimination.

For example, Complainant could establish a case of sex discrimination under a theory of gender stereotyping by showing that she did not get the job as an NIBIN ballistics technician at Walnut Creek because the employer believed that biological men should consistently present as men and wear male clothing.

Alternatively, if Complainant can prove that the reason that she did not get the job at Walnut Creek is that the Director was willing to hire her when he thought she was a man, but was not willing to hire her once he found out that she was now a woman — she will have proven that the Director discriminated on the basis of sex. Under this theory, there would actually be no need, for purposes of establishing coverage under Title VII, for Complainant to compile any evidence that the Director was engaging in gender stereotyping.

In this respect, gender is no different from religion. Assume that an employee considers herself Christian and identifies as such. But assume that an employer finds out that the employee's parents are Muslim, believes that the employee should therefore be Muslim, and terminates the employee on that basis. No one would doubt that such an employer discriminated on the basis of religion. There would be no need for the employee who experienced the adverse employment action to demonstrate that the employer acted on the basis of some religious stereotype — although, clearly, discomfort with the choice made by the employee with regard to religion would presumably be at the root of the employer's actions. But for purposes of establishing a prima facie case that Title VII has been violated, the employee simply must demonstrate that the employer impermissibly used religion in making its employment decision....

Applying Title VII in this manner does not create a new "class" of people covered under Title VII — for example, the "class" of people who have converted from Islam to Christianity or from Christianity to Judaism. Rather, it would simply be the result of applying the plain language of a statute prohibiting discrimination on the basis of religion to practical situations in which such characteristics are unlawfully taken into account.

Thus, we conclude that intentional discrimination against a transgender individual because that person is transgender is, by definition, discrimination "based on ... sex," and such discrimination therefore violates Title VII....

---

## Note

The Employment Nondiscrimination Act ("ENDA"), which would explicitly prohibit employment discrimination against gay and lesbian, and under some drafts transgender, individuals is introduced annually in Congress, most recently as of this writing, in June of 2013. ENDA would provide for prohibitions similar to those under Title VII and the Americans with Disabilities Act. For example, the 2007 bill, which would have prohibited discrimination only on the basis of sexual orientation, would have applied to businesses of fifteen or more people and contained exemptions for religious corporations, associations, societies, or educational institutions, as well as the Armed Forces.

As stated above, a number of states have passed statutes to protect LGBT individuals from employment discrimination. A complete state-by-state presentation of state antidiscrimination statutes is available from the National Gay and Lesbian Task force at http://www.thetaskforce.org/reports_and_research/nondiscrimination_laws (last visited Oct. 6, 2013). States that do not expressly provide such protections may nevertheless permit transgender discrimination claims as sex discrimination.

## Grooming Codes

Employer dress and grooming codes that impose different rules based on a protected trait may violate federal employment discrimination laws. Such issues often arise in cases where an employer policy has different requirements for men and women. Although courts often uphold such policies, they do impose some limits.

---

### Focus Questions: *Jespersen v. Harrah's Operating Company, Inc.*

1. *The trial court resolved the case on the defendant's motion for summary judgment. Why did the plaintiff not cross-move for summary judgment? A three judge panel affirmed the trial court decision, and the opinion below reflects the court's rehearing en banc.*

2. *If you were Jespersen's attorney, how would you have done things differently—to achieve a different outcome?*

---

## Jespersen v. Harrah's Operating Company, Inc.

### 444 F.3d 1104 (9th Cir. 2006)

Chief Judge Schroeder.

We took this sex discrimination case en banc in order to reaffirm our circuit law concerning appearance and grooming standards, and to clarify our evolving law of sex stereotyping claims.

The plaintiff, Darlene Jespersen, was terminated from her position as a bartender at the sports bar in Harrah's Reno casino not long after Harrah's began to enforce its comprehensive uniform, appearance and grooming standards for all bartenders. The standards required all bartenders, men and women, to wear the same uniform of black pants and white shirts, a bow tie, and comfortable black shoes. The standards also included grooming requirements that differed to some extent for men and women, requiring women to wear some facial makeup and not permitting men to wear any. Jespersen refused to comply with the makeup requirement and was effectively terminated for that reason.

The district court granted summary judgment to Harrah's on the ground that the appearance and grooming policies imposed equal burdens on both men and women bartenders because, while women were required to use makeup and men were forbidden to wear makeup, women were allowed to have long hair and men were required to have their hair cut to a length above the collar. The district court also held that the policy could not run afoul of Title VII because it did not discriminate against Jespersen on the basis of the "immutable characteristics" of her sex. The district court further observed that the Supreme Court's decision in *Price Waterhouse*, prohibiting discrimination on the basis of sex stereotyping, did not apply to this case because in the district court's view, the Ninth Circuit had excluded grooming standards from the reach of *Price Waterhouse*. The district court granted summary judgment to Harrah's on all claims.

The three-judge panel affirmed, but on somewhat different grounds. The panel majority held that Jespersen, on this record, failed to show that the appearance policy imposed a greater burden on women than on men. It pointed to the lack of any affidavit in this record to support a claim that the burdens of the policy fell unequally on men and women. Accordingly, the panel did not agree with the district court that grooming policies could never discriminate as a matter of law. [T]the panel also held that *Price Waterhouse* could apply to grooming or appearance standards only if the policy amounted to sexual harassment, which would require a showing that the employee suffered harassment for failure to conform to commonly-accepted gender stereotypes. The dissent would have denied summary judgment on both theories.

... With respect to sex stereotyping, we hold that appearance standards, including makeup requirements, may well be the subject of a Title VII claim for sexual stereotyping, but that on this record Jespersen has failed to create any triable issue of fact that the challenged policy was part of a policy motivated by sex stereotyping. We therefore affirm.

## I. BACKGROUND

Plaintiff Darlene Jespersen worked successfully as a bartender at Harrah's for twenty years and compiled what by all accounts was an exemplary record....

In April 2000, Harrah's amended [its "Personal Best"] policy to require that women wear makeup. Jespersen's only objection here is to the makeup requirement. The amended policy provided in relevant part: ...

**Beverage Bartenders and Barbacks will adhere to these additional guidelines:**

**Overall Guidelines (applied equally to male/female):**

- Appearance: Must maintain Personal Best image portrayed at time of hire.
- Jewelry, if issued, must be worn. Otherwise, tasteful and simple jewelry is permitted; no large chokers, chains or bracelets.
- No faddish hairstyles or unnatural colors are permitted.

**Males:**

- Hair must not extend below top of shirt collar. Ponytails are prohibited.
- Hands and fingernails must be clean and nails neatly trimmed at all times. No colored polish is permitted.
- Eye and facial makeup is not permitted.
- Shoes will be solid black leather or leather type with rubber (non skid) soles.

**Females:**

- Hair must be teased, curled, or styled every day you work. Hair must be worn down at all times, no exceptions.
- Stockings are to be of nude or natural color consistent with employee's skin tone. No runs.
- Nail polish can be clear, white, pink or red color only. No exotic nail art or length.
- Shoes will be solid black leather or leather type with rubber (non skid) soles.
- *Make up (face powder, blush and mascara) must be worn and applied neatly in complimentary colors. Lip color must be worn at all times. (emphasis added).*

Jespersen did not wear makeup on or off the job, and in her deposition stated that wearing it would conflict with her self-image. It is not disputed that she found the makeup requirement offensive, and felt so uncomfortable wearing makeup that she found it interfered with her ability to perform as a bartender. Unwilling to wear the makeup, and not qualifying for any open positions at the casino with a similar compensation scale, Jespersen left her employment with Harrah's.

After exhausting her administrative remedies with the Equal Employment Opportunity Commission and obtaining a right to sue notification, Jespersen filed this action in July 2001. In her complaint, Jespersen sought damages as well as declaratory and injunctive relief for discrimination and retaliation for opposition to discrimination, alleging that the "Personal Best" policy discriminated against women by "(1) subjecting them to terms and conditions of employment to which men are not similarly subjected, and (2) requiring that women conform to sex-based stereotypes as a term and condition of employment."

Harrah's moved for summary judgment, supporting its motion with documents giving the history and purpose of the appearance and grooming policies. Harrah's argued that the policy created similar standards for both men and women, and that where the standards differentiated on the basis of sex, as with the face and hair standards, any burdens imposed fell equally on both male and female bartenders.

In her deposition testimony, attached as a response to the motion for summary judgment, Jespersen described the personal indignity she felt as a result of attempting to comply with the makeup policy. Jespersen testified that when she wore the makeup she "felt very degraded and very demeaned." In addition, Jespersen testified that "it prohibited [her] from doing [her] job" because "[i]t affected [her] self-dignity ... [and] took away [her] credibility as an individual and as a person." Jespersen made no cross-motion for summary judgment, taking the position that the case should go to the jury. Her response to Harrah's motion for summary judgment relied solely on her own deposition testimony regarding her subjective reaction to the makeup policy, and on favorable customer feedback and employer evaluation forms regarding her work.

The record therefore does not contain any affidavit or other evidence to establish that complying with the "Personal Best" standards caused burdens to fall unequally on men or women, and there is no evidence to suggest Harrah's motivation was to stereotype the women bartenders. Jespersen relied solely on evidence that she had been a good bartender, and that she had personal objections to complying with the policy, in order to support her argument that Harrah's "'sells' and exploits its women employees." Jespersen contended that as a matter of law she had made a prima facie showing of gender discrimination, sufficient to survive summary judgment on both of her claims.

## II. UNEQUAL BURDENS

In order to assert a valid Title VII claim for sex discrimination, a plaintiff must make out a prima facie case establishing that the challenged employment action was either intentionally discriminatory or that it had a discriminatory effect on the basis of gender. Once a plaintiff establishes such a prima facie case, "[t]he burden then must shift to the employer to articulate some legitimate, nondiscriminatory reason for the employee's rejection." [citation omitted].

In this case, Jespersen argues that the makeup requirement itself establishes a prima facie case of discriminatory intent and must be justified by Harrah's as a bona fide occupational qualification. Our settled law in this circuit, however, does not support Jespersen's position that a sex-based difference in appearance standards alone, without any further showing of disparate effects, creates a prima facie case.

In *Gerdom v. Cont'l Airlines, Inc.*, we considered the Continental Airlines policy that imposed strict weight restrictions on female flight attendants, and held it constituted a violation of Title VII. We did so because the airline imposed no weight restriction whatsoever on a class of male employees who performed the same or similar functions as the flight attendants. Indeed, the policy was touted by the airline as intended to "create the public image of an airline which offered passengers service by thin, attractive women, whom executives referred to as Continental's 'girls.'" In fact, Continental specifically argued that its policy was justified by its "desire to compete [with other airlines] by featuring attractive female cabin attendants[,]" a justification which this court recognized as "discriminatory on its face." ...

In contrast, this case involves an appearance policy that applied to both male and female bartenders, and was aimed at creating a professional and very similar look for all of them. All bartenders wore the same uniform. The policy only differentiated as to grooming standards.

In *Frank v. United Airlines, Inc.*, we dealt with a weight policy that applied different standards to men and women in a facially unequal way. The women were forced to meet the requirements of a medium body frame standard while men were required to meet only the more generous requirements of a large body frame standard. In that case, we recognized that "[a]n appearance standard that imposes different but essentially equal burdens on men and women is not disparate treatment." [citation omitted]. The United weight policy, however, did not impose equal burdens. On its face, the policy embodied a requirement that categorically "applie[d] less favorably to one gender[,]" and the burdens imposed upon that gender were obvious from the policy itself. [citation omitted].

This case stands in marked contrast, for here we deal with requirements that, on their face, are not more onerous for one gender than the other. Rather, Harrah's "Personal Best" policy contains sex-differentiated requirements regarding each employee's hair, hands, and face. While those individual requirements differ according to gender, none on its face places a greater burden on one gender than the other. Grooming standards that appropriately differentiate between the genders are not facially discriminatory.

We have long recognized that companies may differentiate between men and women in appearance and grooming policies, and so have other circuits.... The material issue under our settled law is not whether the policies are different, but whether the policy imposed on the plaintiff creates an "unequal burden" for the plaintiff's gender.

Not every differentiation between the sexes in a grooming and appearance policy creates a "significantly greater burden of compliance[.]" For example, in [another case], this court upheld Safeway's enforcement of its sex-differentiated appearance standard, including its requirement that male employees wear ties, because the company's actions in enforcing the regulations were not "overly burdensome to its employees[.]"

Similarly, as the Eighth Circuit has recognized, "[w]here, as here, such [grooming and appearance] policies are reasonable and are imposed in an evenhanded manner on all employees, slight differences in the appearance requirements for males and females have only a negligible effect on employment opportunities." [citation omitted]. Under established equal burdens analysis, when an employer's grooming and appearance policy does not unreasonably burden one gender more than the other, that policy will not violate Title VII.

Jespersen asks us to take judicial notice of the fact that it costs more money and takes more time for a woman to comply with the makeup requirement than it takes for a man to comply with the requirement that he keep his hair short, but these are not matters appropriate for judicial notice. Judicial notice is reserved for matters "generally known within the territorial jurisdiction of the trial court" or "capable of accurate and ready determination by resort to sources whose accuracy cannot reasonably be questioned." Fed. R. Evid. 201.

Our rules thus provide that a plaintiff may not cure her failure to present the trial court with facts sufficient to establish the validity of her claim by requesting that this court take judicial notice of such facts. Those rules apply here. Jespersen did not submit any documentation or any evidence of the relative cost and time required to comply with the grooming requirements by men and women. As a result, we would have to speculate about those issues in order to then guess whether the policy creates unequal burdens for women. This would not be appropriate.

Having failed to create a record establishing that the "Personal Best" policies are more burdensome for women than for men, Jespersen did not present any triable issue of fact. The district court correctly granted summary judgment on the record before it with respect to Jespersen's claim that the makeup policy created an unequal burden for women.

## III. SEX STEREOTYPING

In *Price Waterhouse*, the Supreme Court considered a mixed-motive discrimination case. There, the plaintiff, Ann Hopkins, was denied partnership in the national accounting firm of Price Waterhouse because some of the partners found her to be too aggressive. While some partners praised Hopkins's "strong character, independence and integrity[,]" others commented that she needed to take "a course at charm school[.]" [citations omitted]. The Supreme Court determined that once a plaintiff has established that gender played "a motivating part in an employment decision, the defendant may avoid a finding of liability only by proving by a preponderance of the evidence that it would have made the same decision even if it had not taken the plaintiff's gender into account." [citation omitted].

[The Court determined that a plaintiff may introduce evidence that the employment decision was made in part because of a sex stereotype in order to establish] that "gender played a motivating part in an employment decision."

Harrah's "Personal Best" policy is very different [from the *Price Waterhouse* situation]. The policy does not single out Jespersen. It applies to all of the bartenders, male and female. It requires all of the bartenders to wear exactly the same uniforms while interacting with the public in the context of the entertainment industry. It is for the most part unisex, from the black tie to the non-skid shoes. There is no evidence in this record to indicate that the policy was adopted to make women bartenders conform to a commonly-accepted stereotypical image of what women should wear. The record contains nothing to suggest the grooming standards would objectively inhibit a woman's ability to do the job. The only evidence in the record to support the stereotyping claim is Jespersen's own subjective reaction to the makeup requirement.

We respect Jespersen's resolve to be true to herself and to the image that she wishes to project to the world. We cannot agree, however, that her objection to the makeup requirement, without more, can give rise to a claim of sex stereotyping under Title VII. If we were to do so, we would come perilously close to holding that every grooming, apparel, or appearance requirement that an individual finds personally offensive, or in conflict with his or her own self-image, can create a triable issue of sex discrimination.

This is not a case where the dress or appearance requirement is intended to be sexually provocative, and tending to stereotype women as sex objects. In *Sage Realty* the plaintiff was a lobby attendant in a hotel that employed only female lobby attendants and required a mandatory uniform ... that was "short and revealing on both sides [such that her] thighs and portions of her buttocks were exposed." [citation omitted]. Jespersen, in contrast, was asked only to wear a unisex uniform that covered her entire body and was designed for men and women. The "Personal Best" policy does not, on its face, indicate any discriminatory or sexually stereotypical intent on the part of Harrah's.

Nor is there evidence in this record that Harrah's treated Jespersen any differently than it treated any other bartender, male or female, who did not comply with the written grooming standards applicable to all bartenders. Jespersen's claim here materially differs from Hopkins' claim in *Price Waterhouse* because Harrah's grooming standards do not require Jespersen to conform to a stereotypical image that would objectively impede her ability to perform her job requirements as a bartender.

We emphasize that we do not preclude, as a matter of law, a claim of sex-stereotyping on the basis of dress or appearance codes. This record, however, is devoid of any basis for permitting this particular claim to go forward. [T]here is no evidence of a stereotypical motivation on the part of the employer. This case is essentially a challenge to one small part of what is an overall apparel, appearance, and grooming policy that applies largely the same requirements to both men and women.

Affirmed.

Circuit Judge Pregerson, with whom Judges Kozinski, Graber, and W. Fletcher, join, dissenting.

… I agree with the majority that a Title VII plaintiff may make out a prima facie case by showing that the challenged policy either was motivated in part "because of a sex stereotype," or "creates an 'unequal burden' for the plaintiff's gender." In other words, I agree with the majority that a Title VII plaintiff may make out a prima facie case by showing that the challenged policy either was motivated in part "because of a sex stereotype," or "creates an 'unequal burden' for the plaintiff's gender." Finally, I agree with the majority that Jespersen failed to introduce sufficient evidence to establish that Harrah's "Personal Best" program created an undue burden on Harrah's female bartenders.[12] Having failed to create such a record, Jespersen did not present any triable issue of fact on this issue. I part ways with the majority, however, inasmuch as I believe that the "Personal Best" program was part of a policy motivated by sex stereotyping and that Jespersen's termination for failing to comply with the program's requirements was "because of" her sex. Accordingly, I dissent from Part III of the majority opinion and from the judgment of the court.

Circuit Judge Kozinski, with whom Judges Graber and W. Fletcher join, dissenting.

I agree with Judge Pregerson and join his dissent—subject to one caveat: I believe that Jespersen also presented a triable issue of fact on the question of disparate burden.

The majority is right that "[t]he [makeup] requirements must be viewed in the context of the overall policy." But I find it perfectly clear that Harrah's overall grooming policy is substantially more burdensome for women than for men. Every requirement that forces men to spend time or money on their appearance has a corresponding requirement that is as, or more, burdensome for women: short hair v. "teased, curled, or styled" hair; clean trimmed nails v. nail length and color requirements; black leather shoes v. black leather shoes. The requirement that women spend time and money applying full facial makeup has no corresponding requirement for men, making the "overall policy" more burdensome for the former than for the latter. The only question is how much.

---

12. I have little doubt that Jespersen could have made some kind of a record in order to establish that the "Personal Best" policies are more burdensome for women than for men. The cost of makeup and time needed to apply it can both be quantified as can, for example, the cost of haircuts and time needed for nail trimming; had a record been offered in this case to establish the alleged undue burden on women, the district court could have evaluated it.

## Notes

1. Did the court hold that a make-up requirement could never constitute an unequal burden? What additional evidence could Jespersen have presented to persuade the court that Harrah's grooming requirements constituted an equal burden on women?

2. It is common for courts to approve of codes requiring different hair lengths and requiring men to shave facial hair. Rationales for upholding such requirements vary, but include the simple observation that hair length is a personal preference, rather than an immutable characteristic; the fact that such code requirements have a *de minimis* effect on employment opportunities; and the fact that these requirements are customary. In the context of race discrimination claims, courts have concluded that prohibitions against braided hairstyles do not violate Title VII because they represent choices, rather than immutable characteristics. *See Rogers v. American Airlines*, 527 F. Supp. 229 (S.D. N.Y 1981). On the other hand, the *Rogers* court suggested that a grooming policy prohibiting an "Afro/bush style" might constitute employment discrimination because such a natural hairstyle is tied to an immutable characteristic. *Id.* at 232.

3. Some dress code regulations do constitute an impermissible, undue burden on one gender. For example, in the case of *Carrol v. Talaman Federal Savings and Loan*, the court found that requiring women to wear a uniform while allowing men to wear general professional dress was an impermissible undue burden. 604 F.2d 1028 (7th Cir. 1979).

---

## Exercise 9.4

You are a practicing attorney. A law firm reads the *Jespersen* case and wants to apply the Personal Best policy to its attorneys, keeping the make-up requirements and tweaking other requirements to comport with the typical dress of attorneys. As part of the dress code, it wants to add the following:

On Mondays through Thursdays, all attorneys are required to wear suits. Female attorneys are required to wear pantyhose with any suit that shows their legs. Female attorneys may not wear open-toed shoes.

Friday is a casual work day.

On Friday, attorneys may dress casually, unless appearing in court or attending meetings with clients. For men, casual dress means a pair of slacks, with a polo-style shirt or button-down oxford-style shirt. Loafers or other similarly-styled shoes may be worn.

Because women have more options for appropriate casual dress, the following limitations will apply:

No shorts.

Any skirts or dresses must be at or below the knee.

No sleeveless shirts or dresses.

No open-toed shoes.

Pantyhose must be worn with a skirt or a dress.

No inappropriately casual attire, such as T-shirts.

Think about how you would advise the law firm. Is such a policy legal? Is such a policy a good idea? What are the drawbacks? What are the benefits?

Now imagine that you are a plaintiff's attorney challenging this dress and appearance code. List all of the rationales a court might apply in evaluating such a case. Are there any additional arguments you might make? Do you think the law firm dress and appearance policy violates Title VII?

## National Origin

Title VII prohibits employment discrimination because of an individual's national origin. Recall that in *Espinoza v. Farah Manufacturing Co.*, 414 U.S. 86 (1973), the United States Supreme Court held that Title VII's prohibition against national origin discrimination does not encompass citizenship discrimination per se. The violation of Title VII occurs if, regardless of the employee's citizenship or immigration status, the employer takes an adverse employment action against the individual on the basis of his or her foreign birth, foreign ancestry, or characteristics associated with the person's national origin.

This national origin section covers three concepts: (1) how the employer's obligation to verify its employees' work authorization status may sometimes lead to national origin discrimination claims; (2) the employment discrimination rights of undocumented workers; and (3) the interaction between workplace communication rules and national origin discrimination.

### *Verification of Work Authorization Status and National Origin Discrimination*

A person's right to legally work in the United States is not necessarily based on U.S. *citizenship* status. United States citizens are entitled to work in the country. For non-citizens, the right to work legally is based on the person having a U.S. immigration status that *authorizes* the person to work in this country. Under the Immigration Reform and Control Act ("IRCA"), it is illegal for a person to work in the United States unless he or she possesses a status that permits the person to legally work in this country. Authorized legal aliens who have a visa or residency status that permits them to legally work in this country are also entitled to legally work. Aliens who do not have an immigration status that allows them to work legally in this country—undocumented workers—cannot *legally* work. IRCA makes it a crime for undocumented workers to produce fraudulent work authorization documents in an attempt to obtain employment in this country. 8 U.S.C. § 1324c(a). Primarily for economic reasons, millions of undocumented workers do currently work in the United States even though IRCA criminalizes such conduct. *See* Christopher Ho and Jennifer C. Chang, *The 40th Anniversary of Title VII of the Civil Rights Act of 1964 Symposium: Drawing the Line after* Hoffman Plastics Compounds, Inc. v. NLRB: *Strategies for Protecting Undocumented Workers in the Title VII Context and Beyond*, 22 Hofstra Lab. & Emp. L. J. 473, 476–77 (2005).

Federal immigration law places a burden on employers to check whether their employees are legally entitled to work. IRCA prohibits an employer's hiring of an alien "knowing" that the alien is not authorized to work in this country. 8 U.S.C. § 1324a(1)(A). IRCA also imposes a requirement on employers to verify an employee's work-authorization documents at the outset of the employment relationship. 8 U.S.C. § 1324a(b)(1)(A), § 1324a(a)(1)(B)(i). The verification obligation requires the employer to examine the employee's work-authorization documents, such as a Social Security card, state driver's license card, certified copy of a birth certificate, permanent resident card, and to see if the documents appear to be reasonable on their face. *Collins Foods International, Inc. v. INS*, 948 F.2d 546 (9th Cir. 1991).

Title VII's national origin discrimination prohibition and the IRCA requirement that obligates employers to verify a person's work-authorization status may create competing pressures on the employer. Consider in the following case whether the employer found itself stuck between a rock and a hard place.

---

### Focus Questions: *Zamora v. Elite Logistics, Inc.*

1. *How far should an employer "push" an investigation into "suspicious circumstances" regarding an applicant or employee's work-authorization status?*

2. *Does an employer face greater legal exposure if it takes a hard-line approach to checking work-authorization status or if its approach is more lax?*

3. *What might penalizing employers for hiring undocumented workers encourage employers to do?*

---

# Zamora v. Elite Logistics, Inc.

478 F.3d 1160 (10th Cir. 2007) (en banc)

Circuit Judge Ebel.

Plaintiff Ramon Zamora sued his former employer, Elite Logistics, Incorporated, under Title VII of the Civil Rights Act, alleging Elite discriminated against Zamora because of his race and national origin (1) by suspending Zamora from work until he presented documentation establishing his right to work in the United States; and (2) then, after reinstating Zamora, firing him after he requested an apology. The district court granted Elite summary judgment on both claims. A divided panel of this court reversed that decision. After rehearing this appeal en banc, this court vacates the panel's decision. As to Zamora's first claim involving Zamora's suspension, because the en banc court is evenly divided, we simply affirm the district court's decision granting Elite summary judgment. As to the second claim involving Zamora's termination, a majority of this court affirms summary judgment in Elite's favor.

I. Background

Viewing the evidence in the light most favorable to Zamora, the evidence in the record established the following: Elite operates a grocery warehouse in Kansas City, Kansas. In June 2000, Elite needed to hire an additional 300 workers in just a few weeks' time. In doing so, Elite failed to verify that all of its new employees were authorized to work in the United States.

A year later, in August 2001, Elite hired Zamora. At that time, Zamora was a Mexican citizen who had been a permanent legal resident of the United States since 1987. As part of the hiring process and in compliance with the Immigration Reform and Control Act of 1986 ("IRCA"), Zamora showed Elite his social security card, which he had had since 1980 or 1981, and his alien registration card. Zamora also filled out an I-9 form truthfully indicating that he was a Mexican citizen and a lawful permanent resident of the United States.

Four months after hiring Zamora, in December 2001, Elite received a tip that the Immigration and Naturalization Service (INS) was going to investigate warehouses in the area.[13] Elite was particularly concerned about such an investigation in light of its earlier hiring practices in June 2000. Elite, therefore, hired two independent contractors to check the social security numbers of all 650 Elite employees. This investigation indicated that someone other than Zamora had been using the same social security number that he was using. The investigation turned up similar problems with thirty-five other employees' social security numbers.

On May 10, 2002, therefore, Elite's human resources manager, Larry Tucker, met specifically with Zamora and gave him an "Important Memorandum," written in Spanish and English, giving him ten days to produce adequate documentation of his right to work in the United States. Tucker followed this same procedure with the other thirty-five employees whose social security numbers raised concerns.[14] The memorandum Tucker gave Zamora and the other affected workers read:

> It is required by federal law that all employees produce documents, which establish their identity and/or employment eligibility to legally work in the United States when they are hired. This eligibility can be established with a US Passport, a Certificate of Citizenship or Naturalization; or with a combination of other documents, such as a state's driver's license, state or federal ID card, US Social Security card and/or a certified copy of a birth certificate, issued by a state of the United States.
>
> It has come to our attention that the documents you provided us previously are questionable. Therefore, we are asking that you obtain proper documentation, or you may not be permitted to continue working here. Please bring proper evidence of your identity and employment eligibility no later than 5:00 p.m. on Monday, May 20, 2002, to the Department of Human Resources, or you may be terminated.
>
> Thank you.

At the bottom of this memorandum there was a place where Zamora indicated that

> I understand and agree that until and if I provide documents, which establish my identity and/or employment eligibility to legally work in the United States, Elite Logistics may not be able to continue permitting me to work. I also understand and agree that I have until 5:00 p.m. on Monday, May 20, 2002, to produce this documentation.

Zamora signed and dated that section of the memorandum. Zamora testified in his deposition that he understood at that time that he needed to bring in a valid social security card and documents establishing that he had a right to work in the United States. Zamora continued working during this ten-day period.

Zamora did not present Elite with any of the requested documents by May 20, 2002. Therefore, Tucker again met with Zamora and, according to Zamora, Tucker told him that he could not "come to work anymore until you got a different Social Security number." Zamora left Tucker's office and returned that same day with a document from the Social Security Administration showing wage earnings for the years 1978–85 for an "R. Zamora" under Zamora's social security number. This document had been mailed to an address

---

13. INS's duties were transferred to the Department of Homeland Security in 2003 and the INS no longer exists.

14. Most of these thirty-five employees, when asked for this documentation, just quit. Only Zamora eventually provided paperwork verifying his right to work in the United States.

in Washington, which Zamora had scratched out and replaced with his then-current Missouri address. More problematic, however, was that the date of birth for R. Zamora on this earnings statement was different than the date of birth Ramon Zamora had given Elite at the time Elite hired him. After reviewing the earnings statement, Tucker became concerned that yet a third individual had been using Zamora's social security number. Therefore, Tucker informed Zamora that this earnings statement was not "acceptable." Neither was an INS document Zamora showed Tucker that indicated that Zamora had previously applied to become a United States citizen.

At some point, Zamora also showed Tucker his naturalization certificate, indicating that Zamora had in fact become a naturalized citizen of the United States. But Tucker rejected that document as well.

The next day, May 23, Zamora brought Tucker a statement from the Social Security Administration indicating that the social security number Zamora had given Elite was in fact his number. Tucker then told Zamora that "[w]e will check this out ourselves. And if it checks out, you can come back to work." Tucker's assistant verified this document's authenticity and then called Zamora, asking him to return to work on May 29.

On May 29, however, instead of returning to work, Zamora went to Tucker's office and handed him a letter stating that "[b]efore I could consider going back to work I need from you two things: 1) an apology in writing, and 2) a complete explanation of why I was terminated. Please send a response to my home." Tucker refused to apologize. Tucker may then have told Zamora to get out of Tucker's office or the building, or to "[j]ust get the hell out." According to Zamora, Tucker also told him he was fired....

III. DISCUSSION

In alleging that Elite discriminated against him on the basis of his race and national origin, Zamora challenges two separate incidents: 1) Elite's suspending Zamora from work until he was able to produce documentation establishing his right to work in the United States; and 2) after Elite reinstated him, Elite's decision to fire Zamora after he requested an explanation and an apology.

A. Suspension

The district court granted Elite summary judgment on the suspension claim, after applying *McDonnell Douglas*'s burden-shifting analysis and concluding that Zamora had established a prima facie discrimination claim, but that Elite had proffered a legitimate, nondiscriminatory reason for suspending Zamora, and Zamora had failed to create a triable issue of fact as to whether or not Elite's proffered justification was merely a pretext for discrimination. A divided panel of this court reversed that decision, determining that Zamora had presented sufficient evidence to create a triable fact as to whether Elite's stated reason for requiring Zamora to produce this documentation — that Elite was trying to avoid INS sanctions — was merely a pretext for race and national origin discrimination. After rehearing en banc, this court is evenly divided on this issue. For that reason, we simply vacate the earlier panel opinion and affirm the district court's decision granting Elite summary judgment on this claim.

B. Termination

Zamora also alleged that Elite discriminated against him on the basis of his race and national origin when Elite fired Zamora after he requested an apology. [The majority assumed that Zamora established a prima facie case on the discrimination claim]. Zamora concedes that Elite asserted a legitimate, nondiscriminatory reason for firing Zamora — its human resources manager, Tucker, believed that Zamora would not return to work unless Tucker apologized, and Tucker refused to apologize. Elite's proffered justification was sufficient for Elite to meet its "exceedingly light" burden under *McDonnell Douglas* and shift the burden back to Zamora to show that Elite's proffered justification was merely a pretext for race and national origin discrimination.

Zamora argues that Elite's proffered reason for terminating Zamora was not worthy of belief because Tucker could not have reasonably believed that Zamora had actually conditioned his return to work on Zamora apologizing. And the undisputed evidence in this case establishes that, although Elite informed Zamora he could return to work on May 29, Zamora did not return to work but instead went to Tucker's office and gave him the letter. And that letter specifically stated that "[b]efore I could consider going back to work I need from you two things: 1) an *apology in writing*, and 2) a complete explanation of why I was terminated. Please send a response to my home." (Emphasis added). Further, because Zamora had asked that Tucker's written apology be sent to his home, Tucker could have reasonably believed that Zamora was not going to return to work on May 29, as Elite had requested. Based upon these undisputed facts known to Tucker, he could reasonably have believed that Zamora was not going to return to work unless Tucker apologized.

Zamora argues that Tucker's strong reaction to Zamora's request for a written apology and explanation indicates that his proffered reason for terminating Zamora was a pretext for his true discriminatory motive. Zamora testified that when he gave Tucker the letter requesting a written explanation and apology, Tucker grabbed it out of Zamora's hand and told Zamora he was fired "because [Tucker] was not apologizing to anybody." But there is simply no evidence in the record indicating that Tucker's reaction was because Zamora was a Mexican-born Hispanic. In fact, the evidence indicates just the opposite. Once Zamora provided Elite with documentation indicating that he was eligible to work in the United States, and that the social security number he was using was his, Tucker offered Zamora his job back. If Tucker was discriminating against Zamora based upon his race or national origin, Tucker would not have reinstated him. There is nothing in the record to suggest that Tucker was not going to permit Zamora to return to work on May 29; in fact, the undisputed evidence indicates that Zamora could have returned to work that day. Under the facts of this case, then, Tucker's suspending Zamora and his later decision to terminate Zamora's employment must be viewed as discrete, separate events. Tucker did not terminate Zamora until Zamora requested a written explanation and apology as a condition for his returning to work. And even Zamora concedes that Elite had no legal obligation to apologize. We agree with that. Nor is there any suggestion that Tucker had ever treated similarly situated employees who were not Hispanic or Mexican-born any differently. Because Zamora failed to present sufficient evidence establishing a genuinely disputed issue of fact as to whether or not Elite's proffered reason for firing Zamora was a pretext for discrimination, summary judgment for Elite was warranted on this claim.

[Two concurring opinions are omitted.]

Circuit Judge McConnell, joined by several other judges, concurring.

Elite claims that its reason for demanding additional documentation from Mr. Zamora was a good faith—even if flawed—attempt to comply with the Immigration Reform and Control Act of 1986. IRCA is relevant here in two respects. First, the statute prohibits the knowing employment of unauthorized aliens and places affirmative burdens on employers to verify the identity and employment eligibility of employees, at the hiring stage, by examining certain documents specified by statute and regulation. *See* 8 U.S.C. §§ 1324a(a)(1)(A)-(B), 1324a(b); 8 C.F.R. § 274a.2(b)(1)(ii) & (v). The statute provides that, at the time of initial hiring, compliance "in good faith with the[se] requirements ... with respect to the hiring ... for employment of an alien in the United States ... establish[es] an affirmative defense that [the employer] has not violated" the above provisions. 8 U.S.C. § 1324a(a)(3). IRCA also makes it unlawful for an employer "to continue to employ [an] alien in the United States knowing the alien is (or has become) an unauthorized alien with respect to such employment." *Id.* § 1324a(a)(2). It is this latter obligation—combined with the range of civil and criminal penalties that await employers who violate IRCA, *see id.* § 1324a(e)-(f)—that Elite claims prompted its actions in this case.

Second, IRCA has created employer incentives to protect against the significant disruption that may occur when immigration enforcement agents inspect a workplace and find workers out of compliance. As the then-Acting Deputy Director of United States Citizenship and Immigration Services ("USCIS") explained in recent congressional testimony:

> [O]ne of the primary reasons for a human resources manager to push participation in [a voluntary program for employee verification] was to avoid that moment when the INS would come in and raid the place and take away half the workers, and make it impossible to make any kind of production. That's the kind of event that gets the human resources manager fired, and that's the kind of event that they would try to plan against.

[citation omitted]. As recent events around the country illustrate, this is not an obligation that employers can afford to take lightly. One of the principal methods of ensuring employee eligibility is verification of Social Security numbers. Indeed, this is the key feature of the federal government's Basic Pilot Program—a voluntary employment eligibility verification system created by Congress in 1997. Employers who participate in Basic Pilot electronically submit information from a newly hired employee's I-9 form—name, date of birth, SSN, citizenship status (if provided)—for comparison with information on the SSA's primary database, irrespective of the facially compliant documents provided by the employee to satisfy I-9 requirements. If the information submitted by the employer matches SSA data, the employer is notified of the employee's verified, eligible status. If the employer-submitted data and SSA records are inconsistent, or if SSA cannot issue verification for some other reason, the employer-submitted information is then checked by USCIS. If eligibility still cannot be established, the government issues a "tentative nonconfirmation," and the employer must notify the employee of the finding. [citation omitted]. Employees are given eight federal workdays to contact USCIS or SSA and resolve the problem. If the employee chooses not to contest the tentative nonconfirmation, it is considered a "final nonconfirmation" and the employer may terminate the employee. If the employee does choose to contact the relevant agency and the agency resolves the issue, the employee must notify his employer and the employer must confirm the new result through the Basic Pilot computer system. If eligibility is still not established after this period and no further verification instructions are provided by the SSA, the employer is authorized to discharge the employee. If the employer chooses not to terminate an employee after issuance of a final nonconfirmation, it must notify USCIS. Failure to notify constitutes a violation of the Illegal Immigration Reform and Immigrant Responsibility Act of 1996 and may result in legal penalties. Compliance efforts have shifted to Social Security number verification because of the easy availability of forged documents and the prevalence of identity theft, which make other forms of documentation less reliable.... Reliance on data—SSN, name, birthdate, asserted citizenship status—rather than documents ameliorates this problem.

In his dissenting opinion, Judge Lucero writes at length about the anti-discrimination requirements contained within IRCA, 8 U.S.C. § 1324b(a), despite the fact that Mr.

Zamora has not alleged a violation of those provisions. Citing the text, legislative history, and implementing regulations of the IRCA provisions, the dissent seems to imply that our interpretation of Title VII ought to be guided by these provisions. That suggestion is unfounded because — as the dissent acknowledges — the IRCA anti-discrimination provisions were intended to "'broaden[] the Title VII protections against national origin discrimination, while not broadening other Title VII protections.'" [citation omitted]. This case arises under Title VII — not IRCA's anti-discrimination provisions — and the principles we interpret will apply across the board to all Title VII claims. It would be contrary to congressional intent for us to "broaden" Title VII by interpreting it to coincide with the IRCA anti-discrimination provisions. To confine our analysis to Title VII does not "go far in insulating employers from national origin discrimination claims," as the dissent charges. It simply respects the different reach of the two different statutes.

## IV.

Turning first to Mr. Zamora's suspension claim, I am at a loss to see how a reasonable factfinder could construe the sequence of events detailed above as discriminatory.

Through Mr. Zamora's suspension on or about May 22, and up to Mr. Tucker's rejection of Mr. Zamora's proffer of a naturalization certificate when he returned later that day or the next, Elite's actions are free of any taint of discrimination. When the company learned of the impending INS inspection, Elite undertook an examination of the Social Security numbers of all of its employees, without regard to their race or national origin. When it learned that thirty-five employees had irregularities regarding their Social Security numbers, Elite contacted all thirty-five and asked all thirty-five for documentation that would clear up these issues. Although Mr. Zamora complains that the company put the burden on the employees to prove their identity and eligibility rather than contacting the relevant government agencies itself, this approach was lawful, and more importantly was applied to all affected employees without regard to their race or national origin. No one disputes that the company's outside contractors uncovered evidence of irregularities in Mr. Zamora's SSN. No one disputes that it was lawful for the company to ask Mr. Zamora to clear up the discrepancy. No one disputes that the company gave Mr. Zamora sufficient time — ten days — to do so. And no one disputes that, twelve days after receiving notice, Mr. Zamora had failed to do anything to clear up the problem. At the time when Mr. Zamora was suspended from employment on May 22, therefore, no reasonable juror could find that he had been treated differently from any other employee, on the basis of his national origin.

The discriminatory suspension claim arises primarily from Mr. Zamora's allegation that he later presented Mr. Tucker with a certificate of naturalization, and that Mr. Tucker refused to accept it as sufficient resolution of his Social Security number irregularities. Because Mr. Zamora was the only employee of the thirty-five problem cases to reach this juncture, one cannot determine whether he was treated differently from other employees. But one can examine the circumstances for evidence that would allow a reasonable factfinder to draw an inference of discrimination. I find none.

Mr. Zamora argues that once he produced his naturalization certificate, it should have been sufficient to clear the company of any possible liability under IRCA. Any further requests for documentation, he argues, were inconsistent with the company's stated rationale and thus evidence of pretext. Similarly, Mr. Zamora contends that because the memorandum handed to him on May 10 stated that "eligibility can be established with ... a Certificate of Citizenship or Naturalization," Mr. Tucker's rejection of such a document is evidence of pretext. Lastly, Mr. Zamora argues that Mr. Tucker's personal demeanor is evidence of discrimination. I do not find these arguments convincing for several reasons.

A.

First, Mr. Zamora ignores the critical fact that in addition to presenting Mr. Tucker with his naturalization certificate he also presented him a Social Security document that displayed a birth date different from the one he had previously reported to Elite. This new development understandably heightened Mr. Tucker's suspicion regarding whether the SSN used by Mr. Zamora was legitimately his. The contemporaneous presentation of a naturalization certificate, which would not contain Mr. Zamora's SSN, would not have resolved the issue. As Mr. Tucker explained:

> [M]y concern with Mr. Zamora was could I find a document or a couple of documents that had the birthdate he was using, the name he was using, and the social security number he was using that verified that this is truly his? And when he brought [in the document with the different birth date,] in addition to the other concern that had been raised with this different birthdate, it appeared to me as if now we had possibly three individuals using this same card.

It may have been wrong, but it was not unreasonable for Mr. Tucker to believe that, under these circumstances, examination of the naturalization certificate would fail to bring the company into compliance with IRCA. IRCA makes it "unlawful for [an employer], after hiring an alien for employment in accordance with [IRCA's hiring procedures] to continue to employ the alien in the United States knowing the alien is (or has become) an unauthorized alien with respect to such employment." 8 U.S.C. § 1324a(a)(2). Thus, Mr. Tucker may have reasonably believed that while examination of a facially valid naturalization certificate would satisfy Elite's statutory duties at the *hiring stage, see* 8 U.S.C. § 1324a(a)(3), once the company was confronted with a *specific* question about a worker's documentation, it was under a duty to investigate and resolve that specific concern.

Indeed, case law interpreting IRCA supports Elite in this view. The Ninth Circuit has held that 8 U.S.C. § 1324a(a)(2) adopts a "constructive knowledge standard," whereby "a deliberate failure to investigate suspicious circumstances imputes knowledge" to an employer. [citation omitted]. As that court explained, employers share "part of [the] burden" of "proving or disproving that a person is unauthorized to work." Initial verification at the hiring stage is done through document inspection, but "[n]otice that these documents are incorrect places the employer in the position it would have been if the alien had failed to produce documents in the first place: it has failed to adequately ensure that the alien is authorized." [citation omitted]....

Whether or not this Court ultimately agrees with the Ninth Circuit's interpretation— which we need not decide in this case ... Mr. Tucker's diligence in seeking resolution of all reported SSN discrepancies was within the bounds of reasonableness and, therefore, that his continued focus on resolving Mr. Zamora's SSN problem does not constitute strong evidence of pretext.

Mr. Zamora's position appears to be that whenever an employer has "good" documents on file—that is, documents that facially comply with IRCA and for which questions have not been raised—the employer is barred from pursuing any suspicious circumstances that arise concerning other documents on file.... IRCA does not necessarily read that way, and I do not believe an employer should be held to have discriminated under Title VII for failing to adopt this somewhat surprising reading of its responsibilities. Indeed, if any action beyond facial examination of eligibility documents is discriminatory, then the entire Basic Pilot Program—which is designed to curb the growing problems of document fraud and identity theft—might be called into question, since it is premised on the examination of data discrepancies rather than documents.

Circuit Judge Lucero, joined by four judges, dissenting.

... Although half of the members of this court agree that Zamora presented sufficient evidence of pretext as to his continued suspension, the majority opinion concludes that the record contains no evidence that Tucker terminated Zamora because Zamora was a "Mexican-born Hispanic." This ignores the events surrounding Zamora's suspension, which had ended a mere four days before. I fail to understand how we can be evenly divided over whether Tucker was motivated by racial bias against Mexican-Americans on May 25, and yet issue a majority opinion concluding that Tucker had no racial motivations as a matter of law on May 29....

III.

Although the concurrence would hold that Zamora's suspension claim fails as a matter of law, in my view Zamora has presented sufficient evidence to survive summary judgment on this claim. The parties do not dispute that Zamora has satisfied the first step of *McDonnell Douglas* by pleading a prima facie case of discriminatory suspension. Therefore, the burden shifted to Elite to articulate a legitimate nondiscriminatory reason for its actions. Elite contends it was merely attempting to comply with IRCA in suspending Zamora for approximately a week without pay. This case is accordingly decided at the last step of *McDonnell Douglas*, in which Zamora must offer evidence showing that the proffered reason is pretextual.

A.

Because Tucker effectively conceded that his actions were not driven by IRCA—he admitted he no longer had concerns about Zamora's right to work in this country as of May 22, 2002—I see little merit in providing an in-depth discussion of the statute. Nevertheless, because I differ greatly from the concurrence in my view of IRCA's requirements and restrictions, I briefly outline my thoughts on this matter.

IRCA was designed to curb the influx of undocumented immigrants by creating a regime of sanctions against employers that hire them. Toward this end, the Act requires employers to verify the identity and eligibility of employees at the time of hiring by examining certain documents. 8 U.S.C. § 1324a(a)(1)(B), (b). Well-meaning employers are provided with significant legal protection at the hiring stage because they are allowed to assert "good faith" compliance with IRCA as an affirmative defense to liability. *Id.* § 1324a(a)(3). IRCA also declares that requesting "more or additional documents" at hiring than those specifically identified in the Act "shall be treated as an unfair immigration-related employment practice." *Id.* § 1324b(a)(6). After the employment relationship is established, IRCA makes it unlawful to "continue to employ [an] alien in the United States knowing the alien is (or has become) an unauthorized alien with respect to such employment." *Id.* § 1324a(a)(2).

Employer sanctions, however, represent only one side of the IRCA coin. When IRCA was initially debated, advocates and members of Congress voiced widespread concerns that the Act would become a tool of invidious discrimination against Hispanic-Americans and other minorities. Although the original bill introducing IRCA did not contain strong anti-discrimination measures, the full House voted to include a significant anti-discrimination amendment. [citation omitted]. Explaining its support for this amendment, the House Committee on Education and Labor stated:

> The [committee] strongly endorses [the anti-discrimination amendment] and ...
> has consistently expressed its fear that the imposition of employer sanctions will

give rise to employment discrimination against Hispanic Americans and other minority group members. It is the committee's view that if there is to be sanctions enforcement and liability there must be an equally strong and readily available remedy if resulting employment discrimination occurs.

In adopting the House amendment to the bill, the Joint Senate and House Conference Committee ("Conference Committee") agreed "[t]he antidiscrimination provisions of this bill are a complement to the sanctions provisions, and must be considered in this context." [citation omitted]. It went on to explain that the provisions "broaden[] the Title VII protections against national origin discrimination, while not broadening the other Title VII protections, because of the concern of some Members that people of 'foreign' appearance *might be made more vulnerable* by the imposition of sanctions." [citation omitted].

Because members of Congress believed that IRCA might not in fact prompt employers to discriminate and the anti-discrimination provisions could thus be unnecessary, the Conference Committee adopted a clause providing, "[t]he antidiscrimination provisions would ... be repealed in the event of a joint resolution approving a [General Accounting Office] finding that the sanctions had resulted in no significant discrimination." *See* 8 U.S.C. § 1324b(k)(2). In 1990, the General Accounting Office ("GAO") released a report to Congress, finding IRCA had indeed resulted in a "serious pattern" of national origin discrimination. [citation omitted]. Thus, IRCA—as enacted, and as it stands today— declares that "[i]t is an unfair immigration-related employment practice for a person or other entity to discriminate against any individual ... with respect to the hiring, or recruitment or referral for a fee, of the individual for employment or the discharging of the individual from employment ... because of such individual's national origin." 8 U.S.C. § 1324b(a)(1)(A).

The concurrence would go far in insulating employers from national origin discrimination claims. It suggests that because employers face sanctions for knowingly continuing to employ unauthorized aliens, employers should be given a virtual safe-harbor against Title VII claims for investigating an employee, so long as they cite IRCA to defend their actions. Assuredly, employers should undertake meaningful investigation if an employee's lawful work status is legitimately called into question. However, fear of sanction for "knowing" employment of unauthorized aliens cannot justify discriminatory precautionary measures. Indeed, regulations implementing IRCA expressly warn employers:

> Knowledge that an employee is unauthorized may not be inferred from an employee's foreign appearance or accent. Nothing in [the definition of knowing] should be interpreted as permitting an employer to request more or different documents than are required under section 274A(b) of the Act or to refuse to honor documents tendered that on their face reasonably appear to be genuine and to relate to the individual.

Adopting the concurrence's approach would undoubtedly narrow the scope of recovery for national origin discrimination claims. This result thwarts Congress's clear intent in passing IRCA to "broaden[] the Title VII protections against national origin discrimination" and to prescribe a "strong and readily available remedy" for such discrimination. [citation omitted]. Due consideration of IRCA does not and should not preclude examination of whether Zamora presented evidence sufficient to reach a jury on his Title VII claims.

B.

[The dissent explained why sufficient evidence of pretext existed to survive summary judgment.] Zamora has consistently argued that Elite's proffered reason for his suspension—a desire to verify Zamora's right to work in the United States—is pretextual. In support of his allegation of pretext, he identifies four pieces of evidence. First, Zamora points to Tucker's own admission that concern over Zamora's right to work did not underlie his decision to continue Zamora's suspension. Zamora contends that this admission demonstrates that Tucker did not have a good faith belief in the proffered justification of IRCA compliance. Second, Zamora notes that Elite's May 10, 2002 written memorandum informed him that a naturalization certificate would be sufficient to clear up concerns over his work status. In rejecting Zamora's proffer of a naturalization certificate, Elite thus violated its own written policy. Third, although a neutral decisionmaker would realize the fact that someone else had used Zamora's SSN did not resolve whether Zamora was the perpetrator or the victim of identity theft, Zamora testified that Tucker accused him of stealing someone else's SSN despite Zamora's protestations to the contrary. Tucker's immediate conclusion that Zamora stole his SSN could reasonably support an inference of discriminatory intent on the part of Tucker. Finally, Zamora has shown that Elite has acted contrary to its alleged good-faith attempt to comply with IRCA, even during the period of his suspension. After Zamora vigorously asserted that his original social security number was correct and true, Tucker instructed Zamora to return to him with a different SSN. Together this evidence demonstrates "weaknesses, implausibilities, inconsistencies, incoherencies, or contradictions" in Elite's proffered reason of IRCA compliance, such that a reasonable factfinder could find that reason "unworthy of credence." ...

## Notes

1. *Electronic Verification.* Immigration law requires employers to facially examine an applicant's work eligibility document at the hiring stage. As Judge McConnell points out in his concurring opinion, facial examination of an eligibility document is unlikely to uncover document fraud or identity theft. What makes it especially difficult for employers is that there are a wide variety of documents that may lawfully demonstrate eligibility to work in the United States and employers are not counterfeit experts. *See* 8 U.S.C. § 1324a(b)(1) (listing documents). Because it is relatively easy for individuals to obtain fraudulent workplace eligibility documents that look like the real thing, the movement is toward electronic verification of eligibility status by employers. The current name of this electronic verification program is E-Verify. E-Verify is an Internet-based system operated by the Department of Homeland Security in conjunction with the Social Security Administration. Through this system employers can go to E-Verify on-line and compare an employee's Form I-9 information with hundreds of millions of records in the Social Security Administration and Department of Homeland Security databases to check for discrepancies. For most employers, the use of E-Verify is voluntary. Under Executive Order 12,989, as amended, federal contractors are required to electronically verify all employees working on federal contracts. *See* 73 Fed. Reg. 33,285 (2008). More than 200,000 employers are currently participating in the E-Verify program. *See* www.dhs.gov and www.uscis.gov (last visited May 28, 2010). One of the issues in the national debate concerning comprehensive immigration reform is whether to make electronic verification mandatory for all employers.

2. *Federal Government Enforcement.* U.S. Immigrations and Customs Enforcement (ICE), the largest investigative agency in the Department of Homeland Security, is the federal agency that enforces the laws requiring employers to verify work authorization status and prohibiting them from knowingly employing undocumented workers. *See* Homeland Security Act of 2002 §§ 441, 451, 471, 6 U.S.C. §§ 251, 271, 291 (Supp. II 2002).

3. *Public Policy.* It is apparent that the verification requirement puts employers on the front lines of enforcing federal immigration policy. *Zamora* suggests that employers who are aggressively challenging an applicant or employee on suspect documents or suspicious circumstances may run the risk of creating facts that lead to a national origin discrimination claim. Consider the following questions.

- Is the verification requirement an appropriate and necessary tool in the effort to stop the flow of illegal immigration, and is it working? What changes, if any, should be made to verification?

- Are the public policy goals in Title VII and IRCA appropriately balanced and harmonized by the *Zamora* decision?

- Would Elite have treated Mr. Zamora the same way if he spoke English as his first language and his name was John Smith?

### Undocumented Workers and Discrimination

The federal immigration laws aim to prevent undocumented workers from working in the United States. The reality, however, is that millions of undocumented workers perform work each day in this country in contravention of the federal immigration laws. Do the laws prohibiting discrimination in employment — ADA, ADEA, Title VII — apply to protect undocumented workers in the same manner that they protect workers who are citizens or authorized aliens? Stated differently, what employment discrimination rights and remedies apply to undocumented workers? The answer is that undocumented workers generally have the same rights as legal workers to be free from illegal employment discrimination under the federal employment discrimination statutes, but there is some question whether undocumented workers are entitled to the same remedies as legal workers for violations of those statutes. The following excerpt summarizes the current state of the law.

---

### Focus Questions: *Employment Law Remedies for Illegal Immigrants*

1. *What are the policy justifications for precluding undocumented workers from recovering back pay in a Title VII suit? Do you agree with those reasons?*

2. *What effect might allowing employers to discover information regarding Title VII plaintiffs' immigration status under the Federal Rules of Civil Procedure have on employment discrimination litigation?*

---

## Jarod S. Gonzalez, *Employment Law Remedies for Illegal Immigrants*

40 Tex. Tech. L. Rev. 987, 989–993 (2008) (article footnotes omitted)

... In *Hoffman Plastic Compounds, Inc. v. NLRB*, 535 U.S. 137, 151–152 (2002), the Supreme Court of the United States held that the National Labor Relations Board (NLRB) could not award back pay to an undocumented worker who had proven that his employer had discharged him for engaging in union-organizing activities in violation of the National

Labor Relations Act (NLRA). In a 5–4 decision, the Court ruled that the NLRB did not have the authority to award back pay to an undocumented worker because such an award would undermine the IRCA's immigration policies. The Court stated that an illegal immigrant may [not] work in the United States without either the employer or the illegal immigrant violating the IRCA.... The Court found that Congress could not have intended to allow the NLRB discretion to award back pay "to an undocumented worker who did not perform any work during the back pay period, could not legally have worked during the back pay period, and committed a crime by ... obtaining the job through falsified documents." *Id.* at 148–149.

The dissenters saw things differently. They focused on the idea that a back pay remedy has important deterrence purposes for employers who violate federal labor laws. A back pay award requires the employer to pay a monetary penalty for violating the law and thus encourages compliance. If an employer knows that it will not be required to provide back pay when it illegally fires an undocumented worker, the employer might have an incentive to hire undocumented workers instead of authorized workers because the labor law violations will cost it less. Moreover, the dissenters argued that unlawfully earned wages and criminal fraud by undocumented workers do not help resolve the back pay question because an employer might have believed, albeit in error, that the undocumented worker could lawfully work in the United States, and the enforcement of a back pay award makes the employer pay a meaningful monetary penalty for violating an important labor law. The dissenters also noted that the IRCA itself does not state how an IRCA violation affects the enforcement of other laws such as the NLRA.

For the most part, the courts and the Department of Labor (DOL) have distinguished the *Hoffman* decision in the context of the Fair Labor Standards Act (FLSA). The FLSA generally requires that employers pay a minimum wage to all employees and overtime wages to nonexempt employees. The DOL asserts that the FLSA provides core labor protections for vulnerable workers and, thus, that immigration status does not affect the remedies available to a worker who suffers an FLSA violation. The DOL distinguishes the *Hoffman* decision because the Supreme Court in that case was concerned about awarding back pay "for years of work not performed, for wages that could not lawfully have been earned." *U.S. Dep't of Labor, Fact Sheet #48: Application of U.S. Labor Laws to Immigrant Workers: Effect of Hoffman Plastics Decision on Laws Enforced by the Wage and Hour Division,* http://www.dol.gov/esa/regs/compliance/whd/whdfs48.pdf (last visited June 4, 2008). In contrast, under the FLSA, the employee or the DOL may seek back pay "for hours an employee has actually worked, under laws that require payment for such work." *Id.*

The federal district courts that have considered whether undocumented workers are entitled to unpaid wages under the FLSA have generally ruled that such workers are entitled to their earned wages under the law. These courts typically rely on the distinction between the *Hoffman* "no work performed" and the FLSA "work performed" scenarios. These courts also note that the FLSA text does not define covered employees based on immigration status.

The work performed distinction is not available in Title VII discrimination cases brought by undocumented workers. It seems fairly clear that the public policy reasons for precluding back pay recovery in NLRA cases are present to the same degree in Title VII cases. Permitting an undocumented worker to recover back pay under Title VII poses the same problems as it does under the NLRA because it awards back pay to an undocumented worker who did not perform any labor, who will have illegally earned his wages, and who committed fraud by obtaining the job using false documents. Moreover, there is no principled reason for concluding that protecting all individuals equally from unlawful discrimination, regardless of immigration status, is any more important than protecting all individuals equally from retaliation for engaging in union-organizing activities, regardless of immigration status. Both are laudable goals, yet they must yield to immigration policy.

Nonetheless, the courts that have evaluated whether *Hoffman* precludes undocumented workers from seeking Title VII back pay have generally been reluctant to find it unavailable. Sometimes these courts focus on slight textual differences between the NLRA and the relevant statute, and avoid the underlying question of whether providing the same remedies to undocumented workers promotes sound immigration policy. For example, in *Rivera v. NIBCO*, 364 F.3d 1057 (9th Cir. 2004), a national origin discrimination action asserted by plaintiffs suspected by the employer to be undocumented, the Ninth Circuit indicated that *Hoffman* does not control in the Title VII context because of three key differences between the NLRA and Title VII. First, though the availability of private actions under the NLRA is severely limited, Title VII depends primarily on private actions for enforcement. Second, Title VII plaintiffs may seek remedies like compensatory and punitive damages, which are aimed at punishing and deterring employers from engaging in unlawful Title VII discrimination. But similar punitive and deterrent remedies are not available under the NLRA. Finally, *Hoffman* concerned limits on the remedial discretion of an administrative agency—the NLRB. In contrast, a federal court, not an administrative agency, has the authority to decide whether a Title VII statutory violation warrants a back pay award. Due to the broad nature of a federal court's authority to award back pay and interpret Title VII, the *Rivera* court deemed the *Hoffman* rationale irrelevant....

Given the uncertainty encompassing federal and state law in this area, management attorneys have latched on to *Hoffman* to inquire into an employment law plaintiff's immigration status during litigation. The liberal discovery rules under the Federal Rules of Civil Procedure arguably favor discovery of immigration status during pretrial litigation in employment cases. If the *Hoffman* decision applies to a particular employment claim, the relevancy standard is satisfied because a plaintiff's immigration status affects the settlement value of a case. This outcome occurs even though immigration status relates merely to damages, not liability. In general, discovery is not limited to relevant evidence of liability but includes damages as well. Most courts that address whether a defendant is entitled to discovery of a plaintiff's immigration status, however, tend to either bar discovery on relevancy grounds or prevent discovery during the liability phase of litigation because discovery may be reopened after a liability finding to determine damages. *See Avila-Blum v. Casa de Cambio Delgado, Inc.*, 236 F.R.D. 190, 191 (S.D.N.Y. 2006) (barring discovery into immigration status during the liability phase of litigation with prospect that the issue could be reopened at a later stage of the proceeding as appropriate in relation to damages).

### Workplace Communication and National Origin

The ability to communicate proficiently in the English language during working time is a requirement for many jobs. Two important national origin discrimination issues concern foreign accent discrimination and English-only rules.

This section first addresses foreign accent discrimination. Discrimination based on "the linguistic characteristics of a particular national origin group" may constitute national origin discrimination. 29 C.F.R. § 1606.1. For example, discriminating against an employee *just* because the employee speaks with a foreign accent is national origin discrimination in violation of Title VII. *See Carino v. Oklahoma Board of Regents*, 750 F.2d 815, 819 (10th

Cir. 1984). But an employer could have a legitimate reason to make decisions based on a person's foreign accent. The following is an excerpt from the EEOC guidance regarding foreign accent discrimination.

> Employers sometimes have legitimate business reasons for basing employment decisions on linguistic characteristics.... An employment decision based on foreign accent does not violate Title VII if an individual's accent materially interferes with the ability to perform job duties. This assessment depends upon the specific duties of the position in question and the extent to which the individual's accent affects his or her ability to perform job duties. Employers should distinguish between a merely discernible foreign accent and one that interferes with communication skills necessary to perform job duties. Generally, an employer may only base an employment decision on accent if effective oral communication in English is required to perform job duties and the individual's foreign accent materially interferes with his or her ability to communicate orally in English.

EEOC Compliance Manual on National Origin Discrimination, Number 915.003 (Dec. 2, 2002).

---

### Exercise 9.5

Seetha applies for a job as a customer service representative for a large health insurance company, Medcare. Seetha speaks English. The customer service position requires that representatives spend eight hours each working shift answering in English customer questions regarding health insurance claims. Medcare hires Seetha for a probationary term. During the probationary term, Seetha's supervisor monitors her job performance. The supervisor comes to the conclusion that Seetha's heavy Indian accent makes it difficult for customers to understand her over the telephone. This conclusion is partly based on multiple incidents in which Seetha's customers requested to speak to another customer service representative because these customers stated that they were having difficulty understanding her. The supervisor terminates Seetha's employment at the end of the probationary term. Does the termination constitute national origin discrimination in violation of Title VII? What are some types of jobs where effective oral communication in English is especially important?

---

It is becoming increasingly common for employers to adopt policies that limit employees' rights to communicate on the job in languages other than English. These are referred to as "English-only rules." English-only rules tend to disproportionately impact persons based on national origin, but appropriately crafted policies that address situations in which the English-only rule serves a legitimate business purpose do not violate Title VII. The following is an excerpt from the EEOC regarding the legality of English-only rules.

> Title VII permits employers to adopt English-only rules under certain circumstances. As with any other workplace policy, an English-only rule must be adopted for nondiscriminatory reasons. An English-only rule would be unlawful if it were adopted with the intent to discriminate on the basis of national origin. Likewise, a policy that prohibits some but not all of the foreign languages spoken in a workplace, such as a no-Navajo rule, would be unlawful. Even where an English-only rule has

been adopted for nondiscriminatory reasons, the employer's use of the rule should relate to specific circumstances in its workplace. An English-only rule is justified by "business necessity" if it is needed for an employer to operate safely or efficiently.

EEOC Compliance Manual on National Origin Discrimination, Number 915.003 (Dec. 2, 2002).

The EEOC lists several situations in which business necessity would justify an English-only rule including: for communications with customers, co-workers, or supervisors who only speak English; in emergencies or other situations in which workers must speak a common language to promote safety; for cooperative work assignments in which the English-only rule is needed to promote efficiency; and to enable a supervisor who only speaks English to monitor the performance of an employee whose job duties require communication with coworkers or customers. Employers who adopt English-only policies should have evidence to prove that such policies further their communication, supervision, or safety needs. *Id.*

---

### Focus Questions: *Maldonado v. City of Altus*

1. *Why are disparate impact and disparate treatment claims applicable to this challenge to the City's English-only policy?*

2. *Does the English-only policy restrict the plaintiffs from speaking Spanish while on breaks and during nonwork periods?*

3. *What spurred the City to create the English-only policy? Do you believe the City had a legitimate business reason for the policy?*

4. *What steps could the City have taken to prevent the written policy and the implementation of the policy from creating a hostile working environment for the Hispanic employees?*

5. *Why would it be offensive to a non-Spanish speaker to be present when co-employees are speaking Spanish during a non-work related conversation? Even if some non-Spanish speakers are offended or do not like hearing a foreign language, why should that matter?*

---

# Maldonado v. City of Altus

### 433 F.3d 1294 (10th Cir. 2006)

Circuit Judge Hartz.

Plaintiffs are employees of the City of Altus, Oklahoma. They appeal the district court's grant of summary judgment dismissing all their claims against the City, the City Administrator, and the Street Commissioner. All claims arise out of the City's English-only policy for its employees. Asserting claims of both disparate-impact and disparate-treatment, Plaintiffs contend that the English-only policy discriminates against them on the basis of race and national origin in violation of Titles VI and VII of the Civil Rights Act of 1964.... We reverse and remand with respect to Plaintiffs' claims against the City alleging disparate impact and disparate treatment under Title VII....

## I. BACKGROUND

### A. Factual Background

Plaintiffs' claims stem from the City's promulgation of an English-only policy. Approximately 29 City employees are Hispanic, the only significant national-origin minority group affected by the policy. All Plaintiffs are Hispanic and bilingual, each speaking fluent English and Spanish.

In the spring of 2002 the City's Street Commissioner, Defendant Holmes Willis, received a complaint that because Street Department employees were speaking Spanish, other employees could not understand what was being said on the City radio. Willis informed the City's Human Resources Director, Candy Richardson, of the complaint, and she advised Willis that he could direct his employees to speak only English when using the radio for City business.

Plaintiffs claim that Willis instead told the Street Department employees that they could not speak Spanish at work at all and informed them that the City would soon implement an official English-only policy. On June 18, 2002, Plaintiff Tommy Sanchez wrote a letter to Ms. Richardson and the City Administrator, Defendant Michael Nettles, expressing concerns about the new Street Department English-only policy and the proposed citywide policy. Sanchez was particularly concerned that his subordinates, Plaintiffs Ruben Rios and Lloyd Lopez, had been told of a policy that he knew nothing about. Citing the City's Personnel Policies and Procedures Manual, the letter informed Nettles that employees had not been given proper notice if this was a new administrative policy and questioned whether Willis and the City had followed proper procedures in implementing the new policy. Sanchez reported that Willis had told him that the reason Hispanics speak Spanish "is because [of] ... insecurities," and that Willis had suggested that he (Sanchez) "would feel uncomfortable if another race would speak their native language in front of [him]." The letter requested that "the City of Altus understand that we Hispanics are proud of our heritage and do not feel that our ability to communicate in a bilingual manner is a hindrance or an embarrassment. There has never been a time that because I spoke Spanish to another Spanish speaking individual, I was unable to perform our job duties and requirements." At the end of the letter Rios and Lopez signed a paragraph stating that "the purpose of this correspondence is to serve as a discrimination complaint in accordance with the City of Altus Personnel Policies and Procedures Manual Section 102, in which we are requesting that an investigation be conducted into these charges and that a report be issued within two weeks." Another employee (Leticia Sanchez) also complained orally to Richardson about Willis's instructing employees not to speak Spanish in any circumstances during work hours.

In July 2002 the City promulgated the following official policy signed by Nettles:

> To insure effective communications among and between employees and various departments of the City, to prevent misunderstandings and to promote and enhance safe work practices, all work related and business communications during the work day shall be conducted in the English language with the exception of those circumstances where it is necessary or prudent to communicate with a citizen, *business owner, organization or criminal suspect* in his or her native language due to the person or entity's limited English language skills. *The use of the English language during work hours and while engaged in City business includes face to face communication of work orders and directions as well as communications utilizing telephones, mobile telephones, cellular telephones, radios, computer or e-mail transmissions and all written forms of communications.* If an employee or applicant for

employment believes that he or she cannot understand communications due to limited English language skills, the employee is to discuss the situation with the department head *and the Human Resources Director to determine what accommodation is required and feasible.* This policy does not apply to strictly private communications between co-workers while they are on approved lunch hours or breaks or before or after work hours *while the employees are still on City property* if City property is not being used for the communication. *Further,* this policy does not apply to strictly private communication between an employee and a family member *so long as the communications are limited in time and are not disruptive to the work environment.* Employees are encouraged to be sensitive to the feelings of their fellow employees, including a possible feeling of exclusion if a co-worker cannot understand what is being said in his or her presence when a language other than English is being utilized. (emphasis added).

Defendants state three primary reasons for adopting the policy: (1) workers and supervisors could not understand what was being said over the City's radios ... ; (2) non-Spanish speaking employees, both before and after the adoption of the Policy, informed management that they felt uncomfortable when their co-workers were speaking in front of them in a language they could not understand because they did not know if their co-workers were speaking about them; and (3) there were safety concerns with a non-common language being used around heavy equipment.

Although the district court observed "that there was no written record of any communication problems, morale problems or safety problems resulting from the use of languages other than English prior to implementation of the policy," it noted that Willis had testified that at least one employee complained about the use of Spanish by his co-workers before implementation of the policy and other non-Spanish speaking employees subsequently made similar complaints. Those city officials who were deposed could recount no incidents of safety problems caused by the use of a language other than English, but the district court found that some Plaintiffs were aware "that employee safety was one reason for the adoption of the policy." The court also stated that "it does not seem necessary that the City await an accident before acting."

Defendants offered evidence that the restrictions in the written policy were actually relaxed to allow workers to speak Spanish during work hours and on City property if everyone present understood Spanish. But Plaintiffs offered evidence that employees were told that the restrictions went beyond the written policy and prohibited all use of Spanish if a non-Spanish speaker was present, even during breaks, lunch hours, and private telephone conversations. Plaintiff Lloyd Lopez stated in his deposition that "we were told that the only time we could speak Spanish is when two of us are in a break room by ourselves, and if anybody other than Hispanic comes in, we are to change our language." In addition he said, "We no longer can speak about anything in general in Spanish around anybody. Even if we were on the phone talking to our wives and we were having a private conversation with them and somebody happened to walk by, we were to change our language because it would offend whoever was walking by."

Lopez understood, however, that the policy permitted him to speak Spanish if he was alone in a truck with another Spanish-speaking co-worker. Plaintiff Ruben Rios testified in his deposition that he similarly understood the policy to exclude the use of Spanish during breaks and the lunch hour if non-Hispanic co-workers were present. When asked specifically whether he understood that the policy allowed Spanish to be spoken between co-workers during lunch or other breaks, he stated that "as long as there was another Hispanic person, we could speak in Spanish but away from other individuals, non-Hispanic people." And Plaintiff Tommy Sanchez testified that he was told that he could not speak Spanish at all, but added that Richardson explained to him that "that's not the way [the City] meant it." The City has not disciplined anyone for violating the English-only policy.

Plaintiffs allege that the policy created a hostile environment for Hispanic employees, causing them "fear and uncertainty in their employment," and subjecting them to racial and ethnic taunting. They contend "that the English-only rule created a hostile environment because it pervasively — every hour of every work day — burdened, threatened and demeaned the [Plaintiffs] because of their Hispanic origin." Plaintiffs each stated in their affidavits:

> The English-only policy affects my work environment every day. It reminds me every day that I am second-class and subject to rules for my employment that the Anglo employees are not subject to. I feel that this rule is hanging over my head and can be used against me at any point when the City wants to have something to write me [up] for.

Evidence of ethnic taunting included Plaintiffs' affidavits stating that they had "personally been teased and made the subject of jokes directly because of the English-only policy[,]" and that they were "aware of other Hispanic co-workers being teased and made the subject of jokes because of the English-only policy." Plaintiff Tommy Sanchez testified in his deposition that each time he went to the City of Altus he was reminded of the restrictions on his speech by non-Hispanic employees. He stated that these other employees of the City of Altus "would pull up and laugh, start saying stuff in Spanish to us and said, 'They didn't tell us we couldn't stop. They just told you.'" Sanchez also testified that an Altus police officer taunted him about not being allowed to speak Spanish by saying, "Don't let me hear you talk Spanish." He further testified that "some of the guys from the street department would ... poke fun out of it [the policy]" and that when he went to other departments "they would bring it up constantly." As evidence that such taunting was not unexpected by management, Lloyd Lopez recounted in his deposition that Street Commissioner Willis told Ruben Rios and him that he was informing them of the English-only policy in private because Willis had concerns about "the other guys making fun of [them]." Plaintiffs also provided evidence that Mayor Gramling was "quoted in a newspaper article as referring to the Spanish language as 'garbage,'" although the Mayor claims that he used the word *garble* and was misquoted....

## B. Disparate Impact Claims

Plaintiffs remaining disparate impact claims arise under Title VII.... To prevail on these claims, Plaintiffs need not show that the policy was created with discriminatory intent. In the leading case on the subject, *Griggs v. Duke Power Co.*, 401 U.S. 424 (1971), the Supreme Court held that Title VII "proscribes not only overt discrimination but also practices that are fair in form, but discriminatory in operation." These kinds of claims, known as disparate-impact claims, "involve employment practices that are facially neutral in their treatment of different groups but that in fact fall more harshly on one group than another and cannot be justified by business necessity." [citation omitted]. To be sure, claims based on a hostile work environment commonly are disparate-treatment claims, which do require proof of discriminatory intent. Indeed, Plaintiffs here bring such a disparate-treatment claim as well as this discriminatory-impact claim. But there is no reason to prohibit discriminatory-impact claims predicated on a hostile work environment. *See generally* L. Camille Hebert, *The Disparate Impact of Sexual Harassment: Does Motive Matter?*, 53 U. KAN. L. REV. 341 (2005).

[The court set forth the allocation of the burdens of proof in disparate impact cases.]

## 1. Prima-facie case

The district court, relying principally on *Garcia v. Spun Steak Co.*, 998 F.2d 1480 (9th Cir. 1993), concluded that Plaintiffs had "not shown that requiring them to use the English language in the workplace imposed significant, adverse effects on the terms, conditions or privileges of their employment, so as to create a prima facie case of disparate impact discrimination under Title VII." Even under *Spun Steak*, however, English-only policies are not always permissible; each case turns on its facts. Here, Plaintiffs have produced evidence that the English-only policy created a hostile atmosphere for Hispanics in their workplace. As previously set forth, all the Plaintiffs stated that they had experienced ethnic taunting as a result of the policy and that the policy made them feel like second-class citizens. Tommy Sanchez testified to instances of taunting by an Altus Police officer, Street Department employees, and other non-Hispanic employees of the City. As evidence that such harassment would be an expected consequence of the policy, Lloyd Lopez testified that Street Commissioner Willis told him that he was notifying him of the policy in private because of concern that other employees would tease Hispanic employees about the policy if they learned of it.

Some of this evidence, as the district court pointed out, has diluted persuasive power because of the absence of specifics—who made what comment when and where. In a typical hostile-work-environment case, we might conclude that the evidence of co-worker taunting did not reach the threshold necessary for a Title VII claim.

There are, however, other considerations with respect to a *policy* that allegedly creates a hostile work environment. The policy itself, and not just the effect of the policy in evoking hostility by co-workers, may create or contribute to the hostility of the work environment. A policy requiring each employee to wear a badge noting his or her religion, for example, might well engender extreme discomfort in a reasonable employee who belongs to a minority religion, even if no co-worker utters a word on the matter. Here, the very fact that the City would forbid Hispanics from using their preferred language could reasonably be construed as an expression of hostility to Hispanics. At least that could be a reasonable inference if there was no apparent legitimate purpose for the restrictions. It would be unreasonable to take offense at a requirement that all pilots flying into an airport speak English in communications with the tower or between planes; but hostility would be a reasonable inference to draw from a requirement that an employee calling home during a work break speak only in English. The less the apparent justification for mandating English, the more reasonable it is to infer hostility toward employees whose ethnic group or nationality favors another language. For example, Plaintiffs presented evidence that the English-only policy extended beyond its written terms to include lunch hours, breaks, and even private telephone conversations, if non-Spanish-speaking co-workers were nearby. Absent a legitimate reason for such a restriction, the inference of hostility may be reasonable.

Our task in this appeal is not to determine whether Plaintiffs have established that they were subjected to a hostile work environment. Rather, in reviewing the grant of summary judgment to Defendants, we are to decide only whether a rational juror could find on this record that the impact of the English-only policy on Hispanic workers was "sufficiently severe or persuasive to alter the conditions of [their] employment and create an abusive working environment." [citation omitted].

It is in this context that we consider the EEOC guideline on English-only workplace rules, 29 C.F.R. § 1606.7. Under the relevant provisions of the guideline: (1) an English-only rule that applies at all times is considered "a burdensome term and condition of employment," § 1606.7(a), presumptively constituting a Title VII violation; and (2) an English-only rule that applies only at certain times does not violate Title VII if the employer can justify the rule by showing business necessity, § 1606.7(b). The EEOC rationales for the guideline are: (1) English-only policies "may 'create an atmosphere of inferiority, isolation, and intimidation' that could make a 'discriminatory working environment'" § 1606.7(a); (2) "English-only rules adversely impact employees with limited or no English skills ... by denying them a privilege enjoyed by native English speakers: the opportunity to speak at work"; (3) "English-only rules create barriers to employment for employees with limited or no English skills"; (4) "English-only rules prevent bilingual employees whose first language is not English from speaking in their most effective language"; and (5) "the risk of discipline and termination for violating English-only rules falls disproportionately on bilingual employees as well as persons with limited English skills." *Id.*

EEOC guidelines, "while not controlling upon the courts by reason of their authority, do constitute a body of experience and informed judgment to which courts and litigants may properly resort for guidance." *Meritor Sav. Bank, F.S.B. v. Vinson*, 477 U.S. 57, 65 (1986) (internal quotation marks omitted).... For our purposes, it is enough that the EEOC, based on its expertise and experience, has consistently concluded that an English-only policy, at least when no business need for the policy is shown, is likely in itself to "create an atmosphere of inferiority, isolation, and intimidation" that constitutes a "discriminatory working environment." § 1606.7(a). (We recognize that several of the EEOC's other grounds for its guideline do not apply here. For example, there is no evidence that the policy prevented any of the Plaintiffs from speaking at work, because all are bilingual.) We believe that these conclusions are entitled to respect, not as interpretations of the governing law, but as an indication of what a reasonable, informed person may think about the impact of an English-only work rule on minority employees, even if we might not draw the same inference. Assuming the reasonableness of the EEOC on the matter, we cannot say that on the record before us it would be unreasonable for a juror to agree that the City's English-only policy created a hostile work environment for its Hispanic employees. We are not suggesting that the guideline is evidence admissible at trial or should be incorporated in a jury instruction. What we are saying is only that a juror presented with the evidence presently on the record in this case would not be unreasonable in finding that a hostile work environment existed.

2. Business Necessity

... Defendants' evidence of business necessity in this case is scant. As observed by the district court, "There was no written record of any communication problems, morale problems or safety problems resulting from the use of languages other than English prior to implementation of the policy." And there was little undocumented evidence. Defendants cited only one example of an employee's complaining about the use of Spanish prior to implementation of the policy. Mr. Willis admitted that he had no knowledge of City business being disrupted or delayed because Spanish was used on the radio. In addition, "city officials who were deposed could give no specific examples of safety problems resulting from the use of languages other than English...." Moreover, Plaintiffs produced evidence that the policy encompassed lunch hours, breaks, and private phone conversations; and Defendants conceded that there would be no business reason for such a restriction. On this record we are not able to affirm summary judgment based on a business necessity for the English-only policy. A reasonable person could find from this evidence that Defendants had failed to establish a business necessity for the English-only rule.

## C. Disparate Treatment

### 1. Discrimination

To prevail under a disparate-treatment theory, "a plaintiff must show, through either direct or indirect evidence, that the discrimination complained of was intentional." [citation omitted]. Plaintiffs contend that they were intentionally discriminated against by the creation of a hostile work environment. We have already held that there is sufficient evidence to support a finding of a hostile work environment. The issue remaining, therefore, is whether those who established the English-only policy did so with the intent to create a hostile work environment.

To begin with, the disparate impact of the English-only rule (creation of a hostile work environment) is in itself evidence of intent. As the Supreme Court stated in *International Brotherhood of Teamsters* in a disparate-treatment case, "[p]roof of discriminatory motive ... can in some situations be inferred from the mere fact of differences in treatment." [citation omitted].

Here, Plaintiffs can rely on more than just that inference. First, there is evidence that management realized that the English-only policy would likely lead to taunting of Hispanic employees: Street Commissioner Willis allegedly told two Hispanic employees about the policy in private because of concern that non-Hispanic employees would tease them if they learned of it. Also, a jury could find that there were no substantial work-related reasons for the policy (particularly if it believed Plaintiffs' evidence that the policy extended to nonwork periods), suggesting that the true reason was illegitimate. Further, the policy was adopted without prior consultation with Hispanic employees, or even prior disclosure to a consultant to the City who was conducting an investigation of alleged anti-Hispanic discrimination during the period when the English-only policy was under consideration. Finally, there is evidence that during a news interview the Mayor referred to the Spanish language as "garbage."

In our view, the record contains sufficient evidence of intent to create a hostile environment that the summary judgment on those claims must be set aside....

---

### Exercise 9.6

Big Oil Company operates offshore oil rigs in the Gulf of Mexico. Big Oil has a rule that all employees must speak English during an emergency. The rule also requires that employees working on the rig itself must speak English while performing their job duties because of the danger of fire, explosion, or a well blowout if communications are not understood among employees. The rule does not apply to non-work related conversations among employees while working on the rig or to conversations during breaks and while employees are off-duty. Does Big Oil's English-only policy violate Title VII?

# Chapter 10

# Administrative and Litigation Procedures

Up to this point, you have spent the majority of your time in this class focused on learning the *substantive* employment discrimination doctrines. You have learned about the proof methods in garden-variety individual disparate treatment cases, the elements of a retaliation claim, and specialized issues involving sexual harassment claims, as examples. How does the procedural process generally work for litigating these cases? The procedural process of an employment discrimination case is the subject of this Chapter.

This Chapter is organized differently from the other Chapters in this casebook. Instead of using the Core Concepts framework, this Chapter is organized by steps. The Chapter utilizes the chronology of the administrative and litigation processes because the order and timeliness of the various procedures are critical in this area of the law. The easiest way to learn the administrative and litigation procedures in the Chapter is to conceptualize the material through a sequential process.

Most employment discrimination claims are different from many federal and state statutory claims in that the aggrieved employee must first go through an administrative procedure before filing suit in court. The federal agency at the heart of the administrative process is the Equal Employment Opportunity Commission (EEOC).

In this Chapter, you will learn about the various steps in the procedural process. Think about the procedural process as a six-step process.

1. The employee files a *charge* with the EEOC.
2. The EEOC serves the *notice* of the charge on the employer.
3. The EEOC *investigates* the charge.
4. The EEOC makes a *determination* on the charge.
5. The EEOC issues a *right-to-sue letter* to the employee.
6. The plaintiff *files* the employment discrimination claim in court.

The first five steps encompass the administrative procedure. The last step initiates the lawsuit in a federal or state court. Accordingly, if the employment discrimination claim proceeds through the administrative process and is then filed in federal district court, the Federal Rules of Civil Procedure govern the procedure of the case beginning at the date of the filing of the lawsuit in court.

The statutory focus in this Chapter will be on the administrative process for Title VII claims. However, ADEA and ADA claims follow a similar process. The differences between the ADEA and Title VII administrative processes are discussed at the end of the administrative process material. An administrative process does *not* apply in Section 1981 claims. The Chapter also briefly discusses state administrative procedures.

## The Administrative Process

## Step 1: The employee files a charge with the EEOC.

Section 706(e)(1) of Title VII provides:

Time for filing charges

A *charge* under this section shall be filed [with the EEOC] within *one hundred and eighty* (180) *days* after the alleged unlawful employment practice occurred…, except that in a case of an unlawful employment practice with respect to which the person aggrieved has initially instituted proceedings with a State or local agency with authority to grant or seek relief from such practice … such charge shall be filed by or on behalf of the person aggrieved [with the EEOC] *within three hundred* (300) *days* after the alleged unlawful employment practice occurred. (emphasis added).

42 U.S.C. § 2000e-5(e)(1).

Title VII, the ADEA, and the ADA each require that the aggrieved employee file the charge of discrimination with the EEOC by the statutorily imposed deadline. The statutes beg several questions. First, what is a "charge"? Second, in practice, where does one go to file the charge with the EEOC? Where *is* this EEOC that the statute references? Finally, how does one make sense of the deadline language in the statute? Let's take these topics in order.

### What Constitutes a Charge under the Federal Anti-Discrimination Statutes?

What constitutes a charge may seem intuitive, but in certain cases it is not that easy to discern whether a "charge" has been filed with the EEOC. Title VII states that "[c]harges shall be in writing under oath or affirmation and shall contain such information as the Commission requires." 42 U.S.C. § 2000e-5(b). There is a form document called the EEOC Form 5 that is typically used by practitioners to file a charge of discrimination. As you can imagine, the form contains places where the employee can provide information about himself and his employer and a basic allegation of the discrimination that occurred. Nothing in the statute, however, states that this Form must be utilized to constitute a valid charge. Consider in this next case whether the United States Supreme Court has brought any clarity to the issue of what constitutes a "charge" under the federal employment discrimination statutes. The case involves the ADEA. But a similar problem arises under Title VII and the ADA.

---

### Focus Questions: *Federal Express Corp. v. Holowecki*

1. *Does an Intake Questionnaire and a signed affidavit describing the alleged discriminatory treatment constitute a "charge" under the ADEA?*

2. *Do the ADEA and the relevant ADEA regulations promulgated by the EEOC provide a satisfactory definition of what constitutes a charge?*

3. *What is the standard that the U.S. Supreme Court adopts for determining whether a charge has been filed?*

4. *Is the standard adopted by the Court easy to apply?*

5.  *Are most charges filed by attorneys who represent complainants or pro se complainants? Does the answer to this question partly explain the Court's decision?*

6.  *What happens if a formal charge is not timely filed with the EEOC?*

---

# Federal Express Corp. v. Holowecki

## 552 U.S. 389 (2008)

Justice Kennedy delivered the opinion of the Court.

This case arises under the Age Discrimination in Employment Act of 1967 (ADEA or Act), as amended, 29 U.S.C. § 621 *et seq*. When an employee files "a charge alleging unlawful [age] discrimination" with the Equal Employment Opportunity Commission (EEOC), the charge sets the Act's enforcement mechanisms in motion, commencing a waiting period during which the employee cannot file suit. The phrase, "a charge alleging unlawful discrimination," is used in the statute, § 626(d), and "charge" appears in the agency's implementing regulations; but it has no statutory definition. In deciding what constitutes a charge under the Act the Courts of Appeals have adopted different definitions. As a result, difficulties have arisen in determining when employees may seek relief under the ADEA in courts of competent jurisdiction.

As a cautionary preface, we note that the EEOC enforcement mechanisms and statutory waiting periods for ADEA claims differ in some respects from those pertaining to other statutes the EEOC enforces, such as Title VII of the Civil Rights Act of 1964 and the Americans with Disabilities Act of 1990. While there may be areas of common definition, employees and their counsel must be careful not to apply rules applicable under one statute to a different statute without careful and critical examination. This is so even if the EEOC forms and the same definition of charge apply in more than one type of discrimination case.

## I

Petitioner, Federal Express Corporation (FedEx), provides mail pickup and delivery services to customers worldwide. In 1994 and 1995, FedEx initiated two programs, designed, it says, to make its 45,000-strong courier network more productive. The programs, "Best Practice Pays" (BPP) and "Minimum Acceptable Performance Standards" (MAPS), tied the couriers' compensation and continued employment to certain performance benchmarks, for instance the number of stops a courier makes per day.

Respondents are 14 current and former FedEx couriers over the age of 40. They filed suit in the United States District Court for the Southern District of New York on April 30, 2002, claiming, *inter alia*, that BPP and MAPS violate the ADEA. Asserting that their claims were typical of many couriers nationwide, respondents sought to represent a plaintiffs' class of all couriers over the age of 40 who were subject to alleged acts of age discrimination by FedEx. The suit maintains that BPP and MAPS were veiled attempts to force older workers out of the company before they would be entitled to receive retirement benefits. FedEx, it is alleged, used the initiatives as a pretext for harassing and discriminating against older couriers in favor of younger ones.

The immediate question before us is the timeliness of the suit filed by one of the plaintiffs below, Patricia Kennedy, referred to here as "respondent." Petitioner moved to dismiss respondent's action, contending respondent had not filed her charge with the EEOC at least

60 days before filing suit, as required by 29 U.S.C. § 626(d). Respondent countered that she filed a valid charge on December 11, 2001, by submitting EEOC Form 283.

The agency labels Form 283 an "Intake Questionnaire." Respondent attached to the questionnaire a signed affidavit describing the alleged discriminatory employment practices in greater detail. The District Court determined these documents were not a charge and granted the motion to dismiss. An appeal followed, and the Court of Appeals for the Second Circuit reversed. We granted certiorari to consider whether respondent's filing was a charge, and we now affirm.

## II

This case presents two distinct questions: What is a charge as the ADEA uses that term? And were the documents respondent filed in December 2001 a charge?

## A

The relevant statutory provision states:

> No civil action may be commenced by an individual under [the ADEA] until 60 days after a charge alleging unlawful discrimination has been filed with the Equal Employment Opportunity Commission....

> Upon receiving such a charge, the Commission shall promptly notify all persons named in such charge as prospective defendants in the action and shall promptly seek to eliminate any alleged unlawful practice by informal methods of conciliation, conference, and persuasion.

29 U.S.C. § 626(d).

The Act does not define charge. While EEOC regulations give some content to the term, they fall short of a comprehensive definition. The agency has statutory authority to issue regulations, *see* § 628; and when an agency invokes its authority to issue regulations, which then interpret ambiguous statutory terms, the courts defer to its reasonable interpretations. The regulations the agency has adopted—so far as they go—are reasonable constructions of the term charge. There is little dispute about this. The issue is the guidance the regulations give.

One of the regulations, 29 C.F.R. § 1626.3 (2007), is entitled "Other definitions." It says: "charge shall mean a statement filed with the Commission by or on behalf of an aggrieved person which alleges that the named prospective defendant has engaged in or is about to engage in actions in violation of the Act." Section 1626.8(a) identifies five pieces of information a "charge should contain": (1)–(2) the names, addresses, and telephone numbers of the person making the charge and the charged entity; (3) a statement of facts describing the alleged discriminatory act; (4) the number of employees of the charged employer; and (5) a statement indicating whether the charging party has initiated state proceedings. The next subsection, § 1626.8(b), however, seems to qualify these requirements by stating that a charge is "sufficient" if it meets the requirements of § 1626.6— *i.e.*, if it is "in writing and ... name[s] the prospective respondent and ... generally allege[s] the discriminatory act(s)."

Even with the aid of the regulations the meaning of charge remains unclear, as is evident from the differing positions of the parties now before us and in the Courts of Appeals. Petitioner contends an Intake Questionnaire cannot be a charge unless the EEOC acts upon it. On the other hand some Courts of Appeals, including the Court of Appeals for the Second Circuit, take a position similar to the Government's in this case, that an Intake

Questionnaire can constitute a charge if it expresses the filer's intent to activate the EEOC's enforcement processes. A third view, which seems to accord with respondent's position, is that all completed Intake Questionnaires are charges.

## B

In support of her position that the Intake Questionnaire she filed, taken together with the attached six-page affidavit, meets the regulatory definition of a charge, respondent places considerable emphasis on what might be described as the regulations' catchall or savings provision, 29 C.F.R. § 1626.8(b). This seems to require only a written document with a general allegation of discriminatory conduct by a named employer. Respondent points out that, when read together, §§ 1626.8(b) and 1626.6 say that a "charge is sufficient when the Commission receives ... a written statement" that "name[s] the [employer] and ... generally allege[s] the discriminatory act(s)." Respondent views this language as unequivocal and sees no basis for requiring that a charge contain any additional information.

The EEOC's view, as expressed in the Government's amicus brief, however, is that the regulations identify certain requirements for a charge but do not provide an exhaustive definition. As such, not all documents that meet the minimal requirements of § 1626.6 are charges.

## C

This does not resolve the case. While we agree with the Government that the regulations do not state all the elements a charge must contain, the question of what additional elements are required remains. On this point the regulations are silent.

The EEOC submits that the proper test for determining whether a filing is a charge is whether the filing, taken as a whole, should be construed as a request by the employee for the agency to take whatever action is necessary to vindicate her rights. The EEOC has adopted this position in the Government's *amicus* brief and in various internal directives it has issued to its field offices over the years. The Government asserts that this request-to-act requirement is a reasonable extrapolation of the agency's regulations and that, as a result, the agency's position is dispositive under *Auer*.

The Government acknowledges the regulations do not, on their face, speak to the filer's intent. To the extent the request-to-act requirement can be derived from the text of the regulations, it must spring from the term charge. But, in this context, the term charge is not a construct of the agency's regulations. It is a term Congress used in the underlying statute that has been incorporated in the regulations by the agency. Thus, insofar as they speak to the filer's intent, the regulations do so by repeating language from the underlying statute. It could be argued, then, that this case can be distinguished from *Auer*. [citations omitted].

It is not necessary to hold that *Auer* deference applies to the agency's construction of the term charge as it is used in the regulations, however. For even if *Auer* deference is inapplicable, we would accept the agency's proposed construction of the statutory term, and we turn next to the reasons for this conclusion.

## D

In our view the agency's policy statements, embodied in its compliance manual and internal directives, interpret not only the regulations but also the statute itself. Assuming these interpretive statements are not entitled to full *Chevron* deference, they do reflect "'a body of experience and informed judgment to which courts and litigants may properly resort for guidance.'" *Bragdon v. Abbott*, 524 U.S. 624, 642 (1998) (quoting *Skidmore v. Swift & Co.*, 323 U.S. 134 (1944)). As such, they are entitled to a "measure of respect" under the less deferential *Skidmore* standard.

Under *Skidmore*, we consider whether the agency has applied its position with consistency. Here, the relevant interpretive statement, embodied in the compliance manual and memoranda, has been binding on EEOC staff for at least five years. True, as the Government concedes, the agency's implementation of this policy has been uneven. In the very case before us the EEOC's Tampa field office did not treat respondent's filing as a charge, as the Government now maintains it should have done. And, as a result, respondent filed suit before the agency could initiate a conciliation process with the employer.

These undoubted deficiencies in the agency's administration of the statute and its regulatory scheme are not enough, however, to deprive the agency of all judicial deference. Some degree of inconsistent treatment is unavoidable when the agency processes over 175,000 inquiries a year. And although one of the policy memoranda the Government relies upon was circulated after we granted certiorari, the position the document takes is consistent with the EEOC's previous directives. We see no reason to assume the agency's position—that a charge is filed when the employee requests some action—was framed for the specific purpose of aiding a party in this litigation.

The EEOC, moreover, has drawn our attention to the need to define charge in a way that allows the agency to fulfill its distinct statutory functions of enforcing antidiscrimination laws and disseminating information about those laws to the public. The agency's duty to initiate informal dispute resolution processes upon receipt of a charge is mandatory in the ADEA context. *See* 29 U.S.C. §626(d) ("[T]he Commission ... shall promptly seek to eliminate any alleged unlawful practice by informal methods of conciliation, conference, and persuasion"). Yet, at the same time, Congress intended the agency to serve an "educational" function. Providing answers to the public's questions is a critical part of the EEOC's mission; and it accounts for a substantial part of the agency's work. Of about 175,000 inquiries the agency receives each year, it dockets around 76,000 of these as charges. Even allowing for errors in the classification of charges and noncharges, it is evident that many filings come from individuals who have questions about their rights and simply want information.

For efficient operations, and to effect congressional intent, the agency requires some mechanism to separate information requests from enforcement requests. Respondent's proposed standard, that a charge need contain only an allegation of discrimination and the name of the employer, falls short in this regard. Were that stripped-down standard to prevail, individuals who approach the agency with questions could end up divulging enough information to create a charge. This likely would be the case for anyone who completes an Intake Questionnaire—which provides space to indicate the name and address of the offending employer and asks the individual to answer the question, "What action was taken against you that you believe to be discrimination?" If an individual knows that reporting this minimal information to the agency will mandate the agency to notify her employer, she may be discouraged from consulting the agency or wait until her employment situation has become so untenable that conciliation efforts would be futile. The result would be contrary to Congress' expressed desire that the EEOC act as an information provider and try to settle employment disputes through informal means.

For these reasons, the definition of charge respondent advocates—*i.e.*, that it need conform only to 29 C.F.R. §1626.6—is in considerable tension with the structure and purposes of the ADEA. The agency's interpretive position—the request-to-act requirement—provides a reasonable alternative that is consistent with the statutory framework. No clearer alternatives are within our authority or expertise to adopt; and so deference to the agency is appropriate under *Skidmore*. We conclude as follows: In addition to the information required by the regulations, *i.e.*, an allegation and the name of the charged party, if a filing is to be deemed a charge it must be reasonably construed as a request for the agency to take remedial action to protect the employee's rights or otherwise settle a dispute between the employer and the employee.

Some Courts of Appeals have referred to a "manifest intent" test, under which, in order to be deemed a charge, the filing must demonstrate "an individual's intent to have the agency initiate its investigatory and conciliatory processes." If this formulation suggests the filer's state of mind is somehow determinative, it misses the point. If, however, it means the filing must be examined from the standpoint of an objective observer to determine whether, by a reasonable construction of its terms, the filer requests the agency to activate its machinery and remedial processes, that would be in accord with our conclusion.

It is true that under this permissive standard a wide range of documents might be classified as charges. But this result is consistent with the design and purpose of the ADEA. Even in the formal litigation context, *pro se* litigants are held to a lesser pleading standard than other parties. In the administrative context now before us it appears *pro se* filings may be the rule, not the exception. The ADEA, like Title VII, sets up a "remedial scheme in which laypersons, rather than lawyers, are expected to initiate the process." The system must be accessible to individuals who have no detailed knowledge of the relevant statutory mechanisms and agency processes. It thus is consistent with the purposes of the Act that a charge can be a form, easy to complete, or an informal document, easy to draft. The agency's proposed test implements these purposes.

Reasonable arguments can be made that the agency should adopt a standard giving more guidance to filers, making it clear that the request to act must be stated in quite explicit terms. A rule of that sort might yield more consistent results. This, however, is a matter for the agency to decide in light of its experience and expertise in protecting the rights of those who are covered by the Act. For its decisions in this regard the agency is subject to the oversight of the political branches. We find no reason in this case to depart from our usual rule: Where ambiguities in statutory analysis and application are presented, the agency may choose among reasonable alternatives.

. . .

### III.

Having determined that the agency acted within its authority in formulating the rule that a filing is deemed a charge if the document reasonably can be construed to request agency action and appropriate relief on the employee's behalf, the question is whether the filing here meets this test. The agency says it does, and we agree. The agency's determination is a reasonable exercise of its authority to apply its own regulations and procedures in the course of the routine administration of the statute it enforces.

Respondent's completed intake form contained all of the information outlined in 29 C.F.R. § 1626.8, including: the employee's name, address, and telephone number, as well as those of her employer; an allegation that she and other employees had been the victims of "age discrimination"; the number of employees who worked at the Dunedin, Florida, facility where she was stationed; and a statement indicating she had not sought the assistance of any government agency regarding this matter.

Petitioner maintains the filing was still deficient because it contained no request for the agency to act. Were the Intake Questionnaire the only document before us we might agree its handwritten statements do not request action. The design of the form in use in 2001, moreover, does not give rise to the inference that the employee requests action against the employer. Unlike EEOC Form 5, the Intake Questionnaire is not labeled a "Charge of Discrimination." In fact the wording of the questionnaire suggests the opposite: that the form's purpose is to facilitate "pre-charge filing counseling" and to enable the agency to determine whether it has jurisdiction over "potential charges." There might be instances where the indicated discrimination is so clear or pervasive that the agency could infer from the allegations themselves that action is requested and required, but the agency is not required to treat every completed Intake Questionnaire as a charge.

In this case, however, the completed questionnaire filed in December 2001 was supplemented with a detailed six-page affidavit. At the end of the last page, respondent asked the agency to "[p]lease force Federal Express to end their age discrimination plan so we can finish out our careers absent the unfairness and hostile work environment created within their application of Best Practice/High-Velocity Culture Change." This is properly construed as a request for the agency to act.

. . .

IV

The Federal Government interacts with individual citizens through all but countless forms, schedules, manuals, and worksheets. Congress, in most cases, delegates the format and design of these instruments to the agencies that administer the relevant laws and processes. An assumption underlying the congressional decision to delegate rulemaking and enforcement authority to the agency, and the consequent judicial rule of deference to the agency's determinations, is that the agency will take all efforts to ensure that affected parties will receive the full benefits and protections of the law. Here, because the agency failed to treat respondent's filing as a charge in the first instance, both sides lost the benefits of the ADEA's informal dispute resolution process.

The employer's interests, in particular, were given short shrift, for it was not notified of respondent's complaint until she filed suit. The court that hears the merits of this litigation can attempt to remedy this deficiency by staying the proceedings to allow an opportunity for conciliation and settlement. True, that remedy would be imperfect. Once the adversary process has begun a dispute may be in a more rigid cast than if conciliation had been attempted at the outset.

This result is unfortunate, but, at least in this case, unavoidable. While courts will use their powers to fashion the best relief possible in situations like this one, the ultimate responsibility for establishing a clearer, more consistent process lies with the agency. The agency already has made some changes to the charge-filing process. To reduce the risk of further misunderstandings by those who seek its assistance, the agency should determine, in the first instance, what additional revisions in its forms and processes are necessary or appropriate.

The judgment of the Court of Appeals is affirmed.

It is so ordered.

Justice Thomas, with whom Justice Scalia joins, dissenting.

Today the Court decides that a "charge" of age discrimination under the Age Discrimination in Employment Act of 1967 (ADEA) is whatever the Equal Employment

Opportunity Commission (EEOC) says it is. The filing at issue in this case did not state that it was a charge and did not include a charge form; to the contrary, it included a form that expressly stated it was for the purpose of "pre-charge" counseling. What is more, the EEOC did not assign it a charge number, notify the employer of the complainant's allegations, or commence enforcement proceedings. Notwithstanding these facts, the Court concludes, counterintuitively, that respondent's filing is a charge because it manifests an intent for the EEOC to take "some action." Because the standard the Court applies is broader than the ordinary meaning of the term "charge," and because it is so malleable that it effectively absolves the EEOC of its obligation to administer the ADEA according to discernible standards, I respectfully dissent.

## Notes

1. *The Holowecki Aftermath.* In *Holowecki,* the Court considered whether an internal questionnaire along with an affidavit alleging discriminatory acts constituted a charge under the ADEA. The Court established the following standard for determining whether a filing is a charge: A filing that names the charged party, *i.e.,* the employer, and alleges discrimination will be considered a charge if it is reasonably construed as a request for the agency to take remedial action to protect the employee's rights or otherwise settle a dispute between the employer and the employee. This is a request-to-act standard. The internal questionnaire and the affidavit of the employee alleging discrimination in the case sufficed to constitute a charge under this standard. Is this standard problematic? Is it too ambiguous for the application of future situations? Justice Thomas in dissent stressed that the dictionary definition of "charge" is a *formal allegation* of wrongdoing that *initiates legal proceedings* against an alleged wrongdoer. According to Thomas, for there to be a valid EEOC charge the filing party must objectively indicate that the employee intended to initiate the EEOC's formal enforcement processes. This must be done by requesting that the agency take *the particular form* of remedial action that results from filing a charge. The employee in *Holowecki* requested in her affidavit that the EEOC "force Federal Express to end their age discrimination." Does that statement necessarily mean that the employee wanted the EEOC immediately to employ the particular method of enforcement that constitutes filing a charge? Thomas does not think so. He stated that the request to "force Federal Express to end their age discrimination" could have been met by the agency's beginning the interviewing and counseling process that might lead to a charge or by the Agency proceeding to enforcement without a charge. What do you think?

2. *Charge of Discrimination Form.* The question of whether the employee in *Holowecki* filed a charge with the EEOC arose because the employee did not file (at least initially) the standard Charge of Discrimination form established by the EEOC. This is the so-called Form 5 that is referred to in the case. A sample document that includes the basics of the Charge of Discrimination document is included in this chapter. The language in this document leaves no doubt that the employee is filing a charge with the EEOC and thus invoking the enforcement process. Note the language in the form that states "I want this *charge* filed with both the EEOC and the State or local Agency, if any. I will advise the agencies if I change my address or telephone number and I will cooperate fully ..." and the reference to the complainant as the *charging* party. The Intake Questionnaire, however, which the EEOC uses to help an individual determine whether to file a charge, serves a separate purpose and has historically not been viewed as a charge by the Agency. Indeed, the EEOC's Intake Questionnaire system on its website states specifically that

completing the questionnaire is not the same as filing a charge. See http://www.eeoc.gov/
employees/howtofile.cfm (last visited June 28, 2013).

3. *Attorneys should not get tripped up.* Many filings with the EEOC are made by employees
*pro se.* The employees may not know about the law in this area. The Court explained that
one of the reasons for its decision was to insure that charges do not fail on technical
grounds given the fact that many intended charges are filed by non-lawyers. As an attorney
representing an employee in an employment discrimination proceeding, you now should
understand the importance of filing the document with the EEOC—the formal Charge
of Discrimination document—that makes clear that the employee is invoking the EEOC's
formal enforcement mechanisms. You do not want to put your client in a position where
the employer later argues that a valid charge was never filed and so, therefore, the client's
discrimination claim is not valid.

4. *Scope of the Charge.* Care must be taken at the charging stage to make sure that all
possible grounds of discrimination (race, sex, age, etc.) and retaliation are included in
the charge. The circuits have generally held that an employee is limited to suing the
employer on the specific claims asserted in the charge, or at least to those judicial claims
that could reasonably be expected to grow out of the charge of discrimination. The
rationale is that the statutory scheme gives the EEOC the first opportunity to resolve discrimination complaints and thus providing the agency with the type(s) of discrimination
involved, so that it can do a proper investigation, is a necessary part of the statutory
scheme. Suing on the basis of a type of discrimination not alleged in the charge, or one
that could not grow out of the charge, thwarts Title VII's statutory scheme. Under this
line of cases, unsuspecting plaintiffs have had their discrimination claims dismissed on
the basis that the claims were beyond the scope of the charge. *See McClain v. Lufkin
Industries, Inc.,* 519 F.3d 264, 276 (5th Cir. 2008) (plaintiffs' allegations of racially discriminatory assignments in the employer's Foundry Division barred because they were
outside the scope of the charge); *Jorge v. Rumsfeld,* 404 F.3d 556, 564–65 (1st Cir. 2005)
(plaintiff's Title VII claim dismissed because not included in charge; administrative charge
alleged only age discrimination under the ADEA); *Wallin v. Minnesota Department of
Corrections,* 153 F.3d 681, 688–89 (8th Cir. 1998) (Title VII retaliation claim rejected
because not included in the charge).

### The Location for Filing a Charge with the EEOC

The EEOC's main office is in Washington, D.C. However, there are various district and
field offices scattered throughout the nation. The aggrieved employee may file his or her
charge with any EEOC office but it is standard for the employee to file the charge with the
EEOC office nearest to where the alleged discrimination occurred. *See* 29 C.F.R. § 1601.8.
For a map of the EEOC's offices, see http://www.eeoc.gov/field/index.cfm (last visited on
June 28, 2013). As explained later in the Chapter, an EEOC charge may be filed with a
state administrative agency in lieu of filing the charge with the relevant EEOC office.

### The Deadline for Filing the Charge with the EEOC

The deadline for filing a charge differs based on whether the state where the charge is
filed has its own statutory protections against employment discrimination. Many states
have their own state anti-discrimination employment statutes and anti-discrimination
agency, which is similar to the EEOC. States that have anti-discrimination statutes and

agencies are referred to as deferral states because the EEOC defers the investigation to the state agency for a certain time period. The Title VII deferral provisions are supposed to promote efficient processing of claims and give the states the first opportunity to act on discrimination charges. As a practical matter, charges that are dually filed with the EEOC and the state agency are subject to a work-sharing agreement between the two agencies. Accordingly, which agency will conduct the investigation is governed by the work-sharing agreement.

| CHARGE OF DISCRIMINATION | AGENCY | CHARGE NUMBER |
|---|---|---|
| This form is affected by the Privacy Act of 1974. See Privacy Act Statement before completing this form | ☒ FEPA ☒ EEOC | 2509A6206 |

Texas Workforce Commission, Civil Rights Division _____ and EEOC
*State or local Agency, if any*

| NAME(Indicate Mr., Ms., Mrs.) | HOME TELEPHONE (Include Area Code) | |
|---|---|---|
| Mr. Jerome Johnson | (214) 543-8201 | |
| STREET ADDRESS / CITY, STATE AND ZIP CODE | | DATE OF BIRTH |
| 5401 Vickery Lane      Dallas, TX 75202 | | 12/15/78 |

NAMED IS THE EMPLOYER, LABOR ORGANIZATION, EMPLOYMENT AGENCY, APPRENTICESHIP COMMITTEE, STATE OR LOCAL GOVERNMENT AGENCY WHO DISCRIMINATED AGAINST ME *(If more than one list below.)*

| NAME | NUMBER OF EMPLOYEES, MEMBERS | TELEPHONE (Include Area Code) |
|---|---|---|
| Southern Bell Systems, Inc. | 15+ | (972) 433-5820 |
| STREET ADDRESS / CITY, STATE AND ZIP CODE | | COUNTY |
| 2625 Industry Parkway      Dallas, TX 75209 | | Dallas |

| NAME | TELEPHONE NUMBER (Include Area Code) | |
|---|---|---|
| STREET ADDRESS / CITY, STATE AND ZIP CODE | | COUNTY |

| CAUSE OF DISCRIMINATION BASED ON *(Check appropriate box(es))* | DATE DISCRIMINATION TOOK PLACE | |
|---|---|---|
| ☒ RACE ☒ COLOR ☐ SEX ☐ RELIGION ☐ NATIONAL ORIGIN ☒ RETALIATION ☐ AGE ☐ DISABILITY ☐ OTHER (Specify) | 1/17/14      1/18/14 ☐ CONTINUING ACTION | |

THE PARTICULARS ARE *(If additional paper is needed, attach extra sheet(s)):*

Cause of Discrimination is Based on Race and Retaliation

My name is Jerome Johnson. I am thirty-five year-old African-American male. I work in the shipping department at Southern Bell Systems, Inc. and have been employed with the company since 2007. On January 18, 2014, Southern Bell Systems, Inc. terminated my employment. The termination surrounds the following incident. On January 17, 2014, my manager, Tom Green, ordered me to clean up the parts area in the warehouse. The mess that needed to be cleaned up had been caused by my co-worker, James Watson, a Caucasian. I asked Mr. Green why I was told to clean up the mess instead of James given that James caused the mess and was in the same department as myself. He told me that "blacks clean better" and "just do what you are told." I then told him that making such an assignment constituted illegal race discrimination. The company terminated my employment the next day. I allege that the termination occurred because of my race and because I complained of illegal race discrimination. I have a spotless employment history at Southern Bell Systems.

| I want this charge filed with both the EEOC and the State or local Agency, if any. I will advise the agencies if I change my address or telephone number and I will cooperate fully with them in the processing of my charge in accordance with their procedures | NOTARY - (When necessary for State and Local Requirements) Bob Davis, Notary |
|---|---|
| | I swear or affirm that I have read the above charge and that it is true to the best of my knowledge, information and belief. |
| I declare under penalty of perjury that the foregoing is true and correct | SIGNATURE OF COMPLAINANT *Jerome Johnson* |
| *Jerome Johnson* | SUBSCRIBED AND SWORN TO BEFORE ME THIS DATE (Day, month, and year) |
| Date 2-8-14      Charging Party (Signature) | 2-8-14 |

EEOC FORM 5

Texas is an example of a deferral state because it has a state anti-discrimination statute, the Texas Commission on Human Rights Act (TCHRA), which is enforced by the Texas Workforce Commission, Civil Rights Division. *See* Tex. Labor Code § 21.001 *et seq.* For

EEOC charges filed in states that have state or local anti-discrimination statutes and agencies (often referred to as Fair Employment Practice Agencies), the deadline to file the EEOC charge is 300 days from the alleged unlawful employment practice. *See* Title VII § 706(e)(1); 42 U.S.C. § 2000e-5(e)(1). If the EEOC charge is to be filed in a state without a state anti-discrimination statute and agency, the deadline is 180 days. *Id.*

### Commencing the Charge-Filing Period

Title VII states that the charge shall be filed within 300/180 days after the "alleged unlawful employment practice occurred." To calculate the charge-filing period, the period commences on the date the unlawful employment practice occurred and ends 300/180 days later. It is important to understand the judicial gloss on when an "unlawful employment practice occurs."

#### Discrete Discriminatory Acts

The basic rule for disparate treatment cases is that the EEOC charging period is triggered when a discrete discriminatory act takes place. *See National Railroad Corp. v. Morgan*, 536 U.S. 101, 110 (2002) (a discrete retaliatory or discriminatory act "occurs" on the date it happens). Examples of such discrete discriminatory acts include hiring, firing, demotion, and failure to promote. There is a catch, however. The United States Supreme Court held in *Delaware State College v. Ricks* that the charging period commences at the time the employee receives *notice* of the discriminatory action. 449 U.S. 250, 259 (1980). The "notice of decision" date may in some cases be different from the discriminatory action date. The *Ricks* case is a good illustration of this principle. Delaware State College denied Ricks, a college librarian, tenure in March 1974. However, consistent with many tenure systems, after the denial of tenure, the College gave him a final, nonrenewable contract that expired on June 30, 1975. Consequently, as a technical matter, Ricks's employment termination with the College did not occur until June 30, 1975. Nonetheless, the EEOC charging period began on the day in March 1974 when the College denied his tenure application and communicated the denial to Ricks. Under this scenario, Ricks's 300/180 day window to file a charge regarding the alleged discriminatory tenure decision actually ended while he was still working at the College as part of his terminal one-year contract.

The "notice of decision" rule worked to the detriment of Professor Ricks, but in some cases such a rule could help the applicant or employee. For example, if an employer makes an apparent employment decision but does not notify the employee of that decision until a subsequent date, the commencement of the charging period runs from the date of the notification. In *Wright v. AmSouth Bancorporation*, 320 F.3d 1198, 1203 (11th Cir. 2003), the employer took certain actions—such as advising the employee to start looking for another job even though he was still employed by the company—that might lead a reasonable employee to believe that a termination was a *fait accompli*. But the charging period did not commence until a firm, final decision to terminate the employee's employment was made by the employer *and communicated* to the employee.

#### Continuing Violations

A different paradigm applies to hostile work environment claims. In *National Railroad Corp. v. Morgan*, the U.S. Supreme Court held that hostile work environment claims involve continuing violations, and thus, so long as an act contributing to that hostile work environment takes place within the 300/180 day charging period, a charge is timely filed. 536 U.S. 101, 117 (2002). The *Morgan* Court stated:

A hostile work environment claim is comprised of a series of separate acts that collectively constitute one "unlawful employment practice." The timely filing provision only requires that a Title VII plaintiff file a charge within a certain number of days after the unlawful employment practice happened. It does not matter, for purposes of the statute, that some of the component acts of the hostile work environment fall outside the statutory time period. Provided that an act contributing to the claim occurs within the filing period, the entire time period of the hostile environment may be considered by a court for the purposes of determining liability.

Consider this hypothetical to illustrate the point. Sarah works for Company X. George is her supervisor. In January 2002, George first subjects Sarah to some unwelcome sexual conduct. The unwelcome conduct continues over a period of time. In May 2002, the unwelcome conduct has become so egregious and consistent that the "severe or pervasive" standard is satisfied. The unwelcome conduct continues on over the next several years with the last incident occurring on March 1, 2004. Sarah's EEOC charge based on hostile work environment sexual harassment is timely if brought within 300/180 days of March 1, 2004. The prior acts of harassment would also come within the scope of the liability determination. The series of harassing acts comprises a continuing violation under Title VII.

### Discriminatory Compensation Decisions

Imagine the following scenario. Linda and Tom work at Carter Company, the employer. Linda and Tom were both hired to do the same job at Carter on the same day, January 1, 1992. Linda and Tom are clones in the sense that they do the same work for the company and perform at the same level. Assume that in 1993, 1994, and 1995, Linda's supervisors give her poor evaluations because of her sex. As a consequence, she is not given raises that she is entitled to based on her work performance. Tom, the male clone, is given good evaluations and receives appropriate merit-based raises. Assume the discriminatory pay decisions as to Linda stop in 1995, but these past pay decisions continue to affect the amount of pay throughout her employment tenure at Carter. Linda and Tom continue to work and perform in lock-step throughout their career at Carter Company. Linda's pay lags behind her male clone. For comparison purposes, in 2009, Tom's salary is $65,000 per year. Linda's salary is $50,000 per year. The difference in pay can be traced to those tainted performance evaluations from 1993–1995.

Under this scenario, when does the EEOC charging period for the discriminatory pay decisions commence? Technically, the discriminatory pay decisions stopped in 1995, so perhaps the charging period for the discrimination should begin at the very latest in 1995 — the date the last discriminatory act took place. But arguably the prior acts of discrimination are being carried over to every paycheck Linda receives from the company subsequent to the discriminatory acts. Should Linda be able to file a timely charge in 2009 based on discriminatory pay decisions that stopped in 1995?

*Ledbetter v. The Goodyear Tire & Rubber Company, Inc.*, presents essentially the scenario outlined above. 550 U.S. 618 (2007). In *Ledbetter*, the Court held that the EEOC charging period begins when the last discriminatory pay decision is made because pay decisions are discrete discriminatory acts. As you now know, as to discrete discriminatory acts, the charge period begins when the act occurs.

The 111th United States Congress enacted the Lilly Ledbetter Fair Pay Act of 2009 in January 2009. President Barack Obama signed the Act into law on January 29, 2009. It became the first Congressional Act that President Obama signed into law. The Ledbetter

Act amends Title VII (Title VII § 706(e)(3)(A)); 42 U.S.C. § 2000e-5(e)(3)(A)), the ADEA (ADEA § 7(d)(3); 29 U.S.C. § 626(d)(3)), the ADA (ADA § 107(a); 42 U.S.C. § 12117(a)), and the Rehabilitation Act (29 U.S.C. §§ 791(g), 794(d)). The key provision of the Act states:

> [A]n unlawful employment practice occurs, with respect to discrimination in compensation ... when a discriminatory compensation decision or other practice is adopted, when an individual becomes subject to a discriminatory compensation decision or other practice, or when an individual is affected by application of a discriminatory compensation decision or other practice, *including each time wages, benefits, or other compensation is paid, resulting in whole or in part from such a decision or other practice.* (emphasis added).

The Act takes effect as if enacted on May 28, 2007. *See* Lilly Ledbetter Fair Pay Act of 2009 § 6. A two-year back pay period preceding the date of the filing of the charge is provided for in the statute. *See* Lilly Ledbetter Fair Pay Act of 2009 § 3. There is an open question concerning how and whether the two-year lookback applies to the ADEA.

Let's return to our Linda/Tom example. Under the Ledbetter Act, each 2009 paycheck is carrying forward the remnants of the prior discrimination and thus a charge could be filed based on a discriminatory 2009 paycheck. The back pay period extends up to two years preceding the charge.

Despite the presence of the Ledbetter Act, Carter Company may argue that Linda's EEOC charge and subsequent Title VII claim is nonetheless barred based on the equitable defense of laches. After all, Linda's claims are based on discrimination that had its genesis over a decade ago.

The doctrine of laches is based on the idea that equity aids the vigilant and not those that slumber on their rights. Laches requires proof that the claimant unreasonably delayed in asserting a right and such delay disadvantaged the other side. The courts may interpret the plain language of the Ledbetter Act to preclude an employer's laches defense.

*Disparate Impact Claims*

A plaintiff must file a timely EEOC charge prior to filing a Title VII lawsuit. This requirement applies to Title VII disparate impact claims. An EEOC charge alleging disparate impact must be made within 180/300 days "after the alleged unlawful employment practice occurred." 42 U.S.C. § 2000e-5(e)(1). Difficult questions arise regarding the triggering of the charging period for disparate impact claims. Do disparate impact claims involve continuing violations or are they based on discrete acts? When does a cognizable disparate impact claim occur? Consider the following U.S. Supreme Court decision.

---

## Focus Questions: *Lewis v. City of Chicago*

1. *What is an "employment practice" under Title VII?*

2. *When does an "unlawful employment practice based on disparate impact" occur under Title VII?*

3. *How is the* Lewis v. City of Chicago *decision distinguishable from the* Delaware State College v. Ricks *decision?*

4. *What practical problems, if any, are created by the Court's decision?*

---

# Lewis v. City of Chicago

### 560 U.S. 205 (2010)

Justice Scalia delivered the unanimous opinion of the Court.

Title VII of the Civil Rights Act of 1964 prohibits employers from using employment practices that cause a disparate impact on the basis of race (among other bases). 42 U.S.C. § 2000e-2(k)(1)(A)(i). It also requires plaintiffs, before beginning a federal lawsuit, to file a timely charge of discrimination with the Equal Employment Opportunity Commission (EEOC). § 2000e-5(e)(1). We consider whether a plaintiff who does not file a timely charge challenging the *adoption* of a practice—here, an employer's decision to exclude employment applicants who did not achieve a certain score on an examination—may assert a disparate-impact claim in a timely charge challenging the employer's later *application* of that practice.

### I

In July 1995, the City of Chicago administered a written examination to over 26,000 applicants seeking to serve in the Chicago Fire Department. After scoring the examinations, the City reported the results. It announced in a January 26, 1996, press release that it would begin drawing randomly from the top tier of scorers, *i.e.*, those who scored 89 or above (out of 100), whom the City called "well qualified." Those drawn from this group would proceed to the next phase—a physical-abilities test, background check, medical examination, and drug test—and if they cleared those hurdles would be hired as candidate firefighters. Those who scored below 65, on the other hand, learned by letters sent the same day that they had failed the test. Each was told he had not achieved a passing score, would no longer be considered for a firefighter position, and would not be contacted again about the examination.

The applicants in-between—those who scored between 65 and 88, whom the City called "qualified"—were notified that they had passed the examination but that, based on the City's projected hiring needs and the number of "well-qualified" applicants, it was not likely they would be called for further processing. The individual notices added, however, that because it was not possible to predict how many applicants would be hired in the next few years, each "qualified" applicant's name would be kept on the eligibility list maintained by the Department of Personnel for as long as that list was used. Eleven days later, the City officially adopted an "Eligible List" reflecting the breakdown described above.

On May 16, 1996, the City selected its first class of applicants to advance to the next stage. It selected a second on October 1, 1996, and repeated the process nine more times over the next six years. As it had announced, in each round the City drew randomly from among those who scored in the "well-qualified" range on the 1995 test. In the last round it exhausted that pool, so it filled the remaining slots with "qualified" candidates instead.

On March 31, 1997, Crawford M. Smith, an African-American applicant who scored in the "qualified" range and had not been hired as a candidate firefighter, filed a charge of discrimination with the EEOC. Five others followed suit, and on July 28, 1998, the EEOC issued all six of them right-to-sue letters. Two months later, they filed this civil action against the City, alleging (as relevant here) that its practice of selecting for advancement only applicants who scored 89 or above caused a disparate impact on African-Americans in violation of Title VII. The District Court certified a class—petitioners here—consisting of the more than 6,000 African-Americans who scored in the "qualified" range on the 1995 examination but had not been hired.

The City sought summary judgment on the ground that petitioners had failed to file EEOC charges within 300 days after their claims accrued. *See* § 2000e-5(e)(1). The District Court denied the motion, concluding that the City's "ongoing reliance" on the 1995 test results constituted a "continuing violation" of Title VII. The City stipulated that the 89-point cutoff had a "severe disparate impact against African Americans," but argued that its cutoff score was justified by business necessity. After an 8-day bench trial, the District Court ruled for petitioners, rejecting the City's business-necessity defense. It ordered the City to hire 132 randomly selected members of the class (reflecting the number of African-Americans the Court found would have been hired but for the City's practices) and awarded backpay to be divided among the remaining class members.

The Seventh Circuit reversed. It held that petitioners' suit was untimely because the earliest EEOC charge was filed more than 300 days after the only discriminatory act: sorting the scores into the "well-qualified," "qualified," and "not-qualified" categories. The hiring decisions down the line were immaterial, it reasoned, because "[t]he hiring only of applicants classified 'well qualified' was the automatic consequence of the test scores rather than the product of a fresh act of discrimination."

## II

### A

Before beginning a Title VII suit, a plaintiff must first file a timely EEOC charge. In this case, petitioners' charges were due within 300 days "after the alleged unlawful employment practice occurred." § 2000e-5(e)(1). Determining whether a plaintiff's charge is timely thus requires "identify[ing] precisely the 'unlawful employment practice' of which he complains." *Delaware State College* v. *Ricks*, 449 U.S. 250, 257 (1980). Petitioners here challenge the City's practice of picking only those who had scored 89 or above on the 1995 examination when it later chose applicants to advance. Setting aside the first round of selection in May 1996, which all agree is beyond the cut-off, no one disputes that the conduct petitioners challenge occurred within the charging period. The real question, then, is not whether a claim predicated on that conduct is *timely*, but whether the practice thus defined can be the basis for a disparate-impact claim *at all*.

We conclude that it can. As originally enacted, Title VII did not expressly prohibit employment practices that cause a disparate impact. That enactment made it an "unlawful employment practice" for an employer "to fail or refuse to hire or to discharge any individual, or otherwise to discriminate against any individual with respect to his compensation, terms, conditions, or privileges of employment, because of such individual's race, color, religion, sex, or national origin," § 2000e-2(a)(1), or "to limit, segregate, or classify his employees or applicants for employment in any way which would deprive or tend to deprive any individual of employment opportunities or otherwise adversely affect his status as an employee, because of" any of the same reasons, § 2000e-2(a)(2). In *Griggs* v. *Duke Power Co.*, 401 U.S. 424, 431 (1971), we interpreted the latter provision to "proscrib[e] not only overt discrimination but also practices that are fair in form, but discriminatory in operation."

Two decades later, Congress codified the requirements of the "disparate impact" claims *Griggs* had recognized. 42 U.S.C. § 2000e-2(k). That provision states:

> (1)(A) An unlawful employment practice based on disparate impact is established under this subchapter only if—
>
> (i) a complaining party demonstrates that a respondent uses a particular employment practice that causes a disparate impact on the basis of race, color,

religion, sex, or national origin and the respondent fails to demonstrate that the challenged practice is job related for the position in question and consistent with business necessity....

Thus, a plaintiff establishes a prima facie disparate-impact claim by showing that the employer "*uses* a particular employment practice that causes a disparate impact" on one of the prohibited bases. *Ibid.* (emphasis added).

Petitioners' claim satisfies that requirement. Title VII does not define "employment practice," but we think it clear that the term encompasses the conduct of which petitioners complain: the exclusion of passing applicants who scored below 89 (until the supply of scores 89 or above was exhausted) when selecting those who would advance. The City "use[d]" that practice in each round of selection. Although the City had adopted the eligibility list (embodying the score cutoffs) earlier and announced its intention to draw from that list, it made use of the practice of excluding those who scored 88 or below each time it filled a new class of firefighters. Petitioners alleged that this exclusion caused a disparate impact. Whether they adequately proved that is not before us. What matters is that their allegations, based on the City's actual implementation of its policy, stated a cognizable claim.

The City argues that subsection (k) is inapposite because it does not address "accrual" of disparate-impact claims. Section 2000e-5(e)(1), it says, specifies when the time to file a charge starts running. That is true but irrelevant. Aside from the first round of selection in May 1996 (which all agree is beyond the 300-day charging period), the acts petitioners challenge — the City's use of its cutoff score in selecting candidates — occurred within the charging period. Accordingly, no one disputes that if petitioners could bring new claims based on those acts, their claims were timely. The issue, in other words, is not *when* petitioners' claims accrued, but *whether* they could accrue at all.

The City responds that subsection (k) does not answer *that* question either; that it speaks, as its title indicates, only to the plaintiff's "[b]urden of proof in disparate impact cases," not to the elements of disparate-impact claims, which the City says are be found in §2000e-2(a)(2). That is incorrect. Subsection (k) does indeed address the burden of proof — not just who bears it, however, but also what it consists of. It *does* set forth the essential ingredients of a disparate-impact claim: It says that a claim "is established" if an employer "uses" an "employment practice" that "causes a disparate impact" on one of the enumerated bases. That it also sets forth a business-necessity defense employers may raise, and explains how plaintiffs may prevail despite that defense, is irrelevant. Unless and until the defendant pleads and proves a business-necessity defense, the plaintiff wins simply by showing the stated elements.

### B

Notwithstanding the text of §2000e-2(k)(1)(A)(i) and petitioners' description of the practice they claim was unlawful, the City argues that the unlawful employment practice here was something else entirely. The only actionable discrimination, it argues, occurred in 1996 when it "used the examination results to create the hiring eligibility list, limited hiring to the 'well qualified' classification, and notified petitioners." That initial decision, it concedes, was unlawful. But because no timely charge challenged the decision, that cannot now be the basis for liability. And because, the City claims, the exclusion of petitioners when selecting classes of firefighters followed inevitably from the earlier decision to adopt the cutoff score, no new violations could have occurred. The Seventh Circuit adopted the same analysis.

The City's premise is sound, but its conclusion does not follow. It may be true that the City's January 1996 decision to adopt the cutoff score (and to create a list of the applicants above it) gave rise to a freestanding disparate-impact claim. *Cf. Connecticut* v. *Teal*, 457 U.S. 440, 445–451 (1982). If that is so, the City is correct that since no timely charge was filed attacking it, the City is now "entitled to treat that past act as lawful." [citation omitted]. But it does not follow that no new violation occurred — and no new claims could arise — when the City implemented that decision down the road. If petitioners could prove that the City "use[d]" the "practice" that "causes a disparate impact," they could prevail.

The City, like the Seventh Circuit, insists that *Evans* and a line of cases following it require a different result. [citations omitted]. Those cases, we are told, stand for the proposition that present effects of prior actions cannot lead to Title VII liability.

We disagree. As relevant here, those cases establish only that a Title VII plaintiff must show a "present violation" within the limitations period. [citation omitted]. What that requires depends on the claim asserted. For disparate-treatment claims — and others for which discriminatory intent is required — that means the plaintiff must demonstrate deliberate discrimination within the limitations period. But for claims that do not require discriminatory intent, no such demonstration is needed. Our opinions, it is true, described the harms of which the unsuccessful plaintiffs in those cases complained as "present effect[s]" of past discrimination. But the reason they could not be the present effects of present discrimination was that the charged discrimination required proof of discriminatory intent, which had not even been alleged. That reasoning has no application when, as here, the charge is disparate impact, which does not require discriminatory intent.

The Seventh Circuit resisted this conclusion, reasoning that the difference between disparate-treatment and disparate-impact claims is only superficial. Both take aim at the same evil — discrimination on a prohibited basis — but simply seek to establish it by different means. Disparate-impact liability, the Court of Appeals explained, "is primarily intended to lighten the plaintiff's heavy burden of proving intentional discrimination after employers learned to cover their tracks." [citation omitted]. But even if the two theories were directed at the same evil, it would not follow that their reach is therefore coextensive. If the effect of applying Title VII's text is that some claims that would be doomed under one theory will survive under the other, that is the product of the law Congress has written. It is not for us to rewrite the statute so that it covers only what we think is necessary to achieve what we think Congress really intended.

The City also argues that, even if petitioners could have proved a present disparate-impact violation, they never did so under the proper test. The parties litigated the merits — and the City stipulated that the cutoff score caused disparate impact — after the District Court adopted petitioners' "continuing violation" theory. That theory, which petitioners have since abandoned, treated the adoption and application of the cutoff score as a single, ongoing wrong. As a result, the City says, "petitioners never proved, or even attempted to prove, that *use* of the [eligibility] list had disparate impact," (emphasis added), since the theory they advanced did not require them to do so. If the Court of Appeals determines that the argument has been preserved it may be available on remand. But it has no bearing here. The only question presented to us is whether the claim petitioners brought is cognizable. Because we conclude that it is, our inquiry is at an end.

## C

The City and its *amici* warn that our reading will result in a host of practical problems for employers and employees alike. Employers may face new disparate-impact suits for practices they have used regularly for years. Evidence essential to their business-necessity defenses might be unavailable (or in the case of witnesses' memories, unreliable) by the time the later suits are brought. And affected employees and prospective employees may not even know they have claims if they are unaware the employer is still applying the disputed practice.

Truth to tell, however, both readings of the statute produce puzzling results. Under the City's reading, if an employer adopts an unlawful practice and no timely charge is brought, it can continue using the practice indefinitely, with impunity, despite ongoing disparate impact. Equitable tolling or estoppel may allow some affected employees or applicants to sue, but many others will be left out in the cold. Moreover, the City's reading may induce plaintiffs aware of the danger of delay to file charges upon the announcement of a hiring practice, before they have any basis for believing it will produce a disparate impact.

In all events, it is not our task to assess the consequences of each approach and adopt the one that produces the least mischief. Our charge is to give effect to the law Congress enacted. By enacting § 2000e-2(k)(1)(A)(i), Congress allowed claims to be brought against an employer who uses a practice that causes disparate impact, whatever the employer's motives and whether or not he has employed the same practice in the past. If that effect was unintended, it is a problem for Congress, not one that federal courts can fix.

---

### Consequences of Failing to File a Timely EEOC Charge

It is crucial that an aggrieved employee file a timely charge with the EEOC in compliance with the previously discussed legal principles. The Commission will not investigate untimely charges and the courts will dismiss claims in which the charge was not timely filed, at least when the defense is properly brought to the court's attention by the employer.

The U.S. Supreme Court has explained that strict adherence to the statutory deadline for filing a charge is required by the statutes. Title VII says the charge *shall* be filed within the 300/180 day time period. The use of the term *shall* in the statute makes the charging period mandatory. *National Railroad Corp. v. Morgan*, 536 U.S. 101, 109 (2002). Nonetheless, the *Morgan* Court held that filing a charge within the charging period is not a jurisdictional prerequisite to a Title VII suit. Instead, it is a requirement subject to waiver, estoppel, and equitable tolling when equity so requires. *Id.* at 121.

The circumstances in which courts have allowed untimely filed charges on equity grounds are few and far between, and those few cases should not be counted on by plaintiffs as a saving grace. *See National Railroad Corp. v. Morgan*, 536 U.S. 101, 113 (2002) (equitable doctrines such as tolling and estoppel are to be used "sparingly"). In almost all cases, an employment discrimination claim based on an untimely filed charge will be dismissed by a court if the defense is timely and properly presented to the court by the employer.

## Step 2: The EEOC serves the notice of the charge on the employer.

Section 706(b) of Title VII states:

Notice to Respondent

Whenever a charge is filed by or on behalf of a person claiming to be aggrieved ... alleging that an employer ... has engaged in an unlawful employment practice, the Commission shall serve a notice of the charge (including the date, place and circumstances of the alleged unlawful employment practice) on such employer ... (hereinafter referred to as the "respondent") within ten (10) days and shall make an investigation thereof.

The statute requires the EEOC to notify the employer by mail or in person that a charge has been filed against it within ten days of the filing. *See* 29 C.F.R. § 1601.14(a). An example of a Notice of Charge of Discrimination is below.

---

### EQUAL EMPLOYMENT OPPORTUNITY COMMISSION

Ms. Samantha Meadows
Human Resources
Southern Bell Systems, Inc.
2625 Industry Parkway
Dallas, Texas 75209

| | |
|---|---|
| PERSON FILING CHARGE: | Jerome Johnson claims to be aggrieved |
| DATE OF THE ALLEGED VIOLATION: | January 17–18, 2014 |
| PLACE OF THE ALLEGED VIOLATION: | Dallas, Texas |
| CHARGE NUMBER: | 2509A6206 |

---

### NOTICE OF CHARGE OF DISCRIMINATION
(See EEOC "Rules and Regulations" before completing this Form)

You are hereby notified that a charge of employment discrimination has been filed against your organization under Title VII of the Civil Rights Act of 1964.

Please submit by March 14, 2014, a statement of your position with respect to the allegation(s) contained in this charge, with copies of any supporting documentation. This material will be made a part of the file and will be considered at the time that we investigate this charge. Your prompt response of this request will make it easier to conduct and conclude our investigation of this charge.

EEOC has instituted a Mediation program which provides parties with an opportunity to resolve the issue of a charge without extensive investigation or expenditure of resources. If you would like to participate, please indicate that desire on the enclosed form and respond by February 28, 2014 to Isabella Hernandez at (214) 658-9456 or iherandez@eeoc.gov. If you DO NOT wish to participate in Mediation, you must submit a statement of your position to the Commission Representative listed below, by the above date.

For further inquiry on this matter, please use the charge number shown above. Your position statement, your response to our request for information, or any inquiry you may have should be directed to:

| | |
|---|---|
| Dallas District Office | Cecilia B. Pioli, Investigator |
| 207 S. Houston Street, 3rd Floor | Commission Representative |
| Dallas, Texas 75202 | (214) 658-9481 |

A copy of the charge is enclosed. The bases of discrimination are race and retaliation. See enclosed Form 5, Charge of Discrimination for circumstances of the alleged violation.

February 12, 2014    Michael Watson, Director /s/
                     Authorized EEOC Official

## Step 3: The EEOC investigates the charge.

Title VII specifically requires the EEOC to investigate a filed charge. The agency will typically assign an investigator to be in charge of the charge, so to speak. EEOC regulations define the agency's investigative authority and powers. As part of its investigation, it is the EEOC's standard practice to require the employer to provide a *position statement* at the early part of the investigative stage. 29 C.F.R. § 1601.15(a). As the term indicates, the *position statement* provides the employer with its initial opportunity to respond to the charge. In general, the employer explains why the employer contends that discrimination did *not* occur. The EEOC may also require the aggrieved employee to provide a statement describing the facts which lead the employee to believe a discriminatory act took place and how that act harmed the employee. *Id.* at § 1601.15(b). The EEOC has the power to subpoena witnesses for purposes of taking their testimony and to subpoena evidence including items like books, records, correspondence, or other documents. *Id.* at § 1601.16(a). The EEOC may require a fact-finding conference with the parties prior to the determination on the charge. *Id.* at § 1601.15(c). It may even visit the facility where the alleged discrimination occurred, if that is deemed necessary to the investigation.

The employee and employer may voluntarily opt to participate in the EEOC's Mediation Program. Participation in the Mediation Program typically occurs early in the charge process and thus, if successful, could avoid a lengthy investigation period and subsequent judicial involvement. In general, a mediation session lasts about three to four hours. The time, of course, varies depending on the nature and complexity of the case. The session is conducted by a person who is specifically trained and experienced in conducting mediations. Each party to the mediation should have a representative or person with authority to settle the case. Detailed information about the agency's Mediation Program is located on its website, http://www.eeoc.gov/employees/mediation.cfm (last visited on July 18, 2013).

## Step 4: The EEOC makes a determination on the charge.

Section 706(b) of Title VII states:

> If the Commission determines after such investigation that there is not reasonable cause to believe that the charge is true, it shall dismiss the charge and promptly notify the person claiming to be aggrieved and the respondent of its action ... If the Commission determines after such investigation that there is reasonable cause to believe that the charge is true, the Commission shall endeavor to eliminate any such alleged unlawful employment practice by informal methods of conference, conciliation, and persuasion.... The Commission shall make its determination on reasonable cause as promptly as possible and, so far as practicable, not later than one hundred and twenty days from the filing of the charge or, where applicable ... from the date upon which the Commission is authorized to take action with respect to the charge.

42 U.S.C. § 2000e-5(b).

The EEOC's focus during its investigation of a charge is to determine whether there *is* or *is not* reasonable cause to believe that the alleged unlawful discrimination amounts to actual unlawful discrimination in violation of the statute. However, there are a variety of technical issues that may preclude the EEOC from delving into the merits of the alleged discrimination in the charge. First, the EEOC might dismiss the charge without much, if any, investigation if the employer has fewer than 15 employees. Recall that employers with fewer than 15 employees are not covered by Title VII. Second, the charge may be dismissed without investigation if the employee did not file a timely charge. Third, the charging party's lack of responsiveness to Commission requests for information may thwart the Commission's investigation.

The EEOC's determination on whether or not reasonable cause exists is not an adjudication of whether or not the statute has been violated. The EEOC through conciliation and negotiated settlement efforts can urge the parties to settle their dispute and thus preclude court litigation. However, absent a settlement, the EEOC's determination on the merits of the dispute, whatever it may be, does not preclude a lawsuit, which *will* adjudicate whether a violation occurred. If the EEOC makes a no reasonable cause finding, the charge will be dismissed, a right-to-sue letter will be issued, and the charging party may subsequently sue in court. If the EEOC makes a reasonable cause determination and the dispute is not settled by EEOC processes, the EEOC may decide to bring suit on behalf of the charging party in court or may close the case and give the party the go-ahead to sue the employer on its own. Another possibility is that the EEOC gives the employee the right to sue and the EEOC subsequently intervenes as a party in the lawsuit. In that situation, both the private plaintiff and the EEOC are parties to the suit.

If the charge is not settled at the EEOC stage through mediation, conciliation, or negotiated settlement, what is the effect, if any, of the EEOC's determination in a subsequent lawsuit under Title VII, the ADEA, or the ADA? Is the EEOC's determination admissible evidence during the trial of the lawsuit? Should the EEOC's determination be excluded from the evidence? Consider these questions as you read the following Fifth Circuit opinion.

---

## Focus Questions: *EEOC v. Manville Sales Corp.*

1. *Should a federal district court properly exclude an EEOC Letter of Violation in an ADEA trial under Federal Rule of Evidence 403 on the ground that such evidence presents a danger of "unfair prejudice"?*

2. *What is the difference between an EEOC Letter of Violation and an EEOC Reasonable Cause Determination Letter? Should the resolution of the evidentiary question turn on the distinction?*

3. *If an EEOC determination is admitted into evidence, is there a way to try and limit the effects of the "unfair prejudice" issue before the jury?*

4. *Do you think EEOC reasonable cause determinations are "highly probative" of discrimination?*

---

# EEOC v. Manville Sales Corp.

### 27 F.3d 1089 (5th Cir. 1994)

Circuit Judge Goldberg.

Charles Mitte and the Equal Employment Opportunity Commission ("EEOC") brought the instant lawsuit under the Age Discrimination in Employment Act ("ADEA"). The plaintiffs alleged that Mitte had been discriminatorily discharged by his employer, Manville Sales Corporation ("Manville"), in violation of the ADEA. After a jury trial, the district court entered judgment in favor of Manville. The plaintiffs appeal.

...

On March 15, 1988, after his original discharge by Manville, Mitte filed the instant age discrimination suit. The EEOC filed a separate action against Manville in December of the same year. The two cases were subsequently consolidated. In their suit, the plaintiffs charged that in the years leading up to Mitte's termination, he outsold the two younger sales representatives retained by Manville and that he was terminated because of his age. Manville responded that its financial problems necessitated a reduction in the sales force and that it selected Mitte because he was the least effective sales representative in the area. In particular, Manville contended that Mitte had problems getting along with certain customers, that he could not handle large volume accounts, that his expenses were too high, and that he was too inflexible to grasp the opportunities that had become available in the field.

[During the trial, the trial court granted the defendant's request to exclude a letter of violation issued by the EEOC after an investigation of Mitte's claim. Mitte and the EEOC asserted at the trial court level and before the Fifth Circuit that this evidentiary ruling was erroneous.]

...

EEOC Letter of Violation

As to the exclusion of the EEOC letter of violation, Manville argues that this evidence was properly excluded under Federal Rule of Evidence 403 because of the danger of unfair prejudice. In *Gilchrist v. Jim Slemons Imports, Inc.,* the Ninth Circuit held that an EEOC letter of violation is excludable because it "suggests that preliminarily there is reason to believe that a violation has taken place" and therefore results in unfair prejudice to defendant. 803 F.2d 1488, 1500 (9th Cir. 1986). In response, the EEOC notes that this circuit considers EEOC determinations of reasonable cause (as opposed to the letter of violation at issue in *Gilchrist*) to be presumptively admissible because they are "so highly probative of [discrimination] 'that [their probity] outweighs any possible prejudice to defendant.'" [citation omitted].

The problem with the EEOC's argument is that in the instant case the lower court considered a letter of violation, similar to the letter involved in *Gilchrist* rather than the letters of reasonable cause which were evaluated in the *McClure* and *Smith* cases. This difference is significant because a letter of reasonable cause is more tentative in its conclusions whereas a letter of violation states the categorical legal conclusion that a violation has taken place. Additionally, we have held that the *McClure* and *Smith* decisions should not "be read as leaving district courts without discretion under Rule 403 to exclude such reports if their probative value is substantially outweighed by prejudicial effect or other considerations enumerated in the rule." [citation omitted]. We agree with the Ninth Circuit's holding in *Gilchrist* that a letter of violation "represents a determination by the EEOC that a violation of the Act has occurred and thus results in a much greater possibility of unfair prejudice" and that "[t]he probative value of a letter of violation may not, in every case, outweigh the potential for prejudice." In the *de novo* adjudication conducted by the trial court in discrimination cases, the task of weighing a letter of violation's probity versus its possibility for prejudice is best left to the trial judge. Because the plaintiffs have failed to show that the exclusion of the letter of violation was an abuse of discretion, we let this ruling stand.

## Notes

1. *Unfair Prejudice under FRE 403.* The issue presented in the *Manville Sales* case is presented in many Title VII, ADEA, and ADA cases. Apparently, after the EEOC investigation of the charge filed by Mr. Mitte, the EEOC issued a letter that unequivocally stated that Manville violated the ADEA. The letter probably read along these lines: "The Commission has determined that the above-named respondent has discriminated against the Charging Party, Mitte, a person protected under the ADEA, by discharging him from his position of employment in violation of the ADEA." It makes perfect sense that an ADEA plaintiff, like Mr. Mitte, who is the beneficiary of such a determination would want to introduce it into evidence during the trial on the ADEA claim. The question is whether the evidence is admissible.

The federal courts have viewed EEOC determinations (or FEPA determinations) regarding alleged discrimination as an exception to the hearsay rule under Federal Rule of Evidence 803(8)(C) because such determinations are "factual findings resulting from an investigation made pursuant to authority granted by law, unless the sources of information or other circumstances indicate lack of trustworthiness." *See Paolitto v. Brown E.&C., Inc.*, 151 F.3d 60, 64 (2d Cir. 1998). The determinations are viewed as "relevant evidence" under the broad relevancy standard established in Federal Rule of Evidence 401 because they have a tendency to make the underlying discrimination question for a judge or jury more or less probable than it would be without the evidence. *See McClure v. Mexia Independent School District*, 750 F.2d 396, 400 (5th Cir. 1985); Federal Rule of Evidence 401 (Relevant evidence means evidence having any tendency to make a fact that is of consequence to the determination of the action more probable or less probable than it would be without the evidence.). As in the *Manville Sales* case, the admissibility hurdle centers on whether this "relevant evidence" should be excluded because its probative value is substantially outweighed by the danger of unfair prejudice or confusion of the issues. *See* Federal Rule of Evidence 403 (Although relevant, evidence may be excluded if its probative value is substantially outweighed by the danger of unfair prejudice, confusion of the issues, or misleading the jury, or by considerations of undue delay, waste of time, or needless presentation of cumulative evidence.).

One concern is that the jury will take the EEOC's determination as to whether discrimination occurred at face value without independently determining whether discrimination occurred. According to the *Manville Sales* court, this problem is particularly acute when the EEOC's determination categorically states that discrimination occurred. In contrast, a determination that there is reasonable cause to believe that discrimination occurred contains wiggle room and would not be as prejudicial. Do you agree with this distinction?

Most circuits have concluded that the admission of EEOC determinations should be left to the sound discretion of the district court. *See Patten v. Wal-Mart Stores East, Inc.*, 300 F.3d 21, 26–27 (1st Cir. 2002); *Paolitto v. Brown E.&C., Inc.*, 151 F.3d 60, 65 (2d Cir. 1998); *Hall v. Western Prod. Co.*, 988 F.2d 1050, 1057–1058 (10th Cir. 1993); *Barfield v. Orange County*, 911 F.2d 644, 650–51 (11th Cir. 1990); *Johnson v. Yellow Freight Systems, Inc.*, 734 F.2d 1304, 1309 (8th Cir. 1984); *McCluney v. Jos. Schlitz Brewing Co.*, 728 F.2d 924, 929–30 (7th Cir. 1984); *Walton v. Eaton Corp.*, 563 F.2d 66, 74–75 (3d Cir. 1977); *Cox v. Babcock & Wilcox Co.*, 471 F.2d 13, 15 (4th Cir. 1972). Do you agree? The minority view, which the Fifth and Ninth Circuit have historically embraced, adopts a *per se* rule that *reasonable cause* determinations must be admitted into evidence because their high probative value outweighs any possible prejudicial effect. *See Plummer v. Western International Hotels Co.*, 656 F.2d 502, 504 (9th Cir. 1981) (reversible error for the district court to exclude an EEOC probable cause determination from a Title VII trial); *McClure v. Mexia Independent School District*, 750 F.2d 396, 400 (5th Cir. 1985) (EEOC reasonable cause determinations are so highly probative evidence of discrimination that any danger of unfair prejudice is outweighed). The Fifth Circuit seems to have retreated from a *per se* rule, however, in recent years. *See Cortes v. Maxus Exploration Co.*, 977 F.2d 195, 201–02 (5th Cir. 1992) (*McClure* should not "be read as leaving district courts without discretion under Rule 403 to exclude such reports if their probative value is substantially outweighed by prejudicial effect or other consideration enumerated in the rule."). Put yourself in the position of a federal district judge, are you swayed that a letter of violation or reasonable cause determination is unfairly prejudicial to the defendant?

2. The reverse scenario occurs when the EEOC finding is that discrimination did not occur or at least that there is no reasonable cause to believe that discrimination occurred. In this scenario, the defendant-employer wants to introduce this evidence during trial. The plaintiff-employee desires to exclude the information. The analysis is basically the same as described above. It boils down to whether the federal district judge views the evidence as unfairly prejudicial. *See Barfield v. Orange County*, 911 F.2d 644 (11th Cir. 1990) (the district court did not err in admitting an EEOC "no reasonable cause" determination into evidence in a Title VII jury trial. The danger of unfair prejudice was too little to overcome the "highly probative" nature of the evidence).

3. There could be several reasons why a federal district court judge would view an EEOC determination as unfairly prejudicial. First, the state of the evidence at the administrative stage is often quite different than the evidence that exists at the time of trial. Consequently, an EEOC determination that does not have the benefit of the full amount of evidence introduced during the trial could simply be wrong due to an incomplete record. During the course of the pretrial stage of the Title VII suit, both sides will have the ability to engage in full discovery. Second, the quality and thoroughness of the EEOC's investigation may be questioned. The Eight Circuit stated in *Johnson* that employment-agency determinations "are not homogenous products; they vary in quality and factual detail." 734 F.2d at 1309. Third, there are difficulties in challenging the weakness of an EEOC determination during the trial. How would a defendant-employer or plaintiff-employee poke holes in an EEOC determination during a Title VII trial? Fourth, there is the issue of distracting the jury from the actual evidence (or lack thereof) of discrimination. The trial inappropriately centers on how the third-party agency evaluated the case, as opposed to the state of the evidence during the trial and how the fact-finder views that evidence. Finally, there is the point made earlier that a jury might have an inherent tendency to give more credence to an EEOC determination than it is really worth, *i.e.*, rubber-stamping the EEOC's determination without really considering the evidence adduced at trial. This is especially problematic when the EEOC determination is not explained in any substantial way. *Cf. L'Etoile v. New England Finish Systems, Inc.*, 575 F. Supp. 2d 331, 334 (D. N.H. 2008) (FEPA's conclusory findings had little probative force and "would distract the jury from its ultimate task, which is to decide whether the alleged acts of discrimination and retaliation occurred, not whether the [agency] correctly decided that they likely did not.").

4. *A final thought.* To the extent that courts consistently either exclude or admit EEOC determinations in Title VII, ADEA, and ADA suits, what does that say, if anything, about the regard in which the courts hold EEOC investigations?

### Exercise 10.1

In our sample *Johnson v. Southern Bell Systems* case, the EEOC determines after an investigation that there is reasonable cause to believe that the company discriminated against Johnson on the bases of race and retaliation in violation of Title VII. Johnson ultimately files a Title VII suit against the company in federal district court. The suit is tried to a jury. At trial, Johnson moves to introduce the EEOC determination into evidence. The company objects.

You are the federal district court judge who must rule on this evidentiary question.

- Will you admit or exclude the evidence? Why or why not? What factors might impact your decision?

- Let's say you decide that the evidence should be admitted. What can you as the judge do in the jury charge to try and alleviate some of the defendant-employer's concerns about the admission of this piece of evidence? Draft a portion of the jury charge that would address this piece of evidence.

- Are you satisfied a court of appeals will find that you did not err in how you addressed this evidentiary question?

## Step 5: The EEOC issues a right-to-sue letter.

Section 706(f)(1) of Title VII states:

> If a charge filed with the Commission ... is dismissed by the Commission, or if within one hundred and eighty days from the filing of such charge ... the Commission has not filed a civil action ... or entered into a conciliation agreement to which the person aggrieved is a party, the Commission shall so notify the person aggrieved and within *ninety days* after the giving of such notice a civil action may be brought by the person claiming to be aggrieved. (emphasis added).

42 U.S.C. § 2000e-5(f)(1).

### *The Time Frame for the EEOC's Issuance of the Right-to-Sue Letter*

The Title VII administrative scheme requires that an aggrieved party file a charge with the EEOC. The charge triggers an EEOC investigation. The investigation leads to a determination by the agency. The agency ultimately notifies the charging party of its disposition of the charge. The aggrieved employee must not file its lawsuit until after the EEOC has issued its notice of the right to file a civil action to the employee. This notice is called the right-to-sue letter.

Section 706(f)(1) of Title VII requires that the EEOC issue the right-to-sue letter no later than the 180th day after the charge-filing date. The 180-day period exists to prevent the administrative process from continuing on and on without resolution. It requires the EEOC bureaucrats to act on charges efficiently. Despite this statutory requirement, EEOC charges have been known to stack up for long periods of time without any action taken on them. Historically, the standard processing time for a charge has extended past the

180-day period. This problem is probably due in part to the substantial workload on the agency relative to its resources.

In any event, the aggrieved party should not file his or her Title VII lawsuit until after securing the right-to-sue letter from the agency. A party who files a Title VII suit without the agency having issued a right-to-sue letter will typically have his or her claim dismissed by the court for failure to exhaust administrative remedies. *See Bey v. Welsbach Electric Corp.*, 38 Fed. Appx. 690, 692 (2d Cir. 2002) (plaintiff's Title VII claim dismissed for failure to exhaust administrative remedies because plaintiff did not obtain right-to-sue letter from the EEOC).

Fortunately, even if the EEOC delays in resolving a charge past the 180-day time period, there is a procedural mechanism that allows the aggrieved party to secure a right-to-sue letter from the agency so that it can get on about its business of filing suit. EEOC regulations provide that the EEOC will issue a right-to-sue letter to the charging party on the expiration of the 180-day period even if the agency has not finished its investigation if the charging party *requests* the right-to-sue letter. *See* 29 C.F.R. § 1601.28(a)(1). Nonetheless, if no such request is made at the expiration of the 180-day period, then the charge stays in the administrative process until such time as the EEOC makes a determination, closes its investigation, and issues a right-to-sue letter or the charging party *solicits* the letter. Accordingly, the EEOC might not issue a right-to-sue letter for several years from the date of the filing of the charge, but the charging party after it receives such notice will still have the opportunity to file its lawsuit because the agency's inaction cannot take the aggrieved party's substantive Title VII rights. For example, in *Burgh v. Borough Council of Montrose*, 251 F.3d 465, 467–68 (3d Cir. 2001), the charging party filed his EEOC charge on March 20, 1995. The EEOC did not issue the right-to-sue letter until December 1, 1998 — approximately 3 years after the filing of the charge. The plaintiff filed his lawsuit within 90 days of receipt of the right-to-sue letter, however. Consequently, the lawsuit was timely filed. *See also Allen v. Avon Products, Inc.*, 55 FEP Cases 1662 (S.D. N.Y. 1998) (plaintiff's Title VII lawsuit timely filed even though nine years passed between the filing of her EEOC charge and the issuance of the right-to-sue letter).

EEOC regulations also allow the agency to issue a right-to-sue letter on request of the charging party *prior* to the expiration of the 180-day period. The issuance of an *early* right-to-sue letter from the EEOC must be based on the District Director's determination that it is probable that the agency will not be able to complete its administrative processing within the 180-day period. *See* 29 C.F.R. § 1601.28(a)(2). The early right-to-sue provision has been challenged, however. The D.C. Circuit held in *Martini v. Fannie Mae*, that this EEOC rule is beyond the agency's statutory authority. 178 F.3d 1336, 1347 (D.C. Cir. 1999). Thus, in that Circuit, aggrieved parties must wait until 180 days have passed from the charge-filing date to sue. Other circuits have upheld the rule. *See Walker v. United Parcel Service, Inc.*, 240 F.3d 1268, 1277 (10th Cir. 2001); *Sims v. MacMillan*, 22 F.3d 1059, 1061–63 (11th Cir. 1994); *Brown v. Puget Sound Electrical Apprenticeship & Training Trust*, 732 F.2d 726, 729 (9th Cir. 1984).

### The 90-Day Time Period to File a Lawsuit

Title VII establishes two primary time requirements for a charging party to properly exhaust his or her administrative remedies with the EEOC. First, the party must file his or her EEOC charge within 300/180 days from the date of the unlawful employment practice's occurrence. Second, the party must file his or her Title VII lawsuit within 90 days of the issuance of the right-to-sue letter. The federal courts have generally held that these requirements are not jurisdictional. They are best viewed as limitations periods. *See Zipes v. Trans World Airlines*, 455 U.S. 385, 393 (1984); *Baldwin County Welcome Center v. Brown*, 466 U.S. 147 (1984).

Section 706(f)(1) of Title VII states that the Title VII lawsuit must be filed within 90 days of the date that the EEOC "gives" its notice of the right to file a civil action, *i.e.*, right-to-sue letter. This statutory language is open to several possible interpretations. Does the EEOC "give" notice on the date that the right-to-sue letter is signed and issued by an EEOC representative? Perhaps the EEOC "gives" notice on the date that the right-to-sue letter is mailed to the charging party. The courts have generally eschewed these possible interpretations and have instead taken the view that the 90-day time period commences on the date that the charging party or his or her attorney *actually receives* the right-to-sue letter. *See Brzozowski v. Correctional Physician Services, Inc.*, 360 F.3d 173, 180 (3d Cir. 2004) (Title VII sets a 90-day period for filing suit in the district court after receipt of a notice of right to sue letter from the EEOC); *Threadgill v. Moore U.S.A., Inc.*, 269 F.3d 848 (7th Cir. 2001) (same); *Cornwell v. Robinson*, 23 F.3d 694, 706 (2d Cir. 1994) (same); *Irwin v. Department of Veterans Affairs*, 498 U.S. 89, 92 (1990) (receipt of EEOC right-to-sue letter by claimant's attorney commenced the lawsuit filing period). A complaint must then be filed in court within 90 days of actual receipt in order for the Title VII claim to be timely filed.

Cases arise in which there is no evidence of the date of actual receipt. In such cases, a presumption is that the date of actual receipt is within a certain number of days from the date of mailing. The date of issuance of the EEOC right-to-sue letter is typically considered to be the date of mailing when there is no proof of the actual mailing date. The circuits vary concerning the number of days in the presumption. The range generally stretches from three to seven days. *Sherlock v. Montefiore Medical Center*, 84 F.3d 522, 525–26 (2d Cir. 1996) (court presumed actual receipt within three days of mailing of EEOC right to-sue-letter); *Banks v. Rockwell International North American Aircraft Operations*, 855 F.2d 324, 326 (6th Cir. 1988) (five-day presumption); *Ellison v. Northwest Airlines*, 938 F. Supp. 1503, 1509 (D. Haw. 1996) (court applied a seven-day presumption).

There is a good way to avoid problems in this area. The aggrieved party can simply look at the issuance date on the right-to-sue letter and work off of that date as the date that begins the 90-day period, even though as a technical, legal matter the time period will start at a later date because the actual receipt date will usually be at a later date. If the attorney or aggrieved party uses this approach, she will avoid many problems regarding satisfying the 90-day limitations period.

### Equitable Tolling, Estoppel, and Waiver

Because the 90-day limitations period is not jurisdictional but operates instead like a statute of limitations, there are situations in which a court might permit a lawsuit filed outside the 90-day statutory period to go forward. First, a court might decide that even though the plaintiff failed to file the lawsuit within the 90-day period, the defense is waived because the employer did not assert it at the appropriate time in the litigation. *See Zipes v. Trans World Airlines*, 455 U.S. 385, 393 (1984) (court considered whether defendant's failure to raise plaintiffs' untimely filed charge waived the defense). Second, a court might buy an equitable ground for tolling the 90-day limitations period like a plaintiff's mental disability. *See Stoll v. Runyon*, 165 F.3d 1238, 1242 (9th Cir. 1999) (court tolled 90-day period because plaintiff was completely psychiatrically disabled during the relevant time period). Third, a court might preclude the application of the 90-day period when the charging party was misled about the statutory requirements by the EEOC or by the employer's promises. *See Ramirez v. City of San Antonio*, 312 F.3d 178, 183–85 (5th Cir. 2002) (in rare circumstances a court could grant equitable tolling when the delay was caused by the EEOC misleading the plaintiff about the nature of her rights).

The discussion in Step 1 noted that, in general, it is very unlikely that a court will excuse a party from missing the deadline to file an EEOC charge. It happens only in very unusual circumstances. Likewise, it is atypical for a court to apply equitable tolling, estoppel, or waiver principles to excuse the plaintiff from failing to file a Title VII lawsuit within the 90-day time period. A plaintiff should not think that he or she will get bailed out by the judge if the plaintiff does not file suit within 90 days of receipt of the right-to-sue letter.

---

## Exercise 10.2

In our sample *Johnson v. Southern Bell Systems* case, you are an attorney, Bobby Beem, who represents Mr. Johnson during the course of the EEOC proceedings. On April 15, 2014, approximately two months after the EEOC charge was filed, you request a right-to-sue letter from the EEOC. The EEOC Director signs the right-to-sue letter on April 30, 2014, and it is issued on that same day. Assume further that the EEOC mails the right-to-sue letter to your office and to Mr. Johnson. You receive the right-to-sue letter on May 5, 2014. What is your deadline for filing the Title VII lawsuit? When should you file the lawsuit?

You can use the sample EEOC right-to-sue letter below to help you visualize what this document looks like.

---

### ADA, ADEA, and Section 1981 Claims and the Administrative Process

The administrative process for ADA claims is the same as for Title VII claims. The ADA enforcement provision states that the powers, remedies, and procedures set forth in the administrative components of Title VII shall be the same as those under the ADA. *See* ADA § 107(a); 42 U.S.C. § 12117(a) ("The powers, remedies, and procedures set forth in section 705, 706, 707, 709, and 710 of the Civil Rights Act of 1964 shall be the powers, remedies, and procedures [the ADA] provides to the [EEOC] ... or to any person alleging discrimination on the basis of disability in violation of any provision of [the ADA].").

The administrative process for ADEA claims is very similar to the process for Title VII claims. The standard framework applies, which consists of the filing of a charge with the EEOC within 300/180 days, serving notice of the charge on the employer, the EEOC investigation, the EEOC determination, the EEOC's issuance of the right-to-sue letter, and the filing of the ADEA lawsuit within 90 days of the receipt of the right-to-sue letter. *See* 29 U.S.C. § 626(d) (establishing 300/180 day limitations period for filing charge based on age discrimination); 29 U.S.C. § 626(e) (a civil action may be brought against the employer named in the charge within 90 days after the date of the receipt of such notice).

However, there are some differences. For example, an ADEA claim must be filed within 90 days of the receipt of a right-to-sue letter if one is issued, but there is no provision in the ADEA that requires a charging party to receive such a letter before commencing a

---

**Equal Employment Opportunity Commission**

**DISMISSAL AND NOTICE OF RIGHTS**

To:
Mr. Jerome Johnson
5401 Vickery Lane
Dallas, Texas 75202
214-543-8201

From:
Equal Employment Opportunity Commission
Dallas District Office
207 S. Houston Street, Third Floor
Dallas, Texas 75702

| | |
|---|---|
| Certified Mail No.: | Z 857 209 343 |
| Charge No.: | 2509A6206 |
| EEOC Representative: | Cecilia B. Pioli (214) 658-9481 |

**YOUR CHARGE IS DISMISSED FOR THE FOLLOWING REASON:**

Right to Sue (Issued on Request)

**NOTICE OF SUIT RIGHTS**

**Title VII and/or the Americans with Disabilities Act.** This is your NOTICE OF RIGHT TO SUE. If you want to pursue your charge further, you have the right to sue the respondent(s) named in your charge in court. **If you decide to sue, you must sue WITHIN 90 DAYS from your receipt of this Notice; otherwise your right to sue is lost. WITH THE ISSUANCE OF THIS NOTICE OF RIGHT TO SUE, THE COMMISSION IS TERMINATING ITS PROCESS WITH RESPECT TO THIS CHARGE.**

On behalf of the Commission

Date:    April 30, 2014          Michael Watson, District Director

cc:   Bobby Beem
      Bobby Beem & Associates
      248 Gables Parkway, Suite 1200
      Dallas, Texas 75210

Enclosures: Information Sheet and Copy of Charge, EEOC Form 5

---

court action under the ADEA. Consequently, receipt of a right-to-sue letter is not a prerequisite to suit. Unless the EEOC first commences an action on behalf of the charging party, an ADEA plaintiff may file suit at any time from 60 days after timely filing the EEOC charge until 90 days after receipt of the right-to-sue letter. *See* 29 U.S.C. §626(d) ("No civil action may be commenced by an individual under [the ADEA] until 60 days after a charge alleging unlawful discrimination has been filed."); *Francis v. Elmsford School District*, 442 F.3d 123, 126–27 (2d Cir. 2006) (explaining that filing charge and waiting sixty days are the prerequisites to filing an ADEA suit); *Julian v. City of Houston*, 314 F.3d 721, 726 (5th Cir. 2002) ("a complainant who timely files the EEOC charge and then observes the sixty-day waiting period has satisfied the statutory preconditions to filing [an ADEA] suit.").

Section 1981 claims are a different ball of wax entirely. Recall that Section 1981 is a Civil War-Reconstruction era statute that prohibits race discrimination in contracts—including employment contracts. There is no administrative process applicable to Section 1981 claims. Accordingly, a party who suffers race discrimination in employment may simply file a court action under Section 1981. The key is to make sure the Section 1981 claim is filed within the appropriate limitations period. Determining the limitations period for a Section 1981 claim is a bit peculiar and quite complicated. The historical background of the limitations period for Section 1981 claims is instructive.

Section 1981 itself does not contain a statute of limitations. Regrettably, this occurs too often. Many federal statutes do not contain limitations periods. The question is thus how to go about finding the right limitations period. Usually, that involves borrowing an analogous state limitations period. In *Goodman v. Lukens Steel Co.*, 482 U.S. 656 (1987), the Supreme Court held that a single state statute of limitations should govern all § 1981 claims and that the limitations period for personal injury tort claims is the most appropriate state statute of limitations. The effect of the *Goodman* decision was that the limitations period for Section 1981 claims varied depending on the state in which the claim was brought. So, for example, a § 1981 claim brought in Texas was subject to a two-year limitations period because Texas has a two-year statute of limitations for personal injury actions. *See Byers v. Dallas Morning News, Inc.*, 209 F.3d 419, 424 (5th Cir. 2002); *Price v. Digital Equip. Corp.*, 846 F.2d 1026, 1028 (5th Cir. 1988). In contrast, a § 1981 claim brought in Louisiana was subject to a one-year limitation period because Louisiana has a one-year prescriptive period for personal injury actions. *See Taylor v. Bunge Corp.*, 775 F.2d 617, 618 (5th Cir. 1985). This caused more work for attorneys, litigants, and judges in that there was not a uniform limitations period for all jurisdictions, but the law was easy enough to apply after one identified the applicable state's law concerning the limitations period for personal injury actions.

The United States Supreme Court in *Jones v. R.R. Donnelley & Sons*, 541 U.S. 369 (2004), changed the law concerning the limitations period for certain § 1981 actions. Now, a uniform four-year limitations period applies throughout the country to Section 1981 claims involving post-employment conduct. But one still needs to apply the forum state's limitation period for Section 1981 claims involving pre-employment conduct (failure to hire claims and certain categories of failure to promote claims). The following is a brief explanation of how the law reached this point.

Several key developments occurred after the *Goodman* decision. In 1989, the Court decided *Patterson v. McLean Credit Union*, 491 U.S. 164 (1989). In *Patterson*, the Court eviscerated a large portion of § 1981 discrimination claims by ruling that § 1981 did not cover post-formation conduct unrelated to an employee's right to enforce his or her contract, such as incidents relating to the conditions of employment. The ruling precluded Section 1981 claims that alleged the employer terminated the employee's employment because of his or her race. Congress did not like the *Patterson* decision, however, and, in 1991, it amended § 1981 to permit § 1981 claims for discrimination in employment that occurs after contract formation. Between the *Patterson* decision and the amendment to § 1981, Congress also enacted an across-the-board four-year statute of limitations for actions "arising under" federal statutes enacted after December 1, 1990. *See* 28 U.S.C. § 1658(a) ("Except as otherwise provided by law, a civil action arising under an Act of Congress enacted after the date of enactment of this section [enacted Dec. 1, 1990] may not be commenced later than 4 years after the cause of action accrues.").

You can see where this is leading. Post-employment § 1981 claims only became actionable after Congress amended Section 1981 in 1991. Therefore, in *Jones v. R.R. Donnelley & Sons*, the Court concluded that the four-year limitations period in the catchall statute applied to Section 1981 post-employment claims because such claims were made possible by a post-1990 Congressional enactment. The *Jones* holding indicates, however, that Section 1981 claims that were actionable under the pre-1991 version of § 1981 are subject to the *Goodman* rule concerning the appropriate limitations period. Thus, a Section 1981 claim brought in Louisiana that alleges that the employer failed to enter into a new contract with the plaintiff-employee because of race is subject to a one-year limitations period. *See e.g., Johnson v. Crown Enterprises, Inc.*, 398 F.3d 339 (5th Cir. 2005) (Section 1981 claim brought by Louisiana plaintiff that alleged failure to enter into a new employment contract was subject to a one-year limitations period—Louisiana's limitations period for personal injury actions).[1]

### State Antidiscrimination Claims and the Administrative Process

The concept of a deferral state has previously been explained. Deferral states have their own state laws and agencies that also prohibit discrimination in employment. Title VII establishes a floor for prohibiting discrimination in employment, but it does not set a ceiling. *See* Title VII § 708; 42 U.S.C. § 2000e-7 (*Effect of State Laws.* "Nothing in this title shall be deemed to exempt or relieve any person from any liability, duty, penalty, or punishment provided by any present or future law or any State or political subdivision of a State, other than any such law which purports to require or permit the doing of any act which would be any unlawful employment practice under this title."). Therefore, states are free to experiment in this arena and provide more rights than federal law does, such as protection against sexual orientation discrimination or broadening what constitutes a covered employer, *i.e.*, reducing or doing away altogether with the Title VII 15-employee coverage requirement. *See* New Mexico Human Rights Act, N.M. Stat. Ann. § 28-1-2(B) (an "employer" means any person employing four or more persons and any person acting for an employer."). Alternatively, a state antidiscrimination statute could essentially mirror Title VII law without much change. *See, e.g., Quantum Chemical Corp. v. Toennies*, 47 S.W.3d 473, 476 (Tex. 2001) (federal antidiscrimination statutes and court decisions guide the reading of the Texas antidiscrimination statute). State antidiscrimination statutes may also vary from Title VII in terms of the procedural process.

Many state antidiscrimination statutes establish a procedural process that is quite similar to Title VII. The process involves filing a charge with the appropriate state agency, exhaustion of administrative remedies with a stage agency (agency investigates charge), and then suing under the state statute in court. *See* Colo. Rev. Stat. § 24-34-306(14) (Colorado). But this is not always the case. For example, in Illinois, the state administrative procedure under the Illinois Human Right Act entails a true administrative adjudication by an administrative law judge (ALJ) with internal administrative appeal rights to a Commission. Final decisions of the Commission may be judicially reviewed under traditional judicial review standards of agency adjudications. *See Board of Education v. Cady*, 860 N.E.2d 526 (Ill. App. 2006). In Nebraska, employment discrimination plaintiffs may bring suit in state district court for violations of the Nebraska Fair Employment Practice Act without first exhausting administrative remedies with the Nebraska Equal Employment Opportunity Commission. *See* Neb. Rev. Stat. § 20-148. Keep the following in mind: Even in states where the state antidiscrimination statute is substantively and procedurally similar to Title VII, important differences tend to arise between state and federal law.

An effective employment discrimination litigator must understand both the federal administrative procedure (EEOC process) and the state administrative procedure (state agency process) so that strategic choices are made intelligently. To sue under Title VII, the EEOC procedures must be followed. To sue under the state statute, the state procedures must be followed. Failure to follow the appropriate federal procedures should not cut off rights

---

1. The Section 1981 limitations period material is taken from a CLE article written by author Jarod S. Gonzalez for the State Bar of Texas Section on Labor and Employment Law in 2005. *See* Federal Employment Law Update, SBOT Labor and Employment Law Section Annual Update, South Texas College of Law, November 3, 2005, 16–17.

under state law if the state procedures are followed. And, vice versa, failure to follow state procedures should not cut off federal rights. *See EEOC v. Commercial Office Products*, 486 U.S. 107 (1988) (untimely filing of discrimination charge under state law does not impact whether a discrimination charge is timely filed with the EEOC under Title VII). It is standard for a charging party to dually file a charge of discrimination with both the EEOC and the applicable state agency and then follow both the federal and state administrative requirements so that rights under both state and federal antidiscrimination laws are preserved.

Take the State of Texas as an illustration of procedural differences between federal and state administrative procedure. Texas is a deferral state. It has its own antidiscrimination statute that models Title VII, the ADEA, and the ADA, called Chapter 21 of the Texas Labor Code. Texas also has its own antidiscrimination agency, called the Civil Rights Division of the Texas Workforce Commission, which was formerly known as the Texas Commission on Human Rights. The procedures and deadlines for filing a charge with the Texas Workforce Commission (TWC) and suing under the Texas antidiscrimination provision are slightly different than the federal system. However, the overarching framework of filing a charge, exhausting administrative remedies, and suing in court is the same as the federal system. Moreover, the substantive law under Chapter 21 is not significantly different from Title VII, the ADA, and the ADEA.

Under Texas state law, the charging party must file the charge with the TWC within 180 days of the alleged unlawful employment practice. *See* Tex. Lab. Code § 21.201-.202. Accordingly, in Texas, preservation of Chapter 21 rights requires that a TWC charge be filed within 180 days of the alleged discriminatory act, even though preservation of Title VII rights based on the same act permits the party to timely file an EEOC charge within 300 days of the alleged discriminatory act.

Under Chapter 21, unlike Title VII, a charging party is not required to obtain a right-to-sue letter — called a Notice of Right to File a Civil Action in Texas — as a prerequisite to filing suit under Chapter 21. The only limitation on filing suit is that the charging party must wait at least 180 days from the date of the filing of the charge before filing suit. *See* Tex. Lab. Code § 21.208; *City of Houston v. Fletcher*, 63 S.W.3d 920, 922 (Tex. App.-Houston [14th Dist.] 2002, no pet.); *Wilshire v. Humpal Physical Therapy*, P.C., 2005 WL 2091092 (Tex. App.-Corpus Christi 2005). Nonetheless, most practitioners will indeed procure a right-to-sue letter from the TWC before suing. If the TWC does issue a Notice of Right to File a Civil Action, the charging party must sue within 60 days of receipt of the notice. *See* Tex. Lab. Code § 21.254. The 60-day deadline is shorter than the federal 90-day deadline. The other main difference is that the charging party must file suit in court no later than 2 years after the filing of the charge. *See* Tex. Labor Code § 21.256. The federal system has no such outer limitations period, although the doctrine of laches might conceivably have a role in the federal system in an extreme case. *But see Allen v. Avon Products, Inc.*, 55 FEP Cases 1662 (S.D. N.Y. 1998) (plaintiff's Title VII lawsuit timely filed even though nine years passed between the filing of her EEOC charge and the issuance of the right-to-sue letter).

Finally, it is worth noting that factual scenarios that give rise to federal and state antidiscrimination claims could also be the subject of a common law claim against the employer. There are many interesting issues that arise concerning whether common law claims based on discriminatory harassment should be preempted by state antidiscrimination statutes. *See* Jarod S. Gonzalez, *State Antidiscrimination Statutes and Implied Preemption of Common Law Torts: Valuing the Common Law*, 59 S.C. L. Rev. 115 (2006). Common law tort claims may advantage plaintiffs because there is no administrative process to go through and tort-style remedies without caps on damages could be available, depending on the jurisdiction.

## Exercise 10.3

In our sample *Johnson v. Southern Bell Systems* case, you are an attorney, Bobby Beem. Mr. Johnson visits your law office on January 22, 2014, a few days after Southern Bell Systems terminated his employment. Mr. Johnson explains why he thinks discrimination occurred and you agree. You agree to take his case and represent him during the administrative proceedings and any subsequent litigation.

- Explain the initial steps you will take to preserve his substantive rights under state and federal antidiscrimination statutes.

- Assume that you exhaust Mr. Johnson's administrative remedies but his claims are not resolved, where will you file the lawsuit? What claims will you assert against Southern Bell Systems? What are the limitations periods for those claims?

### Procedural Requirements for Public Sector Employees

Federal law prohibits workplace discrimination by public employers as well as by private employers. Many federal employees are protected from race, color, religion, sex, and national origin discrimination by §717 of Title VII and from age discrimination by §15 of the ADEA. *See* 42 U.S.C. §2000e-16; 29 U.S.C. §633a. The Rehabilitation Act or the ADA provides protection for federal employees with a disability. *See* 29 U.S.C. §794(a). In general, the substantive provisions of the antidiscrimination laws covering federal employees are the same as those for private employees. However, the procedural requirements for federal employees differ significantly from the procedures for private employees. Each of the statutory provisions cited above create a unique procedural scheme, the details of which are beyond the scope of this course. In general, a federal employee must first file an administrative complaint with the agency that committed the discrimination. Federal employees must then exhaust their remedies within the agency. After a final decision by the agency, the employee may seek review of the decision by the EEOC or by filing suit in district court. If review is sought with the EEOC, there is an opportunity to seek judicial review after the EEOC adjudication. Important limitation periods relate to each stage of the procedure and these periods may differ from those that apply to private employees.

Many governmental employees at the state and local level are also protected from discrimination in employment by federal antidiscrimination laws. But some state employees, like elected officials, are exempted from coverage under the discrimination laws. *See* 42 U.S.C. §2000e-(f); 29 U.S.C. §630(f). Covered state employees alleging discrimination will typically follow the procedures applicable to private sector employees. The Government Employee Rights Act of 1991 (GERA) is an exception. GERA protects certain appointed officials and policy-making officials of a state, who were previously excluded from coverage under the antidiscrimination laws, from workplace discrimination on the basis of race, color, religion, sex, national origin, age or disability. For state officials covered by GERA, the procedure is different than the private sector procedure. Under GERA, the employee files a charge with the EEOC. The EEOC adjudicates the dispute through a formal agency procedure. An ALJ holds a formal hearing on the charge. The ALJ's findings are reviewed by the EEOC and the EEOC then makes its final decision. The EEOC's final decision is subject to judicial review but it may only be overturned by a court if it was "(1) arbitrary, capricious, an abuse of discretion, or otherwise not consistent with law; (2) not made consistent with required procedures; or (3) unsupported by substantial evidence." 42 U.S.C. § 2000e-16c(d).

## The Court Process

### Step 6: The plaintiff files the employment discrimination claim in court.

Section 706(f)(3) of Title VII states:

> Each United States district court and each United States court of a place subject to the jurisdiction of the United States shall have jurisdiction of actions brought under this title [Title VII]. Such an action may be brought in any judicial district in the State in which the unlawful employment practice is alleged to have been committed, in the judicial district in which the employment records relevant to such practice are maintained and administered, or in the judicial district in which the aggrieved person would have worked but for the alleged unlawful employment practice, but if the respondent is not found within any such district, such an action may be brought within the judicial district in which the respondent has his principal office.

42 U.S.C. § 2000e-5(f)(3).

The Federal Rules of Civil Procedure control the procedure for litigating an employment discrimination case filed in federal district court. Jurisdiction and venue for a Title VII action are provided by Section 706(f)(3). Instead of filing in federal court, a plaintiff may decide to file her Title VII claim in state court. The state court procedures of the state in which the Title VII suit is filed must be followed if the plaintiff chooses to file her Title VII claim in state court. Of course, Title VII claims filed in state court are frequently removed to federal court by the employer on the basis of federal question jurisdiction.

The typical plaintiff in a Title VII suit is a private party. The dominant paradigm in Title VII litigation is the private plaintiff suing the employer after exhaustion of the EEOC administrative process. *See* 42 U.S.C. § 2000e-5(f)(1). But Title VII actions are not restricted to private plaintiffs. Section 707 of Title VII permits the EEOC to bring pattern or practice cases against employers. *See* 42 U.S.C. § 2000e-6(a). The authority to bring § 707 actions previously rested with the Department of Justice. The Department of Justice may sue a governmental employer for violating Title VII pursuant to Section 706. *See* 42 U.S.C. § 2000e-5(f)(1).

Section 706 also permits the EEOC to sue non-governmental employers if certain statutory prerequisites are satisfied. First, the EEOC must make a "cause" determination on the charge. This means that the EEOC finds based on its investigation that there is "reasonable cause" to believe that the employer discriminated against the charging party. Second, the EEOC must attempt to conciliate the dispute. Title VII states that if the EEOC finds reasonable cause it "shall endeavor to eliminate any such unlawful employment practice by informal methods of conference, *conciliation* and persuasion." 42 U.S.C. § 2000e-5(b) (emphasis added). The EEOC attempts to conciliate a charge by negotiating in good faith with the employer a settlement of the charging party's claims. It is only after the EEOC is unable to secure from the employer an acceptable conciliation agreement that the EEOC may bring a civil action against the employer. *See* 42 U.S.C. § 2000e-5(f)(1). In short, an effort to conciliate by the EEOC is a condition precedent to the EEOC's power to sue. Conciliation is not a condition precedent to the institution of a private action for relief under Title VII by an individual plaintiff.

Title VII provides intervention opportunities for both the EEOC and private parties so that all interested entities may participate in the lawsuit regardless of which entity initially sued. If the EEOC sues an employer after conciliation fails, the private party may intervene as a matter of right in the EEOC suit. *See* 42 U.S.C. § 2000e-5(f)(1) ("The [aggrieved private party] shall have the right to intervene in a civil action brought by the [EEOC] …"). If the aggrieved private party, after receiving a right-to-sue letter, sues the employer, the court may allow the EEOC to intervene in the private action. *Id.* ("Upon timely application, the court may, in its discretion, permit the EEOC … to intervene in such civil action upon certification that the case is of general public importance.").

### The Lawsuit

Pleadings, discovery, summary judgment, and trial comprise four important stages in an employment discrimination lawsuit. Consider the following issues that arise at the various stages of employment discrimination litigation.

### Pleadings

Federal Rule of Civil Procedure 8(a)(2) states that a complaint must include "a short and plain statement of the claim showing that the pleader is entitled to relief." Is there a heightened pleading requirement for employment discrimination cases subject to the *McDonnell-Douglas* framework?

---

### Focus Questions: *Swierkiewicz v. Sorema*

1. *Must a complaint in an employment discrimination lawsuit contain specific facts establishing a prima facie case of discrimination under* McDonnell Douglas?

2. *What is the* McDonnell Douglas *burden-shifting framework? How would you describe its function? Does the framework have anything to do with how a discrimination claim is pleaded?*

3. *What are the reasons for the Court's holding?*

4. *What justification, if any, is there for requiring more than "notice pleading" in an employment discrimination lawsuit?*

---

## Swierkiewicz v. Sorema

### 534 U.S. 506 (2002)

Justice Thomas delivered the opinion for a unanimous Court.

This case presents the question whether a complaint in an employment discrimination lawsuit must contain specific facts establishing a prima facie case of discrimination under the framework set forth by this Court in *McDonnell Douglas Corp. v. Green*, 411 U.S. 792

(1973). We hold that an employment discrimination complaint need not include such facts and instead must contain only "a short and plain statement of the claim showing that the pleader is entitled to relief." Fed. Rule Civ. Proc. 8(a)(2).

## I

Petitioner Akos Swierkiewicz is a native of Hungary, who at the time of his complaint was 53 years old. In April 1989, petitioner began working for respondent Sorema N. A., a reinsurance company headquartered in New York and principally owned and controlled by a French parent corporation. Petitioner was initially employed in the position of senior vice president and chief underwriting officer (CUO). Nearly six years later, François M. Chavel, respondent's Chief Executive Officer, demoted petitioner to a marketing and services position and transferred the bulk of his underwriting responsibilities to Nicholas Papadopoulo, a 32-year-old who, like Mr. Chavel, is a French national. About a year later, Mr. Chavel stated that he wanted to "energize" the underwriting department and appointed Mr. Papadopoulo as CUO. Petitioner claims that Mr. Papadopoulo had only one year of underwriting experience at the time he was promoted, and therefore was less experienced and less qualified to be CUO than he, since at that point he had 26 years of experience in the insurance industry.

Following his demotion, petitioner contends that he "was isolated by Mr. Chavel ... excluded from business decisions and meetings and denied the opportunity to reach his true potential at SOREMA." Petitioner unsuccessfully attempted to meet with Mr. Chavel to discuss his discontent. Finally, in April 1997, petitioner sent a memo to Mr. Chavel outlining his grievances and requesting a severance package. Two weeks later, respondent's general counsel presented petitioner with two options: He could either resign without a severance package or be dismissed. Mr. Chavel fired petitioner after he refused to resign.

Petitioner filed a lawsuit alleging that he had been terminated on account of his national origin in violation of Title VII of the Civil Rights Act of 1964 and on account of his age in violation of the Age Discrimination in Employment Act of 1967. The United States District Court for the Southern District of New York dismissed petitioner's complaint because it found that he "ha[d] not adequately alleged a prima facie case, in that he ha[d] not adequately alleged circumstances that support an inference of discrimination." The United States Court of Appeals for the Second Circuit affirmed the dismissal, relying on its settled precedent, which requires a plaintiff in an employment discrimination complaint to allege facts constituting a prima facie case of discrimination under the framework set forth by this Court in *McDonnell Douglas*. The Court of Appeals held that petitioner had failed to meet his burden because his allegations were "insufficient as a matter of law to raise an inference of discrimination." We granted certiorari to resolve a split among the Courts of Appeals concerning the proper pleading standard for employment discrimination cases and now reverse.

## II

Applying Circuit precedent, the Court of Appeals required petitioner to plead a prima facie case of discrimination in order to survive respondent's motion to dismiss. In the Court of Appeals' view, petitioner was thus required to allege in his complaint: (1) membership in a protected group; (2) qualification for the job in question; (3) an adverse employment action; and (4) circumstances that support an inference of discrimination.

The prima facie case under *McDonnell Douglas*, however, is an evidentiary standard, not a pleading requirement. In *McDonnell Douglas*, this Court made clear that "[t]he critical issue before us concern[ed] the order and allocation *of proof* in a private, non-class action challenging employment discrimination." (emphasis added). In subsequent cases, this Court has reiterated that the prima facie case relates to the employee's burden of presenting evidence that raises an inference of discrimination.

This Court has never indicated that the requirements for establishing a prima facie case under *McDonnell Douglas* also apply to the pleading standard that plaintiffs must satisfy in order to survive a motion to dismiss. For instance, we have rejected the argument that a Title VII complaint requires greater "particularity," because this would "too narrowly constric[t] the role of the pleadings." [citation omitted]. Consequently, the ordinary rules for assessing the sufficiency of a complaint apply.

In addition, under a notice pleading system, it is not appropriate to require a plaintiff to plead facts establishing a prima facie case because the *McDonnell Douglas* framework does not apply in every employment discrimination case. For instance, if a plaintiff is able to produce direct evidence of discrimination, he may prevail without proving all the elements of a prima facie case. Under the Second Circuit's heightened pleading standard, a plaintiff without direct evidence of discrimination at the time of his complaint must plead a prima facie case of discrimination, even though discovery might uncover such direct evidence. It thus seems incongruous to require a plaintiff, in order to survive a motion to dismiss, to plead more facts than he may ultimately need to prove to succeed on the merits if direct evidence of discrimination is discovered.

Moreover, the precise requirements of a prima facie case can vary depending on the context and were "never intended to be rigid, mechanized, or ritualistic." Before discovery has unearthed relevant facts and evidence, it may be difficult to define the precise formulation of the required prima facie case in a particular case. Given that the prima facie case operates as a flexible evidentiary standard, it should not be transposed into a rigid pleading standard for discrimination cases.

Furthermore, imposing the Court of Appeals' heightened pleading standard in employment discrimination cases conflicts with Federal Rule of Civil Procedure 8(a)(2), which provides that a complaint must include only "a short and plain statement of the claim showing that the pleader is entitled to relief." Such a statement must simply "give the defendant fair notice of what the plaintiff's claim is and the grounds upon which it rests." *Conley v. Gibson*, 355 U.S. 41 47 (1957). This simplified notice pleading standard relies on liberal discovery rules and summary judgment motions to define disputed facts and issues and to dispose of unmeritorious claims.

Rule 8(a)'s simplified pleading standard applies to all civil actions, with limited exceptions. Rule 9(b), for example, provides for greater particularity in all averments of fraud or mistake. This Court, however, has declined to extend such exceptions to other contexts.... Just as Rule 9(b) makes no mention of municipal liability under 42 U.S.C. § 1983 neither does it refer to employment discrimination. Thus, complaints in these cases, as in most others, must satisfy only the simple requirements of Rule 8(a).

Other provisions of the Federal Rules of Civil Procedure are inextricably linked to Rule 8(a)'s simplified notice pleading standard. Rule 8(e)(1) states that "[n]o technical forms of pleading or motions are required," and Rule 8(f) provides that "[a]ll pleadings shall be so construed as to do substantial justice." Given the Federal Rules' simplified standard for pleading, "[a] court may dismiss a complaint only if it is clear that no relief could be granted under any set of facts that could be proved consistent with the allegations." [citation omitted]. If a pleading fails to specify the allegations in a manner that provides sufficient notice, a defendant can move for a more definite statement under Rule 12(e) before responding. Moreover, claims lacking merit may be dealt with through summary judgment under Rule 56. The liberal notice pleading of Rule 8(a) is the starting point of a simplified pleading system, which was adopted to focus litigation on the merits of a claim.

Applying the relevant standard, petitioner's complaint easily satisfies the requirements of Rule 8(a) because it gives respondent fair notice of the basis for petitioner's claims. Petitioner alleged that he had been terminated on account of his national origin in violation of Title VII and on account of his age in violation of the ADEA. His complaint detailed the events leading to his termination, provided relevant dates, and included the ages and nationalities of at least some of the relevant persons involved with his termination. These allegations give respondent fair notice of what petitioner's claims are and the grounds upon which they rest. In addition, they state claims upon which relief could be granted under Title VII and the ADEA.

Respondent argues that allowing lawsuits based on conclusory allegations of discrimination to go forward will burden the courts and encourage disgruntled employees to bring unsubstantiated suits. Whatever the practical merits of this argument, the Federal Rules do not contain a heightened pleading standard for employment discrimination suits. A requirement of greater specificity for particular claims is a result that "must be obtained by the process of amending the Federal Rules, and not by judicial interpretation." [citation omitted]. Furthermore, Rule 8(a) establishes a pleading standard without regard to whether a claim will succeed on the merits.

For the foregoing reasons, we hold that an employment discrimination plaintiff need not plead a prima facie case of discrimination and that petitioner's complaint is sufficient to survive respondent's motion to dismiss. Accordingly, the judgment of the Court of Appeals is reversed, and the case is remanded for further proceedings consistent with this opinion.

It is so ordered.

---

## Notes

1. *Requirement to plead sufficient factual matter to state a plausible claim.* Although the *Swierkiewicz* Court declined to impose *McDonnell Douglas* as a pleading requirement, subsequent U.S. Supreme Court case law has imposed heightened pleading standards that are applicable to employment discrimination claims. Rule 8(a)(2) of the Federal Rules of Civil Procedure requires a pleading to contain a "short and plain statement of the claim showing that the pleader is entitled to relief." In *Bell Atlantic Corp. v. Twombly*, 550 U.S. 544, 555 (2007), the Supreme Court held that while Rule 8(a)(2) does not require detailed factual allegations, it does demand more than a simple and unadorned accusation that the defendant harmed the pleader. In order to show that the pleader is entitled to relief, a plaintiff must include in the complaint "sufficient factual matter, accepted as true, to 'state a claim to relief that is plausible on its face.'" *Ashcroft v. Iqbal*, 556 U.S. 662, 679 (2009). The *Twombly* pleading standard excludes simple notice pleadings, requiring factual allegations rather than simple assertions or unadorned accusations. *Id.* Although the facts of *Twombly* dealt with an antitrust conspiracy, the Court explained that this standard is consistent with *Swierkiewicz* because it requires a plaintiff to allege only those facts necessary to state a claim, and not any additional facts required to prove a prima facie case. *Twombly*, 550 U.S. at 569–70. Several circuits have applied the *Twombly* pleading standard to employment discrimination claims. *See, e.g., Stevenson v. U.S. Postal Service*, 316 Fed. Appx. 145, 148 (3d Cir. 2009); *Prince-Garrison v. Maryland Dept. of Health and Mental Hygiene*,

317 Fed. Appx. 351, 352 (4th Cir. 2009); *Zokari v. Gates*, 561 F.3d 1076, 1084 (10th Cir. 2009); *Davis v. Coca-Cola Bottling Co. Consol.*, 516 F.3d 955, 974 (11th Cir. 2008).

Accordingly, it is now more important than ever for an employment discrimination plaintiff to plead the facts in sufficient detail such that the claim of discrimination is "plausible" on its face. For example, in a disparate treatment case, the employment discrimination plaintiff should focus on pleading facts that show the employer's discriminatory intent and the causal connection between the discriminatory intent and the adverse employment action. A plaintiff's failure to satisfy the *Twombly/Iqbal* pleading standard opens up an opportunity for the defendant employer to move to dismiss the plaintiff's employment discrimination claim on defective pleading grounds through a Fed R. Civ. P. 12(b)(6) motion. The evidence indicates that employers are taking advantage of these new opportunities, and more employment discrimination cases are being dismissed due to deficient pleadings post-*Twombly/Iqbal*. *See Davis v. Coca-Cola Bottling Co. Consol.*, 516 F.3d 955, 974 (11th Cir. 2008) (Title VII claims were pleaded in a speculative way and therefore did not satisfy *Twombly* pleading standard).

2. *The Plaintiff's Complaint.* As in other types of suits, the plaintiff's complaint in an employment discrimination suit should cover jurisdiction and venue and allege in basic terms the acts that constitute discrimination. Furthermore, the complaint should plead for damages and other remedies desired, attorneys' fees, and should typically assert the right to a jury trial. The 1991 Civil Rights Act provided for jury trials in some Title VII cases.

3. *The Defendant's Answer.* While constructing the employer's answer, any jurisdictional or venue challenges should be considered, as they should be in all cases. The answer should deny the plaintiff's averments of discrimination in compliance with Fed. R. Civ. P. 8(b). Moreover, do not forget to set out in the answer any specific defenses to the employment discrimination claim. Fed. R. Civ. P. 9(c) requires that affirmative defenses must be pleaded. Recall that there are various defenses an employer may have to an employment discrimination claim. Some possible affirmative defenses include the plaintiff's failure to timely file his EEOC charge; the plaintiff's failure to sue within 90 days of the receipt of the right-to-sue letter; and in a sexual harassment case, the employer's two-part affirmative defense from the *Faragher/Ellerth* cases.

4. *Mandatory Pre-Dispute Arbitration Agreements.* Upon being served with the lawsuit, the defendant-employer should evaluate whether the employment discrimination claim is properly heard in a federal district court forum in the first place. Some employers require their employees to sign mandatory pre-dispute arbitration agreements, which apply to employment discrimination claims, at the outset of the employment relationship. *See* Alexander J.S. Colvin, *Empirical Research on Employment Arbitration: Clarity Amidst the Sound and Fury*, 11 Emp. Rts. & Empl. Pol'y J. 405, 410 (2007) (2003 survey of employers in the telecommunications industry revealed that 14.1% had adopted employment arbitration procedures). This type of agreement would say something like "all disputes arising out of the employee's employment relationship with the company shall be exclusively arbitrated." Such agreements are generally enforceable by the courts. Accordingly, the defendant-employer should file a motion to compel arbitration when the plaintiff-employee signed an agreement to arbitrate employment discrimination claims but still filed suit on such claims in court. If granted, the case will be dismissed from the federal district court's docket and heard and decided by an arbitrator.

The enforceability of mandatory pre-dispute arbitration agreements for employment discrimination claims is still controversial, even though the general enforceability of such agreements has been established since the 1990s. In *Gilmer v. Interstate/Johnson Lane Corp.* the United States Supreme Court enforced a pre-dispute arbitration agreement between the employer and the employee as it related to an ADEA claim. 500 U.S. 20 (1991). The Court determined that neither the purposes of the ADEA nor its statutory framework precluded enforcement of the agreement. In a subsequent opinion, *Circuit City Stores, Inc. v. Adams*, the Court clarified that arbitration agreements in employment contracts are enforceable under the Federal Arbitration Act (FAA), 9 U.S.C. § 1 *et seq.*, save for a limited exemption for transportation workers. 532 U.S. 105, 119 (2001). The federal courts have consistently followed the *Gilmer/Circuit City* decisions and enforced mandatory arbitration agreements of employment discrimination claims. *See Gold v. Deutsche Aktiengesellschaft*, 365 F.3d 144, 147–48 (2d Cir. 2004) (Title VII claims are arbitrable).

Prior to the *Gilmer* decision, there were pockets of judicial resistance to the idea that these agreements were generally enforceable, but the *Gilmer* decision stomped out much of this overt resistance. The *Gilmer* decision stood as a watershed event because it gave the Court's blessing to these agreements in the employment law arena. The Court's decision in 1991 was consistent with the rise of arbitration in all areas of the law in the late 1980s, early 1990s, and continuing into the twenty-first century. *See* Colvin, 11 Emp. Rts & Empl. Pol'y J. at 408 ("The contemporary phenomenon of employment arbitration reached its initial major impetus with the Supreme Court's 1991 *Gilmer* decision."). The Court has continued to issue opinions that favor arbitration of employment discrimination lawsuits. *See 14 Penn Plaza LLC v. Pyett*, 556 U.S. 247 (2009) (holding that a provision in a collective bargaining agreement that clearly and unmistakably requires union members to arbitrate claims under the ADEA is enforceable).

The judiciary has decided in favor of enforcing mandatory arbitration agreements in the employment discrimination area. But that does not mean that all such agreements will be enforced. There is still quite a bit of litigation over whether a particular mandatory pre-dispute arbitration agreement is enforceable in a particular lawsuit. A court might decide not to enforce such an agreement if the employee did not accept the agreement, there was no consideration, or the agreement was not conspicuous. *See Gibson v. Neighborhood Health Clinics*, 121 F.3d 1126, 1131–32 (7th Cir. 1997) (employee's promise to submit employment discrimination claims to arbitration was not binding due to lack of consideration). Moreover, an arbitration agreement might not be enforced because it is too one-sided in favor of the employer's interests. *See Ferguson v. Countrywide Credit Indus.*, 298 F.3d 778, 785 (9th Cir. 2002) (arbitration agreement covering Title VII claims unenforceable under unconscionability doctrine because the agreement compelled arbitration for the types of employment law claims employees are likely to bring against employers but exempted from arbitration the types of claims that employers are likely to bring against employees); *Circuit City Stores, Inc. v. Adams*, 279 F.3d 889, 893–895 (9th Cir. 2002) (arbitration agreement unenforceable because agreement required employees to submit claims to arbitration but no such requirement existed for employers, limited the relief available to employees, and imposed onerous arbitrator's fee allocation scheme on employees). Finally, an arbitration agreement between an employer and an employee does not preclude a non-signatory, like the EEOC, from suing the employer. *See EEOC v. Waffle House, Inc.*, 534 U.S. 279 (2002).

Frankly, most folks who are interested in this area of the law do not get upset about the employer and employee agreeing to arbitration *after* a dispute arises. Presumably, the parties can make an informed choice about whether to enter into such an agreement at that point in time. It is the *pre*-dispute arbitration agreements that are imposed by the employer as a condition of employment that cause the furor. For opponents of such agreements, their best hope perhaps lies in Congressional action. And, indeed there has been push-back from Congress on this point. Bills have been introduced in the United States Congress that would amend the FAA to invalidate any pre-dispute arbitration agreement between an individual employee and his or her employer related to the employment relationship. *See* Arbitration Fairness Act of 2007 (S. 1782, H.R. 3010) (in the 110th Congress). It should be interesting to see what action, if any, Congress takes on this issue over the next several years.

5. *Settlements and Releases.* Employers and employees cannot agree to waive substantive rights under federal and state antidiscrimination statutes *in advance* of a cause of action. But, once a claim arises, employer and employee may agree to settle the claim within the bounds of generally accepted contract principles regarding settlements. As you can imagine, the heart of the settlement often is money paid by the employer to the employee in exchange for the employee's releasing the employer from liability as to that claim and other claims that may have arisen. Settlement may take place after litigation between employee and employer has ensued. It may also take place at the termination stage of an employee's employment with the employer, as a means of cutting off future litigation by the employee. The employee receives severance pay in exchange for signing the waiver of rights. It is to the employer's advantage to prevent future litigation, and the money spent by the employer as part of a severance agreement may end up costing the company quite a bit less than the possible expense of future litigation.

Special rules are in place to regulate waivers of ADEA rights. The Older Workers Benefit Protection Act (OWBPA) amended the ADEA to require that *all* waivers of ADEA rights — whether pre-suit as part of a severance agreement or early retirement program, as examples, or post-suit after litigation between the parties has commenced — must satisfy several requirements. The standard for determining whether an ADEA release is valid is a "knowing and voluntary" standard. To be *knowing and voluntary*, the waiver must, at a minimum, meet the following requirements:

(A) be written in a plain and clear way so that the average person can understand it;

(B) specifically refer to rights and claims under the ADEA;

(C) not waive rights or claims that may arise after the date the waiver is executed;

(D) be made in exchange for consideration above and beyond that which the employee is already entitled to;

(E) advise the employee *in writing* to consult with an attorney prior to executing the agreement;

(F) give the employee at least a 21-day period to consider the agreement prior to signing it; and

(G) give the employee a 7-day period after the agreement is executed in which the employee may decide to revoke the agreement and render it unenforceable.

*See* 29 U.S.C. § 26(f)(1). There are additional requirements for waivers made in connection with a reduction-in-force (RIF). *See* 29 U.S.C. § 26(f)(1)(H).

The courts interpret ADEA waivers to make sure that they are strictly OWBPA-compliant. An excellent example of this principle is found in *Oubre v. Entergy Operations, Inc.* 522 U.S. 422 (1998). In *Oubre,* the U.S. Supreme Court considered a case in which an employee accepted a severance package ($6,258) in exchange for releasing all legal claims she had against the company. The release, however, was not OWBPA-compliant in at least three respects: the company did not give the employee the requisite 21 days to consider her options; the company did not provide the employee with a 7-day revocation period; and the release made no specific reference to claims under the ADEA. The employee later sued the company under the ADEA even though she had released any and all ADEA claims in the agreement. The company argued that she could not sue because she had ratified the invalid release by retaining the monies paid to secure it. It also insisted that the noncompliant release barred the action, unless as a precondition to filing suit, the employee tendered back the monies received. The Court rejected the company's arguments. The waiver must satisfy the enumerated requirements to be valid and enforceable. The waiver at issue did not and was therefore not enforceable. The Court reasoned that the statutory language forbids ratification and tender-back because such doctrines would frustrate the purpose and practical operation of the statute. In most cases, the employee will already have spent the consideration and will thus not have the monies to tender back. Employers, however, could assert restitution, recoupment, and set-off as affirmative defenses to ADEA claims brought by employees who have signed non-compliant OWBPA releases. If such defenses are proven, the amount of the consideration could be deducted from the successful ADEA plaintiff's damages award.

OWBPA language is not required to execute enforceable releases of non-ADEA claims.

6. *Jury Waivers.* Title VII, the ADA, and the ADEA provide the right to a jury trial in certain instances. But the employer and employee could enter into a pre-dispute agreement to waive the right to a jury trial. The enforceability of jury-trial waiver agreements is similar to the arbitration issue. In general, the federal courts have tended to enforce jury-trial waiver agreements in the employment discrimination cases, even though waivers of jury trials are subject to a "knowing consent" standard. *See Winiarski v. Brown & Brown, Inc.,* No. 5:07-CV-409-OC-10GRJ, 2008 U.S. Dist. LEXIS 35799 (M.D. Fla. 2008) (federal district court enforced jury-trial waiver as to plaintiff's employment discrimination claims). The policy choice as to whether such agreements should be enforced is similar to the policy discussion surrounding the enforceability of mandatory pre-dispute arbitration agreements.

Procedurally, the plaintiff's original complaint will typically include a jury-trial demand in an employment discrimination suit. *See* Fed. R. Civ. P. 38(b) ("On any issue triable of right by a jury, a party may demand a jury trial by: (1) serving the other parties with a written demand—*which may be included in a pleading*—no later than 14 days after the last pleading directed to the issue is served; and (2) filing the demand in accordance with Rule 5(d).") (emphasis added). The defendant-employer should file a motion to strike the jury demand early on in the pretrial process if the employee signed a jury-trial waiver agreement. *See* Fed. R. Civ. P. 39(a) ("When a jury trial has been demanded under Rule 38, the action must be designated on the docket as a jury action. The trial on all issues so demanded must be by jury unless ... (2) the court, on *motion* or on its own, finds on some or all of those issues there is no federal right to a jury trial.") (emphasis added). If the motion is granted, the employment discrimination claim will be tried to the judge.

An example of a complaint and answer in an employment discrimination lawsuit follow, beginning on the next page. The exact wording and format of the documents may vary according to local practice.

*Sample Complaint in an Employment Discrimination Case*

IN THE UNITED STATES DISTRICT COURT
FOR THE NORTHERN DISTRICT OF TEXAS
DALLAS DIVISION

| | | |
|---|---|---|
| JEROME JOHNSON | § | |
| | § | |
| Plaintiff, | § | CIVIL ACTION NO. |
| | § | |
| vs. | § | 3:14-CV-1154-A |
| | § | |
| SOUTHERN BELL SYSTEMS, INC. | § | |
| | § | |
| Defendant. | § | |

PLAINTIFF'S ORIGINAL COMPLAINT

TO THE HONORABLE UNITED STATES DISTRICT JUDGE:

## INTRODUCTION

1.    This is a civil action seeking money damages and other equitable relief to redress violations of Plaintiff Jerome Johnson's rights under the laws of the United States. Plaintiff has been denied his right to freedom from race discrimination in employment because of the acts of the Defendant Southern Bell Systems and its failure to comply with respective statutory duties to act without racially discriminatory motive and to protect the rights of the Plaintiff.

## JURISDICTION

2.    Subject-matter jurisdiction exists by virtue of 28 U.S.C. § 1331 (the assertion of federal statutory claims) and 28 U.S.C. § 1343 in that this is an action to recover damages under Acts of Congress providing for the protection of employment rights. Plaintiff's claims against Southern Bell Systems arise pursuant to Title VII of the Civil Rights Act of 1964, as amended, 42 U.S.C. § 2000e, *et seq.*, and Section 1981, as amended, 42 U.S.C. § 1981.

## VENUE

3.    Defendant Southern Bell Systems is a business situated within the judicial district of this Court, and all of the events complained of occurred within the judicial district of this Court. The Defendant operates within Dallas County and the Northern District of Texas, Dallas Division. Therefore, venue is proper in this Court. *See* 28 U.S.C. § 1391(b); 42 U.S.C. § 2000e-5(f)(3).

## PARTIES

4.    Plaintiff Jerome Johnson is an African-American male and a citizen of the United States of America. He currently resides in Dallas, Texas, and during all times relevant to this action has been a resident of the Northern District of Texas.

5.    Defendant Southern Bell Systems is a corporation incorporated under the laws of the State of Texas, has its main office located at 2625 Industry Parkway, Dallas, Texas, 75209, and during all times relevant to this action has been a resident of the Northern District of Texas.

6.   Southern Bell Systems conducts business in the Northern District of Texas and is a statutory "employer" as defined by Title VII. *See* 42 U.S.C. § 2000e(b).

## CONDITIONS PRECEDENT TO SUIT

7.   Mr. Johnson has satisfied all conditions precedent necessary to assert his Title VII claims in this Court. Mr. Johnson filed a timely EEOC charge with the Commission.

8.   Mr. Johnson received his right-to-sue letter from the EEOC on or about April 30, 2014.

9.   Mr. Johnson is filing this original complaint within 90 days of his receipt of the right to sue letter. *See* 42 U.S.C. § 2000e-5(f)(1).

## FACTUAL BACKGROUND

10.   Southern Bell Systems hired Mr. Johnson as a clerk in the shipping department in 2007. Mr. Johnson held that job for seven years until the company terminated his employment in 2014. During his tenure at Southern Bell Systems, Mr. Johnson received annual raises and exhibited excellent performance in his job duties.

11.   Mr. Johnson's job duties at Southern Bell Systems entailed data entry and filing work. At no point in time, did Mr. Johnson's duties include janitorial work.

12.   On or around January 17, 2014, Mr. Johnson's boss, Tom Green, ordered Mr. Johnson to clean up the parts area in the warehouse. This type of cleaning work was not part of Mr. Johnson's job duties. Moreover, the person that actually caused the mess was Mr. Watson, Mr. Johnson's co-worker. Mr. Watson is Caucasian.

13.   Upon being given the "clean up" order, Mr. Johnson inquired of Mr. Green as to why he had been ordered to clean up the mess and not his co-worker who had actually created the mess in the first place and was in the same department as Mr. Johnson. Mr. Green responded that "blacks clean better" and "just do what you are told."

14.   Mr. Johnson complained to Mr. Green on the spot that Mr. Green's action constituted illegal race discrimination. For that reason, he refused to follow the "clean up" order.

15.   Southern Bell Systems terminated Mr. Johnson's employment the next day, on or about January 18, 2014, allegedly for refusing to follow an order from a supervisor.

## FEDERAL CLAIMS

### TITLE VII RACE DISCRIMINATION CLAIM

16.   Mr. Johnson repeats and re-alleges each and every allegation set forth in the paragraphs above as if fully set forth at length herein.

17.   Southern Bell System's actions in ordering him to do clean-up work and his subsequent termination from employment were motivated by race in violation of Title VII.

### SECTION 1981 RACE DISCRIMINATION CLAIM

18.   Mr. Johnson repeats and re-alleges each and every allegation set forth in the paragraphs above as if fully set forth at length herein.

19.   Southern Bell System's actions in ordering him to do clean-up work and his subsequent termination from employment were motivated by race in violation of 42 U.S.C. Section 1981.

## TITLE VII RETALIATION CLAIM

20. Mr. Johnson repeats and re-alleges each and every allegation set forth in the paragraphs above as if fully set forth at length herein.

21. Southern Bell Systems unlawfully retaliated against Mr. Johnson by terminating his employment with the company because he complained about race discrimination. Southern Bell System's actions violate the prohibition against retaliation in Title VII.

## SECTION 1981 RETALIATION CLAIM

22. Mr. Johnson repeats and re-alleges each and every allegation set forth in the paragraphs above as if fully set forth at length herein.

23. Southern Bell Systems unlawfully retaliated against Mr. Johnson by terminating his employment with the company because he complained about race discrimination. Southern Bell System's actions violate the prohibition against retaliation in 42 U.S.C. Section 1981.

## RELIEF REQUESTED

24. As a direct and proximate result of the Defendant's actions described above, the Plaintiff, Jerome Johnson, is entitled to the relief provided for by 42 U.S.C. § 2000e-5(g), as well as compensatory and punitive damages as provided for by 42 U.S.C. § 1981a(b).

Plaintiff Jerome Johnson requests that this Court:

(a) Assume jurisdiction of this case.
(b) Grant to Plaintiff a Trial by jury. Plaintiff demands a jury trial pursuant to Fed. R. Civ. P. 38 and 42 U.S.C. § 1981a(c).
(c) Award Plaintiff a judgment against the Defendant for the relief set forth above.
(d) Award attorney's fees and the costs of prosecution of this action to Plaintiff.
(e) Award to the Plaintiff such other additional or alternative relief as the Court deems appropriate.

Dated:   May 24, 2014

Respectfully Submitted,

Bobby Beem /s/
State Bar No. 15083342
Bobby Beem & Associates
248 Gables Parkway, Suite 1200
Dallas, Texas 75210

(214) 576-8883 — telephone
(214) 576-8845 — fax
bbeem@beemlaw.com

ATTORNEY FOR PLAINTIFF

### *Sample Answer in an Employment Discrimination Case*

IN THE UNITED STATES DISTRICT COURT
FOR THE NORTHERN DISTRICT OF TEXAS
DALLAS DIVISION

| | | |
|---|---|---|
| JEROME JOHNSON | § | |
| | § | |
| Plaintiff, | § | CIVIL ACTION NO. |
| | § | |
| vs. | § | 3:14-CV-1154-A |
| | § | |
| SOUTHERN BELL SYSTEMS, INC. | § | |
| | § | |
| Defendant. | § | |

### DEFENDANT'S ORIGINAL ANSWER

TO THE HONORABLE UNITED STATES DISTRICT JUDGE:

SOUTHERN BELL SYSTEMS, INC., DEFENDANT, files its Original Answer to Plaintiff's Original Complaint and states:

### Matters Admitted or Denied

1. Defendant admits that Plaintiff is suing for money damages, legal and equitable relief and that he alleges that he has been denied the right to be free from racial discrimination in employment. Defendant denies that it failed to comply with statutory duties, denies that it acted out of racially discriminatory motive or that it failed to protect the rights of the Plaintiff. Defendant further denies that Plaintiff was discriminated against because of his race or that he is entitled to any money damages or any legal or equitable relief as alleged. Defendant denies any remaining allegations of Paragraph 1 of Plaintiff's Original Complaint.

2. Defendant admits that this Court has subject matter jurisdiction over this case and that Plaintiff is asserting causes of action under the statutes alleged. However, Defendant denies that Plaintiff has been discriminated or retaliated against or that he has any valid or meritorious causes of action under any of these statutes. Defendant denies any remaining allegations of Paragraph 2 of Plaintiff's Original Complaint.

3. Defendant admits that it is situated and does business within the Northern District of Texas and that venue of this case is properly alleged in Paragraph 3 of Plaintiff's Original Complaint.

4. Defendant admits that Plaintiff is an African-American male and a United States citizen. Defendant does not have sufficient knowledge or information to admit or deny the remaining allegations of Paragraph 4 of Plaintiff's Original Complaint; therefore, deny.

5. Defendant admits the allegations of Paragraph 5 of Plaintiff's Original Complaint.

6. Defendant admits the allegations of Paragraph 6 of Plaintiff's Original Complaint.

7. Defendant admits the allegations of Paragraph 7 of Plaintiff's Original Complaint.

8. Defendant admits that Plaintiff's right-to-sue letter in this case was issued on or about April 30, 2014. Defendant does not have sufficient knowledge or information to know when Plaintiff received his right-to-sue letter. Therefore, Defendant denies the remaining allegations of Paragraph 8 of Plaintiff's Original Complaint.

9.   Defendant admits the allegations of Paragraph 9 of Plaintiff's Original Complaint.

10.  Defendant admits that Plaintiff was hired by Southern Bell Systems in 2007 and terminated his employment in 2014. Defendant denies any remaining allegations in Paragraph 10 of Plaintiff's Original Complaint.

11.  Defendant admits that Plaintiff did data entry and file work while employed at Southern Bell Systems. Defendant denies any remaining allegations in Paragraph 11 of Plaintiff's Original Complaint.

12.  Defendant admits that Plaintiff's supervisor, Tom Green, requested that the Plaintiff participate in a cleaning event. Defendant admits that James Watson is Caucasian. Defendant denies any remaining allegations in Paragraph 12 of Plaintiff's Original Complaint.

13.  Defendant denies the allegations in Paragraph 13 of Plaintiff's Original Complaint.

14.  Defendant denies the allegations in Paragraph 14 of Plaintiff's Original Complaint.

15.  Defendant admits that Southern Bell Systems terminated Plaintiff's employment on or about January 18, 2014. Defendant denies the remaining allegations in Paragraph 15 of Plaintiff's Original Complaint. Defendant terminated Plaintiff's employment for a legal reason.

16.  Defendant reasserts its previous admissions or denials set forth in the paragraphs above.

17.  Defendant denies the allegations in Paragraph 17 of Plaintiff's Original Complaint.

18.  Defendant reasserts its previous admissions or denials set forth in the paragraphs above.

19.  Defendant denies the allegations in Paragraph 19 of Plaintiff's Original Complaint.

20.  Defendant reasserts its previous admissions or denials set forth in the paragraphs above.

21.  Defendant denies the allegations in Paragraph 21 of Plaintiff's Original Complaint.

22.  Defendant reasserts its previous admissions or denials set forth in the paragraphs above.

23.  Defendant denies the allegations in Paragraph 23 of Plaintiff's Original Complaint.

24.  Plaintiff's request for relief does not require an admission or denial. Nevertheless, Defendant denies that Plaintiff is entitled to any of the relief requested or to any relief available in the statutes alleged.

## Affirmative Matters or Defenses

25.  Defendant terminated Plaintiff's employment for a legitimate, non-discriminatory reason.

26.  Defendant pleads that there has been no violation of Plaintiff's rights under Title VII of the Civil Rights Act of 1964 or 42 U.S.C. Section 1981.

27.  To the extent Plaintiff may claim that Defendant's legitimate, non-discriminatory reason, while true, is only one of the reasons for its conduct and another motivating factor was Plaintiff's race, then Defendant pleads that the same decision would have been made regardless of any discriminatory reason.

28.  To the extent Plaintiff may claim that Defendant's legitimate, non-discriminatory reason, while true, is only one of the reasons for its conduct and another motivating factor was retaliation for Plaintiff's alleged race discrimination complaint under Section 1981, then Defendant pleads that the same decision would have been made regardless of any retaliatory reason.

29.  Defendant pleads that Plaintiff is not entitled to any relief in this cause.

30. Defendant pleads that Plaintiff is not entitled to recover punitive damages.

31. Defendant pleads that Plaintiff is not entitled to declaratory relief in this cause.

32. Defendant pleads that Plaintiff is not entitled to injunctive relief in this cause.

33. Defendant pleads that Plaintiff is not entitled to compensatory relief in this cause.

34. Defendant pleads any and all applicable damage caps.

35. Defendant pleads that Plaintiff failed to mitigate his damages.

### Prayer

THEREFORE, Defendant asks the Court to enter judgment that Plaintiff take nothing, dismiss Plaintiff's suit with prejudice, assess costs, attorney's fees, and expert witness fees against Plaintiff, and award Defendant all other relief to which it is entitled.

Dated:   June 5, 2014

Respectfully Submitted,

Patricia Suarez /s/
State Bar No. 28511690
Suarez, Locke, and McDonald
5506 Elm Street
Dallas, Texas 75210

(214) 573-1520 — telephone
(214) 573-9971 — fax
psuarez@slmlaw.com

ATTORNEY FOR DEFENDANT

### Certificate of Service

This is to certify that, pursuant to Civil Local Rule 5.1(d) of the Northern District of Texas, on this 5th day of June, 2014, a true and correct copy of the foregoing was served electronically on Bobby Beem by filing this document electronically with the Court pursuant to ECF Administrative Procedures.

Patti Suarez /s/

## Discovery

The critical, but tedious, part of the employment discrimination lawsuit is building (or defending) the case. A substantial part of building a case or defense involves the formal discovery procedure whereby a party requests that the other party provide information through mechanisms such as requests for admissions, interrogatories, requests for production and depositions. These discovery procedures are set forth in the Federal Rules of Civil Procedure. For claims filed in a state court, similar discovery devices are often available. In a disparate treatment case, the plaintiff may focus on securing discovery concerning the alleged decision-maker(s) and how discriminatory intent can be imputed to those individual(s). He or she will likely try to discover information regarding similarly-situated employees who were treated differently. The defendant may focus on securing information from the plaintiff that the plaintiff will use to prove his or her case to aid in preparing for the plaintiff's deposition and then using the statements from the plaintiff's deposition to win a summary judgment motion.

A frequent discovery dispute arises in employment discrimination lawsuits concerning whether the plaintiff-employee is entitled to information regarding company practices, policies, and actions that extend beyond the department or office in which the plaintiff worked. Under the general relevancy discovery standard, arguments can be made in favor of and against permitting such discovery in a particular case. Some courts will not allow discovery beyond the plaintiff's employing unit absent a showing of particularized need and the likely relevance of broader information. *See Earley v. Champion International Corp.*, 907 F.2d 1077, 1084–85 (11th Cir. 1990) (discovery in Title VII case limited to employing unit); *James v. Newspaper Agency Corp.*, 591 F.2d 579, 582 (10th Cir. 1979) (discovery in sex discrimination suit limited to plaintiff's department); *Haselhorst v. Wal-Mart Stores, Inc.*, 163 F.R.D. 10, 11 (D. Kan. 1995) (discovery limited to employing unit). This is not a uniform view held by courts.

## Summary Judgment

Finding an employment discrimination lawsuit in which the employer does *not* file a summary judgment motion is about as rare as a Halley's comet sighting. Of course, this comparison is an exaggeration, but it drives home the point. It is standard operating procedure for an employer to try and win the case by filing a summary judgment motion. The basic contention is that the plaintiff's claim(s) fail as a matter of law under the Fed. R. Civ. P. 56 summary-judgment standard. It is at the summary-judgment stage that the plaintiff will have to produce sufficient evidence of discrimination under the applicable framework to convince the federal judge that the case should go to the jury because there is a fact question. The ruling on the summary-judgment motion in an employment discrimination lawsuit is a game-changing moment. Employers often win these motions. But if an employer loses the motion, the dynamics of the litigation shift dramatically. Often, the employer must face a jury trial. Many employers believe that juries act unpredictably even when the facts are favorable to their position. Many employment discrimination cases settle after an employer's summary judgment motion is denied and prior to the scheduled trial date due to the employer deciding that the risks and expense of going to trial are not worth the possible reward (jury finding in the employer's favor).

## *Trial*

The employment discrimination trial is similar to other civil trials in many ways. If the trial is to a jury, the parties go through the voir dire process—questioning the venire panel for possible bias or prejudice and information that will lead them to successfully exercise challenges for cause and peremptory challenges. The parties make their opening statements and then present their evidence regarding the question of discrimination. Depending on the state of the evidence after the parties rest, the plaintiff and/or the defendant may move for judgment as a matter of law. (Under Fed. R. Civ. P. 50, a court should render judgment as a matter of law when a party has been fully heard on an issue and there is no legally sufficient evidentiary basis for a reasonable jury to find for that party on that issue.) If any such motions are denied, the case is submitted to the jury. The jury is charged on the law and asked whether discrimination occurred. The parties make their closing arguments. In some cases, the jury instructions follow closing arguments. The jury deliberates and returns the verdict. The parties may file post-verdict motions and later the trial court signs the judgment, often in accordance with the jury's verdict. The parties may then appeal.

There is a fine line to charging a jury in an employment discrimination suit. On the one hand, the relevant law must be clearly articulated to the jury. On the other hand, care must be taken not to provide the jury with so much "law" that the jury becomes confused and distracted from the question at hand: whether discrimination occurred. For example, explaining to the jury the entire *McDonnell Douglas* burden-shifting framework and asking the jury to analyze the evidence in light of that framework is not a preferred approach. By the time the employment discrimination case reaches the jury charge stage, it should be a given that the prima facie case is satisfied and that the employer produced a legitimate, non-discriminatory reason for its personnel action. If such burdens were not satisfied, a motion for judgment as a matter of law is the appropriate procedural device to use. That being said, there could be some real value to instructing juries on what they can infer from disbelief of an employer's explanation for the employment action. Some circuits take the position that the jury *must* be given a "pretext" instruction (*i.e.*, "If you disbelieve the reason(s) Defendant has given for its decision, you may infer that Defendant terminated Plaintiff's employment because of her sex."). *See Townsend v. Lumbermens Mutual Casualty Co.*, 294 F.3d 1232, 1238 (10th Cir. 2002); *Ratliff v. City of Gainesville*, 256 F.3d 355, 360–61 (5th Cir. 2001); *Smith v. Borough of Wilkinsburg*, 147 F.3d 272, 280 (3d Cir. 1988). Other circuits view the instruction as permitted, but not mandatory. *See Fite v. Digital Equipment Corp.*, 232 F.3d 3, 7 (1st Cir. 2000); *Gehring v. Case Corp.*, 43 F.3d 340, 343 (7th Cir. 1994). Even in a circuit where a "pretext" instruction is supposedly mandatory, the trial judge's failure to give the jury that instruction is not necessarily reversible error. *See Kanida v. Gulf Med. Coast Med. Pers. LP*, 363 F.3d 568, 577 (5th Cir. 2004). If you were a trial judge in an employment discrimination lawsuit, would you give the jury a "pretext" instruction? Why or why not?

---

## Further Discussion

Delve a little deeper into the structure of a typical employment discrimination charge. The first part of the jury charge includes the general instructions that are given to the jurors in civil cases. This includes, but is not limited to, charging the jury on the burden of proof, consideration of the evidence, and expert witnesses. The second part of the jury charge hones in on the actual dispute in the employment discrimination suit. The jury charge may briefly summarize the nature of the claims and defenses and then focus on what the plaintiff must prove as to his various claims. The court will also instruct the jury that if the Plaintiff has proven his claim(s) against the Defendant by a preponderance of the evidence, it must determine the damages to which the Plaintiff is entitled. The jury charge will specify and describe the damages that are available to be recovered by the Plaintiff in the case if liability is established and that the jury is authorized by the court to consider (such as mental anguish, emotional distress, and punitive damages). The third part of the jury charge is the actual questions that the jury must answer during its deliberations. The questions can be generally grouped into two categories: liability and damages. The jury's answers to the questions constitute the jury's verdict.

## Exercise 10.4

In our sample *Johnson v. Southern Bell Systems* case, Johnson tries his race discrimination case to the jury in federal district court. During the presentation of evidence, Johnson introduces the "comparator" evidence and testifies to the alleged racial comments. The employer contends that it terminated Johnson's employment for insubordination. Mr. Green testifies that he never made the alleged racial comments and assigned multiple employees to do the clean-up work. The comparator, Mr. Watson, was not assigned to do the work because he had an injured wrist, at least according to the company.

You are the law clerk for the federal district court judge in this case. Briefly draft the following portions of the jury charge:

- the nature of the claims and defenses;

- instructions regarding Johnson's burden to prove unlawful race discrimination; and

- the liability question for the jury regarding the termination claim.

Explain the difficulties you encountered during this exercise.

# Chapter 11

# Remedies

For a civil litigation plaintiff, the goal at the end of successfully establishing civil liability is typically the recovery of damages, *i.e.*, money. The defendant "wins," in a sense, if the plaintiff does not recover damages or damages are paid out that are less than expected— given an objective evaluation of the case. Employment discrimination litigants, like all civil litigants, focus on recovering damages or preventing the recovery of damages. This is not to say that it is all about the money. The goal for some litigants could be more about standing up for justice, defending a reputation, or just getting a job back. When a person accuses another person—technically the employer is the entity accused of discrimination, but an employer is simply a group of people—of illegally discriminating based on a protected characteristic, one can understand that the emotions of the parties involved come into play and affect the resulting litigation in a way that is different from a basic commercial law case. Right or wrong, good or bad, there is a unique interpersonal aspect to employment discrimination cases that shapes what both the plaintiff and the defendant are seeking in order to resolve the dispute. Effective lawyering can sometimes help the employee and employer find creative solutions to their differences that may or may not involve the exchange of money. Keep this in mind as you study the Remedies Chapter.

This Chapter considers the remedies a prevailing plaintiff is entitled to recover upon proof of a violation of the various federal antidiscrimination statutes: Title VII of the Civil Rights Act of 1964, as amended (Title VII); the Americans with Disabilities Act of 1990, as amended (ADA); the Age Discrimination in Employment Act of 1967, as amended (ADEA); and 42 U.S.C. Section 1981, as amended. The available remedies are specified in the statutes themselves, except for Section 1981.

The initial and dominant focus of the Chapter is on Title VII remedies, however, for several reasons. First, the ADA remedies are basically the same as Title VII remedies. Consequently, if you learn the Title VII remedies, you will automatically have a solid foundation as to the remedies available under the ADA. Second, although there are some differences between Title VII remedies and ADEA remedies, it is easier to flesh out those differences after the Title VII remedies are learned. Finally, Section 1981 remedies, which are not specified in the statute itself, make more sense after you learn about the remedies in the other statutes. For example, there are limitations on some Title VII remedies that are not present with Section 1981 remedies.

## ✦ Core Concept: Introduction to Remedies

A "remedy" is the "means by which a right is enforced or the violation of a right is prevented, redressed, or compensated." BLACK'S LAW DICTIONARY 896 (abridged 6th ed. 1991). The federal antidiscrimination statutes specify how the discriminatory actions that violate [or may violate] the statutes may be prevented, redressed, or compensated. There are certainly some remedial differences that cut across these statutes, but there are essentially six similar types of remedies recoverable for violating Title VII. Each type of remedy can be further classified as either an equitable remedy or legal remedy. Here are the basic statutory remedies:

1. Back Pay and Retroactive Seniority [Equitable Remedy]
2. Reinstatement [Equitable Remedy]
3. Front Pay [Equitable Remedy]
4. Declaratory and Injunctive Relief [Equitable Remedy]
5. Compensatory Damages like Emotional Pain and Mental Anguish [Legal Remedy]
6. Punitive Damages [Legal Remedy]

Although some of these terms may be unfamiliar to you, a simple example illustrates that the available remedies are fairly intuitive. Consider the scenario in the *Johnson v. Southern Bell Systems* case from the Procedure Chapter. Jerome Johnson sues his former employer Southern Bell Systems for unlawfully terminating his employment in violation of Title VII. If he proves a Title VII violation at trial, what remedies might he be able to recover to compensate him for the violation?

First, if proven, he may recover any lost income due to the employer's discrimination from the date of the discriminatory act until the final judgment. This is called *back pay*. This term is sometimes spelled as one word "backpay." For example, assume Johnson made $40,000.00 per year at Southern Bell Systems. His employment is unlawfully terminated on January 18, 2014. On January 18, 2016, the court signs a final judgment finding that Southern Bell Systems violated Title VII. The back pay award for the lost income for the two years from the date of the discriminatory act until final judgment would be $80,000.00 plus the amount of lost employment benefits, if he was unable to find any employment during that time period. Second, the court may order Southern Bell Systems to *reinstate* Johnson to his former position as a warehouse employee. Third, although perhaps less likely, the court may issue an *injunction* to prohibit Southern Bell Systems from engaging in discriminatory acts in the future. Fourth, if proven, Johnson may recover damages for any *compensatory damages* like emotional pain or mental anguish suffered as a result of the discrimination. For example, perhaps Johnson had $1,000.00 in medical bills for psychological treatment stemming from the discrimination. Finally, if proven, Johnson may recover *punitive damages* to punish Southern Bell Systems if the company's actions were motivated by malice. The final judgment would state the total amount of damages recovered [Back pay + Compensatory Damages + Punitive Damages] and order reinstatement.

Once again, the above example is somewhat simplistic. There is likely more complexity in the case. But the example makes the basic point concerning available remedies in a broad fashion. More difficult issues will be addressed later in the Chapter.

The preceding summary glosses over the historical development of the law in this area. Title VII, as originally enacted, provided only equitable remedies. It was not until the 1991 Civil Rights Act that legal remedies became recoverable in Title VII cases. Since 1991, legal and equitable remedies have been recoverable in Title VII disparate treatment cases. Legal remedies are not available in disparate impact cases.

## ✦ Core Concept: Equitable v. Legal Remedies under Title VII

At its inception, Title VII only permitted the recovery of traditional equitable remedies like injunctive relief and reinstatement or hiring with or without back pay. Section 706(g)(1) of Title VII, as originally enacted in 1964, provided:

If the court finds that the respondent has intentionally engaged in or is intentionally engaging in an unlawful employment practice charged in the complaint, the court may enjoin the respondent from engaging in such unlawful employment practice, and order such affirmative action as may be appropriate, which may include reinstatement or hiring of employees, with or without back pay (payable by the employer, employment agency, or labor organization, as the case may be, responsible for the unlawful employment practice).

The Equal Employment Opportunity Act of 1972 amended Title VII § Section 706(g)(1) to add that the court may "order such affirmative action as may be appropriate, which may include, *but is not limited to*, reinstatement or hiring of employees, with or without back pay (payable by the employer, employment agency, or labor organization, as the case may be, responsible for the unlawful employment practice), *or any other equitable relief as the court deems appropriate.*" *See* Equal Employment Opportunity Act of 1972 Pub. L. No. 92-261, 86 Stat. 103 (1972) (italicized language was added to Section 706(g)(1) in the 1972 amendments).

## Enforcing the Historical Law and Equity Divide

The text of Section 706(g)(1) as originally enacted in 1964 and subsequently amended in 1972 limited the remedies recoverable to traditional equitable remedies. Section 706(g)(1) stated that the *court* may order "reinstatement or hiring of employees with or without back pay ... *or any other equitable relief* as the court deems appropriate." (emphasis added). The statute expressed two important points: (1) reinstatement, ordered hiring, and back pay are equitable remedies; and (2) the only remedies recoverable under Section 706(g)(1) are equitable remedies. *See Albemarle Paper Co. v. Moody*, 422 U.S. 405, 415–16 (1975).

The equitable remedies limitation in Title VII prior to 1991 impacted Title VII plaintiffs in a couple of very important ways. First, the courts took Congress at its word that it intended to separate equitable remedies from legal remedies and provide only for equitable remedies like back pay, reinstatement and front pay, and declaratory and injunctive relief. *See Winsor v. Hinckley Dodge*, 79 F.3d 996, 1002 (10th Cir. 1996). Indeed, the implication from the text of Section 706(g)(1) is that legal remedies are not available under Title VII, in that the court may order "*any other equitable relief* as the court deems appropriate." The statutory reference to the *court* ordering relief also reinforced the equitable remedies limitation. Historically, in equity courts, also known as chancery courts, the chancellor fashioned the remedies based on principles of fairness and achieving justice. *See* DAN B. DOBBS, LAW OF REMEDIES § 2.6(2) (2d. ed. 1993) ("The chancellor acted as trier of fact as well as decision-maker on issues of conscience or rules."). In law courts, the jury awarded damages at law such as compensatory and punitive damages. *See* 1 JOHN N. POMEROY, A TREATISE ON EQUITY JURISPRUDENCE § 237d (5th ed. 1941) ("The award of mere compensatory damages, which are almost always unliquidated, is a remedy peculiarly belonging to the province of the law courts, requiring the aid of a jury in their assessment, and inappropriate to the judicial functions and position of a chancellor."). There is no reference to a *jury* awarding damages in Section 706(g)(1).

The uniform view is that reinstatement, retroactive seniority, declaratory relief, and injunctive relief are indeed all traditionally equitable remedies. There is a good argument, however, that Congressional labeling of back pay as an *equitable* remedy was wrong, at least if Congress intended to adhere to the historical labeling of remedies as either equitable or legal. *See Waldrop v. Southern Co. Services*, 24 F.3d 152, 158 (11th Cir. 2004) (stating that "it has long been the general rule that back wages are legal relief in the nature of compensatory damages."); 2 DAN B. DOBBS, LAW OF REMEDIES § 6.10(5) at 226 (2d. ed. 1993) (explaining back pay is an ordinary damages claim, close to an exemplar of a claim at law); Colleen P. Murphy, *Misclassifying Monetary Restitution*, 55 SMU L. REV. 1577, 1633 (2002) ("[T]he backpay remedy is more appropriately characterized as damages for the plaintiff's losses and thus legal relief."); Jarod S. Gonzalez, *SOX, Statutory Interpretation, and the Seventh Amendment: Sarbanes-Oxley Act Whistleblower Claims and Jury Trials*, 9 U. PA. J. LAB. & EMP. L. 25, 62–63 (2006) (opining that back pay is best viewed as a legal remedy). But that tiny problem did not appear to concern the federal courts prior to 1991. *See Albemarle Paper Co v. Moody*, 422 U.S. 405, 415–16 (1975) (holding back pay is an equitable remedy to be awarded by the district court in its discretion). The courts' point appeared to be that back pay is equitable because it is technically discretionary with the judge even though such discretion is very much constrained. *See Crocker v. Piedmont Aviation, Inc.*, 49 F.3d 735, 748 (D.C. Cir. 1995) ("The characterization of Title VII back pay awards as equitable is bolstered by the fact that judges formally retain some degree of equitable discretion in deciding whether to award back pay in individual cases once violations are proven, even though the [U.S. Supreme Court] has severely constrained the exercise of this discretion."). In any event, prior to 1991, courts uniformly prohibited Title VII plaintiffs from recovering the types of damages that were viewed as legal remedies, *i.e.*, compensatory and punitive damages, and adhered to the position that back pay, reinstatement and front pay, and declaratory and injunctive relief are equitable remedies recoverable under the statute.

The equitable remedies limitation meant that no jury trial right existed for Title VII cases prior to 1991. *See Slack v. Havens*, 522 F.2d 1091, 1094 (9th Cir. 1975) (jury trials not required in Title VII suits); *EEOC v. Detroit Edison*, 515 F.2d 301 (6th Cir. 1975) (same); *Robinson v. Lorillard Corp.*, 444 F.2d 791, 802 (4th Cir. 1971) (same); *Johnson v. Georgia Highway Express, Inc.*, 417 F.2d 1122, 1125 (5th Cir. 1969) (same). The statute itself provided no express or implied right to a jury trial. Moreover, the Seventh Amendment to the United States Constitution did not guarantee a jury trial right because the Title VII statutory remedies were equitable as opposed to legal in nature. Under the historical test to the Seventh Amendment, adopted by the United States Supreme Court, the Title VII action was thus best viewed as an action at equity in which no jury-trial right attached. *See Slack v. Havens*, 522 F.2d 1091, 1094 (9th Cir. 1975); *Chauffeurs, Teamsters & Helpers Local No. 391 v. Terry*, 494 U.S. 558, 565 (1990); *City of Monterey v. Del Monte Dunes at Monterey, Ltd.*, 526 U.S. 687, 718 (1999). The absence of a jury-trial right became an increasingly bitter pill to swallow for Title VII plaintiffs as the years went by from 1964 to 1991.

For many individuals concerned about fulfilling the promise of Title VII, the absence of "make whole" relief in the Title VII remedial provision was a glaring hole in the statute. In 1991, Congress filled in that hole via the 1991 Civil Rights Act. Among other things, the 1991 Civil Rights Act amended Title VII to permit a plaintiff to recover compensatory damages such as mental anguish, emotional distress, loss of enjoyment of life, and other non-pecuniary losses and punitive damages. *See* 42 U.S.C. §§ 1981a(a)(1), 1981a(b)(1). The 1991 amendments completed the current remedial Title VII picture. The equitable remedies provision, Section 706(g)(1), remained in force. Accordingly, here are the key parts of the Title VII remedial picture.

### Title VII Remedial Provision — Title VII § 706(g); 42 U.S.C. § 2000e-5(g) [Equitable Relief]

(g) Injunctions; appropriate affirmative action; equitable relief; accrual of back pay; reduction of back pay; limitations on judicial orders

(1) If the court finds that the respondent has intentionally engaged in or is intentionally engaging in an unlawful employment practice charged in the complaint, the court may enjoin the respondent from engaging in such unlawful employment practice, and order such affirmative action as may be appropriate, which may include, but is not limited to, reinstatement or hiring of employees, with or without back pay (payable by the employer, employment agency, or labor organization, as the case may be, responsible for the unlawful employment practice), or any other equitable relief as the court deems appropriate. Back pay liability shall not accrue from a date more than two years prior to the filing of a charge with the Commission. Interim earnings or amounts earnable with reasonable diligence by the person or persons discriminated against shall operate to reduce the back pay otherwise allowable.

(2) (A) No order of the court shall require the admission or reinstatement of an individual as a member of a union, or the hiring, reinstatement, or promotion of an individual as an employee, or the payment to him of any back pay, if such individual was refused admission, suspended, or expelled, or was refused employment or advancement or was suspended or discharged for any reason other than discrimination on account of race, color, religion, sex, or national origin or in violation of section 2000e-3(a) of this title.

(B) On a claim in which an individual proves a violation under section 2000e-2(m) of this title and a respondent demonstrates that the respondent would have taken the same action in the absence of the impermissible motivating factor, the court—

(i) may grant declaratory relief, injunctive relief (except as provided in clause (ii)), and attorney's fees and costs demonstrated to be directly attributable only to the pursuit of a claim under section 2000e-2(m) of this title; and

(ii) shall not award damages or issue an order requiring any admission, reinstatement, hiring, promotion, or payment, described in subparagraph (A).

### Title VII Remedial Provision — 42 U.S.C. § 1981a [Legal Relief]

#### Section 102 of the Civil Rights Act of 1991
#### Damages in Cases of Intentional Discrimination in Employment

(a) Right of recovery

(1) Civil rights

In an action brought by a complaining party under section 706 or 717 of the Civil Rights Act of 1964 [42 U.S.C. § 2000e-5 or 42 U.S.C. § 2000e-16] against a respondent who engaged in unlawful intentional discrimination (not an employment practice that is unlawful because of its disparate impact) prohibited under section 703, 704, or 717 of the Act [42 U.S.C. §§ 2000e-2, 2000e-3, or 2000e-16], and provided that the complaining party cannot recover under 42 U.S.C. Section 1981 of this title, the complaining party may recover compensatory and punitive damages as allowed in subsection (b) of this section, in addition to any relief authorized by section 706(g) of the Civil Rights Act of 1964, from the respondent.

(2) Disability

In an action brought by a complaining party under the powers, remedies, and procedures set forth in section 706 or 717 of the Civil Rights Act of 1964 (as provided in section 107(a) of the Americans with Disabilities Act of 1990 (42 U.S.C. § 12117(a)), and section 505(a)(1) of the Rehabilitation Act of 1973 (29 U.S.C. § 794a(a)(1), respectively) against a respondent who engaged in unlawful intentional discrimination (not an employment practice that is unlawful because of its disparate impact) under section 501 of the Rehabilitation Act of 1973 (29 U.S.C. § 791) and the regulations implementing section 501, or who violated the requirements of section 501 of the Act or the regulations implementing section 501 concerning the provision of a reasonable accommodation, or section 102 of the Americans with Disabilities Act of 1990 (42 U.S.C. § 12112), or committed a violation of section 102(b)(5) of the Act, against an individual, the complaining party may recover compensatory and punitive damages as allowed in subsection (b) of this section, in addition to any relief authorized by section 706(g) of the Civil Rights Act of 1964, from the respondent.

(3) Reasonable accommodation and good faith effort

In cases where a discriminatory practice involves the provision of a reasonable accommodation pursuant to section 102(b)(5) of the Americans with Disabilities Act of 1990 [42 U.S.C. § 12112(b)(5)] or regulations implementing section 501 of the Rehabilitation Act of 1973 [29 U.S.C. § 791], damages may not be awarded under this section where the covered entity demonstrates good faith efforts, in consultation with the person with the disability who has informed the covered entity that accommodation is needed, to identify and make a reasonable accommodation that would provide such individual with an equally effective opportunity and would not cause an undue hardship on the operation of the business.

(b) Compensatory and punitive damages

(1) Determination of punitive damages

A complaining party may recover punitive damages under this section against a respondent (other than a government, government agency or political subdivision) if the complaining party demonstrates that the respondent engaged in a discriminatory practice or discriminatory practices with malice or with reckless indifference to the federally protected rights of an aggrieved individual.

(2) Exclusions from compensatory damages

Compensatory damages awarded under this section shall not include backpay, interest on backpay, or any other type of relief authorized under section 706(g) of the Civil Rights Act of 1964 [42 U.S.C. § 2000e-5(g)].

(3) Limitations

The sum of the amount of compensatory damages awarded under this section for future pecuniary losses, emotional pain, suffering, inconvenience, mental anguish, loss of enjoyment of life, and other nonpecuniary losses, and the amount of punitive damages awarded under this section, shall not exceed, for each complaining party—

(A) in the case of a respondent who has more than 14 and fewer than 101 employees in each of 20 or more calendar weeks in the current or preceding calendar year, $50,000;

(B) in the case of a respondent who has more than 100 and fewer than 201 employees in each of 20 or more calendar weeks in the current or preceding calendar year, $100,000; and

(C) in the case of a respondent who has more than 200 and fewer than 501 employees in each of 20 or more calendar weeks in the current or preceding calendar year, $200,000; and

(D) in the case of a respondent who has more than 500 employees in each of 20 or more calendar weeks in the current or preceding calendar year, $300,000.

(4) Construction

Nothing in this section shall be construed to limit the scope of, or the relief available under section 1981 of this title [42 U.S.C. § 1981].

(c) Jury trial

If a complaining party seeks compensatory or punitive damages under this section—

(1) any party may demand a trial by jury; and

(2) the court shall not inform the jury of the limitations described in subsection (b)(3) of this section.

(d) Definitions

As used in this section:

(1) Complaining party

The term "complaining party" means—

(A) in the case of a person seeking to bring an action under subsection (a)(1) of this section, the Equal Employment Opportunity Commission, the Attorney General, or a person who may bring an action or proceeding under title VII of the Civil Rights Act of 1964 (42 U.S.C. § 2000e et seq.); or

(B) in the case of a person seeking to bring an action under subsection (a)(2) of this section, the Equal Employment Opportunity Commission, the Attorney General, a person who may bring an action or proceeding under section 505(a)(1) of the Rehabilitation Act of 1973 (29 U.S.C. § 794a(a)(1)), or a person who may bring an action or proceeding under title I of the Americans with Disabilities Act of 1990 (42 U.S.C. § 12111 et seq.).

(2) Discriminatory practice

The term "discriminatory practice" means the discrimination described in paragraph (1), or the discrimination or the violation described in paragraph (2), of subsection (a) of this section.

Revised Statutes § 1977A, as added Pub. L. No. 102-166, Title I, § 102, Nov. 21, 1991, 105 Stat. 1072.

## ✦ Core Concept: Purpose of Remedies

The Title VII remedial scheme is designed to achieve two objectives. First, the scheme aims to prevent discrimination and as much as possible end all discrimination in the workplace. Second, it aims to make the victims of workplace discrimination completely whole from the losses suffered. The United States Supreme Court best explained the underlying purpose of the remedial scheme in *Albemarle Paper Co. v. Moody*, 422 U.S. 405 (1975). The *Albemarle* Court discussed the underlying purpose of the Title VII remedies in the context of the plaintiffs' argument that the district court erred in refusing to award them backpay after they had prevailed on liability.

# Albemarle Paper Co. v. Moody
## 422 U.S. 405 (1975)

Justice Stewart delivered the opinion of the Court.

[The trial court found system-wide race discrimination at Albemarle Paper Company and ordered corrections to the seniority system, but refused to order back pay because it found no bad faith. The appellate court reversed, holding that back pay is available when its award will advance the goals of Title VII.]

The petitioners contend that the statutory scheme provides no guidance, beyond indicating that backpay awards are within the District Court's discretion. We disagree. It is true that backpay is not an automatic or mandatory remedy; like all other remedies under the Act, it is one which the courts "may" invoke. The scheme implicitly recognizes that there may be cases calling for one remedy but not another, and—owing to the structure of the federal judiciary—these choices are, of course, left in the first instance to the district courts. However, such discretionary choices are not left to a court's "inclination, but to its judgment; and its judgment is to be guided by sound legal principles." [citation omitted]. The power to award backpay was bestowed by Congress, as part of a complex legislative design directed at a historic evil of national proportions. A court must exercise this power "in light of the large objectives of the Act." [citation omitted]. That the court's discretion is equitable in nature hardly means that it is unfettered by meaningful standards or shielded from thorough appellate review....

It is true that "[e]quity eschews mechanical rules ... [and] depends on flexibility." [citation omitted]. But when Congress invokes the Chancellor's conscience to further transcendent legislative purposes, what is required is the principled application of standards consistent with those purposes and not "equity [which] varies like the Chancellor's foot." [citation omitted]. Important national goals would be frustrated by a regime of discretion that "produce[d] different results for breaches of duty in situations that cannot be differentiated in policy." [citation omitted].

The District Court's decision must therefore be measured against the purposes which inform Title VII. As the Court observed in *Griggs v. Duke Power Co.*, the primary objective was a prophylactic one: "It was to achieve equality of employment opportunities and remove barriers that have operated in the past to favor an identifiable group of white employees over other employees." Backpay has an obvious connection with this purpose. If employers faced only the prospect of an injunctive order, they would have little incentive to shun practices of dubious legality. It is the reasonably certain prospect of a backpay award that "provide[s] the spur or catalyst which causes employers and unions to self-examine and to self-evaluate their employment practices and to endeavor to eliminate, so far as possible, the last vestiges of an unfortunate and ignominious page in this country's history." [citation omitted].

It is also the purpose of Title VII to make persons whole for injuries suffered on account of unlawful employment discrimination. This is shown by the very fact that Congress took care to arm the courts with full equitable powers. For it is the historic purpose of equity to "secur[e] complete justice." [citation omitted]. "[W]here federally protected rights have been invaded, it has been the rule from the beginning that courts will be alert to adjust their remedies so as to grant the necessary relief." [citation omitted]. Title VII deals with legal injuries of an economic character occasioned by racial or other antiminority discrimination. The terms "complete justice" and "necessary relief" have acquired a clear meaning in such circumstances. Where racial discrimination is concerned, "the [district] court has not merely the power but the duty to render a decree which will so far as possible eliminate the discriminatory effects of the past as well as bar like discrimination in the future." [citation omitted]. And where a legal injury is of an economic character, "[t]he general rule is, that when a wrong has been done, and the law gives a remedy, the compensation shall be equal to the injury. The latter is the standard by which the former is to be measured. The injured party is to be placed, as near as may be, in the situation he would have occupied if the wrong had not been committed." [citation omitted].

The "make whole" purpose of Title VII is made evident by the legislative history. The backpay provision was expressly modeled on the backpay provision of the National Labor Relations Act. Under that Act, "[m]aking the workers whole for losses suffered on account of an unfair labor practice is part of the vindication of the public policy which the Board enforces." [citation omitted]. We may assume that Congress was aware that the Board, since its inception, has awarded backpay as a matter of course—not randomly or in the exercise of a standardless discretion, and not merely where employer violations are peculiarly deliberate, egregious, or inexcusable. Furthermore, in passing the Equal Employment Opportunity Act of 1972, Congress considered several bills to limit the judicial power to award backpay. These limiting efforts were rejected, and the backpay provision was re-enacted substantially in its original form. A Section-by-Section Analysis introduced by Senator Williams to accompany the Conference Committee Report on the 1972 Act strongly reaffirmed the "make whole" purpose of Title VII:

> The provisions of this subsection are intended to give the courts wide discretion exercising their equitable powers to fashion the most complete relief possible. In dealing with the present section 706(g) the courts have stressed that the scope of relief under that section of the Act is intended to make the victims of unlawful discrimination whole, and that the attainment of this objective rests not only upon the elimination of the particular unlawful employment practice complained of, but also requires that persons aggrieved by the consequences and effects of the unlawful employment practice be, so far as possible, restored to a position where they would have been were it not for the unlawful discrimination. 118 Cong. Rec. 7168 (1972).

As this makes clear, Congress' purpose in vesting a variety of "discretionary" powers in the courts was not to limit appellate review of trial courts, or to invite inconsistency and caprice, but rather to make possible the "fashion[ing] [of] the most complete relief possible."

It follows that, given a finding of unlawful discrimination, backpay should be denied only for reasons which, if applied generally, would not frustrate the central statutory purposes of eradicating discrimination throughout the economy and making persons whole for injuries suffered through past discrimination. The courts of appeals must maintain a consistent and principled application of the backpay provision, consonant with the twin statutory objectives, while at the same time recognizing that the trial court will often have the keener appreciation of those facts and circumstances peculiar to particular cases. . . .

---

## ✦ Core Concept: Types of Title VII Remedies and Standards for Awarding Title VII Remedies

### Back Pay

Except in exceptional circumstances, courts award back pay to a plaintiff who has proved that the employer violated Title VII. Back pay is lost income due to the employer's discriminatory action. The back pay award includes all the compensation the aggrieved plaintiff would have received in the absence of discrimination up and until final judgment. This includes, but is not limited to, lost wages, raises, overtime compensation, bonuses, sick leave, vacation pay, and retirement benefits. *See Suggs v. ServiceMaster Educ. Food Mgmt.*, 72 F.3d 1228, 1233 (6th Cir. 1996). A plaintiff is entitled to pre-judgment interest on a back pay award. *See Richardson v. Tricom Pictures & Productions, Inc.*, 334 F. Supp. 2d 1303, 1315–16 (S.D. Fla. 2004). The purpose of awarding pre-judgment interest on back pay is to compensate the plaintiff for the time value (current value plus interest) of lost money and the effects of inflation. *See EEOC v. Joe's Stone Crab*, 15 F. Supp. 2d 1364, 1379 (S.D. Fla. 1998).

### Retroactive Seniority Relief

In some companies, seniority standing in employment, computed from the date of first hire, determines important job rights such as the order of layoff and recall of employees and the opportunity to bid for and win preferred job assignments. An employer's unlawful discriminatory action may cause an employee or applicant to lose these valuable seniority rights. It is understood that the "make whole" objective of the Title VII equitable provision will often require an award of the seniority credit and rights that the plaintiff would have earned but for the wrongful treatment. *See Franks v. Bowman Transportation Co.*, 424 U.S. 747, 766 (1976) ("It can hardly be questioned that ordinarily [an award of seniority] relief will be necessary to achieve the 'make-whole' purposes of the Act.").

### Reinstatement

In addition to back pay, prevailing Title VII plaintiffs are presumptively entitled to either reinstatement or front pay. Reinstatement is preferred over front pay but, when extenuating circumstances warrant, a trial court may award a plaintiff front pay in lieu of reinstatement. In deciding whether to award front pay instead of reinstatement, courts determine whether discord and antagonism between the parties or the lack of a comparable position would render reinstatement ineffective as a make-whole remedy. A trial court should not award front pay unless it first makes factual findings as to why reinstatement is not a viable option. *See E.E.O.C. v. W & O, Inc.*, 213 F.3d 600, 619 (11th Cir. 2000).

## Front Pay

Back pay takes a big step toward making the prevailing Title VII plaintiff whole for the period between the date of the discrimination and the trial. Reinstatement would then put the plaintiff in his or her rightful position absent the unlawful discrimination. But if reinstatement is not an option due to discord or the lack of a comparable position, front pay may be awarded by the trial judge. Front pay is a monetary remedy designed to compensate the plaintiff for the loss of future earnings he or she may suffer because the plaintiff cannot be placed in the position he or she was unlawfully denied. *See Maxfield v. Sinclair International*, 766 F.2d 788, 796 (3d Cir. 1985).

A front-pay determination is by its very nature subjective. The length of the front-pay period is determined by a variety of factors including the plaintiff's work expectancy, life expectancy, and market conditions. A federal district judge is given considerable discretion regarding the front-pay period. *See Schwartz v. Gregori*, 45 F.3d 1017, 1022 (6th Cir. 1995) (explaining the front-pay award is committed to the discretion of the trial court and review by the appellate court is for abuse of discretion).

*Donlin v. Philips Lighting North America Corp.*, 564 F.3d 207 (3d Cir. 2009), addressed the issue of front pay. In *Donlin*, a temporary employee, Colleen Donlin, sued for discrimination in violation of Title VII, claiming that the company failed to hire her as a full-time employee because of her gender. The gender discrimination claim proceeded to a jury. The jury returned a verdict in favor of the plaintiff on liability and damages. Specifically, in an advisory verdict, the jury awarded front pay to Donlin for twenty-five years. At the time of the award, Donlin was approximately 40 years of age and the jury's award of front pay for 25 years meant that such award would cover Donlin's lost earnings until the normal retirement age of 65. The district judge, however, issued a front pay award for a ten-year period. The employer contended on appeal that even the lesser ten-year period was too speculative, but the Third Circuit disagreed. The excerpt on front pay from the *Donlin* opinion is below. Note that other circuit courts have affirmed front-pay periods of 10 years or more.

# Donlin v. Philips Lighting North America Corp.

### 564 F.3d 207 (3d Cir. 2009)

Circuit Judge Hardiman.

. . .

Though back pay makes a plaintiff whole from the time of discrimination until trial, a plaintiff's injury may continue thereafter. Accordingly, courts may award front pay where a victim of employment discrimination will experience a loss of future earnings because she cannot be placed in the position she was unlawfully denied. Front pay is an alternative to the traditional equitable remedy of reinstatement, which would be inappropriate where there is a likelihood of continuing disharmony between the parties or unavailable because no comparable position exists. Because the award of front pay is discretionary, we review the District Court's decision for abuse of discretion and will reverse only if we are left with a definite and firm conviction that a mistake has been committed.

The jury recommended a front-pay award of $395,795 to cover the difference in Donlin's salary and pension earnings for 25 years, adjusted to account for the probability of death and discounted to present value. The District Court modified that award, limiting front pay damages to 10 years, which totaled $101,800. Despite this reduction, Philips asserts that the District Court's award of front pay was erroneous in two respects.

First, Philips claims that Donlin should not be entitled to front pay because she mitigated her damages by reestablishing herself in the workforce before trial. Philips cites *Ford Motor* for the proposition that damages are inappropriate where they "would catapult [the plaintiff] into a better position than they would have enjoyed in the absence of discrimination." [citation omitted]. As we have explained, however, the District Court found that Donlin was *not* in the same position she would have been in had Philips hired her as a full-time employee. Instead, the District Court concluded that her salary would have been higher had she been hired and remained at Philips. When a defendant's front pay objection is predicated upon the same objections regarding mitigation of damages which we have rejected with regard to back pay, we reject the front pay argument as well.

Second, Philips asserts that an award of front pay based on a 10-year period was inappropriate because it involved speculation regarding market conditions, Donlin's future earnings, and her length of employment. The District Court agreed with this argument in part when it reduced the advisory jury's award of front pay from 25 years to 10 years. Philips contends that the time period is still too long, noting that the Mountaintop facility where Donlin was employed is subject to unpredictable market conditions—including adjustments in demand and the availability of exclusive contracts with major suppliers—which cannot be accurately estimated for 10 years.

Because a claimant's work and life expectancy are pertinent factors in calculating front pay, such an award "necessarily implicates a prediction about the future." [citation omitted]. Accordingly, we will not refuse to award front pay merely because some prediction is necessary. Instead, we allow the District Court to exercise discretion in selecting a cut-off date for an equitable front pay remedy subject to the limitation that front pay only be awarded "for a reasonable future period required for the victim to reestablish her rightful place in the job market." *Goss v. Exxon Office Sys. Co.*, 747 F.2d 885, 889–90 (3d Cir. 1984).

In *Goss*, the plaintiff complained that the District Court cut off her front pay after just four months, arguing that front pay should be extended because she was unlikely to earn as much money in her new sales job. Goss's earnings were commission-based and her commissions were likely to be lower in her new position given her lack of familiarity with her new employer's products. Accordingly, Goss argued that her front pay should be extended even though she found new employment. We disagreed, finding that the question whether Goss would be less successful in her new job required unreasonable speculation regarding future market conditions and the company's success. Therefore, we declined to lengthen the front pay damages period.

In *Green v. USX Corp.*, 843 F.2d 1511, 1532 (3d Cir. 1988), however, we distinguished *Goss* and imposed a two-year front pay award for a class of plaintiffs asserting discrimination in the hiring process of a Pennsylvania steel company. Because the plaintiffs presented evidence for the period immediately following trial, we found that calculating front pay damages based on a two-year period was a "reasonable compromise" and not "wild speculation" because it would help offset future harm that "would *certainly* be caused" by past discrimination.

Though the 10-year damages period granted by the District Court exceeds that awarded in *Green*, we note that there will often be uncertainty concerning how long the front-pay period should be, and the evidence adduced at trial will rarely point to a single, certain number of weeks, months, or years. More likely, the evidence will support a range of reasonable front-pay periods. Within this range, the district court should decide which award is most appropriate to make the claimant whole.

Such an exercise of discretion may result in an award different from what one or both of the parties would prefer. This possibility is caused by the inexactness of predictive evidence for front pay, and our standard of review (abuse of discretion) grants considerable leeway to district courts to grant an award that best serves Title VII's remedial purpose.

We have not yet spoken precedentially regarding the precise length of time that is appropriate for an award of front pay. Indeed, in one case, a front-pay award of X years may be appropriate, while on different facts, a front-pay award for that same term of years would be inappropriate. These decisions are left to the sound discretion of the district court and every case must be considered on its particular facts. We note, however, that other courts of appeals have affirmed front-pay awards of 10 years or more. [citations omitted]. Additionally, we note that in *Blum v. Witco Chem. Corp.*, 829 F.2d 367, 376 (3d Cir. 1987), we held that awarding front pay until plaintiffs' projected retirement in eight years did not require unreasonable speculation. We see no reason why a front pay award for eight years would be proper, but an award for 10 years constitutes an abuse of discretion. This is especially true here, where an advisory jury recommended front pay for 25 years.

Accordingly, we find that the District Court did not abuse its discretion when it awarded Donlin front pay for 10 years.

---

## Note

*How long is too long?* Under the right set of facts, is it fair to predict in today's economy that a prevailing Title VII plaintiff would have remained in the job from which she was unlawfully excluded until some generally established retirement age? If the *Donlin* district court judge had accepted the jury's advisory verdict on front pay and awarded front pay to Donlin for twenty-five years until her expected retirement age at 65, would such an award be an abuse of discretion that should be overruled on appeal by the Third Circuit?

---

### Exercise 11.1

On June 1, 2004, Bill Medina, then 55 years of age, signed a five-year contract to be the City of Gainesville, Florida's chief of police. On June 1, 2005, the City terminated Chief Medina's employment as chief of police. Chief Medina sued the City for violating Title VII, claiming that the City unlawfully terminated his employment because of his national origin. On June 1, 2007, Chief Medina prevailed at trial on his Title VII claim and subsequently moved the court for an award of front pay for the period of time Medina would have worked if he had remained in the position until retirement at the age of 65 in 2014.

Both the City of Gainesville and Chief Medina stipulate that, because of antagonism on both sides, reinstatement is not a viable option in this case. During the trial and on post-trial motion, Chief Medina introduces evidence that each of the previous three police chiefs for the City served in that position until they retired at the age of 65, their employment contracts notwithstanding. Is a front-pay award for 7 years proper? If not, for what period of time should Chief Medina receive front pay?

### Declaratory and Injunctive Relief

Section 706(g)(1) of Title VII, 42 U.S.C. § 2000e-5(g)(1), states that:

> If the court finds that the respondent has intentionally engaged in or is intentionally engaging in an unlawful employment practice charged in the complaint, the court may *enjoin* the respondent from engaging in such unlawful employment practice, and order such affirmative action as may be appropriate, ... or any other equitable relief as the court deems appropriate. (emphasis added).

An "injunction" is "a court order prohibiting someone from doing some specified act or commanding someone to undo some wrong or injury.... Generally, it is a protective remedy, aimed at future acts, and is not intended to redress past wrongs." BLACK'S LAW DICTIONARY 540 (abridged 6th ed. 1991).

Upon a finding of an intentional Title VII violation, Title VII permits a court to award injunctive relief in accordance with the principles of equity. *See EEOC v. Novartis Pharmaceutical Corp.*, No. 2:05-cv-404, 2007 U.S. Dist. LEXIS 72831, at *13 (W.D. Pa. 2007) ("[A] finding of intentional discrimination appears to be the only statutory prerequisite to the issuance of an injunction."). Injunctive relief is permissive, not mandatory. Like requests for permanent injunctions in other contexts, the prevailing Title VII plaintiff requesting a permanent injunction should show that she has suffered an irreparable injury; that remedies available at law are inadequate to compensate for that injury; that considering the balance of the hardships between the plaintiff and the defendant, a remedy in equity is warranted; and that the public interest would not be disserved by an injunction. It appears as though the combination of a liability finding under Title VII, Title VII's endorsement of equitable relief, and the public interest in enforcing Title VII satisfy the traditional four-factor permanent injunction test and make an award of injunctive relief "appropriate," even if the Title VII violation has already ceased. *See EEOC v. DCP Midstream*, 608 F. Supp. 2d 107, 109-10 (D. Maine 2009). Where the discrimination is ongoing, an injunction may flow as a matter of course. *See EEOC v. Preferred Labor LLC*, No. 06-40190-FDS, 2009 U.S. Dist. LEXIS 12861, at *14 (D. Mass. Feb. 13, 2009) (holding an award of some injunctive relief is mandatory where the discrimination is ongoing). The point is that, in determining whether to order an injunction upon a liability finding, the courts either tend to presume that the traditional test for determining whether to order a permanent injunction may be met once a Title VII violation is proven or skip over the test entirely.

In determining whether to order an injunction after a liability finding, the trial judge must focus on whether the employer's discriminatory conduct is likely to persist in the future. This is so because the whole point of the injunction is to protect the plaintiff and other employees from future discriminatory acts by that employer. *See Brown v. Trustees of Boston University*, 891 F.2d 337, 361 (1st Cir. 1989). Some appellate courts have stated that the burden is on the *employer* to prove, upon a finding of intentional discrimination, that it is unlikely to violate Title VII again. *See EEOC v. Massey Yardley Chrysler Plymouth*, 117 F.3d 1244, 1253 (11th Cir. 1997); *EEOC v. Harris Chernin, Inc.*, 10 F.3d 1286, 1292 (7th Cir. 1993); *EEOC v. Goodyear Aerospace Corp.*, 813 F.2d 1539, 1544–45 (9th Cir. 1987). At least one appellate court has held, however, that, where a single violation (as opposed to a pattern or series of violations) exists, the burden is on the *party moving for the injunction* (an individual plaintiff or the EEOC) to prove that the employer is likely to engage in future discriminatory conduct. *See EEOC v. General Lines, Inc.*, 865 F.2d 1555, 1565 (10th Cir. 1989). Ultimately, whether to grant an injunction is left to the sound discretion of the trial court. *See EEOC v. Frank's Nursery & Crafts, Inc.*, 177 F.3d 448, 467–68 (6th Cir. 1999).

In the following case, the EEOC sued an employer under Title VII for unlawfully retaliating against an employee who complained about racially offensive conduct. A jury found the defendant liable for illegal retaliation. After the trial, the EEOC and the employee, as intervenor, moved for injunctive relief. (It is not unusual for the EEOC, as the government agency charged with seeking to vindicate the public interest in Title VII cases, to seek injunctive relief after it has successfully proven a Title VII violation). The retaliation in violation of Title VII involved one individual employee (not a class of individuals) and, at the time the EEOC requested injunctive relief after the trial, three years had passed since any reports of further illegal retaliation. The federal district judge nevertheless ordered injunctive relief.

---

### Focus Questions: *EEOC v. DCP Midstream L.P.*

1. *Why is an injunction an appropriate remedy when the plaintiff has not produced evidence of discrimination that goes beyond his case and the discrimination is not ongoing?*

2. *What types of injunctive relief did the EEOC seek in the DCP Midstream case?*

3. *What types of injunctive relief did the judge finally award in the case?*

4. *How long does the injunction last?*

5. *Do you agree with the district judge's decision? Why or why not?*

---

# EEOC v. DCP Midstream L.P.

## 608 F. Supp. 2d 107 (D. Maine 2009)

### ORDER ON INJUNCTIVE RELIEF

District Judge Hornby.

A jury has found that the defendant DCP Midstream, L.P. ("DCP Midstream") illegally retaliated against employee Daniel Mayo when Mayo complained about racially offensive conduct and/or complained about retaliatory conduct that occurred after he made his complaints about the racially offensive conduct. The jury did not find that DCP Midstream engaged in any actual racial discrimination against Mayo or that it permitted a racially hostile environment in the workplace. The jury awarded Mayo $35,000 in compensatory damages for the retaliation. Because of an earlier stipulation, Mayo will also receive a backpay award of $52,275. The jury deadlocked on punitive damages, and that issue will be retried.

The plaintiffs Equal Employment Opportunity Commission ("EEOC") and Mayo (plaintiff-intervenor) (collectively "the plaintiffs") also request injunctive relief against DCP Midstream under Title VII of the Civil Rights Act of 1964, 42 U.S.C. § 2000e-5(g)(1), a decision that I as the judge must make. Because I conclude that DCP Midstream has not met its burden to show that it is unlikely that illegal retaliation will recur, I conclude that injunctive relief is appropriate. However, I choose to limit and alter some of the plaintiffs' requested provisions for reasons that I describe.

Accordingly, I grant the plaintiffs' motion in part.

[The court explained the circumstances in which the jury found the employer liable for retaliation under Title VII. DCP Midstream operates facilities where employees unload propane from railcars and then load the propane into customers' trucks for subsequent distribution. Mayo was an African-American employee at a DCP Midstream facility in Auburn, Maine. Mayo complained to the employer, DCP Midstream, on several occasions about how a customer and co-worker used the term "n*****" in his presence. Mayo introduced evidence to show that his supervisors and Human Resources treated him harshly for making such complaints. Ultimately, Mayo proved that his employer terminated his employment because Mayo complained about the racially discriminatory comments instead of the pretextual reason given by the employer that Mayo had violated a safety rule.]

ANALYSIS

The Supreme Court has stated that "a plaintiff seeking a permanent injunction must satisfy a four-factor test before a court may grant such relief." *eBay Inc. v. MercExchange, LLC*, 547 U.S. 388, 391 (2006) (holding that this general test "appl[ies] with equal force to disputes" under a federal statute "expressly provid[ing] that injunctions 'may' issue 'in accordance with the principles of equity'"). The plaintiff must show:

> (1) that it has suffered an irreparable injury; (2) that remedies available at law, such as monetary damages, are inadequate to compensate for that injury; (3) that, considering the balance of hardships between the plaintiff and the defendant, a remedy in equity is warranted; and (4) that the public interest would not be disserved by a permanent injunction.

Title VII of the Civil Rights Act of 1964 states that:

> If the court finds that the respondent has intentionally engaged in or is intentionally engaging in an unlawful employment practice charged in the complaint, the court may enjoin the respondent from engaging in such unlawful employment practice, and order such affirmative action as may be appropriate, ... or any other equitable relief as the court deems appropriate. 42 U.S.C. § 2000e-5(g)(1).

Similar to the statute in question in *eBay*, Title VII instructs a court to award relief in accordance with the principles of equity; thus *eBay's* four-factor test applies with equal force to awarding injunctive relief in this case. The jury here found an unlawful employment practice, and I agree. This finding of liability, coupled with Title VII's congressional endorsement of equitable relief, is sufficient to meet the first three prongs of the test. The fourth prong is likewise met because, as the First Circuit has recognized, "the public has an interest in the enforcement of federal statutes." [citation omitted]. As a result, injunctive relief is available as "appropriate."

According to the First Circuit Court of Appeals, in an employment discrimination case a district court "has broad power to restrain acts which are of the same type or class as unlawful acts which the court has found to have been committed or whose commission in the future, unless enjoined, may fairly be anticipated from the defendant's conduct in the past." [citation omitted]. The First Circuit has also stated, in a private employee lawsuit, that "[a]n injunction should be narrowly tailored to give only the relief to which plaintiffs are entitled," and the court warned against an injunction that is effectively class-wide relief where no class has been certified. [citation omitted]. Here, however, one of the plaintiffs is the EEOC, a governmental agency recognized by the Supreme Court as "seeking to vindicate a public interest, not simply provide make-whole relief for the employee." [citation omitted]. Accordingly, in determining whether to award injunctive relief, I must keep in mind the public's interests, as well as Mayo's individual interests. *See EEOC v. Frank's Nursery & Crafts, Inc.,* 177 F.3d 448, 468 (6th Cir. 1999) ("[T]he EEOC may obtain equitable relief that protects a class of persons from unlawful employment discrimination without citing numerous instances of such discrimination.... [T]he EEOC may seek it upon proof even of just one instance of discrimination that violates Title VII. In seeking such relief, the EEOC need not identify a class or its numbers, or even identify a pattern or practice of discrimination.").

Generally, "[w]hile the awarding of some injunctive relief is mandatory where the discrimination is ongoing, such relief is not required where the discrimination has ceased and there is no reasonable probability of further noncompliance." [citation omitted]. But in a retaliation case, the burden is on the employer to show that it is unlikely to retaliate against protected activity in the future.

Here, DCP Midstream fails to meet that burden. Only one of the four supervisory employees involved in Mayo's termination has left DCP Midstream since the retaliation occurred. DCP Midstream already had formal policies in place prohibiting retaliation before the Mayo incident, but the jury obviously concluded that the previous training and materials for management personnel failed to prevent illegal retaliation. If DCP Midstream's "upper echelon of management felt free to ignore ... policies in the past, there is no reason to believe that those same members of management will abide by them in the future." It is true that the retaliation against Mayo arose in a constellation of circumstances that may not recur (a complaint that resulted in a customer's job loss, and a complaint about a co-worker who had a close relationship with a supervisor), and three years have passed since Mayo's termination without reports of any other illegal retaliation. Those are grounds to limit the relief, but not deny an injunction altogether. Thus, I will grant appropriately limited injunctive relief.

I address the plaintiffs' specific requests:

1. Injunction. The plaintiffs request an order stating that DCP Midstream "and its managers, officers, agents, successors, and assigns, are enjoined from engaging in retaliation against any individual for engaging in protected activity under Title VII. [DCP Midstream] and its agents are further enjoined from taking any retaliatory action against any individual for participating in this matter in any way or giving testimony in this matter, including, but not limited to, Mayo and other witnesses in this case."

Given the nature of the unlawful employment practice here, this language is appropriate.

2. Reporting. The plaintiffs request a court-imposed requirement that "[i]f any job applicant or employee engages in protected activity under the non-retaliation provisions of Title VII, [DCP Midstream] must report all such activities to the EEOC within seven days of any such activity," as well as report its "response to such activities within seven days of the conclusion of its response." The plaintiffs also request that "[t]he report of [DCP Midstream]'s response to the protected activity must contain, at a minimum, the full name, home address and telephone number, social security number and date of birth of the person engaging in the protected activity, the job title or position of the person engaging in the protected activity, a detailed description of the protected activity, the name(s) and job title of the person(s) engaging in the allegedly discriminatory conduct, the dates of the discriminatory conduct, the dates of the alleged protected activity, a description of the actions [DCP Midstream] took in response to the protected activity, the names and job titles of the persons acting on [DCP Midstream]'s behalf in responding to the protected activity, and the dates of [DCP Midstream]'s actions in response to the protected activity."

I deny the plaintiffs this request. These reporting requirements are unduly burdensome given the excessive detail to be furnished to the EEOC, including unnecessary personal information such as birth dates and social security numbers, which are sensitive information considering current concerns over identity theft. Furthermore, a deadline of seven days is impracticable given the slow pace of business administration in large corporations such as DCP Midstream. Most importantly, however, I conclude that the bureaucracy of this request is excessive, given the other relief I am ordering—letters sent to all employees, training of employees, posting of a notice in DCP Midstream facilities, *etc.* Those will be sufficient to deter retaliatory practices in the future. DCP Midstream employees who suffer retaliation will be encouraged to report it given their knowledge of Title VII's protections and of Mayo's successful lawsuit and substantial money award.

3. Distribution of Policies and Procedures Prohibiting Retaliation. The plaintiffs propose a requirement that DCP Midstream, "[w]ithin seven days after the entry of this Judgment for Injunctive relief, … must send a letter to all of its employees at each of its Northeast Propane Terminals, advising them of the verdict against [it] in this case on the issue of retaliation, enclosing a copy of [its] policy prohibiting retaliation against individuals who engage in protected activity under Title VII, and stating that [it] will not tolerate any such retaliation and will take appropriate disciplinary action against any manager, supervisor or employee who engages in such retaliation. The letter must be printed on [DCP Midstream's] letterhead and must be signed by [its] Chief Executive Officer."

This is appropriate relief, but fourteen days will be allowed for sending out the letter.

4. Posting and Notices. The plaintiffs propose a requirement that DCP Midstream, "[w]ithin seven days after the entry of this Judgment for Injunctive Relief, … must post at each of its Northeast Propane Terminals a copy of [a] remedial notice" detailing the verdict in this case as well as the order providing injunctive relief.

I agree with the plaintiffs that a notice should be posted at each of the Northeast Propane Terminals. The language of that notice, however, must be altered to reflect today's decision. The deadline for posting it shall be fourteen days. The notice must remain posted for two years following the entry of the order providing injunctive relief.

5. Disciplinary Action. The plaintiffs request that DCP Midstream, "[w]ithin seven days after the entry of this Judgment for Injunctive Relief, … will provide one hour of counseling to [certain named supervisory employees] on the provisions in Title VII and [DCP Midstream's] corporate policies prohibiting retaliation against individuals who engage in protected activity under Title VII," and that DCP Midstream "will place and permanently maintain a letter in the personnel file of [these various individuals] regarding the counseling, together with a copy of this Judgment for Injunctive Relief."

I deny this request. These supervisory employees were not parties to this litigation and had no opportunity to defend themselves individually against charges. As such, it would be inappropriate to impose this quasi-disciplinary requirement on them and alter their personnel files. It is sufficient that I order DCP Midstream to undertake retaliation training generally for management and workers.

6. Training. [The plaintiffs asked that the injunction include provisions requiring DCP Midstream supervisory employees to participate in a 4-hour training seminar on the requirements of Title VII and DCP employees in general to participate in a 1-hour seminar].

It is appropriate to require that DCP Midstream personnel receive training, but such training is required only on Title VII's prohibition on retaliation, because that was the only illegal employment practice. Illegal retaliation is not a difficult concept to master. Accordingly, one hour of training will be required on illegal retaliation. (Of course, DCP Midstream may expand this training to include other topics if it so chooses.) The same limitations apply to training for non-management employees. With the exception of these changes, I approve the plaintiffs' language.

7. Daniel Mayo's Personnel File and Information. With respect to Mayo, the plaintiffs request that DCP Midstream "must expunge from Daniel Mayo's personnel record all documents relating to his termination and place in his file a letter stating that his discharge was motivated by [DCP Midstream]'s effort to retaliate against him for engaging in legally protected activity," and that, "[i]f asked by a prospective employer for information or a reference concerning Daniel Mayo, [DCP Midstream] must provide only the dates of his employment and last position held, and must advise the caller that they only provide this limited information pursuant to company policy."

The language is appropriate, except that I will not compel DCP Midstream to prevaricate, and thus I will not order DCP Midstream to say that it is providing the limited information "pursuant to company policy."

8. Monitoring. [The plaintiff requested that the EEOC be given the authority to monitor and review compliance with the injunction. The court agreed. The court ordered that DCP Midstream must, periodically during the term of the injunction, submit written proof via affidavit that it had complied with requirements of the injunction. The employer also had to maintain records regarding compliance. The court gave the EEOC the authority to attend training sessions, review documents related to complying with the injunction, and conduct interviews of company employees, managers, supervisors, and contractors as related to the injunction.]

9. Successors. This language is appropriate to bind DCP Midstream's successors, if any, for the duration of this injunction.

10. Duration of Injunction. Because three years have already passed without incident and because the retaliation here resulted from a modestly unusual combination of events, I find that an injunction with a duration of two years (not the five years requested) is appropriate here.

CONCLUSION

In sum, then, I approve the plaintiffs' requests in paragraphs 1, 3, 4, and 6–10 of their Proposed Judgment for Injunctive Relief, with modifications as described, and I deny their request in paragraphs 2 and 5.

For the above stated reasons, the plaintiffs' Motion for Injunctive Relief is hereby granted in part.

The plaintiffs shall file with the Court a revised proposed judgment on injunctive relief, modified in accordance with my rulings, by April 20, 2009. In light of the pending retrial on punitive damages, they shall also state when they request entry of the Order. The defendant shall file any response by April 27, 2009.

So Ordered.

———————

## Notes

1. *Pattern of Title VII violations.* The EEOC did not contend in the *DCP Midstream* case that the employer engaged in a pattern of discriminatory activity. In cases where the EEOC or private plaintiffs prove a series of Title VII violations (as opposed to a single violation), it is more likely that the courts will order injunctive relief. But, as *DCP Midstream* and the cases cited in the opinion demonstrate, proof of a pattern of Title VII violations is not required for a court to order injunctive relief. *See also EEOC v. Red River Beverage Co.*, No. 3:99-CV-1685-P, 2002 U.S. Dist. LEXIS 27325 (N.D. Tex. Mar. 7, 2003) (finding no evidence of a pattern of discriminatory conduct in a Title VII retaliation case but still ordering a three-year injunction that included employee training requirement).

2. *Preliminary injunctive relief.* The injunction ordered in *DCP Midstream* is best characterized as a *permanent* injunction because the court issued it after a determination of the merits of the lawsuit. *See* Russell L. Weaver, Donald F. Partlett, Donald E. Lively, and Michael B. Kelly, Remedies: Cases, Practical Problems and Exercises 126 (2004) (explaining permanent injunctions are "issued after a determination on the merits of a lawsuit and are designed to apply prospectively and permanently unless modified or resolved"). Section 706(g)(1) clearly provides the judge with the opportunity to order a permanent injunction after a determination on the merits that the employer is liable (*i.e.*, a finding of a Title VII violation). But what about the statutory authority of a district court to order a *preliminary* injunction in a Title VII case? *Id.* ("A preliminary injunction is issued at the beginning of litigation and is designed to prevent irreparable harm from occurring during the pendency of a suit (*i.e.*, before the merits can be decided).").

In *EEOC v. Novartis Pharmaceutical Corp.*, No. 2:05-cv-404, 2007 U.S. Dist. LEXIS 72831, at *49 (W.D. Pa. Sept. 28, 2007), the district court determined that it could not appropriately exercise its discretion to grant or deny injunctive relief under Section 706(g)(1) until it first determined whether an intentional violation of Title VII had occurred. The implication from the case is that Section 706(g)(1) does not present the statutory authority for a court to issue a preliminary injunction to a private plaintiff in a Title VII dispute. The truth of this implication is questionable, although the courts do appear to be reluctant to issue a temporary restraining order or order preliminary injunctive relief under Section 706(g)(1) unless there has first been a finding of a Title VII violation. The best view is that, irrespective of the injunctive relief provisions in Title VII, the federal courts have an inherent equitable power to order preliminary injunctive relief to plaintiffs in Title VII suits so long as the traditional requirements for obtaining a preliminary injunction (likelihood of success on the merits, irreparable harm, balance of equities, and public interest) are met. *See Wagner v. Taylor*, 836 F.2d 566, 570–72 (D.C. Cir. 1987). Regardless, there is clear statutory authority for a court to issue a temporary restraining order or preliminary injunction in favor of the EEOC, as opposed to a private plaintiff, at the charge stage of a Title VII case.

Section 706(f)(2) states that if, during the preliminary stage of its investigation, the EEOC concludes that judicial intervention is necessary to allow it to perform its statutory duties and carry out the purposes of Title VII, the EEOC "may bring an action for appropriate temporary or preliminary relief pending final disposition of such charge." 42 U.S.C. §2000e-5(f)(2). Under this provision, the EEOC has sought and obtained temporary restraining orders and preliminary injunctions against employers deemed to have taken actions that would inhibit the agency's ability to conduct its investigation. *See EEOC v. Astra USA*, 94 F.3d 738 (1st Cir. 1996) (upholding federal district court granting a request for preliminary injunction and enjoining an employer from enforcing the terms of settlement agreements with company employees that thwarted the EEOC's ability to investigate a discrimination charge); *EEOC v. Recruit USA, Inc.*, 939 F.2d 746, 749–50 (9th Cir. 1991) (upholding federal district court granting a temporary restraining order and preliminary injunction to EEOC that precluded employer from destroying, altering, or removing certain documents related to the discrimination claim). In seeking a preliminary injunction under this provision, the best view is that the EEOC must meet the traditional preliminary injunction standard of proving (1) a substantial likelihood of success on the merits; (2) a significant risk of irreparable harm if the injunction is withheld; (3) a favorable balance of interests; and (4) a fit between the injunction and the public interest. *See EEOC v. Anchor Hocking Corp.*, 666 F.2d 1037, 1040–41 (6th Cir. 1981) (showing of irreparable harm is a prerequisite for injunctive relief under Section 706(f)(2)). This is the standard for obtaining a preliminary injunction in federal court. States may have slightly different standards for obtaining a preliminary injunction.

### Compensatory Damages

Section 102 of the Civil Rights Act of 1991 provides that a Title VII plaintiff who proves an unlawful intentional Title VII violation may recover compensatory damages for "future pecuniary losses, emotional pain, suffering, inconvenience, mental anguish, loss of enjoyment of life, and other nonpecuniary losses." *See* 42 U.S.C. § 1981a(b)(3). Compensatory damages are restricted to intentional discrimination claims and so they cannot be obtained in disparate impact suits. *See* 42 U.S.C. § 1981a(a)(1).

A "pecuniary loss" is a loss of money or something of tangible economic value. Under Title VII, *future pecuniary losses* are out-of-pocket expenses that are likely to occur after the litigation concludes. Such losses are recoverable and include "moving expenses, job search expenses, medical expenses, psychiatric expenses, and other quantifiable out-of-pocket expenses that are incurred [by the Title VII plaintiff] as a result of the [employer's] discriminatory conduct." EEOC Policy Guidance No. 915.002 § II(A)(1) (July 14, 1992). A future pecuniary loss is distinct from front pay. Front pay is recoverable under Section 706(g) and therefore does not constitute compensatory damages. *See* 42 U.S.C. § 1981a(b)(2) ("Compensatory damages awarded under this section shall not include backpay, interest on backpay, *or any other type of relief authorized under section 706(g) of the Civil Rights Act of 1964.*") (emphasis added); *Pollard v. E.I. Du Pont de Nemours & Co.*, 532 U.S. 843, 845 (2001) (front pay award is not an element of compensatory damages under Section 1981(a)).

A "nonpecuniary loss" is a loss that stems from the intangible injuries of emotional and reputational harms incurred by a Title VII plaintiff as a result of the employer's discriminatory conduct. Damages are recoverable for intangible injuries like emotional pain, suffering, inconvenience, mental anguish, loss of enjoyment of life, injury to professional standing, injury to character and reputation, injury to credit standing, loss of health, and even lost future earnings. *See* EEOC Policy Guidance No. 915.002 § II(A)(2) (July 14, 1992); *Williams v. Pharmacia, Inc.*, 137 F.3d 944, 952–53 (7th Cir. 1998) (holding that lost future earnings capacity is a nonpecuniary loss that compensates the Title VII plaintiff for a lifetime of diminished earnings resulting from the reputational harms suffered due to the employer's discrimination).

Possible manifestations of emotional harm in Title VII cases include "sleeplessness, anxiety, stress, depression, marital strain, humiliation, emotional distress, loss of self esteem, excessive fatigue, a nervous breakdown ... ulcers, gastrointestinal disorders, hair loss, or headaches." EEOC Policy Guidance No. 915.002 § II(A)(2) (July 14, 1992). A Title

VII plaintiff claiming emotional harm damages must prove that the employer's discriminatory act caused the emotional harm. *See Decorte v. Jordan*, 497 F.3d 433, 442 (5th Cir. 2007) (holding that compensatory damages for emotional distress require specific proof about how the plaintiff was personally affected by the discriminatory conduct and the nature and extent of the harm). Thus, preexisting emotional harm symptoms tend to undermine a claim for emotional harm damages. *See* EEOC Policy Guidance No. 915.002 § II(A)(2) (July 14, 1992). A Title VII plaintiff claiming emotional harm damages should introduce medical evidence and corroborating testimony regarding manifestations of that emotional harm if at all possible. Nonetheless, a plaintiff's testimony by itself may be sufficient evidence to support an award for emotional distress damages in an appropriate case. *See Migis v. Pearle Vision, Inc.*, 135 F.3d 1041, 1046–47 (5th Cir. 1998) (upholding compensatory damages award for emotional distress under Title VII where emotional distress evidence consisted solely of plaintiff's own testimony that her unlawful firing caused her to suffer low self-esteem, anxiety attacks, marital hardship, sleeplessness, and crying). The amount of emotional harm damages awarded should be based on the severity and length of time of the harm suffered. *See* EEOC Policy Guidance No. 915.002 § II(A)(2) (July 14, 1992).

### Punitive Damages

Section 102 of the Civil Rights Act of 1991 states that:

> A complaining party may recover punitive damages under this section against a respondent (other than a government, government agency or political subdivision) if the complaining party demonstrates that the respondent engaged in a discriminatory practice or discriminatory practices with malice or with reckless indifference to the federally protected rights of an aggrieved individual. *See* 42 U.S.C. § 1981a(b)(1).

"Punitive damages" under Title VII are damages designed to punish the employer for intentional wrongdoing and set an example for other employers. The plaintiff demanding punitive damages has the burden to prove that the employer acted both "intentionally" and with the mental state of "malice or reckless indifference." The heightened mental state requirement does not mean, however, that "employers must engage in conduct with some independent, 'egregious' quality before being subject to a [Title VII] punitive award." *Kolstad v. American Dental Association*, 527 U.S. 526, 538 (1999).

Agency principles limit the imposition of vicarious liability for punitive damages on employers. There must be a basis for imputing to the employer liability for the discriminatory actions of the employer's agent. One way this may be accomplished is by proof from the plaintiff that the employee who engaged in discrimination is a managerial agent acting within the scope of his employment.

Even if a basis for imputing liability is established, the employer may still avoid punitive damages if it proves that it engaged in "good-faith efforts" to comply with Title VII (such as adopting and implementing an anti-discrimination policy). *See Kolstad*, 527 U.S. at 545–46; *Monteagudo v. Asociacion de Empleados del Estado Libre Asociado de Puerto Rico*, 554 F. 3d 164, 176 (1st Cir. 2009) (demonstrating good-faith compliance is the employer's affirmative defense); *Sturgill v. UPS*, 512 F.3d 1024, 1035–36 (8th Cir. 2008) (reversing Title VII punitive damages award because no UPS managers acted with malice or reckless indifference in failing to accommodate plaintiff's request for religious accommodation and UPS demonstrated that it followed a nationwide, multi-step protocol for considering employee requests for religious accommodations).

Factors a jury might properly consider in determining whether the plaintiff has proven "malice or reckless disregard" include the degree of egregiousness and nature of the employer's conduct; the nature, extent, and severity of the harm to the plaintiff; the duration of the discriminatory conduct; the existence and frequency of past similar conduct by the employer; evidence that the employer tried to conceal or cover-up the discriminatory practice; and the employer's actions after learning of the discriminatory conduct. *See* EEOC Policy Guidance No. 915.002 § II(B)(1) (July 14, 1992); *Parker v. Gen. Extrusions, Inc.*, 491 F.3d 596, 604 (6th Cir. 2007) (holding employer's repeated "half-hearted" or "sham" efforts to investigate employee's sexual harassment allegations and attempts to drive the employee from her job fulfilled the "malice or reckless indifference" standard).

The majority rule in the circuit courts of appeals is that punitive damages may be awarded without a compensatory damages award. *See Abner v. Kansas City Southern Railroad Co.*, 513 F.3d 154, 160 (5th Cir. 2008); *Timm v. Progressive Steel Treating, Inc.*, 137 F.3d 1008, 1010 (7th Cir. 1998). The amount of a punitive damages award must be tied to the nature and extent of the employer's discriminatory acts and the amount of harm suffered by the plaintiff in order to satisfy constitutional due process concerns. *See, e.g., BMW of North America v. Gore*, 517 U.S. 559 (1996); *State Farm Mutual Insurance Co v. Campbell*, 538 U.S. 408 (2003) (explaining the constitutional limits on punitive damages awards). The financial resources of the employer may be taken into account by the jury in fashioning a punitive damages award. *See Whitney v. Citibank, N.A.*, 782 F.2d 1106, 1119 (2d Cir. 1986). The Title VII cap on punitive damages, which is explained below, renders the issue of *extremely* excessive punitive damages awards, which might be considered by some a problem in other civil contexts, largely a moot point under Title VII. *See White v. Burlington Northern & Santa Fe Railroad Co.*, 364 F.3d 789, 806 (6th Cir. 2004) ("Title VII's own quite substantial restrictions on punitive damage awards guard against excessive awards"). But Title VII punitive damages awards may still be challenged as excessive under the Constitution. *See EEOC v. Harbert-Yeargin, Inc.*, 266 F.3d 498, 514 (6th Cir. 2001) (discussing employer's unsuccessful attempt to argue in Title VII case that $300,000 punitive damages award was so excessive as to violate its constitutional right to the due process of law).

## ✦ Core Concept: Title VII's Compensatory and Punitive Damages Cap

Section 102 of the 1991 Civil Rights Act, which amended Title VII, placed a cap on the combined amount of compensatory and punitive damages recoverable by a Title VII plaintiff. *See* 42 U.S.C. § 1981a(b)(3)(A)-(D). The provision states:

(3) Limitations

The sum of the amount of compensatory damages awarded under this section for future pecuniary losses, emotional pain, suffering, inconvenience, mental anguish, loss of enjoyment of life, and other nonpecuniary losses, and the amount of punitive damages awarded under this section, shall not exceed, for each complaining party—

(A) in the case of a respondent who has more than 14 and fewer than 101 employees in each of 20 or more calendar weeks in the current or preceding calendar year, $50,000;

(B) in the case of a respondent who has more than 100 and fewer than 201 employees in each of 20 or more calendar weeks in the current or preceding calendar year, $100,000; and

(C) in the case of a respondent who has more than 200 and fewer than 501 employees in each of 20 or more calendar weeks in the current or preceding calendar year, $200,000; and

(D) in the case of a respondent who has more than 500 employees in each of 20 or more calendar weeks in the current or preceding calendar year, $300,000.

As you can tell, the cap on compensatory and punitive damages varies by the case. The cap is tied to how many employees the defendant-employer employs. The maximum amount recoverable under the cap is $300,000. The $300,000 cap applies if the employer employs more than 500 employees. For a defendant-employer who employs fewer than 500 employees, the amount of the cap is lower in accordance with the rules outlined above. Under the statute, the "current year" has been interpreted to mean the year in which the discriminatory act took place, not the year in which the case is filed or the judgment is signed. *See Vance v. Union Planters Corp.*, 279 F.3d 295, 297 (5th Cir. 2002).

The statute does not speak specifically to how to identify the relevant employer. There is a possibility in some cases that for purposes of counting the number of employees employed by an "employer" two presumably separate enterprises (like parent and subsidiary corporations) may be treated as one "employer." The typical four-factor balancing test for determining whether distinct entities constitute an integrated enterprise, *i.e.*, a single employer, under § 1981a(b)(3) include interrelation of operations; centralized control of labor relations; common management; and common ownership or financial control. But the ultimate question is which entity or entities made the final decisions regarding employment matters related to the person claiming discrimination. *Vance*, 279 F.3d at 301.

The jury in a Title VII case is not notified of the compensatory and punitive damages cap in the jury charge. *See* 42 U.S.C. § 1981a(c)(2). If the jury awards more than the cap, the defendant will file a post-verdict motion to reduce the compensatory and punitive damages award to reflect the cap and the compensatory and punitive damages amounts in the judgment will then conform to the cap.

---

### Exercise 11.2

In the *Jerome Johnson v. Southern Bell Systems* case, Mr. Johnson receives a compensatory damages award of $400,000 and punitive damages award of $100,000 from the jury for a combined amount of $500,000. The evidence indicates that at the time of the discriminatory act in 2014 Southern Bell Systems employs 150 employees. At the time of trial in 2016, Southern Bell Systems employs 300 employees. Southern Bell Systems is a subsidiary corporation of Baker Wells Corporation, the parent corporation. Baker Wells Corporation employs roughly 1,500 employees during 2014–2016. Southern Bell Systems and Baker Wells have maintained separate corporate formalities. What amount of compensatory damages and punitive damages is Johnson entitled to under the Title VII cap?

---

## ✦ Core Concept: Mitigation of Damages

A Title VII plaintiff who loses her job because of unlawful discrimination should not sit back and refuse to find a new job in the hopes that she will win her Title VII case and be compensated at her former full salary level for the time period between the discrimination and final judgment. The plaintiff has a statutory duty to mitigate damages, back pay included. *See* Title VII § 706(g)(1); 42 U.S.C. § 2000e-5(g)(1) ("Interim earnings or amounts earnable with reasonable diligence by the person or persons discriminated against shall operate to reduce the back pay otherwise allowable.").

The duty to mitigate requires that the plaintiff make a reasonable and good-faith effort to secure and maintain substantially equivalent employment. In the following case, a federal district judge reduced a prevailing Title VII plaintiff's back pay award because the plaintiff did not exercise reasonable diligence in mitigating her damages by maintaining substantially equivalent employment with her new employer.

---

## Focus Questions: *Richardson v. Tricom Pictures & Productions, Inc.*

1.  *What is the back pay amount sought by Plaintiff Richardson?*

2.  *What is the back pay amount awarded by the court?*

3.  *How does the court arrive at this amount?*

4.  *For which period(s) of time was Plaintiff Richardson not entitled to back pay?*

5.  *Do you agree with the trial court's back pay determination? Why or why not?*

---

# Richardson v. Tricom Pictures & Productions, Inc.
## 334 F. Supp. 2d 1303 (S.D. Fla. 2004)

### ORDER ON PENDING MOTIONS

District Judge Altonaga.

This cause came before the Court upon Plaintiff, Marinell Richardson's Motion for Award of Equitable Remedies Pursuant to 42 U.S.C. § 2000e-5(g) and Motion for Entry of Final Judgment Against Defendant; and Defendant, Tricom Pictures & Productions, Inc.'s Cross-Motion to Reduce the Jury's Advisory Verdict and for Remittitur....

I. Background

Plaintiff, Marinell Richardson ("Richardson"), alleged in her Second Amended Complaint that she was employed as a sales representative by Defendant, Tricom Pictures & Productions, Inc. ("Tricom"), between November of 2000 and June 29, 2001. She identified Defendant, James Trainer ("Trainer"), as her immediate supervisor. The Second Amended Complaint alleged various acts of physical and verbal sexual harassment of Richardson by Trainer during the course of Richardson's employment. Richardson also alleged that she was retaliated against by Tricom after she complained about Trainer's conduct, and that Tricom failed to pay her at the time-and-a-half overtime rate for hours she worked in excess of forty per week. These acts, it was alleged, violated Title VII, the Fair Labor Standards Act ("FLSA"), the Florida Civil Rights Act ("FCRA"), and Fla. Stat. § 760.10. Richardson further alleged state law tort claims against Tricom for negligent hiring, negligent training and supervision, negligent retention, and state law tort claims for battery and assault against Trainer. The various state law claims were dismissed prior to trial pursuant to 28 U.S.C. § 1367(c), which permits courts to decline to exercise supplemental jurisdiction over nonfederal claims under certain conditions.

This matter was tried before a jury that rendered a verdict in favor of Tricom on Richardson's FLSA overtime claim (Count VII) and Title VII sexual harassment claim (Count I), and in favor of Richardson on her Title VII retaliation claim (Count I). As to the overtime claim, the jury found that Richardson did not prove by a preponderance of the evidence that she worked in excess of forty hours during any given workweek. As to the sexual harassment claim, the jury found that Richardson did not prove by a preponderance of the evidence that she was subjected to harassment of a sexual nature that was so severe or pervasive that it altered the terms and conditions of her employment and created an intimidating, hostile and abusive working environment.

As to the retaliation claim, the jury found that Richardson proved by a preponderance of the evidence that she was terminated because of her complaints about sexual harassment. The jury also found that Richardson proved by a preponderance of the evidence that she should be awarded damages to compensate her for a net loss of wages and benefits to the date of trial as a result of the retaliation. In an advisory verdict, the jury decided that the total amount of lost wages and benefits, *i.e.,* back pay, that Richardson should receive is $20,000.00. However, the jury found that Richardson should not be awarded damages to compensate her for emotional pain and mental anguish, as she had failed to prove she suffered such damages by a preponderance of the evidence. Finally, in considering punitive damages, once again on an advisory basis, the jury recommended the assessment of punitive damages in the amount of $50,000.00, finding that Richardson proved by a preponderance of the evidence that (1) a higher management official of Tricom acted with malice or reckless indifference to Richardson's federally protected rights, and (2) Tricom did not attempt in good faith to comply with the law by adopting policies and procedures designed to prohibit discrimination in the workplace.

Richardson has now moved for the entry of an order awarding her equitable remedies and for entry of Final Judgment. Richardson seeks a declaration, pursuant to the Declaratory Judgment Act, 28 U.S.C. §§ 2201 and 2202, that Tricom has violated her civil rights and the anti-retaliation provisions of Title VII, as set forth in 42 U.S.C. § 2000e-3(a). Richardson also seeks monetary relief, under 42 U.S.C. § 2000e-5(g), in the form of back pay (net of all interim earnings) in the amount of $59,208.00, or alternatively, if the Court determines that Tricom did present sufficient evidence that Richardson did not adequately mitigate her damages, $20,000.00 as awarded by the jury; prejudgment interest on back pay at the rate of 5.70%, in the amount of $3,374.86; one year of front pay in lieu of reinstatement in the amount of $30,000.00; punitive damages in the amount of $50,000.00 as awarded by the jury; and postjudgment interest in accordance with 28 U.S.C. § 1961(a). Richardson further requests that the Court enter an order entitling her to attorney's fees and costs pursuant to 42 U.S.C. § 2000e-5(k), the amounts of which may be determined by separate motion filed after the entry of judgment.

Tricom has moved to reduce the jury's advisory verdict and for remittitur. Tricom contends that Richardson's requests for declaratory relief, an increase of the back pay award to $59,208.00, and front pay of $30,000.00, should be denied, and the jury's back pay and punitive damages awards should be reduced.

Tricom has presented the following arguments, most of which the Court finds compelling: Richardson is not entitled to a declaratory judgment because a plaintiff cannot maintain an action for declaratory or injunctive relief unless she can demonstrate a good chance of being injured by the defendant in the future, which Richardson has not shown; the jury's advisory verdict of $20,000.00 in back pay should be reduced to $10,961.48 because it appears that the former did not take into account, or did not fully take into account, Richardson's failure to mitigate her damages; even if back pay is awarded, an additional award of prejudgment interest would not be equitable; Richardson is not entitled to front pay based on the same failure to mitigate damages, failure to present evidence that she is entitled to front pay, and failure to provide the necessary information to calculate an award of front pay; and the court should reduce the jury's punitive damages award, also to $10,961.48, because the award violates due process and because the evidence does not support the amount of the verdict.

II. Legal Discussion

A. Back Pay

Title 42, United States Code, Section 2000e-5(g)(1) states:

> If the court finds that the respondent has intentionally engaged in or is intentionally engaging in an unlawful employment practice charged in the complaint, the court may enjoin the respondent from engaging in such unlawful employment practice, and order such affirmative action as may be appropriate, which may include, but is not limited to, reinstatement or hiring of employee, with or without back pay (payable by the employer ... responsible for the unlawful employment practice), or any other equitable relief as the court deems appropriate.

Back pay, and interest on back pay, are not "compensatory damages," and therefore are excluded from an award of compensatory damages for a Title VII violation. 42 U.S.C. § 1981a(b)(2). "[A]n award of back pay is intended to make the claimant whole, not to confer a windfall." [citation omitted]. Towards this end, Title VII specifically provides that "[i]nterim earnings or amounts earnable with reasonable diligence by the person or persons discriminated against shall operate to reduce the back pay otherwise allowable." 42 U.S.C. § 2000e-5(g)(1). Therefore, "in calculating a back pay award, the trial court must determine what the employee would have earned had she not been the victim of discrimination, and must subtract from this figure the amount of actual interim earnings." [citation omitted].

While a successful Title VII claimant, such as Richardson, is generally entitled to an award of back pay, the claimant must make a reasonable and good-faith effort to mitigate her damages. [A claimant must mitigate her damages by seeking employment "substantially equivalent" to the position she was denied.] It is the employer's burden to prove its mitigation defense to a Title VII back pay award.

" 'Substantially equivalent employment' is employment that affords virtually identical promotional opportunities, compensation, job responsibilities, working conditions, and status to those available to employees holding the position from which the Title VII claimant has been discriminatorily terminated.' " [citation omitted]. The employer must show that the claimant failed to exercise "reasonable diligence to locate other suitable employment and [or] maintain a suitable job once it is located." [citation omitted]....

... [*Brady v. Thurston Motor Lines, Inc.,*] addressed the effect that a discharge for misconduct from interim employment should have on a back pay award in this way:

> [W]e are of the opinion the Title VII claimant must also use reasonable diligence to maintain any suitable employment which is secured. To permit otherwise

would force the Title VII defendant to pay for the misconduct of a claimant in subsequent employment. We do not think that such a result is properly related to the make whole objective of back pay.

In determining what reasonable diligence requires, it seems clear that it should not permit all on the job behavior except [willful] or wanton conduct. The standard of reasonable diligence is more discerning. It requires instead that in maintaining subsequent employment, a Title VII claimant act reasonably and responsibly in accordance with employer rules. As noted earlier, the duty of a Title VII plaintiff to mitigate damages includes the obligation to accept a "job substantially equivalent to the one he was denied." *Ford Motor Co. v. EEOC*, 458 U.S. 219, 232 (1982). Such a duty of necessity includes the obligation to make reasonable and good faith efforts to maintain that job once accepted. When either of these obligations are not met, a claimant should be said to have voluntarily removed himself from the job market or the work place and forfeited his right to back pay. *Id.* . . .

We are thus of opinion that the rationale which supports the tolling of the back pay period following a voluntary quit should also apply to those terminations which result from a violation of an employer's rules. It would be incongruous to hold that while Title VII claimants cannot voluntarily terminate suitable, interim employment without suffering a back pay reduction, they may choose without penalty to risk the loss of similar employment by engaging in misconduct. To permit claimants the freedom of substantially unrestrained conduct during interim employment unfettered by the loss of back pay, would serve only to punish the employer for the misconduct of the claimant, and be inconsistent with the requirement of exercising reasonable diligence.

753 F.2d 1269, 1277–79 (4th Cir. 1985).

In *Brady*, two of the plaintiffs were discharged from their subsequent employment for violating the stated rules of their respective employers and the discharges were found to be justified. The court determined that violation of the employer's rules amounted to a lack of reasonable diligence in maintaining interim employment. Accordingly, the court held that these plaintiffs were entitled to back pay from the time of their wrongful discharge by the defendant until the day of their discharge by the subsequent employer, and the defendant would receive a credit for the wages the plaintiffs actually earned during this period. During the period of unemployment following the discharge from the subsequent employment, the plaintiffs were entitled to no back pay. The back pay period commenced to run again upon plaintiffs' reemployment, and for such reemployment period the defendant would receive a credit for the wages plaintiffs earned had they not been discharged for cause from the previous employer at the wage rate effective upon that discharge, or the wages they did earn, whichever was greater.

Other courts, relying on *Brady*, have reduced or offset back pay awards beyond the date of the aggrieved employee's involuntary termination from a new job. [citations omitted]. In all of these cases, the plaintiffs either presented no evidence disputing the reasons given for termination from substantially equivalent employment, or the evidence indisputably showed that the plaintiff was terminated for cause based on intentional conduct in violation of company rules.

Here, the jury heard evidence of Richardson's employment after she was terminated by Tricom. The Court now reviews this evidence in determining whether any adjustments to the jury's advisory back pay award of $20,000.00 are necessary to comport with the law on back pay awards.

Richardson was able to obtain a position as a pledge producer at WLRN, Inc. on November 13, 2001, and later a position at Barton G, both of which paid her a salary of $32,000.00 per year, $2,000.00 more a year than she earned at Tricom. She was terminated or forced to resign from WLRN and was then laid off from Barton G approximately three weeks before the trial. Tricom is not challenging the comparability of Richardson's two post-termination jobs to her Tricom job. Richardson testified at trial that she made reasonable efforts to obtain similar employment. Therefore, the court assumes, as Tricom has, that Richardson's subsequent positions with WLRN and Barton G were "substantially equivalent."

Richardson is seeking an award of back pay in the amount of $59,208.00. While employed at Tricom, during the relevant time period, Richardson earned an annual salary of $30,000.00. This breaks down to $2,500.00 per month. Richardson was terminated from Tricom on June 29, 2001. Thus, 28 months lapsed from Richardson's termination up through the date of trial, which Richardson contends entitles her to a gross back pay award of $70,000.00 ($2,500.00 times 28 months), less applicable interim earnings. According to Richardson, her interim earnings during this time period are $3,900.00 from WLRN and $6,892.00 from Barton G. Thus, Richardson seeks a net back pay award in the amount of $59.208.00 calculated as follows ($70.000.00 − $10,792.00).

Tricom argues that the jury's advisory verdict of $20,000.00 must be reduced because it does not properly reflect Richardson's failure to mitigate her damages. The evidence showed Richardson's employment at WLRN was terminated after three months because of her inability to cooperate with peers; her lack of respect for peers, particularly part-time employees; her inappropriate behaviors in front of members of the general public who were volunteering, reflecting negatively on the name and reputation of WLRN and the non-profit Friends of WLRN; and her alienation of nearly the entire staff of WLRN, forcing her supervisor to act as an intermediary between Richardson and nearly every other staff member with whom she was required to interact, including four employees in the membership department, the Radio Station Manager, the Radio Program Director, and the weekday morning program host. Numerous complaints about Richardson's conduct were received by management from WLRN and Friends of WLRN staff members.

This information regarding Richardson's problems at WLRN was contained in a WLRN letter/memo of termination of Richardson, which was admitted as a business record during the trial, and the testimony of Karen Echols, a corporate representative of WLRN. Ms. Echols testified that WLRN's termination of Richardson was based on performance problems, mainly Richardson's inability to get along with WLRN staff and volunteers. Richardson confirmed, during her own testimony, the testimony of Ms. Echols that Richardson was involuntarily terminated from WLRN, or forced to resign. Richardson did not dispute that she had personal conflicts with other WLRN employees, and that this caused her termination. Thus, it is apparent that Richardson failed to mitigate her damages by acting in a manner that caused her involuntary termination. There was no evidence indicating that her behavior at WLRN resulted from emotional distress or psychological injuries that may be attributed to her termination from Tricom. Indeed, the jury found that Richardson should not be awarded damages to compensate her for emotional pain and mental anguish, presumably because they found she did not suffer such injuries.

Tricom requests that the court deny Richardson back pay for the period of time after her involuntary termination from WLRN. Thus, according to Tricom's calculations, Richardson is entitled to back pay from her last day of employment at Tricom, June 29, 2001, up to her first day of employment at WLRN, November 13, 2001, a period of 19 weeks. Tricom agrees that Richardson's back pay should be calculated at $2,500.00 per month, which breaks down to $576.92 per week ($30,000.00 divided by 52 weeks). Tricom proposes that Richardson is entitled to $10,961.48 (19 weeks times $576.92). However, if the Court were to allow back pay extending beyond Richardson's employment at WLRN, Tricom asserts that the amount earned by Richardson at WLRN was $8,000.00 ($615.38 per week times 13 weeks), and not the $3,900.00 stated in Richardson's Motion. Tricom argues that the evidence shows that Richardson worked for WLRN for 13 weeks, at $615.38 per week ($32,000.00 per year divided by 52 weeks), resulting in earnings of $8,000.00. Tricom requests that this amount, in addition to Richardson's earnings at Barton G, should be deducted from any back pay award extending beyond her employment at WLRN.

The $59,208.00 number suggested by Richardson and the $10,961.48 urged by Tricom were presented to the jury. The jury decided to award $20,000.00 to compensate Richardson for her net loss of wages and benefits to the date of trial, *i.e.*, back pay. Richardson acknowledges that the jury's award supports the reasonable interpretation that the jury may have believed that Richardson did not fully mitigate her damages, but this would simply be an interpretation of the jury's verdict, not an express jury finding. Richardson argues that Tricom did not submit any evidence that she failed to mitigate her damages regarding lost wages. Should the Court conclude that Tricom did prove that Richardson did not fully mitigate her earnings, however, Richardson requests that the Court award a back pay award commensurate with the jury award.

Richardson challenges the testimony from the WLRN representative as not reliable because Ms. Echols was not there when Richardson worked at WLRN and she basically testified from a memo in Richardson's personnel file as to events leading to Richardson's termination from WLRN. Contrary to Richardson's assertions, a review of the testimony indicates that Ms. Echols spoke based on personal knowledge of the circumstances surrounding Richardson's termination from WLRN and read from the WLRN termination letter/memo that was admitted under the business record exception to the hearsay rule. Moreover, as previously mentioned, Richardson herself admitted that she had difficulties getting along with others at WLRN, including one of her supervisors, and that resulted in her termination. She also admitted that she was given the choice of either resigning or being fired, and that she elected to be terminated so that she could receive unemployment benefits. Thus, WLRN's reasons for termination are unrebutted and the involuntary termination was justified on this record.

Based on the foregoing, Tricom has made a showing that Richardson did not exercise reasonable diligence in mitigating her damages by maintaining substantially equivalent employment at WLRN. Even if she was not in direct violation of company rules at WLRN, she was terminated for cause based on repeated behavior that was not accidental, and was, according to the WLRN representative, egregious. However, Tricom did not offer evidence regarding the circumstances surrounding Richardson being laid off by Barton G. Applying *Brady*, the leading case on this issue, Richardson is entitled to back pay from the time of her termination from Tricom, June 29, 2001, until the date of her termination from WLRN. Richardson is then entitled to back pay for the period when she was employed by Barton G and thereafter until trial, since Tricom has not shown that Richardson failed to mitigate her damages during this period. The only period for which Richardson is not entitled to back pay is the period between her jobs at WLRN and Barton G. Tricom will receive credit for Richardson's actual earnings at WLRN and Barton G, which paid her the same annual salary of $32,000.00.

. . .

## Notes

1. *Advisory Jury Verdicts.* The *Richardson* jury came up with a $20,000.00 award for back pay. The plaintiff later filed a post-verdict motion asking the court to award her $59,208.00 in back pay. The plaintiff styled her motion as a "Motion for Award of Equitable Remedies." Given that back pay under Title VII is viewed an equitable remedy and equitable remedies are determined by courts and not juries, why was the jury charged on back pay and asked to determine what, if any, back pay award was appropriate for the plaintiff?

The answer to this question is that the jury's back pay award was simply advisory and did not bind the trial court. *See* Fed. Rule Civ. P. 39(c) (providing for advisory juries). The trial judge remained the final arbiter of how much, if any, back pay was permitted under Title VII. *See Lutz v. Glendale Union High School, District No. 205*, 403 F.3d 1061, 1069 (9th Cir. 2005) (holding that even after the 1991 Civil Rights Act there is no right to have a jury determine the appropriate amount of back pay under either Title VII or the ADA).

2. *Duty to Maintain Substantially Equivalent Employment.* The main point from the *Richardson* case is that the duty to mitigate damages is on-going. It requires both that the plaintiff use reasonable diligence to secure substantially equivalent employment initially and that the plaintiff use reasonable diligence to *maintain* that employment up until the time of final judgment. Does the *Richardson* court establish a rule that termination "for cause" in a subsequent job constitutes a failure to mitigate damages? The *Richardson* judge made a determination that, as a matter of law, the plaintiff's employment was involuntarily terminated from WLRN for egregious behavior and that plaintiff thus failed to satisfy her duty to mitigate. Will future determinations regarding whether such "bad behavior" violates the duty to mitigate in similar cases be so easy for judges to make? In your mind, what should the standard be?

## ✦ Core Concept: Damages under the ADA

### *ADA Remedial Provision — ADA § 107(a); 42 U.S.C. § 12117(a)*

> Powers, Remedies, and Procedures.—The powers, remedies, and procedures set forth in sections 705, 706, 707, 709 and 710 of the Civil Rights Act of 1964 (42 U.S.C. 2000e-4, 2000e-5, 2000e-6, 2000e-8, and 2000e-9) shall be the powers, remedies, and procedures this title provides to the Commission, to the Attorney General, or to any person alleging discrimination on the basis of disability in violation of any provision of the Act, or regulations promulgated under section 106, concerning employment.

ADA remedies are similar to Title VII remedies. Section 107(a) of the ADA, as originally enacted in 1990, provides that the remedial provisions under Section 706(g) of Title VII apply to the ADA. The 1991 Civil Rights Act added a provision that permits ADA plaintiffs to recover compensatory and punitive damages based on the standards applicable to Title VII claims. *See* 42 U.S.C. § 1981a(a)(2). In reasonable accommodation cases, an ADA plaintiff may not recover compensatory or punitive damages if the employer proves that it made good faith efforts to identify and make a reasonable accommodation. *See* 42 U.S.C. § 1981a(a)(3); *EEOC v. Federal Express Corp.*, 513 F.3d 360, 374–75 (4th Cir. 2008) (upholding a punitive damages award because employer did not provide reasonable accommodations to a deaf employee and failed to prove that it made good faith efforts to comply with the ADA's reasonable accommodation requirements). The same caps on compensatory and punitive damages discussed under Title VII apply to the ADA. *See* 42 U.S.C. § 1981a(a)(2); § 1981a(b)(3).

## ✦ Core Concept: Damages under the ADEA

### ADEA Remedial Provisions — ADEA § 7; 29 U.S.C. § 626

(b) Enforcement; prohibition of age discrimination under fair labor standards; unpaid minimum wages and unpaid overtime compensation; liquidated damages; judicial relief; conciliation, conference, and persuasion.

The provisions of this chapter shall be enforced in accordance with the powers, remedies, and procedures provided in sections 211(b), 216 (except for subsection (a) thereof), and 217 of this title [the Fair Labor Standards Act], and subsection (c) of this section. Any act prohibited under section 623 of this title shall be deemed to be a prohibited act under section 215 of this title. Amounts owing to a person as a result of a violation of this chapter shall be deemed to be unpaid minimum wages or unpaid overtime compensation for purposes of sections 216 and 217 of this title: *Provided*, That liquidated damages shall be payable only in cases of willful violations of this chapter. In any action brought to enforce this chapter the court shall have jurisdiction to grant such legal or equitable relief as may be appropriate to effectuate the purposes of this chapter, including without limitation judgments compelling employment, reinstatement or promotion, or enforcing the liability for amounts deemed to be unpaid minimum wages or unpaid overtime compensation under this section. Before instituting any action under this section, the Equal Employment Opportunity Commission shall attempt to eliminate the discriminatory practice or practices alleged, and to effect voluntary compliance with the requirements of this chapter through informal methods of conciliation, conference, and persuasion.

(c) Civil actions; persons aggrieved; jurisdiction; judicial relief; termination of individual action upon commencement of action by Commission; jury trial

(1) Any person aggrieved may bring a civil action in any court of competent jurisdiction for such legal or equitable relief as will effectuate the purposes of this chapter: *Provided*, That the right of any person to bring such action shall terminate upon the commencement of an action by the Equal Employment Opportunity Commission to enforce the right of such employee under this chapter.

(2) In an action brought under paragraph (1), a person shall be entitled to a trial by jury of any issue of fact in any such action for recovery of amounts owing as a result of a violation of this chapter, regardless of whether equitable relief is sought by any party in such action.

### FLSA Remedies Provision — 29 U.S.C. § 216 — Applicable to ADEA Remedies

(b) Damages; right of action; attorney's fees and costs; termination of right of action.

Any employer who violates the provisions of section 206 or section 207 of this title shall be liable to the employee or employees affected in the amount of their unpaid minimum wages, or their unpaid overtime compensation, as the case may be, and in an additional equal amount as liquidated damages. Any employer who violates the provisions of section 215(a)(3) of this title shall be liable for such legal or equitable relief as may be appropriate to effectuate the purposes of section 215(a)(3) of this title, including without limitation employment, reinstatement, promotion, and the payment of wages lost and an additional equal amount as liquidated damages. An action to recover the liability prescribed in either of the preceding sentences may be maintained against any employer (including a public agency) in any Federal or State court of competent jurisdiction by any one or more employees for and in behalf of himself or themselves and other employees similarly situated. No employee shall be a party plaintiff to any such action unless he gives his consent in writing to become such a party and such consent is filed in the court in which such action is brought. The court in such action shall, in addition to any judgment awarded to the plaintiff or plaintiffs, allow a reasonable attorney's fee to be paid by the defendant, and costs of the action. The right provided by this subsection to bring an action by or on behalf of any employee, and the right of any employee to become a party plaintiff to any such action, shall terminate upon the filing of a complaint by the Secretary of Labor in an action under section 217 of this title in which (1) restraint is sought of any further delay in the payment of unpaid minimum wages, or the amount of unpaid overtime compensation, as the case may be, owing to such employee under section 206 or section 207 of this title by an employer liable therefor under the provisions of this subsection or (2) legal or equitable relief is sought as a result of alleged violations of section 215(a)(3) of this title.

The remedies available under the ADEA are those that are generally available under certain parts of the Fair Labor Standards Act and those that are specifically provided for by the ADEA itself. *See* 29 U.S.C. §626(b)-(c)(1). The statute explicitly provides for the right to a jury trial. *Id.* at §626(c)(2).

Although the ADEA speaks of equitable and legal relief, ADEA remedies are a tad different from Title VII remedies. In general, an ADEA plaintiff may recover monetary damages in the form of back pay or liquidated damages for a willful violation; reinstatement or front pay in lieu of reinstatement are also available remedies. *See* 29 U.S.C. §626(b); §216(b); *Downes v. Volkswagen of America, Inc.*, 41 F.3d 1132, 1141 (7th Cir. 1994).

One important difference between ADEA remedies and Title VII remedies is that the ADEA allows for the recovery of liquidated damages in cases of *willful* violations. *Id.* at §626(b) ("[L]iquidated damages shall be payable only in cases of willful violations of this chapter."). The ADEA authorizes an award for back pay and, for *willful* violations, an additional equal amount as liquidated damages. *See* 29 U.S.C. §626(b); 29 U.S.C. §216(b) (allowing for the recovery of lost wages and an additional equal amount as liquidated damages). A "willful" violation occurs when the employer knew or showed reckless disregard for the matter of whether its conduct was prohibited by the ADEA. *See Hazen Paper Co. v. Biggins*, 507 U.S. 604, 617 (1993). Technically, the ADEA does not allow for the recovery of compensatory and punitive damages. *See Kulling v. Grinders for Industry, Inc.*, 115 F. Supp. 2d 828, 846 n. 20 (E.D. Mich. 2000); *Franzoni v. Hartmarx Corp.*, 300 F.3d 767, 773 (7th Cir. 2002) (holding neither punitive damages nor damages for pain and suffering are available under the ADEA). But the liquidated damages award effectively serves the same function as compensatory and punitive damages awards under Title VII. *See Trans World Airlines, Inc. v. Thurston*, 469 U.S. 111, 125 (1985) (holding ADEA liquidated damages provision is punitive in nature).

Consider the following example to illustrate the liquidated damages concept. An ADEA plaintiff is awarded $30,000 in lost wages (back pay). The ADEA plaintiff proves the employer's violation of the ADEA was willful. The plaintiff is entitled to double-damages in the amount of $60,000.

## ✦ Core Concept: Damages under Section 1981

A plaintiff that has a race discrimination claim against his or her employer is wise to sue under 42 U.S.C. § 1981, as well as Title VII, if for no other reason than Congress has not imposed any damages caps on Section 1981 claims. *See Swinton v. Potomac Corp.*, 270 F.3d 794, 820 (9th Cir. 2001) (noting that Congress has had ample opportunity since the 1991 Title VII amendments to impose damages caps in Section 1981 but has not done so). Except for the lack of a damages cap, Section 1981 judicial remedies are similar to Title VII judicial remedies. *See CBOCS West, Inc. v. Humphries*, 128 S. Ct. 1951, 1960 (2008). The courts have created the remedies available under Section 1981 because there is no remedies provision in the statute itself. Back pay, reinstatement, and front pay in lieu of reinstatement are appropriate remedies available under Section 1981. *See Davis v. Integrated Systems Solutions Corps.*, No. 97-C-3774, 2003 U.S. Dist. LEXIS 5092, at *5 (N.D. Ill. Mar. 31, 2003). Compensatory and punitive damages are appropriate legal remedies under Section 1981 and are not limited by statute. *See Pollard v. E.I. du Pont de Nemours & Co.*, 532 U.S. 843, 851 (2001).

Despite the similarities between the remedies available under Title VII and Section 1981, the absence of a damages cap under Section 1981 can make a big difference in a particular case. For example, in *Goldsmith v. Bagby Elevator Co.*, 513 F.3d 1261, 1284 (11th Cir. 2008), the race discrimination plaintiff sued under Section 1981 and Title VII. The plaintiff won a judgment, rendered in accordance with the jury verdict, of $27,160.59 in back pay, $27,160.59 in damages for mental anguish, and $500,000 in punitive damages. Because of the lack of compensatory and punitive damages cap under Section 1981, the plaintiff was able to keep the entire amount of the mental anguish and punitive damages awards, $527,160.59. The Eleventh Circuit ruled that the $500,000 punitive damages amount complied with due process. If the case had been strictly limited to Title VII claims, the $100,000 damages cap would have applied because the employer-defendant employed 150 people. In other words, the maximum amount recoverable for compensatory and punitive damages under Title VII would have been $100,000, the jury award notwithstanding. The Section 1981 claim benefitted the *Goldsmith* plaintiff to the tune of $427,160.59 ($527,160.59 − $100,000 = $427,160.59). That is real value to a race discrimination plaintiff.

## ✦ Core Concept: Recovery of Attorney's Fees

Employment discrimination claims are some of the most difficult federal claims for attorneys to litigate. From a plaintiff's perspective, employment discrimination claims are often difficult to prove and therefore take a lot of time, effort, knowledge and skill on the part of the attorney representing the plaintiff. What incentives should the law provide to encourage competent attorneys to represent plaintiffs in these cases?

For plaintiffs' attorneys inclined to take cases on a contingency fee basis, the cap on compensatory and punitive damages under Title VII may discourage private attorneys from taking employment discrimination cases where the economic damages are relatively low. On the other hand, the fee-shifting provisions of the federal employment discrimination laws are one means of encouraging the plaintiff's bar to represent employees in employment discrimination cases. Indeed, the federal discrimination statutes covered in this casebook all have provisions that require a losing defendant to pay the prevailing party plaintiff's reasonable attorney's fees. Section 706(k) of Title VII states that the prevailing party in a Title VII proceeding may recover attorney's fees and costs. *See* 42 U.S.C. § 2000e-5(k) ("In any action or proceeding under this title the court, in its discretion, may allow the prevailing party, other than the Commission or the United States, a reasonable attorney's fee (including expert fees) as part of the costs, and the Commission and the United States shall be liable for costs the same as a private person."). The ADA incorporates the fee-shifting provision of Title VII. *See* 42 U.S.C. § 12117(a). For Section 1981 claims, attorneys' fees are recoverable under a fee-shifting statute that applies to civil rights cases called the Civil Rights Attorney's Fees Awards Act of 1976. *See* 42 U.S.C. § 1988. The Equal Pay Act and ADEA also contain fee-shifting provisions in the statutes that are modeled on the fee-shifting provision in the Fair Labor Standards Act.

A federal employment discrimination plaintiff that prevails on liability is entitled to have the employer pay his attorney's fees except in the most unusual of situations. In contrast, it is rare that a defendant that prevails on liability in a federal employment discrimination lawsuit will recover its attorney's fees from the plaintiff. Title VII, the ADA, and the fee-shifting provision applicable to Section 1981 crack the door open for the employer to recover its attorney's fees from the plaintiff if the employer is the prevailing party because the statutes state that a "prevailing party" may be entitled to fees. The Equal Pay Act and the ADEA state that only prevailing *plaintiffs* are entitled to fees. However, even where an employer could qualify as a prevailing party entitled to fees, there is a strong presumption against awarding fees to the employer because such awards strongly discourage employment discrimination plaintiffs from suing in the first place. Permitting such recoveries as a matter of course would undercut the federal employment discrimination statutes as "private attorney general" statutes. For this reason, the United States Supreme Court held that a Title VII plaintiff should not be assessed the employer's attorney's fees unless the court hearing the case decides that the Title VII claim was frivolous, unreasonable, groundless, or brought in bad faith. *See Christianburg Garment Co. v. EEOC*, 434 U.S. 412 (1978).

## ➤ Beyond the Basics: Affirmative Action as a Remedy

You have previously studied the legality of voluntary affirmative action plans under Title VII and the U.S. Constitution and the requirement that covered federal contractors engage in affirmative action. Another type of "affirmative action" presents itself in the form of a court-ordered remedy. Title VII states that if the court finds that the employer intentionally engaged in an unlawful employment practice, the court can "order such affirmative action as may be appropriate." 42 U.S.C. § 2000e-5(g)(1). Accordingly, in appropriate instances, courts have sometimes ordered affirmative action as a remedy for past discrimination by the employer.

A court-ordered affirmative action plan, such as a race-conscious affirmative action plan that sets minority hiring goals, is permissible when the court has found a persistent pattern of egregious, pervasive and intentional systemic discrimination by the employer. In structuring an affirmative action plan remedy, a court must take care to adhere to the standards applicable to the voluntary adoption of affirmative action plans by employers. In general, such plans must be reasonable, temporary, and must not unduly trammel the rights of other employees. District courts are sometimes given considerable discretion to fashion appropriate plans. For example, in *United States v. Paradise*, 480 U.S. 149 (1987), the Supreme Court upheld a lower court order that established a race-conscious affirmative action plan as a remedy. The court order required the employer to promote one African-American state trooper for every white trooper promoted as a means of remedying the employer's "long-term, open, and pervasive" intentional race discrimination and its refusal to abide by prior court orders.

Court-ordered affirmative action as a remedy for unlawful discrimination is controversial, and courts typically make such orders only in cases where the employer is a habitual, hard-core discriminator that has consistently demonstrated a refusal to comply with the employment discrimination laws.

## ➤ Beyond the Basics: Job Offers as a Remedy

The Title VII remedial provisions aim to bring an end to employment discrimination and also make victims of employment discrimination whole. They encourage employers to comply voluntarily with Title VII through conciliation and settlement. In general, the courts have fashioned remedial rules that try to serve these statutory objectives. A good example is a rule regarding the remedial effect of offers of employment (or re-employment) made by the employer to the claimant after discrimination is alleged. In *Ford Motor Co. v. EEOC*, 458 U.S. 219 (1982), the Court held that an employer charged with discrimination in hiring can cut off the accrual of backpay liability under Title VII by unconditionally offering the claimant the job previously denied, even if the job offer does not include an offer of retroactive seniority or back pay.

This rule is more easily explained through an illustration. Mary applies for a job with Company X in August 2001 and is rejected. Mary files an EEOC charge alleging Company X refused to hire her for the position because she is a female. In August 2002, Company X offers Mary the job that she applied for in August 2001. Company X's job offer does not give her seniority rights retroactive to August 2001 nor does it give her the backpay she would have earned between August 2001 and August 2002 had she been originally hired.

The job offer is likely very important to Mary. She needs a job and now Company X is offering it to her. Therefore, Mary accepts the job offer and begins work for Company X in August 2002. She has not been made whole by Company X, but the job offer is an important step toward voluntary compliance with the law. Mary could still sue Company X for retroactive seniority and backpay for the period between August 2001 and August 2002.

Assume Mary declines the job offer at Company X. Mary decides to reject the offer because she is already working at Company Y when the offer is made. She has built up some seniority at Company Y, and Company X's job offer does not come with any retroactive seniority. She also thinks the long-term prospects at Y are better than those at X. Therefore, she deems it a better deal to stay at Company Y. Mary will still be able to pursue her sex discrimination claim against Company X, including remedies against Company X that accrued prior to X's job offer, but her right to receive backpay after the job offer is rejected is cut off.

The rule tolling the further accrual of backpay liability if Company X offers Mary the job sought and she rejects it serves the objective of ending discrimination through voluntary compliance because it gives Company X a strong incentive to hire a Title VII claimant like Mary. While Mary may be no more attractive on the merits than other job applicants, a job offer to Mary will free Company X of the threat of liability for further backpay damages. If Company X does not offer Mary the job and ultimately is determined to have violated Title VII, it will have to pay her backpay damages for a person who never came to work. Therefore, the rule gives Mary an edge over other competitors for the job that she sought at Company X.

If Mary is unemployed or underemployed at the time of the job offer from Company X and she rejects the offer, cutting off back pay is consistent with Mary's duty to mitigate damages by accepting substantially equivalent employment with an employer. By refusing to accept the job, she has violated her duty to mitigate damages. If Mary is employed at Company Y when she is offered the Company X job and believes that the Company Y job plus her claim against Company X for backpay prior to X's offer is more valuable to her than the X job and the right to seek other make-whole remedies from X, she may decide to reject the Company X job offer. Continuing to hold Company X responsible for back pay after the decision to reject the job offer is made would put Mary in a better position than she would be in but for the unlawful discrimination and so the accrual of backpay after the date of the conditional job offer is not permitted. Title VII requires that Mary be placed in the position she would have been in but for the unlawful discrimination but does not require her to be placed in a better position. If Mary is employed by Company Y at the time of X's job offer, her decision whether to reject or accept the offer is a difficult one but the decision does not deprive her of the right to seek full compensation for the alleged Title VII violation.

## ➤ Beyond the Basics: Damages and Civil Procedure

### *Pleadings*

This section explores how damages intersect with procedure. The section focuses on Title VII; however, where appropriate, similar issues would occur in other types of discrimination cases.

*Pleading Damages in the Title VII Plaintiff's Complaint.* The Title VII plaintiff's complaint should state all of the types of damages and other relief asserted that the plaintiff desires to recover. Under general principles of pleading damages, "general damages" do not have to be specifically pleaded to be recovered. General damages are those damages that naturally and necessarily flow from the wrong asserted. *See Weyerhauser Co. v. Brantley*, 510 F.3d 1256, 1266 (10th Cir. 2007); 5A CHARLES ALAN WRIGHT & ARTHUR R. MILLER, FEDERAL PRACTICE & PROCEDURE § 1310 (3d ed. 2005). However, "special damages" must be pleaded to be recovered under Federal Rule of Civil Procedure 9(g). *See* Fed. R. Civ. P. 9(g). Special damages are damages "which do not arise from the wrongful act itself, but depend on circumstances peculiar to the infliction of each respective injury." BLACK'S LAW DICTIONARY 273 (abridged 6th ed. 1991).

Some uncertainty exists regarding the categorization of the various types of damages recoverable under Title VII as either general or special damages. According to the standard outlined above, nonpecuniary damages for loss of reputation and mental anguish and punitive damages could be viewed as "special damages," and so must be specifically pleaded to be recovered. Accordingly, there is at least some concern that a Title VII plaintiff that fails to plead a type of damages subsequently viewed as a "special damages" will have waived that type of damages if the defendant brings this pleading failure to the court's attention late in the pretrial stages of litigation or during trial or post-trial.

There are a couple of good arguments against waiver when a Title VII plaintiff fails to plead "special damages." First, Fed. R. Civ. P. 54(c) cuts against waiver because that rule indicates that the failure to plead a type of damages does not preclude the recovery of such damages once they have been proven. Rule 54(c) states that every final judgment (other than a default judgment) shall grant the relief to which each party is entitled, even if the party has *not* demanded that relief in its pleadings. *See Soltys v. Costello*, 520 F.3d 737, 742–43 (8th Cir. 2008) (raising question as to whether punitive damages must be specifically pleaded as "special damages" under Rule 9(c); the Circuit noted the interplay between Rule 54(c) and Rule 9(g) with respect to punitive damages but did not explore the issue on appeal because of the party's failure to raise the issue at the trial court level). Second, even if a court were inclined to rule that some types of Title VII damages must be specifically pleaded because they are "special damages," a motion to amend the pleadings to add such a damages claim even at the late stages of litigation (*i.e.*, post-trial) could be granted to a plaintiff on the ground that the addition of the damages claim did not "surprise or prejudice" the defendant.

The point of this discussion is for you to understand that the attorney representing a Title VII plaintiff should make best efforts to plead all the types of damages the plaintiff desires to recover prior to the deadline for amending pleadings in the case so that the tricky issues outlined above do not come into play.

*Pleading Attorney's Fees, Court Costs, and Interest in the Title VII Plaintiff's Complaint.* The law is nearly uniform that attorney's fees are special damages that must be "specifically stated" in the pleadings to be recovered. *See United Industries, Inc. v. Simon Hartley, Ltd.,* 91 F.3d 762, 764–65 (5th Cir. 1996). Accordingly, the Title VII plaintiff must plead for attorney's fees in the complaint in order to later recover fees as a "prevailing party" after the suit is resolved. *See, e.g., Perry v. Serenity Behavioral Health Systems,* No. CV106-172, 2009 U.S. Dist. LEXIS 38201, at *8 (S.D. Ga. May 6, 2009) (disallowing plaintiffs' attorney's fees claims because plaintiffs failed to specifically plead attorney's fees). To be on the safe side, and within the bounds of ethical constraints on pleadings, the Title VII plaintiff should also specifically plead that it is entitled to pre-judgment interest, post-judgment interest, and court costs. *But see Murray v. Louisiana State Foundation,* 234 B.R. 731, 785 (M.D. La. 1999) (awarding trustee pre-judgment interest in bankruptcy case even though trustee did not specifically plead the right to pre-judgment interest).

*Pleading the Jury Demand in the Title VII Plaintiff's Complaint.* The 1991 Civil Rights Act amended Title VII to explicitly guarantee the Title VII plaintiff or defendant the right to a jury trial when the plaintiff seeks compensatory or punitive damages. *See* 42 U.S.C. § 1981a(c)(1). Procedurally, the Title VII plaintiff seeking a jury trial should plead compensatory or punitive damages in the Original Complaint and include the language "Jury Trial Demanded" in the Complaint to secure the jury-trial right. The case will subsequently be placed on the trial court's jury docket unless the defendant moves to strike the jury demand for some reason. *See* Fed. R. Civ. P. 38(b) ("Demand. On any issue triable of right by a jury, a party may demand a jury trial by: (1) serving the other parties with a written demand—which may be included in a pleading—no later than 14 days after the last pleading directed to the issue is served; and (2) filing the demand in accordance with Rule 5(d).").

*Pleading Affirmative Defenses in the Title VII Defendant's Answer.* Under the Federal Rules of Civil Procedure, the burden is on the party raising an affirmative defense to *plead* and prove the defense. Fed. R. Civ. P. 8(c)(1) states:

> Affirmative Defenses. *In General,* in responding to a pleading, a party must affirmatively state any avoidance or affirmative defense, including: accord and satisfaction; arbitration and award; assumption of risk; contributory negligence; duress; estoppel; failure of consideration; fraud; illegality; injury by fellow servant; laches; license; payment; release; res judicata; statute of frauds; statute of limitations; and waiver.

The items specifically listed as affirmative defenses under Rule 8(c) must be pleaded by the employer in a Title VII suit. You may recall from your reading of the Procedure Chapter that employers often have procedural defenses that relate to the Title VII plaintiff's failure in a timely fashion to file an EEOC charge or sue. These defenses are in the nature of a statute of limitations defense. As such, they qualify as affirmative defenses and must be pleaded by the employer-defendant in the answer in order to avoid waiver.

Do not be fooled into thinking that if a defense is not specifically listed in Rule 8(c) it is not an affirmative defense and therefore need not be pleaded. There are a variety of defenses that Title VII (and the courts interpreting the statute) defines as "affirmative defenses" that may be raised by the employer. Many of these affirmative defenses, such as the *Faragher/Ellerth* affirmative defense to liability in the sexual harassment context, are discussed in other parts of this book. The key point is that whenever the courts have characterized a defense under a federal antidiscrimination statute as an "affirmative defense," the employer should plead the defense specifically in its answer in compliance with Rule 8(c) and then carry its burden of proving that defense at trial. Pleading the affirmative defense will permit the employer to ask for a jury interrogatory or jury instruction on that defense at trial if sufficient evidence is introduced on the defense.

With respect to Title VII remedies, for example, the employer's defense to punitive damages that it engaged in "good faith efforts" to comply with Title VII is an affirmative defense that must be pleaded by the employer. *See Monteagudo v. Asociacion de Empleados del Estado Libre Asociado de Puerto Rico*, 554 F. 3d 164, 176 (1st Cir. 2009). The employer's "same decision" defense to a mixed-motives cases under Section 706(g)(2)(B) is a partial affirmative defense that cuts off the ability of the plaintiff to recover damages and should therefore be pleaded by the employer once a mixed-motives claim has been clearly brought into the case. *See Griffith v. City of Des Moines*, 387 F.3d 733, 742 (8th Cir. 2004) (noting that the same decision test under Section 706(g)(2)(B) is an affirmative defense to damages but not liability). Moreover, although the Title VII plaintiff has the statutory duty to mitigate damages, the failure to mitigate damages is the defendant's affirmative defense that it must plead and prove. *See Robinson v. Southeastern Pennsylvania Transportation Authority*, 982 F.2d 892, 897 (3d Cir. 1993). Finally, the defendant should be sure to plead all applicable damages caps.

The defendant's goal is to try to assert all relevant affirmative defenses applicable to the case prior to the deadline for amending pleadings. As justice requires, the defendant may be granted permission by the court to amend its pleadings to add other affirmative defenses after this deadline — even up to and after trial in some circumstances. But, just as with the plaintiff's pleadings, securing court permission to add a previously unpleaded affirmative defense after the deadline for amending pleadings is not something to be counted on by the employer.

### Discovery

Both the plaintiff and the employer-defendant should investigate the damages alleged during the course of the pretrial proceedings in order to either prove or defend against them, respectively. The plaintiff should be independently gathering information to build its case regarding the amount of damages claimed. The employer-defendant should explore any and all possible defenses to the damages claimed and seek information from the plaintiff regarding the damages alleged and how such damages are being calculated. It is not uncommon for parties to hire expert witnesses to calculate damages. Certainly, the formal discovery methods in the Federal Rules of Civil Procedure should be used by both parties to gather damages-related information from the opposing party. Under the broad relevancy standard for discovery articulated in Fed. R. Civ. P. 26, information regarding damages is discoverable. *See* Fed. R. Civ. P. 26(b) ("Scope in General. Unless otherwise limited by court order, the scope of discovery is as follows: Parties may obtain discovery regarding any nonprivileged matter that is relevant to any party's claim or defense.... Relevant information need not be admissible at the trial if the discovery appears reasonably calculated to lead to the discovery of admissible evidence."); *Hite v. Peters*, No. 07-4492-RMB-AMD, 2009 U.S. Dist. LEXIS 51894, at *8–*14 (D. N.J. June 19, 2009) (ordering plaintiff to produce his employment records to employer because such records related to plaintiff's statutory duty under Title VII to mitigate damages and were thus relevant under Rule 26 standards).

### The Trial

During the trial, the plaintiff and the employer-defendant introduce evidence regarding damages (or lack thereof). The parties then give their damages "pitch" to the jury during closing arguments. Ultimately, the judge and jury will have to determine whether the plaintiff is entitled to the damages claimed and, if so, the amount that will compensate the plaintiff for the loss suffered.

If the parties try the discrimination claims to a jury, difficulties may arise in discerning how to charge the jury on damages. Consider whether the following is a good representation of a possible jury charge and jury interrogatories on damages in *Johnson v. Southern Bell Systems*. Assume that Johnson's race discrimination claim is tried to the jury.

### Jury Instructions Example on Damages

#### DAMAGES

If Plaintiff has proven his race discrimination claim against Defendant by a preponderance of the evidence, you must determine the damages to which Plaintiff is entitled. You are instructed that you should not interpret the fact that I have given instructions about damages as an indication in any way that I believe that Plaintiff should, or should not, prevail in this case. It is your primary task to decide whether Defendant is liable. I am instructing you on damages only so that you will have guidance in the event you decide that Defendant is liable and that Plaintiff is entitled to recover money from Defendant.

In the event that you find the Defendant liable for any of the actions in this case, the parties have agreed that the issue of monetary damages for loss of wages by the Plaintiff, if any, will be decided by the Court.

#### A. MENTAL ANGUISH AND EMOTIONAL PAIN DAMAGES

If Defendant is liable to Plaintiff, Plaintiff is entitled to compensatory damages for the pain and suffering, mental anguish, shock, and discomfort that he has suffered because of Defendant's conduct. You may award compensatory damages only for injuries that Plaintiff proves were proximately caused by Defendant's allegedly wrongful conduct. The damages that you award must be fair compensation for all of Plaintiff's non-economic damages, no more and no less. Compensatory damages are not allowed as a punishment and cannot be imposed or increased to penalize Defendant. You should not award compensatory damages for speculative injuries, but only for those injuries which Plaintiff has actually suffered or that Plaintiff is reasonably likely to suffer in the future.

If you decide to award compensatory damages, such as those for mental anguish, you should be guided by dispassionate common sense. Computing damages may be difficult, but you must not let that difficulty lead you to engage in arbitrary guesswork. On the other hand, the law does not require that Plaintiff prove the amount of his losses with mathematical precision, but only with as much definiteness and accuracy as the circumstances permit.

You must use sound discretion in fixing an award of damages, drawing reasonable inferences where you find them appropriate from the facts and circumstances in evidence.

## B. PUNITIVE DAMAGES

If you find that Defendant is liable for Plaintiff's injuries, you must award Plaintiff the compensatory damages that he has proven. You also may award punitive damages if Plaintiff has proved that Defendant acted with malice or reckless indifference to the rights of others. One acts willfully or with reckless indifference to the rights of others when it acts in disregard of a high and excessive danger about which it knows or which would be reasonably apparent to it.

If you determine that Defendant's conduct was so shocking and offensive as to justify an award of punitive damages, you may exercise your discretion to award those damages. In making any award of punitive damages, you should consider that the purpose of punitive damages is to punish a defendant for shocking conduct and to deter Defendant and others from engaging in similar conduct in the future. The law does not require you to award punitive damages; however, if you decide to award punitive damages, you must use sound reason in setting the amount of the damages.

The amount of an award of punitive damages must not reflect bias, prejudice, or sympathy toward any party. It should be presumed a plaintiff has been made whole by compensatory damages, so punitive damages should be awarded only if Defendant's misconduct, after having paid compensatory damages, is so reprehensible as to warrant the imposition of further sanctions to achieve punishment or deterrence. You may consider the financial resources of the Defendant in fixing the amount of punitive damages.

You may not award punitive damages if you find that the racial discrimination against Plaintiff was contrary to Defendant's good faith efforts to comply with anti-discrimination laws in this country. In making this decision you may consider the entirety of Defendant's conduct as it relates to attempting to prevent racial discrimination in its workplace. Defendant has the burden of proof by a preponderance of the evidence to prove this issue.

### JURY INTERROGATORIES

### Jury Question No. 1

Do you find by a preponderance of the evidence that Defendant terminated Plaintiff's employment in January 2014 because of Plaintiff's race?

Answer "Yes" or "No."

---

If you answered "Yes" to Jury Question No. 1, then answer *Jury Question Nos. 2–3*. If not, proceed *to the end of this document and sign to enter your verdict.*

## Jury Question No. 2

What amount of damages, if any, if now paid in cash would be the reasonable damages for mental anguish and emotional distress and other non-monetary losses suffered by Plaintiff as a result of his termination because of his race?

Answer in dollars and cents, if any.

$_____

## Jury Question No. 3

Do you find by a preponderance of the evidence that Defendant acted with malice or reckless indifference to the rights of the Plaintiff to be free from race discrimination when it terminated his employment because of his race?

Answer "Yes" or "No."

_____

If you answered "Yes" to Jury Question No. 3, then answer *Jury Question No. 4*. If you answered "no," then proceed to *the end of this document and sign to enter your verdict.*

## Jury Question No. 4

Did Defendant prove by a preponderance of the evidence that its termination of Plaintiff's employment because of his race was contrary to Defendant's overall good faith efforts to comply with the laws that prohibit race discrimination by employers against their employees?

Answer "Yes" or "No."

_____

If you answered "Yes" to Jury Question No. 4, then *proceed to the bottom of the end of this document and sign to enter your verdict.* If you answered "No," then answer Jury Question No. 5.

## Jury Question No. 5

What amount of damages, if now paid in cash, has Plaintiff established by a preponderance of the evidence to be an appropriate amount for punitive damages as a result of his termination because of his race?

Answer in dollars and cents, if any.

$_____

In the event that you find the Defendant liable in this case, the parties have agreed that the issue of monetary damages for loss of wages by the Plaintiff, if any, will be decided by the Court.

## Certificate

We, the Jury, in the above-entitled action, *Jerome Johnson v. Southern Bell Systems, Inc.*, Civil Action No. 3:14-CV-1154-A, have unanimously agreed to the answers in the above questions and return such answers to the Court as our verdict. So say we all.

Signed this 24th day of June, 2016.

Robert Bruner

Jury Foreperson

## Exercise 11.3

This is a mediation exercise. Mr. Jerome Johnson has filed suit against Southern Bell Systems for race discrimination and retaliation in violation of Title VII and Section 1981. The parties have engaged in considerable discovery. Southern Bell Systems moved for summary judgment on all claims and the court denied the motion as to all claims. The federal district court has ordered the parties to mediation. The jury trial is scheduled to begin in about three months. An objective view of the facts of the case indicates that a finding of discrimination and/or retaliation by the fact-finder if the case goes to trial is certainly possible and perhaps likely. Consider the sample EEOC documents and sample pleadings from the Procedure Chapter to help think through the liability question.

You will be broken into groups of three. One person will serve as the mediator. Another person will serve as the plaintiff's attorney. The remaining person will serve as the defendant's attorney. Now that you have a background on remedies law in employment discrimination cases try to hammer out a settlement. The mediator controls the negotiations. Use the additional information stated below to aid in negotiations. The parties can frame their positions based on additional factual information that they add to the case so long as the information is fairly inferred from the dispute.

Information for Mediation

- Jerome Johnson was 35 years old at the time of the discrimination. He began working for the company in 2007.
- Johnson's employment was terminated on January 18, 2014.
- Johnson filed the lawsuit in June 2014.
- The trial date is scheduled for June 15, 2016. A one-week trial is expected.
- Johnson's salary at the time of the termination was $40,000 annually.
- During the time between his termination and the present, Johnson worked for 3 months as a trucker driver (approximate annual salary of $30,000 per year). He was laid off due to the recession. He then worked three months at a clothing store selling men's clothes ($12.00 per hour). The job was part-time and he worked approximately 25 hours per week. Once again, his employment ended at the clothing store because he was laid off through no fault of his own. Other than these periods of time, he was not employed.
- Southern Bell Systems has 150 employees.

If you were able to arrive at a settlement agreement, what are its terms? Both sides should be able to explain the bargaining positions taken and how the agreement came together. If you were not able to resolve the case, what were the sticking points?

## Exercise 11.4

Even though remedies are discussed late in this book, they are important in many different stages of a potential or actual employment discrimination claim. List every step in the process of resolving a discrimination claim in which a practicing lawyer needs to be mindful about the available remedies and whether the facts support such remedies.

### Exercise 11.5

In this chapter, you have learned about various ways that a plaintiff's damages may be limited. You also learned about damage-limiting concepts in Chapter 3. Think about how to organize this information so that it will be helpful to you as a practicing attorney. For example, it might make sense to create a list or chart of each of the ways damages might be limited.

# Chapter 12

# Capstone Experience

By the end of this class, you should have a good foundational understanding of the doctrine of federal employment discrimination law. You also should be conversant with the theories that undergird the field, the history of major legal developments, and the practical dynamics that may affect a case. This Chapter is designed to give you a capstone experience, where you can bring all of this knowledge together and test it against real-world hypotheticals. You also may find these capstone exercises helpful in studying for a final examination.

The capstone exercises take you through five different scenarios you might face as an attorney practicing in this field: (1) evaluating a case from a plaintiff's attorney's perspective; (2) performing an initial case evaluation as an attorney for a defendant; (3) undertaking discovery; (4) evaluating a case at the summary judgment stage; and (5) helping an employer evaluate how to resolve a matter.

## Capstone Exercise 1:
## Evaluating a Case from a Plaintiff's Attorney's Perspective

You are a plaintiff's lawyer, and Sally comes to you for legal advice. Sally works at a large law firm with 500 lawyers. Almost half of the firm's associates are women, but the representation of women drops off precipitously at the senior associate, junior partner and partner level. The firm has a 10-person management committee, and nine of its members are men. Several firm departments, such as litigation and bankruptcy, have particularly low numbers of women.

The firm expects its lawyers to work hard. The firm's lawyers are required to bill at least 2,000 hours a year and are often required to work 12-hour days. The lawyers frequently collaborate on cases and transactional projects. Decisions about how to staff cases or transactional projects are subjective and discretionary, with partners or senior associates forming teams to work on them. Associates are evaluated once a year by all partners for whom they have worked, although there are varying levels of participation in the evaluation process by the partners.

Continued advancement within the firm depends largely upon the number of hours billed, as well as the collective, subjective assessments of the partners. At times, a particularly negative evaluation from an influential partner may end the career of an associate at the firm. Partnership decisions are largely made in the same way, although the associate's book of business is also a major factor in the partnership decision. Associate mentoring is rather ad hoc with certain partners choosing to take an associate to interact with clients or providing professional advice and development opportunities.

Sally is a fourth-year associate at the firm. She believes that during her last performance evaluation, she was evaluated on different criteria than male associates. During the evaluation, Sally was told that she was not kind enough to staff members and that she was too aggressive in her handling of cases.

Sally believes that a number of women at the firm have been discriminated against. Sally says she has often seen high-profile assignments given to junior male associates rather than to more qualified, senior female associates. Sally has heard through the grapevine that high-level partners have made sexualized or sex-related comments about women at the firm. One partner asked a female associate who obtained an especially favorable judgment in her client's favor whether she had worn a bikini to court. Another male partner told a female associate that one of the female partners "used to be a good attorney before she had babies."

On several occasions, Sally has not been invited to happy hours arranged by members of her department, and she feels socially isolated. Sally also believes that women are disproportionately asked to take on more non-billable responsibilities than male attorneys, such as providing associate training.

This is information that Sally has told you during a preliminary meeting. You are going to meet with Sally one more time before deciding whether to take her case. Does Sally have a good case? Do you take Sally's case? If you need more information, what information would you need? What questions will you need to ask Sally at your meeting? How would you plead this case?

Before you file a charge with the EEOC and/or a comparable state agency on behalf of Sally, is there any candid advice that you should give Sally about her alternatives to addressing the alleged discrimination that fall short of initiating the EEOC process that may subsequently lead to litigation in court? In addition, what will you tell her, if anything, about the practical ramifications of pursuing the litigation route as a means of resolving her dispute?

Assume that Sally wants to pursue her claims against the firm and that you agree to represent her and take the case. What steps will you take to initiate the administrative process? If you exhaust the administrative process, where will you file the case and what claims will you bring? Assume that you are in a state where the state law mimics the federal law in all significant respects; however, in this particular state, the state law does not have a cap on compensatory or punitive damages. You also know the following information about the local legal system.

You would be able to file your lawsuit in either a state court or a federal court. The state court in which you would file is understaffed and cases often take at least two years to go to trial. At the same time, the trial court judges within the state court system in your locality are known (for the most part) to favor letting cases go to trial. Because the local judges do not have interns or clerks, they are more likely to prefer to hear brief oral arguments on motions, rather than to require lengthy written motions.

In the local federal district court, there is an equal mix of plaintiff friendly and defense friendly judges. Most of the judges in federal district court prefer to consider written motions, rather than oral ones. Cases take approximately 18 months to go to trial. Remember that in making your decision about where to file a lawsuit, removal may be an option if you file a federal claim in a state court. Assume that there is no diversity of citizenship between the parties. Think about your obligation to talk with your client about her options regarding forum and claim choice.

## Capstone Exercise 2:
## Initial Case Evaluation by a Lawyer for a Defendant

You are an attorney working at a large defense firm. You receive a frantic call from one of your clients, Barnes Hospital. Your contact there tells you that the hospital has just been served with a complaint alleging gender discrimination. The client sends a copy of the complaint to your office. The substantive portions of the complaint read as follows:

1. Alicia White worked at Barnes Hospital from August 1995 until the present.

2. Ms. White is employed as a physician's assistant.

3. While employed at Barnes Hospital, Ms. White has been constantly subjected to teasing by doctors about her large breasts.

4. Doctors have repeatedly told Ms. White that she has "nice tits" and looked down her shirt while she files paperwork.

5. On one occasion, Dr. Roman Smith purposively brushed up against her breasts while she was assisting him with a medical procedure.

6. Ms. White continues to be subjected to this treatment.

In her complaint, the plaintiff seeks all remedies available under Title VII. The complaint is filed in a federal district court that has proper subject matter jurisdiction, personal jurisdiction and venue. The plaintiff's lawyer is a well-respected employment discrimination attorney in town, who is known for taking good cases and aggressively prosecuting them.

During the phone call, your client contact, who works in the hospital's personnel office, tells you that Alicia White is a troublemaker and that Alicia's allegations are all false because Dr. Roman Smith is a nice guy.

What should you do? Think about the information you will need, what you will need to do to get it, and what documents you may need to file with the court. Think about how to interact with your client and about any information you need to provide to your client.

## Capstone Exercise 3:
## Discovery

In federal court, lawyers have several discovery tools at their disposal. These include interrogatories (written questions), requests for documents, mental or physical exams of parties (in certain instances), requests for admissions, and depositions. Formal discovery can be sought from parties to the case. In addition, documents can be requested from and depositions can be taken of non-parties. In federal court, parties are also required to exchange initial disclosures, which, among other things, require a party to disclose a computation of each category of damages claimed by the disclosing party and the documents or other evidentiary material, unless privileged or protected from disclosure, on which each computation is based, as well as to make available for inspection and copying any insurance agreement under which part or all of the judgment may be satisfied.

Re-read the Charge of Discrimination and the Complaint in the Jerome Johnson case discussed in the Procedure Chapter. In addition to the information contained therein, the defendant's lawyer has found out that, on his health insurance form, Mr. Johnson has listed two children as his legal children. However, by talking with employees, the lawyer has learned that the two children are not Mr. Johnson's biological children and the lawyer does not know whether Mr. Johnson legally adopted the children. The lawyer also found out that Mr. Johnson went through a bitter divorce five years ago.

First, act as the plaintiff's lawyer. Outline a discovery plan for this case, thinking about how a lawyer might obtain information to learn about the case and then admissible evidence to support the case. In thinking about discovery, write out what you need to prove to establish the claim and the admissible evidence that you will use. Also, think about the story that you will want to tell the jury and what evidence will support this narrative. Think about how you rebut evidence presented by the defendant.

Second, switch points of view, thinking about discovery from the defendant's lawyer's perspective. Remember to think about the evidence you will need to rebut the plaintiff's claims, as well as the evidence that you will need to establish any defenses or affirmative defenses.

## Capstone Exercise 4: Summary Judgment

Bob Graham worked as a computer programmer at Excel Corporation. He had worked for the company for 25 years. Bob worked in a department with 100 employees, all of whom had the same job title as Bob, except for the supervisor of the department. In the department, half of the workers were women and half the workers were men. The company at which Mr. Graham worked undertook a reduction in force. After the RIF, Mr. Graham's department had 75 employees. Fifty of the remaining workers were women, half over the age of 40 and half under. The remaining 25 employees were men under the age of 40. All of the individuals who were terminated were men over the age of 40.

Mr. Graham is 59 years old and was the oldest worker in his department. Mr. Graham was offered early retirement prior to the RIF, but declined. When the offer was made, his supervisor told him, "You should really take this offer Bob. It will save me from making some tough choices." As a result of the RIF, Mr. Graham was terminated. When he asked his supervisor why he was terminated, the supervisor responded, "You made me make a tough choice, and I did." During his deposition, the supervisor testified that he did not take Bob's gender or age into account when he decided to terminate him; rather, Bob was terminated because he was the only individual in his position who did not have a college degree.

Bob properly exhausts his administrative remedies and files a lawsuit in federal district court, alleging that "he was discriminated against on the basis of his age and his gender when he was terminated." He files claims under Title VII and the ADEA and is asserting both single- and mixed-motive claims under both statutes. Bob chooses not to file a disparate impact claim.

You are the attorney for the defendant. Based on this set of facts, draft a memorandum of law in support of a summary judgment motion. Assume that there is admissible evidence to support anything stated in the set of facts listed above. If you need additional information, indicate what such information would be.

## Capstone Exercise 5:
## Resolution of a Matter

Part of your role as an employment discrimination lawyer is preventing discrimination and advising clients on how to resolve discrimination complaints prior to litigation. In the disability context, you may be called upon to assist clients responding to requests for accommodations. You should act as a counselor to your client in the following two scenarios.

### 5.1

Re-read Capstone Exercise 2. Instead of filing a complaint, Ms. White submits a written complaint containing the same allegations to the hospital's personnel department. The hospital seeks your assistance on what to do next. How do you advise the hospital to proceed?

### 5.2

The same hospital employs Jason Harmon. Mr. Harmon is a new employee. Mr. Harmon uses a wheelchair. Mr. Harmon does not work at the hospital itself, but works at a document storage facility. Mr. Harmon comes to the personnel department and requests that he be allowed to start work at 9:00 a.m., rather than 8:00 a.m., because he is unable to drive and must take a bus to work. The earliest bus that can get him to work arrives at the document storage facility at 8:30 a.m.

Mr. Harmon's job responsibilities include filing medical records. Records that are more than 30 years old are stored in a small building that is separated from the main storage facility. There is no sidewalk between the two buildings, and the smaller building is up a small hill. Mr. Harmon requests that a covered sidewalk with a ramp be installed between the two buildings, so that he can complete his filing duties.

Mr. Harmon also requests that a counter and a sink in the employee break room be lowered so that he can reach it.

The client calls you asking for your advice regarding its legal obligations. What should the hospital do?

# Index

Bold indicates a major discussion of the material